Prepare your students with the power of classroom practice

adopt and assign
MyEducationLab today
www.myeducationlab.com

What is MyEducationLab?

MyEducationLab is a powerful online tool that provides students with assignments and activities set in the context of real classrooms. MyEducationLab is fully integrated in your course and provides practice for your students in an easy to assign format.

Children: "Oo"
Teacher: Good job.

ASSIGNMENTS AND IN-CLASS ACTIVITIES:

Each chapter in MyEducationLab includes assignable Activities and Applications exercises that use authentic classroom video, teacher and student artifacts, or case studies to help students understand course content more deeply and to practice applying that content.

PRACTICE TEACHING: Building Teaching Skills and Dispositions exercises use video, artifacts, and/or case studies to help your students truly see and understand how specific teaching techniques and behaviors impact learners and learning environments. These exercises give your students practice in developing the skills and dispositions that are essential to quality teaching.

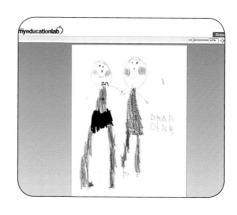

dents really like the videos,
e articles are interesting
levant too. I like how the
nforces the concepts in the
ok in a meaningful way. I am
d the textbook came with this
resource—it's great!"

— Shari Schroepfer,
Adams State College

Does it work?

A survey of student users from across the country tells us that it does!

93% MyEducationLab was easy to use.

70% MyEducationLab's video clips helped me to get a better sense of real classrooms.

79% I would recommend my instructor continue using MyEducationLab.

Percentage of respondents who agree or strongly agree.

Where is it?

- Online at www.myeducationlab .com
- Integrated right into this text! Look for margin annotations and end-of-chapter activities throughout the book.

This program will change teaching! Brilliant!"

— Bob Blake,
SUNY College at Brockport

What do I have to do to use MyEducationLab in my course?

Just contact your Pearson sales representative and tell him/her that you'd like to use MyEducationLab with this text next semester. Your representative will work with your bookstore to ensure that your students receive access with their books.

What if I need help?

We've got you covered 24/7. Your Pearson sales representative offers training in using MyEducationLab for you and your students. There is also a wealth of helpful information on the site, under "Tours and Training" and "Support." And technical support is available 24 hours a day, seven days a week, at http://247pearsoned.custhelp.com.

The ability to track students' performance on the MyEducationLab activities has allowed me to easily keep the students' performance records and devote more time to the development of appropriate in-class activities. The technology has made it possible to design a mastery-based learning system and more easily demonstrate evidence-based practices."

— Daniel E. Hursh,
West Virginia University

ISTE National Educational Technology Standards (NETS•T) and Performance Indicators for Teachers

Effective teachers model and apply the National Educational Technology Standards for Students (NETS•S) as they design, implement, and assess learning experiences to engage students and improve learning; enrich professional practice; and provide positive models for students, colleagues, and the community. All teachers should meet the following standards and performance indicators. Teachers:

1. FACILITATE AND INSPIRE STUDENT LEARNING AND CREATIVITY

   Teachers use their knowledge of subject matter, teaching and learning, and technology to facilitate experiences that advance student learning, creativity, and innovation in both face-to-face and virtual environments. Teachers:
   - promote, support, and model creative and innovative thinking and inventiveness.
   - engage students in exploring real-world issues and solving authentic problems using digital tools and resources.
   - promote student reflection using collaborative tools to reveal and clarify students' conceptual understanding and thinking, planning, and creative processes.
   - model collaborative knowledge construction by engaging in learning with students, colleagues, and others in face-to-face and virtual environments.

2. DESIGN AND DEVELOP DIGITAL-AGE LEARNING EXPERIENCES AND ASSESSMENTS

   Teachers design, develop, and evaluate authentic learning experiences and assessments incorporating contemporary tools and resources to maximize content learning in context and to develop the knowledge, skills, and attitudes identified in the NETS•S. Teachers:
   - design or adapt relevant learning experiences that incorporate digital tools and resources to promote student learning and creativity.
   - develop technology-enriched learning environments that enable all students to pursue their individual curiosities and become active participants in setting their own educational goals, managing their own learning, and assessing their own progress.
   - customize and personalize learning activities to address students' diverse learning styles, working strategies, and abilities using digital tools and resources.
   - provide students with multiple and varied formative and summative assessments aligned with content and technology standards and use resulting data to inform learning and teaching.

3. MODEL DIGITAL-AGE WORK AND LEARNING

   Teachers exhibit knowledge, skills, and work processes representative of an innovative professional in a global and digital society. Teachers:
   - demonstrate fluency in technology systems and the transfer of current knowledge to new technologies and situations.
   - collaborate with students, peers, parents, and community members using digital tools and resources to support student success and innovation.
   - communicate relevant information and ideas effectively to students, parents, and peers using a variety of digital-age media and formats.
   - model and facilitate effective use of current and emerging digital tools to locate, analyze, evaluate, and use information resources to support research and learning.

4. PROMOTE AND MODEL DIGITAL CITIZENSHIP AND RESPONSIBILITY

   Teachers understand local and global societal issues and responsibilities in an evolving digital culture and exhibit legal and ethical behavior in their professional practices. Teachers:
   - advocate, model, and teach safe, legal, and ethical use of digital information and technology, including respect for copyright, intellectual property, and the appropriate documentation of sources.
   - address the diverse needs of all learners by using learner-centered strategies and providing equitable access to appropriate digital tools and resources.
   - promote and model digital etiquette and responsible social interactions related to the use of technology and information.
   - develop and model cultural understanding and global awareness by engaging with colleagues and students of other cultures using digital-age communication and collaboration tools.

5. ENGAGE IN PROFESSIONAL GROWTH AND LEADERSHIP

   Teachers continuously improve their professional practice, model lifelong learning, and exhibit leadership in their school and professional community by promoting and demonstrating the effective use of digital tools and resources. Teachers:
   - participate in local and global learning communities to explore creative applications of technology to improve student learning.
   - exhibit leadership by demonstrating a vision of technology infusion, participating in shared decision making and community building, and developing the leadership and technology skills of others.
   - evaluate and reflect on current research and professional practice on a regular basis to make effective use of existing and emerging digital tools and resources in support of student learning.
   - contribute to the effectiveness, vitality, and self-renewal of the teaching profession and of their school and community.

ISTE National Educational Technology Standards (NETS•S) and Performance Indicators for Students

1. Creativity and Innovation

   Students demonstrate creative thinking, construct knowledge, and develop innovative products and processes using technology. Students:
   - apply existing knowledge to generate new ideas, products, or processes.
   - create original works as a means of personal or group expression.
   - use models and simulations to explore complex systems and issues.
   - identify trends and forecast possibilities.

2. Communication and Collaboration

   Students use digital media and environments to communicate and work collaboratively, including at a distance, to support individual learning and contribute to the learning of others. Students:
   - interact, collaborate, and publish with peers, experts, or others employing a variety of digital environments and media.
   - communicate information and ideas effectively to multiple audiences using a variety of media and formats.
   - develop cultural understanding and global awareness by engaging with learners of other cultures.
   - contribute to project teams to produce original works or solve problems.

3. Research and Information Fluency

   Students apply digital tools to gather, evaluate, and use information. Students:
   - plan strategies to guide inquiry.
   - locate, organize, analyze, evaluate, synthesize, and ethically use information from a variety of sources and media.
   - evaluate and select information sources and digital tools based on the appropriateness to specific tasks.
   - process data and report results.

4. Critical Thinking, Problem Solving, and Decision Making

   Students use critical thinking skills to plan and conduct research, manage projects, solve problems, and make informed decisions using appropriate digital tools and resources. Students:
   - identify and define authentic problems and significant questions for investigation.
   - plan and manage activities to develop a solution or complete a project.
   - collect and analyze data to identify solutions and/or make informed decisions.
   - use multiple processes and diverse perspectives to explore alternative solutions.

5. Digital Citizenship

   Students understand human, cultural, and societal issues related to technology and practice legal and ethical behavior. Students:
   - advocate and practice safe, legal, and responsible use of information and technology.
   - exhibit a positive attitude toward using technology that supports collaboration, learning, and productivity.
   - demonstrate personal responsibility for lifelong learning.
   - exhibit leadership for digital citizenship.

6. Technology Operations and Concepts

   Students demonstrate a sound understanding of technology concepts, systems, and operations. Students:
   - understand and use technology systems.
   - select and use applications effectively and productively.
   - troubleshoot systems and applications.
   - transfer current knowledge to learning of new technologies.

INTEGRATING EDUCATIONAL TECHNOLOGY INTO TEACHING

FIFTH EDITION

M.D. Roblyer
University of Tennessee at Chattanooga

Aaron H. Doering
University of Minnesota

Allyn & Bacon

Boston • New York • San Fancisco
Mexico City • Montreal • Toronto • London • Madrid • Munich • Paris
Hong Kong • Singapore • Tokyo • Cape Town • Sydney

Series Editor:	Kelly Villella Canton
Editotial Assistant:	Annalea Manalili
Senior Development Editor:	Mary Kriener
Senior Marketing Manager:	Darcy Betts
Production Editor:	Gregory Erb
Editorial Production Service:	Nesbitt Graphics, Inc.
Composition Buyer:	Linda Cox
Manufacturing Buyer:	Megan Cochran
Electronic Composition:	Nesbitt Graphics, Inc.
Interior Design:	Nesbitt Graphics, Inc.
Photo Researcher:	Annie Pickert
Cover Designer:	Linda Knowles

For related titles and support materials, visit our online catalog at www.pearsonhighered.com

Between the time website information is gathered and then published, it is not unusual for some sites to have closed. Also, the transcription of URLs can result in typographical errors. The publisher would appreciate notification where these errors occur so that they may be corrected in subsequent editions.

Library of Congress Cataloging-in-Publication Data

Roblyer, M. D.
  Integrating educational technology into teaching / M.D. Roblyer, Aaron H. Doering.
    p. cm.
  Includes bibliographical references and index.
  ISBN 978-0-13-513063-6
  1. Educational technology--United States. 2. Computer-assisted instruction--United States.
  3. Curriculum planning--United States. I. Doering, Aaron Herbert II. Title.

LB1028.3.R595 2010
371.33--dc22

                                          2009006704

Printed in the United States of America

Photo Credits: p. 1, Getty Images/Stockbyte RF; p. 3, PunchStock; p. 10 (L), U.S. Air Force; p. 10 (R), IBM Corporation; p. 11 (TL), Apple Computer; p. 11 (TC), Tom Watson/Merrill Education; p. 11 (TR), Sam Craft/AP Images; p. 11 (B), Pearson Learning Photo Studio; p. 14, Author Provided; p. 16, IndexOpen; p. 20, Bob Daemmrich/PhotoEdit; p. 22, iStockphoto; p. 31, Najlah Feanny/Corbis; p. 35 (L), Corbis/Bettmann; p. 35 (R), Courtesy of Robert Gagne; p. 38, Patrick White/Merrill Education; p. 39 (FL), Courtesy of the Library of Congress; p. 39 (L), Courtesy of the Library of Congress; p. 39 (M), Corbis/Bettmann; p. 39 (R), Courtesy of Jerome Bruner; p. 39 (FR), Basic Books; p. 55, Bob Daemmrich Photography; p. 71, iStockphoto; p. 73, iStockphoto; p. 80, Bill Aron/PhotoEdit; p. 85, Mary Kate Denny/PhotoEdit; p. 91, Ariel Skelley/Stock Market/Corbis, p. 100, A. Ramey/PhotoEdit; p. 109, iStockphoto; p. 110, Dorling Kindersley Media Library, p. 115, Kevin Wolf/AP Images; p. 137, John Berry/ Syracuse Newspapers /The Image Works; p. 141, David Young-Wolff/PhotoEdit; p. 149, John Maniaci/Wisconsin State Journal/AP Images; p. 160, Bonnie Kamin/PhotoEdit; p. 161, Shutterstock; p. 167, Bob Daemmrich Photography; p. 178, Anthony Magnacca/Merrill Education; p. 194, Eckehard Schulz/AP Images; p. 205, Kim Kulish/Corbis; p. 207, Kevin Wolf/AP Images; p. 222, iStockphoto; p. 232, Patrick White/Merrill Education; p. 237, Bob Daemmrich/PhotoEdit; p. 263, Zigy Kaluzny/Stone Allstock/Getty Images; p. 273, Bill Aron/PhotoEdit; p. 275, David Young-Wolff/PhotoEdit; p. 276, UpperCut Images/Alamy Images RF; p. 282, Don Tonge/Alamy Images; p. 289, Patrick White/Merrill Education; p. 295, Courtesy of Leapfrog School Division; p. 299, Michael Newman/PhotoEdit; p. 303, Michael Newman/PhotoEdit; p. 313, Michael Newman/PhotoEdit; p. 319, Bob Daemmrich/The Image Works; p. 333, David Young-Wolff/PhotoEdit; p. 343, Bob Daemmrich/PhotoEdit; p. 348, Valerie Schultz/Merrill Education; p. 363, Hana/Datacraft/Digital Vision/Getty Images; p. 371, Courtesy of Finale/MakeMusic; p. 387, Paco Ayala/AGE Fotostock America; p. 396, Courtesy of Bonnie Mohnsen; p. 397, Courtesy of Bonnie Mohnsen; p. 398, Courtesy of Bonnie Mohnsen; p. 405, Ed Kashi/Corbis; p. 407, Anthony Magnacca/Merrill Education; p. 410, Scott Cunningham/Merrill Education; p. 418, Scott Cunningham/Merrill Education; Adapting for special needs feature, Elizabeth Crews Photography; Design mp3, Don Farrall/Photodisc/Getty Images.

10 9 8 7 6 5 4 3 2 1   WEB 13 12 11 10 09

Allyn & Bacon
is an imprint of

ISBN-10: 0-13-513063-8

ISBN-13: 978-0-13-513063-6

Dedication

For Bill and Paige Wiencke, whose love is, as Arthur Clarke said of advanced technology, indistinguishable from magic.
For Cassie and all of our furry critters, thank you for being on this journey with me.

Brief Contents

Contents

Special Features

Preface

Each year, the computer physically becomes smaller and smaller, yet computing power grows exponentially. Today, we can access the Internet on our cell phone, a device that has quickly morphed into a powerful tool that does more than what a computer could do just ten years ago. We are "connected" with our "friends" throughout social networking environments such as Facebook; we keep friends informed of our everyday movements with Twitter; and we go to a virtual dance with our friends within Second Life. One would think that with all of these technological improvements, technology integration within the field of education would be flourishing and having significant impact on learning, motivation, and pedagogy. Given the speed at which our daily lives have been affected by changes in technology, it is fair to ask ourselves, "Has education made good use of technology's power?"

The research on technology integration is mixed—some studies show educational technology having a "significant" impact on achievement, while the "no significant difference" research also continues to grow. Yet with each new scientific survey and study of technology use in schools, it has become increasingly clear that the technology itself provides *only* the raw materials for enhanced educational strategies. Meaningful technology integration is dependent on how teachers plan for and use these powerful devices.

There are more questions now than ever before about how to meet the varying needs of individual students so that none are left behind, but there are some clearly defined guidelines on what works best when it comes to matching students' needs with technology's capabilities. What have we learned so far that enlightens our use of technology in education?

- **Good pedagogy rules** — Web-based learning in the past ten years has shown that interaction with teachers, flawed and variable as it may be, is more important than ever before. This textbook proposes that technology is, above all, a channel for helping teachers communicate better with students. *It can make good teaching even better, but it cannot make bad teaching good.* Consequently, technology-using teachers never can be a force for improved education unless they are first and foremost informed, knowledgeable shapers of their craft. Before integrating technology into their teaching, educators must know a great deal, for example, about why there are different views on appropriate teaching strategies, how societal factors and learning theories have shaped these views, and how each strategy can address differing needs.

- **Technology is us** — Rather than seeing technology as some foreign invader here to confuse and complicate the simple life of the past, we can recognize that technology is very much our own response to overcoming obstacles that stand in the way of a better, more productive way of life. As Walt Kelly's "profound 'possum" Pogo said, "We have met the enemy, and he is us." Technology is us—our tools, our methods, and our own creative attempts to solve problems in our environment. Turmoil will accompany the transitions as we adapt to the new environment we ourselves have created. But technology is, by definition, intended to be part of our path to a better life, rather than an obstacle in its way.

- **We control how technology is used in education** — As a follow-up to our recognition that "technology is us," we must recognize the truth of Peter Drucker's statement: "The best way to predict the future is to create it." Both individual teachers and teaching organizations must see themselves as enlightened shapers of our future. Each teacher must help to articulate the vision for what the future of education should look like; each should acquire skills to help work toward realizing that vision.

Core Principles at the Center of This Text

The purpose of this book is to show how we are challenged to shape the future of technology in education. How we respond to this challenge is guided by how we see it helping us accomplish our own informed vision of what teaching and learning should be. Our approach to accomplishing this purpose rests on four premises:

- **Technology-based methods should be based in both learning theory and teaching practice** — There is no shortage of innovative ideas in the field of instructional technology; new and interesting methods come forward about as often as new and improved gadgets. Those who would build on the knowledge of the past should know why they do what they do, as well as how to do it. Thus, we have linked various technology-based integration strategies to well-researched theories of learning, and we have illustrated them with examples of successful practices based on these theories.

- **Uses of technology should match specific teaching and learning needs** — Technology has the power to improve teaching and learning, but it can also make a teacher's life more complicated. Therefore, each resource should be examined for its unique qualities and its potential benefits for teachers and students. Teachers should not use a tool simply because it is new and available; each integration strategy should be matched to a recognized need. We do not oppose experimentation, but we do advocate informed use.

- **Old integration strategies are not necessarily bad; new strategies are not necessarily good** — As technologies change and evolve at lightning speed, there is a tendency to throw out older teaching methods with the older machines. Sometimes this is a good idea; sometimes it would be a shame. Each of the integration strategies recommended in this book is based on methods with proven usefulness to teachers and students. Some of the strategies are based on directed methods that have been used for some time; other strategies are based on the newer, constructivist learning models. Each is recommended on the basis of its usefulness rather than its age.

- **Technological Pedagogical and Content Knowledge (TPACK) is necessary** — It has always been assumed that teachers need to know the content they are teaching very well and that teachers must know exceptional pedagogical strategies for teaching this content. Now, the educational technology community, including the authors of this book, argues that teachers need to have not only content and pedagogy knowledge, but also technological knowledge: it should be a perfect union of the three known as technological pedagogical and content knowledge (TPACK).

The goal of this edition is for teachers to see more clearly their role in shaping the future of technology in education. This book illustrates that the real keys to great education lie not in the recesses of an increasingly smaller box of computing power, but in the larger, less well-defined region "out there" that both encompasses and transcends it: the interplay of teacher, student, content, and tools.

What's New in the Fifth Edition

Best known for its technology integration strategies grounded in strong research, the fifth edition of *Integrating Educational Technology into Teaching* offers a total technology integration package across all content areas that gives your students hands-on practice with technology tools as they learn how to incorporate technology into the curriculum to support and shape learning. This edition includes a number of additions that reflect the changes in the field of Educational Technology.

- The newly **updated six-part Technology Integration Planning (TIP) Model** shows teachers how to create an environment in which technology can effectively enhance learning.

- The fifth edition introduces your students to the concept of **Technological Pedagogical and Content Knowledge (TPACK)** and the role it can have in preparing for integrating technology within their future classrooms. Students learn to assess themselves to be more successful at integrating technology within their classroom. This new model is introduced in Chapter 1 and reinforced within each chapter's Technology Integration Example and Workshop, as well as at the beginning of each of the content chapters (Chapters 9–15), where scenarios are provided to assist students in understanding what TPACK looks like within their specific content areas.

- The fifth edition introduces the radically **new ISTE National Educational Technology Standards for Students (NETS-S) and Teachers (NETS-T),** revised in 2007 and 2008, respectively. The new standards and Essential Conditions are thoroughly discussed in the first three chapters and correlated with text throughout. Chapter correlations to the NETS-T and the list of the standards also appear in the front of the book. In addition, the Technology Integration Lesson features in every chapter, as well as on MyEducationLab and referenced in the margins of the book, are correlated to the new NETS-S.

FIGURE 1.2   National Educational Technology Standards for Students and Teachers

NETS-S	NETS-T
1. Creativity and Innovation 2. Communication and Collaboration 3. Research and Information Fluency 4. Critical Thinking, Problem Solving, and Decision Making 5. Digital Citizenship 6. Technology Operations and Concepts	1. Facilitate and Inspire Student Learning and Creativity 2. Design and Develop Digital-Age Learning Experiences and Assessments 3. Model Digital-Age Work and Learning 4. Promote and Model Digital Citizenship and Responsibility 5. Engage in Professional Growth and Leadership

Source: © 2007, 2008 International Society for Technology in Education. ISTE ® is a registered trademark of the International Society for Technology in Education.

- **Web 2.0 technologies and strategies** are discussed and incorporated into every chapter. Ranging from open source applications to digitization to adventure learning to social networking, the fifth edition outlines the growing number of new technological options and opportunities for schools, teachers, and students.

- **MyEducationLab** in-text and end-of-chapter activities in every chapter signal readers to go to the MyEducationLab site for Educational Technology. This rich, assignable online resource offers prospective teachers the opportunity to view live classroom footage, evaluate classroom lessons, access technology tutorials, download valuable assessment resources, and much more.

Features of This Text

For the fifth edition, the authors maintain a cohesive, comprehensive **technology integration framework** that builds on strong research and numerous integration strategies. This Technology Integration Framework:

Introduces Your Students to Technology Integration

Technology Integration Examples, located at the beginning of Chapters 2–15, are classroom-based scenarios that provide a classroom context for chapter content by focusing on the selection and use of specific technology within a classroom environment. Each walks the reader through the steps of the TIP Model and is tied to chapter objectives and linked to the end-of-chapter Technology Integration Workshop.

Making the Case for Technology Integration

Use the following questions to reflect on issues in technology integration and to guide discussions within your class.

1. Some educators object to the use of tools such as test generators and worksheet generators, saying that they encourage teachers to use technology to maintain current methods, rather than using technology in more innovative ways. What case can you make for keeping software tools like these in classrooms?

2. As mentioned in this chapter, the use of online and on-computer testing systems is becoming a popular, albeit controversial, practice (see http://www.fairtest.org/facts/computer.htm). What are the main points raised by critics of these systems? How would you address them?

3. Student information systems, which help track student, class, and school progress and help teachers with decision making, have become increasingly popular in recent years. They have also proven to be a useful tool for communicating with parents. In

Top Ten — Rules for Effective Desktop Publishing

1. **Use a limited number of typefaces (fonts)** — Unusual typefaces can help direct the eye toward text, but too many different fonts on a page can be distracting, and some fancy fonts are difficult to read.

2. **Use different fonts for title and text** — To aid the reader, use a serif typeface (a font with small curves or "hands and feet" that extend from the ends of the letters) for text in the main body of the document. Use a sans serif typeface, a font without extensions, for titles and headlines.

3. **Use appropriate sizes for type** — Make the type large enough to assist the reader (e.g., younger readers usually need large point sizes), but not too large to dominate the page.

4. **Avoid overuse of type styles** — Breaking up text with too many style changes interferes with reading. Avoid excessive underlining, boldfacing, and italics.

5. **Match text and background colors** — Use white or yellow type on a black block to add drama. Avoid color combinations that can be difficult to read (e.g., orange on green or red on blue).

6. **Use visual cues** — Attract reader attention to important information on the page by using frames or boxes around text; bullets or arrows to designate important points; shading of the part of the page behind th... italic type; and captions fo...

7. **Use white space well** ...

Adapting for Special Needs

Young students and students with cognitive impairments are often confused by the complexity of standard productivity software packages such as *Microsoft Office*. One solution is a software product called *Max's Toolbox* (http://www.maxssandbox.com/). Designed for children ages 3 to 10, it provides a child-friendly interface and modified menus for Microsoft *Word, Excel,* and *PowerPoint*. It allows students to learn the basic operation of core productivity tools without being overwhelmed by all the options and advanced features. *Max's Toolbox* is a model learning scaffold that introduces young learners to essential concepts (e.g., save, print) so that they can later move easily into the full-feature version of *Microsoft Office*. A trial version is available for download.

Contributed by Dave Edyburn

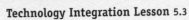

Technology Integration Lesson 5.3

Using Image Editing Software

Title: Bringing the Planets Closer to Home   **Grade Level:** 5 through 12
Content Area/Topic: Math (measurement) and astronomy

NETS for Students: Standards 3 (Research and Information Fluency), 4 (Critical Thinking, Problem Solving, and Decision Making), and 6 (Technology Operations and Concepts)

Description of Standards Applications: This integration lesson offers students the opportunity to research the scale of images of the solar system using an image editing program. Students problem solve with measuring tools to compare images from the solar system.

Instruction: Students begin by downloading NASA photos from the Internet (e.g., images of the solar system at http://spaceart.com/solar) and converting them to an uncompressed TIF format using an image editing program such as Adobe Photoshop. Their task is to learn how to measure the images. First, ... use the software to calibrate the images (determine the scale) by comparing the size of each im... measurement such as the diameter of Mars. Then they multiply the measured distance ... ermine the size of other features they have downloaded. In this way, the students can ... features that change, such as the Martian and Earth polar ice caps. These mea... basis of many projects to study space phenomena.

... hecklist to assess correct completion of required tasks.

... drie, B. (2000). Far out measurements: Bringing the planets closer to home using image-... earning and Leading with Technology, 27(5), 36–41.

- *End-of-Chapter Reviews,* study aids at the end of chapters, summarize and review critical chapter content and extend student learning through interactive Web-Enrichment activities.

Helps Your Students *Plan* for Effective Technology Integration

- *MyEducationLab* activities in-text and at the end of every chapter offer students the opportunity to evaluate classroom lessons, complete concept extension activities, and access resources that can be incorporated into daily planning. In particular, video clips of classroom footage allow prospective teachers to think critically about classroom challenges and possibilities. Software tutorials allow students to become familiar with software they can incorporate as part of classroom instruction. Building Teaching Skills activities help students develop critical skills for the classroom.

Helps Your Students *Practice* Technology Integration

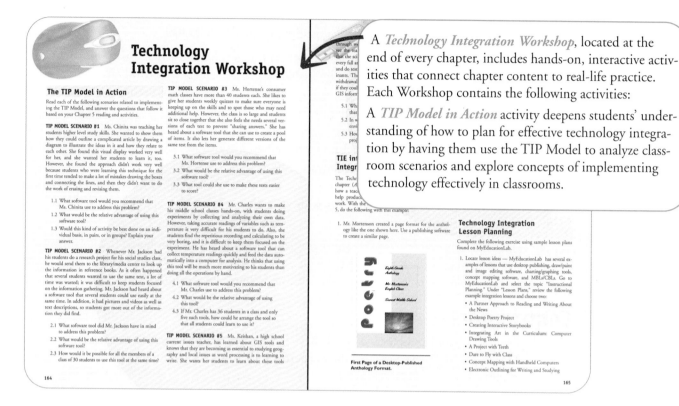

- A *TIE into Practice* hands-on activity, which is connected to the chapter-opening *Technology Integration Example (TIE)*, extends student understanding and experience by giving students the opportunity to analyze the Technology Integration Example and use software tutorials to apply some of the concepts.

- *Technology Integration Lesson Planning*, a hands-on feature aligned with the new ISTE Standards as well as the content standards for each content area, provides students the ability to evaluate a set of technology integration ideas according to the TIP Model; provides modifiable measurement tools such as rubrics and checklists so students can evaluate the lesson plans and software; encourages students to examine sample lessons across the curriculum; and allows students to modify lesson plans to meet their own needs.

- A *For Your Teaching Portfolio* feature directs students to save the material they created in each chapter in a personal portfolio.

Supplemental Materials

Instructor's Manual/Test Bank provides concrete suggestions to promote interactive teaching and actively involve students in learning. Each chapter contains chapter objectives, key terms, key concepts, and group activities, as well as a comprehensive test bank containing multiple choice, true/false, short-answer, and essay questions.

Computerized Test Bank Software This software gives instructors electronic access to the test questions printed in the Instructor's Manual, allowing them to create and customize exams on their computer. The software can help professors manage their courses and gain insight into their students' progress and performance. Computerized test bank software is available on a dual platform CD-ROM for Macintosh and PC/Windows users.

PowerPoint Slides Designed as an instructional tool, the *PowerPoint* presentations for each chapter can be used to present and elaborate on chapter content.

 MyEducationLab is a research-based learning tool that brings teaching to life. Through authentic in-class video footage, interactive simulations, case studies, examples of authentic teacher and student work, and more, MyEducationLab prepares you for your teaching career by showing what quality instruction looks like.

- *Video* Authentic classroom videos show how real teachers handle actual classroom situations. These video clips provide students with immediate access to real classrooms where effective technology integration is happening. Students can watch teachers as they use technology in their classrooms to shape and support learning.
- *Skill Builder Tutorials* These tutorials offer hands-on learning with software applications that teach basic skills such as using spreadsheets, presentation software, layout programs, classroom management and assessment tools, and much more.
- *Resources* The Resources link with numerous assessment tools such as rubrics and checklists, as well as weblinks that provide students with valuable resources that can be incorporated into daily lesson planning.

To start using MyEducationLab, activate the access code packaged with your book. If your instructor did not make MyEducationLab a required part of your course or if you are purchasing a used book without an access code, go to www.myeducationlab.com to purchase access to this wonderful resource!

Contributors

Over the life of this book, a number of people have made valuable contributions to various chapters. The following individuals have provided their expertise and assistance with the Fifth Edition, as well as with previous editions:

	Fifth Edition Contributors	**Previous Editions**
Chapter 3, Teaching with Instructional Software	George Veletsianos, University of Manchester, UK	
Chapter 6, Teaching with Multimedia and Hypermedia	Charles Miller, University of Minnesota	
Chapter 9, Technology in English and Language Arts Instruction	Cassandra Scharber, University of Minnesota	Rebecca Anderson, University of Memphis
Chapter 10, Technology in Foreign and Second Language Instruction	Martha Bigelow, University of Minnesota	Adrienne Herrell, Florida State University-Panama City
		Michael Jordan, California State University-Fresno
Chapter 11, Technology in Mathematics and Science Instruction	Bhaskar Upadhay, University of Minnesota	Ed Dickey, University of South Carolina
		Michael Odell, University of Idaho
Chapter 12, Technology in Social Studies Instruction		Michael Berson, University of South Florida
Chapter 13, Technology in Music and Art Instruction	Scott Lipscomb, University of Minnesota	Barbara Houghton, Northern Kentucky University
		Dan Newson, Berklee School of Music
Chapter 14, Technology in Physical Education and Health Education		Bonnie Mohnsen, Bonnie's Fitware
Chapter 15, Technology in Special Education	Daryl Peterson, University of Minnesota	Dave Edyburn, University of Wisconsin-Madison

Acknowledgments

History shows us that while technology is no panacea for education, it does have its own alchemy when combined appropriately with pedagogy and content. Technology is working its shape-shifting magic in ways we could not have imagined possible just a decade ago, altering completely and irrevocably the features that define modern life: the way we communicate, travel, entertain ourselves, and worship—even the way we think about and relate to each other as social beings. Though it is difficult not to be swept off our feet as our very foundations shift and shudder, and though the pace of technological change often challenges our ability to cope with its demands, we have to acknowledge the possibilities that rapidly improving technologies offer our classrooms. Even as we ask ourselves, "How can we learn to wield this new power? When will there be time?" we must find the courage to respond that we can and that the time is now.

Both the goal and challenge of this book have been to provide the reader with the most up-to-date, yet foundational, theory, research, and practices in educational technology across the disciplines. We believe we have achieved this goal. As in any project, realizing our goal would not have been possible without the assistance of numerous individuals who helped sharpen the focus of this edition. These individuals include reviewers for this edition: Beverly Bohn, Park University; David Bullock, Portland State University; Maël Disseau, Southeastern College at Wake Forest; James Grunwald, Martin Luther College; Alec Peck, Boston College; and Sharon L. Peterson, Western Michigan University.

I would also like to thank graduate student Bjorn Pederson for his assisstance on the project and to acknowledge my academic mentors who believed in me—Simon Hooper, Pennsylvania State University; Cecil Keen, Minnesota State University–Mankato; David Lanegran, Macalester College; and Roger Richman, Moorhead State University.

And finally, the incredible support from the Pearson Education staff is impossible to measure. The vision, expertise, and support of our Senior Development Editor, Mary Kriener, as well as the rest of the editorial and production team—Acquisitions Editor, Kelly Villella Canton; Development Editor, Amy Nelson; Editorial Assistant, Annalea Manalili; Senior Marketing Manager, Darcy Betts; Production Editor, Greg Erb; Photo Coordinator, Annie Pickert; and packager, Kathy Smith—made this version of the book useful, attractive, and meaningful. Thank you very much!

From the Authors:

From M. D. Roblyer: I would like to recognize the enduring love and patience of my family, Bill and Paige Wiencke, and the tenacious loyalty of friends across the country and around the world. Also, I would like to continue to remember and acknowledge the incalculable contributions of those who are with us now only in memory: Servatius L. Roblyer and Catherine P. Roblyer, and Raymond and Marjorie Wiencke.

From Aaron H. Doering: In the early 1990s, M.D. (Peggy) Roblyer had a vision to change the way teachers teach and students learn with technology, and the development of *Integrating Educational Technology into Teaching (IETT)*, published for the first time in 1996, realized this vision. Many years ago, it was a dream of mine to collaborate with great minds that cared about education, technology, and students. Thus, I am greatly humbled to work with her on this version of *IETT*. Thank you, Peggy. As usual, I would like to recognize my wife, Cassie, who has supported me at all costs and was my "personal" editor. Thank you for understanding the many nights, weekends, and holidays of writing it took to make this version one that can hopefully have a major impact in the future of technology in education. I would also like to acknowledge my parents, Royce and Sharon, whose calls to "see how the book was coming along" were much appreciated. Thank you for always being there.

Finally, we would like to acknowledge all the educators whose work embodies the beliefs that education is our future and that our primary responsibility to our students is enabling them to make this earth a better place. Thank you for sharing our vision and making it a daily, living reality.

M. D. Roblyer and Aaron H. Doering

About the Authors

M.D. Roblyer

M.D. Roblyer has been a technology-using teacher, professor, and contributor to the field of educational technology for more than 35 years. She began her exploration of technology's benefits for teaching in 1971 as a graduate student at one of the country's first successful instructional computer training sites, Pennsylvania State University, where she helped write tutorial literacy lessons in the Coursewriter II authoring language on an IBM 1500 dedicated instructional mainframe computer. While obtaining a Ph.D. in instructional systems at Florida State University, she worked on several major courseware development and training projects with Control Data Corporation's PLATO system. In 1981–1982, she designed one of the early microcomputer software series *Grammar Problems for Practice,* in conjunction with the Milliken Publishing Company.

She has written extensively and served as contributing editor and reviewer for numerous educational technology publications. Her other books for Pearson Education include *Starting Out on the Internet: A Learning Journey for Teachers; Technology Tools for Teachers: A Microsoft Office Tutorial* (with Steven C. Mills); and *Educational Technology in Action: Problem-based Exercises for Technology Integration.*

Currently, Dr. Roblyer is a Professor of Learning and Leadership in the Graduate Studies Division at the University of Tennessee at Chattanooga. She serves on the editorial boards of various technology and research journals and is president of AERA's Special Interest Group *Online Teaching and Learning.* Her current research focus centers on understanding student success in virtual environments and exploring ways to increase interactive qualities in virtual courses. She is married to William R. Wiencke and is the mother of a daughter, Paige.

Aaron H. Doering

Aaron Doering is an Assistant Professor of Learning Technologies at the University of Minnesota where he holds the Bonnie Westby-Huebner Endowed Chair in Education and Technology. His teaching and research interests focus on the design and development of effective distance online learning environments, technology integration in K–12 preservice and inservice settings, and the innovative use of technology to support teaching and learning. With a Ph.D. in instructional systems and technology and a M.S. in geography, his latest research and projects have focused on adventure learning environments, online scaffolding environments, and online community-building environments. His focus is on the impact of adventure learning within the K–12 classroom, how to design and develop education courses in technology and how geospatial technologies can be used to enhance learning within science and social studies curricula.

As part of his research, Dr. Doering serves as the Primary Investigator for the GoNorth! Online Adventure Learning program (http://www.polarhusky.com). Each year, he and the GoNorth! team traverse the Arctic region via dogsled to study the environmental issues, peoples, and cultures of the region. As part of their effort to improve geographic, natural, and social science literacy of all students, Dr. Doering and his team connect online with more than 3 million students in 2900 schools throughout the world via interactive technology, such as video podcasts and streaming video. In 2008, he was recognized and honored as a Microsoft Education Award Laureate for his innovative GoNorth! project. Dr. Doering also serves as the Primary Investigator for GeoThentic (http:geothentic.umn.ed), an online multi-scaffolding environment designed and developed on the technological pedagogical content knowledge theoretical framework that assists teachers to teach and students to learn geography using geospatial technologies.

Prior to coming to the University of Minnesota, Dr. Doering taught middle and high school social studies in Rochester, Minnesota. Beginning with his years as a secondary Social Studies teacher, Dr. Doering exudes a passion for teaching, particularly teaching how technology can be used to enhance learning and the important role it has within the classroom and workplace.

Part 1

Introduction and Background on Integrating Technology in Education

As we look today at what is happening with technology—and what the future promises—in classrooms across the country, we see that some of the most innovative and promising practices in education involve technology, and the promise of even more exciting capabilities foreshadows great benefits for teachers. This book presents some of the most powerful and capable educational technology resources available today and demonstrates how teachers can take advantage of them.

However, teachers must make a considerable investment of their time to prepare themselves to use technology resources well. The first two chapters in this book introduce the world of educational technology and review the knowledge and skills teachers need to prepare themselves to apply educational technology—especially computer technology—effectively in their classrooms.

Part 1

Required Background for Teachers

In Part 1, two chapters provide important foundational information and skills to help teachers take the first steps toward using technology in classrooms.

Chapter 1 Educational Technology in Context: The Big Picture

Computer technology in education has a history that spans some 50 years, and other kinds of technology have been in use for much longer. Classroom technology resources have changed dramatically over time, but a broad perspective of the field helps illuminate many of today's concepts, terms, and activities. Chapter 1 gives both an historical and a current context for applications of educational technology to show how they have evolved—and are still evolving—into the tools described later in this book. The chapter also describes current resources, issues, and trends that shape today's educational technology.

Chapter 2 Theory and Practice: Foundations for Effective Technology Integration

This chapter emphasizes the need to reach beyond the "nuts and bolts" of how technology resources work by emphasizing the links among three critical factors: learning theories, integration models, and essential conditions for effective integration. Successful integration requires a connection between how people learn and how teachers employ technology to assist and enhance this learning. Thus, this chapter begins with an overview of learning theories and how they have generated two different perspectives on how to integrate technology into teaching and learning activities: directed models and constructivist models. Secondly, this chapter introduces the Technology Integration Planning (TIP) Model, a systematic procedure for identifying problems and implementing and evaluating technology-based solutions. Finally, the chapter describes a series of conditions that offer essential support for teachers' technology integration.

Chapter 1

Educational Technology in Context: The Big Picture

It is clear that educational technology is essentially the product of a great historical stream consisting of trial and error, long practice and imitation, and sporadic manifestations of unusual individual creativity and persuasion.

Paul Saettler, in *The Evolution of American Educational Technology* (1990)

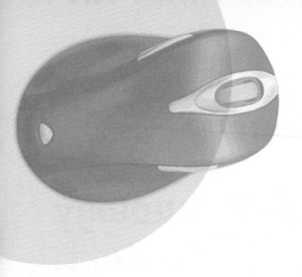

Technology Integration Example

Then and Now

Then . . .

Anna was almost as proud of her new classroom computers as she was of her new teaching degree. She had high hopes for the 1978–1979 school year in her first teaching position, especially since the principal had asked her if she could use two brand-new Apple computer systems that had been donated to the school. As a student teacher, she had helped children use computer-assisted instruction (CAI) on terminals that were located in the school's computer lab and connected by telephone lines to her university's big mainframe computer, but this would be much different. Now the computers would be located right in her classroom, and how she used them would be completely up to her. With her new skills and these marvelous devices at her disposal, she felt a heady sense of power and anticipation.

She found some free and "shareware" drill-and-practice and instructional game software packages, and successfully lobbied the principal to buy others. She planned to buy yet more with money she would raise from bake sales. All the students wanted to use the computers, but with only two machines, Anna quickly devised activities that allowed everyone to have a turn. She had "relay-race math practices" to help students prepare for tests, and she created a computer workstation where they could play math games as a reward for completing other activities and where she could send students in pairs to practice basic skills.

As Anna used her new computers, she coped with a variety of technical problems. Some of the software was designed for an earlier version of the Apple operating system, and each disk required a format adjustment every time it was used. Programs would stall when students entered something the programmers had not anticipated; students had either to adjust the code or to restart the programs. Despite these and other difficulties, by the end of the year Anna was still enthusiastic about her hopes, plans, and expectations. She felt she had seen a glimpse of a time when computers would be an integral part of everyday teaching activities. She planned to be ready for the future.

Now . . .

As she prepared to begin another school year, Anna found it difficult to believe it had been almost 30 years since that first pioneering work with her Apple microcomputers. When she moved to a new school building in 2000, each classroom had a five-computer workstation connected to the school network. Teachers downloaded software and media from the school server, and dozens of titles were available across content areas. Her students used the Internet to do research projects and to collaborate with students in other locations. Her class's favorite activity this year was working with students around the state to gather and compare data on prices for various products and services, but they also liked the spreadsheet software's "Buy a Car" activity.

Anna also marveled at how many other teachers in the school were using technology now. Everyone communicated via email, and many, like herself, had their own web pages so that students and parents could check homework assignments and view class projects. In other classes, students were using graphing calculators and handheld computers to solve problems, and she often heard them talking about the simulations they were doing in science and social studies. A video project to interview war veterans had drawn a lot of local attention, and the student projects displayed on school bulletin boards were ablaze with screen captures from websites and images students had taken with digital cameras.

There were still problems, of course. Computer viruses sometimes shut down the school's server, and there was a growing issue with students plagiarizing work from Internet sources. The firewall that the district had put in place to prevent students from accessing undesirable Internet sites also prevented access to many other, perfectly good sites. Some teachers complained that they had no time for the technology-based group projects students loved because they were too busy preparing them for the new state and national tests.

Yet despite these concerns, Anna was amazed at how far educational technology had come from those first, hesitant steps in the classroom and how much more there still was to try. She knew other teachers her age who were retiring, but she was too interested in what she was doing to think about that. She had been asked to help design a virtual course for homebound students. Not a day went by that a teacher didn't come to her for help on a new Internet page or video project. She couldn't wait to see what challenges lay ahead. She looked forward to the future.

Objectives

After reading this chapter and completing the learning activities for it, you should be able to:

1. Describe four views on how to define the term *educational technology* and identify professional associations that represent each view.

2. Identify periods in the history of educational computing and describe what we have learned from past applications and decisions.

3. Generate a personal rationale for using technology in education based on findings from research and practice.

4. Place a given educational technology resource in one of the following general hardware (stand-alone computer, network, and related device/system) or software (instructional, productivity, and administrative) categories.

5. Identify which one of the following technology resource configurations would be appropriate for a given educational need: laboratories, mobile workstations, mobile PCs (e.g., laptops or handheld computers), classroom workstations, and single-classroom PCs.

6. Identify the general categories of educational technology instructional/productivity resources: instructional software, software tool, multimedia, distance learning, and virtual reality environment.

7. Explain the impact of each of the following types of issues on current uses of technology in education: societal, educational, cultural/equity, and legal/ethical.

8. Identify trends in emerging technologies and the implications they may have for teaching and learning.

9. Identify technology skills teachers and their students need to have to be prepared for future learning and work tasks.

Introduction: Why Do We Need the "Big Picture"?

When a classroom teacher like Anna browses the Internet for new teaching materials or has students use handheld computers to take notes, that teacher is using some of the latest and best of what is commonly called *technology in education* or **educational technology**. But, as Saettler (1990) noted in this chapter's opening quote, educational technology is not new at all, and it is by no means limited to the use of equipment, let alone computer equipment. Modern tools and techniques are simply the latest developments in a field that some believe is as old as education itself.

This chapter explores the link between the early applications of educational technology and those of today and tomorrow. This review serves an important purpose. It helps new learners develop mental pictures of the field, what Ausubel (1968) might call *cognitive frameworks*, through which to view all applications and consider best courses of action. Several kinds of information help form this framework:

- **Key terminology** — Talking about a topic requires knowing the vocabulary relevant to that topic. Yet the term *educational technology* and many related terms are not defined the same way by everyone. Educators who want to study the field must realize that language used to describe technology reflects differing views by various groups on appropriate uses of educational technology.

- **Reflecting on the past** — Showing where the field began helps us understand where it is headed and why. Reviewing changes in goals and methods in the field over time provides a foundation on which to build even more successful and useful structures to respond to the challenges of modern education.

- **Considering the present** — The current role of educational technology is shaped primarily by two kinds of factors: available technology resources and our perspectives on how to make use of them. Available technologies dictate what is possible; a combination of social, instructional, cultural, and legal issues influence the directions we choose to take.

- **Looking ahead to the future** — Technology resources and societal conditions change so rapidly that today's choices are always influenced as much by emerging trends as by current conditions. To be informed citizens of an Information Society, teachers must be futurists.

What Is Educational Technology?

References to educational technology, learning technologies, and **instructional technology** pervade professional journals and magazines throughout education. Yet no single, acceptable definition for these terms serves the field, and there is uncertainty even about the origins of the terms (Reiser & Dempsey, 2006). Educational technology historian Paul Saettler (1990) says that the earliest reference to educational technology seems to have been made by radio instruction pioneer W. W. Charters in 1948, and instructional technology was first used by audiovisual expert James Finn in 1963. Even in those early days, definitions of these terms focused on more than just devices and materials. Saettler notes that a 1970 Commission on Instructional Technology defined it as both "the media born of the communication revolution which can be used for instructional purposes . . ." (p. 6) and "a systematic way of designing, carrying out, and evaluating the total process of learning and teaching . . ." (p. 6).

While today's educators tend to think of educational or instructional technology as equipment—particularly electronic equipment—Saettler (1990) reminds us that such a limited definition would have to change over time as resources change. Only about 20 years ago, Cuban's history of technology in education since 1920 (1986) placed the emphasis on radio and television, with computers as an afterthought. If such a description were written now, the focus might be on the Internet, while 20 years from now, it might be on intelligent computer-assisted instruction or virtual reality or whatever these technologies are called then. As the 1970 commission concluded, a broader definition of educational technology that encompasses both tools and processes "belongs to the future" (Saettler, 1990, p. 6).

Therefore, in the view of most writers, researchers, and practitioners in the field, useful definitions of educational technology must focus both on the process of applying tools for educational purposes and the tools and materials used. As Muffoletto (1994) puts it, "Technology . . . is not a collection of machines and devices, but a way of acting" (p. 25).

Four Perspectives That Define Educational Technology

If educational technology is viewed as both processes and tools, it is important to begin by examining four different historical perspectives on these processes and tools, all of which have helped shape current practices in the field. These influences come to us from four groups of education professionals. Because each of these groups emerged from a different area of education and/or society, each has a unique outlook on what *educational technology* is, and each defines it in a slightly different way. To some degree, these views have merged over time, but each retains a focus that tends to shape the integration practices it considers important. These four views and the professional organizations that represent them are summarized in Table 1.1.

- **Perspective #1: Educational technology as media and audiovisual communications** — This perspective grew out of the audiovisual (AV) movement in the 1930s, when higher education instructors proposed that media such as slides and films delivered information in more concrete, and therefore more effective, ways than lectures and books did. This movement produced audiovisual communications or the "branch of educational theory and practice concerned primarily with the design and use of messages that control the learning process" (Saettler, 1990, p. 9). The view of educational technology as media to deliver information continues to dominate areas of education and the communications industry. As late as 1986, the National Task Force on Educational Technology equated educational technology with media, treating computers simply as another medium (Saettler, 1990).

- **Perspective #2: Educational technology as instructional systems and instructional design** — This view originated with post–World War II military and industrial trainers who were faced with the problem of preparing large numbers of personnel quickly. Based on efficiency studies and learning theories from educational psychology, they advocated using more planned, systematic approaches to developing uniform, effective materials and training procedures. Their view was based on the belief that both human (teachers) and nonhuman (media) resources could be part of an efficient system for addressing any instructional need. Therefore, they equated "educational technology" with "educational problem solutions." As these training personnel began to work with both university research and development projects and K–12 schools, they also influenced practices in both of these areas. Behaviorist theories initially dominated and cognitive theories later gained precedence. In the 1990s, popular learning theories criticized systems approaches as being too rigid to foster some kinds of learning—particularly higher order ones. Thus, the current view of educational technology as instructional systems is continually evolving. (See Chapter 2 for more information on two approaches to educational technology as instructional systems and how each influences methods of integration.)

- **Perspective #3: Educational technology as vocational training** — Also known as **technology education**, this perspective originated with industry trainers and vocational educators in the 1980s. They believed (1) that an important function of school learning is to prepare students for the world of work in which they will use technology and (2) that vocational training can be a practical means of teaching all content areas such as math, science,

TABLE 1.1 Four Perspectives That Shaped Educational Technology

Perspectives: Educational Technology as . . .	Organization and Members	Historical View	Current View
#1: Media and AV communications	Association for Educational Communications and Technology (AECT) *http://www.aect.org* Serves library-media educators	Began with focus on delivering information as alternatives to lectures and books, using devices to carry messages (e.g. films, TV) during instruction. Later added an emphasis on online and computer/information systems as "media."	Still focuses on technologies as media. Most AECT divisions still focus on concerns of library-media educators. AECT state affiliates usually refer to themselves as "media associations."
#2: Instructional systems and instructional design	International Society for Performance Improvement (ISPI) *http://www.ispi.org* Serves higher education and industry instructional designers, trainers	Originally National Society for Programmed Instruction: Emphasized making instruction and training more efficient.	Focus is on creating and validating instructional systems to improve productivity and competence in the workplace.
#3: Vocational training (a.k.a. technology education)	International Technology Education Association (ITEA) *http://www.iteaconnect.org* Serves technology education teachers	Until the 1980s was the American Industrial Arts Association. Focused on skills with manufacturing, printing, woodworking, and metals.	Focuses on technology-related careers and promoting technological literacy through hands-on experiences that use technology in the context of learning mathematics, science, humanities, and engineering concepts.
#4: Computer systems (a.k.a. educational/ instructional computing)	International Society for Technology in Education (ISTE) *http://www.iste.org* Serves technology-using teachers, administrators, and higher education personnel	Until the 1980s, was the International Council for Computers in Education (ICCE). Focused on computer systems to support and deliver instruction.	Merged with the International Association for Computers in Education (IACE; formerly the Association for Educational Data Systems, or AEDS). Advances uses of technology in K–12 education and teacher education and technology skill standards for teachers and students.

and language. This view brought about a major paradigm shift in vocational training in K–12 schools away from industrial arts curricula centered in woodworking/metals and graphics/printing shops toward technology education courses taught in labs equipped with high-technology stations such as desktop publishing, computer-assisted design (CAD), and robotics systems.

• **Perspective #4: Educational technology as computer systems (a.k.a. educational computing and instructional computing)** — This view began in the 1950s with the advent of computers and gained momentum when they began to be used instructionally in the 1960s. As computers began to transform business and industry practices, both trainers and teachers began to see that computers also had the potential to aid instruction. From the time computers came into classrooms in the 1960s until about 1990, this perspective was known as *educational computing* and encompassed both instructional and administrative support applications. At first, programmers and systems analysts created all applications. But by the 1970s, many of the same educators involved with media, AV communications, and instructional systems also were researching and developing computer applications. By the 1990s, educators began to see computers as part of a combination of technology resources, including media, instructional systems, and computer-based support systems. At that point, educational computing became known as *educational technology*.

How This Textbook Defines *Technology in Education*

Each of these four perspectives on technology in education has contributed to the current body of knowledge about processes and tools to address educational needs. But, as Saettler (1990) points out, no single paradigm that attempts to describe educational technology can characterize satisfactorily what is happening with technology in education today and what will happen in the future. Furthermore, all of the organizations described here seem to be engaged in a struggle to claim the high-profile term *educational technology*. Their often-conflicting views of the role of technology in education confuse newcomers to the field, however, and make it difficult for them to learn the role of technology; the resources and issues differ depending on whose descriptions they hear and which publications they read. This textbook attempts to address the disparate views on this topic in the following ways:

- **Processes** — For the processes, or instructional procedures for applying tools, we look to (1) learning theories based on the sciences of human behavior and (2) applications of technology that help prepare students for future jobs by teaching them skills in using current tools as well as skills in "learning to learn" about tools of the future that have not yet been invented—or even imagined.
- **Tools** — Although this textbook looks at technology tools as an overlapping combination of media, instructional systems, and computer-based support systems, it emphasizes a subset of all of these resources, focusing primarily on computers and their roles in instructional systems. There are three reasons for this focus:
  1. **Capabilities** Computers are more complex and more capable than other types of media such as films or overheads and require more technical knowledge to operate.

  2. **Convergence** Computer systems are moving toward subsuming many other media within their own resources. For example, CD-ROMs and DVDs now store images that once were shown on filmstrips, slides, or videotape. Presentation software (e.g., *PowerPoint*) has largely replaced overhead transparencies.
  3. **Complexity** Computer-based materials such as software lessons and computer-driven media traditionally have been more complicated than more traditional media for educators to integrate into other classroom activities. Educators can see much more easily—some would say even intuitively—how to integrate less technical media such as films or overheads because there are fewer operations and less technology knowledge that is needed to operate and teach with such media.

It is with this rationale in mind that this text assigns the following "evolving" definitions:

Educational technology is a combination of the processes and tools involved in addressing educational needs and problems, with an emphasis on applying the most current tools: computers and other electronic technologies.

Integrating educational technology refers to the process of determining which electronic tools and which methods for implementing them are the most appropriate responses to given classroom situations and problems.

Instructional technology is the subset of educational technology that deals directly with teaching and learning applications (as opposed to educational administrative applications).

Looking Back: How Has the Past Influenced Today's Educational Technology?

Many of today's technology-oriented teachers have been using computer systems only since microcomputers came into common use, but as the timeline in Figure 1.1 shows, a thriving educational computing culture predated microcomputers by 20 years.

A Brief History of Educational Computing Activities and Resources

When integrated circuits made computers both smaller and more accessible to teachers and students, microcomputers became a major turning point in the history of the field of educational technology. Thus, most of the history of computer technology in education is told in two periods: before and after the introduction of microcomputers (Niemiec & Walberg, 1989; Roblyer, 1992). In 1994, yet another technological development, the World Wide Web, transformed educational technology. This development marked the beginning of the third and current era of computers in education.

Pre-microcomputer era. Although this era's computer resources were very different from those of today, both computer companies and educators learned much at this time about the role technology was destined to play in education and who could best shape that role. IBM was a pioneer in this field, producing the first instructional mainframe with multimedia learning stations: the IBM 1500. By the time IBM discontinued it in 1975, some 25 universities were using this system to develop CAI materials. The most prominent of these efforts was led by Stanford University professor and "Grandfather of CAI" Patrick Suppes, who developed the Coursewriter language to create reading and mathematics drill-and-practice lessons. Other similar company- and university-led instructional initiatives ensued: Suppes founded the Computer Curriculum Corporation (CCC); the Digital Equipment Corporation created the PDP-1, the first instructional minicomputer; and the Control Data Corporation (CDC) created the Programmed Logic for Automatic Teaching Operations (PLATO) system and the *Tutor* CAI authoring language.

For about 15 years, these mainframe and minicomputer CAI systems dominated the field. Universities also developed instructional applications for use on these systems. Among these were Brigham Young University's Time-shared Interactive Computer-Controlled Information Television, or TICCIT, system and computer-managed instruction (CMI) systems based on mastery learning models, such as the American Institutes for Research's Program for Learning in Accordance with Needs (PLAN) and Pittsburgh's individually prescribed instruction (IPI). However, these systems were both expensive to buy and complex to operate and maintain, and school district offices began to control their purchase and use. But by the late 1970s, it was apparent that teachers disliked the control of CAI/CMI applications by both district data processing and industry personnel; they began to reject the idea that computers would revolutionize instruction on a business office model.

Microcomputer era. The entire picture changed in the late 1970s with the invention of small, stand-alone, desktop microcomputers, which wrested control of educational computers from companies, universities, and school districts and placed them in the hands of teachers and schools. Several initiatives emerged to shape this new teacher-centered control. A software publishing movement that catered to educators quickly sprang up. With National Science Foundation funding, the Minnesota Educational Computing Consortium (MECC) became the single largest microcomputer software provider, and a multitude of other companies and cottage industries soon followed. To offer advice on how to select quality products, organizations emerged to review software (e.g., Northwest Regional Education Laboratory's MicroSIFT Project, the Educational Products Information Exchange or EPIE), and professional organizations, journals, and magazines began to publish software reviews. As teachers clamored for more input into courseware design, companies created authoring languages (e.g., PILOT, SuperPILOT) and menu-based authoring systems (e.g., GENIS, PASS), but teacher authoring soon proved too time consuming, and interest faded. As schools searched for a way to make CAI more cost effective, districts began to purchase networked integrated learning systems (ILSs) with predeveloped curriculum to help teachers address required standards. Control of computer resources moved once again to central servers controlled by school district offices.

Also at this time, *computer literacy* skills began to be required in school and state curricula, spurred on by computer education experts like Arthur Luehrmann. However, this emphasis was soon dropped due to difficulties in defining and measuring these skills. As a result of Seymour Papert's work (1987), products and research based on the Logo programming language became the focus of the field. The Logo view of technology—that computers should be used as an aid to teach problem solving—began to replace traditional instructional computer uses (e.g., drills, tutorials) as the "best use" of technology. Yet despite its popularity and research showing it could be useful in some contexts, researchers could capture no impact from Logo use on mathematics or other curriculum skills, and interest in Logo, too, waned by the beginning of the 1990s.

Internet era. Just as teachers seemed to be losing interest once again in technology's potential for instruction, the first browser software (*Mosaic*) transformed a formerly text-based Internet into a combination of text and graphics. By the last part of the 1990s, teachers and students joined the throng of users on the "Information Superhighway." By the beginning of the 2000s, email, online (i.e., web-based) multimedia, and videoconferencing became standard tools of Internet users, and portable devices such as the Apple iPhone and Palm Treo have made Internet access ubiquitous as the next decade approaches. As more and more individuals add data plans to their cellular phone and utilize texting in their everyday lives, they demonstrate constant connectedness, which could have a major impact on education in the near future. No longer do you need to be tethered to an Ethernet line to be connected to the world. This ease of access to online resources and communications has

FIGURE 1.1 Computer Technology in Education Timeline

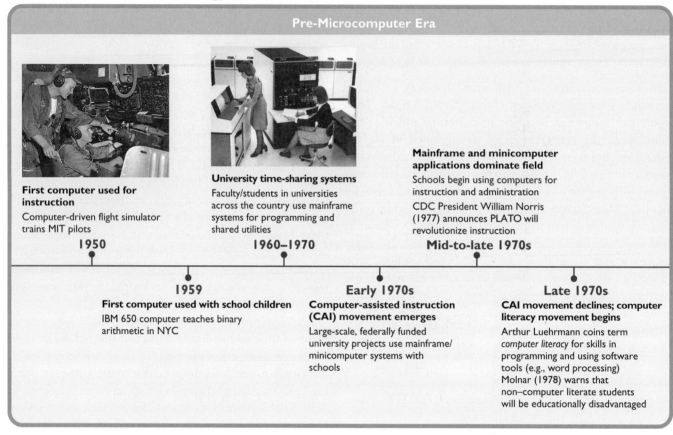

Pre-Microcomputer Era

First computer used for instruction

Computer-driven flight simulator trains MIT pilots

1950

University time-sharing systems

Faculty/students in universities across the country use mainframe systems for programming and shared utilities

1960–1970

Mainframe and minicomputer applications dominate field

Schools begin using computers for instruction and administration

CDC President William Norris (1977) announces PLATO will revolutionize instruction

Mid-to-late 1970s

1959

First computer used with school children

IBM 650 computer teaches binary arithmetic in NYC

Early 1970s

Computer-assisted instruction (CAI) movement emerges

Large-scale, federally funded university projects use mainframe/minicomputer systems with schools

Late 1970s

CAI movement declines; computer literacy movement begins

Arthur Luehrmann coins term *computer literacy* for skills in programming and using software tools (e.g., word processing) Molnar (1978) warns that non–computer literate students will be educationally disadvantaged

---

driven a dramatic increase in distance learning offerings, first in higher education and then in K–12 schools.

As interest in technology in education expanded, the International Society for Technology in Education (ISTE) developed **National Educational Technology Standards (NETS)** for teachers, students, and administrators. These standards are used in every state in the United States and numerous countries throughout the world and have been credited with significantly enhancing learning expectations. As Don Knezek, CEO of ISTE, noted, the NETS have been a symbol of leadership and success.

> Leadership in technology is best illustrated by ISTE's creation of the National Educational Technology Standards (NETS), first published in 1998. ISTE is now leading the creation of the next generation of NETS. In 1998, it was enough to define what students needed to know about and be able to do with technology. Now, we're defining what students need to know and be able to do with technology to learn effectively and live productively in a rapidly changing digital world.
>
> — *Don Knezek, ISTE CEO, 2007*

In 1998, the **National Educational Technology Standards for Students (NETS-S)** were first published,

followed by the most recent version in 2007. These standards communicate "what students should know and be able to do to learn effectively and live productively in an increasingly digital world . . ." The most recent revision of the NETS has been the **National Educational Technology Standards for Teachers (NETS-T)** in 2008 (first published in 2000). These standards "define the fundamental concepts, knowledge, skills, and attitudes for applying technology in educational settings." Figure 1.2 on page 12 outlines ISTE's new NETS-S and NETS-T. Refer to the inside cover of this book for a complete listing of standards and performance indicators. The **National Educational Technology Standards for Administrators (NETS-A)**, first released in 2002, "define what administrators need to know and be able to do in order to discharge their responsibility as leaders in the effective use of technology in our schools."

What Have We Learned from the Past?

In no small part, developments in computer technology have shaped the history of educational technology. However, knowing the history of educational technology is useful only if we apply what we know about the past to future decisions and actions. What have we learned from more than 50 years

FIGURE 1.1 *(continued)*

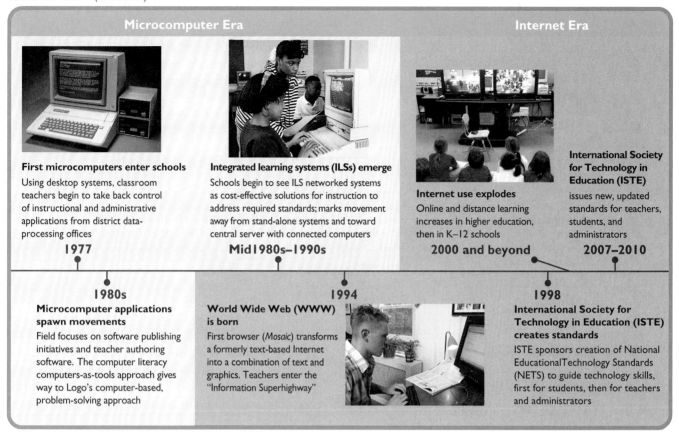

Microcomputer Era

First microcomputers enter schools
Using desktop systems, classroom teachers begin to take back control of instructional and administrative applications from district data-processing offices
1977

Integrated learning systems (ILSs) emerge
Schools begin to see ILS networked systems as cost-effective solutions for instruction to address required standards; marks movement away from stand-alone systems and toward central server with connected computers
Mid1980s–1990s

Internet Era

Internet use explodes
Online and distance learning increases in higher education, then in K–12 schools
2000 and beyond

International Society for Technology in Education (ISTE)
issues new, updated standards for teachers, students, and administrators
2007–2010

1980s
Microcomputer applications spawn movements
Field focuses on software publishing initiatives and teacher authoring software. The computer literacy computers-as-tools approach gives way to Logo's computer-based, problem-solving approach

1994
World Wide Web (WWW) is born
First browser (*Mosaic*) transforms a formerly text-based Internet into a combination of text and graphics. Teachers enter the "Information Superhighway"

1998
International Society for Technology in Education (ISTE) creates standards
ISTE sponsors creation of National EducationalTechnology Standards (NETS) to guide technology skills, first for students, then for teachers and administrators

of applying technology to educational problems that can improve our strategies now? Educators are encouraged to research and develop their own conclusions from the history of educational technology and consider the following points: from these and other descriptions they might read. However, the following points also are important:

- **No technology is a panacea for education** — Great expectations for products such as Logo and ILSs have taught us that even the most current, capable technology resources offer no quick, easy, or universal solutions. Computer-based materials and strategies are usually tools in a larger system and must be integrated carefully with other resources and with teacher activities. Cuban (2001) proposes that technology was "oversold" from the beginning and is not having the system-changing impact many thought it would. Trend (2001) proposes that overuse of distance learning can create more problems than it solves. If we begin with more realistic expectations in mind, we have more potential for success and impact on teaching and learning. Planning must always begin with this question: What specific needs do my students and I have that (any given) resources can help meet?

- **Computer/technological literacy offers a limited integration rationale** — Many parents and educators want technology tools in the classroom primarily because they feel technical skills will give students the technological literacy required to prepare them for the workplace. But an employability rationale provides limited guidelines for how and where to integrate technology. The capabilities of technology resources and methods must be matched to skills that display an obvious need for application in our current system of education (e.g., reading, writing, and mathematics skills); research and information gathering; and problem solving and analysis.

- **Teachers usually do not develop technology materials or curriculum** — Teaching is one of the most time- and labor-intensive jobs in our society. With so many demands on their time, most teachers cannot be expected to develop software or create complex technology-based teaching materials. In the past, publishers, school or district developers, or personnel in funded projects have provided this assistance; this seems unlikely to change in the future.

- **"Technically possible" does not equal "desirable, feasible, or inevitable"** — A popular saying is that today's

FIGURE 1.2 National Educational Technology Standards for Students and Teachers

NETS-S	NETS-T
1. Creativity and Innovation	1. Facilitate and Inspire Student Learning and Creativity
2. Communication and Collaboration	2. Design and Develop Digital-Age Learning Experiences and Assessments
3. Research and Information Fluency	3. Model Digital-Age Work and Learning
4. Critical Thinking, Problem Solving, and Decision Making	4. Promote and Model Digital Citizenship and Responsibility
5. Digital Citizenship	5. Engage in Professional Growth and Leadership
6. Technology Operations and Concepts	

technology is yesterday's science fiction. But science fiction also shows us that technology brings undesirable—as well as desirable—changes. For example, distance technologies have allowed people to attend professional conferences online, rather than by traveling to another location; however, people continue to want to travel and meet face to face. Procedures for human cloning are becoming available, and genetic engineering is increasingly feasible. In education, we can simulate face-to-face communication to an increasingly realistic degree. All of these new technological horizons make it evident that it is time to analyze carefully the implications of each implementation decision. Better technology demands that we become critical consumers of its power and capability. We are responsible for deciding just which science fiction becomes reality.

- **Things change faster than teachers can keep up** — History in this field has shown that resources and accepted methods of applying them will change, often quickly and dramatically. This places a special burden on already overworked teachers to continue learning new resources and changing their teaching methods. Gone are the days—if, indeed, they ever existed—when a teacher could rely on the same handouts, homework, or lecture notes from year to year. Educators may not be able to predict the future of educational technology, but they know that it will be different from the present; that is, they must anticipate and accept the inevitability of change and the need for a continual investment of their time.

- **Older technologies can be useful** — Technology in education is an area especially prone to what

Roblyer (1990) called the "glitz factor." With so little emphasis on finding out what actually works, anyone can propose dramatic improvements. When they fail to appear, educators move on to the next fad. This approach fails to solve real problems, and it draws attention away from the effort to find legitimate solutions. Worse, teachers sometimes throw out methods that had potential but were subject to unrealistic expectations. The past has shown that teachers must be careful, analytical consumers of technological innovation, looking to what has worked in the past to guide their decisions and measure their expectations in the present. Educational practice tends to move in cycles, and "new" methods often are old methods in new guise. In short, teachers must be as informed and analytical as they want their students to become.

- **Teachers always will be more important than technology** — With each new technological development that appears on the horizon, the old question seems to resurface: Will computers replace teachers? The developers of the first instructional computer systems in the 1960s foresaw them replacing many teacher positions; some advocates of today's distance learning methods envision a similar impact on future education. Yet the answer to the old question is the same and is likely to remain so: Good teachers are more essential now than ever. One reason for this was described in Naisbitt's (1984) *Mega Trends:* ". . . whenever new technology is introduced into society, there must be a counterbalancing human response . . . the more high tech (it is), the more high touch (is needed)" (p. 35). We need more teachers who understand the role technology plays in society and in education, who are prepared to take advantage of its power, and who recognize its limitation. In an increasingly technological society, we need more teachers who are both technology savvy and child centered.

Why Use Technology? Using Past Research and Practice to Develop a Sound Rationale

The history of educational technology also teaches us the importance of the "Why use technology?" question. Educators will use new methods if they can see clearly compelling reasons to do so. (See the discussion of relative advantage in Chapter 2.) Many educators look to educational research for evidence of technology's present and potential benefits. However, even though electronic technologies have been in use in education since the 1950s, research results have not made a strong case for its impact on teaching and learning. The number and quality of studies on educational impact have been disappointing (Cradler, 2003; Roblyer, Castine, & King, 1988), and researchers such as Clark (1983, 1985, 1991, 1994) have openly criticized "computer-based effectiveness" research such as meta-analyses to summarize results across studies comparing computer-based and traditional methods. Clark concluded that most such studies suffered from confounding variables that could either increase or decrease achievement. They attempt to show a greater impact on achievement of one delivery method over the other without controlling for other factors such as different instructors, instructional methods, curriculum contents, or novelty. Kozma (1991, 1994) responded to these challenges by proposing that research should look at technology not as an information delivery medium but as "the learner actively collaborating with the medium to construct knowledge" (1991, p. 179).

Although the lack of agreement on integration methods and benefits makes it challenging to state a clear and compelling case for using technology in education, four current conditions combine to make it essential that we do so:

- **Increasing costs of keeping up with technology** — The process of integrating technology effectively into education requires substantial investments in technology infrastructure and teacher training. Educators and policy makers need a solid rationale for why these funds are well spent (Ringstaff & Kelley, 2002).

- **Attacks by technology critics** — Justifying technology expenditures by confirming technology's benefits is increasingly important in light of recent volleys of

criticisms from noneducators (Healey, 1998; Oppenheimer, 2003). These highly publicized attacks focus on the lack of evidence that technology's benefits outweigh the problems it causes (e.g., high costs of updating resources, implementation difficulties, potential dangers to students).

- **Low teacher use** — Recent surveys indicate that even teachers who have sufficient training and access to resources are not using technology as much as had been expected (Cuban, Kirkpatrick, & Peck, 2001; Norris, Sullivan, Poirot, & Soloway, 2003). Clearly, teachers are not hearing a convincing case for technology's benefits.

- **The influence of the accountability movement and the No Child Left Behind (NCLB) Act** — Passed in 2001, the federal NCLB act is predicted to dominate policy and drive funding for some time to come. One of its most controversial requirements is that funding for proposed expenditures must be tied to "scientifically based research" on effectiveness. Like many educational initiatives, technology integration currently lacks this kind of research base.

Research evidence. The **Center for Applied Research in Educational Technology (CARET)**, a funded project of the International Society for Technology in Education (ISTE), has the most comprehensive review of research evidence available on the impact of technology in education (see http://caret.iste.org). The What Works Clearinghouse, established by the U.S. Department of Education's Institute of Education Sciences to provide "high-quality reviews of scientific evidence of the effectiveness of replicable educational interventions," is also a source for this research evidence.

CARET's approach to the rationale for technology use is based on what educators have been saying for years: Simply having students use technology does not raise achievement. The impact depends on the ways the technology is used and the conditions under which applications are implemented. For example, CARET poses the question, "How can technology influence student academic performance?" It answers this question by citing studies that indicate that the application influences performance, not as a delivery system, but as instruction that works under certain circumstances. Table 1.2 summarizes research CARET has found about how and under what conditions technology can enhance teaching and learning.

As the CARET project illustrates, the case for using technology in teaching is one that must be made not just by

Making the Case for Technology Integration

Use the following questions to reflect on issues in technology integration and guide discussions within your class.

1. In his book *High Tech Heretic*, Clifford Stoll (1999) said, "You certainly can get an excellent education without a computer" (p. 32), and "When every student . . . is pressed to become a computer maven, and only the incompetent are allowed to become plumbers, neither our programs nor our pipes will hold water" (p. 123). After reading Chapter 1, how would you respond to this position?

2. Saettler (1990) said, "Computer information systems are not just objective recording devices. They also reflect concepts, hopes, beliefs, attitudes" (p. 539). What concepts, hopes, beliefs, and attitudes do you think our past and current uses of technology in education reflect?

3. Richard Clark's now-famous comment about the impact of computers on learning was that the best current evidence is that media are mere vehicles that deliver instruction but do not influence student achievement any more than the truck that delivers our groceries causes change in our nutrition (Clark, 1983, p. 445). Why do you think this statement has had such a dramatic impact on the field of educational technology? How would you respond to it?

4. In his article on "cybercheating," Gardiner (2001) says, ". . . I understand that the temptation of exchanging hours of research and writing for a few minutes of searching seems like a good deal as the deadline looms. . . . I wondered how I could ever overcome the power of the Internet and the lure of cheating" (p. 174). Can you suggest arguments that would help persuade students that cybercheating, while easy and quick, is not in their best interests?

isolating variables that make a difference, but by combining them. Practitioners have cited over the years a number of reasons why we should integrate technology into teaching.

To Motivate Students

- **Gaining their attention** — Teachers say technology's visual and interactive qualities can direct students' attention toward learning tasks.

- **Supporting manual operations during high-level learning** — Students are more motivated to learn com-

plex skills (e.g., writing compositions and solving algebraic equations) when technology tools help them do the low-level skills involved (e.g., making corrections to written drafts or doing arithmetic).

- **Illustrating real-world relevance through highly visual presentations** — When students can see that high-level math and science skills have real-life applications, it is no longer just "school work"; they are more willing to learn skills that have clear value to their future life and work.

- **Engaging them through production work** — Students who learn by creating their own products with technologies such as word processing, multimedia, hypermedia, and other technology products report higher engagement in learning and a greater sense of pride in their achievements (Doering, Beach, & O'Brien, 2007; Doering & Veletsianos, 2007; Franklin, 1991; Taylor, 1989; Tibbs, 1989; Volker, 1992).

- **Connecting them with audiences for their writing** — Educators say that students are much more motivated to write and do their best production work when they publish it on the web, since others outside the classroom will see their work (Cohen & Riel, 1989; Doering & Beach, 2002; Doering, Beach, & O'Brien, 2007).

- **Engaging learners through real-world situations and collaborations** — Students who see the application of what they are studying as authentic and real world are motivated by the application to their daily lives (Doering & Veletsianos, 2008, p. 8).

To Enhance Instruction

- **Supplying interaction and immediate feedback to support skill practice** — Software such as the drill-

Today's young people interact with technology on a daily basis. Integrating technology and education taps into their comfort zone.

TABLE 1.2 Results from CARET's Reviews of Research

Why Use Technology?	When Does Technology Work Best?
Studies show that it can:	**Studies show that it works best when it:**
• Influence student academic performance;	• Directly supports the curriculum objectives being assessed;
• Develop higher order thinking and problem solving;	• Provides opportunities for student collaboration;
• Improve student motivation, attitude, and interest in learning;	• Adjusts for student ability and prior experience, and provides feedback to the student and teacher about student performance or progress with the application;
• Help prepare students for the workforce; and	• Is integrated into the typical instructional day;
• Address the needs of low-performing and at-risk students and those with learning handicaps.	• Provides opportunities for students to design and implement projects that extend the curriculum content being assessed by a particular standardized test; and
	• Is used in environments where teachers, the school community, and school and district administrators support the use of technology.

Source: The Center for Applied Research in Educational Technology (CARET), http://caret.iste.edu.

and-practice type offers many students the privacy, self-pacing, and immediate feedback they need to comprehend and retain lower level skills.

- **Helping students visualize underlying concepts in unfamiliar or abstract topics** — Simulations and other interactive software tools have unique abilities to illustrate science and mathematics concepts. Highly trained principles become easier to understand.

- **Illustrating connections between skills and real-life applications** — Technology tools support problem-based learning that helps students see where high-level math and science skills apply.

- **Letting students study systems in unique ways** — Students use tools such as spreadsheets and simulations to answer "what if" questions that they would not be able to do easily by hand or that would not be feasible at all without the benefits of technology.

- **Giving access to unique information sources and populations** — The Internet connects students with information, research, data, and expertise not available locally.

- **Supplying self-paced learning for capable students** — Self-directed students can learn on their own with software tutorials and/or distance educational materials. They can surge ahead of the class or tackle topics not offered by the school.

- **Allowing access to learning opportunities** — Students with disabilities depend on technology to compensate for vision, hearing, and/or manual dexterity they need to read, interact in class, and do products to show what they have learned.

- **Providing opportunities and support for cooperative learning** — Although students can do small-group work without technology, teachers report that students are often more motivated to work cooperatively on hypermedia, database, and website production projects.

To Make Student and Teacher Work More Productively

- **Saving time on production tasks** — Software tools such as word processing, desktop publishing, and spreadsheets allow quick and easy corrections to reports, presentations, budgets, and publications.

- **Grading and tracking student work** — Integrated learning systems and handheld computers help teachers quickly assess and track student progress.

- **Providing faster access to information sources** — Students use the Internet and email to do research and collect data that would take much longer to gather by traditional delivery methods.

- **Saving money on consumable materials** — Software tools such as drill-and-practice simulations save schools by taking the place of many materials (e.g., worksheets, handouts, dissection animals) that are used and replaced each year.

To Help Students Learn and Sharpen Their Information Age Skills

- **Technological literacy** — Technology such as word processing, spreadsheets, simulations, multimedia, and the Internet have become increasingly essential in many job areas. Students who use these in school have a head start on what to do in the workplace.

- **Informational literacy** — Students learn skills that Johnson and Eisenberg (1996) call the "Big Six" (task definition, information seeking strategies, location and access, use of information, synthesis, and evaluation).

- **Visual literacy** — Images are increasingly replacing text as communication media. Students must learn to interpret, understand, and appreciate the meaning of visual messages; communicate more effectively through applying the basic principles and concepts of visual design; produce visual messages using the computer and other technology; and use visual thinking to conceptualize solutions to problems (Christopherson, 1997, p. 173).

When viewed together with research findings, these reasons pose a powerful rationale for why technology must become as commonplace in education as it is in other areas of society. They also help point out specific ways to integrate technology into teaching and learning. A summary of the elements underlying a rationale for using technology in teaching is given in Table 1.3.

TABLE 1.3 Why Use Technology? A Summary of Elements Underlying a Rationale

1. Motivation:
- Ways of gaining learner attention
- Support for manual operations in high-level learning
- Illustrations of real-world relevance
- Engagement in production work
- Connections with distance audiences

2. Enhanced instructional methods:
- Interaction and immediate feedback
- Visual demonstrations
- Illustrative connections between skills and applications
- Opportunities to study systems in unique ways
- Unique information sources and populations
- Self-paced learning
- Access to learning opportunities
- Cooperative learning

3. Increased productivity:
- Saving time on production tasks
- Grading and tracking student work
- Faster access to information sources
- Saving money on consumable materials

4. Required Information Age skills:
- Technological literacy
- Information literacy
- Visual literacy

Looking Around: What Factors Shape the Current Climate for Technology in Education?

The history of educational technology shows us that two general characteristics shape the field's direction and the impact it will have on teaching and learning: (1) the capabilities of resources available at a given time in the evolution of technology; and (2) the combination of current societal influences, educational trends and priorities, economic factors, and company marketing initiatives. This section gives an overview of current technology resources, how they are used, and prevailing factors and issues that are shaping their impact.

Current Educational Technology Systems, Configurations, and Applications

Figure 1.3 provides a graphical overview of the technical resources available for teachers to use. Note that all technology integration strategies require a combination of **hardware** or equipment (desktop, **laptop**, or handheld computer, along with appropriate input/output devices such as printers and scanners) and **software** or programs written to perform various kinds of educational applications. As Table 1.4 shows, computer equipment can be arranged or configured in various ways, each of which is suited to supporting specific types of integration strategies. Software to support educational technology applications includes these types:

- **Instructional** — Programs designed to teach students skills or information through demonstrations, examples, explanation, or problem solving
- **Productivity** — Programs designed to help teachers and students plan, develop materials, and keep records

The availability of computers and other technology in classrooms and computer labs encourages proficiency and comfort at a young age.

FIGURE 1.3 The Educational Technology "Tree of Knowledge"

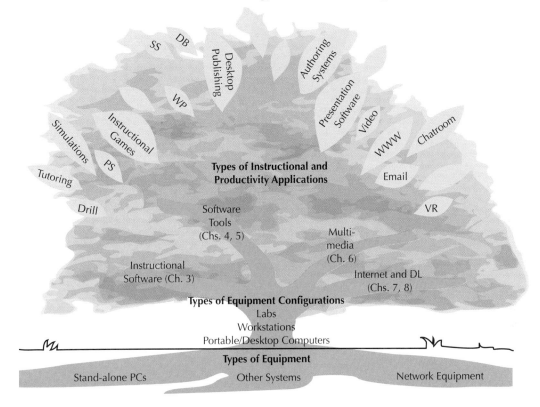

• **Administrative** — Programs that administrators at school, state, and district levels use to support record keeping and exchanges of information among various agencies.

Integration strategies described in this textbook focus on instructional and productivity applications that teachers implement.

An Overview of Today's Big Issues in Education and Technology: Societal, Educational, Cultural/Equity, and Legal/Ethical

One reason that teaching is so challenging is that it occurs in an environment that mirrors—and sometimes magnifies—some of society's most profound and problematic issues. Adding computers to this mix makes the situation even more complex. Yet to integrate technology successfully into their teaching, educators must recognize and be prepared to work in this environment with all of its subtleties and complexities. Some of today's important issues and their implications for technological trends in education are described in the following sections.

Go to MyEducationLab, select the topic "Assessment," and go to the "Assignments, Activities, and Applications" section. Access the video "Student Achievement Increases" and consider how technology can affect what and how students are able to learn. Complete the activity that follows.

Societal Issues Shaping Current Technology Uses

Economic, political, and social trends have a great impact on whether or not innovations take hold, have limited acceptance, or are ignored completely. Societal issues helping to shape the current climate for educational technology include the following:

• **Economic conditions** — Recent economic downturns in the U.S. economy have meant decreased education funding. Experts predict that funds will not return to previous levels when the economy improves.

• **Anti-technology positions** — Some critics say that ubiquitous technology interferes with privacy and complicates daily life. Others feel that teaching/learning benefits have not been clearly established and that technology is not as important as other programs that are being cut (e.g., music, arts). Still others say that computer use poses potential health hazards and that Internet cyberporn and predators pose other risks, especially to young users.

• **Impact of the NCLB Act of 2001** — Among other things, the NCLB act requires that all government-funded programs demonstrate benefits with "scientifically based research" and that schools demonstrate that all students are meeting standards.

TABLE 1.4   Types of Technology Facilities and How They Are Used

Types of Facilities	Uses	Benefits	Limitations/ Problems
Laboratories (usually 20–30 networked computers)			
All labs		Centralized resources are easier to maintain and secure; networking software can monitor individual performance in groups.	Need permanent staff to supervise and maintain resources. Students must leave their classrooms to use them.
Special-purpose labs	• Programming or technical courses • Technology education/ vocational courses (e.g., with CAD, robotics, desktop publishing stations) • MIDI music labs • Labs dedicated to content area(s), e.g., mathematics/ science, foreign languages • For use by Chapter or Title III students • Multimedia production work • Teacher work labs	Permanent setups of group resources specific to the needs of certain content areas or types of students.	Usually exclude groups who do not meet special purpose. Isolate resources.
General-use computer labs (open to all school groups)	Student productivity tasks (e.g., word processing, multimedia production); class demonstrations; student project work	Accommodate varied uses by different groups.	Difficult to schedule specific uses. Usually available to only one class at a time.
Library/media center labs	Same as for general-use labs	Same as for general-use labs, but permanent staff are already present. Ready access to all materials to promote integration of computer and noncomputer resources.	Same as for general-use labs. Staff members need special training. Classes cannot usually do production or group work that might bother other users of the library/media center.

This combination of social conditions means that educators increasingly are forced to set priorities for scarce education dollars. In light of this and recent attacks on technology by those outside education, it is ever more important to use research results and best-practice findings to establish a sound rationale for technology use and justify technology expenses and potential risks to student users. Increasingly, funding for technology-based strategies will be dependent on these results and findings. In light of increasing accountability requirements, it also seems likely that schools will begin emphasizing the use of computer systems to track student progress.

Educational Issues Shaping Current Technology Uses

Trends in the educational system are intertwined with trends in technology and society. Three kinds of educational issues have special implications for the ways technology is used in teaching and learning:

- **Standards movement** — All content areas and states have skill standards students must meet to pass courses and to get degrees and certification. High-stakes tests on standards determine success. This movement may drive a trend toward using technology in ways that help teachers and students pass tests and meet required standards.

TABLE 1.4 *(continued)*

Mobile Computers (a.k.a. computers on wheels or COWs)			
Mobile workstations	Demonstrations, short-term uses	Stretch resources by sharing them among many users; supply on-demand access.	Moving equipment can cause breakage and other maintenance problems. Sometimes difficult to get through doors or up stairs. Can increase security problems.
Mobile labs (complete set of computers, usually 15–30 handhelds or laptops on carts)	Individual student or teacher production and data-gathering tasks; teacher assessment tasks (e.g., with handheld devices)	Same as for mobile work-stations, but serve more students at one time.	Same as for mobile workstations.
Classroom Computers			
Classroom workstations (usually 2–5 computers with a printer)	Learning stations with individual tutoring and drills; whole-class demonstrations; Internet research and production tasks for cooperative learning groups	Easily accessible to teachers and students.	No immediate technical assistance available to teachers. Only part of class can use at one time.
Stand-alone classroom computer (one computer, often connected by network to school server)	Whole-class demonstrations; teacher email; small group tasks	Same as for classroom workstations.	Same as for classroom workstations.

- **Reliance on the Internet and on distance education** — Increasing numbers of virtual K–12 courses are being offered, and virtual high schools are becoming commonplace in U.S. education. This means that students could have increased access to high-quality courses and degrees. However, virtual learning takes special skills not all students have, and dropout rates from distance courses are higher, which could further widen the **Digital Divide**. Some critics say that distance learning is not as empowering as a face-to-face educational experience.

- **Debate over directed vs. inquiry-based, constructivist instructional methods** — Educators disagree on the proper roles of traditional, teacher-directed learning versus student-led, inquiry-based methods. Long-used and well-validated directed uses of technology have been shown to be effective for addressing standards, but many educators see them as passé. Inquiry-based, constructivist methods are considered more modern, but it is less clear how they address required standards.

Cultural and Equity Issues Shaping Current Technology Uses

The following three factors reflect the complex racial and cultural fabric of our society, and they continue to have a great impact on technology use:

- **Digital Divide** — A phrase coined by Lloyd Morrisett, former president of the Markle Foundation, *Digital Divide* refers to a discrepancy in access to technology resources among socioeconomic groups. The single greatest factor determining access is economic status, although race and gender may also play a role, depending on the type of technology. Recent studies (Corporation for Public Broadcasting, 2003) find that while children from all income levels have greatly increased their Internet use, children from underserved populations (e.g., low-income and minority students) still lag far behind other students in home and school access.

- **Racial and gender equity** — Technology use remains dominated by males and certain ethnic groups.

Studies show that when compared with males and whites, females, African Americans, and Hispanic minorities use computers less and enter careers in math, science, and technology areas at lower rates. Many educators believe these two findings are correlated: Lower use of technology leads to lower entrance into technical careers. Even where computers are available in schools, there tends to be unequal access to certain kinds of activities. For example, children in Title I programs may have access to computers, but they use them mainly for remedial work rather than for email, multimedia production, and other personal empowerment activities.

- **Special needs** — Devices and methods are available to help students compensate for their physical and mental deficits and allow them equal access to technology and learning opportunities. However, technological interventions that could help students with special needs are difficult to purchase and implement and often go unused. Parents clamor for the technology resources guaranteed their children by federal laws, but schools often claim insufficient funding to address these special needs.

As Molnar pointed out in his landmark 1978 article "The Next Great Crisis in American Education: Computer Literacy," the power of technology is a two-edged sword, especially for education. While it presents obvious potential for changing education and empowering teachers and students, technology also may further divide members of our society along socioeconomic, ethnic, and cultural lines and widen the gender gap. Teachers will lead the struggle to make sure technology use promotes, rather than conflicts with, the goals of a democratic society.

Technology can be a major equalizer in learning for all students.

Legal and Ethical Issues Shaping Current Technology Uses

In many ways, technology users represent society in a microcosm. The legal and ethical issues educators face reflect those of the larger society. The five major kinds of ethical and legal issues, discussed next, have great impact on how technology activities are implemented:

- **Viruses/hacking** — Illegal activities of two kinds are on the rise: (1) **Viruses**, or programs written to cause damage or do mischief, cause problems ranging from lost files to systems being shut down for weeks. (2) **Hackers** are breaking into online systems to access personal data on students, accomplish identify theft, and do other malicious acts. To combat these problems, schools are forced to install **firewalls** and **virus protection software** to safeguard classroom computers, and to spend larger portions of technology funds each year on preventing and cleaning up after illegal activities.

- **The new plagiarism** — Greater online access to full-text documents has resulted in increased incidents of "cybercheating," or students using materials they find on the Internet as their own. Sites have emerged to help teachers catch plagiarizers, and the number of educational organizations and teachers using them is increasing.

- **Privacy/safety** — Increasing amounts of students' personal information are being placed online, and students are spending more time using online environments — educational and non-educational. Social networking sites such as Facebook and MySpace are incredibly popular with adolescents. At the same time, studies show a high incidence of attempts by online predators to contact students, and objectionable material is readily available and easy to access. To address these concerns, schools are requiring students/parents to sign an Authorized Use Policy (AUP) and putting procedures in place to safeguard access to students' personal information. Schools have also been put on notice to supervise carefully all student use of the Internet and to install filtering software to prevent access to objectionable materials.

- **Copyright** — Online availability of full-text publications is increasing, and distance courses are posting more materials in online course management systems. To make sure they comply with copyright laws, schools are making teachers and students aware of policies about copyright/AUP and fair use of published materials.

- **Illegal downloads/software piracy** — An increasing number of sites offer ways to download copies of software or other media without paying for them, and software and media companies are prosecuting more offenders.

Top Ten

Issues Shaping Today's Technology Uses in Education

1. **Accountability and the standards movement** — Educators want to know (a) how technology can help students meet required curriculum standards and (b) what role technology skills play in children's education.

2. **Funding for educational technology** — As technology costs grow and education funds wane, policy makers ask, "How can we justify spending scarce education dollars on technology?"

3. **The Digital Divide** — Since technology access differs between wealthier and poorer schools, people want to know if technology is deepening the economic chasm between rich and poor.

4. **Racial and gender equity** — Science, technology, and engineering careers remain dominated by males and certain ethnic groups; educators say more student involvement in technology at earlier levels could change this picture.

5. **The role of distance education** — Virtual schools are springing up around the country. Parents wonder: (a) Can all students succeed in online environments? and (b) Will students learn as much as in face-to-face classrooms?

6. **Privacy and safety** — As more student data go online and students spend more time on the Internet, measures have to be put in place to limit access to personal data and to protect students from online predators.

7. **Viruses and hacking** — The online community is seeing an unprecedented number of viruses and illegal entries into networks. Schools are forced to spend precious funds on measures to protect themselves.

8. **Online plagiarism** — Students have easy access to papers and projects they can turn in as their own work. Teachers have to be on the alert for plagiarism and use online sources to check suspicious work.

9. **Anti-technology sentiments** — In light of the scarcity of research on technology's impact on indicators of education quality, critics of educational technology are on the attack.

10. **Information literacy** — Society's increasing dependence on technology to communicate information means that students must learn the skills to use information technologies effectively.

Despite the ease of copying or downloading free materials, teachers are tasked with modeling and teaching ethical behaviors with respect to software and media.

The culture, language, and problems of the larger society also emerge among technology users, and their activities reflect many of the rules of conduct and values of society in general. Teachers who use technology are faced with addressing the problems that arise when people try to work outside those values and rules.

The most important of these issues in terms of their impact in shaping what we can and must do with technology in education are summarized in the *Top Ten* feature. What we are able to do to apply the power of technology to enhance education will be shaped primarily by how we are able to respond to these major issues.

Looking Ahead: What Developments in Technology Integration Are Emerging?

Emerging Trends in Hardware and Software Development

Visions of the future are suffused with images of technologies that may seem magical and far-fetched now, just as cellular phones and fax machines seemed only a few decades ago. And, although the technology images we see when we look into the future of education are murky and ill defined, we know that they will mirror current technical trends and the goals and priorities we set today for tomorrow's education. As with so many "miraculous" technologies, the question is how we will take advantage of their capabilities to bring about the kind of future education systems our society wants and our economy needs.

Future technological developments will have such a profound impact on education that the federally funded Institute for the Advancement of Emerging Technologies in Education (IAETE) at the Appalachian Educational Laboratory (AEL) was founded specifically to study and document leading-edge technologies with promising educational practices. IAETE's latest findings on innovations in education and the emerging technologies associated with them are documented at its website (http://www.iaete.org) and in its annual publication, *INSIGHT*.

Just as the Internet changed communications capabilities in ways that shaped educational practices, other

Wireless technology offers teachers and students endless capabilities.

technological developments will have equally dramatic consequences for schools. One such technology may be **radio-frequency identification (RFID)**, which consists of a computer chip and an electronic monitoring system that tracks the location of the chip and can update information on it. First introduced in department stores to monitor inventory and prevent theft of goods, RFID is already being proposed to track student attendance, increase school security, and monitor the location of library resources (Murray, 2003b). Some educators envision even more school-related RFID uses and say it has the potential to save time that can be redirected to teaching activities. However, six other trends in technological developments, summarized in Table 1.5, promise to have even more direct impact on teaching and learning activities: **wireless connectivity**, merged technologies, handheld devices, high-speed communications, **virtual systems** and **artificial intelligence**.

- **Trend #1: Wireless connectivity** — A universal trend across computer systems, wireless connections are simplifying computer networks by reducing the number of required cables and allowing greater freedom of movement. Instead of each computer having a "drop" or cabled access point to the network, wireless networks have one drop through which many computer devices can access the network. One result is mobile labs on a cart that contains from 10 to 30 laptops and a wireless access point that can be plugged into a network jack. Some schools have "hot spots" or drops around the building so that students can use a portable computer anywhere in the school.

- **Trend #2: Merging of technologies** — An ever-increasing number of devices combine communications capabilities that were once housed in individual devices. For example, cellular phones now allow not only voice communications, but they also can create and send digital images and text messages. Handheld devices often incorporate the power of desktop computers and the capabilities of digital cameras.

- **Trend #3: Developments in portable devices** — Computers are becoming increasingly portable, which allows teachers and students greater flexibility in learning environments. Laptops are becoming more popular, along with **handheld computers** such as the Apple iPhone and extremely portable PCs such as the Asus Eee PC, a 9" laptop, or Apple's MacBook Air. Many schools are replacing their desktop computers with these portable devices so that learning activities need not be confined to classrooms or school buildings.

- **Trend #4: Availability of high-speed communications** — Imitating the gradual spread of electrical

TABLE 1.5 Emerging Technology Trends and Implications for Education

Emerging Trends	Examples	Implications for Technology Integration Strategies
Wireless connectivity	• Mobile labs • School-wide hot spots (wireless connections to networks)	• Mobility makes it easier for teachers to plan for and implement activities. • Easier access to networks makes it easier to obtain materials, update assessments.
Merging of technologies	• Handheld devices with built-in communications and digital imaging capabilities	• Combined capabilities mean fewer devices to buy and keep track of during instruction.
Developments in portable devices	• Laptops • Multiple-function handheld devices • Tablet PCs	• Portability makes it easier for each student to have a computer; thus allowing individualized strategies. • Students can write and do research from any location. • Teachers can do continuous monitoring and assessment.
Availability of high-speed communications	• In homes: Digital Subscriber Lines (DSL) and cable modems • In schools: TI lines, DSL, and cable modems	• High-quality, reliable voice and visual communications make distance learning more like face-to-face classrooms. • More students have access to virtual courses and degree programs.
Visual immersion systems	• Head-mounted VR systems • Augmented reality systems • 3-D imaging systems	• Students with physical limitations can simulate movement in real situations. • Simulated systems allow more realistic and authentic presentations of information.
Intelligent applications	• Intelligent grading systems • Intelligent tutors	• Computer systems grade complex performances (e.g., writing) more quickly and reliably than teachers. • Computer tutors adapt more quickly to individual students' learning needs.

power and telephone access into all parts of the United States during the early 1900s, high-speed Internet connections are becoming increasingly ubiquitous in the 2000s. Faster connections made possible by Digital Subscriber Lines (DSLs), cable modems, high-speed wifi, enhanced mobile networks speeds (e.g., Edge and 3G) mean higher quality, more reliable voice and video communications, which are the necessary ingredients in making distance learning environments emulate face-to-face ones.

• **Trend #5: Visual immersion systems** — Once only dreamed of in science fiction, computer-generated environments that immerse students in simulated worlds are becoming increasingly available. Current applications include full-immersion systems with head-mounted displays, augmented reality systems, and 3-D models on computer screens. Although full-immersion systems are still too expensive for most schools, experimental applications continue to appear sporadically. Virtual 3-D models on computer screens are becoming more prevalent (Parham, 2003; Thatcher, 2003). Some experts predict increased use of augmented reality systems, which allow people with computer-powered goggles to view real-world images with overlays from **global positioning system (GPS)** satellites (Augmented reality, 2002).

• **Trend #6: Intelligent applications** — Artificial intelligence (AI) has never had the same degree of impact on education as it has had on activities such as chess playing and industrial training and problem solving. However, applications of so-called "intelligent programs" (software that emulates human thought processes and responses to situations) continue to appear in education as researchers explore ways to use AI-type capabilities to solve persistent problems in instruction and assessment.

Implications of New Technologies for Teachers and Students

The six trends just discussed promise significant changes in the way education is carried out. The changes in educational practices are gradual, and current examples are usually limited to pilot programs and studies. However, the technologies described here are advancing so quickly in other areas of society, it is easy to imagine a future where they are commonplace in education.

- **Flexible learning environments** — No longer do students have to leave classrooms for "pull-out" activities in labs. With wireless communications and portable devices, now the lab comes to the students, and learning environments can be located beyond the walls of classrooms and schools. Students can take notes, gather data, or do research from wherever they are and have easy, fast access to resources such as writing labs and digital production labs. Tinker, Staudt, and Walton (2002) describe an example of the power this flexibility offers on a field trip to do scientific observations, and Curtis, Williams, Norris, O'Leary, and Soloway (2003) describe how to manage and carry out lessons that maximize the flexibility of handheld devices. One study has already indicated that teachers find handheld devices easy to integrate into classroom activities (Branigan, 2002a).

- **Adaptable assessment options** — New technologies are already having an impact on how educators assess students, and more changes seem likely in the future. Teachers are beginning to use handheld devices to make monitoring students' progress more immediate and continuous (Hudgins, 2001). As standards and accountability loom ever larger on the horizon, continuous assessment becomes more important, making it easier to guide student progress and to ensure success on tests. Scharber, Dexter, and Riedel (2005) studied the design, development, and effectiveness of an automated essay scorer with preservice teachers solving technology integration cases where the computer automatically graded and gave feedback to the teachers' responses. The Pennsylvania Department of Education found that an intelligent system for scoring the essay portion of state-mandated tests matched an expert reviewer's scores more often than reviewers matched each other (Branigan, 2000). This indicates that faster, cheaper updates to current methods of as-

sessing complex performances such as writing may not be far away.

- **Reliance on distance learning** — As high-speed connections become more readily available to schools and homes, the number of students learning through virtual systems is steadily increasing (Zucker & Kozma, 2003). Many states sponsor a virtual high school, and many organizations offer courses for junior high and even elementary students (NACOL, 2008; Roblyer, 2003b; Setzer, Lewis, & Greene, 2005). Though currently fraught with controversy, distance learning for K–12 students eventually will have the same degree of impact on reshaping schools as it has had on redefining higher education.

- **Support for people with disabilities** — New technologies continue to make the most dramatic advances in opportunities for people with disabilities. Kurzweil (2003) describes immersion systems and intelligent programs that help people with sensory impairments and physical disabilities function effectively in learning situations. Branigan (2002b) describes a **virtual reality (VR)** project that has dramatically improved the performance of students with hearing impairments. Because the No Child Left Behind Act requires that all students, including those with disabilities, meet high standards of achievement, it seems likely that schools will increase their investments in new assistive technologies (Assistive technologies, 2003).

Skills for the Future: ISTE NETS for Students, Teachers, and Administrators

Clearly, 21st-century educators will have to deal with issues that their predecessors could not even have imagined. Both they and the students they teach must have skills and knowledge that will prepare them to meet these new challenges.

The National Council for the Accreditation of Teacher Education (NCATE), the agency responsible for accrediting colleges of education, has joined with ISTE not only in establishing standards for teaching about technology in education but also in saying that schools of education should increase their emphasis on the use of technology in teacher training (NCATE, 1997). Thus, the ISTE National Educational Technology Standards (NETS) for Teachers have become the benchmark for technology infusion in teacher education programs. NETS for Teachers are specified for each chapter and in technology integration idea activities in this text. It is important to note the relationship between the NETS for Teachers and NETS for Students, as shown in Figure 1.2 on page 12 and in the front of this book. NETS for Students are considered to be the basic skills that students—and their teachers—should meet.

FIGURE 1.4 Electronic Teaching Portfolios: How to Create and Use Them

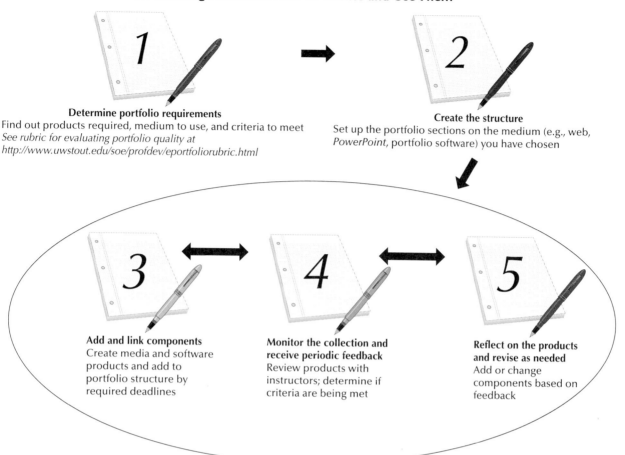

1 Determine portfolio requirements
Find out products required, medium to use, and criteria to meet
See rubric for evaluating portfolio quality at http://www.uwstout.edu/soe/profdev/eportfoliorubric.html

2 Create the structure
Set up the portfolio sections on the medium (e.g., web, *PowerPoint*, portfolio software) you have chosen

3 Add and link components
Create media and software products and add to portfolio structure by required deadlines

4 Monitor the collection and receive periodic feedback
Review products with instructors; determine if criteria are being met

5 Reflect on the products and revise as needed
Add or change components based on feedback

How Teachers Can Demonstrate Their Skills: Electronic Portfolios

Many teacher preparation programs require their candidates to develop a teaching *portfolio* as they go through the program. Portfolios are a collection of the student's work products over time, arranged so that they and others can see how their skills have developed and progressed. They also include criteria for selecting and judging content. The portfolio concept originated in higher education with colleges of arts, music, and architecture, areas in which work could not be measured well through traditional tests. Instead of final exams, these students had to have a professional portfolio when they graduated to demonstrate their level of accomplishment in their field. For today's technology-integrated curriculum, which often calls for multimedia work products, many teachers are turning to student **electronic portfolios** as the assessment strategy of choice. Although older students could decide on their own portfolio format, teachers usually provide the portfolio structure and tell students how to fill in the content. Teachers can choose from several kinds of resources for these structures:

- **"Ready-made" software packages** — These include *Learner Profile* (Sunburst), *Grady Profile* (Auerbach), and *My ePortfolio* (Learning Quest). Teachers can use these packages instead of creating their own structure. These systems usually are built on database software, with fields for attaching files of written and visual products.

- **PDF documents** — To store and display documents (with or without graphics), teachers can use *Adobe Acrobat* to create electronic versions of pages. These are essentially "pictures of pages" and are easy to store and share with others.

- **Multimedia authoring software** — Early multimedia structures were in programs such as *HyperStudio*, but some teachers now structure portfolios with packages such as Microsoft *PowerPoint*, Apple *Keynote*, Macromedia *Director*, Travantis *Lectora*, or eZedia's *eZediaQTI*. These packages allow for advanced, sophisticated video and audio presentations.

- **Databases** — Relational database software such as *FileMaker Pro* is helpful to teachers who must keep track of many students' work. They offer teachers the advantage of cataloguing work and creating profiles of achievement across groups of students.

- **Websites** — Portfolios can be posted on the Internet, where they can be more easily shared with others. Like multimedia packages, these portfolios can offer sophisticated video and audio presentations. Companies that act as hosts for electronic portfolios are listed at http://electronicportfolios.com/portfolios/bookmarks.html#vendors.

- **Video** — Although analog video offered only a low-cost, linear format, digital video offers much more flexible, interactive formats for displaying portfolio elements.

Figure 1.4 shows a suggested sequence to follow in creating an electronic portfolio. Also see Barrett (2000) and her collection of portfolio resources at http://electronicportfolios.com/ for more advice on portfolio development and Hanfland (1999) for tips on portfolio development for young children.

Interactive Summary

The following is a summary of the main points covered in this chapter.

1. **Four perspectives that define educational technology:** The following educational technology organizations represent the four views of educational technology described in this chapter:

   - **AECT** — Technology as media and AV communications

   - **ISPI** — Technology as instructional systems and instructional design

   - **ITEA** — Technology as vocational training (a.k.a., technology education)

   - **ISTE** — Technology as computer systems.

2. **History of educational computing technology and what we have learned from it:** The three eras in the history of educational computing/technology were:

   - **Pre-microcomputer era (1950–late 1970s)** — University projects use mainframe and minicomputer systems to deliver instruction in schools; the computer literacy movement begins.

   - **Microcomputer era (late 1970s–1994)** — Microcomputers enter schools and spawn the software publishing, Logo, and ILS movements.

   - **Internet era (1994–present)** — The first web browser (*Mosaic*) makes possible travel on the Information Superhighway.

3. **A rationale for using educational technology:** Elements of a rationale for using technology in education include increased motivation, unique instructional capabilities, support for new instructional approaches, increased productivity, and required skills for the Information Age. The research rationale for using technology in teaching is documented at the CARET website.

4. **Current educational technology systems, configurations, and applications:** One of the primary concerns in setting up and maintaining any computer lab is accessibility for all users.

5. **Factors shaping the climate for technology integration:** These include current educational technology systems, configurations, and applications. Issues include

   - **Societal** (economic, anti-technology positions, impact of the No Child Left Behind Act)

   - **Educational** (standards movement, reliance on Internet and distance education, and debate over directed vs. constructivist methods)

   - **Cultural and equity** (Digital Divide, racial and gender equity, special needs)

   - **Legal and ethical** (viruses/hacking, online plagiarism, privacy/safety, copyright, illegal downloads/software piracy).

6. **Emerging trends in hardware/software development:** These include:

   - Wireless connectivity

   - Merging of technologies

   - Developments in portable devices

   - Increasingly high-speed communications (e.g., through cable modem and DSL)

   - Visual immersion systems

   - Intelligent applications

7. **New skills for the future:** The International Society for Technology in Education established the National Educational Technology Skills (NETS) for students, teachers, and administrators. These standards document skills that will be essential in order to take advantage of emerging technology capabilities. People often use electronic portfolios to demonstrate technology and other skills they have attained.

Key Terms

- artificial intelligence
- Center for Applied Research in Educational Technology (CARET)
- Digital Divide
- educational technology
- electronic portfolio
- firewall
- global positioning system (GPS)
- hacker
- handheld computer
- hardware

- instructional technology
- laptop computer
- National Educational Technology Standards (NETS)
- National Educational Technology Standards for Students (NETS-S)
- National Educational Technology Standards for Teachers (NETS-T)
- National Educational Technology Standards for Administrators (NETS-A)
- No Child Left Behind (NCLB) Act

- radio-frequency identification (RFID)
- software
- software piracy
- technology education
- virtual reality (VR)
- virtual system
- virus
- virus protection software
- wireless connectivity

Web-Enrichment Activities

1. **Research on uses of educational technology** — Use the ISTE Center for Applied Research in Educational Technology (CARET) website at http://caret.iste.org/ to learn what research can teach us about effective uses of technology for learning. Use the Search feature to do a keyword search for research related to a specific subject area, such as science or writing. From the list of results, read three of the article reviews or answers. Summarize what you learned about using technology to teach that subject.

2. **The role of technology in the No Child Left Behind Act** — The federal Elementary and Secondary Education Act of 2001, also called No Child Left Behind, spotlights technology in Title 2, Part D, Enhancing Education Through Technology. Read this part of the act at http://www.ed.gov/policy/elsec/leg/esea02/pg34.html, paying attention to the goals of the act. Give two examples of how these goals might affect a classroom teacher in a public school in the United States.

3. **Technology Integration** — Visit Edutopia at http://www.edutopia.org/index.php. At the Edutopia website, click on the Video Library tab to access the video collection. In the Search by Topic window, use the menu to browse videos by topic, and select Technology Integration. Watch one of the videos. (a) Which of the four perspectives that shaped educational technology is evident in the video? (b) Refer to Table 1.3 in the textbook, and list elements that show why technology is being used in the video.

Go to MyEducationLab to complete the following exercises.

Video Select the topic "Music and Art Integration," and go to the "Assignments, Activities, and Applications" section. Access the video "Parent Pleased with Son's Opportunities" to watch one parent discuss how her son has benefited from technology integration. Complete the activity that follows.

Building Teaching Skills Select the topic "Professional Development," and go to the "Building Teaching Skills and Dispositions" section. Access the activity "Using Technology Appropriately" and complete the full activity.

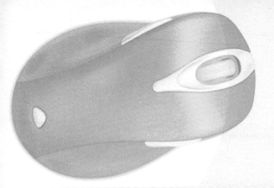

Technology Integration Workshop

TIE into Practice: Technology Integration Examples

Read each of the following scenarios related to implementing the TIP Model, and answer the questions that follow it based on your Chapter 1 reading and activities.

TIP MODEL SCENARIO #1: PERSPECTIVES ON EDUCATIONAL TECHNOLOGY A federal grant that the Paradigm School District wanted to apply for required that applicants have a district-wide technology plan in place. The superintendent appointed a Technology Committee to develop the plan. In the first meeting, veteran high school computer-assisted design (CAD) teacher Redd Borders said, "Of course, it's obvious that our plan must be structured around the technology education skills students need to learn in order to get a job. We can justify all the materials and equipment we'll need by listing them under the job skills." Curriculum coordinator Edna Gaines said, "Wait a minute, what about using computers for teaching and for helping students learn better?" "Oh, that stuff is just frills," said Redd. "What we really need to focus on is how technology can help our students get a job after they graduate!" "Well, personally, I think we should let the audiovisual department develop this plan," said media specialist Twyla Jennings. "They're the ones who have always helped schools use all their equipment." When the meeting adjourned 2 hours later, the committee was still arguing about what the plan's focus should be and who should be in charge of it.

1.1 Based on what you read in this chapter about the four perspectives on educational technology, explain what could have caused this disagreement on the basics of the technology plan.

1.2 Was one of the members' perspectives most correct? Explain why.

TIP MODEL SCENARIO #2: HISTORY Ruie Frey was the social studies coordinator for a large urban school district. After attending a state workshop on using videos to help teach social studies, she proposed to the superintendent that the district develop its own set of video-based materials to support high school social studies instruction. She said that the district social studies teacher council could meet and outline a series of videos to support the district's required curriculum, and district media center personnel could train teachers to develop the videos. She requested that the district budget funds to award a stipend to each social studies teacher who agreed to develop one or more of the videos. She said this plan would be cost effective because it would be far cheaper to have teachers develop their own video materials than to buy the ones that were commercially available, and the district would be more certain that the videos were what the teachers would need, want, and use in their classrooms.

2.1 Describe what we have learned from the history of technology in education that could help the superintendent react appropriately to this proposal.

2.2 Based on what you read in Chapter 1, propose a more workable way to meet the needs of the district's social studies teachers.

TIP MODEL SCENARIO #3: A "WHY USE TECHNOLOGY" RATIONALE A school district instructional technology coordinator wanted the district to buy a new computer lab for a local foreign languages magnet school. She asked the magnet school coordinator to give her a summary of "hard research" to show how various technologies improve achievement and attendance in high school language learning courses, which she felt would help her "sell" this purchase to the school board.

3.1 Describe the assumption the coordinator is making about the benefits of technology use for instruction. Based on what you read at the CARET website about educational technology research, explain why this "selling strategy" may not be a sufficient rationale.

3.2 What societal and economic conditions described in Chapter 1 may have led to the coordinator's requiring "hard research" of this kind? How does the NCLB Act refer to "hard research"?

TIP MODEL SCENARIO #4: CURRENT TECHNOLOGY RESOURCES Lennie, a high school journalism teacher, was contemplating how to justify five multimedia production stations (each consisting of a computer and multimedia production software) he wanted to purchase for the journalism lab. This year, the district had funds available for instructional materials but not for equipment. Lennie felt he could justify the stations as instructional materials because they couldn't do the task of multimedia production without the multimedia software. Therefore, he reasoned that in his purchase justification statement to buy the five stations, he could list the purchase category as "instructional materials."

4.1 Explain how and why the purchasing agent in the district business office probably would react to this justification statement.

4.2 Find out and explain why it is necessary for schools to divide technology purchases into equipment and materials.

TIP MODEL SCENARIO #5: SOCIETAL ISSUES

Over the summer, the Empire School District installed computers connected to the Internet in every school classroom. In the district-wide faculty meeting at the beginning of the year, the district technology coordinator made a pitch to teachers to allow students to use their classroom computers after school whenever possible. He said that this would help give students access to computers they might not get at home, possibly lessening the Digital Divide. When one teacher asked who could help these students use the computers, he replied, "These kids know more about computers than we do. They will do just fine helping each other." One teacher remarked that, since each school has a computer club, they might call on the members to help supervise after-school users.

5.1 Based on what you read in Chapter 1, describe the kinds of problems that could arise from the kind of access the technology coordinator was advocating.

5.2 Explain why this strategy would or would not help address the Digital Divide.

TIP MODEL SCENARIO #6: LEGAL/ETHICAL ISSUES

One of the school board members in your district has become alarmed at the increasing number of stories in the news about students using the Internet to plagiarize other people's work. She has asked for a district-wide policy that students not be permitted to access the Internet in schools unless they do so in a library media center under the supervision of a trained library media specialist. The board has asked you, the district technology coordinator, to react to this proposal.

6.1 After reading Gardiner's article (2001) about online plagiarism and McNabb's article (2001) on appropriate usage guidelines, what would you say about the feasibility and desirability of the school board member's proposal?

6.2 What other proposals could you make to the board that would address the potential problem of online plagiarism in your district?

TIP MODEL SCENARIO #7: EQUITY ISSUES

You are a math/science resource teacher in an elementary school. Your principal has just returned from a seminar on gender equity issues, where she learned about the long-standing trend of females entering science and engineering fields in far fewer numbers than males. She also learned that girls shape opinions on their career options beginning in early levels of school. She asks you to recommend some hardware, software, and materials she could purchase that would encourage girls to consider going into technical fields as well as hands-on activities such as science simulations that might interest girls at this age.

7.1 After reading the AAUW report *Tech-Savvy: Educating Girls in the New Computer Age* (2000) and the Margolis and Fisher article (2002), what positives and negatives could you tell your principal about the approach she has recommended?

7.2 What other, perhaps more effective, strategies could you suggest to address the problems she has identified?

TIP MODEL SCENARIO #8: DISTANCE EDUCATION ISSUES

The superintendent of the large school district in which you are a high school math teacher has been talking to administrators of a virtual high school consortium. He has decided the district should offer its high-level math and science courses, especially the advanced placement courses, in a "virtual" environment. He feels this will save money and offer more equitable access to the courses since it is hard to find qualified teachers for all schools. Most courses have already been developed by the virtual school consortium and are available for students to use. The superintendent has asked all the high school math and science teachers to come to a meeting to discuss how to replace the current course offerings with online ones.

8.1 Based on your experience and knowledge about delivering courses face to face and online, what should the superintendent consider before going ahead with this plan?

8.2 Assume that the decision is made to do what he has recommended. What could you suggest to make the proposed change work most effectively for students?

TIP MODEL SCENARIO #9: ANTI-TECHNOLOGY ISSUES

A parent of a child in your school has read a report called *Fool's Gold: A Critical Look at Computers in Childhood* by the Alliance for Childhood (1999), which is highly critical of using computers in schools. Another parent has read Oppenheimer's *The Flickering Mind* (2003), which also takes a negative view. The parents passed the report and book on to all of the school board members, who found them very disconcerting. They were especially upset since a bond issue had just been placed on the ballot to pay for technology upgrades and Internet connections for the schools. One board member suggested that perhaps the bond issue should be removed from the ballot until the question of the benefits of using computers in education could be clarified. The issue was put on the agenda for discussion at the next school board meeting. Your superintendent knows you are an advocate for using technology in education and asks you to speak to the board at the meeting.

9.1 What could you tell the school board members that might give them a context for understanding this and other similar reports?

9.2 What evidence could you provide to support your belief that technology has an important role to play in education? (Limit your comments to the three strongest points.)

TIP MODEL SCENARIO #10: PRIVACY/SAFETY ISSUES One of the teachers in your school told you about a project for which his students were doing research on the Internet. One of the students said he had "met" someone in a chatroom who was an astronaut in the NASA program. The teacher encouraged several other students who were interested in space careers to contact that same person in the chatroom and to do a group presentation of their findings.

10.1 Does this sound like a good strategy to you? Why or why not?

10.2 After looking at the information at the University of Delaware website on writing an AUP, what should a school be sure to include in its AUP that addresses situations like this?

For Your Teaching Portfolio

At the end of each of Chapters 2 through 15 in this textbook, you will have an opportunity to add products to your teaching portfolio to show what you know about and are able to do with technology in education. In this introductory chapter, review the information on teaching portfolios in the section titled How Teachers Can Demonstrate Their Skills: Electronic Portfolios (page 25); determine the portfolio requirements for your program; and begin creating your portfolio structure.

Chapter 2
Theory and Practice: Foundations for Effective Technology Integration

Students are conducting original research on the weather, for instance, using some of the same tools as professional scientists, then sharing their data and results with others all over the globe. Astronauts on the space shuttle and explorers in the jungles of Peru have involved students in the excitement of their discoveries as they happen. . . . Instead of asking, "Should schools have computers?" we need to focus on a more productive question: "How are technologies best used in education to help students achieve and prepare for the world outside of school?"

J. Hawkins, in *The World at Your Fingertips* (1997)

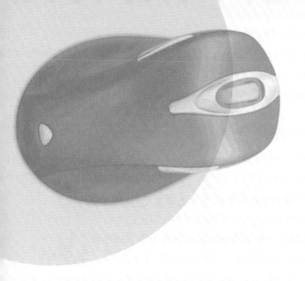

Technology Integration Example

The Role of Context

Strategy A: Preparing students for state tests

One of Bill's responsibilities as mathematics department chair was helping all teachers make sure their students did well on the mathematics portion of the state's Test of Essential Skills for Success (TESS). Because students could not go on to high school unless they passed the TESS, Bill and the other math teachers were determined that every student in the school would pass TESS-M, the math portion. They were also determined that they would not just "teach to the test." They wanted the students to have a good grounding in math skills that would serve them well in their future education.

From practice test scores he had seen, Bill realized that there were too many students who needed help to provide individual coaches or tutors for each one, and he disliked the idea of making all students work on skills only some of them needed. At a school he had visited in another district, Bill had been impressed with how teachers relied on a computer-based system that included drills, tutorials, simulations, and problem-solving activities that they could access in their rooms or from the computer lab.

One of the benefits of the system was that students could take practice tests and teachers could get a list of skills with which they were having problems. Then the system would recommend specific activities, on and off the system, matched to each child's needs. The activities ranged from practice in very basic math skills to solving real-life problems that required algebra and other math skills. Bill persuaded his principal to purchase a year's subscription to this system, and he and the other math teachers agreed on ways they would use it to supplement their classroom instruction.

That year, every student at the school passed TESS-M. The math teachers agreed that the computer-based activities had played a key role in students' preparation. They liked the way it helped them target students' specific needs more efficiently while not overemphasizing test taking. Bill asked the principal to make the system a permanent part of the school's budget.

Strategy B: A simulated family project

Mayda's seventh-grade math students are usually fairly good at math skills; almost none of them have any trouble passing the state's criterion-referenced test. However, she likes to do at least one ongoing project each year to show students how their math skills apply to real-life situations. She also wants them to learn to work together to solve problems, just as they would be doing in college and in work situations when they graduated.

The first activity she does at the beginning of each year is to have her students work in small groups to simulate "families." They select a type of "job" their "wage earner" will have and create a monthly budget in a spreadsheet template she set up that shows income earned from an imaginary job versus estimated monthly expenses for each of them and for the "family." To select jobs, the groups consult online newspaper Help Wanted sections to get an idea of what positions are available and how much they pay.

To estimate expenses, they look at online newspaper and real estate ads to see how much it costs to rent a house or an apartment in an area where they would like to live. Throughout the year, she gives each group unexpected expenses (e.g., the dog gets sick, the roof is leaking); the students must then adjust their spreadsheet budget to compensate for the extra expenses. If a group gets too far out of line with its budgeted expenses, she makes the students get a "loan," which they do by researching available interest rates and adding a loan payment to their spreadsheet budgets that will pay off their "debt."

Toward the end of the year, Mayda has students download a 1040 tax return form from the IRS website and do estimated taxes. Finally, they prepare a report using *PowerPoint* software that shows charts of their spending and what they learned about "making ends meet." The students always tell her this is the most meaningful math activity they have ever done.

Objectives

After reading this chapter and completing the learning activities for it, you should be able to:

1. Match directed and constructivist integration strategies with their learning theory foundations.

2. Identify technology integration strategies as directed, constructivist, or combinations of these.

3. Describe the six phases of the Technology Integration Planning (TIP) Model.

4. Match descriptions of instructional problems with technology-based solutions that have the potential for high relative advantage to teachers and students.

5. Create outcome objectives and assessment plans for technology integration strategies.

6. For a given technology integration strategy, create an instructional plan that is pedagogically sound and addresses equity and classroom implementation needs.

7. For a given technology integration plan, create a logistical plan that addresses ethical, legal, equipment, scheduling, and technical issues.

8. Develop a plan to evaluate the impact of a given technology integration strategy.

9. Describe essential conditions to support effective classroom integration of technology.

10. Use the six-phase TIP Model to develop a sample classroom technology integration strategy.

Ingredients for Successful Technology Integration: A Look at the Theory

This chapter describes the four factors that help create the recipe for effective technology integration strategies, as depicted in Figure 2.1:

- **Learning theory foundations** — Since technologies are used to carry out learning strategies, it is important to begin with a look at two very different, competing theories of how learning should take place and examine how various kinds of integration strategies were derived from them.

- **Technological pedagogical content knowledge** — Identifying one's strengths and weaknesses in technol-

ogy integration is crucial. Thus, a framework for guiding teachers' knowledge assessment and development is discussed.

- **Integration planning model** — For the procedural and "people" issues involved in technology integration, we look to a six-phase planning model and discuss how teachers can use it to plan technology-based lessons.

- **Essential conditions for integration** — The International Society for Technology in Education (ISTE) emphasizes that technology-based strategies work best when optimal conditions are in place to support them. Thus, a review of these conditions is the final piece in the foundation.

FIGURE 2.1 A Recipe for Technology Integration

Technology Integration

Special Ingredients for Successful Technology Integration

Ingredient 1: A Foundation of Learning Theories
Ingredient 2: Technological Pedagogical Content Knowledge (TPACK)
Ingredient 3: Technology Integration Planning Model (TIP)
Ingredient 4: Essential Conditions for Integration
Directions: Use all of these ingredients wisely. Prepare yourself by obtaining knowledge in all of these areas, and then use them together to see students actively engaged with technology in your classroom.

Learning Theories for Technology Integration

Directed and Constructivist Instruction Models: What Can We Learn from Each Other?

Prior to about 1980, there seemed little question about the appropriate instructional role for technology, particularly computer technology. According to respected writers of the time (Taylor, 1980), there were three acceptable roles: computers as tools to support learning (e.g., word processing, calculations), as tutors to deliver instruction (e.g., drill and practice, tutorials), and as "tutees" (e.g., learning to program computers).

FIGURE 2.2 Objectivism and Constructivism: How Are We Different?

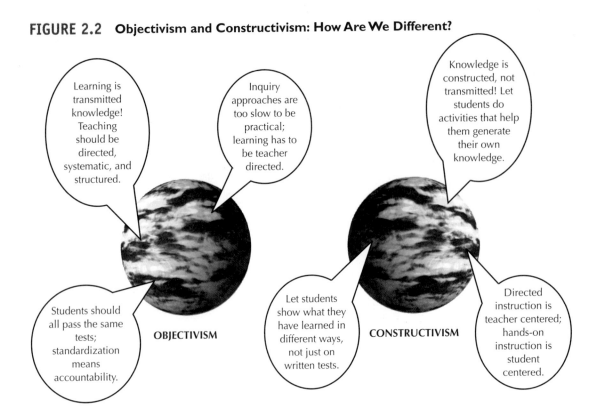

However, as technology has become more capable and complex, everyday life has changed, and with it our views of education and appropriate teaching strategies. In the past, educational goals reflected society's emphasis on the need for basic skills—such as reading, writing, and arithmetic—and an agreed-on body of information considered essential for everyone. Many educators now believe that the world is changing too quickly to define education in terms of specific information or skills; they believe it should focus instead on more general capabilities, such as "learning to learn" skills, that will help future citizens cope with inevitable technological change.

While everyone seems to agree that changes are needed to respond to modern challenges, they seem to disagree on which strategies will serve today's educational goals. One view, **directed instruction** or **objectivism**, is grounded primarily in behaviorist learning theory and the information-processing branch of the cognitive learning theories. The other view, **constructivist** or **inquiry-based learning**, evolved from other branches of thinking in cognitive learning theory. A few technology applications, such as drill and practice and tutorials, are associated only with directed instruction; most others (problem solving, multimedia production, web-based learning) can enhance either directed instruction or constructivist learning, depending on how they are used.

This book is based on the premise that there are meaningful roles for both directed instruction and constructivist strategies and the technology applications associated with them. Both can help teachers and students meet the many and varied requirements of learning in today's Information Age society.

Theoretical Foundations of Directed and Constructivist Models

Like most people with radically different views on the same issue, **objectivists** and **constructivists** frequently use different terms to describe essentially the same things. Sfard (1998) says that differences in the language used to describe learning spring from two different metaphors used for learning: the acquisition metaphor and the participation metaphor. She notes that "...the acquisition metaphor is likely to be more prominent in older writings, [and] more recent studies are often dominated by the participation metaphor" (p. 5). These differences in language signal fundamental differences in thinking about how learning takes place and how we can foster it. Figure 2.2 gives examples of how educators use different terms to describe the same things because of their differing views.

How did these differences come about? It is important to recognize that both people who espouse directed instruction and those who take constructivist approaches are attempting to identify what Gagné (1985) called the *conditions of learning* or the "sets of circumstances that obtain when learning occurs" (p. 2). Both approaches are based on the work of respected learning theorists and psychologists who have studied both the behavior of human beings as learning organisms and the behavior of students in schools and classrooms.

FIGURE 2.3 Theories Underlying Directed Technology Integration Strategies

| Objectivist Learning Theories | → | Directed Integration Strategies |

Behaviorist Theory: B. F. Skinner Learning as Stimulus–Response Chains	**Information-Processing Theory: Atkinson and Shiffrin** The Mind as Computer	**Cognitive-Behavioral Theory: Robert Gagné** Providing Conditions for Learning	**Systems Theory and Systematic Instructional Design** Managing the Complexity of Teaching
	Sensory Register / Short-Term Memory / Long-Term Memory		
• **Learning is** an activity that occurs inside the mind and can be inferred only by observed behaviors. • Behaviors are shaped by "contingencies of reinforcement" to shape desired responses: *positive reinforcement* (increases desired behaviors with rewards); *negative reinforcement* (increases desired behaviors by withholding rewards); *punishment* (decreases undesirable behaviors with aversive stimuli).	• **Learning is** encoding information into human memory, similar to the way a computer stores information. • There are three kinds of stores: *sensory registers* to receive information; *short-term* or *working memory* (STM) to hold it temporarily; and *long-term memory* (LTM) to store information indefinitely.	• **Learning is** shaped by providing optimal *instructional conditions*. • Conditions include the nine *Events of Instruction* that differ according to the type of skill being taught and a *skills hierarchy* approach that presents simple skills and builds to complex ones.	• **Learning is** fostered by using a *system of instruction* based on behaviorist information processing, and cognitive behaviorist theories. • An instructional system is designed by stating goals and objectives; doing task analysis to set a learning sequence; matching assessment and instruction to objectives; creating materials; and field testing and revising materials.

Educators' views diverge, however, in the ways they define learning, how they identify the conditions required to make learning happen, and how they perceive the problems that interfere most with learning. They disagree because they attend to different philosophies and learning theories and, consequently, they take different perspectives on improving current educational practice.

The two sets of learning theories have very different underlying epistemologies: beliefs about the nature of human knowledge as well as how to develop it. *Constructivists* (those who espouse inquiry-based methods based on cognitive, developmental, and generative/discovery theories) and *objectivists* (those who espouse directed methods based on behavioral, cognitive-behavioral, and information-processing theories) come from separate and different epistemological "planets," although both nurture many different tribes or cultures (Molenda, 1991; Phillips, 1995). The characteristics and theoretical origins of these philosophical differences can be summarized in the following way:

• **Objectivists** — *Knowledge has a separate, real existence of its own outside the human mind.* Learning happens

when this knowledge is transmitted to people and they store it in their minds.

• **Constructivists** — *Humans construct all knowledge in their minds by participating in certain experiences.* Learning occurs when one constructs both mechanisms for learning and one's own unique version of the knowledge, colored by background, experiences, and aptitudes.

Learning theories underlying objectivist methods. As Figure 2.3 shows, objectivists attend to concepts that evolved from behavioral, information-processing, and cognitive behaviorist learning theories and the **systems approaches to instructional design** that were based on them. The basic concepts associated with these theories are described briefly here, and their implications for education and for technology integration are summarized in Figure 2.4 on page 36.

• **Behaviorist theories: B. F. Skinner** — Called by some "the most influential psychologist of the 20th century" (Eggen & Kauchak, 2004, p. 200), Skinner's **operant conditioning** concepts built on the **classical conditioning** concepts of Russian physiologist Ivan Pavlov.

FIGURE 2.4 How Objectivist Learning Theories Lead to Directed Technology Integration Strategies

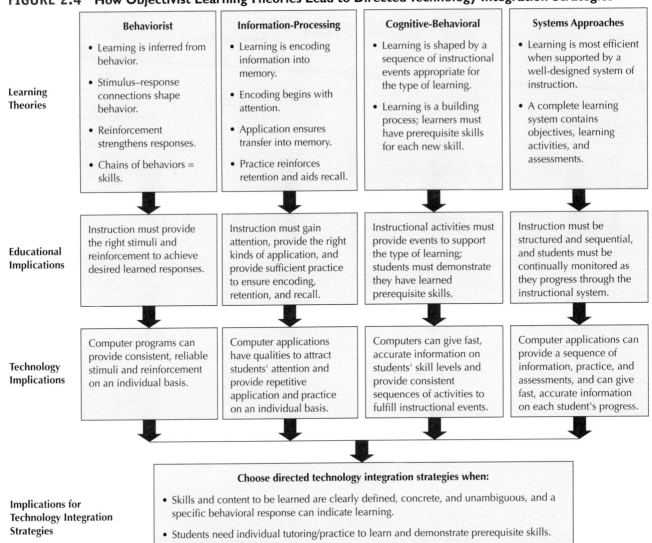

While Pavlov viewed learning as involuntary *physical* responses to outside stimuli (e.g., dogs salivate at the sight of a dog food can), Skinner said that people can have voluntary *mental* control over their responses and that the consequences of their past actions can act as stimuli in shaping future behaviors. He said that since learning processes occur inside the mind and we cannot see them directly, learning can only be inferred by observing behaviors. He believed learned behaviors could be shaped by **contingencies of reinforcement** set up to shape desired responses: Positive reinforcement (e.g., praise for correct answers) and negative reinforcement (e.g., avoiding detention by being on time to school) increase behaviors, while punishment decreases behaviors (e.g., refraining from violence after being expelled for fighting). Skinner used reinforcement principles to develop **programmed learning** techniques for training and instruction. Later,

Benjamin Bloom used Skinner's principles in his **mastery learning** concepts, an approach that gave students a sequence of objectives that defined mastery of a subject. Students had to pass tests on each objective to demonstrate they had mastered a skill before proceeding to the next one. Today, many classroom management techniques are based on behavior modification principles derived from Skinner's reinforcement principles (e.g., students get praise or an entertaining graphic for correct answers; students memorize important basic skills by increasing the frequency of correct responses to problems).

• **Information-processing theories** — Because many people found Skinner's "learning as behavior-shaping concepts" insufficient to guide instruction, the first cognitive (as opposed to behavioral) learning theorists began to hypothesize processes *inside the brain* that allow human beings to learn and remember. Much of the work of the information-processing theorists is based on a model of memory and storage proposed by Atkinson and Shiffrin (1968), who said that the brain contains three kinds of memory, or "stores," to process information—much like a computer. **Sensory registers** receive information a person senses through receptors (i.e., eyes, ears, nose, mouth, and/or hands). After a second or so, the information is either lost or transferred to **short-term memory (STM)**, or working memory. STM holds new information for about 5 to 20 seconds. Unless it is processed or practiced in a way that causes it to transfer to **long-term memory (LTM)**, it also is lost. LTM can hold information indefinitely, but for new information to be transferred to LTM, it must be linked in some way to prior knowledge already in LTM. Common teaching practices based on these concepts include the use of (1) interesting questions and eye-catching material to help students pay attention to a new topic; (2) instructions that point out important points in new material to help students remember them by linking them to information they already know; and (3) practice exercises to help transfer information from STM to LTM. Guidelines for enhancing attention, encoding, and storage processes include (1) Gagné's hierarchical "bottom-up" approach, in which students learn lower order or prerequisite skills first (e.g., multiplication skills required to learn long-division skills) and build on them; and (2) Ausubel's "top-down" approach, in which "advance organizers" or topic overviews give students mental frameworks on which to "hang" new information. Computer programs provide ideal environments for the highly structured cueing, attention-getting, and practice features that information-processing theorists have found so essential to learning.

- **Cognitive-behavioral theory: Robert Gagné** — An educational psychologist who translated principles

from behavioral and information-processing theories into practical instructional strategies for teachers and trainers, Gagné used research on information-processing models of learning to derive guidelines for arranging optimal "conditions of learning." Guidelines included **learning hierarchies** and the **Events of Instruction** for several types of learning. (See Table 2.1.) Gagné, Wager, and Rojas (1981) showed how Gagné's Events of Instruction could be used to plan lessons using each kind of instructional software (drill, tutorial, simulation). They said that only a tutorial could "stand by itself" and accomplish all of the necessary Events of Instruction; the other kinds of software required teacher-led activities to accomplish events before and after software use.

- **Systems approaches: instructional design model** — These methods have their roots in the collaborative work of educational psychologists Robert Gagné and Leslie Briggs, who created a way to apply principles learned from military and industrial training to developing curriculum and instruction for schools. They believed that learning was most efficient when it was supported by a carefully designed system of instruction. Gagné promoted *instructional task analysis* to identify required learning hierarchy subskills and conditions of learning for them. Briggs offered systematic methods of designing training programs to save companies time and money in training their personnel. When combined, these areas of expertise became a set of step-by-step processes known as a *systems approach to instructional design*, or *systematic instructional design*, which came into common use in the 1970s and 1980s. Other names associated with this era include Robert Mager (instructional objectives), Glaser (criterion-referenced testing), Cronbach and Scriven (formative and summative evaluation),

TABLE 2.1 Gagné's Nine Events of Instruction

Events of Instruction and Their Relation to Processes of Learning

Instructional Event	Relation to Learning Process
1. Gaining attention	*Reception* of patterns of neural impulses
2. Informing the learner of the objective	Activating a process of *executive control*
3. Stimulating recall of prerequisite learning	*Retrieval* of prior learning to working memory
4. Presenting the stimulus material	Emphasizing features for *selective perception*
5. Providing learning guidance	*Semantic encoding*; cues for *retrieval*
6. Eliciting the performance	Activating *response organization*
7. Providing feedback about performance correctness	Establishing *reinforcement*
8. Assessing the performance	Activating *retrieval*; making *reinforcement* possible
9. Enhancing retention and transfer	Providing cues and strategies for *retrieval*

David Merrill (component display theory), and Charles Reigeluth (elaboration theory). Since instructional design results in a highly structured sequence of instruction, computer tutorials and self-paced distance learning courses offer ideal delivery systems for instructional design through these approaches.

Teaching methods and technology integration strategies that reflect objectivist theories. A considerable body of research indicates that directed methods work well for addressing certain kinds of teaching/learning problems. For example, Kirshner, Sweller, and Clark (2006) argue that direct instruction is more effective and efficient than minimally guided instruction when learners do not have enough prior knowledge to be self-guided. They state that minimally guided instruction ignores the fundamentals of human cognition and overloads working memory; as such, minimal guidance during instruction is ineffective in altering long-term memory (i.e., learning). Kirshner et al. cite a large body of literature that supports their arguments (pp. 79–83), and other scholars echo their claims. For example, Doering (2007) found that social studies preservice teachers learned how to effectively use and teach geography using geospatial technologies when they were taught using a directed versus a minimally guided approach. Carnine, Silbert, and Kameenui (1997) and Stein, Silbert, and Carnine (1997) determined that directed drill and practice can help teach basic reading and mathematics skills. Spence and Hively (1993) note that increased fluency practice supports precision teaching of basic reading and math skills to young learners. Mallott (1993) found that using reinforcement principles can improve the study habits and achievement of college students, and Carnine (1993) ascertains that structured, teacher-directed techniques were effective in teaching problem-solving and

Directed technology integration strategies let students master skills at their own pace.

higher order thinking skills to at-risk students. Finally, Hirsch (2002) comments that "one minute of explicit (directed) learning can be more effective than a month of implicit (exploratory) learning."

Objectivists focus primarily on technology integration strategies for systematically designed, structured learning products such as drills, tutorials, and integrated learning systems (ILSs; discussed in Chapter 3). When they do use other, more open-ended materials such as simulations and problem-solving software, the integration strategies are very structured, providing a step-by-step sequence of learning activities matched to specific performance objectives. When objectivists evaluate these products, they typically look for a match among objectives, methods, and assessment strategies and how well they help teachers and students meet curriculum standards. To reflect objectivist principles, materials and integration strategies must have clearly defined objectives and a set sequence for their use.

Learning theories underlying constructivist methods. Figure 2.5 shows that constructivist beliefs and methods were derived from a combination of concepts in **social activism**, **scaffolding**, stages of development, and **multiple intelligences** theories. The basic concepts of these theories are described briefly here, and their implications for education and for technology integration are summarized in Figure 2.6 on page 42.

- **Social activism theory: John Dewey** — An early proponent of racial equality and women's suffrage, John Dewey's radical activism shaped his beliefs about education. Identified closely with the Progressive Education reform initiative popular in the first half of the 1990s, many of his principles of education were in direct opposition to those of that period. Dewey deplored standardization and believed that curriculum should arise from students' interests. He also believed that curriculum topics should be integrated, rather than isolated, since teaching isolated topics prevented learners from grasping the whole of knowledge. He felt that education is growth, rather than an end in itself and that the common view that education is preparation for work separated society into social classes. Instead, Dewey believed education should be a way of helping individuals understand their culture and should develop their relationship to and unique roles in society. Since he felt that social consciousness was the ultimate aim of all education, learning was useful only in the context of social experience. He found reading and mathematics had become ends in themselves, disconnected from any meaningful social

FIGURE 2.5   Theories Underlying Inquiry-Based Technology Integration Strategies

Inquiry-Based
Integration Strategies

Constructivist Learning
Theories

Social Activism Theory:
John Dewey
Learning as Social Experience

- **Learning is** individual growth that comes about through social experiences.
- Growth is fostered through hands-on activities connected to real-world issues and problems.
- School curriculum should arise from students' interests and be taught as integrated topics, rather than as isolated skills.

Scaffolding Theory:
Lev Vygotsky
Learning as a Cognitive Building Process

- **Learning is** cognitive development shaped by individual differences and the influence of culture.
- Adults (experts) and children (novices) perceive the world differently. The difference between them is the *Zone of Proximal Development.*
- Adults support learning through *scaffolding*, or helping children build on what they already know.

Child Development Theory:
Jean Piaget
Stages of Development

- **Learning is** cognitive growth through neurological and social maturation.
- Children go through stages of cognitive development *(sensorimotor, preoperational, concrete,* and *formal operations)* by interacting with their environment.
- When they confront unknowns, they experience *disequilibrium;* they respond with *assimilation* (fitting it into their views) or *accommodation* (changing their views).

Discovery Learning:
Jerome Bruner
Instructional Support for Child Development

- **Learning is** cognitive growth through interaction with the environment.
- Children are more likely to understand and remember concepts that they *discover* during their interaction with the environment.
- Teachers support *discovery learning* by providing opportunities for exploring and manipulating objects and doing experiments.

Multiple Intelligences Theories:
Howard Gardner
The Role of Intelligence in Learning

- **Learning is** shaped by innate *intelligences:*
 –Linguistic—Uses language effectively, writes clearly and persuasively.
 –Musical—Communicates by writing and playing music.
 –Logical-mathematical—Reasons logically, recognizes patterns; formulates and tests hypotheses; solves problems in math and science.
 –Spatial—Perceives the world visually, can recreate things after seeing them.
 –Bodily-kinesthetic—Uses the body and tools skillfully.
 –Intrapersonal—Is an introspective thinker; has heightened metacognitive abilities.
 –Interpersonal—Notices moods and changes in others, can identify motives in others' behavior, relates well with others.
 –Naturalist—Can discriminate among living things.

context. Dewey believed that learning should be hands-on and experience-based, and that meaningful learning resulted from students working together on tasks related to their interests. Though considered by many to be the Grandfather of Constructivism, Dewey also advocated a merging of "absolutism" and "experimentalism," just as this chapter calls for combining directed and constructivist methods. Although he probably would deplore the current standards movement and the use of high-stakes testing programs, today's interdisciplinary curriculum and hands-on, experience-based learning are in tune with Dewey's lifelong message.

- **Scaffolding theories: Lev Semenovich Vygotsky** — Until the end of the Cold War in the 1990s, the writings of Russian philosopher and educational psychologist Lev Vygotsky had more influence on educational theory and practice in the United States than they did in his own country. His landmark book, *Pedagogical Psychology*, written in 1926, was not published in Russia until 1991 (Davydov, 1995). Since he viewed learners as individuals rather than as part of a "collective," his educational concepts were threatening to a communistic state but found a warm reception in a democracy. He felt that how children learn and think derives directly from the culture around them. An adult perceives things much differently than a child does, but this difference decreases as children translate their social views into personal/psychological ones. Vygotsky used the term **zone of proximal development (ZPD)** to refer to the difference between adult/expert and child/novice levels of cognitive functioning. He felt that teachers could provide good instruction by finding out where each child was in his or her development and building on the child's experiences, a process he called *scaffolding*. Ormrod (2001) said that teachers promote students' cognitive development by presenting some classroom tasks that "they can complete only with assistance, that is, within each student's zone of proximal development" (p. 59). Many visual technology tools, from video-based scenarios to virtual reality, are designed to scaffold students' understanding through graphic examples and real-life experiences relevant to their individual needs.

- **Child development theory: Jean Piaget** — Piaget referred to himself as a "genetic epistemologist," or a scientist who studies how knowledge begins and develops in individuals. He believed that, while the ages at which children mature vary somewhat, all children go through four stages of cognitive develop-

ment, that each stage occurs only after certain genetically controlled neurological changes, and that all children develop higher reasoning abilities in the same sequence:

- **Sensorimotor stage (birth–2 years)** — They explore the world around them through their senses and motor activity.

- **Preoperational stage (2–7 years)** — They develop speech and symbolic activities (e.g., drawing objects, pretending, imagining), numerical abilities (e.g., assigning numbers and counting), increased self-control, and ability to delay gratification, but they cannot do conservation tasks (recognizing that shape is not related to quantity).

- **Concrete operational stage (7–11 years)** — They increase abstract reasoning, can generalize from concrete experiences, and can do conservation tasks.

- **Formal operations stage (12–15 years)** — They form and test hypotheses, organize information, and reason scientifically; they can show results of abstract thinking with symbolic materials (e.g., writing, drama).

Piaget believed children develop through these stages by interacting with their environment. When they confront new and unfamiliar features of their environment that do not fit with their current views of the world, they experience "disequilibrium." They learn by fitting the new experiences into the existing view of the world (i.e., **assimilation**) or by changing their views of the world to incorporate the new experiences (i.e., **accommodation**). He felt that children are active and motivated learners whose knowledge of the world becomes more integrated and organized over time. Although Piaget himself repeatedly expressed a lack of interest in how his work applied to school-based education, calling it "the American question," his pupil, MIT mathematician Seymour Papert (1980), used Piaget's theories as the basis of his work with Logo, a language designed to let young students solve design problems using an on-screen "turtle." This environment provided the vital link that Papert felt would allow children to move more easily from the concrete operations of earlier stages of Piaget's hypothesis to more abstract (formal) ones. Papert's 1980 book *Mindstorms* challenged then-current instructional goals and methods for mathematics and became the first constructivist statement of educational practice with technology.

- **Discovery learning: Jerome Bruner** — Some of the principles associated with educational theorist Jerome Bruner seem to coincide with those of

Vygotsky and Piaget. Like Piaget, Bruner believed children go through various stages of intellectual development. But unlike Piaget, Bruner supported intervention. He was primarily concerned with making education more relevant to student needs at each stage, and he believed that teachers could accomplish this by encouraging active participation in the learning process. Active participation, he felt, was best achieved by providing **discovery learning** environments that would let children explore alternatives and recognize relationships between ideas (Bruner, 1973). Bruner felt that students were more likely to understand and remember concepts they had discovered in the course of their own exploration. However, research findings have yielded mixed results for discovery learning, and the relatively unstructured methods recommended by Bruner have not found widespread support. Teachers have found that discovery learning is most successful when they provide some structured experiences first.

- **Multiple intelligences theory: Howard Gardner** — The only learning-developmental theory that attempts to define the role of intelligence in learning, Gardner's work is based on Guilford's pioneering work on the structure of intellect (Eggen & Kauchak, 2004) and Sternberg's view of intelligence as influenced by culture (Ormrod, 2001). Gardner says there are at least eight different and relatively independent types of intelligence: *linguistic* (e.g., writers, journalists, poets use language effectively, are sensitive to the uses of language, and write clearly and persuasively); *musical* (e.g., composers, pianists, conductors understand musical structure and composition, and communicate by writing or playing music); *logical-mathematical* (e.g., scientists, mathematicians, doctors reason logically in math terms, recognize patterns in phenomena, formulate and test hypotheses, and solve problems in math and science); *spatial* (e.g., artists, sculptors, graphic artists receive the world in visual terms, notice and remember visual details, and can recreate things after seeing them); *bodily-kinesthetic* (e.g., dancers, athletes, watchmakers see the body skillfully, manipulate things well with hands, and use tools skillfully); *intrapersonal* (e.g., self-aware/self-motivated persons are introspective thinkers, aware of their own motives, and have heightened metacognitive abilities); *interpersonal* (e.g., psychologists, therapists, salespersons notice moods and changes in others, can identify motives in others' behavior, and relate well with others); and *naturalist* (e.g., botanists, biologists can

discriminate well among living things). According to Gardner's theory, IQ tests (which tend to stress linguistic/logical-mathematical abilities) cannot judge all students' ability to learn, and traditional academic tasks may not reflect true ability. This theory supports doing group work on multimedia products, assigning students group roles based on their type of intelligence (e.g., those with high interpersonal intelligence are project coordinators, those with high logical-mathematical ability are technical experts, and those with spatial ability are designers).

Teaching methods and technology integration strategies that reflect constructivist theories. As Figure 2.6 illustrates, constructivist methods are designed to make learning more visual and experiential and to allow students more flexibility in how they learn and demonstrate competence. These qualities were designed to address a problem John Seely Brown called *inert knowledge,* a term introduced by Whitehead in 1929 to mean skills that students learned but did not know how to transfer later to problems that required them (Brown, Collins, & Duguid, 1989). Brown said that inert knowledge resulted from learning skills in isolation from each other and from real-life application; thus, he advocated *cognitive apprenticeships,* or activities that called for authentic problem solving, that is, solving problems in settings that are familiar and meaningful to students (CTGV, 1990). These ideas were based on the theories of Dewey, Vygotsky, Piaget, and Bruner.

The first technology integration strategies based on these ideas were Papert's Logo-supported "microworlds," in which children worked with a very visual programming language to create on-screen designs. Later, other technology-based materials, such as the *Jasper Woodberry Problem Solving Series,* videodisc-based mathematics materials created by the now-disbanded Cognition and Technology Group at Vanderbilt (CTGV), and more recently, *GeoThentic,* were designed to provide learning environments that reflected *situated cognition,* or instruction **anchored** in experiences that learners considered authentic because they emulated the behavior of adults. The CTGV and Doering and Veletsianos felt that, with their materials, teachers could help students build on or "scaffold" from experiences they already had to generate their own knowledge in an active, hands-on way, rather than receiving it passively. Today's constructivist integration strategies often focus on having students use data-gathering tools (e.g., handheld computers) to study problems and issues in their locale and on creating multimedia products to present their new knowledge and insights.

FIGURE 2.6 How Constructivist Learning Theories Lead to Inquiry-Based Technology Integration Strategies

	Social Activism	Scaffolding	Child Development	Discovery Learning	Multiple Intelligences
Learning Theories	• Learning requires social interaction among students on problems and issues of direct concern to them.	• Learning works best when students get assistance from experts to build on what they already know. • Each learner's background shapes how he/she learns.	• Learning abilities differ at each developmental stage. • Children progress through the stages through exploration of their environment.	• Children understand and remember concepts better when they discover the concepts themselves through exploration.	• Learning can occur on many levels and be demonstrated in different ways, depending on a student's preferred mode of intelligence.
Educational Implications	Instruction should stress collaborative activities and real-world connections.	Instruction should be tailored to each student's individual needs and preferences.	Instruction must be matched to students' developmental stage and must provide opportunities for exploration.	Students must be given opportunities for unstructured exploration and self-discovery.	Instruction must allow for different ways of learning and showing competence in the same topics and materials.
Technology Implications	Technology supports opportunities for collaboration; visual presentations help students connect abstract concepts with real-world applications.	Technology can support multiple paths to studying the same material and can provide "visual scaffolds" to help students understand complex concepts.	Technology can supply "electronic manipulatives" that support exploration activities for various stages of development.	Technology can make possible a rich array of information and complex environments for students to explore.	Multimedia supports many channels for learning the same content; students can demonstrate learning by doing different roles in a group technology project.

Implications for Technology Integration Strategies

Choose inquiry-based technology integration strategies when:

• Concepts to be learned are abstract and complex; teachers feel that hands-on, visual activities are essential to help students see how concepts apply to real-world problems and issues.
• Teachers want to encourage collaboration and/or allow alternative ways of learning and showing competence.
• There is time to allow unstructured exploration to motivate students and help them discover their own interests.

Conflicting Views of Directed and Constructivist Methods

Not surprisingly, educators who attend to objectivist theories have dramatically different ideas about curriculum and teaching/learning methods than those who espouse constructivist theories. Sometimes these differences of opinion have generated strident debate in the literature (Baines & Stanley, 2000; Kirschner, Sweller, & Clark, 2007; Kuhn, 2007; Schmidt, Loyens, van Gog, & Paas, 2007; *Educational Technology*, 1991a, 1991b). The debate continues because proponents of directed and constructivist views of learning focus on different kinds of problems (or different aspects of the same problems) confronting teachers and students in today's schools.

Problems and needs addressed by directed and constructivist integration strategies. As Table 2.2 illustrates, the characteristics of each model are specifically targeted to certain teaching and learning problems. Directed models stress individual work using traditional teaching and learning methods because they are designed to address problems of accountability and quality assurance in our educational system. Constructivist models stress cooperative work and nontraditional exploration methods because they are designed to help students think on their own, work with diverse groups, and see the relevance of skills to their daily lives.

Assessment measures and grading strategies for directed and constructivist integration strategies. Table 2.2 also shows the contrast in assessment methods used to support directed and constructivist methods. Because directed strategies are also mastery learning strategies and teachers require clear, easily observable evidence that students have adequately mastered the skills, typical assessments for directed models are written objective tests (e.g., multiple choice, true/false, matching, short answer) and essays. Essays often are used to assess higher level performances such as writing a composition. Measures are graded according to preset criteria for what constitutes acceptable performance. Very often, a software package includes tests and built-in criteria for passing them. Essays usually are graded with a criteria checklist or writing **rubric**, an instrument consisting of a set of descriptions that define important components and qualities of the work.

Constructivists tend to eschew traditional assessment strategies as being too limiting to measure real progress in complex learning and too removed from real-life tasks to be authentic. However, teachers recognize that even the most innovative activities require a reliable and valid means of measuring student progress. Commonly used assessment strategies are project assignments (e.g., web pages, multimedia products, desktop-published publications), self-report instruments (e.g., student-prepared journals or other descriptions), and portfolio entries.

Criticisms of each model. It is because they have such different views of reality and theory bases that educators who espouse objectivist and constructivist beliefs take very different views of appropriate technology-based methods. Objectivists say constructivist methods are unrealistic; constructivists consider directed methods to be outmoded. Table 2.2 expands on these criticisms.

The Future of Technology Integration: Merging the Two Approaches

We must be open minded in finding ways to merge these two integration approaches that will benefit both learners and teachers. Of course, the most effective approach will depend on the topics and problems that define the learning activity and individual learning needs.

Clearly, instructional problems identified by objectivists and constructivists are common to most schools and classrooms, regardless of grade level, type of student, or content. Teachers will always use some directed instruction as the most efficient means of teaching required skills; teachers will always need motivating, cooperative learning activities to ensure that students want to learn and that they can transfer what they learn to problems they encounter. Tinker (1998) warns, "It is a fallacy to think that technology will make traditional content outdated. . . . The corollary to this thinking that traditional content is less important than learning to learn . . . is a dangerous doctrine" (p. 2). Proficient technology-oriented teachers must learn to combine directed instruction and constructivist approaches and to select technology resources and integration methods that are best suited to their specific needs.

These two ostensibly different views of reality will merge to form a new and powerful approach to solving some of the major problems of the educational system, each contributing an essential element of the new instructional formula. Hirsch (2002) believes that directed learning is best for providing a foundation of skills, while inquiry-based learning is probably best for developing global skills slowly over time. Other theorists and practitioners believe that constructivism will eventually dominate overall educational goals and objectives such as learning to apply scientific methods, while systematic approaches will ensure that specific prerequisite skills are learned. This is not currently the case, however, especially in light of the tension between the constructivist view of reality and the current standards and testing movement.

TABLE 2.2   A Comparison of Directed and Constructivist Models and the Problems They Address

	Directed Instructional Models	Constructivist Models
Teaching/Learning Methods	• Stress individualized work. • Have specific skill-based instructional goals and objectives; same for all students. • Teachers transmit a set body of skills and/or knowledge to students. • Students learn prerequisite skills required for each new skill. • Sequences of carefully structured presentations and activities to help students understand (process), remember (encode and store), and transfer (retrieve) information and skills. • Traditional teacher-directed methods and materials are used: lectures, skill worksheets.	• Stress group-based, cooperative work. • Have global goals such as problem solving and critical thinking; sometimes differ for each student. • Have students generate their own knowledge through experiences anchored in real-life situations. • Students learn lower order skills in the context of higher order problems that require them. • Learning through problem-oriented activities (e.g., "what if" situations); visual formats and mental models; rich, complex, learning environments; and learning through exploration. • Nontraditional materials are used to promote student-driven exploration and problem solving.
Assessment Methods	• Traditional assessments (e.g., multiple choice, short answer) with specific expected responses; student products (e.g., essays) graded with checklists of rubrics.	• Nontraditional assessments (e.g., group products such as web pages, multimedia projects) with varying contents or portfolios; student products graded with self-report instruments, rubrics.
Instructional Needs and Problems Targeted	• *Accountability:* All students must meet required education standards to be considered educated. • *Individualization:* Help meet individual needs of students working at many levels. • *Quality assurance:* Quality of instruction must be consistently high across teachers and schools in various locations. • *Convergent thinking:* All students must have the same skills.	• *Higher level skills:* All students must be able to think critically and creatively and solve problems. • *Cooperative group skills:* Help students learn to work with others to solve problems. • *Increase relevancy:* Students must have active, visual, authentic learning experiences that relate to their own lives. • *Divergent thinking:* Students must think on their own and solve novel problems as they occur.
Criticisms	• Breaking topics into discrete skills and teaching them in isolation from each other is directed more at basic skills than at higher level ones; students cannot apply skills later (i.e., knowledge is inert). • Learning is repetitive and predictable: students often find it uninteresting and irrelevant; lack of motivation leads to lower achievement and higher dropout rates. • Not all topics lend themselves to directed approaches. • Students cannot solve novel problems or work cooperatively with others to solve problems.	• When students are allowed to demonstrate knowledge in varying ways, teachers cannot certify students' individual skill levels, as required by today's accountability standards. • Letting students generate their own knowledge is time consuming and inefficient; students may lack prerequisite skills to handle constructivist problem-solving environments effectively. • Not all topics lend themselves to constructivist approaches. • Despite learning being anchored in authentic problems, students may not transfer skills to real-life situations.

FIGURE 2.7 Technology Integration Strategies for Directed, Constructivist, or Both Models

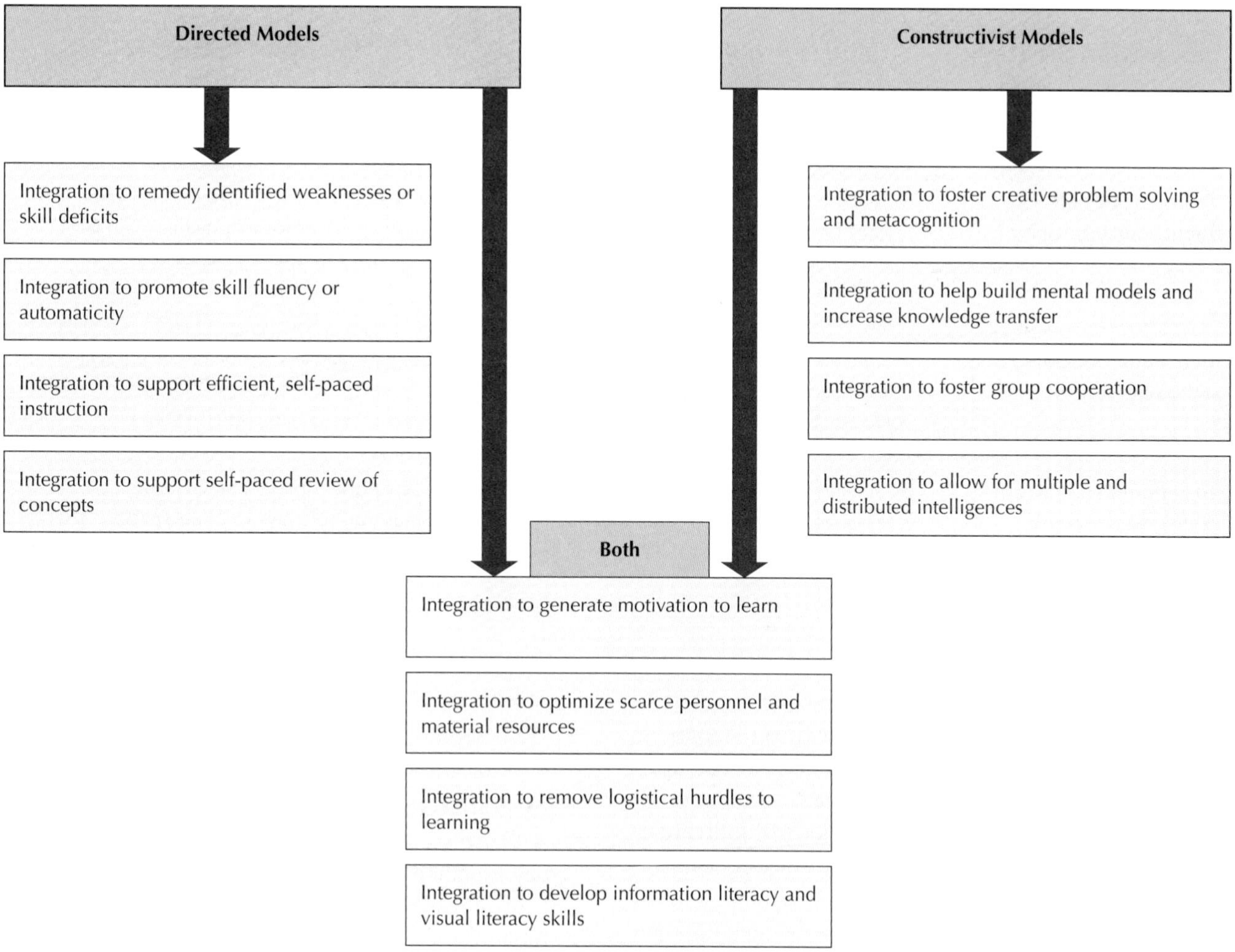

Directed Models	Constructivist Models
Integration to remedy identified weaknesses or skill deficits	Integration to foster creative problem solving and metacognition
Integration to promote skill fluency or automaticity	Integration to help build mental models and increase knowledge transfer
Integration to support efficient, self-paced instruction	Integration to foster group cooperation
Integration to support self-paced review of concepts	Integration to allow for multiple and distributed intelligences

Both

Integration to generate motivation to learn

Integration to optimize scarce personnel and material resources

Integration to remove logistical hurdles to learning

Integration to develop information literacy and visual literacy skills

Technology Integration Strategies Based on Each Model

Subsequent chapters in this book describe and give examples of integration strategies for various types of courseware materials and technology media. All of these strategies implement a group of general integration principles. Some strategies draw on the unique characteristics of a technology resource to meet certain kinds of learning needs. Others take advantage of a resource's ability to substitute for materials lacking in schools or classrooms. Teachers may use many or all of these strategies at the same time.

It is important to recognize that each of the integration strategies described here addresses specific instructional needs identified by educational theorists and practitioners. Strategies are not employed because technology is the wave of the future or because students should occasionally use computers because it is good for them. This text advocates making a conscious effort to match technology resources

to problems that educators cannot address in other, easier ways.

As Figure 2.7 shows, four technology integration strategies are based primarily on directed models, four are based on constructivist ones, and four are strategies that could help address either model.

Technology integration strategies based on directed models. As Table 2.3 and the following list show, the four integration strategies based on directed methods are all designed to address individual instruction and practice:

- **Integration to remedy identified weaknesses or skill deficits** — Constructivists say that students should learn prerequisite skills as they see the need for them in a group or individual project. However, experienced teachers know that even motivated students do not always learn skills as expected. These failures occur for a variety of reasons, many of which are related to learners' internal capabilities and not all of which are thoroughly understood. When the absence of prerequisite

TABLE 2.3 Technology Integration Strategies Based on Directed Teaching Models

Integration Strategy	Needs/Problems Addressed	Example Activities
To remedy identified weaknesses or skill deficits	• At-risk students need individual instruction and practice. • Students fail parts of high-stakes tests.	Tutorial or drill-and-practice software is targeted to identified skills.
To promote skill fluency/automaticity	• Students need to be able to recall and apply lower level skills quickly, automatically. • Students need to review for upcoming tests.	Drill-and-practice or instructional game software lets students practice math facts, vocabulary, or spelling words.
To support efficient, self-paced learning	• Students are motivated and able to learn on their own. • No teacher is available for the content area.	Use tutorial software or distance learning courses for foreign languages, higher level science or math, or other elective subjects.
To support self-paced review of concepts	• Students need help studying for tests. • Students need make-up instruction for missed work.	Use tutorial, drill-and-practice, or simulation software to cover specific concepts.

skills presents a barrier to higher level learning or to passing tests, directed instruction usually is the most efficient way of providing them. Materials such as drill-and-practice and tutorial software have proven to be valuable resources for providing this kind of individualized instruction. When students have failed to learn required skills, they frequently find technology-based materials more motivating and less threatening than teacher-delivered instruction.

- **Integration to promote skill fluency or automaticity** — Some prerequisite skills must be applied quickly and without conscious effort in order to be most useful. Gagné (1982) and Bloom (1986) referred to this automatic recall as **automaticity**. Students need rapid recall and performance of a wide range of skills throughout the curriculum, including simple math facts, grammar and usage rules, and spelling. Some students acquire automaticity through repeated use of the skills in practical situations. Others acquire it more efficiently through isolated practice. Drill-and-practice, instructional games, and sometimes simulation courseware can provide practice tailored to individual skill needs and learning pace.

- **Integration to support efficient, self-paced learning** — When students are self-motivated and have the ability to structure their own learning, the most desirable method is often the one that offers the fastest and most efficient path. Sometimes these students are interested in topics not being covered in class or for which there is no instructor available. Directed instruction for these

students can frequently be supported by well-designed, self-instructional tutorials and self-paced distance learning workshops and courses.

- **Integration to support self-paced review of concepts** — When students cover a number of topics over time, they usually need a review prior to taking a test to help them remember and consolidate concepts. Sometimes students are absent when in-class instruction was given or need additional time going over the material to understand and remember it. In these situations, drill-and-practice and tutorial software materials are good ways to provide these kinds of self-paced reviews.

Technology integration strategies based on constructivist models. Table 2.4 and the following list summarize the four integration strategies identified with constructivist methods:

- **Integration to foster creative problem solving and metacognition** — Although most people acknowledge the importance of students having a knowledge base of specific skills and information, it is also becoming evident that our world is too complex and technical for students to learn ahead of time everything they may need for the future. Thus, our society is beginning to place a high value on the ability to solve novel problems in creative ways. If students are conscious of the procedures they use to solve problems, they often can more easily improve on their strategies and become more effective, creative problem solvers. Consequently, teachers often try to present students with novel problems to solve and

TABLE 2.4 Technology Integration Strategies Based on Constructivist Models

Integration Strategy	Needs/Problems Addressed	Example Activities
To foster creative problem solving and metacognition	• Students need to be able to solve complex, novel problems as they occur. • Teachers want to encourage students' self-awareness of their own learning strategies.	• Video-based scenarios pose problems, help support student problem solving. • Graphic tools illustrate concepts and support student manipulation of variables. • Simulations allow exploration of how systems work.
To help build mental models and increase knowledge transfer	• Students have trouble understanding complex and/or abstract concepts. • Students have trouble seeing where skills apply to real-life problems.	• Video-based scenarios pose problems. • Students create multimedia products to illustrate and report on their research. • Simulations, problem-solving software illustrate and let students explore complex systems.
To foster group cooperation skills	• Students need to be able to work with others to solve problems and create products.	Students collaborate to: • Do Internet research. • Create multimedia/web page products. • Compete in instructional games.
To allow for multiple and distributed intelligences	• Teachers want to allow students multiple ways to learn and to demonstrate achievement.	Students have varying roles in group work to create: • Multimedia products. • Web pages. • Desktop-published newsletters, brochures.

to get them to analyze how they learn to solve them. Resources such as problem-solving courseware and multimedia applications often are considered ideal environments for getting students to think about how they think and for offering opportunities to challenge their creativity and problem-solving abilities.

• **Integration to help build mental models and increase knowledge transfer** — The problem of inert knowledge is believed to arise when students learn skills in isolation from problem applications. When students later encounter problems that require the skills, they do not realize how the skills could be relevant. Problem-solving materials in highly visual formats allow students to build rich mental models of problems to be solved (CTGV, 1991). For example, visual information allows users to easily recognize patterns (CTGV, 1990). Students need not depend on reading skills, which may be deficient, to build these mental models. Thus, supporters hypothesize that teaching skills in these highly visual, problem-solving environments helps ensure that knowledge will transfer to higher order skills. These technology-based

methods are especially desirable for teachers who work with students in areas such as mathematics and science, where concepts are abstract and complex and where inert knowledge is frequently a problem.

• **Integration to foster group cooperation skills** — One skill area currently identified as an important focus for schools' efforts to restructure curriculum (U.S. Department of Labor, 1992) is the ability to work cooperatively in a group to solve problems and develop products (Johnson & Johnson, 2004, 2005; Johnson, Johnson, & Holubec, 1992; Kirshner, 2001). Although schools certainly can teach cooperative work without technology resources, a growing body of evidence documents students' appreciation of cooperative work as both more motivating and easier to accomplish when it uses technology.

• **Integration to allow for multiple and distributed intelligences** — Integration strategies with group cooperative activities also give teachers a way to allow students of widely varying abilities to make valuable contributions on their own terms. Since each student is seen as an important member of the group in these activities, the

TABLE 2.5 Technology Integration Strategies to Support Either Model

Integration Strategy	Needs/Problems Addressed	Example Activities
To generate motivation to learn	• Due to past failures, at-risk students need more than usual motivation. • Students need to see the relevance of new concepts and skills to their lives. • Students need to be active, rather than passive, learners.	• Visual and interactive qualities of the Internet and multimedia resources draw and hold students' attention. • Drill-and-practice/tutorial materials give students private environments for learning and practice. • Video-based scenarios, simulations show relevance of science and math skills. • Hands-on production work (e.g., multimedia, web pages) gives students an active role in learning.
To optimize scarce personnel and materials resources	• Schools have limited budgets, must save money on consumables. • Teachers are in short supply in some subject areas.	• Simulations allow repeated science experiments at no additional cost. • Distance courses can offer subjects for which schools lack teachers.
To remove logistical hurdles to learning	• Students find repetitive tasks (handwriting, calculations) boring and tedious. • Students lack motor skills to show their designs. • Students cannot travel to places to learn about them. • Some social and physical phenomena occur too slowly, too quickly, or at too great a distance to allow observation.	Students can use: • Word processing to make quick, easy revisions and corrections to written work. • Calculators and spreadsheets to do low-level calculations involved in math/science problem solving. • Computer-assisted design (CAD) and drawing software to try out and change designs. • Virtual tours to see places they could not go physically. • Simulations to allow study of social systems (e.g., voting) and physical systems (chemical reactions).
To develop information literacy/visual literacy skills	Students need to learn: • Modern methods of communicating information. • How to analyze the quality of visual presentations.	Students can: • Do research reports as multimedia products or web pages. • Become media savvy by using information on the Internet and video.

activities themselves are viewed as problems for group—rather than individual—solution. This strategy has implications for enhancing students' self-esteem and for increasing their willingness to spend more time on learning tasks. It also allows students to see that they can help each other accomplish tasks and can learn from each other as well as from the teacher or from media.

Enabling integration strategies useful with either model. Some integration strategies have a more general support role for instruction and can address the needs of either model. These "enabling" strategies seem to be appearing with increasing frequency in combination with other directed or constructivist strategies described in this chapter. They seem to support the other strategies and make them more feasible and practical. The four strategies are summarized in Table 2.5 and the following list:

• **Integration to generate motivation to learn—** Teachers who work with at-risk students say that capturing students' interest and enthusiasm is key to success; frequently, they cite it as their most difficult challenge. Some educators assert that today's television-oriented students are increasingly likely to demand more motivational qualities in their instruction than students in previous generations did. Constructivists argue that instruction must address students' affective needs as well as their cognitive ones, saying that students will learn more if what they are learning is interesting and relevant to their needs. They recommend the highly visual and interactive qualities of Internet and multimedia resources as the basis of these strategies. Proponents of directed methods make similar claims about highly structured, self-instructional learning environments. They say that some students find it very motivating to learn at their own pace in a private environment because they receive immediate feedback on their progress. It seems evident that appropriate integration strategies to address motivation problems depend on the needs of the student; either constructivist or directed integration strategies can be used to increase motivation to learn.

- **Integration to optimize scarce resources** — Current resources and numbers of personnel in schools are rarely optimal. Many of the courseware materials described in later chapters can help make up for the lack of required resources in the school or classroom—from consumable supplies to qualified teachers. For example, drill-and-practice programs can replace worksheets, a good distance program can offer instruction in topics for which local teachers are in short supply, and a simulation can let students repeat experiments without depleting chemical supplies or other materials.

- **Integration to remove logistical hurdles to learning** — Some technology tools offer no instructional sequence or tasks but help students complete learning tasks more efficiently. These tools support directed instruction by removing or reducing logistical hurdles to learning. For example, word processing programs do not teach students how to write, but they let students write and rewrite more quickly, without the labor of handwriting. CAD software does not teach students how to design a house, but it allows them to try out designs and features to see what they look like before building models or structures. A calculator lets students do lower level calculations so they can focus on the high-level concepts of math problems. A CD-ROM might contain only a set of pictures of sea life, but it lets a teacher illustrate concepts about sea creatures more quickly and easily than he or she could with books.

- **Integration to develop information literacy and visual literacy skills** — A rationale underlying many

of the most popular directed and constructivist integration strategies is the need to give students practice in using modern methods of communicating information. For example, when students use presentation software instead of cardboard charts to give a report, they gain experience for college classrooms and business offices, where computer-based presentations are the norm. Using technology to communicate visually represents Information Age skills that students will need both for higher education and in the workplace.

Developing Teacher Knowledge: Technological Pedagogical Content Knowledge (TPACK)

An Overview of the TPACK Framework

Before we discuss a planning model for technology integration in classrooms, there is one additional theory to consider that complements the learning theories and instructional strategies described earlier in this chapter. Teachers must consider the different knowledge domains they bring to the classroom that impact the teaching and learning strategies they use and the ways in which they choose to integrate technology into the classroom.

As discussed, teaching is a complex combination of what teachers know about the content they teach and how they decide to teach that content. Historically, teacher education has centered on two things—content knowledge and pedagogy. Shulman (1986) provides an analysis of these components (pedagogical content knowledge) and stresses the importance of looking at how these components work together rather than separately. Hughes (2000) extends Shulman's scholarship by adding technology as another component of knowledge that is needed by teachers. Most recently, Mishra and Koehler (2006) discuss in-depth the conceptual and theoretical framework of **technological pedagogical content knowledge (TPACK)** while others (e.g., Doering & Veletsianos, 2007; Hughes & Scharber, 2007) have focused on the impact of TPACK within content-specific domains.

The TPACK framework strives to "capture some of the essential qualities of knowledge required by teachers for technology integration in their teaching, while addressing the complex, multifaceted and situated nature of teacher knowledge" (Mishra & Koehler, 2006).

Technological pedagogical content knowledge is an understanding that emerges from an interaction of content, pedagogy, and technology knowledge. Underlying truly meaningful and deeply skilled teaching with technology, TPCK is different from knowledge of all three components individually. . . . TPCK is the basis of effective teaching with technology and requires an understanding of the representation of concepts using technologies; pedagogical techniques that use technologies in constructive ways to teach content; knowledge of what makes concepts difficult or easy to learn and how technology can help redress some of the problems that students face; knowledge of students' prior knowledge and theories of epistemology; and knowledge of how technologies can be used to build on existing knowledge and to develop new epistemologies or strengthen old ones (Koehler & Mishra, 2008).

Initially referred to simply as *TPCK*, the model evolved as it gained momentum and acceptance and continued to flourish as a theoretical construct. In the *Journal of Computing in Teacher Education*, TPCK became TPACK as Thompson and Mishra (2007–2008) argued that the insertion of the "A" better represents the interdependence of the three knowledge domains (T, P, C) and the framework better explains the "Total PACKage" of teacher knowledge.

Technology integration is a complex and "wicked" problem (Mishra & Koehler, 2006) that the educational technology field has long struggled to understand, define, and explain; the TPACK framework is a metacognitive tool teachers can use to enhance technology integration into their classrooms by helping them visualize how their technology knowledge and skills work in tandem with their other knowledge domains

about teaching and learning. This framework "attempts to capture some of the essential qualities of knowledge required by teachers for technology integration in their teaching, while addressing the complex, multifaceted and situated nature of teacher knowledge" (Mishra & Koehler, 2006). Theoretically and practically, teaching requires an intricate combination of content, pedagogy, and technology knowledge. As noted in Figure 2.8, teachers must understand more than technology alone, more than pedagogy (teaching/learning) alone, and more than content alone. They need to continue to move towards the center where they can use all knowledge domains to design and deliver instruction effectively with technology. For example, Doering and Veletsianos (2007) note that a geography teacher should understand the complex relationships and interconnections among all three of these components of teacher knowledge rather than isolating what they know about Google Earth (technology), structured problem solving (pedagogy), and cultural geography (content).

Go to MyEducationLab and select the topic "Technology Integration Models." Under "Rubrics/Checklists," access the activity "TPACK Identification Model" to investigate where you might fit within the TPACK model.

A Technology Integration Planning (TIP) Model for Teachers

An Overview of the TIP Model

In addition to developing their metacognitive awareness of their TPACK strengths and weaknesses and identifying the integration strategy they intend to use, teachers need a planning approach to ensure their strategy will be successful. The Technology Integration Planning (TIP) Model, shown in Figure 2.9, benefits teachers by giving them a general approach to address challenges involved in integrating technology into teaching. Each of the model's six phases outlines a set of planning and implementation steps that help ensure technology use will be meaningful, efficient, and successful in meeting needs. Experienced technology-using teachers tend to move through these steps intuitively. However, for new teachers or those just beginning to integrate technology, the TIP Model provides a helpful guide on procedures and issues to address. After giving an overview of the model, we will discuss each phase in more depth and present a classroom example (the "Online Multicultural Project") of how to implement the tasks.

FIGURE 2.8 Technological Pedagogical Content Knowledge Model (TPACK)

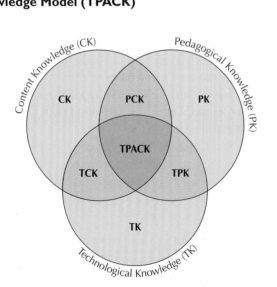

FIGURE 2.9 The Technology Integration Planning (TIP) Model

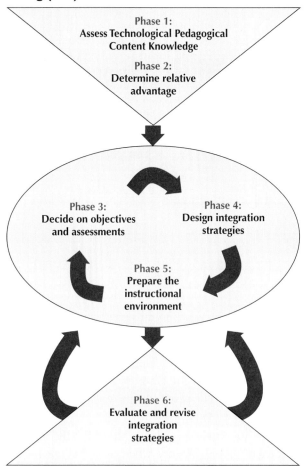

- **Phase 1 focus:** *What is my technological pedagogical content knowledge?* — Teachers need to identify where they believe they see themselves within the TPACK framework. Pope and Golub (2000) emphasize that preservice teachers need "to be critical consumers of technology, to be thoughtful users who question, reflect, and refract on the best times and ways to integrate technology." In order to be "critical consumers," all teachers need to be explicitly aware of their current knowledge bases in the areas of TK, TCK, TPK, and TPACK (Hughes & Scharber, 2008). This metacognitive awareness of TPACK enables teachers to set learning goals for themselves and, in turn, to make thoughtful decisions for technology integration.

- **Phase 2 focus:** *Why should I use a technology-based method?* — Teachers look at their current teaching problems and identify technology-based methods that may offer good solutions. In his best-selling book on how and why innovations get adopted, Everett Rogers (2004) says that people resist changing how they do things, even if new ways are better. However, people are more likely to change if they see clearly the benefits of a new method over an old one. He calls this seeing a **relative advantage**.

- **Phase 3 focus:** *How will I know students have learned?* — Teachers decide on the skills they want students to learn from the technology-integrated lesson(s) and design ways to assess how well students have learned and how effectively the activity has been carried out.

- **Phase 4 focus:** *What teaching strategies and activities will work best?* — Teachers decide on instructional strategies and how to carry them out. When teachers create an instructional design for technology integration, they consider the characteristics of their topic and the needs of their students and decide on an instructional course of action that addresses both within the constraints of their classroom environment.

- **Phase 5 focus:** *Are essential conditions in place to support technology integration?* — Teachers organize the teaching environment so that technology plans can be carried out effectively. Since research on effective technology uses shows that teachers can integrate technology successfully *only* if they have adequate hardware, software, and technical support available to them, ISTE (2008) lists a set of *essential conditions* for unleashing the potential power of technology tools and methods. The school and district must provide many of these essential conditions, but for each technology integration strategy, the teacher considers which conditions are in place and to what degree. This helps shape the kind of integration possible for the situation.

- **Phase 6 focus:** *What worked well? What could be improved?* — Teachers review outcome data and information on technology-integrated methods and determine what should be changed to make them work better next time. In addition to collecting formal data on instructional and other outcomes, teachers sometimes interview students and observers to ask what they think could be improved. Some teachers keep daily notes or logs on implementation problems and issues. As they review all the information, teachers can use the *Technology Impact Checklist* (located in MyEducationLab) to help them reflect on whether the problems they identified in Phases 1 and 2 have, indeed, been addressed successfully.

Phase 1: Reflect on Technological Pedagogical Content Knowledge

All teachers can place themselves within the Technological Pedagogical Content Model. Some are skilled in using technology; some are very knowledgeable within their content

Classroom Example: Online Multicultural Project

Phase 1: Reflect on technological pedagogical knowledge. Mia wanted to include more meaningful multicultural activities in the social studies curriculum. She and the other social studies teachers in her school focused primarily on studying various holidays and foods from other cultures. They sponsored an annual International Foods smorgasbord event that was very popular with the students, but she doubted it taught them much about the richness of other cultures or why they should respect and appreciate cultures different from their own. She sometimes overheard her students making disparaging comments about people of other nationalities. Mia felt a better approach to multicultural education might help, but she wasn't sure she had enough background knowledge to be able to develop a more meaningful project.

Analysis Questions
1. What does Mia want to accomplish in her classroom?
2. How might Mia reflect on her technological pedagogical content knowledge?
3. What is the purpose of this reflection?

area, while others have a toolbox of teaching methods that they can employ at anytime. What is important is that teachers continually reflect on where they are located in this model so that their technology integration planning can complement their abilities.

Phase 1 questions. The first phase in integrating technology requires teachers to self-assess their knowledge domains by asking themselves the following questions:

- **What is my knowledge of technology (TK)?** — It is very important that teachers be cognizant of their attitudes toward and skills with technology. In addition, teachers need to be aware of the various technologies they could integrate within their content area. Attitude, skills, and awareness all affect the success of technology integration within a classroom. Do you need to improve your technology knowledge before employing the lesson you have developed?

- **What is my knowledge of pedagogy (PK)?** — Teachers' choices of pedagogy influence their everyday ability to foster learning within a classroom. Teachers must be aware of the ways they stimulate learning through the teaching methods they employ. By being aware of the tools and strategies they use in addition to the theoretical foundations that guide their practice, teachers can understand how their pedagogy will affect their use of technology. Do you need to expand your pedagogical knowledge before employing the lesson you developed?

- **What is my knowledge of content (CK)?** — Knowing the content of a specific discipline is necessary to de-

velop meaningful learning experiences within the classroom. Assessing your knowledge of your content area(s) is important in fostering the meaningful use of technology within the classroom. Do you need to update your content knowledge before employing the lesson you developed?

- **Where do I see myself in the TPACK model?** — Teachers should identify where they believe they currently reside within the TPACK model. In addition, teachers should consider how they might foster their movement to the center of the model where technology, pedagogical, and content knowledge overlap and intertwine. How do you believe your teaching would improve if you were at the center of the TPACK model?

Phase 2: Determine Relative Advantage

Every teacher has topics—and sometimes whole subject areas—that he or she finds especially challenging to teach. Some concepts are so abstract or foreign to students that they struggle to understand them; students find some topics so boring, tedious, or irrelevant that they have trouble attending to them. Some learning requires time-consuming tasks that students resist doing. Good teachers spend much time trying to meet these challenges—making concepts more engaging or easier to grasp, or making tasks more efficient to accomplish.

Recognizing relative advantage. Technology-based strategies offer many unique benefits to teachers as they look for instructional solutions to these problems. Time and effort are required to plan and carry out technology-based methods, however, and sometimes additional ex-

Classroom Example: Online Multicultural Project

Phase 2: Determine relative advantage. After reflecting on her technological pedagogical content knowledge, Mia concluded that she could follow a model she heard about while attending a workshop the previous summer. At the workshop, teachers at another school district described an online project with partner schools in countries around the world. One teacher told about her partners in Israel and Spain. She said students exchanged information with designated partners and answered assigned questions to research each other's backgrounds and locales. Then they worked in groups on travel brochures or booklets to email to each other. They even took digital photos of themselves to send. It sounded like a great way for kids to learn about other cultures in a meaningful way while also learning some geography and civics. The teachers in the workshop remarked that it was difficult to demean people who look and talk differently from you when you've worked with them and gotten to know them. Mia was so impressed with the online project they described that she decided to try it out in her own classroom.

Analysis Questions

1. What is the problem Mia wants to address?
2. What evidence does she have that there is a problem?
3. What would be the relative advantage of the method she is proposing?
4. How does she hope this method will be better than previous ones?

---

pense is involved as well. Teachers have to consider the benefits of such methods compared to their current ones and decide if the benefits are worth the additional effort and cost.

As mentioned earlier, Everett Rogers (2004) refers to this decision as seeing the **relative advantage** of using a new method. Table 2.6 lists several kinds of learning problems and technology solutions with potential for high relative advantage to teachers. However, these lists are really just general guidelines. Being able to recognize specific instances of these problems in a classroom context and knowing how to match them with an appropriate technology solution require knowledge of classroom problems, practice in addressing them, and an in-depth knowledge of the characteristics of each technology. Chapters 3 through 15 of this textbook provide the latter information, as well as many examples of matching technology to various needs.

Phase 2 questions. The second phase in integrating technology requires answering the following two questions about technology's relative advantage in a given situation:

- **What is the problem I am addressing?** — To make sure a technology application is a good solution, begin with a clear statement of the teaching and learning problem. This is sometimes difficult to do. It is a natural human tendency to jump to a quick solution rather than to recognize the real problem. Also, everyone may not see a problem the same way. Use the following guidelines when answering the question "What is the problem?"

- **Do not focus on technologies** — Remember that knowing how to use a technology appropriately is part of a solution, not in itself a problem to solve. Therefore, avoid problem statements like "Students do not know how to use spreadsheets efficiently" or "Teachers are not having their students use the Internet." Not having the skills to use a technology (e.g., a spreadsheet or the Internet) is an instructional problem, but not the kind of teaching/learning problem to be considered here. It is sometimes true that teachers are given a technology and told to implement it. In these situations, they must decide if there is a real teaching or learning problem the new resource can help meet. If teachers have a technology available and choose not to use it, however, it may mean they can see no relative advantage to using it; nonuse of a technology is not in itself a problem to address with the TIP Model.

- **Look for evidence** — Look for observable indications that there really is a problem. Examples of evidence include the following: Students consistently achieve lower grades in a skill area, a formal or informal survey shows that teachers have trouble getting students to attend to learning tasks, or teachers observe that students are refusing to turn in required assignments in a certain area.

TABLE 2.6 Technology Solutions with Potential for High Relative Advantage

Learning Problem	Technology Solutions	Relative Advantage
Concepts are new, foreign (e.g., mathematics, physics principles).	Graphic tools, simulations, video-based problem scenarios	Visual examples clarify concepts and applications.
Concepts are abstract, complex (e.g., physics principles, biology systems).	Math tools (Geometer's *SketchPad*), simulations, problem-solving software, spreadsheet exercises, graphing calculators	Graphics displays make abstract concepts more concrete; students can manipulate systems to see how they work.
Time-consuming manual skills (e.g., handwriting, calculations, data collection) interfere with learning high-level skills.	Tool software (e.g., word processing, spreadsheets) and probeware	Takes low-level labor out of high-level tasks; students can focus on learning high-level concepts and skills.
Students find practice boring (e.g., basic math skills, spelling, vocabulary, test preparation).	Drill-and-practice software, instructional games	Attention-getting displays, immediate feedback, and interaction combine to create motivating practice.
Students cannot see relevance of concepts to their lives (e.g., history, social studies).	Simulations, Internet activities, video-based problem scenarios	Visual, interactive activities help teachers demonstrate relevance.
Skills are "inert," i.e., students can do them but do not see where they apply (e.g., mathematics, physics).	Simulations, problem-solving software, video-based problem scenarios, student development of web pages, multimedia products	Project-based learning using these tools establishes clear links between skills and real-world problems.
Students dislike preparing research reports, presentations.	Student development of desktop-published and web page/multimedia products	Students like products that look polished, professional.
Students need skills in working collaboratively, opportunities to demonstrate learning in alternative ways.	Student development of desktop-published and web page/multimedia products	Provides format in which group work makes sense; students can work together "virtually"; students make different contributions to one product based on their strengths.
Students need technological competence in preparation for the workplace.	All software and productivity tools; all communications, presentation, and multimedia software	Illustrates and provides practice in skills and tools students will need in work situations.
Teachers have limited time for correcting students' individual practice items.	Drill-and-practice software, handheld computers with assessment software	Feedback to students is immediate; frees teachers for work with students.
No teachers available for advanced courses.	Self-instructional multimedia, distance courses	Provides structured, self-paced learning environments.
Students need individual reviews of missed work.	Tutorial or multimedia software	Provides structured, self-paced environments for individual review of missed concepts.
Schools have insufficient consumable materials (e.g., science labs, workbooks).	Simulations, CD-ROM-based texts, ebooks	Materials are reusable; saves money on purchasing new copies.
Students need quick access to information and people not locally available.	Internet and email projects; multimedia encyclopedias and atlases	Information is faster to access; people are easier, less expensive to contact.

Classroom Example: Online Multicultural Project

Phase 3: Decide on objectives and assessments. Mia reflected on the problems she saw with her current methods of addressing multicultural education and what she wanted her students to learn about other cultures that they didn't seem to be learning now. She decided on the following three outcomes: better attitudes toward people of other cultures, increased learning about similarities and differences among cultures, and knowledge of facts and concepts about the geography and government of the other country they would study. So that she could measure the success of her project later, she created objectives and instruments to measure the outcomes:

- Attitudes toward cultures — At least 75% of students will demonstrate an improved attitude toward the culture being studied with a higher score on the post-unit attitude measure than on the pre-unit measure. **Instrument**: She knew a good way to measure attitudes was with a semantic differential. Before and after the project, students would answer the question: "How do you feel about people from _____?" by marking a line between sets of adjectives to indicate how they feel.

- Knowledge of cultures — Each student group will score at least 90% on a rubric evaluating the brochure or booklet that reflects knowledge of the cultural characteristics (both unique and common to our own) about the people being studied. **Instrument**: After listing characteristics she wanted to see reflected in the products, she found a rubric to assess them. (See sample in Table 2.7.) She decided they should get at least 15 of the 20 possible points on this rubric.

- Factual knowledge — Each student will score at least 80% on a short-answer test on the government and geography of the country being studied.

Analysis Questions

1. How do you think Mia should use the product rubric to assign grades?
2. What kinds of questions could Mia include in a survey to measure how much students liked this way of learning?

- **Do technology-based methods offer a solution with sufficient relative advantage?** — Analyze the benefits of the technology-based method in light of the effort and cost to implement it, and then make a final decision. Use the following guidelines to answer the question "Is technology a good solution?"

  - **Estimate the impact** — Consider the benefits others have gained from using the technology as a solution. Is it likely you will realize similar benefits?

  - **Consider the required effort and expense** — How much time and work will it take to implement the technology solution? Is it likely to be worth it?

Phase 3: Decide on Objectives and Assessments

Writing objectives is a good way of setting clear expectations for what technology-based methods will accomplish. Usually, teachers expect a new method will improve *student behaviors*—for example, that it will result in better achievement, more on-task behaviors, improved attitudes. Sometimes, however, changes in *teacher behaviors* are important—for example, saving time on a task. In either case, objectives should focus on *outcomes* that are observable (e.g., demonstrating, writing, completing), rather

than on internal results that cannot be seen or measured (e.g., being aware, knowing, understanding, or appreciating).

After stating objectives, teachers create ways to assess how well outcomes have been accomplished. Sometimes, they can use existing tests and rubrics. In other cases, they have to create instruments or methods to measure the behaviors.

The new NETS for teachers calls for educational leaders to model technology integration and affect change.

TABLE 2.7 Sample Brochure Rubric

Category	(4) Excellent	(3) Good	(2) Almost	(1) Not Yet
Attractiveness & Organization (Organization)	The brochure has exceptionally attractive formatting and well-organized information.	The brochure has attractive formatting and well-organized information.	The brochure has well-organized information.	The brochure's formatting and organization of material are confusing to the reader.
Content–Accuracy (Ideas)	The brochure has all of the required information (see checklist) and some additional information.	The brochure has all of the required information (see checklist).	The brochure has most of the required information (see checklist).	The brochure has little of the required information (see checklist).
Writing–Mechanics (Conventions)	All of the writing is done in complete sentences. Capitalization and punctuation are correct throughout the brochure.	Most of the writing is done in complete sentences. Most of the capitalization and punctuation are correct throughout the brochure.	Some of the writing is done in complete sentences. Some of the capitalization and punctuation are correct throughout the brochure.	Most of the writing is not done in complete sentences. Most of the capitalization and punctuation are not correct throughout the brochure.
Graphics/Pictures	The graphics go well in the text and there is a good mix of text and graphics.	The graphics go well with the text, but there are so many that they distract from the text.	The graphics go well with the text, but there are too few.	The graphics do not go with the accompanying text or appear to be randomly chosen.
Sources	There are many citations from a variety of sources accurately listed.	There are some citations from a variety of sources accurately listed.	There are a few citations accurately listed on the brochure.	Incomplete citations are listed on the brochure.

Source: Reprinted by permission of Kent School District, 12033 SE 256 St., Kent, WA 98030, (253) 373-7000 (www.kent.k12.wa.us).

Example outcomes, objectives, and assessments. Here are a few examples of outcomes; objectives, which are used to state outcomes in a measurable form; and assessment methods matched to the outcomes:

- **Higher achievement outcome** — Overall average performance on an end-of-chapter test will improve by 20%. (Assess achievement with a test.)

- **Cooperative work outcome** — All students will score at least 15 out of 20 on the cooperative group skill rubric. (Use an existing rubric to grade skills.)

- **Attitude outcome** — Students will indicate satisfaction with the simulation lesson by an overall average score of 20 of 25 points. (Create an attitude survey to assess satisfaction.)

- **Improved motivation** — Teachers will observe better on-task behavior in at least 75% of the students. (Create and use an observation sheet.)

Phase 3 questions. This phase in integrating technology requires answering two questions about outcomes and assessment strategies:

- **What outcomes do I expect from using the new methods?** — Think about problems you are trying to solve and what would be acceptable indications that the technology solution has succeeded in resolving them. Use the following guidelines:

- *Focus on results, not processes* — Think about the *end results* you want to achieve, rather than the *processes* to help you get there. Avoid statements, like "Students will learn cooperative group skills," that focus on a process students use to achieve the outcome (improved cooperative group skills). Instead, state what you want students to be able to do as a result of having participated in the multimedia project —for example, "Ninety percent of students will score 4 out of 5 on a cooperative groups skills rubric."

- ***Make statements observable and measurable*** — Avoid vague statements, like "Students will understand how to work cooperatively," that cannot be measured.

- **What are the best ways of assessing these outcomes?** — The choice of assessment method depends on the nature of the outcome. Note the following guidelines:

  - ***Use written tests to assess skill achievement outcomes*** — Written cognitive tests (e.g., short answer, multiple choice, true/false, matching) and essay exams remain the most common classroom assessment strategy for many formal knowledge skills.

  - ***Use evaluation criteria checklists to assess complex tasks or products*** — When students must create complex products such as multimedia presentations, reports, or web pages, teachers may give students a set of criteria that specify the requirements each product must meet. Points are awarded for meeting each criterion.

  - ***Use rubrics to assess complex tasks or products*** — Rubrics fulfill the same role as evaluation criteria checklists and are sometimes used in addition to them. Their added value is giving students descriptions of various levels of quality. Teachers usually associate a letter grade with each level of quality (Level 5 = A, Level 4 = B, etc.).

  - ***Use Likert scale–type surveys or semantic differentials to assess attitude outcomes*** — When the outcome is improved attitudes, teachers design a survey in **Likert scale** format or with a **semantic differential**. A Likert scale is a series of statements that students use to indicate their degree of agreement or disagreement. For example:

    I like writing more when I use word processing. (Circle one of the following numbers.)

Strongly Agree	Agree	No Opinion	Disagree	Strongly Disagree
1	2	3	4	5

    In a semantic differential, students respond to a question by checking a line between each of several sets of bipolar adjectives to indicate their level of feeling about the topic of the question. For example:

    "How do you feel about math?"

    Warm __ __ __ __ __ Cold?

    Happy __ __ __ __ __ Sad?

  - ***Use observation instruments to measure frequency of behaviors*** — For example, if teachers wanted to see an increase in students' use of scientific language,

they could create a chart to keep track of this use on a daily basis.

Phase 4: Design Integration Strategies

Teachers make many design decisions as they integrate technologies into teaching, including single-subject vs. interdisciplinary approach, grouping strategies, and sequence of learning activities. What usually drives these design decisions is whether the learning environment will be primarily directed (a teacher or expert source presents information for students to absorb) or primarily inquiry based or constructivist (students do activities to generate their own learning). To make this decision, examine the needs and integration strategies described in Tables 2.3 through 2.5, and determine which one(s) apply for the situation.

Deciding on teaching/learning methods. Use the following guidelines to help determine whether your methods should be primarily directed or constructivist:

- **Use directed strategies** — when students need an efficient way to learn specific skills that must be assessed with traditional tests.

- **Use constructivist strategies** — when students need to develop global skills and insights over time (e.g., cooperative group skills, approaches to solving novel problems, mental models of highly complex topics) and when learning may be assessed with alternative measures such as portfolios or group products.

Phase 4 questions. This phase in integrating technology requires answering three questions—about instructional strategies, technology materials, and implementation strategies. These questions are listed here, with suggestions for answering them in actual classroom situations:

- **What kinds of instructional methods are needed in light of content objectives and student characteristics?** — After determining whether integration strategies will be primarily directed or constructivist, also consider the following:

  - ***Content approach*** — Should the approach be single subject or interdisciplinary? Sometimes school or district requirements dictate this decision, and sometimes teachers combine subjects into a single unit of instruction as a way to cover concepts and topics they may not otherwise have time to teach. Most often, however, interdisciplinary approaches are used to model how real-life activities require the use of a combination of skills from several content areas.

Classroom Example: Online Multicultural Project

Phase 4: Design integration strategies. Mia knew that her students would not achieve the insights she had in mind through a strategy of telling them information and testing them on it. They would need to draw their own conclusions by working and communicating with people from other cultures. However, she felt she could use a directed approach to teach them the Internet and email skills they would need to carry out project activities. The project website had good suggestions on how to set up groups of four with designated tasks for each group member. It also suggested the following sequence of activities for introducing and carrying out the project:

Step 1: Sign up on the project website; obtain partner school assignments.

Step 2: Teachers in partner schools make contact and set a timeline.

Step 3: Teachers organize classroom resources for work on project.

Step 4: Introduce the project to students: Display project information from the project website and discuss previous products done by other sites.

Step 5: Assign students to groups; discuss task assignments with all members.

Step 6: Determine students' email and Internet skills; begin teaching these skills.

Step 7: Students do initial email contacts/chats and introduce themselves to each other.

Step 8: Teacher works with groups to identify information for final product.

Step 9: Students do Internet searches to locate required information; take digital photos and scan required images; exchange information with partner sites.

Step 10: Students do production work; exchange final products with partners.

Step 11: Do debriefing and assessments of student work.

Analysis Questions

1. Is Mia's approach primarily directed or constructivist?
2. Why did she decide to take this approach?
3. At which point should Mia do the preassessments to measure students' skills and attitudes prior to the project?
4. How should Mia determine students' levels of required Internet and email skills?

- *Grouping approach* — Should the students work as individuals, in pairs, in small groups, or as a whole class? This decision is made in light of how many computers or software copies are available, as well as the following guidelines:

  - Whole class: For demonstrations or to guide whole-class discussion prior to student work

  - Individual: When students have to demonstrate individual mastery of skills at the end of the lesson or project

  - Pairs: For peer tutoring; higher ability students work with those of lesser ability

  - Small group: To model real-world work skills by giving students experience in cooperative group work

- **How can technology best support these methods?** — Think about the steps that will be required to carry out the technology-based solution you identified in Phase 3.

- **How can I prepare students adequately to use technologies?** — When designing a sequence of activities that incorporates technology tools, be sure to leave enough time for demonstrating the tools to students and allowing them to become comfortable using them before they do a graded product.

Phase 5: Prepare the Instructional Environment

If teachers could obtain all of the teaching resources they needed whenever they wanted them, they would make all Phase 5 planning decisions after they had decided on the

Classroom Example: Online Multicultural Project

Phase 5: Prepare the instructional environment. As soon as Mia knew that her students would be able to participate in the Internet project, she began to get organized. First, she examined the timeline of project activities so she would know when her students needed to use computers. She made sure to build in enough time to demonstrate the project site and to get students used to using the browser and search engine. Then she began the following planning and preparation activities:

- Handouts for students — To make sure groups knew the tasks each member should do, Mia created handouts specifying timelines and what should be accomplished at each stage of the project. She also made a checklist of information students were to collect and made copies so that students could check off what they had done as they went. She wanted to make sure everyone knew how she would grade their work so she made copies of the assessments (the rubric and a description of the country information test), handed them out, and discussed them with the students.

- Computer schedule — Mia had a classroom workstation consisting of five networked computers, each with an Internet connection, so she set up a schedule for small groups to use the computers. She knew that some students would need to scan pictures, download image files from the digital camera, and process those files for sending to the partner schools, so she scheduled some additional time in the computer lab for this work. She thought that students could do other work in the library/media center after school if they needed still more time.

Analysis Questions

1. If Mia wanted to do a demonstration and display of the project website to the whole class at once, what resource would she have to arrange to do this?
2. Mia was concerned about students revealing too much personal information about themselves to people in their partner schools. What guidelines should she give them about information exchanges to protect their privacy and security?
3. If the network or Internet access were interrupted for a day, what could Mia have the students do to make good use of their time during the delay?

---

best instructional strategies in Phase 4. In practice, however, teachers make many Phase 4 and 5 decisions at the same time. Most teachers usually decide how they will teach something in light of what is available for teaching it.

Essential conditions for effective technology uses. In Phase 5, teachers make sure their instructional environment meets all of the following essential conditions required for successful technology integration:

- **Adequate hardware, software, and media** — Enough computers are available, and there are sufficient legal copies of instructional resources.

- **Time to use resources** — Hardware and enough legal copies of software have been obtained or scheduled for the time needed.

- **Special needs of students** — Provisions have been made for access by students with disabilities and for all students' privacy and safety.

- **Planning for technology use** — Teachers are familiar enough with the hardware and software to use it efficiently

and do necessary troubleshooting; they have allowed time for testing and backup of files; they have a backup plan in the event technology resources fail to work as planned.

Phase 5 questions. This integrating technology phase requires answering three questions about preparing an instructional environment that will support technology integration:

- **What equipment, software, media, and materials will I need to carry out the instructional strategies?** — As you create ways to stretch scarce resources, be sure that your strategies are ethical and in keeping with the reasons you chose a technology-based solution in the first place. Some guidelines:

  - *Computers* — If there are not enough computers available to support the individual format you wanted, consider organizing the integration plan around student pairs or small groups. Also consider having computer and noncomputer learning stations that individuals or groups cycle through, completing

Classroom Example: Online Multicultural Project

Phase 6: Evaluate and revise integration strategies. Mia was generally pleased with the results of the multicultural project. According to the semantic differential, most students showed a major improvement in how they perceived people from the country they were studying. Students she had spoken with were very enthusiastic about their chats and email exchanges. Some group brochures and booklets were more polished than others, but they all showed good insights into the similarities and differences between cultures, and every group had met the rubric criteria on content. The web searches they had done seemed to have helped a lot. One thing that became clear was that production work on their published products was very time consuming; in the future the schedule would have to be changed to allow more time. Mia also realized she had to stress that the deadlines are firm. Students would search for and take digital photos forever if she let them, and that put them behind on doing their products and left little time to discuss their findings on comparisons of cultures. Results varied on the short-answer test on the government and geography of the country being studied. Only about half the students met the 80% criterion. Mia realized she would have to schedule a review of this information before the test. She decided to make this a final group task after the production work was done.

Analysis Questions

1. Although all of Mia's groups did well on context overall, rubric scores revealed that most groups scored lower in one area: spelling, grammar, and punctuation in the products. What steps could Mia add to the production work checklist that might improve this outcome next time?

2. If Mia found that only five of the seven groups in the class were doing well on their final products, what might she do to find out more about why this was happening?

3. One teacher who observed the project told Mia that it might be good to have the school district media/materials production office do the final work on the products for the students. Does this seem like a good idea? Why or why not?

---

various activities at each one. However, if students must master skills on an individual basis, consider scheduling time in a computer lab when all students in the class can use resources at once.

- *Copies of software and media* — Unless a software or media package specifically allows it, making copies of published software or media is illegal, even if copies are used on a temporary basis. Inquire about education-priced lab packs and site licenses.

- *Access to peripherals* — In addition to computers, remember to plan for adequate access to printers, printer paper, and any other needed peripherals (e.g., probes, handhelds).

- *Handouts and other materials* — Prepare and copy (or post) necessary support materials. Unless learning to use the software without guidance is a goal of the project, consider creating summary sheets to remind students how to do basic operations.

- **How should resources be arranged to support instruction and learning?**

  - *Access by students with disabilities* — For students with visual or hearing deficits, consider software or adaptive devices created especially to address these disabilities.

  - *Privacy and safety issues* — Students should never use the Internet without adult supervision and should never participate in unplanned chat sessions. If possible, **firewall software** should be used to prevent accidental access to inappropriate sites.

- **What planning is required to make sure technology resources work well?**

  - *Troubleshooting* — Computers, like all machines, occasionally break down. Learn simple diagnostic procedures so you can correct some problems without assistance.

  - *Test-runs and backup plans* — Leave sufficient time to learn and practice using resources before students use them, but also try out the resources again just before class begins. Have a backup plan in case something goes wrong at the last minute.

Phase 6: Evaluate and Revise Integration Strategies

As teachers complete a technology-based project with students, they begin reviewing evidence on how successful the strategies and plans were in solving the problems they identified. They use this information to decide what should be changed with respect to objectives, strategies, and implementation tasks to ensure even more success next time.

Evaluation issues.   In Phase 6, teachers look at the following issues:

- **Were the objectives achieved?** — This is the primary criterion of success for the activity. Teachers review achievement, attitude, and observation data they have collected and decide if the technology-based method solved the problem(s) they had in mind. These data help them determine what should be changed to make the activity work better.

- **What do students say?** — Some of the best suggestions on needed improvements come from students. Informal discussions with them yield a unique "consumer" focus on the activity.

- **Could improving instructional strategies improve results?** — Technologies in themselves do not usually improve results significantly; it is the way teachers use them that is critical. Look at the design of both the technology use and the learning activities surrounding it.

- **Could improving the environment improve results?** — Sometimes a small change, such as better scheduling or access to a printer, can make a big difference in a project's success.

- **Have I integrated technology well?** — Use the *Technology Impact Checklist* (see MyEducationLab) to determine if the activity has been "worth it."

Phase 6 questions.   This phase in integrating technology requires answering two summary questions about evaluating and revising technology integration strategies:

- **How well has the technology integration strategy worked?** — Review the collected data to answer this question.
  - *Achievement data* — If the problem was low student achievement, do data show students are achieving better than they were before? If the goal was improved motivation or attitudes, are students achieving at least as well as they did before? Is higher achievement consistent across the class, or did some students seem to profit more than others?
  - *Attitude data* — If the problem was low motivation or students refusing to do required work, are there indications this behavior has improved? Has it improved for everyone or just for certain students?

- *Students' comments* — Be sure to ask both lower achieving and higher achieving students for their opinions. Even if achievement and motivation seem to have improved, what do students say about the activity? Do they want to do similar activities again?

- **What could be improved to make the technology integration strategy work better?** — The first time you do a technology-based activity, you can expect it will take longer and you will encounter more errors than in subsequent uses. The following areas are most often cited as needing improvement:
  - *Scheduling* — If students request any change, it is usually for more time. This may or may not be feasible, but you can review the schedule to determine if additional time can be built in for learning software and/or for production work.
  - *Technical skills* — It usually takes longer than expected for students to learn the technology tools. How can this learning be expedited or supported better?
  - *Efficiency* — From the teacher's point of view, the complaint is usually that the activity took longer than expected to plan and carry out. Review the schedule to see if there is any way the activity can be expedited.

Theory and practice are essential ingredients in recipes for successful technology planning and integration. The theoretical concept of teacher knowledge can be used as a metacognitive tool for teachers that informs and affects their strategies and planning approaches for technology integration (practice). Typically, teachers are more cognitively aware of their planning strategies than they are of the theory they are intuitively using to inform the design of instruction and learning experiences for their classrooms. The TPACK framework is useful for teachers in aiding their awareness of what knowledge tools they are currently utilizing together when thinking about integrating technology into their classrooms as well as in visualizing growth and future possibilities in their teaching with technology. As a planning tool, TIP makes concrete the questions teachers need to think through when designing instruction that uses technology. Used together, TPACK and TIP are the theory and practice tools that make technology integration purposeful, effective, and meaningful for teachers and students alike.

Go to MyEducationLab, select the topic "Instructional Planning," and under "Rubrics/Checklists," access the "Technology Integration Planning Checklist" when planning integrated lessons.

FIGURE 2.10 Essential Conditions for Effective Technology Integration

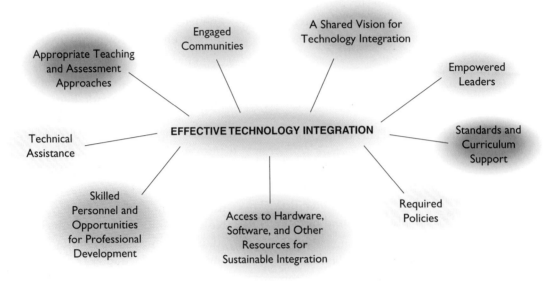

When Technology Works Best: Essential Conditions for Technology Integration

When ISTE established National Education Technology Standards (NETS) for teachers, students, and administrators, they also described the conditions necessary for teachers to exploit the potential power of technology. As ISTE leaders introduced NETS in forums around the country, teachers spoke of barriers they had encountered when they attempted to implement technology in their schools or classrooms. The essential conditions were distilled from these comments. These conditions are summarized in ISTE's *NETS for Teachers* (2008) book, as well as online at http://www.ISTE.org. Once teachers complete an effective preparation program and take positions in schools, their ability to use technology to good advantage is determined in large part by whether the school district and/or school have provided the conditions described here. A summary of the essential conditions for effective technology integration is shown in Figure 2.10.

Essential Condition: A Shared Vision for Technology Integration

Teachers need system-wide support to implement technology. This means that the school, district, local community, and state share with teachers a commitment to using technology to support teaching and learning. As Kwajewski (1997b) says, educational leaders must view technology as a "core value." Usually, this commitment is documented in the form of a statewide and/or district-wide plan created as a cooperative effort of teachers, administrators, and community business partners. The National Center for Technology Planning offers guidelines for planning strategies and examples of school and district plans. Kimball and Sibley (1997–1998) have provided a comprehensive rubric for assessing these plans. To ensure that teachers and administrators have a shared vision for how technology should be supported, all technology plans should reflect the qualities discussed next.

Coordinate school and district planning, and involve teachers and other personnel at all levels. Plans at the school and district levels should be coordinated with each other. It is helpful if each school has a technology liaison/coordinator to act as the school's representative on a district-wide planning committee. To obtain widespread support, planning should involve parents, community leaders, school and district administrators, and teachers.

Budget yearly amounts for technology purchases, and make funding incremental. Technology changes too rapidly for schools to expect that one-time purchases of equipment or software will suffice. A technology plan should allow for yearly upgrades and additions to keep resources current and useful. The plan should identify a specific amount to spend each year and a prioritized list of activities to fund over the life of the plan.

Emphasize teacher training. Knowledgeable people are as important to a technology plan as up-to-date technology resources are. Successful technology programs hinge on well-trained, motivated teachers. A technology plan should acknowledge and address this need with appropriate training activities.

Match technology to curriculum needs. Rather than asking, "How can we use this equipment and software?" an effective vision focuses on questions such as these:

- What are our current unmet needs, and can technology address them?
- What are we teaching now that we can teach better with technology?
- What can we teach with technology that we could not teach before but that should be taught?

It is difficult to identify unmet needs since the emergence of new technology has a way of changing them. Many educators did not realize they needed faster communications, for instance, until the fax machine, email, and cellular telephones became available. However, technology should become an integral part of new methods to make education more efficient, exciting, and successful.

Keep current and build in flexibility. Leading-edge technology solutions can quickly become outdated as new resources and applications emerge. To keep up with these changes, educators must constantly read and attend conferences, workshops, and meetings. School and district technology plans should address how schools will obtain and use technology resources over a 3- to 5-year period but should also incorporate new information through annual reviews.

Essential Condition: Empowered Leaders

To see change with technology occur, all invested parties must be part of the equation, be empowered, and share a vision. Stakeholders at all levels must be informed about the goals of the community, district, and school. This means holding public forums, bringing community members into the classroom, and educating those who can affect change. To make a difference in achieving systemic success with technology, the entire community must be involved.

Essential Condition: Standards and Curriculum Support

The new NETS for Students, published in 2007, identify higher order thinking skills and digital citizenship as critical for students to learn effectively for a lifetime and live productively in our emerging global society (ISTE, 2007). However, as the example lessons throughout this textbook indicate, students do not learn these standards as a separate subject area. Rather, they achieve them in the context of

their work in content-area courses. Therefore, it is critical to situate NETS for Students in content-area curriculum in ways that support both the subject-area content and the technology skills and that align with the shared vision so implementation can lead to goals such as enhanced learning and motivation. Fortunately, many content-area standards already address appropriate technology resources and applications, and others seem poised to do so. Thus, this essential condition is met best when technology and content-area standards are designed to support each other.

Essential Condition: Required Policies

As discussed in Chapter 1, legal, ethical, and equity conditions in our society profoundly affect educational uses of technology in schools. Effective technology integration that supports student learning requires school and district policies that ensure appropriate behavior, safety, equitable treatment of all students, financial assistance, incentives, and accountability at all levels of integration.

Internet use policies. The increasing use of the Internet for communications and research also means increased risks for students. A recent national survey reported that 19% of all young people using the Internet had been approached by predators. The situation is so alarming that the U.S. Congress passed the Children's Internet Protection Act to encourage schools to take measures that keep children away from Internet materials that could be harmful to them (McNabb, 2001). Most schools have students sign an **acceptable use policy (AUP)** that stipulates the risks involved in Internet use; outlines appropriate, safe student behavior on the Internet; and asks students if they agree to use the Internet under these conditions and if they agree to certain information about themselves being posted on the school's website.

Legal/ethical use polices. Schools also have policies and materials in place to address several common issues: illegal access to school servers (hacking), viruses, and software/media piracy. Districts usually address illegal access problems by placing *firewall software* on district and school networks. Firewall software prevents access to specific website addresses or to websites that contain certain keywords or phrases. (Unfortunately, firewalls and filtering software also create a new set of problems for schools by preventing their users from connecting to many legitimate educational sites.) Other districts or schools choose to use commercially available filtering software. Districts and schools also safeguard computers by using virus protection software and posting warnings to students and teachers about the hazards of opening downloaded files. Simpson (2001) gives an excellent summary of laws related to software copying, recommendations on publicizing software policies, and example copyright statements that schools and districts can use.

He emphasizes that software companies are serious about enforcing software copyright laws and that districts and schools can protect themselves against copyright infringement lawsuits by stating and publicizing a policy regarding software copying, requiring teacher and staff training on the topic, requiring hard drive and network programs that discourage users from making illegal copies, and providing adequate numbers of copies for their users (e.g., site licenses, lab packs, or networkable versions).

Policies to ensure equity.   Schools are also responsible for ensuring equitable access to and use of technology resources by all students, especially those who are traditionally underserved or underrepresented in mathematics, science, and technology occupations.

Financial assistance, incentives, and accountability policies.   Schools need to support teachers in their efforts to integrate technology effectively. Important aspects of this support include financial assistance for purchasing software for use in their classrooms and attending professional development opportunities; offering incentives to teachers for trying to integrate technology—these may range from monetary incentives to release time; and accountability for teachers who do and do not support district technology initiatives.

Essential Condition: Access to Hardware, Software, and Other Resources for Sustainable Integration

Finding funding.   Experts agree that adequate funding can determine the success or failure of even the best technology plans. The summary of guidelines on funding shown in Table 2.8 is based on recommendations from Ritchie and Boyle (1998) and Soloman (2001). Schools will never have the budgets for technology that they want or need. Strategies for optimizing available funds include requiring competitive bids, scheduling hardware and software upgrades, using donated equipment, and using broken computers for spare parts.

Purchasing hardware and software.   Although teachers depend on their schools and district offices to take leadership in providing necessary resources, teacher input in this process is critically important. When schools and districts make hardware and software purchases, they are making curricular decisions. Therefore, it is important for purchases to begin with those that fulfill the curriculum needs for which teachers most need technology support.

Setting up and maintaining physical facilities.   Schools have developed several arrangements to help ensure that computer equipment supports teachers' various curriculum needs. Schools can minimize technology repair problems if users follow good usage rules and conduct preventive maintenance procedures. In addition, education organizations usually choose one of the following maintenance options: maintenance contracts with outside suppliers, an in-house maintenance office, built-in maintenance with each equipment purchase, or a repair and maintenance budget. Each of these methods has its problems and limitations, and debate continues over which method or combination of methods is most cost effective depending on an organization's size and the number of computers and peripherals involved. Securing equipment is an equally important maintenance issue. Loss of equipment from vandalism and theft is a common problem in schools. Again, several options are available for dealing with this problem: monitoring and alarm systems, security cabinets, and lock-down systems.

Sustainability.   Fortunately and unfortunately, technology is constantly improving. It is fortunate because improvements in technology lead to more opportunities for integration in the classroom and to technology that is more aesthetically pleasing and user-friendly. However, as technology improves outside of the classroom walls, schools find that the computers that were new just four years ago are now running extremely slowly and cannot run the latest software programs. Thus, sustainability means that a plan for initial and sustained funding over time must be in place. School professionals must make wise choices related to when and how they spend technology funds.

Essential Condition: Skilled Personnel and Opportunities for Professional Development

As a result of the high-profile U.S. DOE initiative Preparing Tomorrow's Teachers to Use Technology (PT3), most preservice teacher training programs include at least some training in how to integrate technology effectively into teaching. However, because technology resources and applications change so quickly, continuing staff development in technology resources and applications remains an essential condition for effective technology integration. Roblyer and Erlanger (1998) have summarized findings from the literature on what makes teacher training programs most effective in helping teachers get to higher stages of awareness about technology:

- **Hands-on, integration emphasis** — Technology integration skills cannot be learned by sitting passively in a classroom, listening to an instructor, or watching demonstrations. Participants must have an opportunity to navigate through a program and complete a set of steps to create a new product. The focus must be on

TABLE 2.8 Finding Funding for Technology

Funding Sources

Hundreds of sources can be found under each of these five categories: *federal, state, corporate, private,* and *community*. The first four usually have budgets for funding larger projects. Schools and teachers usually have smaller projects and seek funding from community sources (e.g., companies, individuals, and groups). General funding sources include:

- **Federal funding sources:** http://www.grants.gov
- **Sources specific to your state:** Links from your state Department of Education website
- **Foundations of large companies:** Look for links from company websites
- **Issues of professional education magazines**
- **Issues of educational technology:** Columns on funding sources and deadlines

Writing Successful Proposals

1. **Read and follow the guidelines.** Your idea MUST address directly the primary goals of the agency (e.g., some agencies cannot fund equipment; some accept only proposals from K–12 groups, and some only from higher education).
2. **Organize the proposal.** Have these components: a concise overview (one to two pages maximum), a statement of the needs the proposal addresses, statements of specific goals and objectives, a narrative summary (as brief as possible), a budget spreadsheet that identifies costs in categories, and a budget narrative that explains the costs.
3. **Write in clear and compelling language.** Ask as many people as possible to read the proposal and suggest changes before you submit it.

Online Grant Writing Guides

Take a "short course" on how to write effective proposals. Most of these courses have links to sources as well as basics on how to write proposals.

- About.com's Advice for Secondary School Educators (http://www.7-12educators.about.com/education/7-12educators/cs/grantwriting/)
- Eisenhower National Clearinghouse Guidelines and Opportunities (http://www.enc.org/professional/funding/)
- Guide for Proposal Writing Created at Michigan State University (http://www.LearnerAssociates.net/proposal)
- Guidelines for Beginners—An Educator's Guide (http://www.uml.edu/College/Education/Faculty/lebaron/GRANTBEGIN)
- Proposal Writing Short Course (http://foundationcenter.org/getstarted/tutorials/shortcourse/index.html)

Characteristics of Successful Applicants

Schools and projects that obtain funding have several characteristics in common:

- They have ideas for how to make things better.
- They keep in constant touch with funding opportunities.
- They have things already written up so they are able to respond quickly when opportunities arise.
- They have one or more good writers handy.
- They are passionate about their work and know how to describe what they do.

Building on Success

To continue receiving outside funding educators who have a funded project must do three things on a continuing basis:

1. **Carry out what you proposed.** Show you did good things with what you already received.
2. **Publicize your success.** Publicize through school and district public relations personnel. Create publications and websites to document accomplishments. Ask the local newspaper or TV and radio stations to come for a show-and-tell session. Give talks and presentations to local groups, and get your project on the agendas of school meetings.
3. **Generate new funding opportunities.** View funded projects as seeds for new opportunities rather than one-time activities.

---

how to use the technology resources in classrooms rather than just on technical skills.

- **Training over time** — Many schools are discovering that traditional models of staff development, particularly "one-shot" inservice training for the entire faculty, are ineffective for teaching skills and for helping teachers develop methods to use computers as instructional

tools (Benson, 1997). Inservice training about technology must be ongoing.

- **Modeling, mentoring, and coaching** — Instructors who model the use of technology in their own teaching long have been acknowledged as the most effective teacher trainers (Handler, 1992; Wetzel, 1993). Research also indicates that one-to-one mentoring and coaching programs are effective for new teachers (Benson, 1997). Linking teachers to each other and to staff developers has also been shown to be effective (Office of Technology Assessment, 1995; Ringstaff & Yocam, 1995). Most teachers seem to learn computer skills through colleague interaction and information sharing (Oliver, 1994).

- **Post-training access** — Teachers not only need adequate access to technology to accomplish training; they also need access after training to practice and use what they have learned.

The road to trained personnel involves professional development for all professionals invested in technology within the schools—teachers, media specialists, administrators, and so on. Schools must have a plan for continued professional development for teachers to learn not only the latest technology, but more importantly the most effective pedagogy related to integrating the technology into the classroom.

Essential Condition: Technical Assistance

Each teacher needs training in simple troubleshooting procedures, such as what to do if a computer says a disk is "unreadable." Teachers should not be expected to address more complicated diagnostic and maintenance problems, however. Nothing is more frustrating than depending on access to a computer to complete an important student project only to discover that it is broken or malfunctioning. Cuban, Kirkpatrick, and Peck (2001) cite equipment problems as a major obstacle to effective technology integration. Schools must support teachers by replacing and repairing equipment designated for classroom use.

Essential Condition: Appropriate Teaching and Assessment Approaches

As Chapters 3 through 15 in this textbook illustrate, models of technology integration range from relatively passive uses (e.g., teachers reviewing a topic with a *PowerPoint* presentation) to more interactive, hands-on ones (e.g., students using word processing for student reports or calculators for supporting mathematics problem solving, doing Internet searches for research, or creating hypermedia products to communicate research findings). Each of these models is appropriate depending on the instructional need, and teachers should be encouraged to use all of them. Assessment practices will vary with the technology integration model. The critical factor is matching the teaching strategy with an appropriate assessment strategy.

For example, if students are creating web pages, a grading rubric would measure their achievement better than a traditional written test would. Depending on the integration model, teachers may want to use a combination of assessment strategies (e.g., written tests as well as products evaluated with a rubric).

Essential Condition: Engaged Communities

Now more than ever partnerships are being encouraged between schools, business, corporations, and individuals. It is very common for businesses within a community to partner with school programs, initiatives, and individuals to make a dream a reality. The partnerships normally benefit all partners—through financial return or exposure. For example, the GoNorth! Adventure Learning Series was developed at the University of Minnesota in partnership with a small business, NOMADS Adventure & Education, Inc., and the delivery is the result of a multiyear partnership with the Best Buy Children's Foundation. The project has reached millions of students worldwide as a result of Best Buy's financial support, and the project has also shown Best Buy's investment in children, learning, and technology.

Making the Case for Technology Integration

Use the following questions to reflect on issues in technology integration and to guide discussions within your class.

1. Sheingold (1991) said that teachers will have to confront squarely the difficult problem of creating a school environment that is fundamentally different from the one they themselves experienced (p. 23). In what ways is the current K–12 environment different from the one you experienced? Do you feel this presents an obstacle to the effective use of technology in your teaching? What are some strategies you feel might help teachers overcome this obstacle?

2. NCATE's document *Technology and the New Professional Teacher* (1997) said that, in addition to technology skills, teachers need an attitude that is fearless in the use of technology, encourages them to take risks, and inspires them to be lifelong learners. What factors and activities can help teachers develop such an attitude? What factors make it difficult for them to acquire it?

Interactive Summary

The following is a summary of the main points covered in this chapter.

1. **Learning theory foundations**: Two lines of learning theories have given rise to two kinds of integration models: directed and constructivist.

   - *Directed models* were shaped by objectivist theories: behaviorist (Skinner), information-processing, cognitive-behavioral (Gagné), and systems theories.

   - *Constructivist models* were shaped by constructivist theories: social activism (Dewey), scaffolding (Vygotsky), child development (Piaget and Bruner), and multiple intelligences (Gardner) theories.

2. **Technological pedagogical content knowledge**: The Technological Pedagogical Content Knowledge (TPACK) framework is a metacognitive tool teachers can use to enhance technology integration into their classrooms by helping them visualize how their technology knowledge and skills work in tandem with their other knowledge domains about teaching and learning. This framework "attempts to capture some of the essential qualities of knowledge required by teachers for technology integration in their teaching, while addressing the complex, multifaceted and situated nature of teacher knowledge" (Mishra & Koehler, 2006, p. 1). Theoretically and practically, teaching requires an intricate combination of content, pedagogy, and technology knowledge. Teachers must understand more than technology alone, more than pedagogy (teaching/learning) alone, and more than content alone. They need to continue to move towards the center where they can use all knowledge domains to design and deliver instruction effectively with technology.

3. **The Technology Integration Planning Model**: This model is designed to help teachers (especially those new to technology) plan for effective classroom uses of technology. The model consists of six phases:

   - **TIP Model Phase 1: Technological pedagogical content knowledge** — To be "critical consumers," all teachers need to be explicitly aware of their knowledge development in the areas of TK, TCK, TPK, and TPACK (Hughes & Scharber, 2008). This metacognitive awareness enables teachers to set learning goals for themselves and, in turn, to make thoughtful decisions for technology integration.

   - **TIP Model Phase 2: Relative advantage** — Deciding on instructional problems and whether or not a technology-based solution would be better than other ways of addressing the problems.

   - **TIP Model Phase 3: Objectives and assessments** — Stating desired outcomes in terms of better student achievement, attitudes, and performance; matching appropriate assessment strategies to each outcome.

   - **TIP Model Phase 4: Integration strategies** — Deciding on teaching activities that incorporate technology resources to enhance student learning.

   - **TIP Model Phase 5: Instructional environment** — Deciding on resources and conditions to put into place to support the activities.

   - **TIP Model Phase 6: Evaluation and revision** — Collecting achievement data and other information to determine if the activities were successful in meeting desired outcomes and what could be improved next time.

4. **Essential conditions for technology integration** — For technology to have the desired impact on improved teaching and learning, several conditions must be in place:

   - **A shared vision for technology integration** — This requires coordinated school and district planning with teachers and other personnel at all levels, budgeting yearly amounts for technology purchases with incremental funding, emphasizing teacher training, matching technology to curriculum needs, and keeping current and building in flexibility.

   - **Empowered leaders** — To see change with technology occur, all invested parties must be part of the equation, be empowered, and share a vision.

   - **Standards and curriculum support** — Technology and content-area standards are designed to support each other.

   - **Required policies** — Policies are in place to ensure legal/ethical use, safe Internet use, and equity of access.

   - **Access to hardware, software, and other resources for sustainable integration** — There is adequate funding, purchasing procedures are organized and effective, and procedures are in place to set up and maintain technology resources.

   - **Skilled personnel and opportunities for professional development** — Staff development that includes hands-on, integration emphasis; training over time; modeling, mentoring, and coaching; and post-training access to technology resources.

   - **Technical assistance** — Continuing support for diagnostic and maintenance problems for teachers' and students' computers.

   - **Appropriate teaching and assessment approaches** — Teaching strategies that are matched to needs and assessment strategies that are matched to the type of learning being measured.

- **Engaged communities** — Now more than ever partnerships are being encouraged between

schools, business, corporations, and individuals. See the ISTE website for more explanation of essential conditions for teachers' optimal use of technologies.

Key Terms

- acceptable use policy (AUP)
- accommodation
- anchored instruction
- assimilation
- automaticity
- classical conditioning
- constructivist learning
- constructivists
- contingencies of reinforcement
- directed instruction
- discovery learning
- Events of Instruction

- firewall software
- inquiry-based learning
- learning hierarchies
- Likert scale
- long-term memory (LTM)
- mastery learning
- multiple intelligences
- objectivism
- objectivists
- operant conditioning
- programmed learning
- relative advantage

- rubric
- scaffolding
- semantic differential
- sensory registers
- short-term memory (STM)
- social activism
- systems approaches to instructional design
- technological pedagogical content knowledge (TPACK)
- zone of proximal development (ZPD)

Web-Enrichment Activities

1. ***Learning theory in technology-integrated lessons*** — Identify the learning theory addressed in a WebQuest. Locate a WebQuest at http://webquest.org/. Click on Find WebQuests, then use the Curriculum x Grade Level Matrix to view a WebQuest for a selected grade level and subject area. As you read the instructions and materials included in the WebQuest, make a list of five aspects of the WebQuest that are informed or supported by learning theory. Refer to Figures 2.3 to 2.6 as you complete the activity.

2. ***Assessment of learning with rubrics*** — To see an example of rubrics developed for a student project, read about Mrs. Gaines' language arts lesson at http://ali.apple.com/ali_sites/hpli/Exhibits/1000734. Click on The Lesson to read the instructions to students, and click on Assessment to see the rubrics used by the students (developed on the Rubistar website used by teachers to create custom rubrics). Search for the rubric Multimedia Project: Rappin' with Beowulf to view Mrs. Gaines' assessment instrument. Refer to Table 2.2 in the chapter, and discuss the model that best applies to Mrs. Gaines' lesson and assessment. List three reasons for selecting the model you did.

3. ***Essential Conditions*** — Visit Kathy Schrock's Guide for Educators for good samples of assessment instruments (http://schooldiscoveryeducation.com/schrockguide/). Open the San Diego Public Schools: K-12 Technology

Competency Rubrics. For what would these rubrics be used? How might they be used to ensure that the essential conditions for technology integration are being met?

Go to MyEducationLab to complete the following exercises.

Video Select the topic "Ethical, Legal, and Social Issues," and go to the "Assignments, Activities, and Applications" section. Access the video "Managing Technology in the Classroom" to explore acceptable use policies and how technology is used to enhance intermediate school curricula. Complete the activity that follows.

Video Select the topic "Instructional Planning," and go to the "Assignments, Activities, and Applications" section. Access the video "Technology Manages the Flow of Activities." Consider how one teacher uses technology to manage the flow of time and materials in her classroom. Complete the activity that follows.

Building Teaching Skills Select the topic "Instructional Planning," and go to the "Building Teaching Skills and Dispositions" section. Access the activity "Developing Technology Integration Skills" and complete the full activity.

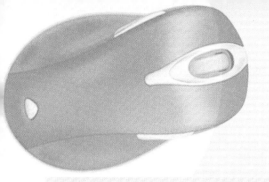

Technology Integration Workshop

TIE into Practice: Technology Integration Examples

Read each of the following scenarios related to implementing the TIP Model, and answer the questions that follow it based on your Chapter 2 reading activities.

TIP MODEL SCENARIO #1: PHASE 1—REFLECTING ON TECHNOLOGICAL PEDAGOGICAL CONTENT KNOWLEDGE Jim, a new English teacher at Maple High School, decided it was time to start integrating technology into his teaching. Although he had been given numerous opportunities to use technology, he had always decided it was not for him. He had been teaching for 15 years, and he felt that his lessons had always worked. "So," he thought, "why should I change?" But now the time had come for a change. He decided he was going to take the time to identify what he knew about his TPACK. He did some self-evaluations and realized he was very strong in content knowledge but weak in both technology and pedagogical knowledge.

1.1 If you were Jim, how would you respond to your TPACK analysis?

1.2 How might you use this information to influence your future lesson planning?

TIP MODEL SCENARIO #2: PHASE 2—DETERMINING THE RELATIVE ADVANTAGE The superintendent of the Wellmade School District felt that every student should be "connected to the Information Superhighway," so he decided to install Internet connections in every school classroom in the district. The hardware and installations were funded through a federal grant and local business sponsors. Two years later, it became apparent that only about 25% of the teachers were using the Internet with students and that most uses amounted to "casual surfing."

2.1 Why do you think the teachers did not see the relative advantage of this technology?

2.2 If you were responsible for integrating this technology into instructional activities, how would you translate the superintendent's rationale into problems and solutions for which the relative advantage would be clear to teachers?

TIP MODEL SCENARIO #3: PHASE 3—DECIDING ON OBJECTIVES AND ASSESSMENTS As a school district science coordinator, you would like the high school biology teachers to begin using a dissection simulation program in lieu of actual dissections of pigs, which has always been done in the past. You feel this will save both time and money for materials. Some biology teachers are reluctant to make this change; they say that students cannot learn as much about anatomy and dissection techniques from a simulation as they can from the "real thing." However, they agree to a test of the software in a couple of classes.

3.1 What would be the expectations of the simulation method in terms of general outcomes?

3.2 If you were one of the biology teachers, how would you word objectives to match these outcomes?

3.3 What instruments or information would you use to assess the "saving time and money" objective?

TIP MODEL SCENARIO #4: PHASE 4—DESIGNING INTEGRATION STRATEGIES Luella is a language arts teacher who uses a software package with vocabulary practice items to improve students' performance on a college entrance exam. Before she has the students use the software, she describes test-taking tips and strategies, and then she shows them how to use the software. Since she feels students can help each other with difficult words, she has them work in groups of three to practice the software. They take turns practicing for about 15 minutes at the end of each class period for the last 2 weeks of the grading period.

4.1 Are Luella's methods primarily directed or inquiry based?

4.2 Do you think this group-based strategy is a good one for the activity? Why or why not?

4.3 Do you think 15 minutes of group practice at the end of each class period will be enough to increase students' performance? Why or why not?

TIP MODEL SCENARIO #5: PHASE 5—PREPARING THE INSTRUCTIONAL ENVIRONMENT Esmerelda is having her students do a social studies project in which they do "virtual interviews" of experts on various periods in U.S. history. She schedules time in the computer lab and has students locate experts by searching Internet sites. She gives them an initial list of sites, but she encourages them to branch out from there, looking for additional sites on their own. There is no lab manager, and she has to go back to the classroom for periods of time while the students work in the lab, but she knows they are competent Internet users and can be trusted not to leave the lab without permission. For their contacts with experts, she has them prepare a standard email with the school name; their names, ages, addresses, and personal email addresses if they have one; and a description of what they would like to know.

5.1 Assuming she is correct that students will not leave the lab without permission, is Esmeralda's plan for having students use the Internet a good one? Why or why not?

5.2 Do you see any problems with the email she is having students send?

5.3 How would you change her plan to improve it?

TIP MODEL SCENARIO #6: PHASE 6—EVALUATING AND REVISING INTEGRATION STRATEGIES Wilfred was a special education resource teacher who wanted to give students with dysgraphia (nonwriting behavior) an alternative way to do homework and class assignments. He showed a couple of the students how to use a small portable "computer companion" with a keyboard and word processing program. They did their work wherever they were and downloaded it to a computer later and printed it out. Students quickly learned how to do this activity and were delighted with their new ability. For the first time, they turned in all their assignments on time. On a brief survey he gave to the special education teachers, however, four of the five teachers indicated they would not use it for their own students with dysgraphia.

6.1 Would you say that findings indicate the project was a success? Why or why not?

6.2 What should he do to find out why teachers responded in this way to his survey?

6.3 What other data or information could he gather about the quality of students' written assignments that could help him decide how to improve the strategy?

For Your Teaching Portfolio

For this chapter's contribution to your teaching portfolio, do the following project and add it to your portfolio:

• Teachers choose technology-based methods over other methods when they see the "relative advantage" of them—that is, when the new method offers enough benefits to convince them to use it instead of the old one. Relative advantage is a perception or belief shaped by teachers' experience and by information they receive. One way teachers learn that a technology-based method has relative advantage is through reading research results. The Center for Applied Research in Educational Technology (CARET) website summarizes "best evidence" research results on the impact of technology in education. Look at the results for the Student Learning area. List the five questions CARET says teachers can ask to determine if technology-based methods have an impact on student learning. Describe two or more studies at the CARET website that offer convincing evidence that a technology-based method has more impact on student learning than another method does.

Part 2

Integrating Software Tutors and Tools into Teaching and Learning

A s the chapters in Part 1 illustrated, the field of educational technology is characterized by controversy and change, due in no small part to the dynamic nature of computer technology itself. In an area as complex and fluid as educational technology, it is helpful to discuss technology resources in categories. In 1980, as microcomputers began to enter K–12 classrooms, Taylor proposed categorizing computer resources as "tutor, tool, and tutee" functions. The tutor functions included those in which the "computer [was] programmed by experts in both programming and in a subject matter . . . and the student [was] then tutored by the computer" (p. 3). In its tool functions, the computer "had some useful capability programmed into it such as statistical analysis . . . or word processing" (p. 3). Tutee functions helped the student learn about logic processes or how computers worked by "teaching" (programming) computers to perform various activities in languages like BASIC or Logo.

Many educators still use this function-based classification system. Because many resources can serve more than one function, however, those new to the field often find it helpful to supplement and overlay this classification system with one based on technical characteristics. This text adopts such a system, classifying resources as software (Part 2) and Internet based (Part 3). The chapters in Part 2 deal with technology resources that revolve around using a computer program (software). Software resources are grouped as instructional software (Chapter 3), software tools (Chapters 4 and 5), and multimedia/hypermedia tools (Chapter 6).

Part 2

Required Background for Teachers

In Part 2, four chapters help teachers build the technology skills they will need to take advantage of software resources.

Chapter 3 Teaching with Instructional Software

Most people think of instructional software as performing a "tutor" function common to that of directed instruction models. However, some software also functions as a tool in integration strategies based on constructivist models. Software described in this chapter fulfills the following instructional roles: tutorial, drill and practice, simulation, instructional games, and problem solving. Chapter 3 also covers networked delivery systems, called *integrated learning systems (ILSs)*, that provide these software functions and keep track of students' usage of them.

Chapter 4 Teaching with the Basic Three Software Tools: Word Processing, Spreadsheet, and Database Programs

Chapter 4 describes and gives integration strategies for three of the most commonly discussed computer programs in the category of classroom technology tools: word processing, spreadsheet, and database software. These were among the first tools to be developed and used in education, especially with microcomputers; thus, the literature documents more uses and classroom integration strategies for them than for most of the tools developed later. Also, these three functions are commonly found as components of so-called *integrated software packages* or *software suites.* (These are different from the integrated learning systems, or ILSs, discussed in Chapter 3.) Even though these three tools have come to be known as *productivity software*, Chapter 4 describes and illustrates both productivity and instructional applications for them.

Chapter 5 Teaching with Software Tools: Beyond the Basic Programs

Since computers came into common use outside of the business office, software tools have emerged to fill a variety of functions. They support students with many repetitive and/or mechanical operations involved in learning—for example, handwriting (when the focus of instruction is writing a story or a composition); arithmetic calculations (for lessons on solving algebra problems); organizing information (for lessons on how to classify animals according to common features); and presenting information clearly and attractively (for presentations on the results of a research project). Software tools contribute to teaching in the same way that power tools contribute to designing and building a house as compared to using hand tools. They make it easier to carry out the mechanics of building the house, but they can also profoundly affect the complexity of the designs that builders may attempt. Similarly, technology tools not only make learning faster and easier, but they also make possible more complex, higher level methods than would be achievable without such tools.

Chapter 6 Teaching with Multimedia and Hypermedia Tools

The final chapter in Part 2 focuses on some of the most exciting technology resources in education today. Multimedia and hypermedia applications can be done with a variety of hardware and software combinations, ranging from simple uses of presentation software to sophisticated multimedia authoring systems. Perhaps more than any other technology resources, these applications help teachers and students reflect on and draw from the diversity of images and motion that characterize the world around us. This chapter describes each of the configurations that can be used in classrooms, including commercial multimedia software and three kinds of authoring software: presentation software, digital video editing systems, and multimedia/hypermedia authoring systems.

Reference

Taylor, R. (1980). *The computer in the school: Tutor, tool, and tutee.* New York: Teachers College Press.

Chapter 3

Teaching with Instructional Software

The fact that individuals bind themselves with strong emotional ties to machines ought not to be surprising. The instruments [we] use become . . . extensions of [our] bodies.

Joseph Weizenbaum, in *Computer Power and Human Reason* (1976, p. 9)

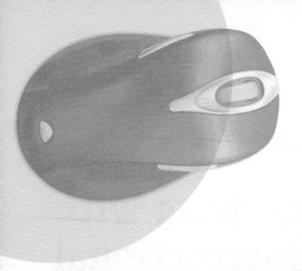

Technology Integration Example

The Alien Rescue® Project

Grade Level: Middle school • Content Area/Topic: Science, solar system • Length of Time: Three weeks

Phases 1 and 2: Assess technological pedagogical content knowledge; Determine relative advantage

Mr. Leroy was a veteran middle school science teacher who had won many awards for his teaching. However, he felt that, despite his efforts to make his class hands-on and project based, his students tended to see science as facts and procedures unrelated to practical problems. He felt most students left middle school without learning why scientific inquiry was useful. One day, he saw a conference presentation on software for middle school students. The software began with a video clip in which a problem scenario was presented as if it were a real live newscast. The video said that an alien spaceship was orbiting Earth and broadcasting a plea for help. Aliens on board the ship were from several planets in a galaxy whose sun had exploded. They escaped but now needed new habitats that would meet the needs of their various species. They asked Earth for help in matching them with planets and moons that each species might find habitable. The software provided an array of information and images on the planets and moons of our solar system, and students could find out about the characteristics of each by doing searches and activities like designing and "sending out" probes. After Mr. Leroy reviewed the software himself and decided it met all criteria for what he believed to be excellent software, he decided to have his students do this project for his solar system unit instead of building models of planets. He felt it would be a good way to generate enthusiasm for using scientific inquiry to help solve complex problems.

Before jumping immediately into the project, however, Mr. Leroy assessed his technological pedagogical content knowledge to see where he might be deficient and also how he might capitalize on his strengths. He realized that his content and pedagogical knowledge was very strong as compared to his technological knowledge. However, he also believed that the software he would be using guided the teacher enough that he could definitely integrate it within his classroom.

Phase 3: Decide on objectives and assessments

Mr. Leroy decided that, in addition to passing his usual test on solar system information, he wanted students to accomplish several other outcomes. Also, he wanted to make sure students enjoyed this new approach. He developed the following outcomes, objectives, and assessments for his project:

- **Outcome:** Demonstrate a problem-solving approach to assigned problems. **Objective:** All students, working in small groups, will create well-designed problem statements, solutions steps, and workable solutions for at least one of three assigned problems. **Assessment:** A checklist based on steps and criteria from the *Alien Rescue Teacher Manual* (TM).

- **Outcome:** Create and present new problems and methods to solve them. **Objective:** All groups will achieve a rubric score of at least 80% on presentations of a new problem and solution related to the alien simulation software. **Assessment:** A rubric to assess the content and quality of the presentation.

- **Outcome:** Use scientific inquiry language outside the unit. **Objective:** At least 80% of students will use the language of scientific inquiry outside of the unit. **Assessment:** An observation checklist.

- **Outcome:** Enjoy using inquiry methods. **Objective:** At least 90% of students will demonstrate positive attitudes

Source: From Alien Rescue Software © The Alien Rescue Team 2001–2004, www.alienrescue.com. Reprinted by permission.

toward the work. **Assessment:** A five-item survey that students will complete anonymously.

Phase 4: Design integration strategies

Mr. Leroy realized that his students would learn inquiry-based methods only by seeing them in action and practicing them over time. He would have to facilitate, rather than direct, student learning, which would take more time than usual. He also realized that students had to answer questions about the solar system on the state's required exams, so he would have to provide diagnostic testing and if necessary, remedial practice about these concepts and facts. Luckily, the *TM* provided test items like this to cover background information, which he could supplement with his own questions. With these things in mind, he created the following activity sequence:

- **Day 1:** Show the opening video to the whole class. Assign students to groups, and let them log on to computers. Allow them to explore the software environment on their own.

- **Day 2:** Have the class review the problem presented in the video by asking the probing questions listed in the *Alien Rescue TM*. Let groups explore the software further, and answer any additional questions they might have.

- **Days 3–5:** Hold discussions about how to work in groups, and use inquiry approaches to solve problems. Ask students to develop their own problem statements, and discuss procedures they will use to solve them. Students will demonstrate the software features they will need. Students practice using the software features and define lists of alien needs.

- **Days 6–10:** Students use software features to explore planets and moons and develop hypotheses about the best matches for each alien species. They use word processing software to document their notes so they can update them easily throughout the activity.

- **Days 11–13:** Groups present their findings on the best places for each species and write up final selections in the required format. Individual students complete the fact worksheets and get remedial practice as necessary.

- **Days 14–16:** Final reflections, assessments, and remedial practice where necessary.

Phase 5: Prepare the instructional environment

Mr. Leroy decided to take the *TM*'s advice and resist the tendency to overdirect students. He knew he had to keep to a timeline to complete the project on schedule, but he also realized that the software designers were warning that too much structure would work against the purpose and design of the software. Keeping this in mind, he began his planning:

- **Software skills:** The software was quite rich with features, tools, and resources, but it was so complex that Mr. Leroy knew he couldn't be expert on all of it. He also realized that some of his students would probably become more expert than he in a very short time. He wanted to become as familiar with it as possible, however, so he could answer students' initial questions. So he went through it carefully and took notes.

- **Handouts:** The *TM* provided a chart to help students keep track of each species' needs. Mr. Leroy prepared a group task sheet and inserted this and other helpful notes on it.

- **Lesson planning:** Mr. Leroy was such a veteran that he usually didn't use lesson plans. But this project was so new and different from his usual teaching methods that he felt he needed to prepare a written sequence. He left space for items he would add as the project progressed so that he would be even more prepared when he taught it next time.

- **Software copies:** Mr. Leroy knew the software was available to teachers only from the university where it was developed. It was free, but he had to sign an agreement that only his class would be using it. He completed the paperwork and obtained the software. He made sure each copy worked on the available equipment.

- **Computer scheduling:** The trickiest part would be scheduling time on computers in the computer lab, which he would be using since he had only one computer in his room. Mr. Leroy arranged with the lab coordinator to have the lab on the days he needed it. He also spoke with the principal, who agreed to give him an extra computer for his room so that more students could work there if necessary.

Phase 6: Evaluate and revise

Mr. Leroy was impressed with the impact the project had on his students' enthusiasm for inquiry skills. Rubric scores indicated that they did better with each probe they designed and each set of data they analyzed. Perhaps best of all, Mr. Leroy documented that about half of the students were talking like scientists, using "inquiry speak" in other work. Some girls asked about careers in space exploration, so Mr. Leroy sent them to look at the NASA and Space Camp sites on the Internet. The problem-solving checklists reflected good progress, too. Scores on the first ones the students did were a little low, but the last ones were really fine in all groups. Mr. Leroy observed only two real problems. One was that some group members had to leave for special school events, leaving a "hole" in the group, which then had to improvise. The other problem was access to computers. Mr. Leroy resolved to ask the principal for a five-computer workstation and printer like the English teacher had. Students' scores on the solar system test varied a lot, so he interviewed students informally to determine why some did so much better than others. In general, attitudes toward science seemed way up, and students were more on task than he had ever seen them.

Objectives

After reading this chapter and completing the learning activities for it, you should be able to:

1. Define five software functions (*drill and practice, tutorial, simulation, instructional game,* and *problem solving*) according to their unique features, benefits, and limitations, and identify examples of each.

2. Define *integrated learning systems (ILSs)* according to their unique features, benefits, and limitations, and identify examples of ILS products.

3. Identify one or more types of instructional software functions that could meet classroom needs.

4. Plan lesson activities that integrate instructional software using a directed learning strategy.

5. Plan lesson activities that integrate instructional software using a constructivist or combination learning strategy.

What Is Instructional Software?

Weizenbaum (1976) called using computers "extensions of [our] bodies." Reeves and Nass (1996) showed the intimate and inherently social relationships between computers and humans, calling computers "social actors." Such metaphors have a long history in education. At the same time as people began to realize that computers could help them do many clerical tasks more quickly and accurately, they also began thinking, "If **computer programs** can be created to do essentially anything, why not program computers to teach?" Educators and developers alike began to pursue this idea in the 1960s and 1970s. Some, like William Norris (1977), who developed Control Data's PLATO teaching system, believed that computer-based education was the only logical alternative to education's "outdated, labor-intensive ways" (p. 451). He believed that education would be more efficient if computers took over the traditional role of teachers.

Today, after more than 30 years of development and experimentation, there is less talk of computers replacing teachers. Instead, there is more conversation about computer programs helping perform various teaching functions, essentially transforming the teaching process. This chapter shows how software programs empower rather than replace teachers.

Software is another word for programs written in programming languages. Software designed and developed to make computers function is called **systems software**, whereas programs written to perform tasks such as word processing or tutoring are called **applications software** or **applications programs**. **Instructional software** is applications software designed specifically to deliver or assist with student instruction on a topic. Although applications software such as word processing and spreadsheets can also enhance instructional activities, this textbook differentiates between applications software and instructional software. Software tools serve many purposes other than teaching; instructional software packages are developed for the *sole* purpose of supporting instruction and/or learning.

In the early days—when instructional software was used primarily to tutor students—it was called **computer-assisted instruction (CAI)**. The term is still in common use, but some kinds of instructional software are designed with more constructivist purposes in mind; they support, rather than deliver, instruction. Therefore, many people consider the term *CAI* outdated and misleading. Teachers may hear instructional software referred to as *computer-based instruction (CBI), computer-based learning (CBL),* or *computer-assisted learning (CAL),* or in more generic terms such as *software learning tools.*

Instructional Roles for Software: Past and Present

It used to be easy to designate a software package by the type of teaching function it served. It was a **drill-and-practice**, **tutorial**, **simulation**, **instructional game**, or **problem-solving** program. (See descriptions in Table 3.1.) These terms originated because each package had clearly different characteristics and served a different instructional purpose. In contrast, much of today's software defies easy classification because many software packages contain several different activities, each of which may perform a different function. For example, language-learning software may have a number of straight drill activities along with activities that fulfill problem-solving and game functions. Also, developers use the terms interchangeably; there seems to be no consensus among developers about the terms used to describe various types of programs. Some developers refer to a drill program that gives extensive feedback as a tutorial. Others refer to simulations or problem-solving functions as games.

Software still reflects the same five functions, but in light of current trends toward multiple-function software

TABLE 3.1 Five Instructional Software Functions

Function/Examples	Description
Drill and Practice	Allows learners to work problems or answer questions and get feedback on correctness.
Tutorial	Acts like a human tutor by providing all the information and instructional activities a learner needs to master a topic: information summaries, explanation, practice routines, feedback, and assessment.
Simulation	Models real or imaginary systems to show how those systems or similar ones work or to demonstrate underlying concepts.
Instructional Game	Increases motivation by adding game rules to drills or simulations.
Problem Solving	(a) Teaches directly (through explanation and/or practice) the steps involved in solving problems or (b) helps learners acquire problem-solving skills by giving them opportunities to solve problems.

packages, teachers may have to analyze a package to determine which instructional function(s) it serves so as to ensure it supports their specific teaching needs. They may not be able to refer to an entire package as a drill or a simulation, but it is possible and desirable to identify whether it provides, for example, science vocabulary skill practice and/or opportunities for studying plant growth in action. As this chapter will show, each software function serves a different purpose during learning and, consequently, has its own appropriate integration strategies.

Learning Theory Connections

The first instructional software reflected the behavioral and cognitive learning theories that were popular at the time. Some software functions (e.g., drill and practice, tutorial) remain focused on *directed* strategies that grew out of these theories, delivering information to help students acquire and retain information and skills. Later instructional software was designed to support the more *constructivist* aims of helping students explore topics and generate their own knowledge. Therefore, some software functions (e.g., simulation, games) can be used in either directed or constructivist ways, depending on how they are designed. Table 3.2 summarizes the strategies underlying each of the five software functions described in this chapter.

Gagné, Wager, and Rojas (1981) suggested a way to look at software that can help educators analyze a given product with respect to its instructional function(s) and design appropriate integration strategies that make use of these functions. Gagné et al. said that drills, tutorials, and simulations each accomplish a different combination of the Events of Instruction. (See the description of Gagné's Events of Instruction in Chapter 2.) The nine events are guidelines identified by Gagné

TABLE 3.2 Types of Integration Strategies for Each Instructional Software Function

Software Function	Instructional Uses	Strategy	
		Directed	**Constructivist**
Drill and practice	Skill practice	X	
Tutorial	Information delivery	X	
Simulation	Demonstration	X	
	Exploration		X
Instructional game	Skill practice	X	
	Exploration		X
Problem solving	Skill practice	X	
	Exploration		X

Technology Integration Lesson 3.1

Example Strategy for Using Programming Languages

Title: A Window on Learning Logo   **Grade Level:** Middle school

Content Area/Topic: Logic and analysis skills

 NETS for Students: Standards 1 (Creativity and Innovation) and 4 (Critical Thinking, Problem Solving, and Decision Making)

Description of Standards Applications: This integration idea offers exploration and creativity in the Logo programming environment. Students use creativity, critical thinking, problem solving, and decision making as they create a Gothic rose using the on-screen "turtles" while they are learning how to develop and analyze patterns. Logo's graphic qualities make it a natural choice to explore the design qualities of symmetry, repetition, and precision. Logo's powerful language structure allows students to create intricate designs quickly and dramatically. With other methods, modifications would be more time consuming, and students would not be able to pinpoint the exact reasons and ways that designs were made different.

Instruction: Begin by reviewing basic Logo commands and exploring the Logo programming environment. Make sure students know that designs are programmed using the "turtle's" on-screen perspective and not their own. Have them practice developing simple procedures, and review debugging procedures line by line to determine how designs are drawn. Begin with an easy problem, such as analyzing the steps in drawing a simple square, to get children used to the logistics. Give students pictures of the Gothic rose window from Notre Dame Cathedral. Ask them to analyze the window, looking for patterns, shapes, and structures. Help them see that complicated designs are made up of simple geometric shapes. Then assign them the task of drawing their own window using three such shapes. Show them how to adjust basic designs by changing variable numbers. The best moments in the project occur when a student displays a window for the first time and a gasp of delight fills the room.

Assessment: Use a rubric on programming language use and creativity.

---

that can help teachers arrange optimal "conditions for learning" for various types of knowledge and skills. By determining which of the events a software package fulfills, he said, educators can determine the teaching role it serves and where it might fit in the instructional process. However, Gagné's approach was primarily for directed uses, rather than constructivist ones. This chapter describes both kinds of strategies for instructional software.

Programming Languages as Instructional Software

This chapter focuses on software designed solely for instructional purposes, whereas Chapters 4 and 5 address the uses of tool software in education. Unlike instructional software described in this chapter, the uses of tool software (e.g., word-processing, computer-assisted design or CAD software) are not limited to education. However, a few programming languages were designed especially for educational purposes and thus may be considered hybrid software, since they merge the capabilities of instructional and tool software. One of the most widely known of the programming languages used for instruction is **Logo**. Logo is used to introduce young children to problem solving through programming and to explore concepts in content areas such as mathematics, science, and language arts (Galas, 1998; Gonsalves & Lopez, 1998; Weinstein, 1999). See Technology Integration Lesson 3.1 for a sample use of Logo as instructional software.

The work of Seymour Papert (1980) (see Chapter 2) and his colleagues at the Massachusetts Institute of Technology made Logo "widely used throughout the world as an introductory programming language and mathematical learning environment for students in elementary and secondary schools" (Watt, 1992, p. 615). Although not as popular as they were in the 1980s, Logo and some of its derivative materials are still used for instructional purposes.

Recent Trends in Software Design and Delivery

Although instructional software resources have been around since the 1960s, the following are the most recent developments in their features and uses:

- **Online access and components** — The Internet is playing an increasingly prominent role in software. Much software is now delivered online with students using web-based applications that can be accessed from virtually any Internet-enabled device (e.g., a computer or a cell phone).

- **Web 2.0 technologies** — Web 2.0 (pronounced "two point Oh") refers to the transition of the web from a collection of related websites to a computing platform that emphasizes user collaboration and contribution. Examples of Web 2.0 applications are blogs, wikis, and social networking sites. At the time of writing, Web 2.0 technologies are being widely adopted in educational circles as user-centered and empowering tools. (See Chapter 6 for a complete discussion of Web 2.0 technologies.)

- **Rich user experiences** — Software design and development has advanced from a focus on information dissemination to providing experiences (as opposed to "products") that are user friendly, engaging, fun, and aesthetically pleasing.

- **Renewed emphasis on directed strategies and networked systems** — The recent emphasis on educational accountability as reflected in the No Child Left Behind (NCLB) Act has breathed new life into strategies that were once considered passé. Even in research circles, some authors have claimed that directed teaching strategies are more effective than minimally guided teaching techniques (Kirshner, Sweller, & Clark, 2006). As constructivist methods became more popular in the 1980s and 1990s, the demand for drill-and-practice and tutorial instructional software waned and use of simulation and problem-solving software increased. Now directed strategies made possible by drills and tutorials—which are ideal for preparing students for tests—are once again on the rise. The same accountability emphasis has created new demand for networked instructional software products called **integrated learning systems (ILSs)**, networked or online systems that provide both computer-based instruction and summary reports of student progress, described later in this chapter. These systems became popular in the late 1980s and early 1990s as an efficient way for many students to access instructional software from a central source (e.g., a school or district server), and educators often employed them to support directed instruction for remedial programs (e.g., Title III programs that provide special resources for disadvantaged students). Although de-emphasized in the late 1990s, today's ILSs are becoming valued not only for their centralized access, but also for their ability to track and report on student progress. Data on individual and group progress in a given classroom, school, or district is a central feature of the new NCLB Act accountability requirements.

Drill-and-Practice Software Functions

Drill-and-practice software provides exercises in which students work example items, usually one at a time, and receive feedback on their correctness. Programs vary considerably in the kind of feedback they provide in response to student input. Feedback can range from a simple display like "OK" or "No, try again" to elaborate animated displays or verbal explanations. Some programs simply present the next item if the student answers correctly.

Types of drill and practice are sometimes distinguished by how the program tailors the practice session to student needs (Merrill & Salisbury, 1984). Types of drill functions, described below, include flash card activities, branching drills, and extensive feedback activities:

- **Flash card activity** — This is the most basic drill-and-practice function, arising from the popularity of real-world flash cards. A student sees a set number of questions or problems, presented one at a time. The student chooses or types an answer, and the program responds with positive or negative feedback depending on whether the student answered correctly.

- **Branching drill** — This is a more sophisticated form of drill and practice. In branching drills, the software moves students on to advanced questions after they get a number of questions correct at some predetermined mastery level; it may also send them back to lower levels if they answer a certain number wrong. Some programs automatically review questions that students get wrong before going on to other levels. Students may not realize that branching is happening, since the program may do it automatically

A popular use of drill software is preparing for important tests.

without alerting them to this fact. Sometimes, however, the program may congratulate students on good progress before proceeding to the next level, or it may allow them to choose their next activities. More recently, educational software designers have attempted to use learners' cognitive status to decide what task learners should be presented with next (Salden, Paas, & van Merriënboer, 2006).

- **Extensive feedback activities** — In these drills, students get more than just correct/incorrect feedback. Some programs give detailed feedback on why the student got a problem wrong. This feedback is sometimes so thorough that the software function is often mistaken for a tutorial. (See the next section for a description of tutorial functions.) However, the function of a drill is not instruction, but rather practice. Consequently, the integration strategies for drill and tutorial functions differ.

Selecting Good Drill-and-Practice Software

In addition to meeting general criteria for good instructional software, well-designed drill-and-practice programs should also meet specific criteria:

- **Control over the presentation rate** — Unless the questions are part of a timed review, students should have as much time as they wish to answer and examine the feedback before proceeding to later questions. A student usually signals readiness to go to the next question by simply pressing a key.

- **Answer judging** — If programs allow students to enter a short answer rather than simply choosing one, a good drill program must be able to discriminate between correct and incorrect answers.

- **Appropriate feedback for correct and incorrect answers** — If students' responses are timed, or if their session time is limited, they may find it more motivating simply to move quickly to the next question. When drills do give feedback, they must avoid two common errors. First, feedback must be simple and display quickly. Students rapidly tire of elaborate displays, and the feedback ceases to motivate them. Second, some programs inadvertently motivate students to get wrong answers by giving more exciting or interesting feedback for wrong answers than for correct ones. The most famous example of this design error occurred in an early version of a popular microcomputer-based math drill series. Each correct answer got a smiling face, but two or more wrong answers produced a full-screen, animated crying face that students found amusing. Consequently, many students tried to answer incorrectly so they could see it. The company corrected this flaw, but this classic error still exists today in other programs.

Go to MyEducationLab and select the topic "Instructional Planning." Under "Rubrics/Checklists," obtain the "Essential Criteria Checklist for Evaluating Instructional Software."

Benefits of Drill and Practice

Research has shown that drill-and-practice software activities can allow the effective rehearsal students need to transfer newly learned information into long-term memory (Merrill & Salisbury, 1984; Salisbury, 1990). Many teachers feel that such practice gives students more rapid recall and use of basic skills as prerequisites to advanced concepts. They like students to have what Gagné (1982) and Bloom (1986) call *automaticity*, or automatic recall of these lower order skills, to help them master higher order ones faster and more easily. The usefulness of drill programs in providing this kind of practice has been well documented, but the programs seem especially popular among teachers of students with learning disabilities (Hasselbring, 1988; Higgins & Boone, 1993; Okolo, 1992).

Although curriculum increasingly emphasizes problem solving and higher order skills, teachers still give students on-paper practice (e.g., worksheets or exercises) for many skills to help them learn and remember correct procedures. Drill software provides the following acknowledged benefits as compared to paper exercises (Kahn, 1998–1999):

- **Immediate feedback** — When students practice skills on paper, they frequently do not know until much later whether or not they did their work correctly. To quote a common saying, "Practice does not make perfect; practice makes permanent." As they complete work incorrectly,

Adapting for Special Needs

Given the diverse level of student abilities in every classroom, teachers need products that anticipate and engage a broad range of skills. Early-learning products like *Bailey's Book House*, *Sammy's Science House*, and *Millie's Math House* (all from Riverdeep) give students opportunities to play, explore, and interact with a variety of pre-academic instructional skills.

Also, many instructional software products support special access devices like switches and alternative keyboards. These are useful to students who have disabilities that prevent them from using instructional software via the standard keyboard.

Contributed by Dave Edyburn

students may actually be memorizing the wrong skills. Drill-and-practice software informs them immediately whether their responses are accurate so they can make quick corrections. This helps both "debugging" (identifying errors in their procedures) and retention (placing the skills in long-term memory for future access).

- **Motivation** — Many students refuse to do the practice they need on paper, either because they have failed so much that the whole idea is abhorrent, they have poor handwriting skills, or they simply dislike writing. In these cases, computer-based practice may motivate students to do the practice they need. Computers don't get impatient or give disgusted looks when a student gives a wrong answer.

- **Saving teacher time** — Since teachers do not have to present or grade drill and practice, students can practice on their own while the teacher addresses other student needs. The curriculum has dozens of areas in which the benefits of drill and practice apply. Some of these are:
  - Math facts
  - Typing skills
  - English- and foreign-language vocabulary
  - Countries and capitals
  - SAT and TOEFL skills
  - Musical keys and notations.

Limitations and Problems Related to Drill and Practice

Although drill and practice can be extremely useful to both students and teachers, it is also the most maligned of the

software activities, sometimes informally referred to among its critics as "drill and kill." This criticism comes from the following two sources:

- **Perceived misuses** — Some authors have criticized teachers for presenting drills for overly long periods or for teaching functions that drills are ill suited to accomplish. For example, teachers may give students drill-and-practice software as a way of introducing new concepts rather than just for practicing and reinforcing familiar ones.

- **Criticism by constructivists** — Since it is identified so closely with traditional instructional methods, drill-and-practice software has become an icon for what many people consider an outmoded approach to teaching. Critics claim that introducing isolated skills and directing students to practice them contradicts the trend toward restructured curriculum in which students learn and use skills in an integrated way within the context of their own projects that specifically require the skills.

Despite these criticisms, it is likely that some form of drill-and-practice software will be useful in many classrooms for some time to come. Rather than ignoring drill-and-practice software or criticizing it as outmoded, teachers should seek to identify needs that drills can meet and use the software in ways that take advantage of its capabilities. See Figure 3.1 for examples of drill software and a summary of drill features.

Using Drill and Practice in Teaching

Classroom integration strategies for drill functions. Drill-and-practice programs may be used whenever teachers feel the need for on-paper exercises such as worksheets. On some occasions, even the most creative and innovative teacher may take advantage of the benefits of drill-and-practice software to give students practice using isolated skills. Integration strategies include:

- **Supplement or replace worksheets and homework exercises** — Whenever students have difficulty with higher order tasks ranging from reading and writing to mathematics, teachers may have to stop and identify specific prerequisite skills that these students lack and provide the instruction and practice they need to go forward. In these cases, learning may require a rehearsal activity to make sure information is stored in long-term memory so students can retrieve it easily. Drills' motivation, immediate feedback, and self-pacing can make it more productive for students to practice required skills on the computer than on paper.

- **Prepare for tests** — Despite the new emphasis on student portfolios and other authentic assessment measures, students can expect to take several kinds of objec-

FIGURE 3.1 · Drill-and-Practice Summary Information

Description of Drill and Practice

Characteristics	Criteria for Effective Drill Software	Benefits
• Presents items for students to answer • Gives feedback on correctness • Sometimes gives explanation of why answers are incorrect	• User control over presentation rate • Good answer judging • Appropriate feedback for correct, incorrect answers	• Gives immediate, private feedback • Motivates students to practice • Saves teacher time correcting student work

Sample Software with Drill-and-Practice Functions

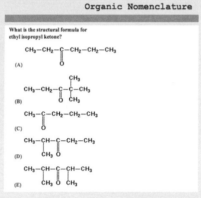

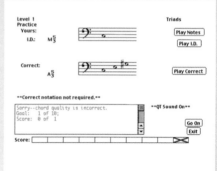

Earobics®
by Cognitive Concepts, Inc.
http://www.earobics.com/

Practice in phonological awareness and other reading readiness skills.

© 1997–2004 by Cognitive Concepts, Inc. All rights reserved.

Organic Nomenclature®
by the *Journal of Chemical Education*
http://www.jce.divched.org/

Practice in naming organic compounds and identifying structural formulas.

Used with permission from the *Journal of Chemical Education*, Vol. 80, No. 10, 2003, pp. 1223–1224; copyright © 2003, Division of Chemical Education, Inc.

MacGAMUT®
by Music Software International
http://www.macgamut.com/

Practice in recognizing intervals, scales, chords, melodic dictation, harmonic dictation, and rhythmic dictation.

MacGAMUT 2003 for Mac and Windows.
© 2003, MacGAMUT Music Software, Inc.
http://www.macgamut.com/

---

tive examinations in their education careers. When they need to prepare to demonstrate mastery of specific skills in important examinations (e.g., for end-of-year grades or for college entrance), drill-and-practice software can help them focus on their deficiencies and correct them. An example integration strategy for drill functions is shown in Technology Integration Lesson 3.2.

Guidelines for using drill and practice. Use the following guidelines to make best use of drill capabilities when designing integration strategies for drill-and-practice functions:

• **Set time limits** — Teachers should limit the time devoted to drill assignments to 10 to 15 minutes per day. This ensures that students will not become bored and that the drill-and-practice strategy will retain its effectiveness. Also, teachers should be sure students

have been introduced previously to the concepts underlying the drills. Drill software should serve mainly to debug and to help students retain their grasp of familiar concepts.

• **Assign individually** — Most drills are designed to allow self-pacing and personalized feedback. Therefore, these activities usually work best for individual computer use. However, some teachers with limited technology resources have found other, ingenious ways to capitalize on the motivational and immediate feedback capabilities of drills. If all students in a class benefit from practice in a skill using a drill program, the teacher may divide them into small groups to compete with each other for the best group scores. The class could even be divided into two groups for a "relay race" competition to see which group can complete the assignment the fastest with the most correct answers.

Technology Integration Lesson 3.2

Example Strategy for Drill-and-Practice Software

Title: Organic Nomenclature

Content Area/Topic: Chemistry

Grade Level: High school

NETS for Students: Standard 4 (Critical Thinking, Problem Solving, and Decision Making)

Description of Standards Applications: This integration idea offers practice in critical thinking and decision making as students strive to understand organic compounds and how they are represented by the formulas that show how their components combine. Using software that presents a name or formula, students need to select correct formulas or names.

Instruction: Begin by introducing the topic of organic compounds and how they are represented by the formulas that show how their components combine. Demonstrate to the whole class how to do these formulas for one or two compounds. Then ask students to respond to others as a whole-class exercise. Next, turn the problem around by presenting one or two formulas and asking students to name the compound. Since it is important for each student to be able to identify and do formulas for these compounds quickly as a prerequisite to further work on organic compounds, the software is designed for use by individual students. The software presents a name or a formula, and the student selects the correct formula or name from a list of five options. Students do a set of these, and the software gives them feedback on their correctness. They do as many sets as needed to master the concept. Both students and teachers can use these exercises to gauge their readiness to proceed with other work.

Assessment: Use a multiple-choice test formatted similar to items in software.

Source: From Shaw, D. B., & Yindra, L. (2003). Organic nomenclature. *Journal of Chemical Education, 80* (10), 1223–1224. Used with permission from the *Journal of Chemical Education;* copyright © 2003, Division of Chemical Education, Inc. Software available from the *Journal of Chemical Education,* http://www.jce.divched.org.

- **Use learning stations** — If not all students need the kind of practice that a drill provides, the teacher may make software one of several learning stations to serve students with identified weaknesses in one or more key skills. Drill-and-practice functions are used best when matched to the specific learning needs of individual students.

Tutorial Software Functions

Tutorial software is an entire instructional sequence on a topic, similar to a teacher's classroom instruction. This instruction usually is expected to be a self-contained instructional unit rather than a supplement to other instruction. Students should be able to learn the topic without any other help or materials. Unlike other types of instructional software, tutorials are true teaching materials. Gagné et al. (1981) said that good tutorial software should address all

nine instructional events. (See the discussion of Gagné's Events of Instruction in Chapter 2.)

People may confuse tutorial and drill activities for two reasons. First, drill software may provide elaborate feedback that reviewers may mistake for tutorial explanations. Even software developers may claim that a package is a tutorial when it is, in fact, a drill activity with detailed feedback. Second, a good tutorial should include one or more practice sequences to check students' comprehension. Since this is a drill-and-practice function, reviewers can become confused about the primary purpose of the activity.

Tutorials often are categorized as linear or branching tutorials (Alessi & Trollip, 2001), as described below:

- **Linear tutorial** — A simple, linear tutorial gives the same instructional sequence of explanation, practice, and feedback to all learners regardless of differences in their performance.

- **Branching tutorial** — A more sophisticated branching tutorial directs learners along alternate paths depending on how they respond to questions and whether they show mastery of certain parts of the material. Branching tutorials can range in complexity by the number of paths they allow and how fully they diagnose the kinds of instruction a student needs. More complex tutorials may also have computer-management capabilities; teachers can place each student at an appropriate level and get progress reports as each one goes through the instruction.

Tutorials are usually geared toward learners who can read fairly well and who are older students or adults. Since tutorial instruction is expected to stand alone, it is difficult to explain or give appropriate guidance on-screen to a nonreader. However, some tutorials aimed at younger learners have found clever ways to explain and demonstrate concepts with graphics, succinct phrases or sentences, or audio directions coupled with screen displays.

Selecting Good Tutorial Software

Being a good teacher is a difficult assignment for any human, let alone a computer. However, software must accomplish this task to fulfill tutorial functions. In addition to meeting general criteria for good instructional software, well-designed tutorial programs should also meet the following standards:

- **Extensive interactivity** — Good tutorials, like good teachers, should require students to give frequent and thoughtful responses to questions and problems and should supply appropriate practice and feedback to guide students' learning. The most frequent criticism of tutorials is that they are "page-turners"—that is, they ask students to do very little other than read. Interactive tutorials have been shown to present cognitive benefits for learners (e.g., Schwan & Riempp, 2004).

- **Thorough user control** — User control refers to several aspects of a tutorial program. First, students should always be able to control the rate at which text appears on the screen. The program should not go on to the next information or activity screen until the user has pressed a key or has given some other indication of having completed the necessary reading. Next, the program should offer students the flexibility to review explanations, examples, or sequences of instruction or to move ahead to other instruction. The program should also provide frequent opportunities for students to exit the program if they like.

- **Appropriate pedagogy** — The program's structure should provide a suggested or required sequence of instruction that builds on concepts and covers the content adequately. It should provide sufficient explanation and examples in both original and remedial sequences. In

sum, it should compare favorably to an expert teacher's presentation sequence for the topic.

- **Adequate answer-judging and feedback capabilities** — Whenever possible, programs should allow students to answer in natural language and should accept all correct answers and possible variations of correct answers. They should also give appropriate corrective feedback when needed, supplying this feedback after only one or two tries rather than frustrating students by making them keep trying indefinitely to answer something they may not know.

- **Appropriate graphics** — Although some authors insist that graphics form part of tutorial instruction (Baek & Layne, 1988), others warn that graphics should be used sparingly and not interfere with the purpose of the instruction (Eiser, 1988). Where graphics *are* used, they should fulfill an instructional, aesthetic, or otherwise supportive function.

- **Adequate recordkeeping** — Depending on the purpose of the tutorial, teachers may need to keep track of student progress. If the program keeps records on student work, teachers should be able to get progress summaries quickly and easily.

Benefits of Tutorials

Since a tutorial includes drill-and-practice activities, helpful features include the same ones as for drills (immediate feedback to learners, motivation, and time savings) plus the additional benefit of offering a self-contained, self-paced unit of instruction. Many successful uses of tutorials have been documented over the years. For examples, see Arnett (2000), CAI in Music (1994), Cann and Seale (1999), Graham (1994, 1998), Kraemer (1990), Murray et al. (1988), and Steinberg and Oberem (2000).

Limitations and Problems Related to Tutorials

Tutorials can fulfill many much-needed instructional functions, but like drill and practice, they also attract their share of criticism, including:

- **Criticism by constructivists** — Constructivists criticize tutorials because they deliver directed instruction rather than allowing students to generate their own knowledge through hands-on projects. Thus, they feel tutorials are trivial uses of the computer.

- **Lack of good products** — Software publishers describe fewer packages as tutorials than any other kind of microcomputer software. This is partly due to the difficulty and expense of designing and developing tutorial software. A well-designed tutorial sequence emerges from extensive research into how to teach the topic well. Designers must know what learning tasks the topic requires, the best sequence for students to follow, how best to explain and demonstrate essential concepts, common errors students are likely to make, and how to provide instruction and feedback to correct those errors. Therefore, programming and graphics can become fairly involved.

- **Reflect only one instructional approach** — Tutorial problems become still more difficult because teachers frequently disagree about what should be taught for a given topic, how to teach it most effectively, and in what order to present the learning tasks. A teacher may choose not to purchase a tutorial with a sound instructional sequence, for instance, because it does not cover the topic the way he or she presents it. Not surprisingly, software companies tend to avoid programs that are difficult to develop and market.

Although tutorials have considerable value and are popular in military and industrial training, schools and colleges have never fully tapped their potential as teaching resources. However, recent trends toward combining tutorial software with audiovisual media and distance education initiatives may bring tutorial functions into more common use. See Figure 3.2 for examples of tutorial software and a summary of tutorial features.

Using Tutorials in Teaching

Classroom integration strategies for tutorial functions. Self-instructional tutorials should in no way threaten teachers, since few conceivable situations make a computer preferable to an expert teacher. However, the tutorial's unique capability of presenting an entire interactive instructional sequence can assist in several classroom situations:

- **Self-paced reviews of instruction** — Students often need to repeat instruction on a topic after the teacher's initial presentation. Some students may be slower to understand concepts and need to spend additional time on them. Others may learn better in a self-paced mode without the pressure to move at the same pace as the rest of the class. Still others may need a review before a test. Tutorials can provide self-paced instruction to address all these needs.

- **Alternative learning strategies** — Some students, typically those at advanced levels, prefer to structure their own learning activities and proceed at their own pace. With a good tutorial, advanced students can glean much background material prior to meeting with a teacher or others to do assessment and/or further work assignments.

- **Instruction when teachers are unavailable** — Some students have problems when they surge ahead of their class. The teacher cannot leave the rest of the class to provide the instruction that such an advanced student

needs. It is also true that many schools, especially those in rural areas, may not offer certain courses because they cannot justify the expense of hiring a teacher for the comparatively few students who need physics, German, trigonometry, or other lower demand courses. Well-designed tutorial courses, especially in combination with other methods such as distance learning, can help meet these students' needs.

Guidelines for using tutorials. Use the following guidelines to make the best use of tutorial capabilities when designing integration strategies for tutorial functions:

- **Assign individually** — Like drill-and-practice functions, tutorial functions are designed for use by individuals rather than by groups of students.

- **Use learning stations or individual checkout** — Depending on which of the above strategies it promotes, a tutorial may be used in a classroom learning station or may be available for checkout at any time in a library/media center. Sometimes teachers send students to learning stations with tutorials in order to review previously presented material while the teacher works with other students. (See Technology Integration Lesson 3.3 on page 87.)

Simulation Software Functions

A simulation is a computerized model of a real or imagined system that is designed to teach how the system works. Unlike tutorial and drill-and-practice activities, in which the teaching structure is built into the package, learners using simulations usually must choose tasks to do and the order in which to do them. Alessi and Trollip (2001) identify two main types of simulations: those that teach *about* something and those that teach *how to do* something. They further divide the "about" simulations into physical and iterative types and the "how to" simulations into procedural and situational types.

Simulations can be used instead of or in conjunction with certain science activities such as dissections.

FIGURE 3.2 **Tutorial Summary Information**

Description of Tutorial Software

Characteristics
- Presents an entire instructional sequence
- Is complete, rather than supplemental, instruction
- Includes drill-and-practice functions
- Can be either linear or branching

Criteria for Effective Tutorial Software
- Extensive interactivity
- Thorough user control
- Appropriate pedagogy
- Adequate answer judging and feedback
- Appropriate graphics
- Adequate record keeping

Benefits
- Same as drill and practice (immediate, private feedback, time savings)
- Offers instruction that can stand on its own

Sample Software with Tutorial Functions

PhysicaElementa®
by Intellectum Plus, Inc.
http://www.mathandscience4u.com/

Instruction in states of matter: A sequence of screens gives explanations, descriptions, and animated examples of solids, liquids, and gases.

© Intellectum Plus, Inc. Used with permission.

Congress for Kids®
Sponsored by the Dirksen Congressional Center
http://www.congressforkids.net

Instruction in various aspects of U.S. government: Sequences of screens give explanations of how government works, with assessment items to review concepts and check comprehension.

© The Dirksen Congressional Center, Pekin, Illinois. Used with permission.

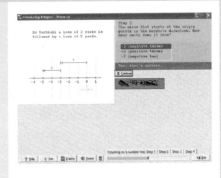

Basic Algebra Shapeup®
by Merit Software, Inc.
http://www.meritsoftware.com/

Instruction in algebra concepts: A series of screens explains a concept, then assessment items check students' knowledge.

© Merit Software, Inc. Used with permission.

Simulations That Teach about Something

- **Physical simulations** — These simulations allow users to manipulate things or processes represented on the screen. For example, students might see selections of chemicals with instructions on how to combine them to see the result, or they might see how various electrical circuits operate. More recent investigations of simulation software include the use of three-dimensional models (e.g., Kim, 2006).

- **Iterative simulations** — These simulations speed up or slow down processes that usually happen either so slowly or so quickly that students cannot see the events unfold. For example, software may show the effects of changes in demographic variables on population growth or the effects of environmental factors on ecosystems. Alessi and Trollip (2001) refer to this type as "iterative" because students can run it over and over again with different values, observing the results each time. Biological simulations, such as those on genetics, are popular since they help students experiment with natural processes. Genetics simulations let students pair animals with given characteristics and see the resulting offspring.

Simulations That Teach How to Do Something

- **Procedural simulations** — These activities teach the appropriate sequences of steps to perform certain procedures. They include diagnostic programs, in which students try to identify the sources of medical or mechanical problems, and flight simulators, in which students simulate piloting an airplane or other vehicle.

Technology Integration Lesson 3.3

Example Strategy for Tutorial Software

Title: The *ActivStats* Statistics Tutorial
Content Area/Topic: AP Statistics

Grade Level: High school

 NETS for Students: Standards 3 (Research and Information Fluency) and 4 (Critical Thinking, Problem Solving, and Decision Making)

Description of Standards Applications: This integration idea offers the opportunity to research raw data, analyze the data, and then interpret the findings through an interactive statistics program, *ActivStats*. The *ActivStats* tutorial software has 26 lessons that cover the basics of introductory statistics.

Instruction: A teacher can use the short animated clips at the beginning of each lesson to introduce the topic to the whole class. The teacher continues the introduction with a review of the lesson's basic concepts by using an animation to illustrate the uses of the statistic and how changing the raw data can alter it. After this demo, students work individually on the remaining lesson activities. For example, most lessons allow the user to import pre-existing data files and provide instructions on how to plot them in a chart or in three dimensions.

Assessment: Students use the built-in quizzes to gauge their comprehension and determine if they are ready to take the teacher's final test on the topic.

Source: Based on Ashbacher, C. (2003). ActivStats. *Mathematics and Computer Education, 37*(2), 254–255. Reprinted with permission of *Mathematics and Computer Education* journal. Software available from Addison-Wesley, http://www.aw-bc.com/activstats/.

- **Situational simulations** — These programs give students hypothetical problem situations and ask them to react. Some simulations allow for various successful strategies, such as letting students play the stock market or operate businesses. Others have most desirable and least desirable options, such as choices when encountering a potentially volatile classroom situation.

The preceding descriptions serve to clarify the various forms a simulation might take, but teachers need not feel they should be able to classify a given simulation into one of these categories. Simulations usually emphasize learning about the system itself rather than learning general problem-solving strategies. For example, a program called *The Factory* has students build products by selecting machines and placing them in the correct sequence. Since the program emphasizes solving problems in correct sequence rather than manufacturing in factories, it should probably be called a problem-solving activity rather than a simulation. Programs such as *SimCity*™ (Electronic Arts), which let students design their own cities, provide more accurate examples of building-type simulations (Adams, 1998). (See Technology Integration Lesson 3.4 for a classroom example using *SimCity*.)

Selecting Good Simulation Software

Simulations vary in type and purpose, so a uniform set of criteria is not possible. For some simulations, a realistic and accurate representation of a system is essential (Reigeluth & Schwartz, 1989), but for others, it is important only to know what the screen elements represent. Since the screen often presents no set sequence of steps, simulations need good accompanying documentation—more than most software. A set of clear directions helps the teacher learn how to use the program and show the students how to use it rapidly and easily. See Figure 3.3 for examples of simulation software and a summary of simulation features.

Benefits of Simulations

The field of science seems to include more simulations than any other area (Andaloro, 1991; Lunce & Bailey, 2007; Mintz, 1993; Richards, 1992; Ronen, 1992; Simmons & Lunetta, 1993; Smith, 1992), but the use of simulations is also popular in teaching social science topics (Adams, 1998; Allen, 1993; Clinton, 1991; Estes, 1994). However, more simulations are currently in development that feature on-line delivery or supplements to combine the control, safety,

Technology Integration Lesson 3.4

Example Strategy for Simulation Software

Title: Community Planning Projects with *SimCity™*

Grade Level: Middle school

Content Area/Topic: Social studies—citizenship/group cooperation in social projects

NETS for Students: Standards 1 (Creativity and Innovation), 2 (Communication and Collaboration), 3 (Research and Information Fluency), 4 (Critical Thinking, Problem Solving, and Decision Making), and 5 (Digital Citizenship)

Description of Standards Applications: This integration idea offers the opportunity for students to work together to develop a city using the *SimCity™* software. Students will use their creativity as they research the many alternatives for developing a city that has the qualities of an environment where they and others would like to live. This lesson helps raise students' awareness of their responsibility to become informed citizens, shows how they can participate in local decision making, and gives practice in working cooperatively with a group to carry out a social project. The software allows the development of a comprehensive plan for the township.

Instruction: A representative from the county planning and zoning office talks with students about factors of concern to community development. The teacher then introduces students to the *SimCity™* software. They form teams of four to five students each and start their own community planning projects with *SimCity*. Each group meets every week to discuss and develop its plan. As a group, they decide how to select and place features such as roads, homes, and utilities. After recording their decisions on paper, they enter them into the program and observe the results. The groups discuss feedback that the program provides on areas such as taxes, crime rates, and public opinion. After the groups' plans are complete, each group presents its plan to the teacher and explains and defends its choices.

Assessment: Papers are graded by a rubric.

Source: From Jacobson, P. (1992). Save the cities! *SimCity* in grades 2–5. *The Computing Teacher, 20* (2), 14–15.

---

and interactive features of computer simulations with the visual impact of pictures of real-life devices and processes. Depending on the topic, a simulation can provide one or more of the following benefits (Alessi & Trollip, 2001):

- **Compress time** — This feature is important whenever students study the growth or development of living things (e.g., pairing animals to observe the characteristics of their offspring) or other processes that take a long time (e.g., the movement of a glacier). A simulation can make something happen in seconds that normally takes days, months, or longer, so that students can cover more variations of the activity in a shorter time.

- **Slow down processes** — Conversely, a simulation can also model processes normally invisible to the human eye because they happen so quickly. For example, physical education students can study the slowed-down

movement of muscles and limbs as a simulated athlete throws a ball or swings a golf club.

- **Get students involved** — Simulations can capture students' attention by placing them in charge of things and asking, "What would you do?" The results of their choices can be immediate and graphic. Users can also interact with the program instead of just seeing its output.

- **Make experimentation safe** — Whenever learning involves physical danger, simulations are the strategy of choice. This is true when students are learning to drive vehicles, handle volatile substances, or react to potentially dangerous situations. They can experiment with strategies in simulated environments that might result in personal injury to themselves or others in real life. For example, the First Responders Simulation and Training Environment (FiRSTE) allows for the training of civilian

FIGURE 3.3 Simulation Summary Information

Description of Simulation Software

Characteristics
- Models a real or imaginary system
- Can model physical phenomena (e.g., growth), procedures (e.g., dissections), and hypothetical situations (e.g., stock market)
- Users can see the impact of their actions

Criteria for Effective Simulation Software
- System fidelity and accuracy (for some simulations)
- Good documentation to explain system characteristics and uses

Benefits
- Compresses time or slows down processes
- Gets students involved
- Makes experimentation safe
- Makes the impossible possible
- Saves money and other resources
- Allows repetition with variations
- Allows observation of complex processes

Sample Software with Simulation Functions

Virtual Labs: Electricity®
by Riverdeep, Inc.
http://web.riverdeep.net

Simulated electrical circuit board: Provides a safe means for students to apply electrical concepts to simulated devices.

Oregon Trail®
by The Learning Company
http://www.learningcompany.com

Simulated trip in the Old West of the 1890s: Students learn about pioneer days by taking roles in a simulated wagon train journey.

SimCity 3000®
by Electronic Arts, Inc.
http://www.maxis.com/

Simulated city: Lets users build their own cities, create a budget for them, populate them, and run them, including responding to intermittent disasters.

first responders to respond to attacks employing weapons of mass destruction (Tichon et al., 2003).

- **Make the impossible possible** — Very often, teachers simply cannot give students access to the resources or situations that simulations can. Simulations can show students, for example, what it would be like to walk on the moon or to react to emergencies in a nuclear power plant. They can see cells mutating or hold countrywide elections. They can even design new societies or planets and see the results of their choices. For example, one researcher at Davis (UCDavis) re-created a mental health treatment ward in a virtual world and gave each of his students a taste of what it means to experience schizophrenia in the real world. As students' virtual characters walked the hallways, they were overcome by hallucinations including "the floor disappearing from underfoot, writing on posters that morphs into derogatory words, a pulsating gun that suddenly appears on a table, and menacing voices that laugh" (UCDavis, 2007).

- **Save money and other resources** — Many school systems are finding dissections of animals on a computer screen to be much less expensive and just as instructional as using real frogs or cats. (It is also easier on the animals!) Depending on the subject, a simulated experiment may be just as effective a learning experience as an actual experiment is, at a fraction of the cost.

- **Allow repetition with variations** — Unlike in real life, simulations let students repeat events as many times as they wish and with unlimited variations. They can pair any number of cats or make endless spaceship landings in a variety of conditions to compare the results of each set of choices.

- **Allow observation of complex processes** — Real-life events often are so complex that they are confusing—especially to those seeing them for the first time. When many things happen at once, students find it difficult to focus on the operation of individual components. Who could understand the operation of a stock market by looking at the real thing without some introduction? Simulations can isolate parts of activities and control background noise. This makes it easier for students to see what is happening when, later, all the parts come together in the actual activity.

Limitations and Problems Related to Simulations

Most educators acknowledge the instructional usefulness of simulations. There are some concerns, however, which include the following:

- **Accuracy of models** — When students see simplified versions of systems in a controlled situation, they may get inaccurate or imprecise perspectives on the systems' complexity. For example, students may feel they know all about how to react to driving situations because they have experienced simulated versions of them. Many educators feel strongly that situational simulations must be followed at some point by real experiences. In addition, many teachers of very young children feel that learners at early stages of their cognitive development should experience things first with their five senses rather than on computer screens.

- **Misuse of simulations** — Sometimes, simulations are used to teach concepts that could just as easily be demonstrated on paper, with manipulatives, or with real objects. For example, students usually are delighted with the simulation of the food chain called *Odell Lakes*, a program that lets students see which animals prey on other animals in a hypothetical lake. However, some educators wonder whether such a computer simulation is necessary or even desirable for teaching this concept. Hasselbring and Goin (1993) point out that students often can master the activities of a simulation without actually developing effective problem-solving skills; on the contrary, such applications actually can encourage counterproductive behaviors. For example, some simulations initially provide little information with which to solve problems, and students are reduced to "trial-and-error guessing rather than systematic analysis of available information" (p. 156). Teachers must structure integration strategies carefully so that students will not use simulations in inappropriate ways.

How to Use Simulations in Teaching: Integration Strategies and Guidelines

Simulations are considered among the most potentially powerful computer software resources; as with most software, however, their usefulness depends largely on the program's purpose and how well it fits in with the purpose of the lesson and student needs. Teachers are responsible for recognizing the unique instructional value of each simulation and for using it to its best advantage.

Classroom applications of simulation functions. Real systems are usually preferable to simulations, but a simulation is useful when the real situation is too time consuming, dangerous, expensive, or unrealistic for a classroom presentation. Simulations should be considered in the following situations:

- **In place of or as supplements to lab experiments** — When adequate lab materials are not available, teachers should try to locate computer simulations of the required experiments. Many teachers find that simulations offer effective supplements to real labs, either to prepare students for making good use of the actual labs or as follow-ups with variations of the original experiments without using consumable materials. Some simulations actually allow users to perform experiments that they could not otherwise manage or that would be too dangerous for students.

- **In place of or as supplements to role-playing** — Many students either refuse to role play in front of a class or get too enthusiastic and disrupt the classroom. Computerized simulations can take the personal embarrassment and logistical problems out of the learning experience, make classroom role playing more controllable, and spark students' imagination and interest in the activities.

- **In place of or as supplements to field trips** — Seeing an activity in its real setting can be a valuable experience, especially for young children. Sometimes, however, desired locations are not within reach of the school, and a simulated experience of all or part of the process is the next best thing. As with labs, simulations provide good introductions or follow-ups to field trips.

- **Introducing and/or clarifying a new topic** — Software that allows students to explore the elements of an environment in a hands-on manner frequently provides students' first in-depth contact with a topic. This seems to accomplish several purposes. First, it is a non-threatening way to introduce new terms and unfamiliar settings. Students know they are not being graded, so they feel less pressure than usual to learn everything right away. A simulation can be simply a get-acquainted look at a topic; it can also build students' initial interest in a topic. Highly graphic, hands-on activities draw them in and whet their appetite to learn more. Finally, some software helps students see how certain prerequisite skills relate to the topic; this may motivate students more strongly to learn the skills than if the skills were introduced in isolation from the problems to which they apply. For example, Tom Snyder's *Decisions! Decisions!* software helps students see the relevance of topics such as the U.S. Constitution and elections.

- **Fostering exploration and process learning** — Teachers often use content-free simulation/problem-solving software (e.g., *The Factory*) as motivation for students to explore their own cognitive processes. Since this kind of software requires students to learn no specific content, it is easier to get them to concentrate on problem-solving steps and strategies. However, with content-free products, it is even more important than usual that teachers draw comparisons between the skills used in the software activities and those in the content areas to which they want to transfer the experience. For example, *Virtual Lab* (Riverdeep) presents an implicit emphasis on science-process skills that the teacher may want to point out. It seems best to use these kinds of activities just prior to content-area activities that will require the same processes.

- **Encouraging cooperation and group work** — Sometimes a simulated demonstration can capture students' attention quickly and effectively and interest them in working together on a product. For example, a simulation on immigration or colonization might be the "grabber" a teacher needs to launch a group project in a social studies unit.

Guidelines for using simulation functions. Simulations offer more versatile implementation than tutorials or drills do. They usually work equally effectively with a whole class, small groups, or individuals. A teacher may choose to introduce a lesson to the class by displaying a simulation or to divide the class into small groups and let each of them solve problems. Because they instigate discussion and collaborative work so well, simulations usually are considered more appropriate for pairs and small groups than for individuals. However, individual use certainly is not precluded.

Instructional Game Software Functions

Technology-based games bridge the worlds of gaming, entertainment, and education in an attempt to deliver fun and effective learning. Simply defined, instructional games add game-like rules and/or competition to learning activities. Even though teachers often use them in the same way as they do drill-and-practice or simulation software, games usually are listed as a separate software activity because their instructional connotation to students is slightly different. When students know they will be playing a game, they expect a fun and entertaining activity because of the challenge of the competition and the potential for winning (Gee, 2004; Raessens & Goldstein, 2005; Randel, Morris, Wetzel, & Whitehill, 1992; Squire, 2005). Teachers frequently intersperse games with other activities to hold students' attention or as a reward for accomplishing other activities, even though games, by themselves, could be powerful teaching tools.

It is important to recognize the common characteristics that set instructional games apart from other types of software: game rules, elements of competition or challenge, and amusing or entertaining formats. These elements generate a set of mental and emotional expectations in students that make game-based instructional activities different from nongame ones.

Selecting Good Instructional Games

Since instructional games often amount to drills or simulations overlaid with game rules, these three types of software often share many of the same criteria (e.g., better reinforcement for

Instructional games are one way to engage students in learning.

correct answers than for incorrect ones). Teachers should use the following criteria in choosing instructional games:

- **Appealing formats and activities** — When Malone (1980) examined the evidence on what makes things fun to learn, he found that the most popular games included elements of adventure and uncertainty and levels of complexity matched to learners' abilities.

- **Instructional value** — Teachers should examine instructional games carefully for their value as both educational and motivational tools. While a number of researchers argue for the benefits of educational games (e.g., Gee, 2004; Squire, 2005), others question their value (e.g., Clark, 2007).

- **Physical dexterity is reasonable** — Teachers should ensure that students will be motivated rather than frustrated by the activities.

- **Social, societal, and cultural considerations** — Games may be inappropriate for children if they are not designed with a respectful outlook. For instance, games that call for violence or combat require careful screening, not only to avoid students' modeling this behavior, but also because girls often perceive the attraction of these activities differently than boys do. In addition, games may present females and various ethnic and cultural groups in stereotypical roles. Ideally, teachers should choose games that do not perpetuate stereotypes, while at the same time highlighting positive messages (e.g., peace and friendship) rather than unnecessary violence (e.g., aggression).

Benefits of Instructional Games

A classroom without elements of games and fun would be a dry, barren landscape for students to traverse. In their review of the effectiveness of games for educational purposes, Randel et al. (1992) found "[the fact] that games are more interesting than traditional instruction is both a basis for using them as well as a consistent finding" (p. 270). They also observed that retention over time favors the use of simulations/games. Successful uses of games have been reported in many content areas (Flowers, 1993; Muckerheide, Mogill, & Mogill, 1999; Trotter, 1991). The appeal of games seems to center around students' desire to compete and play. Games provide teachers with opportunities for taking advantage of this innate desire to get students to focus on a curriculum topic. See Figure 3.4 for examples of instructional game software and a summary of game features.

Limitations and Problems Related to Instructional Games

Some teachers believe that any time they can sneak in learning under the guise of a game, it is altogether a good thing

(McGinley, 1991). However, games are also frequently criticized from several standpoints:

- **Learning versus having fun** — Some schools forbid any use of games because they believe games convince students that they are escaping from learning, thus drawing attention away from the intrinsic value and motivation of learning. Critics also feel that winning the game becomes a student's primary focus and that the instructional purpose is lost in the pursuit of this goal. Observers disagree about whether getting lost in the game is a benefit or a problem.

- **Confusion of game rules and real-life rules** — Some teachers have observed that students can become confused about which part of the activity is the game and which part is the skill; they may then have difficulty transferring their skill to later nongame situations. For example, the teacher's manual for Sunburst's *How the West Was One + Three × Four* reminds teachers that some students can confuse the math operations rules with the game rules and that teachers must help them recognize the need to focus on math rules and use them outside the game. Recent studies seem to indicate that instructional games can be useful in fostering higher order skills but that their usefulness hinges on how teachers employ them (DiPietro, Ferdig, Boyer, & Black, 2007; Henderson, Klemes, & Eshet, 2000; Rieber, Smith, & Noah, 1998).

- **Inefficient learning** — Although students obviously find many computer games exciting and stimulating, it is sometimes difficult to pinpoint their educational value. Teachers must try to balance the motivation that instructional games bring to learning against the classroom time they take away from nongame strategies. For example, students may become immersed in the challenge of the *Carmen Sandiego* series, but more efficient ways to teach geography may be just as motivating.

Using Instructional Games in Teaching

Classroom applications for instructional games. Several kinds of instructional opportunities invite teachers to take advantage of the motivational qualities of games. Instructional games should be considered in the following situations:

- **In place of worksheets and exercises** — As with drill-and-practice software, teachers can use games to help students acquire automatic recall of prerequisite skills.

- **To teach cooperative group working skills** — Like simulations, many instructional games serve as the basis for or introduction to group work. In addition, some games can be played collaboratively over the Internet (e.g., via an Internet-enabled game console). A game's competitive qualities can present opportunities for competition among groups. (See Technology Integration Lesson 3.5.)

FIGURE 3.4 Instructional Game Summary Information

Description of Instructional Game Software

Characteristics	Criteria for Effective Instructional Game Software	Benefits
• Opportunities for content skill practice or problem solving in a fun, entertaining environment • Has game rules • Challenges students to compete and win	• Appealing formats and activities • Obvious instructional, as opposed to entertainment, value • Reasonable required levels of physical dexterity • Minimal violence/aggression	• Fun activities motivate students to spend more time on the topic

Sample Software with Instructional Game Functions

Arthur's® Math Games™
by The Learning Company
http://www.learningcompany.com

Game to practice math skills: Students do adventures that require essential math skills in counting, logic, geometry.

© 2001 Riverdeep Interactive Learning Limited, and its Licensors. All rights reserved. Used with permission.

Where in the USA Is Carmen Sandiego?®
by The Learning Company
http://www.learningcompany.com

Mystery game to study geography/history: Students answer geography and history questions that yield clues as to where the mystery character (Carmen) is hiding.

© 2001 Riverdeep Interactive Learning Limited, and its Licensors. All rights reserved. Used with permission

Alice in Vivaldi's Four Seasons
by Kids Music Stage
http://www.kidsmusicstage.com/

Adventure game to practice music skills: Students must answer puzzles with music questions to free Alice, who is trapped in the magical music clock.

© Music Games International. Used with permission.

• **As a reward** — Perhaps the most common use of games is to reward good work. This may be a valid role for instructional software, but teachers should avoid overuse of it. Otherwise, the game can lose its motivational value and become an "electronic babysitter." In addition, using games as rewards disregards the power of games to be teachable software, limiting them to a behaviorist tool. Some schools actually bar games from classrooms for fear that they overemphasize the need for students to be entertained.

Guidelines for using instructional games. Use the following guidelines to make the best use of game capabilities when designing integration strategies for game functions:

• **Use appropriately** — Some educators believe that games—especially computer-based ones—are overused, misused, and used inappropriately. Use games appropriately so that students effectively learn from them while they continue to stay motivated by the game play.

• **Involve all students** — Make sure that girls and boys alike are participating and that all students have a meaningful role.

• **Emphasize the content-area skills** — Before students begin playing, make sure they know the relationship between game rules and content-area (e.g., math) rules. Students should recognize which rules they will be using in their later work and which are merely part of the game environment.

Technology Integration Lesson 3.5

Example Strategy for Instructional Game Software

Title: Problem Solving and Geography
Content Area/Topic: Geography

Grade Level: Elementary to high school

NETS for Students: Standards 1 (Creativity and Innovation), 2 (Communication and Collaboration), 3 (Research and Information Fluency), and 4 (Critical Thinking, Problem Solving, and Decision Making)

Description of Standards Applications: This integration idea offers the opportunity for students to work, compete, and collaborate as they use the software *Carmen Sandiego* to maneuver through towns and track a thief. It is the research with the atlas software and the creativity and decision making of the teams that will illuminate the winners. *Carmen Sandiego* (The Learning Company) can be used as the basis for learning geography and research skills. The game becomes a more powerful activity for improving research and reference skills when it is paired with use of an online atlas.

Instruction: The class is divided into teams, and each team member is assigned a role: field operative (runs the game software), researcher (runs the atlas software), or recorder (records information and coordinates team activities). Members switch roles every class period to give everyone a turn at each. A bar graph is posted in the classroom to show how many "cases" each class has solved. Within the class, teams are encouraged to help and coach each other. Thus, competition is fostered between classes, but collaboration is fostered within classes. To guide their work, the students receive data sheets and maps similar to those provided with the game software. The recorder uses the map to circle each city the team "goes through" and draws a line indicating the direction they traveled from one city to the next. This information is recorded on another sheet, which the researcher uses to try to find the next location to track the thief. At the end of each case, information is filled in on a matrix on a final sheet.

Assessment: The teacher checks the final sheet to grade each group's work.

Source: Greenman, M. (1991). A computer-based problem solving geography unit. *The Computing Teacher, 18*(2), 22–24.

Problem-Solving Software Functions

Although simulations and instructional games are often used to help teach problem-solving skills, problem-solving software is designed especially for this purpose (Hmelo-Silver, 2004). Problem-solving software functions may focus on fostering component skills in or approaches to general problem-solving ability, or it may provide opportunities to practice solving various kinds of content-area problems (e.g., Doering & Veletsianos, 2007). However, defining the activity of problem solving seems elusive. One way to think about problem solving is through three of its most important components (Sherman 1987–1988): recognition of a goal (an opportunity for solving a problem), a process (a sequence of physical activities or operations), and mental activity (cognitive operations to pursue a solution).

Problem solving covers a wide variety of desired component behaviors. The literature mentions such varied subskills for problem solving as metacognition, observing, recalling information, sequencing, analyzing, finding and organizing information, inferring, predicting outcomes, making analogies, and formulating ideas. Although there are many opinions about the proper role of instructional software in fostering these abilities, there seem to be two main approaches:

- **Content-area skills** — Some problem-solving software focuses on teaching content-area skills, primarily in mathematics and science. For example, *The Geometric Supposer* by Sunburst encourages students to learn strategies for solving geometry problems by drawing and manipulating geometric figures. Others, like *Alien Rescue* developed by the University of Texas, are what might be called problem-solving "environments." These complex, multifaceted packages offer a variety of tools that allow students to create solutions to science-related problems presented by a scenario. Still others provide opportunities to practice solving specific kinds of math or science problems.

Making the Case for Technology Integration

Use the following questions to reflect on issues in technology integration and guide discussions within your class.

1. Drill-and-practice software is often referred to by the derogatory term "drill and kill." Do you believe this is because the number of situations is diminishing in which drill-and-practice software would be the strategy of choice or because people fail to recognize the appropriate situations for using it? Explain your reasoning.

2. Some schools, such as those with a college preparatory focus, do not allow the use of instructional games of any kind. Is there a compelling case to be made for allowing the use of instructional game software to achieve specific educational goals? That is, can games do something in an instructional situation that no other strategy is able to do? If so, what? Can you give examples?

• **Content-free skills** — Some educators feel that general problem-solving ability can be taught directly by specific instruction and practice in its component strategies and subskills (e.g., recalling facts, breaking a problem into a sequence of steps, or predicting outcomes). Others suggest placing students in problem-solving environments and, with some coaching and guidance, letting them develop their own heuristics for attacking and solving problems.

Although the purposes of the two views overlap somewhat, the first is directed more toward supplying prerequisite skills for specific kinds of problem solving whereas the second view aims more toward motivating students to attack problems and to recognize problem solving as an integral part of everyday life.

Selecting Good Problem-Solving Software

Qualities to look for in good problem-solving software depend on the purpose of the software. In general, problem formats should be interesting and challenging, and software should have a clear link to developing a specific problem-solving ability. Software documentation should state clearly which specific problem-solving skills students will learn and how the software fosters them. See Figure 3.5 for examples of problem-solving software and a summary of problem-solving features.

Benefits of Problem-Solving Software

Problem-solving software can help students in the following ways:

• **Improved interest and motivation** — Students are more likely to practice solving problems in activities they find interesting and motivating. Some educators also feel that students will become more active, spontaneous problem solvers if they experience success in their initial problem-solving efforts.

• **Prevents inert knowledge** — Content-area problem-solving environments can make knowledge and skills more meaningful to students because they illustrate how and where information applies to actual problems. Students learn both the knowledge and its application at the same time. Also, students gain opportunities to discover concepts themselves, which they frequently find more motivating than being told or, as constructivists might say, being programmed with, the information (McCoy, 1990).

Limitations and Problems Related to Problem-Solving Software

Problem-solving software packages are among the most popular of all software functions; however, the following issues are still of concern to educators:

• **Names versus skills** — Software packages use many terms to describe problem solving, and their exact meanings are not always clear. Terms that appear in software catalogs as synonyms for problem solving include thinking skills, critical thinking, higher level thinking, higher order cognitive outcomes, reasoning, use of logic, and decision making. In light of this diversity of language, teachers must identify the skills that a software package addresses by looking at its activities. For example, for a software package that claims to teach inference skills, one would have to see how it defines *inference* by examining the tasks it presents, which may range from determining the next number in a sequence to using visual clues to predict a pattern.

• **Software claims versus effectiveness** — It would be difficult to find a software catalog that did not claim that its products foster problem solving, yet few publishers of software packages that purport to teach specific problem-solving skills have data to support their claims. When students play a game that requires skills related to problem solving, they do not necessarily learn these skills. They may enjoy the game thoroughly—and even be successful at it—without learning any of the intended skills. Teachers may have to use problem-solving software themselves to confirm that it achieves the results they want.

• **Possible negative effects of directed instruction** — Some researchers believe that direct attempts to teach problem-solving strategies can actually be counterproductive for some students. Mayes (1992) reports on studies that found "teaching sequenced planning to solve prob-

FIGURE 3.5 Problem-Solving Summary Information

Description of Problem-Solving Software

Characteristics

Four different types:

1. Tools to help students solve problems
2. Environments that challenge students to create solutions to complex problems
3. Problems to help develop component problem-solving skills (e.g., recalling facts, following a sequence)
4. Opportunities for practice in solving content-area problems

Criteria for Effective Problem-Solving Software

- Challenging, interesting formats
- Clear links to developing specific problem-solving skills or abilities

Benefits

- Challenging activities motivate students to spend more time on the topic
- Prevents inert knowledge by illustrating situations in which skills apply

Sample Software with Problem-Solving Functions

Alien Rescue®
by The Alien Rescue Team
http://www.alienrescue.com

Challenge activity to teach scientific inquiry: Students must use software tools and information to locate new home planets in the solar system to match the needs of various aliens.

From *Alien Rescue Software* © The Alien Rescue Team 2001-2004, www.alienrescue.com. Reprinted by permission.

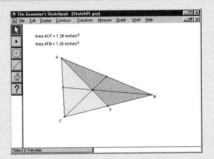

The Geometer's Sketchpad®
by Key Curriculum Press, Inc.
http://www.keypress.com/sketchpad

A dynamic construction and exploration tool: Students use software features to draw objects, investigate their mathematical properties, analyze problems, propose solutions, and do proofs to test their hypotheses.

The Geometer's Sketchpad®, Courtesy of Key Curriculum Press, 1150 65th Street, Emeryville, CA 94608; 1-800-955-MATH, www.keypress.com.

---

lems to high-ability learners could interfere with their own effective processing" (p. 243). In a review of research on problem solving in science, Blosser (1988) also found indications that problem-solving instruction may not have the desired results if the instructional strategy does not suit certain kinds of students. For example, students with high math anxiety and low visual preference or proportional reasoning abilities will profit from instruction in problem solving only if it employs visual approaches.

- **Transfer** — Although some educators feel that general problem-solving skills, such as inference and pattern recognition, will transfer to content-area skills, scant evidence supports this view. In the 1970s and 1980s, for example, many schools taught programming in mathe-

matics classes under the hypothesis that the planning and sequencing skills required for programming would transfer to problem-solving skills in math. Research results never supported this hypothesis. In general, research tends to show that skill in one kind of problem solving will transfer primarily to similar kinds of problems that use the same solution strategies. Researchers have identified nothing like "general thinking skills," except in relation to intelligence (IQ) variables.

Using Problem-Solving Software in Teaching

Classroom integration strategies for problem-solving software. Integration strategies for problem-solving software

FIGURE 3.6 Problem-Solving Log for the Logical Journey of the Zoombinis

Role/Date	Problem	Solution Tried	Outcome	Strategy
Monitor	What to do?	Click on screen	Not much happens	Trial and error
12.10.05			When click on dice, Zs appear	
		Quit and start again	Listen to introduction for clues!	Pay attention to detail

vary considerably depending on whether the desired approach is a directed or a constructivist one. The following are guidelines for both kinds of integration strategies. Problem-solving software is appropriate for the following instructional needs:

- **To teach component skills in problem-solving strategies** — Many problem-solving packages provide good, hands-on experience with one or more of the skills required to use a problem-solving approach. These include identifying and following a logical sequence, identifying relevant information to solve problems, not jumping to conclusions too quickly, and remembering relevant information.

- **To provide support in solving problems** — Some software packages are specifically designed to scaffold students as they practice solving complex problems. For example, *Geometer's Sketchpad* helps students draw objects and investigate their mathematical properties.

- **To encourage group problem solving** — Some software provides environments that lend themselves to solving problems in small groups. For example, wiki software provides capabilities for collaborative problem solving.

Guidelines for directed teaching. Usually, teachers want to teach clearly defined skills. To teach problem solving, they must decide which particular kind of problem-solving ability students need to acquire and how best to foster it. For example, Stokes (1999) recommends that students use a teacher-designed reflection sheet and keep a log of problem-solving strategies and outcomes. (See Figure 3.6 for Stokes' example log.) With clearly identified skills and a definite teaching strategy, problem solving software has unique abilities to help focus students' attention on required activities. This kind of software can get students to apply and practice desired behaviors specific to a content area or more general abilities in problem solving.

The following six steps can help you integrate software for directed teaching:

1. Identify problem-solving skills or general capabilities to build or foster skills in:
   - solving one or more kinds of content-area problems (e.g., building algebra equations);

- using a scientific approach to problem solving (identifying the problem, posing hypotheses, planning a systematic approach); and
- identifying the components of problem solving such as following a sequence of steps or recalling facts.

2. Decide on an activity or a series of activities that will help teach the desired skills.

3. Examine software to locate materials that closely match the desired abilities, remembering not to judge capabilities on the basis of vendor claims alone.

4. Determine where the software fits into the teaching sequence (for example, to introduce the skill and gain attention, as a practice activity after demonstrating problem solving, or both).

5. Demonstrate the software and the steps to follow in solving problems.

6. Build in transfer activities and make students aware of the skills they are using in the software.

Guidelines for using constructivist strategies. Like many technology resources, some software with problem-solving functions is designed for more constructivist approaches to learning. These models give students no direct training in or introduction to solving problems; rather, they place students in highly motivational problem-solving environments and encourage them to work in groups to solve problems. Bearden and Martin (1998) describe such a strategy using problem-solving software combined with a listserv email (an email feature that allows a message to be sent to a group) for students to share their results. (Also see Martin and Bearden, 1998.) The following seven steps can help you integrate problem-solving software according to constructivist models:

1. Allow students sufficient time to explore and interact with the software, but provide some structure in the form of directions, goals, a work schedule, and organized times for sharing and discussing results.

2. Vary the amount of direction and assistance provided, depending on each student's needs.

3. Promote a reflective learning environment; let students talk about the methods they use.

Technology Integration Lesson 3.6

Example Strategy for Problem-Solving Software

Title: Geometry with *Geometers Sketchpad*   **Grade Level:** Middle school

Content Area/Topic: Beginning geometry

NETS for Students: Standards 3 (Research and Information Fluency) and 4 (Critical Thinking, Problem Solving, and Decision Making)

Description of Standards Applications: This integration idea involves using software that supports many kinds of learning activities ranging from highly structured student work to free exploration. These activities encourage students to utilize digital tools as they develop critical thinking skills through problem solving.

Instruction: An example of a structured activity with a pre-made sketch requires a teacher to demonstrate a *Sketchpad* sketch and lead students to understand the underlying concepts with guided observations and questions. A more open-ended, constructivist approach to the same objective would have students explore the sketch themselves using guidelines the teacher provides (e.g., they make measurements of it and/or add new constructions). *Sketchpad* also supports activities called "black box tasks" for students with more sophisticated knowledge of the software. In these activities, students use the software tools to re-create a given figure or deduce the underlying properties that two or more objects have in common.

Source: From Ng, K., & Teong, S. (2003). The *Geometer's Sketchpad* for primary geometry: A framework. *Micromath* 19(3), 5–9. Used with permission.

---

4. Stress thinking processes rather than correct answers.

5. Point out the relationship between software activities and other kinds of problem solving.

6. Let students work together in pairs or small groups.

7. For assessments, use alternatives to traditional paper-and-pencil tests.

For an example of a problem-solving software that supports both directed and constructivist applications, see Technology Integration Lesson 3.6.

Integrated Learning Systems

Integrated learning systems (ILSs) are systems that offer computer-based instruction and other resources to support instruction, along with summary reports of student progress through the instruction; all are provided through networked or online sources. The most powerful—and the most expensive—of available instructional software products, ILSs were introduced in the early 1970s and, until recently, were delivered via computer network from a central computer (server), usually located in the school. Initially, students and teachers used the instructional and management systems from terminals or microcomputers connected to the server. More recently, ILS-type capability is provided by offering the curriculum online via the Internet rather than through a local network.

Regardless of the delivery system, an ILS is characterized as a "one-stop shopping" approach to providing software. Each ILS offers a variety of instructional techniques in one place, usually as a curriculum package complete with technical maintenance and teacher training. In addition to providing a combination of drill-and-practice, tutorial, simulation, problem-solving, reference, and tool software, an ILS is capable of maintaining detailed records on individual student assignments and performance and supplying printouts of this information to teachers. Bailey and Lumley (1991, p. 21) include the following as characteristics of an ILS:

- Instructional objectives specified, with each lesson tied to those objectives;
- Lessons integrated into the standard curriculum;
- Software that spans several grade levels in comprehensive fashion; and
- A management system that collects and records results of student performance.

Top Ten

Integration Strategies for Instructional Software

The best kinds and uses of instructional software depend on the content area and skills teachers need to address. The ten uses given here are among the most popular described in the literature.

1. Use simulation software such as Tom Snyder's *Operation Frog* or The Digital Frog International's online *Digital Frog* to replace or supplement hands-on dissections to help teach anatomy.

2. Use ExploreLearning's *Mouse Genetics* online simulation software to let students explore basic principles of genetics and heredity.

3. Use Electronic Arts, Inc.'s *SimCity* simulation software to give students hands-on opportunities to see environmental and other consequences of city policy and planning decisions.

4. Use Tom Snyder's *Decisions, Decisions: The Constitution* to let students take a scenario approach to learning how separation and balance of power works in the U.S. federal government.

5. Use Key Curriculum Press's *Geometer's Sketchpad* or the Center for Educational Technology's *Geometric Supposer* problem-solving software to let students explore geometric principles and proofs.

6. Use Sunburst's *The Factory Deluxe* problem-solving software to give young children a visual environment for analyzing processes, predicting outcomes, and learning the importance of sequence in solving complex problems.

7. Use Sunburst's *How the West Was One + Three × Four* instructional game software to give students a highly motivating format for practicing the correct mathematical order of operations when solving math problems.

8. Use GeoThentic, an online scaffolding learning environment from the University of Minnesota, to learn how to use geospatial technologies to learn geography.

9. Use Byki Deluxe, drill-and-practice software available from Transparent Software, to let students practice foreign language vocabulary and phrase translations.

10. Use tutorial instructional sequences such as Odyssey K-5 from CompassLearning to give students detailed reviews of basic math or science topics or to let advanced students surge ahead.

The teacher usually makes initial assignments for work on the system, monitors student progress by reviewing ILS reports, and provides additional instruction or support where needed. As each student signs on to a microcomputer connected to the server or Internet, the file server sends (or downloads) student assignments and software to the station and proceeds to keep records on what the student does during the time spent on the system.

The software component of an ILS. Instructional activities available on an ILS range from simple drill and practice to extensive tutorials. Many ILSs are moving toward complete tutorial systems intended to replace teachers in delivering entire instructional sequences. An ILS usually includes instruction on the entire scope and sequence of skills in a given content area; for example, it may cover all discrete mathematics skills typically presented in grades 1 through 6.

Integrated learning systems software is even more accessible with portable computers.

The management system component of an ILS. The capability that differentiates ILSs from other networked systems is the emphasis on individualized instruction tied to records of student progress. A typical ILS gives teachers progress reports across groups of students as well as the following kinds of information on individual performance:

- Lessons and tests completed;
- Questions missed on each lesson by numbers and percentages;
- Numbers of correct and incorrect tries;
- Time spent on each lesson and test; and
- Pretest and post-test data.

Selecting ILSs

One way to ensure the appropriate use of ILSs is to have a careful, well-planned initial review process that involves both teachers and school administrators. Criteria for the selection process are usually based on the curriculum coverage and pedagogical strategies in the ILS, as well as perceptions about the usefulness of the reports that the system produces and to what extent they meet the needs of the district. See Figure 3.7 for examples of ILSs and a summary of ILS features.

Benefits of ILSs

Brush (1998) estimated that as of 1998, between 11% and 25% of all U.S. schools owned ILSs. Two recent developments have caused a rapid rise in these numbers (Readers' Choice Awards, 2004):

- **District- and state-adopted academic standards —** An increased emphasis on educational accountability in

the 1990s caused states to set curriculum standards and to create tests to measure students' progress on them. Integrated software and management assessments aligned with these standards helps schools prepare for meeting these standards.

- **Accountability requirements of the No Child Left Behind (NCLB) Act —** The NCLB Act stipulated that schools who fail to meet Adequate Yearly Progress (AYP) for 3 years in a row must use a portion of their Title I funds for out-of-school tutoring, which the NCLB Act refers to as Supplemental Educational Services. ILS materials are ideal for providing these services.

Since an ILS provides a combination of the materials described previously in this chapter, its potential benefits duplicate the benefits of those functions. In addition to those benefits, ILS networked or online materials are easy for teachers and students to access and can provide entire curricula from one location. Prepared curricula and ease of use mean that school personnel need not know a great deal about technology to use an ILS. Consequently, they usually simplify integration decisions by defining schoolwide curriculum rather than individual lessons. When teachers assign some students to use ILS activities, it frees time for them to help other students who need their personal assistance. In addition, teachers can personalize instructional activities for each student by reviewing the extensive information on student and class progress provided by the ILS management system.

Limitations and Problems Related to ILSs

Teachers should note that although many educators still refer to these multifaceted systems as "integrated learning systems," the vendors of the systems tend to refer to them as "educational solutions," "accountability solutions," or "supplemental educational services" (Readers' Choice Awards, 2004). By whatever name, several items are ongoing concerns:

- **The costs of ILSs —** The primary criticism of ILSs centers on their expense as compared to their impact on improving learning. ILS proponents feel that the students who experience the most success with ILSs are those whose needs are typically most difficult to meet (Becker, 1994; Bender, 1991; Bracy, 1992; Shore & Johnson, 1992). Proponents also say there is value in any system that helps potential dropouts stay in school or helps students with learning disabilities. They point to studies and personal testimony from teachers over the years that ILSs motivate students by allowing them to work at their own pace and to experience success each time they are on the system.

FIGURE 3.7 Integrated Learning Systems Summary Information

Description of Integrated Learning Systems

Characteristics

- Networked or online systems of instruction
- Provide complete curricula on a topic area
- Monitor and provide reports on student progress
- Summarize data by student, class, or school

Criteria for Effective ILSs

- Good curriculum coverage
- Good pedagogical strategies
- Several different report formats
- Easily read and interpreted reports

Benefits

- Can help provide Supplemental Educational Services required by the NCLB Act
- Benefits of drill, tutorials, simulations, instructional games, and problem solving, depending on which activities are used
- Easier to access via network or online
- Entire curriculum at one source
- Personalized instruction matched to student needs
- Summary progress data help meet teacher/district accountability requirements

Sample Integrated Learning System (ILS) Software

Sample Screens:
The CompassLearning Odyssey® Manager
http://www.compasslearning.com

Sample Screens:
The PLATO® Learning Systems ILS
http://www.plato.com

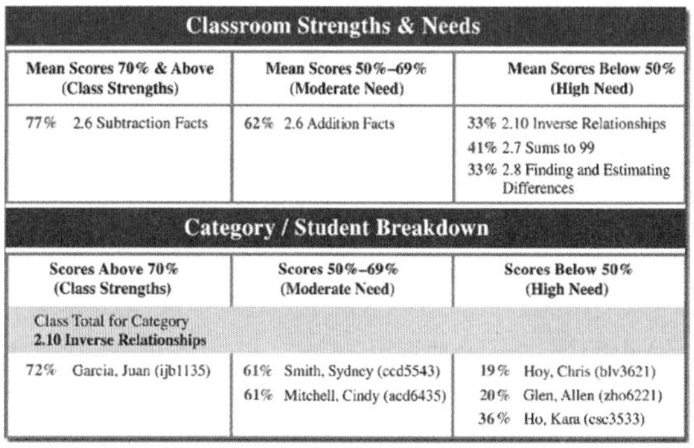

Sample Reports

Classroom Strengths & Needs		
Mean Scores 70% & Above (Class Strengths)	**Mean Scores 50%–69%** (Moderate Need)	**Mean Scores Below 50%** (High Need)
77% 2.6 Subtraction Facts	62% 2.6 Addition Facts	33% 2.10 Inverse Relationships 41% 2.7 Sums to 99 33% 2.8 Finding and Estimating Differences

Category / Student Breakdown		
Scores Above 70% (Class Strengths)	**Scores 50%–69%** (Moderate Need)	**Scores Below 50%** (High Need)
Class Total for Category 2.10 Inverse Relationships		
72% Garcia, Juan (ijb1135)	61% Smith, Sydney (ccd5543) 61% Mitchell, Cindy (acd6435)	19% Hoy, Chris (blv3621) 20% Glen, Allen (zho6221) 36% Ho, Kara (csc3533)

- **Research on ILS impact** — Studies of a variety of ILSs in a number of different locations reached generally the same conclusion as Van Dusen and Worthen (1995) did: The impact of an ILS on student achievement varies greatly with implementation methods. Kulik's (2003) meta-analysis of ILS studies published between 1990 and 1997 shows modest gains for schools using ILSs. Becker's (1992) summary of some 30 studies of ILS effectiveness found wide variation in results with various implementation methods and systems. Students generally tended to do somewhat better with ILSs than with other methods, and results were sometimes substantially superior to non-ILS methods. But Becker found no predictable pattern for successful and unsuccessful ILSs. Subsequent large-scale studies of ILS use in the United Kingdom (Wood, Underwood, & Avis, 1999), Indiana (Estep, McInerney, & Vockell, 1999–2000), and New York (Miller, 1997; Paterson, Henry, & O'Quin, 2003) duplicated this finding. However, Brush, Armstrong, and Barbrow (1999) found that two different resources offered in the same ILS had different impacts on achievement. Individualized software designed to provide foundations instruction had less impact than software that could be selected by teachers to supplement their own instruction.

- **Concerns about the role of ILSs** — In a follow-up to his literature review on ILS uses, Becker (1994) criticized uses of ILSs that encourage "mindless adherence to the principle of individualized instruction" (p. 78). Brush

(1998) agreed with Becker, finding that ". . . lack of teacher involvement (in ILS use) has led to improper coordination between classroom-based and computer-based instructional activities . . . and lack of teacher understanding regarding effective strategies and procedures for using ILSs" (p. 7). An early concern expressed by many educators (White, 1992) that the cost of ILSs combined with the comprehensive nature of their curricula might cause schools to view them as replacements for teachers has not yet proven to be a real problem.

Using ILSs in Teaching

When used only as a teacher replacement to provide individual student instruction, ILSs seem to be less effective. When viewed as a supplement to other teaching methods and carefully integrated into a total teaching program, they seem more likely to have the desired impact on raising achievement. One way to ensure appropriate and cost-effective uses of ILS products may be through a careful, well-planned purchasing process that involves both teachers and administrators. One such process was developed by the California Department of Education (Armstrong, 1999). This five-stage process (planning, pre-evaluation, evaluation, selection, and implementation/post-evaluation) is designed to "establish selection procedures that ensure that . . . curricular goals remain at the heart of the selection process" (p. 3). Guidelines for potential ILS purchasers based on those offered by Chrisman (1992), Smith and Sclafani (1989), and Vaille and Hall (1998) are summarized here:

- Clearly identify the problem the ILS is supposed to solve, and understand the instructional theory on which the system is based.
- Determine whether the ILS is a closed system (one that provides 80% or more of the instruction for a given course) or an open system (one linked to the school's resources).
- Find out if the system's scope and sequence are matched to that of the school.
- Determine the target population for which the system was designed and whether it closely matches the characteristics of students who will be using the ILS.
- Consider the adequacy of the reporting and management system for the school's needs.
- Consider how much of its resources the school must spend on hardware and software.
- Project the educational benefits to the school from the system, and compare them with the costs.
- Request that vendors inform the school of ILS updates.

- Carefully evaluate the grade-level software, management system, customization, and online tools, and be sure that they match the school's expectations.
- Set up reasonable terms of procurement, and calculate the personnel and fiscal impact of the ILS.

Successful uses of ILSs have been reported for both directed and constructivist teaching approaches.

Directed applications for ILSs. In a directed teaching approach, an ILS system can be used for remediation and as a mainstream delivery system. With either of these applications, teachers still have important roles to play. They must assign initial levels of work, follow up on student activities on the system, and give additional personal instruction when needed.

- **For remediation** — Although ILSs are expensive alternatives to other kinds of delivery systems, the requirements of the NCLB Act have provided new motivation—as well as new funding sources—for using them. Even when new funding and the motivation to use ILSs are present, schools must determine how ILS functions coordinate with and complement those of the classroom teacher. ILS uses serve target populations that have typically presented the most difficult problems for traditional classroom activities: Title I groups, English for Speakers of Other Languages (ESOL) students, special education students, and at-risk students. Schools have tried and usually failed to reach these students with other methods.

- **As a mainstream delivery system** — Rather than using an ILS only as a backup system to address educational problems, a school may let an ILS do the initial job of teaching whole courses for all students in a grade level. In light of the expense of ILSs, this type of use is more rare. However, some alternative projects, like the Edison Project (Walsh, 1999), predict that the costs of using technology in this way will amount to substantially less over time than teacher salaries. Using ILSs to increase student-to-teacher ratios has stimulated ongoing debate and study.

Constructivist applications for ILSs. An ILS can also combine several kinds of technology resources to support constructivist learning approaches. This kind of ILS can provide what Perkins (1991) called a "rich environment" that students can use to construct their own knowledge. ILS products useful for constructivist purposes typically have an information bank (electronic encyclopedias), symbol pads (word processing and/or desktop publishing software), construction kits (Logo or other graphic languages or tools), and phenomenaria (computer simulations and/or problem-solving resources). They also usually have data-

TABLE 3.3 Technology Integration Strategies for Directed, Constructivist, or Either Models

Integration Strategies for Instructional Software	Directed Models				Constructivist Models					Either Model		
	Remedy identified weaknesses or skill deficits	Promote skill fluency or automaticity	Provide efficient, self-paced instruction	Support self-paced review of concepts	Foster creative problem solving and metacognition	Build mental models, increase knowledge transfer	Foster group cooperation	Allow for multiple intelligences	Generate motivation to learn	Optimize scarce personnel and material resources	Remove logistical hurdles to learning	Develop information literacy and visual literacy skills
Drill and Practice												
Supplement or replace worksheets, homework exercises	X	X										
Prepare for tests	X	X										
Tutorials												
Self-paced reviews			X	X								
Alternative learning strategies			X	X								
Instruction when teachers are unavailable			X	X								
Simulations												
Replace or supplement labs										X	X	X
Replace or supplement role playing								X	X			
Replace or supplement field trips						X			X	X	X	
Introduce a new topic						X			X			
Foster exploration, process learning					X	X	X					
Encourage cooperation and group work							X	X	X			
Instructional Games												
Supplement or replace worksheets, homework exercises	X	X										
Teach cooperative skills							X	X				
As a reward									X			
Problem Solving												
Teach component skills in problem-solving strategies					X	X						
Provide support in solving problems					X			X				
Encourage group problem solving					X		X					

collection systems to track student usage of the system (Mageau, 1990).

A Summary of Instructional Software Integration Strategies

Although descriptions of instructional software in the literature are changing, many references to software evaluation criteria and evaluation methods focus on products to be used with directed instruction. While many criteria are appropriate for software designed for both directed and constructivist kinds of uses, additional details are often lacking on what to look for in software that will be used with constructivist methods.

Constructivist activities tend to emphasize learner-centered, collaborative, and open-ended products rather than drill or tutorial software. For example, Litchfield (1992) lists criteria for "inquiry-based science software and interactive multimedia programs." Checklists by Hoffman and Lyons (1997) and Vaille and Hall (1998) are among those that include criteria for more open-ended products. Further criteria and methods for evaluating multimedia and online multimedia products are discussed in Chapters 6 through 8. For a summary of all instructional software uses matched to directed and constructivist integration strategies, see the matrix in Table 3.3.

Interactive Summary

The following is a summary of the main points covered in this chapter.

1. **Types of instructional software** — Instructional software packages are computer programs designed specifically to deliver or support one or more kinds of learning activities. These programs can serve one or more of the following five functions:

   - **Drill and practice** — Students work example items, usually one at a time, and receive feedback on their correctness.

   - **Tutorial** — These provide an entire instructional sequence similar to a teacher's classroom instruction on a topic.

   - **Simulation** — These computerized models of real or imagined systems are designed to teach how the system works.

   - **Instructional games** — These activities are designed to increase motivation by adding game rules and/or competition to learning activities. Probably the most famous instructional games are *Math Blaster*® and the *Carmen Sandiego*® series.

   - **Problem solving** — These programs serve one of three purposes: (1) to foster component skills involved in solving problems, (2) to teach or provide practice in general approaches to problem solving, or (3) to teach or provide opportunities to practice solving various problems in specific content areas.

2. **Integrated learning systems** — These products offer computer-based instruction and other resources to support instruction, along with summary reports of student progress through the instruction; all are provided through networked or online sources. Now often referred to as "software solutions" or "technology solutions," the top software solutions or ILS programs offer a range of resources from assessment system features that help diagnose and remedy student deficits to helping teachers use the products more effectively.

3. **Using instructional software to meet classroom needs** — Instructional software functions can meet each of the following classroom needs:

   - **Drill and practice** — Supplementing or replacing work-sheets and homework exercises, preparation for tests

   - **Tutorial** — Self-paced reviews of instruction, alternative learning strategies, and instruction when teachers are unavailable

   - **Simulation** — In place of or as supplements to lab experiments, in place of or as supplements to role playing, in place of or as supplements to field trips, to introduce or clarify a new topic, to foster exploration and problem solving, and to encourage cooperation and group work

   - **Instructional game** — In place of worksheets and exercises, to teach cooperative group working skills, and as a reward

   - **Problem solving** — To teach component skills in problem-solving strategies, to provide practice in solving problems, and to encourage group problem solving

Key Terms

- applications programs
- applications software
- computer-assisted instruction (CAI)
- computer programs
- drill and practice

- instructional game
- instructional software
- integrated learning systems (ILSs)
- Logo
- problem solving

- simulation
- software
- systems software
- tutorial

Web-Enrichment Activities

1. **Software reviews online** — Visit the following software review websites, and compare the information they present.
   - SREB EvaluTech http://www.evalutech.sreb.org/
   - California Learning Resource Network http://www.clrn.org/home/
   - SuperKids http://www.superkids.com
   - Education World http://www.educationworld.com

   Which sites evaluate the largest number of titles? Which sites are most recently updated? Which sites include reviews submitted by site visitors? Which sites would you use to learn about software you were considering for your students?

2. **Simulations** — Go to www.edutopia.org, and go to the Video Library. View the video "No Gamer Left Behind." Describe how technology, such as simulations and games, can be used as a motivator in the classroom. How might this affect student learning?

Go to MyEducationLab to complete the following exercises.

Video   Select the topic "Instructional Strategies," and go to the "Assignments, Activities, and Applications" section. Access the video "Drill and Practice" to see how two different teachers utilize online drill-and-practice websites as part of instruction. Note how the teachers familiarize the students with the software.

Tutorials   Select the topic "Assessment" and access the practical tutorial and skill-building activity titled "Rubistar Tutorial." Use the tutorial to learn how to create a rubric. This skill will be reviewed again in the Technology Integration Workshop.

Technology Integration Workshop

The TIP Model in Action

Read each of the following scenarios related to implementing the TIP Model, and answer the questions that follow it based on your Chapter 3 reading and activities.

TIP MODEL SCENARIO #1   Ms. Andie uses a program called *Spelling Bee* to give her students practice before a spelling test or the language arts part of a standardized test. She knows the secret to her students doing well in spelling is getting them to spend time thinking about the words; she finds she can get them to spend more time with helpful practicing than she can with a paper-and-pencil exercise or other format. The software presents words via audio prompt and lets students enter spellings. They get points for every correct answer. If they play alone and attain a score they are shooting for, they win the spelling bee. They can also compete against each other in pairs.

1.1 What type of software function is Ms. Andie using? What does it offer that makes it a good match for the problem?

1.2 If Ms. Andie wanted to have students practice in pairs to compete against each other, how could she set up the activity to make sure some students wouldn't become too frustrated by losing all the time?

1.3 Since the software gives audio prompts and feedback, what would Ms. Andie have to do if she wanted to use this effectively in a classroom of 30 students?

TIP MODEL SCENARIO #2   Mr. Sydney's students are not interested in learning about the U.S. Constitution. He wants to show them that it is a document that affects their lives every day and in many situations they or people they know might encounter. Rather than just telling them about it, he found a software package that lets them practice applying it. Using the package, students role-play various people faced with creating articles of confederation to deal effectively with issues such as threats to their borders, needs for currency, trade disputes, internal disagreements about key issues, and separate rights for states versus central power. As they work in groups on various problems, students come to understand why laws are necessary and how they affect their lives. As a final activity,

each group presents an article of confederation and illustrates how it works in practice.

2.1 What software function is Mr. Sydney using? What did it offer that made it a good match for the problem?

2.2 What outcomes would you want to assess after this activity? How would you state these outcomes?

2.3 How would you measure students' progress in achieving these outcomes?

TIP MODEL SCENARIO #3   In her Spanish I class, Ms. Sharon is having her students write an email newsletter describing in Spanish their school and events in their community to students in a classroom in Puerto Rico. She finds that her students' Spanish vocabulary is very limited, and she wants to give them practice in using Spanish equivalents for many English words. She locates a software package that provides vocabulary practice by presenting words in English or Spanish to which students must supply equivalents in the opposite language. If they supply the correct word, the program pronounces both words. The Teacher's Manual gives a list of all the words.

3.1 What kind of software function does this software provide, and why does Ms. Sharon think her students need it?

3.2 Would it be best for students to use this package individually, in small groups, or as a whole class?

3.3 How would you assess whether this program was helping students learn enough vocabulary?

TIP MODEL SCENARIO #4   Mr. Carson finds that students in his honors algebra class can solve algebra equations, but they can't identify situations in everyday life that require them to set up and solve a simple equation. He finds a software package that has "virtual stores" in which students must solve various problems in order to "buy" items. They must use algebra equations to solve these problems. Mr. Carson has his students work in small groups to practice solving the problems and stating the strategies they used.

4.1 What kind of software function does this software provide, and why does Mr. Carson think his students will benefit from it?

4.2 What outcomes should Mr. Carson expect, and how should he state them?

4.3 What are the best ways to assess these outcomes?

TIP MODEL SCENARIO #5 Ms. Walker's science class is an academically diverse group, with some students learning concepts very quickly and others needing much more time to review and work on them. She has found a software series that provides a complete teaching sequence (instruction, practice items, testing) on each topic in the middle school physical sciences. Some students use it for review of topics they find particularly difficult; others use it to catch up when they have been absent. The students who learn quickly also use it to jump ahead and learn advanced topics on their own.

5.1 What kind of software function does this software provide, and what problem does Ms. Walker have that it addresses?

5.2 Would one copy of the software meet Ms. Walker's needs? Why or why not?

5.3 How could Ms. Walker find out if most students enjoy using the software?

TIE into Practice: Technology Integration Examples

The Technology Integration Example that opened this chapter (*Alien Rescue*) showed how a teacher might use an educational simulation package to give students highly motivational, hands-on experience with a scientific inquiry approach to problem solving. In the following activities, use the knowledge you have gained from Chapter 3 to do the following with this example:

1. Mr. Leroy created a rubric like the one shown on page 108 to assess students' presentations of new problems and the methods they use to solve them. Having completed the Rubistar tutorial in MyEducationLab, use Rubistar to create this rubric.

2. Answer the following questions about the *Alien Rescue* lesson:
   - Phase 1 — How did the *Alien Rescue* software offer relative advantage in comparison to other ways of teaching scientific inquiry that Mr. Leroy had used in the past?
   - Phase 2 — Mr. Leroy designed a five-item survey to assess students' attitudes toward using this approach to learning science. What kind of items would you include on such a survey?

   - Phase 3 — What roles could you assign to individuals in each working group of students to help focus their tasks and make their work more efficient?
   - Phase 4 — One of the tasks students completed to collect information was to design and send out space probes, which the Teacher's Manual said was a fairly complex activity. Why shouldn't Mr. Leroy create a directions sheet for students on how to do such a complex task?
   - Phase 5 — Mr. Leroy found that students' scores on the solar system test varied across the class. What could he do to make sure that students were more uniformly successful on this kind of test?

3. What NETS for Students skills would students learn by completing the *Alien Rescue* project? (See the front of this book for a list of NETS for Students.)

Technology Integration Lesson Planning

Complete the following exercise using sample lesson plans found on MyEducationLab.

1. Locate lesson ideas — MyEducationLab has several examples of lessons that use the simulation, instructional game, and problem-solving software. Go to MyEducationLab and select the topic "Instructional Planning." Under "Lesson Plans" review the following example integration lessons and choose two:
   - Problem-Solving and Geography
   - GeoGame
   - Geometry with *Geometer's Sketchpad*
   - Building a Simulated City
   - Laptops go to Middle School
   - Earth on Fire

2. Evaluate the lessons — Use the *Evaluation Checklist for a Technology-Integrated Lesson* (located on MyEducationLab under the topic "Instructional Planning") to evaluate each of these lessons

3. Modify a lesson — Select one of the lesson ideas and adapt its strategies to meet a need in your own content area. You may choose to use the same approach in the original or adapt it to meet your needs.

4. Add descriptors — Create descriptors for your new lesson like those found within the sample lessons (e.g., grade level, content and topic areas, technologies used, relative advantage, objectives, NETS standards).

5. Save your new lesson — Save your modified lesson with all its descriptors.

Category	Excellent Work	Very Good Work	Poor Work	No Credit
Problem and Solution Content	Reflected comprehensive knowledge of solar system; all facts and ideas were completely accurate; there was a good match of problem and solution.	Reflected fairly good knowledge of solar system; most facts and ideas were completely accurate; there was a good match of problem and solution.	Reflected some knowledge of solar system, but there were several factual inaccuracies; the solution was not the best match for the problem.	Reflected limited and/or inaccurate knowledge of solar system; there was little or no relationship between the problem and solution.
Clarity of Problem and Solution	Both problem and solution were clearly stated; other students could readily understand both.	Both problem and solution were fairly well stated but needed some clarification.	Either the problem or the solution required extensive clarification.	Both the problem and the solution required extensive clarification.
Presentation Organization	Presentation was extremely well organized; content was divided into logical sections for presentation, and transitions were smooth.	Presentation was usually well organized; content was divided into logical sections for presentation, but transitions were somewhat uneven and choppy.	Presentation was somewhat organized, but there were no transitions within the presentation.	Presentation was choppy, confusing, and difficult to follow.
Presentation Mechanics	Presentation was interesting and compelling; visual aids and/or multimedia were used and were well designed to support content.	Presentation was fairly interesting; some visual aids and/or multimedia were used and were well designed to support content.	Presentation was acceptable but could have been more interesting and could have used visual aids and/or multimedia better.	Presentation was uninteresting; no visual aids and/or multimedia were used.
Cooperative Group Work	Project and . presentation work was divided equally; each student had a clearly defined role in the work; it was clear that students worked well together.	Project and . presentation work seemed to have been divided equally, but exact roles needed clarification; students seemed to work well together.	Project and presentation work was not divided equally; roles were unclear, but students seemed to work together.	Only one or two students did all the work of the project and presentation; there was little evidence of cooperative work.

Rubric to assess students' presentations of new problems and methods for solving them.

For Your Teaching Portfolio

For this chapter's contribution to your teaching portfolio, add the following products you created in the Technology Integration Workshop:

1. The rubric you created to assess the *Alien Rescue* presentations.

2. The evaluations you did using the *Evaluation Checklist for a Technology-Integrated Lesson.*

3. The new lesson plan you developed, based on the ones you found on the MyEducationLab.

Chapter 4

Teaching with the Basic Three Software Tools: Word Processing, Spreadsheet, and Database Programs

> Technologies should not support learning by attempting to instruct the learners, but rather should be used as knowledge construction tools that students learn *with*, not *from*. In this way, learners function as designers, and the computers function as mindtools for interpreting and organizing their personal knowledge.
>
> Jonassen, D., Carr, C, & Yueh, H. (1998), in Computers as mindtools for engaging learners in critical thinking. *TechTrends, 43*(2), 24

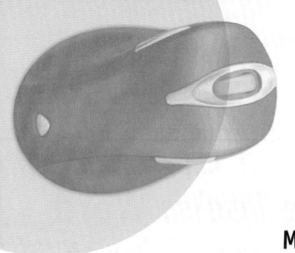

Technology Integration Example

Money Management with Spreadsheets: Can You Afford Your Dream Car?

Grade Level: Middle to high school. Content Area/Topic: Applied math skills. Length of Time: One week

Phases 1 and 2: Assess technological pedagogical content knowledge and determine relative advantage

Whenever Ms. Kiley teaches her Applied Mathematics Problem-Solving class for grades 9 through 12, she has teenagers of many ages and ability levels. She wants all of them to have experience applying math skills to real problems they will encounter in their daily lives. She tries to include projects that are interesting and relevant to all of them and that require a combination of research, mathematical problem solving, and production skills. One activity she found that meets all her criteria is called "Can You Afford Your Dream Car?" She selected this project because almost all of her students are beginning drivers and are interested in car purchases. So that they can do calculations quickly and focus on the underlying concepts (e.g., the relationship among down payment, interest rate, and loan period), Ms. Kiley designed a spreadsheet template for students to use. Each student does Internet research to locate the best price on a car he or she would like to buy, enters the information into the spreadsheet template Ms. Kiley created, and answers various questions about loan amounts and car payments.

Prior to creating this project, Ms. Kiley realized she needed to assess her own technological pedagogical content knowledge (TPACK) so she could evaluate her strengths and weak-

nesses and understand where to locate herself within the TPACK model. Through this assessment, she realized that her knowledge of the content she was teaching was weak whereas her knowledge of the instructional methods she planned to use and her understanding of how to use technology effectively for learning were strong. She felt that her strengths could support her lack of content knowledge, however, so she decided to brush up on some of the latest research about money management and move forward with the project.

Phase 3: Decide on objectives and assessments

To keep her students on track and to make sure they learn what she has in mind for this project, Ms. Kiley created objectives and assessments to measure their research, problem-solving, and production outcomes. The outcomes, objectives, and assessments are:

- **Outcome:** Select a car to purchase and complete background research on it. **Objective:** Each student completes all required steps to select a car to "buy"; completes a list of the activities required to research and locate comparison information about its price, loan, and features; and enters the information into a spreadsheet template. **Assessment:** A checklist with points for each required activity.

- **Outcome:** Do mathematical problem solving. **Objective:** Each student uses the spreadsheet to answer a series of questions about the amount of the car loan and the payments at various interest rates and time periods. **Assessment:** Worksheet questions with points for each one; 80% is passing.

- **Outcome:** Do a final report. **Objective:** Each student achieves a rubric score of at least 90% on a word-processed report that describes and illustrates the car, tells why it is a cost-effective purchase, and includes a spreadsheet (based on the template provided) showing how he or she will pay for it. **Assessment:** Rubric on report quality and accuracy.

Phase 4: Design integration strategies

Ms. Kiley wanted to make sure each student had hands-on experience with the research and production activities and was able to master each of the skills she outlined, so she decided to make this an individual activity. She designed the following activity sequence to carry out the project:

- **Day 1:** Introduce the project. Encourage students to talk about cars they have already purchased or are considering purchasing, and ask them to describe how they went about selecting one and, if they actually bought it, how they decided on a loan amount, term, and payment size. Demonstrate the spreadsheet template, and show students how the payments and total amount paid change automatically depending on the loan amount, interest, and period entered into the spreadsheet. Review the project checklists and rubrics as well as the timeframe for completing the work. Introduce the problems students are to work using their completed spreadsheets.

- **Day 2:** Take students to the computer lab, and demonstrate some of the sites they may want to use to check out makes and models of cars. Also, demonstrate once again how to use the spreadsheet template. Have students do some calculations with the spreadsheet, and answer any questions they have. Let them begin researching cars they want to buy.

- **Day 3:** In the computer lab, allow students to continue their research. Some students may have completed research on their home computers. These students can begin work on their final reports or complete the problem-solving exercise.

- **Day 4:** In the computer lab, allow students to continue work on their reports and the exercises with the spreadsheet template.

- **Day 5:** Back in the classroom, let selected students present their "dream car purchase." Use the classroom computer workstation to show an online example of the car model and the dealer from which they would buy it. Students who need more time can go to the computer lab.

- **Day 6:** Students turn in their projects and exercises.

Phase 5: Prepare the instructional environment

The first time Ms. Kiley taught this project, she had to create the spreadsheet template and handouts of the checklists and rubric for students to use. For subsequent times, she had to do the following:

- **Handouts:** Ms. Kiley made copies of the project requirements and grading criteria sheets (i.e., checklists and rubrics) to hand out to students. She also made sure these handouts were online at her classroom website as PDF files, so students could download additional copies if needed.

- **Software skills:** Although Ms. Kiley demonstrated how to use the spreadsheet template, she checked with students individually as they worked in the lab to make sure they knew how to enter the required information in the cells and could copy and paste their completed worksheet into their report.

- **Computer scheduling:** Ms. Kiley made sure she could have her whole class in the computer lab for the 3 days she would need it; she also made sure individual students could come to the lab for the 2 subsequent days to complete their research and reports.

- **Template copies:** Ms. Kiley made sure that a copy of the template was on the classroom website so that students could download it to their own disks.

Phase 6: Evaluate and revise

Each time she taught the project, Ms. Kiley reviewed students' work and asked for their comments on how she could make the project even more meaningful. She quickly realized that students who did not have a home computer were at a disadvantage in completing the work in a timely way. Therefore, she made a special effort to help these students during their time in the lab and made sure they knew they could have additional lab time outside class or before or after school to use the classroom workstation. She found that, although students usually completed their spreadsheets correctly and could answer questions about them, their reports varied considerably in quality. She decided to consider other ways of having students present their work.

Objectives

After reading this chapter and completing the learning activities for it, you should be able to:

1. Use correct terminology to identify features and capabilities of word processing, spreadsheet, and database software tool programs.

2. Identify productivity applications for software tools that educators would find valuable in making their work more efficient and productive.

3. Describe specific kinds of teaching and learning tasks for both teachers and students that each kind of tool can support.

4. Develop instructional activities that integrate the functions and capabilities of the software tools.

Introduction to the Basic Three Software Tools

Why Use Software Tools?

In education and, indeed, in most other areas of our Information Society, three of the most widely used software support tools are word processing, spreadsheet, and database programs. Word processing and other software tools have become not only very popular and extremely useful; they are also an indispensable part of our daily work. Teachers choose them for the qualities and benefits they bring to the classroom and for the potential they offer not only to make more productive use of our time but also to shape and guide the kinds of activities we are able to undertake. Depending on the capabilities of the tool and the needs of the situation, these programs can offer several benefits:

- **Improved productivity** — Getting organized, producing instructional materials, and accomplishing paperwork tasks all go much faster when software tools are used. Using a technology tool to do these tasks can free up valuable time that can be rechanneled toward working with students or designing learning activities.

- **Improved appearance** — Software tools help teachers and students produce polished-looking materials that resemble the work of professional designers. The quality of classroom products is limited only by the talents and skills of the teachers and students using the tools. Students appreciate receiving attractive-looking materials and find it rewarding and challenging to produce handsome products of their own.

- **Improved accuracy** — Software tools make it easier to keep precise, accurate records of events and student accomplishments. More accurate information can support better instructional decisions about curriculum and student activities.

- **More support for interaction and collaboration** — Software tools have capabilities that promote interaction and collaboration among students, allowing input from several people at once. These qualities can encourage creative, cooperative group-learning activities.

Introduction to the "Basic Three"

Since the early days of microcomputers, word processing, spreadsheet, and database programs have served as the most basic components in the teachers "technology toolkit." As Table 4.1 shows, each of these performs a specific type of function and each helps support specific productivity and teaching/learning activities. However, the three programs are usually designed to work together. For example, in the Technology Integration Example at the beginning of this chapter, a student completes a spreadsheet that demonstrates a mathematical concept such as loan terms, and then he or she inserts this spreadsheet into a word-processed report.

Overview of productivity uses. These three software products are often referred to as the "basic productivity tools," because they were the first such tools to be designed to save time on clerical types of tasks and, thus, to make work proceed more efficiently. In schools, word processing is the most frequently used of the three for productivity purposes, since teachers and students use it across all subject areas whenever they need to do typed work such as a composition or report. Spreadsheet and database software tend to be used primarily to enhance teacher productivity rather than student productivity.

Overview of instructional uses. Word processing is used primarily to support English and foreign language exercises, such as learning vocabulary and punctuation. Spreadsheets are used most often for demonstrations in mathematics and

TABLE 4.1 An Overview of the "Basic Three" Software Tools

Software Tool	Software Function	Sample Products
Word Processing **Example:** *Microsoft Word*	**Creates documents consisting of pages with text and graphics.**	**Student compositions, poetry, and reports: flyers; simple newsletters; letters**
Spreadsheet **Example:** *Microsoft Excel*	Puts numerical information in row/column format; allows quick calculations and recalculations.	Budgets, checkbooks, gradebooks, illustrations of mathematics concepts
Database **Example:** *FileMaker Pro*	**Organizes and stores collections of information; allows items to be easily and quickly retrieved.**	**Data from surveys, inventories of materials, student information**

business education areas, but they also support instructional activities such as science experiments or social studies surveys. At one time, creating and searching databases was a popular strategy for teaching students organization, research, and study skills and for demonstrating how information is organized to serve various important functions in our society (e.g., census and tax records). With the emergence of Internet search engines such as Google, student creation of databases has given way to an emphasis on **data mining** techniques, which call for collecting data from all the information available and searching it to see relationships among the data elements.

Recent Development in Software Tools

Although software tools have been in existence for many years, they are constantly being updated with new features and capabilities. Most of the following recent developments have made these tools even more useful in the classroom:

- **Web-based software tools** — There has been a surge of software tools that are now available via the Internet, and many are free of charge. **Google Docs**, for instance, provides users access to online programs for word processing, spreadsheets, and presentations. The site offers easy storage and sorting of documents online and allows for sharing of documents among multiple users.

- **Open-source software** — **Open-source software**, computer software the source code for which is made available in the public domain and that permits users to use, change, and improve the software and to redistribute it in modified or unmodified form, is also becoming more popular, with open-source alternatives to many of the most popular programs. OpenOffice.org provides users with free access to software that you download and use on your local computer.

- **PDA tools** — All of the basic software tools are now available on personal digital assistants (PDAs) or handheld computers. This portable format makes them easily accessible and flexible to use for both teachers and students. Since these basic software tools have been transferred to handheld format, the handhelds themselves have become more popular.

- **Web-enabled features** — All of the basic tools, like many tools described in other chapters, now allow insertion of "live" web page links in documents, and most allow documents to be saved in Hypertext Markup Language (HTML) or web page formats. This makes it even easier to connect documents to web page resources that embellish or add to the document's content. For example, students may include links in a project report to some of the resources they consulted during their research.

- **Better file-exchange compatibility** — In the early days of software tools, programs were often incompatible. That is, documents created in one program could not be opened in another program. Incompatibility was especially problematic between programs on Macintosh and Windows (PC) computers. This problem limited file sharing and hindered collaborative work since people often had different **computer platforms** (types of computers) and tool programs. Today's software tools, both online and on a local computer, are designed to be much more compatible across programs and platforms, making it much easier for teachers and students to transfer documents and to work together on projects.

- **Software suites and integrated packages** — Because it is usually cheaper to buy several tools at once rather than separately, software tools are increasingly used as parts of **software suites** or **integrated packages**. Keizer (1997) differentiates between integrated packages, which combine several functions such as word processing, spreadsheet, database, and graphics working under one program, and software suites, which are separate programs that companies place in the same package. An example of the latter, *iWork*, developed by Apple, includes *Pages* for word processing, *Keynote* for presentations, and *Numbers* for a spreadsheet. Similarly, *Microsoft Office* has several separate applications that work well together. While any of these packages may be useful, depending on the needs of the classroom and the types of software included, the current trend is toward using *Microsoft Office* since it includes Microsoft *Word* and Microsoft *PowerPoint,* two of the most popular applications.

Go to MyEducationLab and select the topic "Software." Under "Assignments, Activities, and Applications," select "Exploring Google Docs and OpenOffice.org" and consider what each site has to offer educators.

Using Word Processing Software in Teaching and Learning

Word processing programs allow people to produce typed documents on a computer screen. Although the lines between word processing and desktop publishing have become increasingly blurred, the programs still differ in the way they produce documents. Word processing programs essentially produce documents as a stream of text, whereas desktop publishing produces them as individual pages. Despite this difference, most word processing programs allow at least some desktop publishing capabilities, such as inserting text boxes and graphics at any location on a page. Word processing features are listed in Table 4.2.

TABLE 4.2   A Summary of Word Processing Features

Feature Categories/General Benefits	Word Processing Features	Description
Basic features save time writing text and make changing text easier and more flexible.	Store documents for later use.	Documents saved to disk can be changed without reentering text.
	Store in many formats (e.g., RTF, PDF, HTML).	• Rich Text format (RTF) removes all or most formatting commands so other word processors can read the file. • PDF format allows files to be read as formatted documents with Adobe *Acrobat Reader*. • HTML format allows documents to be placed on the Internet.
	Erase and insert text.	Allows easy insertion of additional letters, spaces, lines, paragraphs, or pages.
	Search and replace.	One command allows all occurrences of a word or phrase to be changed as specified.
	Move or copy text.	Allows cutting and pasting (deleting text and inserting it elsewhere) or copying and pasting (repeating text in several places).
	Allow word wraparound.	Automatically goes to next line at end of a line without pressing Enter or Return (Also hyphenates words, as needed.)
Desktop publishing features make flyers, reports, newsletters, brochures, and student handouts more attractive and professional looking.	Alignment	Centers or right- or left-justifies text.
	Change styles/appearance.	Allows a variety of fonts, type styles, font colors, margins, line spacing, tabs, and indentations in the same document.
	Insert automatic headers, footers, and pagination.	Automatically places text at the top (header) or bottom (footer) of each page in a document with or without page numbering (pagination).
	Insert graphics.	Inserts clip art or image files into documents and formats them; some programs allow image editing.
	Insert colors and shading.	Graphics can be filled with color or degrees of shading.
	Insert tables.	Organizes information into rows and columns without using tabs or indentations.
	Insert text boxes.	Allows text blocks to be inserted in any location in or around a document.
	Insert drawn figures.	Allows inserting shapes, callouts, and other figures to enhance documents.
Language features help teachers and students correct their work and do various language, spelling, and usage exercises.	Check and correct spelling.	Spell-checker feature compares words in a document to those stored in the program's dictionary files.
	Suggest words.	Thesaurus feature suggests synonyms for any word.
	Check grammar and usage.	Grammar checkers review documents for items such as sentence length, frequency of word use, and subject–verb agreement. Also marks phrases or sentences to be corrected.
Web features allow teachers and students to connect documents with Internet resources and create web page announcements, reports, and projects.	Insert "live" URLs.	Allows person reading the document to click on text and go automatically to a website. (*Note:* Web browser must be active.)
	Create web pages.	Acts as simple web page development software and creates HTML pages.
Support features make using the program easier and more flexible.	Use templates.	Users can easily adapt preformatted models of résumés, newsletters, and brochures to their own needs.
	Offer voice recognition.	Allows text to be received and entered via dictated words rather than as typed entries.
	Merge text with data files.	• Automatically inserts words (e.g., names and addresses) into documents such as letters. • Lists of data can be stored within the word processing program or merged from a database.

Today, word processing is a necessary basic skill ... in school and life in general.

The Impact of Word Processing in Education

Why teachers use word processing. Perhaps no other technology resource has had as great an impact on education as word processing. Not only does word processing offer high versatility and flexibility, it also is "model-free" instructional software; that is, it reflects no particular instructional approach. A teacher can use it to support any kind of directed instruction or constructivist activity. Since its value as an aid to teaching and learning is universally acknowledged, word processing has become the most commonly used software in education. It offers many general relative advantages (unique benefits over and above other methods) to teachers and students:

- **Saves time** — Word processing helps teachers use preparation time more efficiently by letting them modify materials instead of creating new ones. Writers can also make corrections to word processing documents more quickly than they could on a typewriter or by hand.

- **Enhances document appearance** — Materials created with word processing software look more polished and professional than handwritten or typed materials do. It is not surprising that students seem to like the improved appearance that word processing gives to their work (Harris, 1985). This is especially possible with the many templates that are part of the software suites today.

- **Allows sharing of documents** — Word processing allows materials to be shared easily among writers. Teachers can exchange lesson plans, worksheets, or other materials on disk and modify them to fit their needs. Students can also share ideas and products among themselves.

- **Allows collaboration of documents** — Especially since the release of Google Docs, teachers and students can now create, edit, and share documents synchronously.

Adapting for Special Needs

Young students and students with cognitive impairments are often confused by the complexity of standard productivity software packages such as *Microsoft Office*. One solution is a software product called *Max's Toolbox* (http://www.maxssandbox. com/). Designed for children ages 3 to 10, it provides a child-friendly interface and modified menus for Microsoft *Word, Excel,* and *PowerPoint.* It allows students to learn the basic operation of core productivity tools without being overwhelmed by all the options and advanced features. *Max's Toolbox* is a model learning scaffold that introduces young learners to essential concepts (e.g., save, print) so that they can later move easily into the full-featured version of *Microsoft Office.* A trial version is available for download.

Contributed by Dave Edyburn

Research on the impact of word processing. Research on the benefits of word processing in education yields contradictory findings. Results of studies of the effects of word processing on quality and quantity of writing are mixed (Bangert-Drowns, 1993). Three reviews of research (Bangert-Drowns, 1993; Hawisher, 1989; Snyder, 1993) found that these differences in findings may reflect differences in researchers' choices of types of word processing systems, prior experience and writing ability of students, and types of writing instruction evaluated. Generally, word processing seems to improve writing and attitudes toward writing only if it is used in the context of good writing instruction and if students have enough time to learn word processing procedures before the study begins.

When Goldberg, Russell, and Cook (2003) updated these findings with a meta-analysis of studies from 1992 to 2002, they focused not only on whether word processing had more impact than handwritten methods but also on identifying when word processing could have the most impact on the quantity and quality of students' writing. Their meta-analysis showed a stronger relationship between computers and quality of writing than previous such analyses had. Students who use computers during writing instruction produce written work that is about 0.4 standard deviation better than students who develop writing skills on paper. Their analysis also suggested that when students write with computers, they "engage in the revising of their work throughout the writing process, more frequently share and receive feedback from their peers, and benefit from teacher input earlier in the writing process" (p. 19). Table 4.3 summarizes some of the findings of all four research reviews.

TABLE 4.3 Findings from Reviews of Word Processing in Education

	Hawisher (26 studies) (1989)	Snyder (57 studies) (1993)	Bangert-Drowns (32 studies) (1993)	Goldberg, Russell, and Cook (14 studies) (2003)
Better quality of writing	No conclusion	No conclusion	Positive results	Positive results
Greater quantity of writing	Positive results	Positive results	Positive results	Positive results
More surface (mechanical) revisions	No conclusion	Positive results	No conclusion	Not reviewed
More substantive (meaning) revisions	No conclusion	No improvement	No conclusion	Not reviewed
Fewer mechanical errors	Positive results	Positive results	Not reviewed	Not reviewed
Better attitude toward writing	Positive results	Positive results	No improvement	Not reviewed
Better attitude toward word processing	No conclusion	Positive results	Not reviewed	Not reviewed

Issues in using word processing. Educators seem to agree that although word processing is a valuable application, its use in education can be controversial:

- **When should students start word processing?** — Word processing software designed for young children is available, and schools can introduce word processing to students as young as 4 or 5 years old. Some educators feel that word processing will free students from the physical constraints of handwriting and free them to develop written expression skills. Others worry that it will make students unwilling to spend time developing handwriting abilities and other activities requiring fine-motor skills.

- **Is it necessary to teach keyboarding skills?** — Discussion is ongoing about whether students need to learn keyboarding ("10-finger typing" on the computer) either prior to or in conjunction with word processing activities. Some educators feel that students will never become really productive on the computer until they learn 10-finger keyboarding. Others feel that the extensive time spent on keyboarding instruction and practice could be better spent on more important skills and that students will pick up typing skills on their own.

- **What effects does word processing have on handwriting?** — While no researchers have conducted formal studies of the impact of frequent word processing use on handwriting legibility, computer users commonly complain that their handwriting isn't what it used to be, ostensibly because of infrequent opportunities to use their handwriting skills.

- **What impact does word processing have on assessment?** — Some organizations have students answer essay-type test questions with word processing rather than in handwriting. Many school districts also allow students to word process their writing tests. This practice introduces several issues. Roblyer (1997) reviewed research that found that students' word-processed compositions tend to receive lower grades than handwritten ones do. This surprising finding indicates that educational organizations that allow students to choose either handwriting or word processing must be careful to establish guidelines and special training to ensure that raters do not inadvertently discriminate against students who choose word processing.

Teachers and administrators are still deciding how best to deal with these issues. Despite these obstacles, education's dependence on word processing continues to grow.

Word Processing in the Classroom: Productivity and Teaching Strategies

Productivity strategies. Word processing can help teachers prepare classroom materials they otherwise would have to type or write out by hand. These include handouts or other instructional materials, lesson plans and notes, reports, forms, letters to parents or students, flyers, and newsletters. Word processing saves preparation time, especially if a teacher uses the same documents every year. For example, a teacher may send the same let-

Technology Integration Lesson 4.1

Using Word Processing to Support Learning of Writing Processes

Title: Cartoon Commentaries on the Computer   **Grade Level:** Middle school
Content Area/Topic: Writing persuasive essays

NETS for Students: Standards I (Creativity and Innovation), 2 (Communication and Collaboration), and 4 (Critical Thinking, Problem Solving, and Decision Making)

Description of Standards Applications: This integration lesson offers students the opportunity to work in groups to analyze a comic strip and/or editorial cartoon, striving to understand the idea behind it. Upon the analysis, students decide if they agree with the author's perspective and if the comic strip/cartoon is effective.

Instruction: Two computers are set up—one with drawing software and one with word processing software. The class is divided into small groups of three to four students each, and the teacher distributes newspapers to the groups. The students go through the papers, selecting at least two comic strips and/or editorial cartoons. They "write the story" or idea of the comic, using either dialog, narrative, or essay form. Each group reports to the class on its analysis. Ask the groups to add another paragraph to their write-ups that expresses their own opinions about the comics' purposes. To elicit their responses, ask questions such as these: Do you support the purpose and point of view of the cartoonist? Why or why not? What mix of images and text does the artist use to make his or her point? Is this mix effective? Again, these write-ups are shared with the class and used as the basis for discussions.

Assessment: Use rubrics to assess cartoon quality.

Source: Reissman, R. (1994). Computer cartoon commentaries. *The Computing Teacher, 21*(5), 23–25.

---

ter to parents each year simply by changing the dates and adding new information. Teachers may want to keep electronic templates or model documents they can easily update and reuse. See Table 4.4 for a suggested list of reusable word-processed documents teachers may want to have on hand.

Instructional integration strategies for word processing. Students can use word processing for almost any written work, regardless of subject area, that they would otherwise write by hand. Research shows that word processing alone cannot improve the quality of student writing but can help students make corrections more efficiently; this can motivate them to write more and take more interest in improving their written work. Some current word processing integration strategies include the following:

- **Supporting the learning of writing processes** — Students can use word processing to write, edit, and illustrate stories; to produce reports in content areas; to

TABLE 4.4   Suggested Word Processing Items for a Teacher's File of Reusable Documents

- Beginning of the year welcome letter
- Permission letters for field trips and other events
- Flyers and other announcements
- Request for fee payments letter
- Fund-raising letter
- List of class rules
- Posted flyer of class rules
- Letterhead stationeries
- Periodic student progress letters to parents
- Lesson plans and notes
- Students information sheets and handouts
- Newsletters
- Annual reports required by the school
- Frequently used worksheets and exercises

keep notes and logs on classroom activities; and for any written assignments. Using word processing in the classroom can make it easier for students to get started writing as well as to revise and improve writing drafts. (See Technology Integration Lesson 4.1.)

- **Using a dynamic group product approach** — Teachers can assign group poems or letters to various students, allowing students to add and change lines or produce elements of the whole document in a word processing program. Using word processing software, students find it easier to share, exchange, and add onto drafts, as well as to work together on written projects at a distance.

- **Assigning individual language, writing, and reading exercises** — Special word processing exercises allow for meaningful, hands-on practice in language use as individual students work on-screen combining sentences, adding or correcting punctuation, or writing sentences for spelling words. Word processing may also make possible a variety of reading/language-related activities ranging from decoding to writing poetry and enjoying literature. Identifying and correcting errors becomes a more visual process. Viau (1998) points out that adding colors to text can be the basis for activities that enhance critical thinking during writing instruction.

- **Encouraging writing through the curriculum** — A recent trend in education is to encourage writing skills in courses and activities other than those designed to teach English and language arts. This practice of writing-through-the-curriculum is in keeping with the new emphasis on integrated, interdisciplinary, and thematic curricula. Word processing can encourage these integrated activities. Its font and graphics features allow students to represent concepts in mathematics, science, and other content areas. Word processors are also available in other languages to support foreign language learning.

Teaching Word Processing Skills: Recommended Skills and Activities

Students new to word processing must have adequate time to develop skills in using the software before teachers can begin to grade their word-processed products. Many online tutorials are available for teaching various software packages, but these may not always be accessible to students. Also, younger or less independent learners may not have the ability to use these self-instructional methods and may need teacher-led instruction.

For all of these reasons, teachers who would like to use word processing in classroom lessons may have to introduce their students to word processing and show them the features

and uses of the software. Table 4.5 shows a recommended strategy you can use to introduce word processing to students in elementary and middle grades. Note that some features and steps are labeled "optional." You may choose to introduce these on an "as-needed" basis or only with older, more experienced students.

Using Spreadsheet Software in Teaching and Learning

Spreadsheets are programs designed to organize and manipulate numerical data. The term *spreadsheet* comes from the pre-computer word for an accountant's ledger: a book for keeping records of numerical information such as budgets and cash flow. Unlike the term *word processing,* which refers only to the computer software or program, the term *spreadsheet* can refer either to the program itself or to the product it produces. Spreadsheet products are sometimes also called **worksheets**. The information in a spreadsheet is stored in rows and columns. Each row–column position is called a **cell** and may contain numerical values, words or character data, and **formulas** or calculation commands.

A spreadsheet helps users manage numbers in the same way that word processing helps them manage words. Bozeman (1992) described spreadsheets as a way to "word process numbers" (p. 908). Spreadsheet software was the earliest application software available for microcomputers. Some people credit spreadsheets with starting the microcomputer revolution, since the availability of the first spreadsheet software, *Visicalc,* motivated many people to buy a microcomputer. Spreadsheet features are listed in Table 4.6 on page 120.

The Impact of Spreadsheets in Education

Why teachers use spreadsheets. Spreadsheet programs are in widespread use in classrooms at all levels of education. Teachers use them primarily to keep budgets and gradebooks and to help teach mathematical topics. They offer teachers and students several kinds of unique benefits:

- **Save time** — Spreadsheets save valuable time by allowing teachers and students to complete essential calculations quickly. They save time not only by making initial calculations faster and more accurate, but their automatic recalculation features also make it easy to update products such as grades and budgets. Entries also can be changed, added, or deleted easily, with formulas that automatically recalculate final grades.

- **Organize displays of information** — Although spreadsheet programs are intended for numerical data,

TABLE 4.5   Tips on Teaching Word Processing
(Also see links to tutorials at http://www.internet4classrooms.com/on-line2.htm)

Suggested Steps	Tasks Under Each Step
Step 1—Prepare for teaching.	**Arrange for:** • A big screen or projection system • A disk for each student • Copying sample file(s) onto student disks • One computer per student • Alternative keyboards or other adaptive devices for students with disabilities. **Create or obtain:** • Handouts or wall posters on word processing features and common errors.
Step 2—Demonstrate the basics.	**Using a big screen or projection system, show how to:** • Load a disk into a computer disk drive (if needed) • Open a file from a disk • Move around in a document using the cursor and scroll bars • Add and delete text; undo changes • Name, save, and close document. **Point out common errors:** • Forgetting to move cursor before typing • Forgetting about automatic wraparound (pressing Enter or Return at end of lines) • "Losing" part of document on the screen by scrolling up or down • Forgetting to save all changes before closing a file.
Step 3—Assign individual practice.	**Give students a sample word processing file on disk and have them:** • Insert the disk and open the file • Do a list of changes to the file (e.g., inserting spaces, deleting lines, undoing changes) • Name, save, and close document.
Step 4—Demonstrate formatting features.	**Using big screen or projection system, show how to:** • Change fonts, styles, and alignment • Add clip art • Spell-check a document • Print a document • **Optional:** Search and replace procedures • **Optional:** Add bullets and numbering. **Point out common errors:** • Inserting too many spaces at top or bottom of document (by pressing Enter or Return) • Unexpected errors from Search and Replace feature (failing to predict results).
Step 5—Assign more individual practice.	**Have students open their sample word processing file from Step 3 and do the following:** • Change fonts, styles, and alignment • Add clip art • Spell-check a document • Print a document • **Optional:** Search and replace text • **Optional:** Add bullets and numbering.
Step 6— Demonstrate procedures with new files.	**Show students how to:** • Open a new file • Name and save under different names (Save vs. Save As) • **Optional:** Set up a new document (e.g., set margins and line spacing) • **Optional:** Do headers, footers, and pagination.
Step 7—Assign more individual practice.	**Do the following:** • Assign a product for them to copy (for younger students) or create (for older students) • Monitor students as they work, and give individual help as needed.

TABLE 4.6 A Summary of Spreadsheet Features

Feature Categories/ General Benefits	Spreadsheet Features	Description of Features
Basic features make it easier to display and manipulate budget, grade, or survey data; and do mathematics problem solving.	Line up information in rows and columns.	Row–column format makes numerical and other information easier to read and digest at a glance.
	Do basic calculations.	Use formulas in cells to do: • Basic arithmetic functions: adding, subtracting, multiplying, dividing • Weighted averages by combining these functions.
	Do complex calculations.	Use formulas in cells to do: • Mathematical functions such as logarithms and roots • Statistical functions such as sums and averages • Trigonometric functions such as sines and tangents • Logical functions such as Boolean comparisons • Financial functions such as periodic payments and rates • Special-purpose functions such as looking up and comparing data entries with other information (e.g., counting the number of grades above a certain number).
	Do automatic recalculation.	When a number in one cell changes (e.g., a grade) a spreadsheet formula automatically updates all calculations related to that number (e.g., an average grade).
	Copy cells.	Numbers, formulas, or other information in cells can be copied and pasted to any other cells.
	Sort data.	Data can be organized alphabetically or numerically.
	Search and replace.	One command allows all occurrences of a specified word, phrase, number, or formula to be changed.
Formatting features	Alignment.	Centers or right- or left-justifies cell entries.
	Changes styles/appearance.	Allows: • A variety of fonts, sizes, font colors, and type styles in the same document • Cells and graphics to be filled with color or degrees of shading
	Insert automatic headers, footers, and pagination.	Allows text to be automatically placed at the top (header) or bottom (footer) of each page in a worksheet with or without page numbering (pagination).
Graphics/interactive features allow spreadsheet data to be shown in more visual formats.	Charting.	Creates charts and graphs automatically from spreadsheet data.
	Insert graphics or movies.	Clip art or other still or moving images can be pasted into cells to illustrate concepts or to change document appearance.
	Insert drawn figures.	Allows inserting shapes, callouts, and other figures to enhance worksheet appearance.
Web features allow teachers and students to connect documents with Internet resources and create web page announcements, reports, and projects.	Insert "live" URLs.	Allows person using the spreadsheet to click on text and go automatically to a website. (*Note:* Web browser must be active.)
	Save as web pages.	Allows worksheets to be displayed online.
Support features make using the program easier and more flexible.	Read and save to other formats.	Spreadsheet can: • Read and use other data files such as those produced by Statistical Packages for the Social Sciences (SPSS) software • Save documents in formats (e.g., tab-delimited) for use in SPSS or other programs.
	Use templates.	Users can easily adapt preformatted models of worksheets (e.g., budgets, checkbooks, and gradekeepers) to their own needs.

their capability to store information in columns makes them ideal tools for designing informational charts such as schedules and attendance lists that may contain few numbers and no calculations at all.

- **Support asking "what if" questions** — Spreadsheets help people visualize the impact of changes in numbers. Since values are automatically recalculated when changes are made in a worksheet, a user can play with numbers and immediately see the result. This capability makes it feasible to pose "what if" questions and to answer them quickly and easily.

- **Increase motivation to work with mathematics** — Many teachers feel that spreadsheets make working with numbers more fun. Students sometimes perceive mathematical concepts as dry and boring; spreadsheets can make these concepts so graphic that students express real delight with seeing how they work.

Research on the impact of spreadsheet use. Although spreadsheets are widely believed to help students visualize numerical concepts better than other, nondynamic tools, few studies have attempted to capture their comparative impact on achievement. Studies show, however, that spreadsheets can be useful tools for teaching concepts in many areas, including algebra problem solving (Sutherland, 1993), meteorology (Sumrall & Forslev, 1994), statistics (Black, 1999), and calculus (Hauger, 2000). The literature contains numerous testimonials by teachers who have used spreadsheets successfully in teaching topics ranging from mathematics to social studies.

Issues in using spreadsheets. One of the few disagreements about spreadsheets in education is whether to use them to keep grades or to rely instead on grade-keeping packages (gradebooks) designed especially for this purpose. (See a discussion of gradebooks in Chapter 5.) Spreadsheets usually offer more flexibility in designing formats and allowing special-purpose calculation functions, while gradebooks are simpler to use and require little setup other than entering students' names and assignment grades. Teachers appear to be about evenly divided on this issue; the choice comes down to personal preference.

Spreadsheets in the Classroom: Productivity and Teaching Strategies

Productivity strategies. Teachers can use spreadsheets to help them prepare classroom materials and complete calculations that they would otherwise have to do by hand or with a calculator. The most common uses of spreadsheets are for keeping club and classroom budgets, preparing performance checklists, and keeping gradebooks.

 Making the Case for Technology Integration

Use the following questions to reflect on issues in technology integration and to guide discussions within your class.

1. Word processing is a software program valued by many teachers, but it is criticized by some who feel that overreliance on it is ruining students' handwriting and that increasing the quantity of what students write is not improving the quality of their writing. How would you respond to these critics?

2. The increasing use of databases in our society, combined with pervasive use of the Internet, is making it easy to access personal information about anyone. However, teachers need specific information about students' learning problems in order to meet their needs. What implications regarding safety and privacy arise from "data mining" information about students in our schools? What do you think is the teacher's role in these privacy and security issues?

3. Spreadsheets, like calculators, can support rapid computations as students work on higher level problems. Some educators feel that using either kind of technology results in students with poor knowledge of underlying math principles. How would you respond to these criticisms?

Instructional integration strategies for spreadsheets. Teachers can use spreadsheets in many ways to enhance learning. The literature, in fact, reflects an increasing variety of applications. Although their teaching role focuses primarily on mathematics lessons, spreadsheets have also effectively supported instruction in science, social studies, and even language arts. Lewis (2001) offers 40 lessons to help teach various curriculum topics in grades K–8.

- **Making possible visual teaching demonstrations** — Whenever concepts involving numbers can be clarified by concrete representation, spreadsheets contribute to effective teaching demonstrations. Spreadsheets offer an efficient way of demonstrating numerical concepts such as multiplication and percentages and numerical applications such as the concept of electoral votes versus popular votes. A worksheet can make a picture out of abstract concepts and provide a graphic illustration of what the teacher is trying to communicate. (See Technology Integration Lesson 4.2.)

- **Supporting student products** — Students can use spreadsheets to create neat timelines, charts, and graphs as well as products that require them to store and calcu-

Technology Integration Lesson 4.2

Using Spreadsheets for Visual Teaching Demonstrations

Title: How the Electoral Vote Works

Content Area/Topic: Civics

Grade Level: 5

NETS for Students: Standards 2 (Communication and Collaboration), 3 (Research and Information Fluency), and 4 (Critical Thinking, Problem Solving, and Decision Making)

Description of Standards Applications: This integration lesson offers students the opportunity to work with mock election data as a class and to analyze electoral and popular votes while critically thinking about the impact of electoral votes. Teachers can use a spreadsheet to display data from a U.S. presidential election that show how popular votes and electoral votes differ and how it is possible for a person to win the popular vote and still lose the election.

Instruction: After the class holds a mock election and assigns electoral votes to each class in the school based on enrollment numbers, a spreadsheet is set up by the teacher to match the list of classes and their popular and electoral votes. Data on election results are entered after the election is held, and the spreadsheet is displayed on a large monitor so the whole class can see the results as they are entered. Through this activity, students are able to see that if very few of the popular votes in key areas are changed, the results of the election would be reversed. The class discusses these results as well as the possibility that a candidate could win the popular vote and lose the electoral vote.

Assessment: Answer questions on the electoral vote as part of an end-of-unit test.

Source: Goldberg, K. (1991). Bringing mathematics to the social studies classroom: Spreadsheets and the electoral process. *The Computing Teacher, 18*(1), 35–38.

late numbers. Creating graphic displays of data in a spreadsheet program can save time, particularly when changes or corrections are made to the data.

- **Supporting mathematical problem solving** — Spreadsheets take over the task of doing arithmetic functions so that students can focus on higher level concepts (Black, 1999; Hauger, 2000; Ploger, Rooney, & Klingler, 1996). By answering "what if" questions in a highly graphic format, spreadsheets help teachers encourage logical thinking, develop organizational skills, and promote problem solving. (See Technology Integration Lesson 4.3.)

- **Storing and analyzing data** — Whenever students must keep track of data from classroom experiments or online surveys, spreadsheets help organize these data and allow students to perform required descriptive statistical analyses on them. (See Technology Integration Lesson 4.4.)

- **Projecting grades** — Students can be taught to use spreadsheets to keep track of their own grades. They can do their own "what if" questions to see what scores they need to make on their assignments to achieve desired class grades. This simple activity can play an important role in encouraging students to take responsibility for setting goals and achieving them.

Teaching Spreadsheet Skills: Recommended Skills and Activities

Just as with word processing, students new to spreadsheets must have time to develop skills in using the software before teachers can begin to grade their work. Some lessons require students to know only the most basic operations, as shown in Step 2 of Table 4.7 on page 125. Other activities require students to create their own spreadsheets and formulas, as shown in Step 4. In the latter case, if students are not able to use the online tutorials that are available for teaching spreadsheet software, teachers can use the strategies outlined in Table 4.7. Even when teaching these advanced concepts, teachers may choose to introduce more complex functions and features on an as-needed basis, depending on the needs of the lesson.

Using Database Software in Teaching and Learning

Databases are computer programs that allow users to store, organize, and manipulate information, including both text and numerical data. Database software can perform some calculations, but its real power lies in allowing

Technology Integration Lesson 4.3

Using Spreadsheets to Teach Problem Solving

Title: Solving Problems with Dimensions and Area   **Grade Level:** 4 through 12
Content Area/Topic: Geometry/algebra

 NETS for Students: Standards 3 (Research and Information Fluency) and 4 (Critical Thinking, Problem Solving, and Decision Making)

	A	B	C
1	width	length	area
2	1	94	94
3	2	92	184
4	3	90	270
5	4	88	352
6	5	86	430
7	6	84	504
8	7	82	574
9	8	80	640
10	9	78	702
11	10	76	760
12	11	74	814
13	12	72	864
14	13	70	910
15	14	68	952
16	15	66	990
17	16	64	1,024
18	17	62	1,054
19	18	60	1,080
20	19	58	1,102
21	20	56	1,120
22	21	54	1,134
23	22	52	1,144
24	23	50	1,150
25	24	48	1,152
26	25	46	1,150
27	26	44	1,144
28	27	42	1,134
29	28	40	1,120
30	29	38	1,102
31	30	36	1,080
32	31	34	1,054
33	32	32	1,024
34	33	30	990
35	34	28	952
36	35	26	910
37	36	24	864
38	37	22	814
39	38	20	760
40	39	18	702

Description of Standards Applications: This integration lesson offers students the opportunity to use the software *Geometer's Sketchpad* to research and analyze mathematical equations based on an authentic scenario and then to make a decision with their data. Problems that engage students and teachers in mathematical problem solving are exciting because they encourage students to develop and test their own conjectures. Without technology, however, these explorations would be much more difficult, if not impossible.

Instruction: Present a problem such as the following: "Sabine will use her house as one side of a new fenced area she is making for her dog. If she has 96 meters of fencing, what are the dimensions of the largest rectangular pen she can make?" Use *Geometer's Sketchpad* to draw the figure with the known numbers, and then help the students create an algebra equation for this problem. Lead them to see that a pen that uses 96 meters of fencing has to have a width of x and a length of $96 - 2x$ since the total fencing available is 96 meters and there are two sides with the same length and one of a different length. (The house serves as the fourth side.) Help students create a spreadsheet that calculates the possible dimensions, based on this information.

Assessment: After working in pairs to do several problems similar to this, students take a test with other problems.

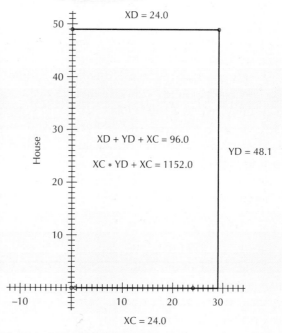

Source: Both figures reprinted with permission from Brown, S., Galloway, C., Orrill, C., & Umberger, S. (2002). Lead your students in mathematical discovery. *Learning and Leading with Technology, 29*(5), 22–27, 64. Copyright © 2002 ISTE (International Society for Technology in Education), iste@iste.org, www.iste.org. All rights reserved.

Technology Integration Lesson 4.4

Using Spreadsheets to Store and Analyze Data

Title: Analyzing Data from an Online Survey　　**Grade Level:** 3 through 12

Content Area/Topic: Language arts—writing assignments

NETS for Students: Standards 3 (Research and Information Fluency) and 4 (Critical Thinking, Problem Solving, and Decision Making)

Description of Standards Applications: This integration lesson offers students the opportunity to research and develop an online survey followed by posting it online and collecting the final data, which can then be analyzed. Creating questions for the survey gives students good practice with writing for an intended audience. An online survey allows students to collect data more easily, and spreadsheets work to store data for easier analysis.

Instruction: Introduce the project and demonstrate the Internet survey tool. You can either decide on the survey topic or allow students to brainstorm one. The class creates a few of the items together as the teacher illustrates principles of item writing. Then the class breaks up into groups to write items in an assigned content area. Once the survey is put online, data are collected automatically in a comma-delimited file—that is, items are separated by commas as they are stored. When the collection is complete, download the file into a spreadsheet and have students do the desired totals and other formulas to analyze the data.

Assessment: Use a rubric to grade the quality of students' project work.

Source: Timmerman, A. (2003). Survey says.... *Learning and Leading with Technology, 31*(2), 10–13, 55.

people to locate information through keyword searches. Unlike word processing software, which can be compared to a typewriter, or a spreadsheet, which can be compared to a calculator, a database program has no electronic counterpart. It is most often compared to a file cabinet or a Rolodex card file. Like these pre-computer devices, the purpose of a database is to store important information in a way that makes it easy to locate later. This capability has become increasingly important as society's store of essential information grows in volume and complexity.

People often use the term *database* to refer both to the computer program and to the product it creates; however, database products are also called **files**. Whereas a spreadsheet stores an item of data in a cell, a database stores one item of data in a location usually called a **field**. Although each field represents one item of information in a database, perhaps the more important unit of information is a **record**, which stores all items of information related to a particular database entry. For example, in a database of student records, each record corresponds to a student, and a record consists of several

fields of information about the student, such as name, address, age, and parent' names. In a database of information about a school's inventory of instructional resources, each record represents one resource and consists of several fields describing aspects such as title, publisher, date published, and location. A summary of database features is shown in Table 4.8 on page 126.

The Impact of Databases in Education

Why teachers use databases. The uses of databases in education have changed in recent years, due to shifts in instructional focuses and data-keeping requirements. Current uses are described later in this chapter. Databases continue to offer educators the following benefits:

- **Reducing data redundancy** — In education, as in business and industry, many different organizations need access to the same kinds of information about the same people or resources. In pre-computer days, it was often the case that each school office and school district

TABLE 4.7 Tips on Teaching Spreadsheets
(Also see links to tutorials at http://www.internet4classrooms.com/on-line2.htm)

Suggested Steps	Tasks Under Each Step
Step 1—Prepare for teaching.	**Arrange for:** • A big screen or projection system • A disk for each student • Copying sample file(s) onto student disks • One computer per student • Alternative keyboards or other adaptive devices for students with disabilities. **Create or obtain:** • Handouts or wall posters on spreadsheet features and common errors.
Step 2—Demonstrate the basics.	**Using a big screen or projection system, show how to:** • Open a spreadsheet file from a disk • Select a worksheet to work on in the file by clicking a tab at the bottom • Select any given cell location by row–column position. **Then demonstrate:** • Spreadsheet "magic": Show how it recalculates automatically when a number is changed. **Finally, show how to:** • Enter new information into a cell • Format given cells for appearance and as various kinds of numbers • Change column width • Copy information in a cell down the column or across a row. **Point out a common error:** • Forgetting to highlight cells to be formatted before selecting a format option.
Step 3—Assign individual practice.	**Give students a sample spreadsheet file on disk and have them:** • Insert the disk and open the file • Do a list of changes to the file (e.g., insert new data, copy down a column or across a row, format cells) • Name, save, and close the document.
Step 4—Demonstrate formatting features.	**Using a big screen or projection system, show how to:** • Create a formula to add a column • Copy a formula across the row to add other columns • **Optional:** Functions such as SUM and AVERAGE • **Optional:** Charting functions • **Optional:** Adding graphics and URLs. **Point out common errors with formulas:** • Forgetting to place the cursor in the cell where you want the formula • Pressing the Right Arrow key (instead of the Return or Enter Key) to leave the cell while creating a formula (Show that this action adds something to the formula, rather than exiting the cell.) • Including the formula cell itself in the formula's calculation (i.e., circular reference error).
Step 5—Assign more individual practice.	**Have students open their sample spreadsheet file from Step 3 and do the following:** • Enter and format various new formulas • **Optional:** Create a chart based on the data • **Optional:** Add a graphic and/or a URL. Monitor students as they work, and give individual help as needed.

TABLE 4.8   A Summary of Database Features

Feature Categories/ General Benefits	Database Features	Description of Features
Basic features make it easier to store large amounts of data in an organized, easily accessible way; allow easy changes to information.	Store data.	Text, numerical, and graphic information in a database is organized by records (e.g., one student in a student information database) and fields (e.g., names, ages, and birth dates of all students).
	Do updates.	Items of information can be called up and easily edited (e.g., changing a student's address after a move or changing the name of a teacher assigned to a group of students).
	Sort data.	Data can be organized alphabetically or numerically by any desired field (e.g., by students' last names or by ages).
Search features make it easy to locate single items of information or all items that meet certain criteria.	Do queries.	Locates and lists all information that matches certain keywords or criteria; allows searches based on Boolean logic.
	Do reports.	Produces formatted summaries of information retrieved from a database (e.g., a teacher creates a report listing students whose scores made them eligible for tutoring on a state-mandated test and the report tells their name, address, and Social Security number).
Calculation features allow data to be analyzed and the results of the analysis to be displayed.	Do formulas.	Allows arithmetic calculations based on numerical information stored in fields (e.g., calculates the average age or grades of students in a certain group).
Web features allow teachers and students to connect documents with Internet resources and to create web page announcements, reports, and projects.	Insert "live" URLs.	Allows person using the database to click on a URL and go automatically to a website. (*Note:* Web browser must be active.)
Other features make the program useful with other programs.	Merge with word-processed documents.	Database files can be used to insert fields automatically into letters and other documents (e.g., inserting student names to personalize letters to parents).

office kept duplicate files on teachers and students. Nowadays, since databases can be accessed from multiple locations, an organization needs to keep only one actual copy of these kinds of information. This cuts down on both the expense and the physical space needed to store the information.

- **Saving time locating and/or updating information** — People need to locate information and keep it accurate—time is money. It takes time to find information and to keep it updated for everyone who needs it. Since a database stores information in a central computer instead of in several different file folders in various offices, users can find information more quickly and make changes more easily whenever updates are needed. For example, if a student's address or legal guardian changes, updating the information in a student information database is both quicker and easier than locating and changing it in many file folders.

- **Allowing comparisons of information through searches across files** — Electronic databases also offer

the important capability of locating information that meets several criteria at once. For example, a teacher may want to locate all of the resources in video format at a certain grade level that focus on a certain topic. A database search would make locating these materials an easy task compared to a lengthy search of library shelves. For a large collection of information, this kind of search is possible only if information is stored in a database.

- **Helping reveal relationships among data** — Databases have the potential to make the concepts underlying data easier to spot. By asking questions and doing searches to answer them, students can see relationships among information elements they otherwise might not have been able to perceive. For example, students might create a database on U.S. presidents. By adding a field on which states entered the Union during each administration, they could ask questions about the number of years each party was in power and how fast the country grew under each administration.

Research on the instructional uses of databases. Collis (1990) summarized six studies on the instructional uses of databases. She found that students can use databases to acquire useful skills in searching for and using information, but they need guidance in asking relevant questions and analyzing results. If allowed to proceed on their own, students may regard a simple printed list of results as a sufficient measure of success. Studies by Maor (1991) in science and Ehman, Glenn, Johnson, and White (1992) in social studies yielded essentially the same results. Databases are most helpful when they are embedded in a structured problem-solving process and when the activity includes class and small-group discussion of search results.

In a review of technology in social studies, Berson (1996) reported that databases are one of the tools with demonstrated usefulness in teaching inquiry and problem-solving skills. Finally, Pugalee and Robinson (1998) found that training in database use and search techniques can increase teachers' Internet skills and their skill in designing lessons and applications that use the Internet. This latter finding indicates that the quality of teachers' Internet use may hinge on their grasp of database concepts.

Issues in using databases. Databases are a permanent and pervasive part of life in the Information Age. They allow users to locate bits of important data in a landscape crowded with information; they support decisions with confirmed facts rather than assumptions; and they put the power of knowledge at our fingertips. Yet this power is not without its dangers, and knowing how to find information is not the same as knowing what one can or should do with it. The following are concerns about the use of databases in education:

- **Simplified access versus privacy** — Each of our names is listed, along with much of our personal information, on literally dozens of databases. This cataloging begins when we are born—even before we are named—when we appear on the hospital's patient database. Whenever we apply for credit cards, driver's licenses, or jobs, we enter still more databases. These information entities reside on computers that can communicate and exchange notes, so information in one database can be shared with many information systems. Education, like other systems in our society, has come to depend on ready access to these information sources. However, easy access to information about people long has been recognized as a threat to personal privacy. If information is easy to access, it may also be easy for unauthorized people to obtain and possibly misuse or for organizations to use in ways that violate basic human rights. As educators use information from school and district databases, they are responsible for safeguarding this private information and protecting it from unauthorized access.

This means making sure passwords remain secret and being sensitive to who is looking at screens or printouts containing personal student information.

- **Coping with information overload** — The recent calls for improved accountability in education have led to more data collection on student characteristics and achievement. However, the sheer amount of available information may make it difficult to locate and to use parts of. Before constructing student information databases, schools and school districts have to think carefully about how they want to use them. They also have to obtain or create database management systems that merge with their testing systems and that have tools to allow **disaggregation** or grouping of students by desired characteristics. These tools make it easier for teachers to identify groups of students that need special instruction and to evaluate the impact of certain kinds of instructional methods or materials.

Databases in the Classroom: Productivity and Teaching Strategies

Productivity strategies. Productivity uses of databases for teachers have not proven as popular as those with tools such as word processing have. Most teachers don't need to create their own management systems to keep inventories of classroom materials or records on student performance; they rely instead on systems in the main office for such vital information. Teachers use prepared databases much more widely than ever before, but they do not usually create them. Current uses of databases for productivity and record keeping include the following:

- **Inventorying and locating instructional resources** — Teachers can look up titles and descriptions of instructional resources in a database system to help them identify materials that meet certain instructional needs. If a school has a large collection of resources used by all of the teachers, the school's library/media center probably catalogs this collection in a database designed for this purpose.

- **Data mining for planning and reporting** — Student records information allows teachers to meet the needs of individual students in several ways. For example, a teacher might access information on student reading levels or learning problems in order to create appropriate instruction. Schools also use databases to create reports for accountability purposes. Locating information from databases in ways that reveal relationships among the data elements has come to be called *data mining*. This activity uses data to track achievement over time and to make appropriate plans for future instruction (Salpeter, 2004). Data mining involves pulling data together from several databases and plac-

Top Ten

Integration Strategies for the Basic Three Software Tools

The best kinds and uses of software tools such as word processing, spreadsheets, and databases depend on the content area and skills teachers need to address. The ten uses given here are among the most popular ones described in the literature.

1. **Sweet hypothesis testing** — Have students predict the average number of M&Ms or Skittles of each color in a package. Then count various packages and build a spreadsheet to display and chart the numbers and calculate averages.

2. **Paragraph coherence** — Show students how good paragraphs are put together by using word processing software to scramble sentences in a paragraph and having students use the copy–cut–paste feature to put the sentences in correct order.

3. **Process writing** — Have students use word processing software to do drafts of their compositions; have them email drafts to you, and send them corrections and suggestions in a different color type.

4. **Colorful writing** — Have students use the word processor's font color option to highlight and discuss various functions in compositions (e.g., topic sentences, emotion-evoking content, factual content, descriptive words and phrases).

5. **Elections concepts** — Use spreadsheet software to demonstrate how many ways a presidential candidate could win the popular vote but lose the electoral vote.

6. **Pizza problem solving** — Students use a spreadsheet to calculate the most cost-effective pizza purchases to serve various numbers of people.

7. **Presidential comparisons** — Use database software to build a database of U.S. presidents in order to compare characteristics such as an individual's background and experience before becoming president.

8. **Online surveys** — Show students how to do survey research by collecting data online and using a spreadsheet to receive and analyze it.

9. **Political cartoons** — Students use word processing and clip art to create political cartoons that illustrate various concepts and current events.

10. **Grave thoughts** — Have students collect birth–death date information from tombstones, enter it into a database, and query it to answer questions about life spans in various decades.

ing it in **data warehouses** or central collection points for collected data. Educators then use data analysis tools, report writers, and decision support tools to analyze data and compile summaries.

- **Using information on students to respond to questions or perform required tasks** — Teachers often are asked to supply personal information on students or to deal with situations relating to their personal needs, yet it is difficult to remember everything about dozens of students. For example, some students require special medication, and the teacher is responsible for reminding them to take it. Or a teacher might need to decide quickly whether a particular adult is authorized to take a child from the school. A school database containing this type of information enables the teacher to access it quickly.

- **Sending personalized letters to parents and others** — The capability to merge database information with a word processing document is convenient whenever a teacher wants to send personalized notes to parents or to the students themselves. The teacher has to create only one letter or note; the database program then takes care of the personalizing.

Instructional integration strategies for databases. When database software became available for microcomputers in the 1980s, instructional activities that made use of these tools quickly became popular. Thus, the literature reflects a variety of applications for databases. The heaviest use seems to be in social studies, but effective applications have been designed for topics in other content areas as well, from language arts to science.

- **Teaching research and study skills** — Skills in locating and organizing information to answer questions and learn new concepts have always been as fundamental as reading and writing skills. Students need good research and study skills not only for school assignments but also to help them learn on their own outside school. As the volume of information in our society increases, the need to learn how to locate important information quickly also grows. Before they owned computers, families bought reference tools such as a good dictionary and a set of encyclopedias so that children could do research for their school reports and other assignments. Today, these and other sources are stored on electronic media, and students need to know how to do computer searches of these references. Many database activities are designed to instruct students in these kinds of searches. Database exercises help students realize how many organizations store data and provide them with practice in looking for information in various sources. These skills are useful across all content areas.

- **Teaching organization skills** — Students need to understand concepts related to handling information. To solve problems, they must locate the right information and organize it in such a way that they can draw relationships between isolated elements. One way to teach these skills is to have students develop and use their own databases; many examples of this kind of activity have been reported. Even very young students can learn about organizing information by creating databases of information about themselves, including birth dates, heights, weights, eye colors, pets, and parents' names. They can then do simple searches of their databases to summarize information about the members of their class. These kinds of activities

help students understand what information is and how to use it. In later grades, they can design and create databases related to areas of study. For example, a class might create a database of descriptive information on candidates running for office in their state or in a national election.

- **Understanding the power of information "pictures"** — Students need to be able to do their own data mining, and to do that, they need to understand the persuasive power of information organized into databases. Learning to use a database can help students recognize how the organization of data can reveal new ideas and concepts. Sometimes a database can generate information "pictures" or relationships among bits of information that may not be visible in any other way. Although these pictures may or may not be completely accurate, many decisions are based on them. For example, the U.S. government uses information databases on those who have been convicted of past income tax offenses to generate descriptive profiles of people who may be likely to try to defraud the government in the future. Students can learn to use database information to generate these types of pictures.

- **Posing and testing hypotheses** — Many problem-solving activities involve asking questions and locating information to answer them. Using databases is an ideal way to teach and provide practice with this kind of problem solving. Students can either research prepared databases full of information related to a content area, or they can create their own databases, which is not as common nowadays. Either way, these activities encourage them to look for information that will support or refute a position. In lower grades, the teacher may pose the question and assign students to search databases to answer it. Later, the activity may call for students to both pose and answer appropriate questions. For example, the teacher may ask students to address popular beliefs concerning artistic or gifted people. The students formulate questions, form debate teams, and design searches of databases on famous people to support their positions. (See Technology Integration Lesson 4.5.)

- **Searching for information during research** — Much of the world's information is stored in databases, and these "information banks" are becoming more available to students and other nontechnical people for everyday use. As they develop their skills in locating and analyzing information during research, students need practice in using standard searching procedures to locate information in databases. (See Technology Integration Lesson 4.6.)

Technology Integration Lesson 4.5

Using Databases to Pose and Test Hypotheses

Title: A Nutrition Database

Grade Level: 5 through 12

Content Area/Topic: Science and Health

NETS for Students: Standards 3 (Research and Information Fluency) and 4 (Critical Thinking, Problem Solving, and Decision Making)

Description of Standards Applications: This integration lesson offers students the opportunity to learn how to ask good, scientific questions and to test possible answers to them by analyzing available data.

Instruction: Show students how to build a database of the nutritional elements of various foods. (See example below.) They can derive their data from another, larger nutrition database, such as the one at the U.S. Department of Agriculture website (http://fnic.nal.usda.gov). Once the database is set up, demonstrate its use and lead students to ask questions such as "Which food has the most protein?" Show them that, to do this, they must divide the Protein field by the Weight field and create a new field to hold the result. They do this as a whole class and examine the result. Then assign small groups to create other questions and the procedures to answer them using the database.

Assessment: Grade students with a checklist of required activities, with points assigned to each one.

Protein Calculation : Select Query

Food Name	Weight	Common Measure	Fat	Calories	Protein	Calcium	Vitamin C	Protein Per Gram
egg	33.4	1 large egg	0.000	16.70	3.514	2.004	0.000	0.105209580838323
orange	131.0	1 orange	0.157	61.57	1.231	52.400	69.692	0.009396946564886
orange juice	248.0	1 cup	0.496	111.60	1.736	27.280	124.000	0.007
hamburger (fast food)	106.0	1 sandwich	9.773	272.42	12.317	126.140	2.226	0.116198113207547
fried chicken (fast food, white meat)	163.0	2 pieces	29.519	493.89	35.713	60.310	0.000	0.219096159509202
milk (whole)	244.0	1 cup	8.150	148.84	8.028	290.360	2.196	0.032901639344262
milk (2%)	244.0	1 cup	4.665	122.00	8.125	297.680	2.440	0.033299180327869
apple	138.0	1 apple	0.497	81.42	0.262	9.660	7.866	0.001898550724638
broccoli	88.0	1 cup	0.308	24.64	2.622	42.240	82.016	0.0297954545455
chocolate chip cookie	10.0	1 medium cookie	2.260	48.10	0.540	2.500	0.000	0.054
	0.0		0.000	0.00	0.000	0.000	0.000	

Record: [◄◄] [◄] 1 [►] [►►][►*] of 10

Source: From "Q&A with Microsoft Access" by David M. Marcovitz (2002), as appeared in *Learning and Leading with Technology.* Reprinted by permission of David M. Marcovitz.

Teaching Database Skills: Recommended Skills and Activities

Unlike word processing and spreadsheet tools, learning to use database features is a key focus of using the software. It is only by seeing how databases work that students are able to understand their power and usefulness. If students are not able to use the online tutorials that are available to teach spreadsheet software, teachers can use the strategies outlined in Table 4.9. Even when teaching these advanced concepts, teachers may choose to introduce more complex functions and features on an as-needed basis, depending on the needs of the lesson.

A Summary of Software Tool Integration Strategies

Software tools are increasingly popular, in part because they address both productivity and instructional needs and in part because they can support either directed or constructivist learning activities. Their primary benefits to instruction are to reduce the labor involved in preparing student products and to remove logistical barriers to learning. For a summary of all software tool uses discussed in this chapter matched to directed and constructivist integration strategies, see the matrix in Table 4.10.

Technology Integration Lesson 4.6

Using Online Databases to Search for Information During Research

Title: Hunting for Celestial Bodies **Grade Level:** 6 and up
Content Area/Topic: Astronomy

NETS for Students: Standard 4 (Critical Thinking, Problem Solving, and Decision Making)

Description of Standards Applications: This integration lesson offers students the opportunity to investigate the night's sky by analyzing the *Starry Night* database to compare what is known about celestial bodies to what may not be discovered yet. Throughout the history of astronomy, ordinary people have discovered new comets and asteroids. Now databases of existing celestial bodies are available to help people determine if they have identified a previously unnamed object in the sky.

Instruction: You can have your students choose an area of the night sky, download from the Internet two or more images taken on different evenings, and compare them to see if they have different objects in them. Students can then use a database such as *Starry Night* (a planetarium program available from Sienna Software) to see if the "new" objects are already identified. If they are not, students can contact astronomers to find out if they have discovered a new nova, asteroid, or comet.

Assessment: Grade students with a checklist of required activities with points assigned to each one.

Source: Erickson, D. (1999). Hunting for asteroids, comets, and novas. *Learning and Leading with Technology, 26*(6), 22–24.

Interactive Summary

The following is a summary of the main points covered in this chapter.

1. **Overview of the "Basic Three"** — Three software tools that are considered basic educational resources are:

   - **Word processing** — Programs that allow people to produce typed documents on a computer screen. Benefits of using them include saving time, improving document appearance, and allowing easy exchange of work.

   - **Spreadsheets** — Programs designed to organize and manipulate numerical data. Benefits of using them include saving time, organizing displays of information, and increasing motivation to work with mathematics.

   - **Databases** — Programs that allow users to store, organize, and manipulate information, including both text and numerical data. Benefits of using them include reducing data redundancy (the number of places data must be stored), saving time locating and/or updating important information, allowing comparisons of information through searches across files, and revealing relationships among data.

2. **Productivity applications for the three basic software tools** — These include:

   - **For word processing** — Creating handouts or other instructional materials, lesson plans and notes, reports, forms, letters to parents or students, flyers, and newsletters

   - **For spreadsheets** — Keeping club and classroom budgets, preparing performance checklists, and keeping gradebooks

   - **For databases** — Inventorying and locating instructional resources, data mining for planning and reporting, using information on students to respond to questions or perform required tasks, and sending personalized letters to parents and others.

TABLE 4.9 Tips on Teaching Databases
(Also see links to tutorials at http://www.internet4classrooms.com/on-line2.htm)

Suggested Steps	Tasks Under Each Step
Step 1—Prepare for teaching.	**Arrange for:** • A big screen or projection system • A disk for each group of students with sample file(s) copied onto the disks OR access to an online database • One computer per student group • Alternative keyboards or other adaptive devices for students with disabilities. **Create or obtain:** • Handouts or wall posters on database features and how to use Boolean operations to complete searches.
Step 2—Demonstrate the basics.	**Using a big screen or projection system, show how to:** • Open a database file from disk or go to an online database • Show various views of the data (e.g., by records or by fields in one record). **Point out a common error:** • Confusing a database file with a spreadsheet file, because they look similar. **Then demonstrate:** • How data can be sorted by various fields • How to use keywords and criteria to locate items of information from a database that match them • **Optional:** Show how to structure Boolean searches to solve problems (e.g., create a diagram or picture that displays the expected results) • **Optional:** Point out common errors with Boolean searches (e.g., using AND and OR combinations without appropriate parentheses).
Step 3—Assign individual practice.	**Give student groups a sample database file on disk or online and have them:** • Do a series of searches to locate items of information and/or to answer a set of questions.
Step 4—Demonstrate database creation and use.	**Discuss with students how to:** • Think through how to create a database to meet a certain need • Decide on how to structure it according to records • Decide on fields to include. **Using a big screen or projection system, show how to:** • Add fields to create the database • Add records of information to the database • **Optional:** How to create a report after a search • **Optional:** How to do calculation functions.
Step 5—Assign more individual practice.	**Have students:** • Create their own database to meet a given need • Enter new data into the structure • Do searches to answer questions • **Optional:** Enter graphics and URLs • **Optional:** Create a report based on the data. Monitor students as they work, and give individual help as needed.

TABLE 4.10 Software Tool Technology Integration Strategies for Directed, Constructivist, or Either Models

Integration Strategies for Basic Software Tools: Word Processing, Spreadsheets, or Databases	Directed Models				Constructivist Models				Either Model			
	Remedy identified weaknesses or skill deficits	Promote skill fluency or automaticity	Provide efficient, self-paced instruction	Support self-paced review of concepts	Foster creative problem solving and metacognition	Build mental models, increase knowledge transfer	Foster group cooperation	Allow for multiple intelligences	Generate motivation to learn	Optimize scarce personnel and material resources	Remove logistical hurdles to learning	Develop information literacy and visual literacy skills
Word Processing — Supporting the learning of writing processes									X		X	
Using a dynamic group process approach							X		X		X	
Assigning individual language, writing, and reading exercises		X							X		X	
Encouraging writing through the curriculum									X		X	
Spreadsheets — Making possible visual teaching demonstrations					X	X			X		X	
Supporting student products											X	
Supporting mathematical and "what if" problem solving					X	X					X	
Storing and analyzing data											X	
Projecting grades					X						X	
Databases — Teaching research and study skills							X		X			X
Teaching organization skills					X	X					X	X
Understanding the power of information "pictures"					X	X						
Posing and testing hypotheses					X	X	X				X	
Searching for information during research											X	X

3. **Teaching and learning tasks that each kind of tool can support —**

- **For word processing** — Supporting the learning of writing processes; using a dynamic group process approach; assigning individual language, writing, and reading exercises; and encouraging writing through the curriculum

- **For spreadsheets** — Making possible visual teaching demonstrations, supporting student products, sup-

porting mathematical and "what if" problem solving, storing and analyzing data, and projecting grades

- **For databases** — Teaching research and study skills, teaching organization skills, understanding the power of information "pictures," posing and testing hypotheses, and searching for information during research.

Key Terms

- cell
- computer platforms
- data mining
- data warehouses
- databases
- disaggregation

- field
- files
- formulas
- Google Docs
- integrated packages
- open-source software

- record
- software suites
- spreadsheets
- worksheets

Web-Enrichment Activities

1. **Lesson activities for software tools** — Visit the Lesson Plans website at http://www.lessonplanspage .com, and search for lesson plans for "word processing," "spreadsheet" and "database."

2. **Explore software options for education** — Go to Microsoft Education at http://www.microsoft.com/ education, and explore the different software tutorials available. Then go to http://www.apple.com/iwork/, and check out the applications available from Apple Education. Finally, visit OpenOffice at http://www .OpenOffice.org, and explore the open-source software available. After examining the various applications on all three sites, what are some creative ways you might integrate word processing, spreadsheets, and databases into a classroom activity?

Go to MyEducationLab to complete the following exercises.

Building Teaching Skills Select the topic "Hardware," and go to the "Building Teaching Skills and Dispositions" section. Access the activity "Using Essential Learning Tools in the Classroom" and complete the full activity.

Tutorials Select the topic "Software" and access the practical tutorial and skill-building activity titled "Excel for PC, Basics." Use the tutorial to learn how to create a spreadsheet. This skill will be reviewed again in the Technology Integration Workshop.

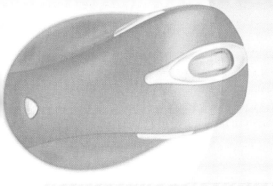

Technology Integration Workshop

The TIP Model in Action

Read each of the following scenarios related to implementing the TIP Model, and answer the questions that follow each one based on your Chapter 4 reading and activities.

TIP MODEL SCENARIO #1   Mr. Gilbert wanted to demonstrate various principles of probability to his junior high advanced math students and then to let them test hypotheses on data sets to show the principles in action. However, the exercises he had them do required a series of calculations on a set of numbers. It took the students a long time to do these calculations with a calculator because they had to keep reentering the numbers and they made a lot of entry errors. All the time spent on entering figures and correcting errors made it difficult for them to focus on the hypothesis testing.

   1.1 What software tool would you recommend Mr. Gilbert use to address this problem?

   1.2 What would be the relative advantage of using this software tool?

   1.3 Would it be better to have the students work individually or in groups to do the exercises? How would you arrange the computer systems to carry out this strategy?

TIP MODEL SCENARIO #2   Mr. Hern has his class work in small groups to create a short story. As a whole class, they discuss the plot and characters; then each group writes a part of the story. The groups exchange sections and critique each other's work. Then they do a final version. After the draft is complete, they post the story on the school's web server along with stories posted from past classes.

   2.1 What would be the relative advantages for Mr. Hern's students of using word processing for their drafts instead of doing typed or handwritten drafts?

   2.2 What would be the relative advantages of posting the story on the Internet when it is completed?

   2.3 What outcomes would Mr. Hern probably want to assess in addition to the quality of writing in the final product? Suggest a way to carry out this assessment.

TIP MODEL SCENARIO #3   Ms. Sanchez is a high school AP composition teacher. She wants her students to do more spelling and grammar proofreading of their own written work and to make required revisions on their papers before they turn them in to her for grading. She feels word processing features will help them learn this habit, so she introduces the software to them in class. Her students have never used word processing before, but she feels AP students can learn word processing on their own. She does a demonstration of word processing features on Monday and then tells the students to go to the computer lab for the next two class periods, do a word-processed paper, and turn it in to her at the end of the class period on Wednesday. When she grades the papers, she realizes they are far worse than usual. Not only are the ideas not well developed, but the spelling and grammar are worse as well.

   3.1 What about Ms. Sanchez's teaching sequence might explain why word processing did not provide the benefit she expected?

   3.2 Why do you think the ideas in the student papers were not as well developed as usual?

   3.3 What are two things you would suggest she do differently if she tries this again?

TIP MODEL SCENARIO #4   Mr. Borodin was trying to show his teenage students in the business education program how they could figure out quickly how much car they could buy with the money they had. He wanted to show them the relationship among the down payment, interest rate, and length of the loan and how this all affected monthly payments and the total they would spend on the car by the end of the loan period. However, he wanted them to be able to do the calculations quickly so they could focus on the underlying math concepts.

   4.1 What technology-based tool could Mr. Borodin use to help address this problem?

   4.2 What would be the relative advantage of using this strategy?

   4.3 Describe the steps you might use to carry out a simple lesson using this strategy.

TIP MODEL SCENARIO #5   Mr. David wants his students to compare the types of bills passed in each of several categories (e.g., technology, human rights) during the last five U.S. presidencies and then to draw conclusions about the bills' impact in each administration. His students can get all the information they need on bills from legislative websites he knows. However, he feels that compiling the information is not enough. He needs a way for his students to compare the features of the bills in ways that will let them ask questions about them, discover relationships between them, and assess the kind of impact they achieved (e.g., the number of people they affected).

5.1 What kind of software tool could Mr. David use to assist with organizing the information for this project?

5.2 Would this kind of work best be done individually or in small groups? What might be a good way to organize this work in a classroom with a three-computer workstation?

5.3 In what ways might he assess students' work on such a project?

TIE into Practice: Technology Integration Examples

The Technology Integration Example that opened this chapter (*Can You Afford Your Dream Car?*) showed how a teacher might use a spreadsheet to help students analyze all the decision variables in making a large purchase. With the knowledge you have gained from Chapter 4, do the following with this example:

1. Ms. Kiley created a spreadsheet like the one shown here for students to use to calculate loan amount, term, and payment for a car purchase. Having completed the Excel basic tutorial, create this spreadsheet.

2. Answer the following questions about the *Dream Car* example:
   - Phase 2: How did a spreadsheet project like this offer relative advantage in comparison with other ways of teaching students about money management?
   - Phase 3: Ms. Kiley created a rubric to assess the quality and accuracy of the final report students did. What kinds of elements would you assess in such a rubric?
   - Phase 4: Ms. Kiley chose to have students work individually on their spreadsheets. What might be some benefits of having students work in groups, rather than individually, on this project?
   - Phase 5: Given that Ms. Kiley demonstrated the use of the spreadsheet in the classroom, why did she take the trouble to check with each student individually as they worked in the lab to make sure they knew how to use it?

Buying a Car	
Car Price	$20,000.00
Down Payment	200
Loan Amount	19,800
Interest Rate	8%
Months	48
Payments	$483.38
Total Paid	$23,202.04
Additional Paid	$3,402.04

- Phase 6: What strategies might Ms. Kiley use to improve the quality of students' final reports? (*Hint*: Consider interdisciplinary projects with other teachers and having students use tools to facilitate writing their reports.)

3. What NETS for Students skills would students learn by doing the *Dream Car* project? (See the front of the book for a list of NETS for Students.)

Technology Integration Lesson Planning

Complete the following exercise using sample lesson plans found on MyEducationLab.

1. Locate lesson ideas — MyEducationLab has several examples of lessons that use word processing, spreadsheet, and database software. Go to MyEducationLab and select the topic "Instructional Planning." Under "Lesson Plans," review the following example integration lessons and choose two:
   - A Cross-Age Collaborative Electronic Book Project
   - Modeling and Scaling with Spreadsheets
   - A Database Project with Rocks
   - Using Databases, Spreadsheets, and Word Processing to Study Genetics
   - A Class Literary Paper
   - Activities for Gifted Students: Grades 4–5

2. Evaluate the lessons — Use the *Evaluation Checklist for a Technology-Integrated Lesson* (located on MyEducationLab under the topic "Instructional Planning") to evaluate each of these lessons.

3. Modify a lesson — Select one of the lesson ideas and adapt its strategies to meet a need in your own content area. You may choose to use the same approach in the original or adapt it to meet your needs.

4. Add descriptors — Create descriptors for your new lesson like those found within the sample lessons (e.g., grade level, content and topic areas, technologies used, relative advantage, objectives, NETS standards).

5. Save your new lesson — Save your modified lesson with all its descriptors.

For Your Teaching Portfolio

For this chapter's contribution to your teaching portfolio, add the following products you created in the Technology Integration Workshop:
- The spreadsheet you created for the *Dream Car* project.
- The evaluations you did using the *Evaluation Checklist for a Technology-Integrated Lesson*.
- The new lesson plan you developed.

Chapter 5
Teaching with Software Tools: Beyond the Basic Programs

Computers are useless. They can only give you answers.

Pablo Picasso, Spanish Cubist painter (1881–1973)

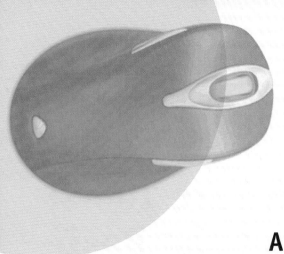

Technology Integration Example

A Desktop-Published Literary Anthology

Based on: Scharf, E. and Cramer, J. (2002). Desktop poetry project. *Learning and Leading with Technology, 29*(6), 28–31, 50–51.

Grade Level: Middle to high school • Content Area/Topic: Language arts, poetry • Length of Time: Year-long project

Phases 1 and 2: Assess technological pedagogical content knowledge; Determine relative advantage

Mr. Mortenson was the English teacher in charge of compiling the school's annual eighth-grade literary anthology. It always took a lot of work to prepare the copy for the printing company to format and typeset; that meant Mr. Mortenson had to limit the number of entries in order to keep the size of the task manageable. However, he felt that it would motivate more students to do their best work if everyone knew at least one of their pieces would be included. An English teacher in another school told him how they prepared their literary anthology using desktop publishing software called Adobe *PageMaker*. They were even able to add graphics and page numbering themselves, which meant that all the printing company had to do was print copies. Mr. Mortenson discussed the use of *PageMaker* with the English teachers in his school, and they were enthusiastic about it. They decided that all of the eighth-grade classes would prepare word-processed drafts of poetry and short stories throughout the first part of the year and that the teachers would upload students' drafts to the school's network server so all students could see them. The computer applications teacher would prepare a desktop-published format for the pages, and all classes would use the format to finalize their own pages.

The teachers decided that they would each tell their students about the anthology at the beginning of the school year and that they then would teach them the various literary forms in a directed way (e.g., showing examples, pointing out structure and devices, taking tests). For each form, each student would prepare a draft and work on refining it. In the spring, teachers would ask students to decide on what they considered to be their best work in each category, with the assurance that at least one item from each student would be published. Finally, each class would help prepare the desktop-published pages.

Prior to beginning the project, however, Mr. Mortenson realized he needed to assess his technological pedagogical content knowledge (TPACK) so that he could evaluate his strengths and weaknesses and understand where he might locate himself within the TPACK model. He realized that his knowledge of the content he was teaching was extremely strong but that his knowledge of the technology and the pedagogy related to using the technology in the classroom was very weak. Thus, he decided he would work with his fellow English teacher who had used Adobe *PageMaker* in the classroom to understand the program and more importantly, how to use it in the classroom for desktop publishing anthologies.

Phase 3: Decide on objectives and assessments

To make sure all students were clear on the expectations for their work, Mr. Mortenson worked with the other English teachers to create common objectives and assessment methods to measure students' knowledge of each literary form and to evaluate the quality of their written products. The outcomes, objectives, and assessments they decided on were as follows:

- **Outcome:** Identify poetry forms. **Objective:** Each student has to identify at least two examples of each poetry form they studied. **Assessment:** A test consisting of a set of example poems for students to label.

- **Outcome:** Identify short story components and language devices. **Objective:** Each student has to identify structural components (e.g., plot, characters, theme) of any given short story and give at least one example of language devices (e.g., metaphor and simile) it used. **Assessment:** A take-home test to read an assigned short story and complete a worksheet identifying the structural components and language devices.

- **Outcome:** Create a poem of each type. **Objective:** Each student writes a poem in the correct form for each genre. **Assessment:** Rubric on poem structure and creativity.

- **Outcome:** Create a short story. **Objective:** At least 90% of the students achieve a rubric score of 15/20 on a short story they create and revise based on teacher feedback. **Assessment:** Rubric on short story structure, required revisions, and creativity.

- **Outcome:** Create desktop-published pages. **Objective:** Students work in pairs to complete all assigned tasks required to format their anthology entries onto predesigned page formats. **Assessment:** Checklist of required tasks.

Phase 4: Design integration strategies

So that they could plan their classroom time, the teachers worked with Mr. Mortenson to design a timeline and sequence for completing the work on the anthology by late spring. They decided on the following:

- **September–February:** In their classes, English teachers introduce the concept of an anthology and show examples from another school, review the literary forms to be covered, have students take tests on structures, and have students write their word-processed drafts. Computer applications classes submit designs for anthology pages as a class project and vote on which one to adopt.
- **March:** Students in all English classes finish their revisions and decide on which work they want to include in the anthology. The computer applications teacher shows English teachers how to paste students' word-processed drafts into the desktop-published pages.
- **April:** English teachers introduce the desktop-publishing software to the students in the computer lab and show them how to change fonts, styles, sizes, and colors to communicate meaning. Students also learn how to insert clip art and other graphics to illustrate their work. After completing small practice projects, students work in pairs in the lab to enter their poems and stories into the desktop-published pages. As they complete their pages, the teachers upload them to the school's server.
- **First 2 weeks in May:** Mr. Mortenson downloads the pages and compiles the anthology. He works with a committee consisting of students from the computer applications classes, the computer applications teacher, and one other English teacher.
- **Last 2 weeks in May:** The printing company produces the copies in time for teachers to distribute during the final week of classes.

Phase 5: Prepare the instructional environment

Mr. Mortenson and the computer applications teacher collaborated to prepare everything the teachers and students would need to do their work. They did the following:

- **Software copies:** Mr. Mortenson worked with the computer applications teacher to make sure the computer lab had copies of Adobe *PageMaker* on each computer. They obtained some wall charts of *PageMaker* shortcuts and hung the charts in the computer lab. Students used these as reminders of how to do common functions.
- **Example anthologies:** Mr. Mortenson obtained copies of past desktop-published anthologies for the students to review.
- **Software skills:** After the computer applications teacher gave a workshop to the English teachers on how to use the *PageMaker* pages her classes had designed, Mr. Mortenson asked her to be available to answer teachers' questions about *PageMaker*. He also made sure teachers knew he was always available to discuss ideas for design items to include in the anthology.
- **Computer scheduling:** The computer applications teacher helped the teachers determine how much time their students would need to complete their work and assisted them with scheduling time in the computer lab.

Phase 6: Evaluate and revise

At the end of the school year, Mr. Mortenson and the other teachers reviewed the work on the anthology and agreed it had been a success. Teachers, administrators, students, and parents were thrilled with the completed anthology, and English teachers reported that students were much more motivated than they had been in previous years. Rubric grades reflected generally good progress in students' writing skills. They all agreed that they could use more time in the computer lab with the desktop-publishing software. Although students had revised their work prior to entering the lab, the teachers found that even more revision went on after students started seeing each other's work and became more motivated to show off their best work. Teachers asked if they could get *PageMaker* software for their classroom workstations so that more revision work could go on there, and Mr. Mortenson and the computer applications teacher agreed to request it.

Objectives

After reading this chapter and completing the learning activities for it, you should be able to:

1. Use correct terminology to identify features and capabilities of several software tools.

2. Describe teaching and learning tasks for both teachers and students that each kind of tool can support.

3. Identify applications for software tools that educators would find valuable in making their work more efficient and productive.

4. Develop lesson activities that integrate the functions and capabilities of each of several software tools.

Introduction to Other Software Support Tools

Chapter 4 discussed three of the most widely used software support tools: word processing, spreadsheet, and database programs. These have come to be viewed as the "basic three." However, many other software tools are available for supporting teachers' and students' work. These tools vary greatly in their purposes, the kinds of benefits they offer, and their utility for teachers.

Each software tool described in this chapter has unique and powerful features, but each may require additional classroom resources and time to learn and to implement within the classroom. Teachers should choose them for the qualities and benefits they bring to the classroom rather than simply because they are available. Depending on the capabilities of the particular tool and the needs of the situa-

tion, a software support tool can offer the same kinds of benefits described for the basic tools in Chapter 4:

- Improved efficiency and productivity
- Improved appearance of product
- Better accuracy and timeliness of information
- More support for interaction and sharing.

The tools described in this chapter range in importance from nearly essential to "nice to have," and in function from presenting instruction to supporting background tasks that make a classroom run smoothly. As you will see throughout this chapter, Picasso was one of the best painters of all time, but he was not correct when it came to computers. Although it is great that computers can give answers, they can do much more than that. They can engage, motivate, and extend the way we think, act, and feel.

TABLE 5.1 Overview of Software Tool Categories

Tool Category	Software Tools	Purposes and Benefits
Materials generators	• Desktop publishing software • Test generators and test item banks • Worksheet and puzzle generators • IEP generators • Graphic document makers • PDF and forms makers	Allow creation and use of documents, tests, exercises, IEPs, certificates, PDFs, and forms.
Data collection and analysis tools	• Electronic gradebooks • Statistical packages • Student management systems • Online and computer-based testing systems • Student response systems	Collect data from students; track progress and support decision making; analyze data from experiments and research.
Graphics tools	• Draw/paint programs • Image editing software • Charting/graphing software • Clip art, animation, sound, and font collections	Illustrate documents and web pages; create visual data summaries.
Planning and organizing tools	• Outlining and concept mapping software • Lesson planning software • Scheduling and time management tools	Help organize ideas for writing; help organize, plan, and schedule activities.
Research and reference tools	• Electronic encyclopedias • Electronic atlases and mapping tools • Electronic dictionaries and thesauruses	Help students research assigned topics.
Content-area tools	• CAD systems • MIDI tools: music editors and sequencers • Reading tools • MBLs/CBLs • GPS and GIS systems	Support tasks specific to content areas such as technology education, music, reading, science, math, geography, and social studies.

Types of Software Support Tools

This chapter describes six general categories of software support tools. Table 5.1 provides examples of software products under each of the following categories:

- **Materials generators** — Help teachers and students produce instructional materials.
- **Data collection and analysis tools** — Help teachers collect and organize information that indicates student progress.
- **Graphics tools** — Allow manipulation of images to illustrate documents and web pages.
- **Planning and organizing tools** — Help teachers and students conceptualize, organize, and communicate their ideas.
- **Research and reference tools** — Let students look up information in electronic versions of encyclopedias, atlases, and dictionaries.
- **Content-area tools** — Support teaching and learning activities in various content areas.

Software Support Tools Covered in Other Chapters: Multimedia, Web, and Video Tools

The purpose of this chapter is to provide a comprehensive overview of software tools used in education, but two categories of tools are addressed in other parts of this textbook. Authoring software and other software tools (e.g., presentation software such as *PowerPoint* and video development tools such as *iMovie* and *FinalCut Pro*) associated with developing multimedia and hypermedia products are described in Chapter 6. Software tools used with distance learning and the Internet, either to develop materials for use on the Internet or to allow people to use the Internet, are covered in Chapter 7.

Recent Developments in Software Support Tools

Although these tools have been in existence for many years, they are constantly being updated with new features and capabilities. Most of the following recent developments have made these tools even more useful in the classroom.

- **Netbooks, PDAs, and Cell Phones** — As with the basic three software tools, many other tools are now available on Netbooks, personal digital assistants (PDAs), handheld computers, and cell phones. This portable format increases accessibility and flexibility of use for both teachers and students. Since these basic software tools were transferred to a more portable format, the portable technologies have become even more popular. Since PDA technology has also meshed with the cell phone industry, such as the Palm Treo and Pre and Apple iPhone, schools are researching how these technologies can be used, especially now that many students have access to them and there are literally thousands of software applications that are being developed for the Treo and the iPhone.

- **Web-connectivity features** — All of the basic tools, like many tools described in other chapters, now allow "live" web page links, interactive Flash programs, movies, and audio to be inserted in documents, and most allow documents to be exported to be viewed on the Internet. This makes it even easier to connect documents to Internet resources that embellish or add to the document's content. For example, when students are developing a concept map, they can add photos, sounds, and links to support documents outside of the concept map.

- **Software suites** — Increasingly, software tools are being packaged as software suites in order to combine their capabilities and make them easier to use together. One of the most popular of the software tool suites is desktop publishing software, which is being packaged with graphic software tools that work well with it and allow faster, more full-featured design of print or web pages. For example, Adobe's *Creative Suite* combines high-end desktop publishing software (*Adobe InDesign*) with *Adobe Photoshop* (image editor), *Adobe Illustrator* (drawing software), *Adobe Dreamweaver* (web page editor), *Adobe Flash* (web application software), and *Adobe Acrobat* (portable document software).

Teachers and students alike use PDAs for organizing and communicating, as well as to share information through special broadcasts like podcasts.

TABLE 5.2 Overview of Materials Generator Software Tools

Software Tools	Sample Products	Description/Sample Classroom Uses
Desktop publishing software	• Adobe: *InDesign*, and *PageMaker* http://www.adobe.com/ • Microsoft *Publisher* http://www.microsoft.com/ • *Quark Express* http://www.quark.com/	Students create their own letterhead; brochures, flyers/posters, newsletters, newspapers, and books.
Test generators and rubric generators	• *Exam View Learning Series* http://www.fscreations.com/learningseries.php • Exam View Assessment Suite http://www.fscreations.com/examview.php • *Test Generator* http://www.testshop.com • *Test Creator* http://www.centronsoftware.com • *Easy Test Maker* http://www.easytestmaker.com/ • *RubricBuilder* http://landmark-project.com/rubric_builder/index.php • *RubiStar* http://rubistar.4teachers.org • *Rubric Generator* http://teach-nology.com/web_tools/rubrics/general/	Teachers create test item banks and generate various versions of tests from them; they can administer tests online.
Worksheet and puzzle generators	• *Puzzlemaker* http://puzzlemaker.discoveryeducation.com/ • *Worksheet Generator* http://school.discoveryeducation.com/ teachingtools/worksheetgenerator/ • Centron *Crossword Puzzle Maker* http://www.centronsoftware.com/ • Teach-nology *Crossword Puzzle Maker* http://www.teach-nology.com/web_tools/crossword/	Teachers produce exercises and games for student skill practice.
IEP generators	• SchoolMAX *Enterprise* http://www.schoolmax.net/ • *IEP Online* http://www.xperts.com/products/educational-product-suite/iep-online.aspx • *EasyIEP* http://www.publicconsultinggroup.com/education/ Technology/EasyIEP/	Teachers create individualized education programs (IEPs) for special education students.
Graphic document makers	• *Printshop 23 Deluxe* http://www.broderbund.com • Teach-nology *Certificate Maker* http://www.teach-nology.com/web_tools/certificates/ • *Smart Draw* http://www.smartdraw.com	Teachers and students create awards, recognitions, flyers, cards, and other decorated documents.
PDF and forms makers	• *Adobe Acrobat* http://www.adobe.com • *PDF Maker Pilot* http://www.colorpilot.com/pdfmaker.html • *Form Artist* http://www.quask.com/survey/products.asp	Teachers and students create PDF files to send formatted documents, and documents and web pages with forms that can be filled in on-screen.

Using Materials Generators

Materials generators include desktop publishing software, test generators and rubric generators, worksheet and puzzle generators, IEP generators, graphic document makers, and PDF and forms makers. A summary of these, with sample products and classroom uses, is shown in Table 5.2.

Desktop Publishing Software

It is perhaps ironic that one of the most useful and widely used of the technology tools is one that communicates information in a traditional medium: the printed page. By allowing teachers and students to design elaborate printed products, however, desktop publishing tools give them the important advantage of complete control over a potentially powerful form of communication. This control over the form and appearance of the printed page is the defining quality of **desktop publishing**, a term coined in 1984 by Paul Brainerd, founder of the Aldus Corporation (Norvelle, 1992), to mean using a combination of software, microcomputers, and printers to allow individuals to be their own publishers.

Desktop publishing versus desktop publishing software. It is possible to do desktop publishing with word processing software. Just as with desktop publishing, word processing allows users to mix text and graphics on each page. However, desktop publishing software offers more control over the design and production of a document. You can use any available word processing software package to create most of the desktop publishing products you want to produce in a school environment (e.g., classroom brochures and newsletters). The more advanced layout features offered by desktop publishing software (e.g., elaborate layering of text and graphics elements) are needed only if you are teaching students how to design and lay out large, complex documents such as newspapers and books.

From a technical standpoint, the primary difference between word processing software and desktop publishing tools is that the latter are designed to create documents as separate pages that are then linked together; the user clicks on icons for each page, and only one page or facing pages display. Word processing "flows" pages in a continuous stream through a document; the user scrolls down to view pages in the document. Because desktop publishing software allows pages to be viewed as separate units, it provides more flexibility with the placement and formats of both text and graphics on individual pages. Word processing is designed to flow text from page to page as it is typed in. Text boxes can be created with word processing software, but they are harder to manage.

Making the most of desktop publishing software: Skills and resources. Like other technology tools, desktop publishing is most effective if the user knows something about the activity before applying the tool. Designing effective print communications is an entire field of expertise in itself with its own degree programs. Graduates frequently are in high demand in business and industry. As Knupfer and McIsaac (1989) observe, many aspects of page design can influence reading speed and comprehension. They describe four different categories of variables that have been researched: graphic design, instructional text design, instructional graphics, and computer screen design. Although the last category focuses on reading from a computer screen, Knupfer and McIsaac note that some of its features apply to both electronic and print-based research, including text density and uppercase versus lowercase type.

However, even with this in mind, teachers and students need not be professional designers to create useful desktop publishing products, and their skills will improve with practice. According to Parker (1989) and Rose (1988), desktop publishing products have greater impact and communicate more clearly if they reflect some fairly simple design criteria. Beginners may want to use the suggestions in the Top Ten Rules for Effective Desktop Publishing feature.

Example classroom applications. Desktop publishing software can be used for many of the same classroom activities and products as word processing software. Desktop publishing is the tool of choice, however, to produce elaborate, graphic-oriented documents (e.g., flyers and posters, brochures, newsletters and magazines, and books and booklets), and teachers can structure some highly motivating classroom projects around these products. Hermann (1988), McCarthy (1988), Newman (1988), Reissman (2000), and Willinsky and Bradley (1990) have reported instructional benefits for desktop publishing that include increases in children's self-esteem when they publish their own work, heightened interest in writing and motivation to write for audiences outside the classroom, and improved learning through small group collaboration. Here is a list of common classroom applications and ideas for implementing them:

- **Practice in grammar, spelling, and communication** — The activity of creating a flyer or brochure can become an opportunity to learn about designing attractive and interesting communications and to apply language usage skills.

- **Methods of reporting research findings** — Popular examples of using desktop publishing projects to report on students' research include creating travel brochures that report on student exploration during field trips, descriptions of the local region, and creative descriptions of organizations or activities. Sometimes this type

Top Ten Rules for Effective Desktop Publishing

1. **Use a limited number of typefaces (fonts)** — Unusual typefaces can help direct the eye toward text, but too many different fonts on a page can be distracting, and some fancy fonts are difficult to read.

2. **Use different fonts for title and text** — To aid the reader, use a **serif typeface** (a font with small curves or "hands and feet" that extend from the ends of the letters) for text in the main body of the document. Use a **sans serif typeface,** a font without extensions, for titles and headlines.

3. **Use appropriate sizes for type** — Make the type large enough to assist the reader (e.g., younger readers usually need large point sizes), but not too large to dominate the page.

4. **Avoid overuse of type styles** — Breaking up text with too many style changes interferes with reading. Avoid excessive underlining, boldfacing, and italics.

5. **Match text and background colors** — Use white or yellow type on a black block to add drama. Avoid color combinations that can be difficult to read (e.g., orange on green or red on blue).

6. **Use visual cues** — Attract reader attention to important information on the page by using frames or boxes around text; bullets or arrows to designate important points; shading of the part of the page behind the important text; different text styles (e.g., boldface or italic type); and captions for pictures and diagrams.

7. **Use white space well** — There is a saying in advertising that "white space sells." Don't be afraid to leave areas in a document with nothing in them at all to help focus attention on areas that do contain information.

8. **Create and use graphics carefully** — Use pictures and designs to focus attention and convey information, but remember that too many elaborate pictures or graphic designs can be distracting.

9. **Avoid common text format errors** — Common desktop design pitfalls include using irregularly shaped text blocks and angled type, both of which are difficult to read (Parker, 1989).

10. **Avoid common text break errors** — Use desktop publishing software features to control for widows and orphans (leftover single words and phrases at the tops or bottoms of pages) and excessive hyphenation (Parker, 1989).

of activity represents the culmination of a large project such as a series of science experiments or a social studies research unit; sometimes it simply is a way for every student to contribute writing for a class project. All of these projects are highly motivational to students, and they attract "good press" for the teacher and the school.

• **Opportunities for creative works** — Even very young students are thrilled to produce and display their own personal books, which sometimes represent work produced over the course of a school year. Sometimes the books show creative works resulting from a competition; frequently, examples of students' best work are collected for a particular topic or time period. Students can sell their

Technology Integration Lesson 5.1

Encouraging Creative Language Projects with Desktop Publishing

Title: Desktop-Published Gifts

Grade Level: 5 through 9

Content Area/Topic: Language arts

NETS for Students: Standards 1 (Creativity and Innovation), 2 (Communication and Collaboration), 3 (Research and Information Fluency), 4 (Critical Thinking, Problem Solving, and Decision Making), 5 (Digital Citizenship), and 6 (Technology Operations and Concepts)

Description of Standards Applications: This integration lesson offers students the opportunity to use desktop publishing software to create gifts for people who have been a part of their life. Students research the gifts they would like to give to the recipients, creatively design and develop the gifts using desktop publishing software, and present them to the recipients describing how and why they were developed.

Instruction: Students begin by brainstorming a list of potential recipients. These can include professionals that help them throughout the year—for example, doctors, dentists, teachers, and scout troop leaders. The teacher shows some gifts created by students in previous classes: personalized stationery with individuals' names or "World's Greatest Mom" on it; business cards; coupon books with special services or favors the student could do for the recipients; magnets or key rings with photos; scrapbooks with a series of pictures telling about a special event. Students work in small design teams to decide on their gifts. After the gifts are completed, students present them to the class in a Priceless Gifts Showcase.

Assessment: Use a rubric to assess creativity and small group work.

Source: Reissman, R. (2000). Priceless gifts. *Learning and Leading with Technology, 28*(2), 28–31.

---

publications as a fund-raising activity, but this kind of project also reaps other benefits for students of all abilities. Teachers report that getting published increases students' pride in their work and makes them want to spend more time on it (Reissman, 2000; Scharf & Cramer, 2002).

The Technology Integration Example at the beginning of this chapter (*A Desktop-Published Literary Anthology*) is one example of a powerful desktop publishing project. See Technology Integration Lesson 5.1 for another good example.

Test Generators and Rubric Generators

Software tools help teachers with what many consider to be one of the most onerous and time-consuming instructional tasks: producing tests and other assessments. Test generators and rubric generators have become common software tools. Table 5.2 lists where to locate several of these tools.

Test generators. Teachers use **test generators** to create and enter questions, and then they have the program prepare

the test. The teacher either may print the required number of copies on the printer or print only one copy and make the required copies on a copy machine. The features of test generators vary, but the following capabilities are common and offer several advantages, even over word processing programs:

- **Test creation and revision procedures** — The software produces tests in a standard layout; the teacher need not worry about arranging the spacing and format of the page. The software prompts teachers to create tests item by item in formats such as multiple choice, fill in the blank, true/false, matching, and—less often—short answer and essay. Changes, deletions, and updates to questions are also easy to accomplish, again without concern for page format.

- **Random generation of questions** — Test items are selected randomly from an item pool to create different versions of a test. This is especially helpful when a teacher wants to prevent "wandering eye syndrome" as students take a test.

- **Selection of questions based on criteria** — Programs usually allow teachers to specify criteria for generating a test. For example, items can be requested in a specific content area, matched to certain objectives, or set up in a certain format such as short-answer items only.

- **Answer keys** — Most programs automatically provide an answer key at the time the test is generated. This is helpful with grading, especially if different versions of the test are used.

- **Test item banks** — Many test generators allow use of existing question pools, or **test item banks**, and some offer these banks for purchase in various content areas. Some programs also import question banks prepared on word processors.

Most test generators offer only on-paper versions of tests, but some allow students to take tests on-screen after they are prepared. The latter type is discussed later in this chapter under Data Collection and Analysis Tools since on-screen testing systems also collect and summarize data as they grade tests.

Online rubric generators. The popularity of rubrics has grown to such an extent that several Internet sites offer free rubric generators. The teacher follows a set of prompts, and the system creates a rubric that can be printed out or referred to online. See a list of rubric generation sites in Table 5.2, and review an example rubric and tutorial on how to use a rubric generator in the end-of-chapter exercises for Chapter 3.

Worksheet and Puzzle Generators

Teachers also use software to produce worksheets, in much the same way as they do to generate tests. **Worksheet generators** help teachers produce exercises for practice rather than test items. Like test generator software, worksheet generator software prompts the teacher to enter questions of various kinds, but it usually offers no options for completing exercises on-screen or for grading them. In many cases, test generator software and worksheet generator software are similar enough to be used interchangeably, and some packages are intended for both purposes. **Puzzle generators** automatically format and create crosswords, word search puzzles, and similar game-like activities. The teacher enters the content, and the software formats the puzzle. Refer to Table 5.2 for popular worksheet and puzzle generation sites. Common uses of worksheet and puzzle generators include:

- Practice for lower level skills such as math facts

- Cloze exercises (fill-in-the-blank comprehension checks)

- Exercises to review words and definitions.

Individualized Education Program (IEP) Generators

Education is placing increasing emphasis on school and teacher accountability. With this emphasis comes an increase in paperwork on student progress. Teachers of students with special needs seem to have the most paperwork requirements of all. Federal legislation such as the Individuals with Disabilities Education Act (IDEA) and the Americans with Disabilities Act requires that schools prepare an individualized educational program, or IEP, for each special needs student. These IEPs serve as blueprints for each special student's instructional activities, and teachers must provide documentation that such a plan is on file and that it governs classroom activities. **IEP generator** software assists teachers in preparing IEPs (Lewis, 1993). Like test and worksheet generators, IEP generators provide on-screen prompts that remind users of the required components in the plan. When a teacher finishes entering all the necessary information, the program prints out the IEP in a standard format. Some IEP generation programs also accept data updates on each student's progress, thus helping teachers with required record keeping as well as IEP preparation.

Graphic Document Makers

Graphic document makers are software tools that simplify the activity of making highly graphic materials such as

Making the Case for Technology Integration

Use the following questions to reflect on issues in technology integration and to guide discussions within your class.

1. Some educators object to the use of tools such as test generators and worksheet generators, saying that they encourage teachers to use technology to maintain current methods, rather than using technology in more innovative ways. What case can you make for keeping software tools like these in classrooms?

2. As mentioned in this chapter, the use of online and on-computer testing systems is becoming a popular, albeit controversial, practice (see http://www.fairtest.org/facts/computer.htm). What are the main points raised by critics of these systems? How would you address them?

3. Student information systems, which help track student, class, and school progress and help teachers with decision making, have become increasingly popular in recent years. They have also proven to be a useful tool for communicating with parents. In what ways do they serve this purpose?

awards certificates and greeting cards. They offer sets of clip art and predesigned templates to which teachers and students can add their own content. For example, teachers have found certificates to be a useful kind of recognition. Certificates congratulate students for accomplishments, and the students can take them home and share them with parents and friends. Most certificate makers include templates for various kinds of achievements. You can select the template that is appropriate for the kind of recognition intended (e.g., completing an activity, being a first-place winner) and enter the personal information for each recipient. Also, students frequently find it motivating to use these packages to design their own certificates, cards, and flyers. The most popular of these document makers is *Printshop* (Broderbund). This and similar software tools are listed in Table 5.2.

PDF and Forms Makers

Acrobat **Portable Document Format (PDF) file** software was created by Adobe to permit the viewing and sending of documents as images. With free *Acrobat Reader* software, documents can be viewed with all of the formatting and design elements (e.g., margins, graphics) of the original document showing, without requiring that the viewer have access to the desktop publishing or word processing software used to create the original. The ability to make PDF documents has improved greatly in the past years and is now a standard in Apple Computer's operating systems. PDF software is often used in conjunction with **forms makers** such as *PDF Maker Pilot*, a software tool that creates documents and web pages with forms that can be filled in on-screen. Teachers find forms makers useful because they make it easier to create forms to collect information from students, parents, or faculty or to implement surveys as part of research projects. Formatting even the simplest form can be time consuming on a word processor. These software tools structure the process and make the design simple to accomplish. As you create these forms, you can store them as templates for later use, perhaps with revisions. Many other non-PDF forms maker tools exist, but *PDF Maker Pilot* is so simple to use and meshes so well with the already-popular *Acrobat* software that it is quickly becoming an indispensable forms software tool for teachers and others.

Using Data Collection and Analysis Tools

Data collection and analysis tools include electronic gradebooks, statistical packages, student information systems, online and computer-based testing systems, and student response systems. A summary of these tools, with sample products and classroom uses, is shown in Table 5.3 on page 148.

FIGURE 5.1 **Sample Screen from the *Class Action Gradebook* Package**

Classroom	Grade Summary	Homework	Classwork	Tests	Student Report	Parent Lette

Student Information	Assignment Information	What If?	Display Student ID's	Points Points/Per

Assignment:	Ch 1	Q 1	Ch 2	Q 2	Ch 3	Q 3
Maximum Score:	100	35	100	35	100	35
Brown, Watson	B/85	A-/32	B/85	B-/28	C-/73	B-/28
de Oliveria, Miguel	C-/71	D+/24	A+/100	B-/29	B/84	B/30
del Aguila, Jose	B-/80	A/33	A-/91	B/30	A+/100	B/30
Figg, Ingrid	F/48	B-/29	B-/83	B/30	C/75	D-/22
Hubbard, La Vette	A+/100	B-/28	A+/100	F/20	F/51	F/20
Jones, Bobbette	C+/79	B-/28	C+/79	D-/21	D+/69	D-/21
Jones, Bobby	C-/71	A/34	D/65	A-/32	B+/88	A-/32
Le, Hortense	F/57	B/30	F/57	D+/24	D-/63	D+/24

Source: Courtesy of CalEd Software.

Electronic Gradebooks

Although some teachers prefer to keep their grades on flexible spreadsheet software, many prefer to use software designed exclusively for this purpose. An **electronic gradebook** (electronic grade-keeping) program allows a teacher to enter student names, test/assignment names, data from tests, and weighting information for specific test scores. The program then analyzes the data and prints reports based on this information. Some gradebooks even offer limited-purpose word processing capabilities to enter notes about tests. The software automatically generates averages and weighted averages for each student and averages across all students on a given test. Gradebooks require less teacher setup time than spreadsheets do, but they also allow less flexibility on format options. Many schools today are using district-wide gradebooks for uniformity across all grading programs. See a sample gradebook screen in Figure 5.1.

Statistical Packages

As Gay (1993) once joked, many teachers believe that the field of statistics should be renamed "sadistics." Yet teachers may find several uses for statistical analyses. If they choose to do action research in their classrooms, as this text encourages, teachers must collect and analyze data on student performance. Depending on the type of research, several typical analyses yield helpful information, including descriptive statistics (e.g., means and standard deviations) and inferential statistics (e.g., t-tests and analyses of variance). **Statistical software packages** can also help with qualitative data collection and analysis and analysis of student performance on tests. Finally, teachers may have to teach beginning statistics to their students in, for example, a business education course.

Statistical software packages perform the calculations involved in any of these kinds of procedures. Naturally, a teacher must have considerable knowledge of the proper applications of various statistical procedures; the software merely handles

TABLE 5.3 Overview of Data Collection and Analysis Tools

Software Tools	Sample Products	Description/Sample Classroom Uses
Electronic gradebooks	• *Class Action Gradebook* http://www.classactiongradebook.com • *Grade Pro* http://www.edline.com/solutions/gradebook_and_classroom_management/ • *Gradekeeper* http://www.gradekeeper.com/ • *Easy Grade Pro* http://easygradepro.com/	Teachers keep track of and calculate student grades.
Statistical packages	• SPSS Inc. http://www.spss.com/ • XLStat http://www.xlstat.com • FlexPro http://weisang.com/ • NCSS Stat System http://www.ncss.com/ • Stata Statistical Software http://www.stata.com/	Teachers and students use statistical procedures to analyze data from experiments and research projects.
Student information systems	• *PowerSchool* http://www.powerschool.com • *Pinnacle* http://www.excelsiorsoftware.com • *Pearson Digital Learning* http://www.pearsonschool.com/index.cfm?locator=PSZ1Aq • *eSIS* http://www.aalsolutions.com	Teachers, administrators, and parents keep track of student and class progress on required curriculum objectives; teachers give online tests and use data to support decision making.
Computer-based testing systems	• *LaserGrade* http://www.lasergrade.com/ • *ExamBuilder* http://www.exambuilder.com/	Teachers have students take tests on a computer screen; software grades tests and compiles data.
Student response systems	• *Hyper Interactive Teaching Technology* http://www.h-itt.com • *Classroom Performance System* http://www.einstruction.com • *Qwizdom Interactive Learning System* http://www.qwizdom.com • Turning Point http://turningtechnologies.com	All students answer a question at the same time, and the system summarizes/displays results immediately; teachers use these systems to engage students and check comprehension.

the arithmetic. But this alone can save considerable time. Popular statistical software tools are listed in Table 5.3.

Student Information Systems

Student information systems (SIS) are networked software systems that help educators keep track of student, class, and school data (e.g., attendance, test scores) to maintain records and support decision making. Schools purchase various operations they want the system to keep track of. Depending on what they choose, the system may do any or all of the following:

• Track and report on attendance

• Maintain records on student demographic data (e.g., birth date, address)

• Develop class scheduling

- Track and report on test scores and achievement by objective
- Allow parents to have online access to student grades and attendance information
- Notify parents about problems with grades or attendance.

In the 1970s, these systems were known by the general term **computer-managed instruction (CMI) systems**. At that time, there was a burgeoning interest in mastery learning in which teachers specified a sequence of objectives for students to learn and prescribed instruction to help the students master each objective. The teacher had to keep track of each student's performance on each objective—a mammoth record-keeping task. CMI systems, such as the Teaching Information Processing System (TIPS) and the Program for Learning in Accordance with Needs (PLAN), ran on large, mainframe computers and were designed to support teachers in these efforts.

Today's educators also must be concerned about monitoring student progress, but the concern now is in complying with accountability requirements such as those specified by the No Child Left Behind Act. Also, these systems can make it easier for teachers to keep parents notified about student progress. Systems such as Pearson's *PowerSchool* and Excelsior Software's *Pinnacle Plus* system allow online access to students' grade reports.

Some SISs are components of integrated learning systems (ILSs). Integration with ILSs allows instruction to be tailored to each student's needs and collects data as students go through the instruction. Reports show the teacher what students have accomplished and point out areas where they may still need assistance and off-computer work.

Computer-Based Testing Systems

Also known as computer-assisted testing, computer-based testing systems allow students to take tests onscreen or to put test answers on optically scanned "bubble sheets" and provide reports on performance data afterward. Some current testing systems overlap with the function of true test generators (see earlier description under Materials Generators), which are designed to produce tests from data banks. Some of the major standardized tests, such as the SAT and GRE, are now given on computerized testing systems, which offers benefits such as immediate knowledge of results. The capabilities of computerized testing systems let educators go beyond the limits of multiple-choice tests and make possible alternative assessments. These systems also simplify test scheduling, because everyone need not take tests at the same time.

With testing systems, tests can be shorter, since the software assesses each person's ability level with fewer questions. The software continuously analyzes performance and presents more or less difficult questions based on the student's performance, a capability known as **computer adaptive**

By having students use "clickers" or some form of Student Response System in the classroom, teachers are able to obtain immediate feedback on student comprehension and knowledge.

testing (CAT) (Strommen, 1994). CAT is being used more and more frequently for testing in professional courses like those in nursing education. Computer-based testing is often controversial, however. Some people feel that computer-based testing is not equivalent to other kinds of testing and that it actually discriminates against some students.

Student Response Systems

Unique among data collection resources, **student response systems** (also called *personal response systems, clickers,* or *classroom response systems*) are a combination of handheld hardware and software that permits each student in a classroom to answer a question simultaneously and permits the teacher to see and display a summary of results immediately. Johnson and McLeod (2004–2005) describe 11 such systems as well as a variety of instructional uses for them. These uses range from vocabulary games to comprehension checks during a classroom presentation and are an easy way to engage all students at once. The "clickers" have ranged from those sold with a textbook to new technologies where cellular phones can be used to respond to questions posed by the instructor.

Using Graphics Tools

Graphics tools include draw/paint programs; image editing tools; charting/graphing tools; and clip art, photo, animation, sound, video, and font collections. A summary of these, with sample products and classroom uses is shown in Table 5.4.

Draw/Paint Programs

Drawing and painting software tools help teachers and students create their own graphics to insert into documents or web pages. In simpler draw/paint programs such as *Kid Pix*,

TABLE 5.4 Overview of Graphics Tools

Software Tools	Sample Products	Description/Sample Classroom Uses
Draw/paint programs	• *Adobe Illustrator* http://www.adobe.com • *Kid Pix* http://www.learningcompany.com/	Teachers and students create their own drawings and illustrations to show on-screen or to print.
Image editing tools	• *Adobe Photoshop* http://www.adobe.com • *GIMP* http://www.gimp.org/	Teachers and students create, modify, and combine images (e.g., clip art, photos, drawings) to illustrate documents, web pages.
Charting/graphing tools	• Tom Snyder's *Graph Master* and *The Graph Club 2.0* http://www.teachtsp.com/ • *Advanced Grapher* http://www.serpik.com/ • *NetCharts Reporting Suite* http://www.visualmining.com	Students create charts and graphs to illustrate and study data summaries.
Clip art, animation, sound, video, and font collections	• *Graphics for Teachers* http://www.teachingheart.net/ graphicl.html • Microsoft's *Clip Art and Media Collection* http://office.microsoft.com/en-us/ clipart/default.aspx • *Flaming Text* http://www.flamingtext.com/ • *Animation Factory* http://www.animationfactory.com/en	Teachers and students insert these into documents and media they create.

users select graphics components (e.g., colors, shapes, lines) from menus and toolbars, making the programs so easy to use that anyone can sit down and create an image in a matter of minutes. Students may use these programs to illustrate their work or to help convey information in reports. One example product, created with *Kid Pix* software and described in Technology Integration Lesson 5.2, illustrates how draw/paint programs can be useful in a science lesson. Catchings and MacGregor (1998) are among those who believe that draw/paint programs allow many students to develop their visual–verbal literacy and creativity. O'Bannon, Krolak, Harkelroad, and Dick (1999) show how students can practice this creativity by designing banners and images for school web pages. Other programs, such as *Adobe Illustrator* and *Adobe Flash* (Figure 5.2), make possible more complex drawings and require more knowledge of art and graphic techniques. These are usually used in high school level communications and technology education courses.

FIGURE 5.2 Sample *Adobe Flash* Image

Source: Artwork courtesy of Erik Natzke.

Image Editing Tools

To modify photographic images, **image editing programs** are the technology software tool of choice. These tools usually are used to enhance and format photos that are then imported into desktop publishing systems or

Technology Integration Lesson 5.2

Using Draw/Paint Graphics Tools to Illustrate Science Concepts

Title: Weaving Art Throughout the Curriculum   **Grade Level:** 4
Content Area/Topic: Science—nature

NETS for Students: Standards 1 (Creativity and Innovation), 2 (Communication and Collaboration), 3 (Research and Information Fluency), and 6 (Technology Operations and Concepts)

Description of Standards Applications: This integration lesson offers students the opportunity to create geometric patterns as the basis for their drawings as they use the *Kid Pix* drawing program. Students research geometric patterns from nature, recreate them using the drawing program, and then share them with their classmates.

Instruction: The teacher demonstrates some example products by artists who use geometric patterns as the basis of a collection of paintings and drawings. Then he or she asks the students to think about collections of their own and to bring in anything they have collected that has to do with nature (e.g., rocks, seashells). Students design their own nature sculptures based on these collections. They use digital cameras to take pictures of their works and then use *Kid Pix* to add special effects to the images to create a final product to share with the class.

Assessment: A rubric is used to assess the creativity and concepts demonstrated by the final product.

Source: Lach, C., Little, E., & Nazzaro, D. (2003). From all sides now: Weaving technology and multiple intelligences into science and art. *Learning and Leading with Technology, 30*(6), 32–35, 59.

---

web page products. Image editing programs are known for their sophistication and wide-ranging capabilities. Many of these packages, such as *Adobe Photoshop*, require considerable time to learn if one wants to become familiar with all facets of the technology, but the basic operations are still very powerful, easy to learn, and effective in the K–12 classroom. Technology Integration Lesson 5.3 shows how these programs could be used in a math/astronomy lesson.

Charting/Graphing Tools

Charting/graphing tools automatically draw and print desired charts or graphs from data entered by users. The skills involved in reading, interpreting, and producing graphs and charts are useful both to students in school and adults in the workplace. However, people with limited artistic ability usually find it difficult to draw charts and graphics freehand. Fortunately, chart-

ing and graphing software takes the mechanical drudgery out of producing these useful "data pictures." If students do not have to labor over rulers and pencils as they try to plot coordinates and set points, they can concentrate on the more important aspects of the graphics: the meaning of the data and what they represent. This kind of activity supports students in their efforts at visualizing mathematical concepts and engaging in inquiry tasks.

Graphing activities in science, social studies, and geography also profit from applications of these kinds of software tools. Moersch (1995) lists and gives example instructional applications for nine kinds of software-produced graphs: bar, pie, stacked bar, *X/Y*, scatter, box, stem and leaf, best fit, and normal curve. Figure 5.3 shows how graphing software supports learning in various content areas. Also, see Technology Integration Lesson 5.4 on page 153 for an example lesson with graphing software.

Technology Integration Lesson 5.3

Using Image Editing Software

Title: Bringing the Planets Closer to Home   **Grade Level:** 5 through 12

Content Area/Topic: Math (measurement) and astronomy

 NETS for Students: Standards 3 (Research and Information Fluency), 4 (Critical Thinking, Problem Solving, and Decision Making), and 6 (Technology Operations and Concepts)

Description of Standards Applications: This integration lesson offers students the opportunity to research the scale of images of the solar system using an image editing program. Students problem solve with measuring tools to compare images from the solar system.

Instruction: Students begin by downloading NASA photos from the Internet (e.g., images of the solar system at http://spaceart.com/solar) and converting them to an uncompressed TIF format using an image editing program such as Adobe Photoshop. Their task is to learn how to measure the images. First, they use the software to calibrate the images (determine the scale) by comparing the size of each image to a known measurement such as the diameter of Mars. Then they multiply the measured distance by the scale to determine the size of other features they have downloaded. In this way, the students can measure and compare features that change, such as the Martian and Earth polar ice caps. These measurements can be the basis of many projects to study space phenomena.

Assessment: Use a checklist to assess correct completion of required tasks.

Source: Slater, T., & Beaudrie, B. (2000). Far out measurements: Bringing the planets closer to home using image-processing techniques. *Learning and Leading with Technology, 27*(5), 36–41.

Clip Art, Photo, Animation, Sound, Video, and Font Collections

Clip art packages were originally collections of still pictures drawn by artists and graphics designers and placed in a book or on a disk for use by others. Nowadays, the idea of clip art has expanded to include drawings, cartoons, photos, and animations—all of which are found easily on the Internet. For example, high-quality photos, illustrations, and videos can be found online at www.istockphoto.com as well as on

FIGURE 5.3   Sample *Graph Club 2.0* Screens

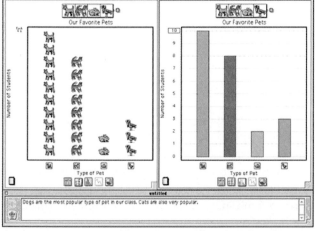

Students can see the same data represented differently side by side.

Source: The Graph Club 2.0. Courtesy of Tom Snyder.

Standards-aligned activities are an interactive and fun way for students to master graphing skills.

Technology Integration Lesson 5.4

Illustrating Math Concepts with Charting/Graphing Tools

Title: A Project with Teeth

Content Area/Topic: Math concepts—data collection and analysis

Grade Level: K–3

NETS for Students: Standards 2 (Communication and Collaboration), 3 (Research and Information Fluency), and 4 (Critical Thinking, Problem Solving, and Decision Making)

Description of Standards Applications: This integration lesson offers students the opportunity to use email to communicate and collaborate with students around the world as they use "lost" teeth data to graph and communicate their results. In addition to graphing, students can research tooth fairy traditions and geographic locations.

Explanation: Teachers use email to connect their K–3 students with "keypals" around the world in order to exchange information on how many teeth children lose during the year. This activity is used as a springboard for learning geography (where the keypals reside), literature and culture (tooth fairy traditions and other stories from their regions), art (creating pictures or murals illustrating tooth fairy traditions), creative writing (email messages to participants, poems and rhymes on teeth), and mathematics (graphing data on lost teeth).

Instruction: After they have at least 3 months of data on lost teeth, students learn how to use a graphing program to compile the data and prepare line or bar graphs. Each student or small group may choose a part of the data to graph; then they compose a letter explaining the results to their keypals. As a cumulative or final whole-class activity, students may use a calculator to add up all the teeth data for each month from all the schools and then enter all the data into one common spreadsheet. Results can be shared among the participants through email.

Assessment: Use a rubric to assess small-group work and demonstration of graphing concept knowledge.

Source: Boehm, D. (1997). I lost my tooth! *Learning and Leading with Technology, 24*(7), 17–19.

---

the Microsoft homepage. When preparing presentations, you can use available art instead of drawing your own original images or taking your own photos. Most word processing, desktop publishing, image editing, and draw/paint programs can import these items from a disk or a website. Font collections are also available to expand the font options that come with a computer or software.

These collections offer valuable resources that help illustrate and decorate written products. Teachers find that such pictures help make flyers, books, and even letters and notices look more polished and professional. Some teachers feel that students are more motivated to write their own stories and reports when they can also illustrate them.

For teachers and students who want to develop their own websites or multimedia presentations, collections of sound effects and video clips (e.g., MPEG files) are also becoming common on the Internet, and many are free of charge. However, a system may need special software

plug-ins, such as *Quicktime* or *Adobe Flash*, to incorporate these elements.

Using Planning and Organizing Tools

Planning and organizing tools include outlining and concept mapping software, lesson planning software, and scheduling/time management tools. A summary of these, with sample products and classroom uses, is shown in Table 5.5.

Outlining Tools and Concept Mapping Software

Several kinds of technology tools are available to help students learn writing skills or to assist accomplished writers in setting their thoughts in order prior to writing. **Outlining tools** are designed to prompt writers as they develop outlines. For example,

TABLE 5.5 Overview of Planning and Organizing Tools

Software Tools	Sample Products	Description/Sample Classroom Uses
Outlining and concept mapping software	• *Inspiration* http://www.inspiration.com • *VisiMap* http://www.coco.co.uk/ • *StoryWeaver* http://www.storymind.com/	Help students organize their ideas in outline or concept map form to prepare for writing; help create story structures.
Lesson planners	• Centron's *Lesson Power* http://www.centronsoftware.com/lesson%20power.html • *Freemind* http://freemind.sourceforge.net/wiki/index.php/Main_Page • *Cmap* http://cmap.ihmc.us/ • *Teacher Planet* http://www.TeacherPlanet.com	Help teachers prepare and document lesson plans.
Scheduling and time management tools	• *ThoughtManager* for Teachers http://www.handshigh.com • *Reel Logix* http://www.thecalendarplanner.com/	Help teachers organize their time and plan activities.

the software may automatically indent and/or supply the appropriate number or letter for each line in the outline. Outliners are offered either within word processing packages or as separate software packages for use before word processing.

Other writing aids include software designed to get students started on writing reports or stories: a story starter. This kind of program provides a first line and invites students to supply subsequent lines. Other tools give students topic ideas and supply information about each topic that they can use in a writing assignment. Sometimes a software package combines outlining tools and other writing aids.

Concept mapping software tools are designed to help people think through and explore ideas or topics by developing concept maps. Concept maps are visual outlines of ideas that can offer useful alternatives to the strictly verbal representations provided by content outlines. The number of concept mapping software programs has grown over the past few years, with many of the programs being web-based or even free of charge. *Inspiration* is one of the most popular of these tools (see Figure 5.4), and *Kidspiration* is a version of this software designed for younger users. Anderson-Inman and Zeitz (1993), Dabbagh (2001), and Kahn (1997b) discuss the learning theory behind using these powerful instructional tools and give good examples of classroom applications. (See Technology Integration Lesson 5.5.)

 **PEARSON** **myeducationlab** The Power of Classroom Practice

Go to MyEducationLab and select the topic "Software." Under "Assignments, Activities, and Applications," select "Uses for Inspiration and Kidspiration" and consider the possible uses for this software.

Lesson Planning Software

Not all teachers rely heavily on written lesson plans to guide their teaching activities. However, many occasions demand

FIGURE 5.4 Sample *Inspiration* Screen

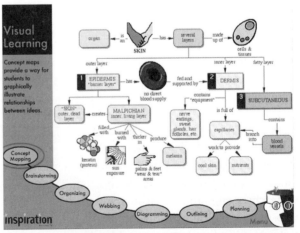

Source: © 2004 Inspiration Software®, Inc. Diagram created in *Inspiration*® by Inspiration Software®, Inc. Used with permission.

Technology Integration Lesson 5.5

Supporting Writing Processes with Concept Mapping

Title: Authors in Residence and Online Mentors

Grade Level: Elementary

Content Area/Topic: Writing process skills

NETS for Students: Standards 1 (Creativity and Innovation), 2 (Communication and Collaboration), 3 (Research and Information Fluency), 4 (Critical Thinking, Problem Solving, and Decision Making)

Description of Standards Applications: This integration lesson offers students the opportunity to be creative and to use a graphic organizer and a word processor to write a story they share with their mentors using collaboration software such as email or blogs.

Instruction: Students first use *Kidspiration* or *Inspiration* software to create a graphic organizer for their written work. After they complete a word-processed first draft, they email the files to their mentors and receive comments, suggestions for improvements, and encouragement. For example, one mentor suggested that a young writer expand her story by playing a "what if" game. She asked what the characters in the story might do in response to the events she had already written. Then she could describe these responses in order to embellish her story. Students and mentors bond through this process, and students are more motivated to revise their writing. Word processing software makes revisions easier and faster, which further encourages students to improve their work.

Assessment: Use a rubric to assess final drafts.

Source: Hagins, C., Auston, J., Timmons, T., & Weeg, P. (2004). Authors "in residence" make writing fun: Online mentors help fourth graders compose original stories. *Learning and Leading with Technology, 31*(6), 36–39.

some form of documentation to show what teachers are teaching and how they are teaching it. Tools that help teachers develop and document their descriptions of lessons are sometimes called *lesson makers* or *lesson planners*. Most of these programs simply provide on-screen prompts for specific lesson components such as objectives, materials, and activity descriptions. They also print out lessons in standard formats, similar to the way test generators format printouts of tests.

Scheduling and Time Management Tools

Several kinds of tools have been designed to help teachers organize their time and plan their activities. Schedule makers help formulate plans for daily, weekly, or monthly sequences of appointments and events. Calendar makers are similar planning tools that actually print graphic calendars of chosen months or years with the planned events printed under each day. Other time management tools are available to help remind users of events and responsibilities. The teacher enters activities and the dates

on which they are to occur. Then, when he or she turns on the computer each day, the software displays on the screen a list of things to do. Some integrated packages combine all of these tools. Time management tools are an especially popular application on handheld computers since people can update their calendars at any time and place.

Using Research and Reference Tools

Research and reference tools include electronic versions of the following tools: encyclopedias, atlases and mapping tools, and dictionaries and thesauruses. A summary of these, with sample products and classroom uses, is shown in Table 5.6.

Electronic Encyclopedias

For many years, American families kept sets of encyclopedias to support their children's education. Young people

TABLE 5.6 Overview of Research and Reference Tools

Software Tools	Sample Products	Description/Sample Classroom Uses
Electronic encyclopedias	• *Encarta* http://encarta.msn.com • *HighBeam Encyclopedia* http://www.encyclopedia.com/ • *Britannica* http://www.britannica.com/	Help students research any topic.
Electronic atlases and mapping tool	• WorldAtlas.com http://www.worldatlas.com/ • U.S. Atlas http://www.nationalatlas.gov/ • *Political World Atlas* http://www.sitesatlas.com/Atlas/PolAtlas/ • *Atlas of the Universe* http://www.atlasoftheuniverse.com/	Help students learn local, national, world, and extraterrestrial geography.
Electronic dictionaries and thesauruses	• Technology words: *Webopedia* http://www.webopedia.com/ • Any words: *Merriam-Webster* http://www.merriam-webster.com/ dictionary.htm • Any words: *Dictionary.com* http://dictionary.reference.com • Thesaurus: *Thesaurus.com* http://thesaurus.reference.com/	Give definitions and synonyms.

FIGURE 5.5 Sample Screen from WorldandISchool.com Encyclopedia

Source: Courtesy of The World & I Online.

FIGURE 5.6   Sample Screen from the WorldAtlas.com Site

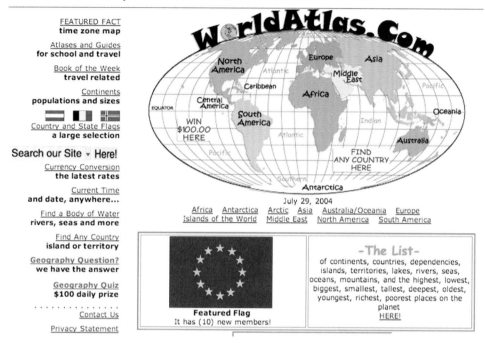

Source: Courtesy of WorldAtlas.com.

used these books for research on school projects, and parents used them to take advantage of "teachable moments" when their children required more than quick answers. Now most major encyclopedias come on CD-ROM or on websites with some kind of database structure. (See an example online encyclopedia in Figure 5.5.) These electronic encyclopedias have several advantages over books. Users can search to locate either one specific item or all references on a given topic. They usually offer multimedia formats that include sound and/or film clips as well as hypertext links to related information on any topic. Because electronic encyclopedias are considered a form of multimedia, Chapter 6 presents more information on and examples of these applications.

Electronic Atlases and Mapping Tools

Like encyclopedias, atlases are popular educational reference tools for families as well as schools. They summarize geographic and demographic information ranging from population statistics to national products. CD-ROM versions of these atlases are especially helpful because they are so interactive. Students can either see information on a specific country or city or gather information on all countries or cities that meet certain criteria. Some atlases even play national songs on request! See a sample online atlas in Figure 5.6. Mapping sites such as *MapQuest* also help teach geographic concepts by showing distances between points.

Electronic Dictionaries (Word Atlases)

Sometimes called **word atlases**, electronic dictionaries and thesauruses give pronunciations, definitions, and example uses for each word entry. They also offer many search and multimedia features similar to those of encyclopedias and atlases. Many electronic dictionaries can play an audio clip of the pronunciation of any desired word, which helps young users and others who cannot read diacritical marks.

Using Tools to Support Specific Content Areas

Numerous content-specific technologies support teaching within a content area. Some of these tools are described within this chapter, and you will find additional content-specific tools within each subject-matter chapter (Chapters 9 through 15). Examples of content-area tools are CAD systems; music tools such as music editors, sequencers, and MIDI tools; reading tools; microcomputer-based labs, graphing calculators and calculator-based labs; and Geographic Information Systems and Global Positioning Systems. A summary of these, with sample products and classroom uses, is shown in Table 5.7.

CAD and 3-D Modeling/Animation Systems

A **computer-assisted design (CAD)** system is a special kind of graphics production tool that allows users to prepare

TABLE 5.7 Overview of Content-Area Specific Tools

Software Tools	Sample Products	Description/Sample Classroom Uses
CAD systems	• *AutoCAD* http://usa.autodesk.com • *Alibre Design* http://www.alibre.com	Students create visual models of houses and other structures as they study design concepts.
Music editors, sequencers, and MIDI tools	• Korg MIDI products http://www.korg.com/ • Apple *GarageBand* http://www.apple.com • Emagic's *MicroLogic Sequencer* http://www.emagic.de • *MIDI Maestro* http://www.tomdownload.com	Students create and revise their own musical pieces.
Reading tools	• Readability calculation software http://www.readabilityformulas.com • Renaissance Learning's *Accelerated Reader* http://www.renlearn.com/ar/	Support reading instruction.
Microcomputer-based labs, graphing calculators, and calculator-based labs	• TI graphing calculators http://education.ti.com/ • Vernier LabPro Packages http://www.vernier.com/	Students collect and analyze data from experiments.
Geographic Information Systems and Global Positioning Systems	• GPS Products for Education http://www.gps4fun.com/ • ARCView GIS http://www.esri.com/software/arcview • GIS products for U.S. Census data http://www.census.gov/geo/www/maps/ • *Google Earth* http://earth.google.com • *Magellan GPS* http://www.magellangps.com/	Students study geographical and social studies information and concepts.

sophisticated, precise drawings of objects such as houses and cars. Like presentation tools, CAD systems began to appear in classrooms after they had been introduced in business and industry. This kind of software is usually employed in vocational-technical classrooms to teach architecture and engineering skills. However, some teachers use CAD software to teach drawing concepts in art and related topics. (See Figure 5.7 for an example of CAD software.) More advanced graphics students may use 3-D modeling and animation software systems to do fancy visual effects such as **morphing**. This term is short for *metamorphosing* and refers to an animation technique in which one image gradually turns into another.

Music Editors, Sequencers, and MIDI Tools

Music editor software provides blank musical staffs on which the user enters the musical key, time, and notes that constitute a piece of sheet music. This software is designed to help people develop musical compositions on-screen, usually in conjunction with hardware such as a **Musical Instrument Digital Interface (MIDI) device**, a standard adopted by the electronic music industry for controlling devices that play music (for example, **music synthesizers**). Music editors allow a user either to hear the music after it is written or to create music on the keyboard and automatically produce a written score.

Music sequencers are software packages that support the creation of music scores with several parts. Steinhaus (1986–1987) explained that music editors offer powerful assistance in the processes of precomposing, composing, revising, and even performing. Forest (1993) offers examples of these activities in a school setting as well as a list of good music-related software and media. Ohler's (1998) thorough review of MIDI technology and its current applications for teaching mu-

FIGURE 5.7 Sample *AutoCAD* Screen

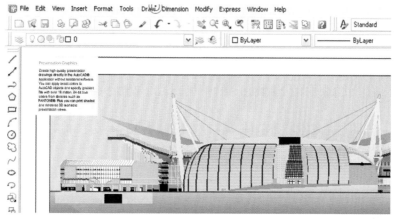

sic reminds us that technology tools can help students "flex the musical muscle that [Howard] Gardner reminds us has always been there" (p. 10). (See Chapter 13, Technology in Music and Art Instruction, for more classroom uses of these tools.)

Reading Tools

Both reading teachers and teachers of other topics occasionally need to determine the approximate reading level of specific documents. A teacher may want to select a story or book for use in a lesson or to confirm that works are correctly labeled as appropriate for certain grade levels. Several methods are available for calculating the reading level of a written work; all of them are time consuming and tedious to do by hand. Readability analysis software automates calculations of word count, average word length, number of sentences, or other measures of reading difficulty.

Another software tool related to reading instruction, Cloze software, provides passages with words missing in a given pattern, for example, every fifth word or every tenth word. Students read the sentences and try to fill in the words. Cloze passages have been found to be good measures of reading comprehension. Some teachers also like to use them as exercises to improve reading comprehension.

Many books for children as well as adults are available in interactive CD-ROM versions called *interactive storybooks* or *electronic books* (Truett, 1993). Some of these allow children to hear narrations in English or Spanish. Others, like the *Living Books* series (*Just Grandma and Me*), let children explore the screen, activating animations and sounds when they click in various locations. These books are designed to provide an interesting, interactive way to read and to increase reading fluency.

A product called *Accelerated Reader* or *AR* (Lopez, 2000; Poock, 1998), designed to track students' reading skills, has become increasingly popular. The purpose of the *AR* system is to motivate students to increase the amount of reading they

Adapting for Special Needs

To support students who are struggling with reading and writing, teachers can use websites, such as *StarChild*, that provide text-to-speech so readers can listen to what they type. If students have difficulty reading text, they can copy and paste it into a specialized program that will read it to them (e.g., see *ReadingBar2* at www.readplease.com). This strategy is especially helpful for students when they are reading on the Internet or when they are typing papers in a word processor to proofread (hear) what they have written (e.g., see Don Johnston's *Write: OutLoud* at http://www.donjohnston.com).

Contributed by Dave Edyburn

do for enjoyment. It keeps track of the number of books they read and tests them on comprehension. Teachers can get individual or aggregate data on books read at each readability level. This gives them a better idea of how students are progressing in their reading abilities and whether they are spending enough time reading at desired levels. Though they caution that further study is needed to draw reliable conclusions, Topping and Paul (1999) found that schools using *AR* for longer periods of time show higher rates of reading, which may correlate with higher tested reading levels.

Microcomputer-Based Labs (Probeware)

A technology tool that has proven particularly useful in math and science classrooms is the **microcomputer-based lab (MBL)**, sometimes referred to as **probeware**. MBL packages

Technology Integration Lesson 5.6

Studying Slope with MBLs/Probeware

Title: Exploring the Relationship Between Science and Mathematics

Grade Level: High school

Content Area/Topic: Concept of slope

NETS for Students: Standards 1 (Creativity and Innovation), 3 (Research and Information Fluency), and 6 (Technology Operations and Concepts)

Description of Standards Applications: This integration lesson offers students the opportunity to use probeware to research a linear equation as they apply their creativity to calculating the relationship between the input to the computer from the probe and the value that the measurement represents.

Instruction: For example, if the MBL is measuring voltage, the probe is calibrated by connecting it to an AA battery previously confirmed by a multimeter to output 1.5 volts. The computer registers 215 counts for 1.5 volts. The beginning point of 0 counts and the ending point of 215 define a line. This line is used to calibrate the probe. After the probe is calibrated, an equation is developed for the line (0, 0 and 215, 1.5). Students sketch the graph of the line defined by these points, using either paper or graphing software. They predict values for counts given specific voltages, using their graph by locating the value on the x axis and finding the corresponding y value for the counts. They use the general linear equation $y = mx + b$ to discuss the slope of the line as the rise (vertical distance between the two points) divided by the run (horizontal distance between the points). The teacher has the students calculate the slope for their lines. They enter the value for the slope into the general linear equation and do the final equation for the example calibration. Once the equation has been determined, students calculate counts for specific voltages. When the probe is ready to be used, students bring in samples to be tested.

Assessment: Use a checklist to assess completion and accuracy of required processes.

Source: Ladelson, L. (1994). Calibrating probeware: Making a line. *The Computing Teacher, 21*(6), 46–47.

consist of software accompanied by special hardware sensors designed to measure light, temperature, voltage, and/or speed. The probes are connected to the microcomputer, and the software processes the collected data. Bitter, Camuse, and Durbin (1993) said that microcomputer probeware actually can replace several traditional items of lab equipment, such as oscilloscopes and voltmeters, because MBLs outperform them. Ladelson (1994) points out that probeware achieves a dual purpose of gathering empirical data and revealing the relationship between science and math. Stanton (1992) describes a variety of MBLs, covering their capabilities and prices along with grade levels and science subjects they can help teach. Walsh (2001) refers to these devices as stand-alone, microprocessor-based data acquisition devices or SAMDADS. He reviews 13 data-gathering devices and describes their uses in various classroom experiments in mathematics and science. (See Technology Integration Lesson 5.6.)

Graphing calculators allow students and teachers to extend their research capabilities by allowing the user to create customizable programs.

Technology Integration Lesson 5.7

Using CBLs to Study Ellipses

Title: Graphing the Ellipse

Content Area/Topic: Math—geometry

Grade Level: 10 through 12

NETS for Students: Standards 1 (Creativity and Innovation), 4 (Critical Thinking, Problem Solving, and Decision Making), and 6 (Technology Operations and Concepts)

Description of Standards Applications: This integration lesson offers students the opportunity to use a graphing calculator to add interest to the study of ellipses as they explore ellipses in the real world and define a macro to create the actual figures.

Instruction: The teacher begins by demonstrating occurrences of ellipses in the real world: orbits of planets and comets, arches of stone bridges (semi-ellipses), elliptical gears, various artworks. Then he or she challenges the students to use the calculators to create their own ellipses. As they add points to construct their ellipses, the teacher discusses the mathematical properties needed to build them. After they understand these properties, they can use the graphing software such as Microsoft Excel or graphing calculators to define a macro to create the actual figures so they will be able to focus more time on exploring proofs and on investigation and problem-solving activities with the calculators.

Assessment: Use a checklist to assess completion of required steps.

Source: Davis, J., & Hofstetter, E. (1998). A graphing investigation of the ellipse. *Learning and Leading with Technology,* 26(2), 32–36.

Graphing Calculators and Calculator-Based Labs

For many years, calculators have played a widespread—and often controversial—role in mathematics education. Even more capable, software-programmed devices called **graphing calculators** have emerged and have become indispensable tools in both mathematics and higher level science curricula. Albrecht and Firedrake (1997) describe uses in physics instruction for these devices in conjunction with the Internet and what they call "data-grabbing devices" (probeware, MBLs, or CBLs). Borenstein (1997) reviews uses of graphing calculators to make possible various experiments and concept demonstrations in algebra. Manouchehri and Pagnucco (1999–2000) and Plymate (1998) describe the use of graphing calculators to explore linear properties of real-world data sets and to make concepts like slope more visual and understandable. (See Technology Integration Lesson 5.7.) When probes or sensors are connected to a graphing calculator rather than to a computer (as described in the previous section on MBLs), they also are called **calculator-based labs (CBLs)**.

GPS technology is popular for both personal and professional use. Used for more than just finding direction, GPS technology is even being incorporated into classroom use.

Geographic Information Systems and Global Positioning Systems

The world of geographic information systems and global positioning systems has grown exponentially over the past few years. Both of these powerful tools are useful in teaching science and the social studies. A **Geographic Information System (GIS)** is a computer system that is able to store in a database a variety of information about geographic locations. After it has stored all the data that describe a given location, the GIS can then display the data in map form. According to Parmenter and Burns (2001), the three primary uses of GISs are (1) to record and maintain large amounts of geographic information, (2) to produce up-to-date, customized maps, and (3) to allow analysis and comparison of information on different locations. A **Global Positioning System (GPS)** is a worldwide radionavigation system made possible by a bank of 24 satellites and their ground stations. Using satellites as reference points, a GPS unit can calculate positions of anything on earth accurate to a matter of feet or inches. A GPS receiver connected to mapping software is what most people think of as a GPS; however, the use of these systems is growing, from finding your way in an unfamiliar community to guiding farmers as they plant and harvest their crops. These small devices can be useful in a car, agricultural equipment, the home, or even a portable laptop. (See Chapter 12 for a detailed look at a GIS and a GPS in the classroom.)

Interactive Summary

The following is a summary of the main points covered in this chapter.

1. **Benefits of software tools are the same as those described for the tools introduced in Chapter 4** — Benefits include improved efficiency and productivity, improved appearance, better accuracy and timeliness of information, and more support for interaction and sharing.

2. **Recent developments in software tools** — These include increased use of PDAs, more web connectivity features, and more collections of tools available in software suites.

3. **Materials generators** — These are tools that help teachers and students produce instructional materials. They include desktop publishing software, test generators and rubric generators, worksheet and puzzle generators, IEP generators, graphic document makers, and PDF and forms makers.

4. **Data collection and analysis tools** — These are tools that help teachers collect and organize information that indicates student progress. They include electronic gradebooks, statistical packages, student information systems, online and computer-based testing systems, and student response systems.

5. **Graphics tools** — These are tools that allow the manipulation of images to illustrate documents and web pages. They include draw/paint programs; image editing tools; charting/graphing tools; and clip art, photo, animation, sound, video, and font collections.

6. **Planning and organizing tools** — These are tools that help teachers and students conceptualize, organize, and communicate their ideas. They include outlining and concept mapping software, lesson planning software, and scheduling/time management tools.

7. **Research and reference tools** — These are tools that let students look up information in electronic versions of encyclopedias, atlases, and dictionaries. They include electronic versions of the following tools: encyclopedias, atlases and mapping tools, and dictionaries and thesauruses.

8. **Content-area tools** — These are tools that support teaching and learning activities in various content areas. They include CAD systems, music tools such as music editors and sequencers, reading tools, microcomputer-based labs, graphing calculators and calculator-based labs, and Geographic Information Systems and Global Positioning Systems.

Key Terms

- calculator-based lab (CBL)
- charting/graphing tool
- clip art
- computer adaptive testing (CAT)
- computer-assisted design (CAD)
- computer-managed instruction (CMI) system
- concept mapping software
- desktop publishing
- electronic gradebook
- forms maker
- Geographic Information System (GIS)

- Global Positioning System (GPS)
- graphic document maker
- graphing calculator
- IEP generator
- image editing program
- microcomputer-based lab (MBL)
- Musical Instrument Digital Interface (MIDI) device
- morphing

- music editor
- music sequencer
- music synthesizer
- outlining tool
- Portable Document Format (PDF) file
- probeware
- puzzle generator
- sans serif typeface

- serif typeface
- statistical software package
- student information system (SIS)
- student response system
- test generator
- test item bank
- word atlas
- worksheet generator

Web-Enrichment Activities

1. ***Materials generators online*** — Use a teacher materials generator at one of the websites listed below to create a puzzle or worksheet for the key terms in one of this textbook's chapters. Swap puzzles and worksheets with another student to review the chapter terms.
   - Puzzlemaker http://puzzlemaker.discoveryeducation.com/
   - TeAch-nology Crossword Puzzle Maker http://www.teachnology.com/web_tools/crossword

2. ***Develop a rubric*** — Use a rubric creator at one of the websites listed below to develop a rubric for a student publishing project. Incorporate the guidelines in the Top Ten Rules for Effective Desktop Publishing.
   - RubiStar http://rubistar.4teachers.org
   - Rubric Generator http://teachnology.com/web_tools/rubrics/general

Go to MyEducationLab to complete the following exercises.

Video Select the topic "Software," and go to the "Assignments, Activities, and Applications" section. Access the video "Classroom Management Software" to explore how one program helps teachers individualize assignments aligned to standards and keep parents informed as well. Complete the activity that follows.

Building Teaching Skills Select the topic "Software," and go to the "Building Teaching Skills and Dispositions" section. Access the activity "Supporting Instruction with Technology" and complete the activity that follows.

Technology Integration Workshop

The TIP Model in Action

Read each of the following scenarios related to implementing the TIP Model, and answer the questions that follow it based on your Chapter 5 reading and activities.

TIP MODEL SCENARIO #1 Ms. Chinita was teaching her students higher level study skills. She wanted to show them how they could outline a complicated article by drawing a diagram to illustrate the ideas in it and how they relate to each other. She found this visual display worked very well for her, and she wanted her students to learn it, too. However, she found the approach didn't work very well because students who were learning this technique for the first time tended to make a lot of mistakes drawing the boxes and connecting the lines, and then they didn't want to do the work of erasing and revising them.

1.1 What software tool would you recommend that Ms. Chinita use to address this problem?

1.2 What would be the relative advantage of using this software tool?

1.3 Would this kind of activity be best done on an individual basis, in pairs, or in groups? Explain your answer.

TIP MODEL SCENARIO #2 Whenever Mr. Jackson had his students do a research project for his social studies class, he would send them to the library/media center to look up the information in reference books. As it often happened that several students wanted to use the same text, a lot of time was wasted; it was difficult to keep students focused on the information gathering. Mr. Jackson had heard about a software tool that several students could use easily at the same time. In addition, it had pictures and videos as well as text descriptions, so students got more out of the information they did find.

2.1 What software tool did Mr. Jackson have in mind to address this problem?

2.2 What would be the relative advantage of using this software tool?

2.3 How would it be possible for all the members of a class of 30 students to use this tool at the same time?

TIP MODEL SCENARIO #3 Ms. Hortense's consumer math classes have more than 40 students each. She likes to give her students weekly quizzes to make sure everyone is keeping up on the skills and to spot those who may need additional help. However, the class is so large and students sit so close together that she also feels she needs several versions of each test to prevent "sharing answers." She has heard about a software tool that she can use to create a pool of items. It also lets her generate different versions of the same test from the items.

3.1 What software tool would you recommend that Ms. Hortense use to address this problem?

3.2 What would be the relative advantage of using this software tool?

3.3 What tool could she use to make these tests easier to score?

TIP MODEL SCENARIO #4 Mr. Charles wants to make his middle school classes hands-on, with students doing experiments by collecting and analyzing their own data. However, taking accurate readings of variables such as temperature is very difficult for his students to do. Also, the students find the repetitious recording and calculating to be very boring, and it is difficult to keep them focused on the experiment. He has heard about a software tool that can collect temperature readings quickly and feed the data automatically into a computer for analysis. He thinks that using this tool will be much more motivating to his students than doing all the operations by hand.

4.1 What software tool would you recommend that Mr. Charles use to address this problem?

4.2 What would be the relative advantage of using this tool?

4.3 If Mr. Charles has 36 students in a class and only five such tools, how could he arrange the tool so that all students could learn to use it?

TIP MODEL SCENARIO #5 Ms. Keishan, a high school current issues teacher, has learned about GIS tools and knows that they are becoming as essential to studying geography and local issues as word processing is to learning to write. She wants her students to learn about these tools through work on a meaningful project that will let them see the real-life applications of the tools. She has learned that the science class does an environmental studies project every fall at a local river in which they collect water samples and do tests to analyze sources of degradation and contaminants. Then they try to determine the sources of these withdrawals and contaminants. She asks the science teacher if they could work together on a project that would provide GIS information to help students with these water analyses.

5.1 What instructional problems did Ms. Keishan see that she wanted to address in the new project?

5.2 In what ways could a GIS system help with the environmental studies project?

5.3 How might GPS tools also be useful with the project?

TIE into Practice: Technology Integration Examples

The Technology Integration Example that opened this chapter (*A Desktop-Published Literary Anthology*) showed how a teacher might use desktop publishing software to help produce the annual literary anthology of student work. With the knowledge you have gained from Chapter 5, do the following with this example:

1. Mr. Mortenson created a page format for the anthology like the one shown here. Use a publishing software to create a similar page.

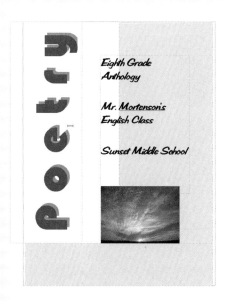

First Page of a Desktop-Published Anthology Format.

2. Answer the following questions about the *Anthology* example:

- Phase 1 — How did using desktop publishing for the anthology offer relative advantage in comparison with the way the teachers had done it before?

- Phase 2 — Mr. Mortenson created a rubric to assess students' work on short story structure, required revisions, and creativity. How would you structure the levels of performance for the "creativity" element?

- Phase 3 — How might Mr. Mortenson involve the art classes in the preparation of this anthology? What software tools might they use that would work well with the desktop publishing software?

- Phase 4 — Online tutorials on software tools can be used to help train teachers and/or students in the use of various desktop publishing software tools. Where might you direct Mr. Mortenson and the computer applications teacher to locate such tutorials?

- Phase 5 — If the principal said no funds were available to purchase the desktop publishing software the teachers wanted, how might the teachers raise the money they need?

3. What NETS for Students skills would students learn by working on the *Anthology* project? (See the front of this book for a list of NETS for Students.)

Technology Integration Lesson Planning

Complete the following exercise using sample lesson plans found on MyEducationLab.

1. Locate lesson ideas — MyEducationLab has several examples of lessons that use desktop publishing, draw/paint and image editing software, charting/graphing tools, concept mapping software, and MBLs/CBLs. Go to MyEducationLab and select the topic "Instructional Planning." Under "Lesson Plans," review the following example integration lessons and choose two:

- A Partner Approach to Reading and Writing About the News
- Desktop Poetry Project
- Creating Interactive Storybooks
- Integrating Art in the Curriculum: Computer Drawing Tools
- A Project with Teeth
- Dare to Fly with Class
- Concept Mapping with Handheld Computers
- Electronic Outlining for Writing and Studying

2. Evaluate the lesson — Use the *Evaluation Checklist for a Technology-Integrated Lesson* (located on MyEducationLab under the topic, "Instructional Planning") to evaluate each of your lessons.

3. Modify a lesson — Select one of the lesson ideas and adapt its strategies to meet a need in your own content area. You may choose to use the same software as in the original or to use a different software package.

4. Add descriptors — Create descriptors for your new lesson similar to those found within the sample lessons (e.g., grade level, content and topic areas, technologies used, relative advantage, objectives, NETS standards).

For Your Teaching Portfolio

For this chapter's contribution to your teaching portfolio, add the following products you created in the Technology Integration Workshop:

- The desktop-published pages you created for the *Anthology* project
- The evaluations you did using the *Evaluation Checklist for a Technology-Integrated Lesson*
- The new lesson plan you developed, based on the one you found on MyEducationLab.

Chapter 6
Teaching with Multimedia and Hypermedia

From an educational perspective, each medium represents the world in different ways.

Tony Bates and Gary Poole, in *Effective Teaching with Technology in Higher Education* (2003)

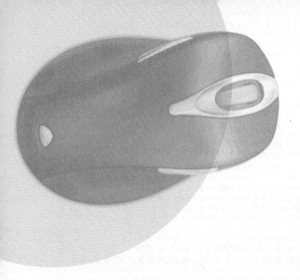

Technology Integration Example

Interactive Multimedia Storybooks

Adapted from: Frederickson, S. (2002). Interactive multimedia storybooks. *Learning and Leading with Technology, 25*(1), 6–10.

Grade Level: 7–8 and 1–2 (working together) • **Content Area/Topic: Language arts, literature** • **Length of Time: Nine weeks**

Phases 1 and 2: Assess technological pedagogical content knowledge; Determine relative advantage

Ms. Dubey was the language arts department chair for her small, rural, K–8 school. While watching first- and second-grade students using interactive storybooks on the Internet and CD-ROM, she was struck by how absorbed they were in the use of language and by their level of engagement with the content of the stories. She realized that they seemed to be learning a great deal about story elements and structure as well as enjoying the reading activity. As she reflected on the difficulties that the seventh- and eighth-grade teachers were having in capturing their students' interest in reading and language, she had an idea for a project that could benefit both the elementary and the middle school students. She decided to ask the grade 7–8 teachers if they would like to have their students create interactive storybooks for the grade 1–2 students. She knew that the school had several copies of *Adobe Flash®*, a popular multimedia design and development software package and that the technology coordinator had been looking for curriculum projects for which this software might be useful. *Adobe **Flash*** is the industry standard for creating interactive web-based animations, websites, and online software tools. Its effectiveness can be attributed to two primary reasons: first, *Flash* merges a powerful, yet easy-to-use visual environment with a robust programming language (i.e., *ActionScript*), thereby allowing developers to combine aesthetically pleasing interfaces with powerful programming techniques; and second, *Flash* files are very small and download quickly over the Internet. Although *Flash* development is often viewed as requiring sophisticated proficiency accessible only to those with extensive programming backgrounds, creating interactive frame-by-frame narratives can be an uncomplicated design process due to *Flash's* visual timeline and stage for organizing imagery and buttons. Additionally, *Flash* has a built-in Script Assist wizard to help beginners learn basic programming skills. When Ms. Dubey approached the grade 7-8 teachers about this idea, they were excited about it, and the technology coordinator promised to help support their work. They decided

that the grade 1–2 students would create storylines that the grade 7–8 students would turn into online interactive books, presenting each group with a meaningful role in the project.

Prior to the beginning of the project, however, Ms. Dubey realized she needed to assess her own technological pedagogical content knowledge (TPACK) so that she could evaluate her strengths and weaknesses and understand where she might locate herself within the TPACK model. She realized that her knowledge of the content she was teaching, her knowledge of the instructional methods she planned to use, and her understanding of how to use technology effectively for learning all positioned her in the middle of the TPACK model. She was excited to move forward to give her students a unique opportunity.

Phase 3: Decide on objectives and assessments

The teachers worked together to decide on what they wanted students to achieve as a result of this project. In addition to acquiring or increasing *Flash* skills and creating completed products, they wanted to make sure grade 7–8 students were learning about story structure and components. They stated project objectives for each grade level and created assessment methods to measure each skill. The outcomes, objectives, and assessments they decided on were as follows:

- **Grade 1–2 Outcome:** Create story lines. **Objective:** Working with the teacher as a whole class, students verbally outline stories to be turned into interactive storybooks. **Assessment:** Rubric to assess on-task behaviors, communications skills, and creativity.

- **Grade 7–8 Outcome:** Demonstrate basic *Flash* design skills. **Objective:** Each student completes all steps to create five to seven frames on the *Flash* timeline (a visual organization of a file's content over time separated into individual frames) to demonstrate the following skills: creating new frames, entering text, inserting graphics, creating buttons, and linking frames with basic *ActionScript* for the buttons. **Assessment:** Checklist of required frames, interactive story elements, and *Flash* skills.

- **Grade 7–8 Outcome:** Design an interactive multimedia story. **Objective:** Students work in groups to prepare an interactive story structure based on the grade 1–2 students' story line, place it on **storyboards** (planning blueprints from which the multimedia product will be designed), create and link the *Flash* frames, and revise it based on feedback. Each group achieves at least 20 of 25 points on the rubric. **Assessment:** Rubric on story structure, completion of *Flash* tasks, completion of required revisions, and creativity.

- **Grade 7–8 Outcome:** Work effectively in small groups. **Objective:** All students demonstrate effective group work behaviors by scoring at least 90% on a group work rubric. **Assessment:** Rubric to assess group behaviors.

- **Grade 7–8 Outcome:** Identify story components on a test. **Objective:** Each student demonstrates a grasp of story structure and components (e.g., plot, sequence, characters) by identifying all of them in at least one completed story. **Assessment:** Checklist of correctly identified story elements.

Phase 4: Design integration strategies

The teachers knew that this project would take some coordination among classes as well as substantial planning and outlining work before students would be able to begin their story production work. They decided on the following timeline for the project:

- **Week 1: Story outlining:** Grade 1–2 classes work with their teachers to create outlines of stories. After the teachers introduce one of their favorite stories, they ask students to brainstorm ideas for a new story. The students dictate the stories as the teachers write them down. Then they read them together and revise them as they like. Each class prepares two stories in this way.

- **Weeks 2–4: Multimedia skill building:** The technology coordinator works with the grade 7–8 teachers and their classes to help them learn the *Flash* skills they will need for this project. Together they do small projects (e.g., basic timeline graphic animations, a linear photograph slideshow, an interactive map of their school, and so on) to build the required technical skills. At the same time, the technology coordinator begins assigning areas of expertise to individual students so that there will be "experts" working on each part of the final product. Some students are assigned to produce graphics to illustrate the story; others become experts on animations, buttons, sounds, or text.

- **Week 5: Storyboarding:** The grade 7–8 students begin their work by interviewing the grade 1–2 students to see what they have in mind for the stories. Working together as a whole class, they identify the story elements for one story. Then, working in small groups, each group identifies elements for an additional story. After students review the structure in this way, the grade 7–8 teachers help their students make the story outlines into frames for the storybook. They design frames on 4- by 6-in. note cards,

which serve as their storyboards. They place the storyboards in the order in which they will go in the interactive book and place "button" stickers on the cards to show where the decision points will be.

- **Weeks 6–8:** The grade 7–8 students work in teams to create interactive stories based on their storyboard blueprints. The technology coordinator again provides help as students work with the *Flash* program to develop their products.

- **Week 9: Assessment and presentation:** After drafts are completed, each team reviews the work of another team. Each team makes revisions to its product, as needed. Finally, the grade 7–8 students present their work to the grade 1–2 students, who interact with the digital stories and give their feedback.

Phase 5: Prepare the instructional environment

To make sure they had all of the resources they would need for the project, the teachers did the following:

- **Lab scheduling:** Ms. Dubey and the teachers knew that much of the work would need to be done in the computer lab, so Ms. Dubey confirmed lab time for the classes.

- **Software copies:** The technology coordinator knew that the computer lab had only one "five-pack" (five copies) of *Flash* software. However, because he had sufficient notice, he was able to obtain a lab-pack, or 30 additional copies on one site license. This allowed him to place one legal copy on each lab computer, as well as two copies for each grade 7–8 class computer.

- **Handouts:** The technology coordinator obtained wall posters and handouts that summarized the *Flash* features and how to use each one. He also placed copies of these on the school website so that anyone could download additional copies later.

- **Other equipment:** So that students would be able to create images for use in *Flash*, the technology coordinator made sure the optical scanner was working in the lab and gave each class the use of a digital camera.

Phase 6: Evaluating and revising

As Ms. Dubey and the teachers looked at the rubric results and interviewed the students, they knew the project had been a success. For the most part, students had worked well together in small groups, and the resulting products were of high quality. The grade 1–2 students were thrilled with the interactive stories created by the grade 7–8 students. Results of the story component identification task indicated that grade 7–8 students had a good grasp of the structure and parts of their stories. Additionally, the grade 7–8 students gained valuable insights into project storyboarding and interactive design, experience that they would be able to develop further in future classes. The teachers decided to repeat the project the following year, this time to focus on producing and comparing various genres of stories.

Objectives

After reading this chapter and completing the learning activities for it, you should be able to:

1. Define *multimedia* and *hypermedia* from historic and current perspectives.

2. Evaluate the quality and capabilities of commercial multimedia and hypermedia products.

3. Describe resources and skills required for multimedia/hypermedia design, development, and integration.

4. Use a multimedia/hypermedia authoring package to design and develop a product that meets visual, navigational, and instructional criteria.

5. Design lesson activities appropriate for each kind of multimedia/hypermedia product.

Introduction to Multimedia and Hypermedia

We live in a multimedia world, surrounded by complex images, photographs, video, and audio. So perhaps it is not surprising that part of our human evolution has focused on making our technology reflect the color and clamor of our surroundings. In educational technology, multimedia has been a steadily growing presence for some time. Computer-based multimedia learning stations have been used since 1966, and non-computer multimedia methods have been around even longer. This chapter examines current classroom uses of electronic multimedia and its companion concept, hypermedia.

Multimedia vs. Hypermedia

Like other educational technology concepts, definitions for *multimedia* and *hypermedia* defy consensus (Moore, Myers, & Burton, 1994; Tolhurst, 1995); people find the two concepts either too close to distinguish between or too slippery to get words around. Tolhurst quoted one source as saying, "By its very nature, [multimedia] is an invertebrate. You poke it and it slithers away" (p. 21). The definitions used in this chapter come to us from two paths that were separate initially but have converged over time.

Multimedia simply means "multiple media" or "a combination of media." The media can be still graphics and photographs, sound, motion video, animation, and/or text items combined in a product whose purpose is to communicate information in multiple ways.

Hypermedia refers to "linked media" or "interactive media," terms that have their roots in a concept developed by Vannevar Bush (1986) in his landmark article "As We May Think." In 1945, Bush proposed a "memex" machine that would let people quickly access items of information

whose meanings were connected but that were stored in different places. In the 1960s, Ted Nelson coined the term *hypertext* to describe a proposed database system, called *Xanadu*, based on Bush's idea (Boyle, 1997). In this system, items of information from all over the world were to be logically connected with hypertext links. For example, one could select "apple" and get information on all related concepts such as trees and fruit—even the Garden of Eden. The technology at that time was inadequate to produce Xanadu, but the idea was the forerunner of today's hypermedia systems in which information stored in various media are connected (often via the Internet)—thus the term *hypermedia*.

In current technologies, such as Internet browsers (see Chapter 7) and design/development software packages, most multimedia products also are hypermedia systems. That is, contemporary media elements are linked together by buttons and navigation menus and often exist as components in a larger, immersive environment. Clicking on or selecting one item sends the user to other, related items. This chapter provides many examples of hypermedia products; all also are multimedia. The combination of media such as video and audio with text makes them multimedia; the ability to get from one media/information element to another makes them hypermedia. It is important to note that the term *multimedia* has become somewhat of an over-arching descriptor for most Internet-based media, interactive or static (i.e., a linear, fixed progression of content). Also, as of this edition's publication, many professionals in the design and development community use the term *new media* to describe the various types of interactive online work they create. Because most of these tools nowadays are actually online linked media, and in order to preserve the term's use throughout the cited references, subsequent discussion in this chapter will refer to them as *hypermedia* unless the term *multimedia* is more appropriate, as in the case of digitized video products.

Types of Hypermedia Systems

Hypermedia systems come in a variety of hardware, software, and media configurations and, until recently, were usually classified according to their primary storage equipment: interactive videodiscs (IVDs), CD-ROMs (compact disc–read-only memory), digital versatile discs (DVDs), Blu-ray discs (Blu-ray), and other technologies. However, dramatic changes in the capabilities of presentation software, multimedia design and development tools, and Internet multimedia formats, as well as the decline in use of videodisc systems, have changed the focus of this classification system from the delivery medium to the purpose and type of capability the products offer.

This chapter focuses on the following six kinds of hypermedia formats: commercial hypermedia software packages, presentation software, video production and editing systems, hypermedia design and development software, virtual reality environments, and Web 2.0. The first represents products developed by companies and sold to educational consumers; the other five are design and development tools (or software packages) that educators and others can use to create their own multimedia and hypermedia products.

Current and Future Impact of Hypermedia on Education

The current widespread educational use of hypermedia systems predicts an even heavier reliance on these products in classrooms of the future. Educators recognize and use these systems when they see the powerful capabilities they offer to enhance classroom learning.

- **Increased motivation** — Hypermedia programs offer such varied options that most people seem to enjoy using them. Students who usually struggle to complete a project or term paper often will tackle a hypermedia project enthusiastically. Many educators believe the most important characteristic of hypermedia is its ability to encourage students to be proactive learners.

- **Flexible learning modes** — Hypermedia programs can draw on such diverse tools that they truly offer something for students who excel in any of what Gardner calls "intelligences" (see Chapter 3). For example, a student who may not be good at written expression but has visual aptitude can document learning with sound or pictures.

- **Development of creative and critical thinking skills** — The tremendous access to hypertext and hypermedia tools opens up a multitude of creative avenues for both students and teachers. Creation of hypermedia products requires that the learner constantly make decisions and evaluate progress, thus encouraging students to apply higher order thinking skills. Brown (2007) suggests that

Adapting for Special Needs

Hypermedia environments have often posed barriers for student learners who are deaf or hard-of-hearing, blind or vision-impaired, or who have difficulty using a mouse to control the computer. As a result, access to multimedia and hypermedia has been an area of concern for the disability community, which has challenged designers to use tools that create accessible lessons and activities. Most design and development tools (e.g., *Adobe Flash, Adobe DreamWeaver,* and so on) provide developers with a wide range of options for improving accessibility in their designs; however, the accessibility capabilities of such software packages often require sophisticated levels of expertise and programming knowledge. Alternatively, there are several authoring tools available that simplify the process of creating accessible content. One such software package is *IntelliPics Studio* (www.intellitools.com). Comparable to other multimedia authoring tools in its ease of use; ability to manipulate text, graphics, and media; and multiple platform availability, *IntelliPics Studio* includes features that provide speech output; single-switch scanning; and access via a standard keyboard, an IntelliKeys alternative keyboard, a mouse, or a touch screen. *IntelliPics Studio* is an essential multimedia design tool for teachers and students committed to developing accessible hypermedia products that can be used by everyone.

Contributed by Dave Edyburn

multimedia design is a complex and generative activity for learners and supports the development of metacognitive skills, problem-solving strategies, creative freedom, and self-awareness of individual learning styles under demanding project-based conditions.

- **Improved writing and process skills** — Carlin-Menter and Shuell (2003) find that by engaging students in multimedia design during the writing process, two-dimensional linear thinking is replaced with multidimensional thinking with regard to story, characters, and context. Multimedia and hypermedia authoring tools can help students generate new and different perspectives on organizing and presenting information, ultimately formulating new insights into the writing process. Instead of viewing writing as one long stream of text, students now see it as chunks of information to be linked.

Hypermedia tools also permit sophisticated evaluations of learning through incorporation of databases to record and archive student use and progress. In the process of using hypermedia, people are said to "leave a track" (Simonson & Thompson, 1994), which may be useful for teachers in analyzing how students approach learning tasks and the various paths learners explore within an array of content. At present, Internet-based learning environments are being designed to apply pattern-recognition techniques from the field of artificial intelligence to help schools assess student mastery of higher order cognitive skills. Bagui (1998) says that multimedia "may have unique capabilities to facilitate learning because of the parallels between multimedia and the natural way people learn" (p. 4), that is, through visual information and imagery.

Research on the Impact of Multimedia and Hypermedia Systems

Roblyer (1999) found that the benefit of multimedia and hypermedia use in the classroom seems to center on the ability to offer students multiple channels through which to process information. Reviews of research by Mayer (1997) from studies of hypermedia use supported this position. He found that students who received explanations in both visual and verbal format (as opposed to students who received verbal presentations only) tended to generate more creative solutions on problem-solving transfer tests. Ultimately, Mayer found that effects were strongest for students with high spatial ability and low prior knowledge. Subsequent studies (Mayer & Moreno, 1998; Moreno & Mayer, 2002) also found that learners exhibited greater comprehension and retention of learned materials when pictures were accompanied by spoken words rather than by written words. Mayer and Moreno observed that this "split attention" effect was consistent with a model of working memory that had separate visual and auditory channels.

Swan and Meskill (1996) examined how effectively current hypermedia products support the teaching and acquisition of critical thinking skills in reading and language. They reviewed hypermedia products in terms of how well they made possible response-based approaches to teaching and learning literature—that is, instructional activities that "place student-generated questions at the center of learning . . . (and encourage) a problem-finding as well as a problem-solving approach to critical thinking" (p. 168). They evaluated 45 hypermedia literature programs using criteria in three areas: technical items, response-based concerns, and classroom issues. The majority of the 45 products used a CD-ROM format, but 10 used a combination of CD-ROM and videodisc, and 4 used computer software. They found that most products were technically sound and linked well with classroom topics, but few were designed to promote the response-based methods that promote critical thinking. "Programs designed for elementary students . . . equated literature education with reading instruction; programs designed for high school . . . generally adopted a traditional text-centered approach" (p. 187). These findings indicate that teachers who want to use multimedia/hypermedia products specifically to promote higher level skills must select products judiciously and warily.

In another review of the impact of hypermedia on learner comprehension and learner control, Dillon and Gabbard (1998) echo the caution voiced by Swan and Meskill (1996). They conclude that:

- Hypermedia's primary advantage is allowing rapid searches through lengthy or multiple information resources. For other purposes, non-hypermedia resources seem equally useful.

- Increased learner control is more useful to higher ability students; lower ability students experience the greatest difficulty with hypermedia.

- Learner style helps determine whether certain hypermedia features are effective in various learning situations. Passive learners may profit more from the cueing offered by hypermedia, whereas more capable learners who are willing to explore may be more capable of exploiting other hypermedia features.

Research on the Design and Use of Multimedia and Hypermedia Systems

Stemler (1997) reviewed findings on various multimedia/hypermedia characteristics that could have an impact on the potential effectiveness of these systems: instructional design, screen design, learner control and navigation, use of feedback, student interactivity, and video and audio elements. Her findings are too extensive to treat adequately here, but educators who are committed to high-quality multimedia development should review the full text of her article.

- **Instructional design** — Stemler recommends that developers analyze each element in a multimedia product to determine which of Gagné's nine Events of Instruction (see Chapter 2) it aims to achieve and how well it achieves those events (p. 342).

- **Screen design** — Well-designed screens focus learners' attention, develop and maintain interest, promote processing of information, promote engagement between learner and content, help students find and organize information, and support easy navigation through lessons (p. 343).

Use the following questions to reflect on issues in technology integration and to guide discussions within your class.

1. In his essay in *Wired* magazine ("*PowerPoint* Is Evil: Power Corrupts. *PowerPoint* Corrupts Absolutely"), Edward Tufte (2003) opines, "Alas, slideware often reduces the analytical quality of presentations. In particular, the popular *PowerPoint* templates (ready-made designs) usually weaken verbal and spatial reasoning, and almost always corrupt statistical analysis.... Particularly disturbing is the adoption of the *PowerPoint* cognitive style in our schools. Rather than learning to write a report using sentences, children are being taught how to formulate client pitches and infomercials." What do you think causes poor classroom use of *PowerPoint*? What would you recommend that teachers do to make sure students use *PowerPoint* effectively?

2. Sherry Turkle (2004) says, "Information technology is identity technology. Embedding it in a culture that supports democracy, freedom of expression, tolerance, diversity, and complexity of opinion is one of the decade's greatest challenges (p. B28)." What role could multimedia instructional materials and student multimedia projects play in bringing about this culture? How can teachers' use of multimedia support the development of such a culture?

- **Interaction and feedback** — Keep feedback on the same screen with the question and student response, and provide immediate feedback. Verify correct answers, and give hints and another try for incorrect answers. Tailor feedback to the response, and provide encouraging feedback; but do not make it more entertaining for students to provide wrong answers than to provide correct ones. If possible, provide students with the option to print out feedback (p. 345).

- **Navigation** — Support navigation with orientation cues, clearly defined procedures, clearly labeled back-and-forward buttons, and help segments (pp. 346–347).

- **Learner control** — In general, provide older and more capable students with more control over the sequence of instructional tasks; younger, less experienced students should have a more guided sequence (p. 348).

- **Color** — Use color sparingly, and employ it primarily for cueing and highlighting certain elements to bring them to the learner's attention. Use a consistent color scheme throughout to promote ease of use (pp. 350–351).

- **Graphics** — Use graphics as well as text to present information that serves students who prefer one kind of presentation over the other. Use graphics sparingly for other purposes (to entertain or amuse); in other words, don't use graphics for the sake of using graphics (p. 351).

- **Animation** — Use animation sparingly and only to present dynamic processes or to highlight key information (p. 352).

- **Audio** — Use audio for short presentations of program content, but do not let it compete with video presentation. Do not require long readings on each screen. Separate material into chunks on each of several screens (p. 353).

- **Video** — Use video sequences for broader, abstract material (that with emotional impact) and for advance organizers rather than for presenting detailed information (p. 354).

Kirschner, Strijbos, Kreijns, and Beers (2004) offer a contemporary perspective of design for online learning environments based on **interaction design**, a discipline focused on creating pleasurable experiences that appeal to and benefit the learner. Interaction design is anchored in the design framework of utility, usability, and aesthetics. This framework provides designers and developers, as well as technology integration specialists and teachers, with a simple set of principles to consider when designing or selecting hypermedia and multimedia applications for use in the classroom (Kirschner et al., 2004):

- **Utility** — **Utility** is concerned with the assortment of functionalities and features incorporated in a hypermedia system or application that satisfy the outlined pedagogical objectives and requirements. In other words, does the hypermedia system provide learners with the content, tools, and necessary scaffolding they need to accomplish their instructional tasks?

- **Usability** — **Usability**, essentially a system's ease-of-use, is defined as the effectiveness, efficiency, and satisfaction with which learners can accomplish a series of tasks in the hypermedia application. Together, the utility and usability of a hypermedia design represent the *usefulness* of the system.

- **Aesthetics** — The **aesthetics** of a hypermedia or multimedia application represent those elements of the design that enhance and heighten the learner experience, as opposed to elements designed merely to satisfy the pedagogical or technical needs of the instructional objectives. Aesthetics may represent the graphic or visual design of the system, the pleasure of use between the learner and the materials, and/or the personal satisfaction or reflection experienced by the learner when using and learning with the system (Norman, 2004).

Although many agree that aesthetics is an essential and vital element in our everyday learning experiences (Lavie & Tractinsky, 2004; Wilson, 2005), contemporary research on emotion suggests that aesthetically pleasing objects affect our emotions positively (e.g., happiness, pleasure, satisfaction, and so on) (Jordan, 2000) and facilitate enhanced curiosity, creativity, and decision-making skills by broadening our thought processes, ultimately promoting learning (Ashby, Isen, & Turken, 1999; Norman, 2004). In addition, research has demonstrated a strong positive correlation between perceived aesthetics and perceived usability, both in product use and software interaction (Hassenzahl, 2004).

Finally, an ongoing series of studies by Mayer focuses on design and usage characteristics for educational multimedia that can optimize impact on student achievement (e.g., Mayer, Fennell, & Farmer, 2004; Mayer & Moreno, 2003). These include methods of reducing *cognitive load* (in which the required cognitive processing of materials exceeds the learner's available cognitive capacity) during multimedia learning, and personalizing multimedia presentations to help students process material more actively.

Recent Developments in Hypermedia Systems

The following three trends in hypermedia system use in education are evident:

- **Web 2.0: Users as designers** — Much of the current development, implementation, and research in the educational technology integration world is focused on *Web 2.0*: an Internet trend that puts the design and authorship of online content into the hands of a website's users. Examples of Web 2.0 online spaces include blogs, wikis, and social-networking sites where users add, modify, and share content, ultimately acting as editors to create the infrastructure of the website. Web 2.0 examples will be discussed later in this chapter as well as in several other chapters in this book.

- **Convergence of offline (disc) and online (Internet) development** — Because of the migration to Internet-based delivery for most hypermedia and multimedia instructional products, educators and researchers currently view hypermedia and online web pages as synonymous.

- **Increasing ease of use** — Hypermedia and multimedia development used to be a fairly technical enterprise. However, thanks to user-friendly design and development systems (e.g., *Adobe DreamWeaver* and *HyperStudio* for authoring hypermedia, *Quicktime VR Authoring Studio*

for the design of virtual environments, Apple *iMovie* and *Windows Movie Maker* for multimedia production and editing) in addition to photography and graphics software tools (e.g., Apple *iPhoto*, *Adobe Photoshop Elements*), the development of all forms of hypermedia and multimedia from presentation software to video production has become accessible to nontechnical teachers and students. This user-friendly trend will likely continue, with future versions of existing software and the development of new hypermedia and multimedia development suites entering both corporate and educational realms.

Commercial Hypermedia Software Packages

As noted in Chapter 3, instructional software is becoming increasingly more like hypermedia in nature. The software tools discussed in Chapters 4 and 5 also reflect this trend. The increased storage capability and availability of CD and DVD media has made it easier to store complex programs with motion graphics, movies, audio, and links to the Internet. Several types of commercial hypermedia products are also readily available, including instructional software (e.g., tutorials, drills, simulations), interactive books and ebooks, reference materials, and collections of development materials. Additionally, Internet bandwidth connection speeds are increasing at a rapid rate in homes and school districts, allowing designers to incorporate CD- and DVD-quality video and multimedia artifacts on the web. Increasing bandwidth availability is one of the key factors in the steadfast merger of multimedia and hypermedia. Examples of commercial hypermedia and multimedia are discussed here and summarized in Table 6.1.

Instructional Software

As described in Chapter 3, instructional software packages, once primarily text-based materials, now often have an extensive assortment of hypermedia features with broadcast-quality multimedia content. Hypermedia features have increased the capability and value of these programs. For example:

- **Tutorials** — Descriptions and explanations can be visual in nature and can be presented with screen capture videos (i.e., video recordings of another user's screen when demonstrating a task), digitized video played in the browser, spoken to the student through use of audio files, and/or presented in text format with supportive imagery.

- **Drill and practice** — Practice items can be posed in audio or video, as well as text, and feedback for correct and incorrect answers can be presented in any combination of these modes.

TABLE 6.1 Summary of Commercial Multimedia Products

Type of Multimedia Product	Sample Sources of Materials	Description

Instructional software	• **MCH Multimedia Developers of Interactive Software**
	  http://mchmultimedia.com/
	• **Tutorial Finder**
	  http://www.tutorialfind.com
	• **DK Multimedia at educate-me.net**
	  http://www.educate-me.net/
	• ***A.D.A.M. The Inside Story***
	  http://adam.com/Our_Products/
	  School_and_Instruction/Educators/K-8/atis.html
	• **Lynda.com**
	  http://www.lynda.com
		• Tutorials
		• Drills
		• Simulations
		• Instructional games
		• Problem solving

Interactive books and eBooks	• **Clifford Interactive Storybooks**
	  http://teacher.scholastic.com/clifford1
	• **All Educational Software interactive storybooks**
	  http://www.alleducationalsoftware.com/
	  interactive-storybooks.html
	• **PBS Kids interactive storybooks**
	  http://pbskids.org/lions/stories/
	• **Grimm Fairy Tales**
	  http://www.grimmfairytales.com/en/main
	• **StoryPlace: Children's Digital Library**
	  http://www.storyplace.org/
		• Interactive storybooks

	• **Listing of books online**
	  http://digital.library.upen.edu/books/
	• **Free downloadable ebooks**
	  http://www.free-ebooks.net/
	• ***Google Books***
	  http://books.google.com/
	• **Project Gutenberg Collection**
	  http://www.gutenberg.org/wiki/Main_Page
		• Ebooks

Reference materials	• **Encarta**
	  http://encarta.msn.com
	• **Encyclopedia.com**
	  http://www.encyclopedia.com/
	• **Encyclopedia Britannica**
	  http://www.britannica.com/
	• **Wikipedia.org**
	  http://www.wikipedia.org
		• Encyclopedia

	• **The Old Farmer's Almanac**
	  http://www.almanac.com/
	• **World Almanac for Kids**
	  http://www.worldalmanacforkids.com/
	• **Nation by Nation Almanac**
	  http://www.nationbynation.com/
		• Almanacs

	• **World Atlas**
	  http://www.graphicmaps.com/aatlas/world.htm
	• ***Google Maps***
	  http://maps.google.com
		• Atlases

TABLE 6.1 **Summary of Commercial Multimedia Products** *(continued)*

Type of Multimedia Product	Sample Sources of Materials	Description
	• *Google Earth* http://earth.google.com • Microsoft *Virtual Earth* http://www.microsoft.com/VirtualEarth/ • **USA Today** http://usatoday.com • **New York Times** http://www.nytimes.com	• Newspapers and newsletters
Collections of development resources	• **Microsoft's Clip Art and Media Collection** http://office.microsoft.com/clipart • **Flaming Text** http://www.flamingtext.com/ • **Animation Factory** http://www.animationfactory.com/en/ • **iStockphoto** http://www.istockphoto.com • **dafont Free Font Collection** http://www.dafont.com • **Freesound Project** http://www.freesound.org/	• Clip art • Audio clips • Video clips • Animations

- **Simulations** — Because multimedia presentations can include movement and sound, simulations can be even more realistic than textual narratives and imagery of a concept or context.

- **Instructional games** — Motion and sound can make presentations more attractive and can further enhance the motivational qualities of games.

- **Problem solving** — Problems may be presented to learners in video format, thus clarifying the problems to be solved and demonstrating visually the relationship among the items of information required for solution generation.

Interactive Books and ebooks

Two kinds of interactive books are currently available: interactive storybooks and interactive texts. The first type targets primarily younger students, whereas the second is most often used by older students and adult learners (e.g., inservice teachers).

On-screen stories have become extremely popular with primary teachers and students (Glasgow, 1996, 1996–1997, 1997; Grimshaw, 2007; Kahn, 1997a), even toddlers (Robinson, 2003). On the audio tracks, narrators read pages as the words are highlighted on screen for the learner. If a stu-

dent needs to hear a word again, just clicking on it with the mouse pointer activates the audio. Some electronic storybooks have a straightforward approach, allowing students to read them at their own pace. Other books are structured to be more interactive and open ended—some allowing students to choose the story path and to end where they want each time the story is read. A study by Doty, Popplewell, and Byers (2001) found that students' ability to answer comprehension questions was higher when they read stories in an electronic storybook format than when they read them in a traditional book format. Similarly, Grimshaw (2007) found a significant increase in enjoyment and comprehension on the part of students when comparing an electronic storybook to the traditional text, as well as increased comprehension when the book was narrated in the electronic version.

ebooks have become a valuable resource for students and teachers alike since they offer more flexibility than print texts do. Because they are no longer copyrighted, many of the classics are available as free downloads for teachers and students. (See Table 6.1 for notes on ebook download sites.)

Reference Materials

Many reference materials are available on CD and DVD at very reasonable cost; in addition, there is increased availability of reference materials on the Internet for little to no cost. To add still more value, these resources are accompanied by search tools that make searching for information in the application both easy and efficient. Some materials have Internet links to still more material. The following are just a few of the categories and example titles:

- **Encyclopedias** — Most of the major encyclopedias are no longer published exclusively in book format; they are available on CD, DVD, and the Internet. Some, like Microsoft's *Encarta,* were designed solely for the electronic format and are available only on disc or the Internet. Others, such as the *World Book Encyclopedia,* now have a version on disc after having been published for many years in book format.
- **Almanacs** — Popular information collections, such as *The Time Almanac,* are increasingly shifting to electronic format. Most are currently available for free on the Internet.
- **Atlases** — Online interactive map utilities, such as *Google Earth,* allow teachers and students to do a variety of interactive activities, such as determining distances and routes from one location to another or exploring the Earth in 3D and utilizing layers of visual data that can be superimposed over the Earth. Others, like the CIA's *The World Factbook,* summarize many kinds of geographical information—from reference maps to population, economical, communication, and transportation data.
- **Newspapers and newsletters** — Most newspapers have searchable online sites, and many, including the *New York Times,* have special educational programs for students. These can be indispensable sources of news and other current events information as well as of great lesson ideas and support materials.
- **Proceedings and other conference materials** — Major education conferences, like the National Educational Computing Conference (NECC), distribute to each registrant proceedings, presenter handouts, vendor samples, and shareware on a CD-ROM. Additionally, many conferences are now making this information available and searchable on their websites.

Some new commercial multimedia products combine instructional software functions with a set of reference materials to create a multifaceted product that can meet a variety of educational needs. One example of this combination approach is the *A.D.A.M. Interactive Anatomy 4.0* software series. It combines simulations of dissections, animated body images, sets of reference images, and notes on anatomy and physiology in single software packages. (See Figure 6.1.)

FIGURE 6.1   Sample screenshot using *A.D.A.M. InterActive Physiology*

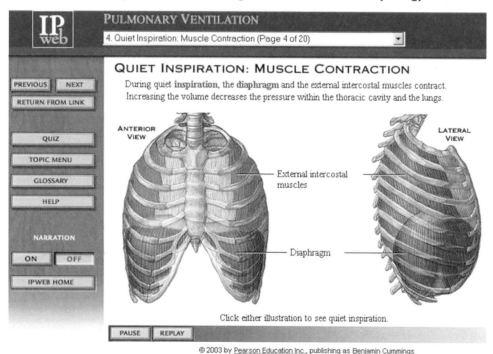

Source: Copyright © 2003, Pearson Education, Inc.

Students use commercial multimedia products as reference materials.

Collections of Development Resources

Many collections of resources used to develop multimedia are available on CD-ROM and the Internet. These include col-

lections of clip art, sound effects, photographs, flowcharts, concept maps, video clips, fonts, *Adobe Flash* animations, and document templates. These are discussed in Chapter 5 in the Using Graphics Tools section (see p. 149).

Evaluating Commercial Hypermedia Products

Because there are so many hypermedia products on the market, teachers must become savvy consumers of these materials. Gibbs, Graves, and Bernas (2000) used Delphi surveys of a panel of instructional technology experts to derive criteria for evaluating software. Perhaps not surprisingly, the list of criteria emphasizes the instructional and pedagogical aspects of the products rather than their hypermedia characteristics. The result is a list similar to that found in Chapter 4 for instructional software (see Table 6.2). Criteria include the following:

- **Instructional planning and support** — The product or documentation that comes with the product speci-

TABLE 6.2   Criteria for Evaluating Commercial Multimedia Software Products

_____ **Instructional planning.** Target audience and prerequisite skills are specified.
Comments:

_____ **Support.** Computer hardware and software requirements are specified.
Comments:

_____ **Instructional adequacy.** Instructional objectives are clearly stated. Practice activities are provided that actively involve the learner. Instructional activities needed to complete learning tasks are made explicit.
Comments:

_____ **Information content.** Information is current and accurately represents the topic. Examples, practice exercises, and feedback are meaningful and relevant.
Comments:

_____ **Information reliability.** Information is accurate, i.e., presented in a truthful, valid way.
Comments:

_____ **Clear, concise, and unbiased language.** Courseware content is presented clearly. (Text, pictorial, graphical, auditory, and video information all are presented clearly.)
Comments:

_____ **Interface design and navigation.** Courseware screen elements (titles, text areas, navigation buttons, and so on) are easy to understand. Directions are understandable.
Comments:

_____ **Feedback and interactivity.** If tests are present, they are matched to objectives. Feedback is appropriate to content, learning tasks, learner response, and learning environment.
Comments:

_____ **Evidence of effectiveness.** During student uses of courseware, there was evidence of learning/performance gains. The courseware supplies information to teachers and students on how it measures student learning.
Comments:

Technology Integration Lesson 6.1

Interactive Storybooks

Title: CD-ROM and Online Interactive Storybooks Enhance Reading Centers

Content Area/Topic: Language arts/reading
Grade Level: K–4

NETS for Students: Standards 2 (Communication and Collaboration) and 4 (Critical Thinking, Problem Solving, and Decision Making)

Description of Standards Applications: This integration lesson offers students the opportunity to use an interactive book to listen to a narrative while they become aware of new vocabulary while writing about their favorite story within their journals. Interactive books play some of the same roles that parents and teachers do for children who cannot yet read well. By reading aloud to young students and asking questions about the content, interactive books provide support to build students' developing literacy skills.

Instruction: Teachers often begin by reading aloud a story from a print book to the whole class, discussing the main components of the narrative and explaining items as needed. They place the interactive version of the story at a classroom reading center, making sure that the learning station has headphones plugged into the computer so that students will not disturb the class as they listen to the story. Each student has a turn at the reading center computer. The teacher asks each student to listen to the story all the way through before completing the interactive (and fun) branching activities. He or she gives students 3 by 5 in. cards and asks them to copy down any words they see and hear that are new to them. In their writing journals (or for nonwriting students, during sharing time), students describe their favorite part of the story.

Assessment: Rubrics are used to assess writing and participation skills.

Source: Adapted from Kahn, J. (1997a). Scaffolding in the classroom: Using CD-ROM storybooks at a computer reading center. *Learning and Leading with Technology, 25*(2), 17–19.

fies the target audience and the prerequisite skills required to use the product successfully.

- **Instructional design** — The objectives are clearly specified, and the instructional activities are well designed to accomplish them. Examples, practice exercises, and feedback are relevant and useful.

- **Content** — Facts, data, and depictions of events are current and accurate. Information is presented in a truthful way and is not misleading or biased.

- **Interface design and navigation** — The product is easy to use, and directions are clear and understandable. Screen elements (e.g., titles, text areas, buttons, or links) are clear and easy to use.

- **Feedback and interactivity** — User input is an integral part of the product. Users receive helpful feedback in response to input.

Integration Strategies for Commercial Hypermedia Products

Because products in this category vary so widely, instructional uses for them are also varied and rich. Integration strategies for instructional software are discussed in detail in Chapter 3, and strategies for software tools are described in Chapters 4 and 5. Technology Integration Lesson 6.1 illustrates ways in which interactive storybook resources can be used in classrooms. Technology Integration Lesson 6.2

Technology Integration Lesson 6.2

Electronic Encyclopedias and Presentation Software

Title: Selling a Space Mission   **Grade Level:** Middle school

Content Area/Topic: History/science

NETS for Students: Standards 1 (Creativity and Innovation), 2 (Communication and Collaboration), 3 (Research and Information Fluency), 4 (Critical Thinking, Problem Solving, and Decision Making), and 6 (Technology Operations and Concepts)

Description of Standards Applications: This integration lesson offers students, after in-depth research using multiple sources, the opportunity to use desktop publishing software to create a brochure and presentation software (i.e., *PowerPoint* or *Keynote*) to develop a presentation to encourage their audience to accept their space research project. Students design, write, edit, and publish a brochure and prepare a *PowerPoint* or *Keynote* presentation to "sell" a space research project.

Instruction: Students pair up to form space mission planning teams. Each team conceptualizes a mission that would accomplish both scientific and social goals that the public could enthusiastically support, given the right encouragement. Then students "sell" their space mission. The teacher uses the Microsoft *Encarta* encyclopedia or another such resource, along with an overhead projection device or large monitor, to take a journey through the history of space exploration, from the *Sputnik* days of the 1960s through the *Apollo* moon mission, the *Challenger* disaster, and the recent remote-robot exploration of Mars. When students design their brochures, they can paste pictures from the encyclopedia into their presentations to illustrate their slides and help "sell" their ideas.

Assessment: Rubrics are used to assess group work skills and the quality of the final projects.

Source: Based on a lesson from *Microsoft Productivity in the Classroom.* Copyright 1997 by the Microsoft Corporation.

shows how an electronic encyclopedia and *PowerPoint* presentation (discussed in the next section) can provide important support for a student project.

Introduction to Multimedia and Hypermedia Design and Development

One of the most amazing things about how multimedia and hypermedia systems have evolved is that people with fairly nontechnical skill levels now can develop complex, professional-looking hypermedia products. Perhaps most importantly for schools, hypermedia authoring may play a major role in preparing students for the information-intensive and visually oriented world of the future. In today's digital world, powerful personal computers and ubiquitous electronic networking allow people to incorporate a variety of media into their

communications. Indeed, hypermedia publishing may eventually supersede paper publishing in importance and impact; moreover, the students in today's classrooms will be on the forefront of this succession, both in use and development. Five kinds of multimedia/hypermedia design and development tools, for use by both teachers and students, are:

- Presentation software,
- Video production and editing systems,
- Hypermedia development software,
- Virtual environments and immersion tools, and
- Web 2.0 authoring tools.

Although these systems vary in capability, sophistication, and authoring procedures, all of them allow people to summarize and display information and knowledge using a combination of text, video, animation, music, graphics, and sound effects. The various skills and resources that students and teachers need in order to use any of these five categories of authoring tools, as well as integration strategies common to all of these authoring formats, are described here.

Multimedia and Hypermedia Authoring Resources

Over time, multimedia/hypermedia programs have become increasingly more powerful and user friendly, and features and capabilities are being added with every new version released. Authors now can draw on a wide variety of resources to put a full range of sound and motion in their multimedia/hypermedia products. The newest feature available in hypermedia authoring is the ability to insert Internet links into products. Users can click on these links and go immediately from the software screen to an Internet site. Hypermedia resources include audio, video, photographs, graphic images, and text. Table 6.3 summarizes sources of multimedia/hypermedia authoring materials under each of these categories.

TABLE 6.3 Summary of Hypermedia Design and Development Resources

Types of Resources	Items of Each Type	Instructional Roles in Multimedia, Products
Audio	• **CD audio**—Digitized music, speech, or sound effects captured from audio CD or video DVD • **Recorded sounds**—Voice recordings • **Prerecorded sounds**—From collections of sound effects offered in multimedia software or from CD-ROM collections	• Background music for presentations • Illustrations of musical types • Portions of famous speeches • Readings of poetry • Directions to students • Sound effects to add interest or humor or to signal transitions • Teacher and student generated podcast audio files
Video	• **Digitized videos**—Imported from DVD or VCR using video digitizer, or from camcorder and edited with movie software (e.g., Apple *iMovie, Windows Movie Maker*) • **Collections of prerecorded video clips**—Available on CD-ROM or DVD	• Demonstrations of procedures (e.g., labs, sport movements) • Recorded lectures • Illustrative examples of topics being discussed • Video decision-making simulations • Video problem-solving situations • Screen capture video for software demonstration
Photographs	• **Scanned photos**—Digitized from print photographs using scanners • **Captured from video sources**—Freeze-frames from DVD or VCR • **Digital camera images**—Downloaded from camera to computer • **Commercial collections**—From CD-ROM and stock photography collections	• Historical events, documents, or famous people • Geographical locations or objects in outer space • Illustrative tools (e.g., machines or art implements)
Graphic images	• **Created or imported**—Using draw/paint software, from clip art collections, or images scanned from drawings or hard copy images • **Animations**—From CD-ROM collections or created using animation tools	• Illustrative cartoons (e.g., political) • Attention-getting cues • Introductory animations for websites and software • Charts and visualizations
Text	• **Entered by author**—Typed into product or added as a graphic item • (e.g., Apple *iWork*, Microsoft *Office*) • **Imported**—From word processing files and graphic design software	• Signs or titles • Summaries of written procedures or explanations • Definitions

Audio resources. Hypermedia authoring programs offer users a number of ways to incorporate audio clips. These include audio from CD, recording sounds, and prerecorded sounds.

Video resources. Motion video clips can add a new and engaging dimension to a software application or website and provide authors with a wide assortment of communication possibilities. As with audio resources, authors have several options for incorporating video displays into a product, including digitized and prerecorded videos as well as video captured from a webcam.

Photographs. As in other settings, in hypermedia a picture is worth a thousand words. Photographs provide a powerful resource for authors in all subject areas not only to enhance but also to amplify the messages communicated to learners. Photos can be scanned, captured from video, taken with digital cameras, imported from a CD-ROM, or downloaded from a stock photography website.

Graphic images. Graphic elements, drawings, charts, and animations offer other tools for authors to communicate their ideas through visual means. Illustrations can demonstrate or support a point that may be difficult to express with text alone. This aspect of hypermedia authoring is particularly appealing to artistically inclined users. Images can be created by authors, imported from clip art collections, scanned from hard copy, or imported from CD-ROM and online stock photography collections. In addition, animations can be created with animation software. With the ever-increasing capability to search for and download images from the Internet, it is important to stress with students the principles of fair use so that they become aware of the need to cite their resources and avoid potential copyright infringement (especially as they move forward in their academic and professional careers). Go to the U.S. Copyright Office (http://www.copyright.gov/fls/fl102.html) for more information on fair use in education.

Text. Despite the attention paid to other components of hypermedia, text remains one of the most powerful ways to communicate ideas. Text can be generated as a multimedia project develops or can be imported from word-processed files.

Hardware Requirements for Hypermedia Design and Development

Although hypermedia authoring can be accomplished with a fairly minimal computer system, more complex products require additional hardware and software capabilities.

Depending on the complexity of the product, some or all of the following hardware resources are needed:

- **Computer with keyboard, mouse, and monitor** — Hypermedia and multimedia development can be done on any platform as long as the system has a hard drive and sufficient random-access memory (RAM). The minimum requirements for running programs such as Apple *iMovie*, *Adobe Flash*, or *Adobe DreamWeaver* are much more affordable for the average classroom than they used to be.

- **Digital cameras** — These let users take digital photographs and store them as digital files. The images then can be incorporated into hypermedia and multimedia projects. Students of all ages enjoy using their own digital photographs in projects. Typically, digital cameras with sensors greater than 5 megapixels are sufficient for use in most classroom projects.

- **Scanners** — If no digital camera is available, scanners can be used to digitize printed photos so they can be saved to a disk. Scanners also can capture digitized images from magazines or books.

- **Video digitizers** — Video digitizers, also known as *digitizing boards*, are devices that capture full-motion video from video cameras, VCRs, videodisc players, or live TV. The device that provides the video must be connected to the computer via a cable. Once video segments are transferred, they are stored as digitized computer files and can be edited using software such as *Adobe Premier* and Apple *iMovie*. Both teachers and students should recognize copyright restrictions when digitizing and editing video.

- **Camcorders and other video input** — Video cameras or camcorders, VCRs, webcams, videodiscs, CD-ROMs,

The availability of technology resources makes it possible for anyone to create amazing movies or presentations.

and DVDs are possible sources of motion video sequences to include in a hypermedia production.

- **Microphones** — To incorporate sound, an audio source such as a microphone is needed. Most computer systems sold in recent years have built-in audio cards, and most new webcams and laptops have built-in microphones.

- **Audio speakers** — To monitor quality and simply to hear the audio parts of a program, speakers are mandatory for hypermedia development. Many newer computers are shipped with either external or internal speakers. For use in the classroom, individual headphones provide students with privacy and prevent a noisy computer lab.

Hypermedia Design and Development Procedures

Whether teachers are developing their own skills or those of their students, the hypermedia authoring process involves two distinct phases. Initially, authors need to learn the mechanics of the programs they plan to use and develop their understanding of the concepts of hypermedia and multimedia. No one can develop a quality product without first being reasonably comfortable with the tools. However, at the next level, hyper-

media authors must develop insights into the complexities of the various media and knowledge of visual and navigation design. This is a long-term process that will emerge through a great deal of experience. A number of strategies can aid the classroom teacher in helping students use their time efficiently and focus on developing quality products. Consider the following steps, shown in Figure 6.2, that students should take when engaging in hypermedia development:

1. **Review existing products** — An effective way of developing authoring and design skills for beginners is to look at what others have done. It is also helpful to examine some effective uses of commercial media; Ken Burns's series on the Civil War, for example, demonstrates the power of images and sound when melded together in the context of a story.

2. **Perform research first** — Most hypermedia development projects require research to locate materials and data, analyze the findings, and summarize them in a format for use in the hypermedia product. It is important to allow adequate time for this research phase because it is the heart of the learning activity and ultimately will lead to higher-quality, more informed hypermedia products.

FIGURE 6.2 Sequence of Development Steps for Multimedia Resources

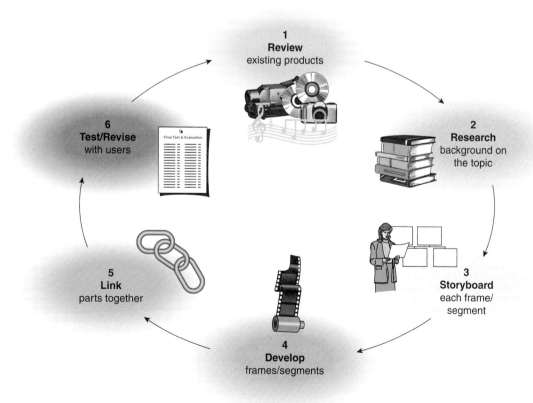

3. **Storyboard** — Storyboarding helps students make good use of their time. On index cards or sticky notes, students can lay out what they want their users to interact with and the necessary content and navigation that must be designed for each section of the hypermedia product. However, planning is the most difficult phase of hypermedia and multimedia development for students; they want to get right to the "fun stuff." Most students prefer to develop only on the computer. Teachers must insist that on-paper planning be done first. It may help to explain that professional media creators practice storyboarding and that even famous movie directors, such as Alfred Hitchcock and Steven Spielberg, storyboarded entire movies before capturing a single camera shot. This saves time in the long run, and it helps to conceptualize the end result first.

4. **Develop individual frames and segments** — In the case of hypermedia products using authoring software (e.g., *Adobe Flash, Adobe DreamWeaver, HyperStudio*), students should develop each frame or website page, including text fields, before adding links or graphics (e.g., clip art, photos, animations, video, and other media). For video productions, students should shoot video footage in segments as opposed to in one long recording. The segments can be edited together at a later time to communicate the story.

5. **Add links and/or scripts** — For software-authored products, links or buttons should be added last. Most design and development software allows the creator to see most or all of the frames at one time. Paired with the note-card or sticky-note storyboards, this feature helps students keep the links organized among sections and web pages. For both software and video products, now is the stage for adding transitions and special effects between frames or segments and additional audio to the final product.

6. **Test and revise the product** — After their products are complete, students should be encouraged to test them, preferably with the help of others who have not been involved in their development. The aim is to revise the products and meet the criteria outlined in a later section of this chapter, Evaluating Student-Developed Hypermedia and Multimedia Projects. Rembelinsky (1997–1998) offers a development sequence designed specifically for creating multimedia summaries of project-based research. She recommends that students go through a development sequence in each of the following general headings: written summary, historical background, creative narrative, scanned images, video, and self-evaluation.

Authoring Skills to Develop over Time

The beauty of hypermedia authoring is that students can create products with skills that range from basic to extraordinarily complex and sophisticated. Teachers have a growing number of online tutorials at their disposal to help students learn the basics of authoring software packages. (See a vast list of tutorials at Lynda.com or the Internet4Classrooms site for links to many of these tutorials.) Students can begin with these tutorials, and teachers can help them move on to advanced techniques in several areas.

Media literacy. Given the complexities and proliferation of various media, an understanding of media basics is a fundamental skill for the Information Age. Because most people have tremendous capabilities to adapt and alter existing media in our present online world, a critically important part of instruction in hypermedia authoring must focus on how to be critical and ethical producers and consumers of media (Roblyer, 1998).

Using music and art. Visual arts and music play major roles in the effectiveness of hypermedia and multimedia products. As students gain more knowledge in the theory and aesthetics of music and art, they will use these resources more productively in the authoring process, ultimately enhancing the quality of their hypermedia and multimedia development.

Print and graphic design principles. Many principles of desktop publishing also apply to hypermedia designs. When students first see the array of graphics and sound options available, they typically overindulge and use so many colors, graphics, and sounds that content is overshadowed. A selection of design principles that can help guide judicious use of these options is described later in the Evaluating Student-Developed Hypermedia and Multimedia Projects section.

Video design principles. For video projects, students learn over time the best ways to illustrate concepts using motion and camera effects. They also learn how to intersperse print and animated titles in their projects.

Creativity and novel thinking. When assessing student projects, look for and encourage creative uses of the potential of hypermedia. Too many student projects resemble glorified paper-based projects, essentially replications of existing materials; they do not take advantage of the true power and affordances (i.e., opportunities for action and interactivity) of this medium. Classroom activities that encourage creative and critical thinking in all subject areas help develop skills and a mindset that naturally enhance the authoring process.

Considering the audience. Whenever possible, teachers should try to give students an opportunity to display their projects. Students are much more motivated when they believe their work is valued. Research on writing has shown that students invest more effort in the writing process when they know others will read their writing. Turner and Dipinto (1992) and others have observed that this sense of audience carries over to hypermedia authoring. However, teachers sometimes find that components of a student project make sense only to the author. Younger students in particular should be reminded constantly that they need to think of their projects from the user's point of view. Encourage them to test their projects on other students, family members, or friends and to focus on the usability of the project in addition to the embedded content.

Evaluating Student-Developed Hypermedia and Multimedia Projects

When students create their own multimedia/hypermedia products, Dipinto and Turner (1995) suggest that student self-assessment may be the most important component of the assessment process. They say that it may enable students to construct a "microworld" in which assessment becomes a feedback mechanism, leading to further exploration and collaboration (p. 11). Brunner (1996), Clark (1996), Litchfield (1995), and Royer and Royer (2002) describe qualities to look for in effective hypermedia products. These are summarized in the Checklist for Assessing Multimedia Products in Table 6.4, which also can be found on MyEducationLab under the topic, "Instructional Planning." You can use this and other such instruments to grade student projects as well as to encourage students to self-assess their work and critique the work of their peers.

TABLE 6.4   Checklist for Assessing Multimedia Products

Content

_____ All information is the most current, up-to-date available.

_____ All information is factually accurate.

_____ Content is free from typos and misspellings, and from punctuation and grammatical errors.

_____ No ethnic, slang, or rude names are used; content is presented in a professional way.

_____ No questionable vocabulary, slang terms, or curse words are used.

_____ Content sources (including sources of graphics) are properly referenced.

Instructional Design

_____ Instructional objectives are clear; the instructional purpose is aligned with school curriculum rather than being for entertainment.

_____ All necessary information is provided in the product to make concepts clear; users are able to understand what is being presented from the information provided.

_____ If tests or other assessments are provided, they are matched directly to objectives.

_____ To add interest and motivation for users, information is presented in an innovative and creative way.

Organization and Navigation

_____ Screens are designed for easy navigation; it is clear how to get to and from various parts of the product.

_____ To aid navigation and use, the product has a consistent look and feel throughout.

_____ Buttons and links all work as indicated.

Appearance

_____ Use of varying fonts and type sizes is controlled so as not to interfere with readability.

_____ Type is large enough to read when projected.

_____ Color contrasts with background for easy reading.

_____ Bold or plain style is used for main text; no shadow and outline if text is more than a few words long. Fancy fonts and type styles are readable.

_____ Only brief main ideas are listed in a single frame, rather than paragraphs of text.

Graphics, Videos, and Sound

_____ Graphics, videos, and sound are included as appropriate to help communicate information on the topic; they are not included just for show.

_____ No obscene or rude graphics or visuals are included.

_____ Use of graphics (e.g., animations, screen changes) is controlled and does not distract from reading.

_____ Pictures and sounds associated with buttons and links are appropriate to the purpose and content of the frames.

Multimedia Authoring Tools, Type 1: Presentation Software

Presentation software tools help users create on-screen descriptions, demonstrations, and summaries of information. A prime example of a design and development technology that migrated from business and industry to the realm of education, these tools were first adopted by business executives and salespeople, who used them to give reports at meetings and presentations to clients. Their capabilities for demonstrating, illustrating, and clarifying information became evident, and presentation tools began to make their way into K–12 and university classrooms.

Presentation tools began exclusively as **electronic slide shows**, sequences of frames shown in a linear way. They have evolved into multimedia authoring tools that allow users to incorporate motion sequences from CD-ROM, DVD, the Internet, and other video media into their presentations. Originally designed to display in a linear sequence, presentation software now offers branching by allowing authors to include clickable buttons or "hot spots" to jump to any location in the presentation, thus avoiding a staccato presentation of content and allowing the presenter to manipulate the flow (and timing) of the presentation as needed. Presentation software also allows authors to include graphics of all kinds, audio and video clips, and links to supportive content on the Internet. For large classes and other groups, presentation software products typically are used in conjunction with computer projection systems, which may be devices such as large high-definition monitor panels, LCD projectors and wall mounted screens, or systems that operate as stand-alone devices. All of these devices enlarge the image produced by the software by projecting it from a computer screen onto a wall screen.

As the most popular of these presentation software tools, Microsoft *PowerPoint* (Apple has a similar presentation software called *Keynote* that is available as part of the *iWork* Suite) presentations have attracted much criticism in recent years for their tendency to be linear and overly simplistic (Tufte, 2003). However, the effectiveness of a presentation tool depends largely on the communications skills of the presenter. While presentation software makes it possible for students and teachers to communicate in the "grammar of multimedia," new users make some common "grammatical mistakes." Ten of the most common mistakes and tips on how to avoid them are described in the *Top Ten* feature.

Integration Strategies for Presentation Software

Because it is readily available and relatively easy to use, *PowerPoint* or *Keynote* software is often the multimedia tool of choice for classroom integration and use. A variety of integration strategies have emerged for these versatile tools; some are described here and summarized in Table 6.5. Technology Integration Lesson 6.3 illustrates how students can create group-based presentations to enhance their understanding of content.

- **Support for lectures or presentations of content** — By far the most popular use of these tools is for supporting and strengthening classroom presentations. Teachers use them to focus student attention and to guide note-taking.

- **Practice screens** — Many teachers set up presentations of spelling or vocabulary words or objects to identify (e.g., lab equipment, famous names or places) to run automatically in the classroom, knowing that students' eyes are drawn to the moving slides.

- **Assessment screens** — When teachers need students to identify pictures of items (e.g., lab equipment, famous people), presentation screens can enable visual assessment strategies.

- **Brief tutorials** — Teachers can create *PowerPoint* or *Keynote* reviews of simple concepts (e.g., grammar

TABLE 6.5 Presentation Software Authoring Tools

Types of Products	Instructional Uses
• **Microsoft *PowerPoint*** http://www.microsoft.com • **OpenOffice.org** (free productivity software) http://www.openoffice.org/ • **Apple *Keynote*** http://www.apple.com/iwork/keynote/ • ***Google Docs* Presentation Software** (free online productivity software) http://www.google.com/docs	• Support for lectures or presentations of content • Practice screens (e.g., spelling words, new vocabulary) • Assessment screens (e.g., identification of objects) • Brief tutorials • Book reports • Student-created presentations

Top Ten

Tips for Effective *PowerPoint* and *Keynote* Presentations

All of the following are qualities that can greatly enhance readability, audience engagement, and/or communication of content during a *PowerPoint-* or *Keynote*-type presentation.

1. **Use large type** — Use at least a 32-point font; use a larger type size if the audience is large and a long distance away from the presenter. Smaller type (no less than a 20-point font) may be used to provide citations, references, and sources, which are typically positioned in the lower-left or -right corner of the appropriate slide.

2. **Contrast the text and background colors** — The audience cannot see text that is too similar in hue to the background on which it appears. Use text with high contrast to the background (e.g., dark text on light-colored backgrounds, white text on dark-colored backgrounds).

3. **Minimize the amount of text on each frame** — Use text to focus attention on main points, not to present large amounts of information. Summarize ideas in brief phrases and make sure that you, not the projection screen, are the focus of the presentation. In other words, use the presentation to enhance, strengthen, and expand upon points that are outlined briefly on each frame.

4. **Keep frames simple** — Frame designs should be simple, clear, and free of distractions. Too many items on one frame can interfere with reading, especially if some items are in motion. In addition, try to employ photographs and images in place of lengthy text when describing a context or event. Finally, try to minimize the number of bullet points (not to exceed three to five points) on each individual slide.

5. **Avoid using too many "fancy" fonts** — Many fonts are unreadable when projected on a screen. Use a plain *sans serif* (straight lines with no "hands" and "feet") font for titles and a plain *serif* font for other text. Avoid using more than three different fonts throughout the presentation to maintain consistency of headings, body text, and pull-out text.

6. **Avoid using gratuitous graphics and clip art** — Graphics interfere with communication when used solely for decoration. Use graphics to help communicate and expand upon the content, not for the sake of using graphics alone.

7. **Avoid using gratuitous sounds** — Sounds interfere with communication when used solely for effect. They should always help communicate the content and not be used as a transition effect.

8. **Use graphics, not just text** — Well-chosen graphics can help communicate messages. Text alone does not make the best use of the capabilities of presentation software. However, with the ever-increasing ease of finding and downloading photographs and images from online sources, it is important that you encourage students to document where images come from and to cite the proper sources in their presentations.

9. **Present in a dark room** — Frames can fade away if the room is too bright. Make sure to cover windows and turn off lights during a presentation.

10. **Avoid reading text aloud** — Do not read what the audience can read for themselves. Use text to guide the main points of discussion. This will help you focus on presenting to the audience as opposed to speaking at the screen. Remember, you—not the *PowerPoint* or *Keynote*—are doing the presenting.

Technology Integration Lesson 6.3

Presentation Software Projects

Title: Presentation Projects Enhance Learning About Biomes

Grade Level: 9 through 10

Content Area/Topic: Science/ecology

NETS for Students: Standards 1 (Creativity and Innovation), 2 (Communication and Collaboration), 3 (Research and Information Fluency), 4 (Critical Thinking, Problem Solving, and Decision Making), and 6 (Technology Operations and Concepts)

Description of Standards Applications: This integration lesson offers students the opportunity to use presentation software to research and present information on organisms living in selected biomes. As students take on the role of a member of the National Academy of Sciences, they perform research, answer key questions, and present information to their peers. The aim of having students create *PowerPoint* or *Keynote* presentations to document and present their findings is to make their learning experience more meaningful and engaged. To accomplish this, teachers assign projects that call for creation of multiple solutions, inquiry, and decision making around a theme or "big idea." One example of such a project is the Biome Inquiry Project.

Instruction: The teacher tells students the "big idea" for the project: "Organisms live in a selected biome because they are adapted to the conditions there." He or she begins by discussing essential background questions: What is a biome? What are the characteristics of various biomes? How are organisms adapted to conditions in each one? Which species in each are threatened and why? The assigned task for the *PowerPoint* presentation is to simulate the work of members of the National Academy of Sciences, who have been asked to appear before the United Nations (UN) and present a plan to reduce human impact on one of the world's biomes. Students select a biome to research, answer key questions about it (e.g., What is the significance of this biome?), and present information about it as though they were making a presentation to the UN. Students are placed in small groups with assigned roles and work together to do the research and create the presentation. The primary emphasis of the lesson is on student exploration of the biomes and the presentation of their research, not simply on learning the presentation software. Students ultimately will learn the *PowerPoint* or *Keynote* software and best practices presentation techniques; however this will occur within the context of authentic problem-based projects such as this one.

Assessment: Student presentations are assessed using a rubric created especially for this project (see the article).

Source: Royer, R., & Royer, J. (2002). Developing understanding with multimedia. *Learning and Leading with Technology, 29*(7), 40–45.

---

rules) or "how-to" procedures (e.g., a lab procedure, computer software demonstration) so that students can review these on their own to make up work or to prepare for tests.

- **Book reports** — Instead of presenting book reports verbally or as written summaries, it is becoming increasingly common for students to report on their reading using *PowerPoint* or *Keynote* slideshows. Teachers often design a standard format or template, and students fill in the required information and add their own illustrations.

- **Student-created presentations** — As Technology Integration Lessons 6.2 and 6.3 illustrate, the most powerful strategy for integrating presentation multimedia is for students to create individual or small-group presentations to document and display the results of research they have done and/or to practice making persuasive presentations. Having learners become the designers and experts of content, in the end presenting their work to the class, can serve as a powerful Technology Integration Lesson for any domain of learning—from art history to math to science to social studies and beyond.

Recent advances in presentation software, such as Apple *Keynote* and *Google Docs* Presentation Software (a free online productivity suite), have afforded significant enhancements in the presentation authoring realm, including sophisticated yet easy-to-use capabilities for creating cinema-quality presentations and collaborating online to create and share presentations on the Internet, respectively. In addition, *PowerPoint*-type presentations have become so popular that many assessment instruments matched to them have been designed.

Go to MyEducationLab, select the topic "Software." Review the "PowerPoint Rubric" for a rubric that can be used to evaluate students' *PowerPoint* presentations.

Multimedia Authoring Tools, Type 2: Video Production and Editing Systems

Once the exclusive domain of Hollywood, video production is now a growing presence in school activities. **Video editing software** is to motion images what word processing is to text. The next decade likely will see an explosion in video editing and production to rival the rapid increase in word processing of documents. As Howard (2001) observed, video production can be very time consuming for anyone who wants to create high-quality videos, and especially so for novice users of video editing software. However, schools across the country are beginning to use these systems to produce school news programs and to develop digitized video for use in the design and development of various hypermedia products (Hoffenburg & Handler, 2001).

Video can be imported onto a computer from a source such as a camcorder or a VCR with a USB or Firewire connection and converted into digital format [**Audio Video Interleave (AVI) format, Moving Picture Experts Group (MPEG) format**, or *QuickTime* **movie (MOV) format**], or it may be transferred in digital form from a digital camera. Once digital video is stored on a computer, the resulting digitized video clips can be inserted into a multimedia package or uploaded to the Internet. Video clips stored in this way are often called **QuickTime® movies,** since Apple provides free player software that frequently is used to view them. Video editing software allows these movies to be edited and combined with special effects such as titles, screen fades, transitions, and voice-over audio/sound effects. Several video production and editing packages are listed in Table 6.6, along with sample integration strategies.

When Apple included a free copy of its video production software *iMovie* with some of its computer systems, it heralded the beginning of widespread interest in video editing among educators and other consumers. An example of an *iMovie* video editing software screen is shown in Figure 6.3. At the bottom of the figure is the sequence of images and videos as well as the audio track. By sliding markers on these tracks and dragging the video clips to their intended destinations in the file, students can cut, copy, and/or paste sections of a video and/or combine them with special effects such as fades or background music. The end result can then be uploaded to an Internet website or output and shared on DVD-based media.

Integration Strategies for Video Production and Editing Systems

Students and teachers are using computer-based video production and editing systems for a variety of purposes, ranging from presenting the daily school news to teaching professional-grade video production skills. Some of these strategies are described here. Technology Integration Lesson 6.4 illustrates one of these uses.

TABLE 6.6 **Video Production and Editing Software**

Types of Products	Instructional Uses
• *FinalCut Pro* http://www.apple.com • *Apple's iMovie* http://www.apple.com • *Avid Xpress Pro* http://www.avid.com • *Adobe Premier Pro* http://www.adobe.com • *Pinnacle Studio* http://www.pinnaclesys.com	• Demonstrations of procedures (e.g., science experiments) • Student-created presentations • Video lectures • Video portfolios • Video decision-making/problem-solving simulations • Documenting of school activities (e.g., yearbooks) • Visual literacy demonstrations • Teaching of video production

FIGURE 6.3 *iMovie* **Editing Screen**

Source: Screen shot reprinted with permission from Apple, Inc.

- **Demonstrations of procedures** — For frequently repeated activities (for example, procedures for science experiments), teachers can film themselves or others completing the steps. These short clips provide demonstrations that can be viewed and repeated as many times as desired by students. For example, Jacobsen, Moore, and Brown (2002) describe a CD-ROM of 600 movie clips that illustrate chemistry laboratory techniques and procedures.

- **Student-created presentations** — Although students can produce a video as a way of documenting research findings (as they do with *PowerPoint* and *Keynote* presentations), they often create videos that illustrate real-life examples of concepts they have learned (e.g., showing how algebra applies to everyday situations) or document conditions they want to bring to light (e.g., social issues in their community).

- **Video lectures** — Teachers can capture video of themselves or other experts explaining key concepts (e.g., a video interview with a DNR expert in the local community for a unit on environmental awareness). These videos can support and extend in-class discussions; they also come in handy if students miss the original presentation or want to review material in a visual way. *Note:* Make sure speakers are aware you will be taping them, and get their permission to reuse the video for future classes.

- **Video portfolios** — Student portfolios have become more common for assessment purposes, and video systems have assumed a central role in portfolio development. Additionally, many teachers are required to develop portfolios to document their teaching methods in preparation for a promotion or additional certification.

- **Video decision-making/problem-solving simulations** — This strategy was made popular with the *Adventures of Jasper Woodbury* videodiscs in the mid-1990s and more recently with the *GeoThentic: Learning Geography through Geospatial Technologies* online environment designed at the University of Minnesota in collaboration with The National Geographic Society (see *Technology Integration Lesson 6.6* later in this chapter). Videos are used to depict problem scenarios that require math, science, or geography skills, and students can review information in the videos as they create solutions to the problems.

- **Documentation of school activities** — Many middle and secondary schools use video cameras and video editing software to produce a daily news show or morning announcements. These productions "star" the students themselves, and students control the camera and perform the necessary editing work. News shows offer valuable opportunities to help students develop their research and interviewing skills, on-camera presentation skills, and technical production skills. When schools create video yearbooks, students capture video clips of events and merge them into a collage of the year's events (Kwajewski, 1997a).

- **Visual literacy instruction** — Now that video, and more recently online video, has established itself as

Technology Integration Lesson 6.4

Video Projects

Title: A Monarch Butterfly Movie Project

Content Area/Topic: Science/biology

Grade Level: Elementary

NETS for Students: Standards 2 (Communication and Collaboration), 3 (Research and Information Fluency), and 6 (Technology Operations and Concepts)

Description of Standards Applications: This integration lesson offers students the opportunity to use video-editing software to document, research, and present the process of metamorphosis. This project helps students gain more insight into the process of metamorphosis than would be possible viewing it via traditional methods. They collect monarch butterfly eggs and create a digital movie of the stages as the eggs grow to become butterflies.

Instruction: Students begin by visiting several Internet sites to learn about monarch butterflies. Then they collect the eggs and set up the environment in which the cocoons will grow. The teacher helps them position the camera to film the development of the butterfly as it goes through the four stages of metamorphosis. After they capture the process, the teacher shows students a speeded up version, and they discuss what they are seeing, using correct scientific terms. They write up their findings and place them and the movie on a web page to share with other classes.

Assessment: A rubric is used to evaluate students' group work skills and involvement in the learning activities.

Sources: Stuhlmann, J. (1997). Butterflies: Using multimedia to capture a unique science project. *Learning and Leading with Technology, 25*(3), 22–27; and Hoffenburg, H., & Handler, M. (2001). Digital video goes to school. *Learning and Leading with Technology, 29*(2), 10–15.

playing a significant role in our society, visual literacy is a requirement. Through analyzing information in video format, students learn how people can use visual images to communicate biases and make persuasive arguments in advertisements and news stories. This enables students to become more thoughtful (and sometimes more cautious) consumers of digital information and marketing.

- **Teaching video production** — Technology education labs typically feature video production as one of the required learning stations. Students in these labs usually create the school's news shows and morning announcements.

- **Real-time video communication, collaboration, and presentation** — Through recent software applications such as Apple *iChat, Adobe Acrobat Connect Pro,* and *Skype,* students can connect with their peers, teachers, and off-site experts through the use of webcams and audio headset/microphones to communicate with one another, collaborate on and present school projects, and perform distance interviews.

Multimedia Authoring Tools, Type 3: Hypermedia Development Software

In the late 1980s, early hypermedia authoring programs included *HyperCard* for Macintosh, *LinkWay* for MS-DOS machines, and *TutorTech* for Apple II computers. These programs represented a major leap forward in technology, but because designers had to invest major time commitments to learn and use the software, their use was limited. Things began to change when Roger Wagner's *HyperStudio* was released in 1988. This program used the same basic "card and stack" metaphor as *HyperCard* did, but it eliminated much of the need for extensive scripting or for programming commands. In recent years, many programs have become available that emulate *HyperStudio*'s easy-to-use format, including *Adobe DreamWeaver.*

Most recently, *Adobe Flash* has become the industry standard for creating interactive web-based animations, websites, interactive storybooks, and online software tools. Its effectiveness can be attributed to two primary reasons: first,

Technology Integration Lesson 6.5

Hypermedia Authoring

Title: Quilting Our History

Content Area/Topic: U.S. history and multimedia design

Grade Level: High school

NETS for Students: Standards 1 (Creativity and Innovation), 2 (Communication and Collaboration), 3 (Research and Information Fluency), 4 (Critical Thinking, Problem Solving, and Decision Making), 5 (Digital Citizenship), and 6 (Technology Operations and Concepts)

Description of Standards Applications:
This integration lesson offers students the opportunity to use a multitude of technology and research skills as they develop an online quilt describing local history. Using technologies such as *Adobe Director, Adobe Photoshop,* and the audio editing program *Audacity,* students carry out multimedia design and production tasks.

Instruction: This schoolwide project requires a great deal of planning and collaboration among teachers in several content areas. The basic goal is to document the history of the local area and the families whose personal histories were intertwined with the history of the region. After all of the content-area teachers have worked together to decide on the project design and how it should be carried out, students form teams to accomplish the production tasks: researching information about the history and families of the local region, creating the geometric design of quilted squares to represent various families, gathering video documentation, and multimedia design. This project uses high-end multimedia software (*Adobe Director*) along with *Adobe Photoshop,* as well as 3D and audio packages. The technology education classes carry out the actual multimedia design and production tasks.

Assessment: Rubrics can be used to evaluate the quality of students' participation and final products.

Source: van Buren, C., & Aufdenspring, D. (1998). Quilting our history: An integrated schoolwide project. *Learning and Leading with Technology,* 26(2), 22–27.

Flash merges a powerful yet easy-to-use visual environment with a robust programming language (i.e., *ActionScript*), thereby allowing developers to combine aesthetically pleasing interfaces with powerful programming techniques; and second, *Flash* files are very small and download quickly over the Internet. Although *Flash* development is often viewed as a sophisticated proficiency accessible only to those with extensive programming backgrounds, creating interactive frame-by-frame narratives can be a simple and uncomplicated design process due to *Flash*'s visual timeline and stage for organizing imagery and buttons. Additionally, *Flash* has a built-in Script Assist wizard to help beginners learn basic programming skills.

Integration Strategies for Hypermedia Authoring Software

Multimedia and hypermedia development projects are taking the place of many traditional activities to accomplish the same purposes. Some common classroom applications of multimedia and hypermedia are described here and

TABLE 6.7 Hypermedia Authoring Software Tools

Types of Products	Instructional Uses
• *HyperStudio* http://www.mackiev.com/hyperstudio/ • *Adobe DreamWeaver* http://www.adobe.com/products/dreamweaver/ • *Adobe Flash* http://www.adobe.com/products/flash/	• Brief tutorials • Student-created presentations • Interactive storybooks • Student-designed websites • Student-designed mini-games

summarized in Table 6.7. See Technology Integration Lesson 6.5 for an illustrative curriculum lesson.

- **Brief tutorials** — Both teachers and students can create multimedia instructional sequences that step the user through the components of a subject. Figure 6.4 shows a screen from an *Adobe Flash* tutorial for learning the note scales on a guitar. In this website, the user may select any note, string, and scaletype to learn the necessary string tuning and frets for playing the scale.

- **Student-created presentations** — Bennett and Diener (1997), Scholten and Whitmer (1996), and Stuhlmann (1997) point out that hypermedia and multimedia presentations not only let students present their findings attractively and with impact, but the act of producing and sharing their presentation helps them learn even more about the topics and enhances their research, study, and communication skills.

- **Interactive storybooks** — Frederickson (1997) describes a use that builds on the book report integration idea. Students document existing stories or write their own so they can be read interactively by others. Those reading these hypermedia and multimedia stories can click on various places on the screen to hear or view parts of a story. This format also lets students go beyond one basic sequence and create their own branches and endings to stories. Wilkerson (2001) describes how teacher-created interactive books can help support mathematics instruction.

- **Student-designed websites and mini-games** — Having students design websites is a challenging and complex problem-solving process. It encourages reflective and critical thinking in which students not only experience and work with new media in an authentic setting but also have the opportunity to explore new forms of expression by designing key elements that best organize and communicate their desired content or goal (Eagleton, 1999). Parallel to website design, having students design online mini-games (i.e., small competitive applications or website components developed in *JavaScript*, *Flash*, or *Java*) can also serve as challenging projects with significant potential in the math, literacy, art, and social sciences

domains. When learners are in the role of designer/developer, enhanced creativity, heightened problem-solving skills, increased motivation, and widened thought processes are only a taste of the potential benefits that may be encountered in K–16 classrooms.

Multimedia Authoring Tools, Type 4: Virtual Environments and Immersion Tools

Once only dreamed of in science fiction, some types of **virtual reality (VR)** are now seen frequently in classrooms. Through various visual and tactile devices, VR can represent real or imaginary worlds in which the user interacts through multiple senses: a true multimedia environment. Although the first VR systems, created for the military and the aerospace industry, required sophisticated computers with advanced computer graphics, other types of VR have been developed that require less sophisticated capabilities and less expensive technology.

Virtual Environments and Immersion Tools

The potential of VR systems to make cyberspace seem real has been talked about since William Gibson's 1984 novel

FIGURE 6.4 **Sample Screens from Multimedia Tutorial**

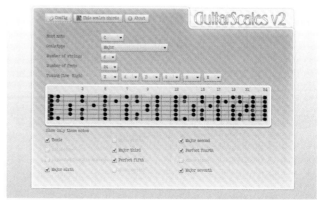

Source: *Guitar Scales*, http://www.rozengain.com/guitar-scales/ Courtesy of Dennis Ippel.

Neuromancer, in which people used **avatars**, or graphic icons, to represent themselves in virtual environments. Until recently, however, that potential has been tapped more for video games than for education. Five types of VR are described here, three of which are commonly used in K–12 classrooms. Educational uses of the other two types are usually limited to university research settings.

- **Full immersion systems** — Though not often used in education, this is what people typically envision when they think of VR. In **full immersion systems**, the user places a headset (e.g., goggles or a helmet) over the eyes. Known as a **head-mounted display (HMD)**, this headset is the channel through which the wearer "sees" the computer-generated environment. Other configurations use a large curved projection screen to immerse the user in the environment. In both VR systems, views of the "real" world are replaced with views of the virtual one, and the senses create an illusion of actually being in the environment the system displays. Other devices for full immersion systems include sound and tactile or **haptic interfaces**. Sound usually is presented to the user through stereo headphones that may or may not be built into the HMD. The user wears a glove or brace-like device that provides tactile feedback when the user "grasps" an object in the virtual world.

- **Web-based VR (K-12)** — This type of VR is made possible by **Virtual Reality Modeling Language (VRML)** and **Extensible Mark-up Language (XML)**. Just as Hypertext Mark-up Language (HTML) describes what a web page will look like in a browser (see Chapter 7),

The world of Virtual Reality in video and computer games has improved greatly with the introduction of real-life avatars. Now, as the social networking capacity of these programs improves, organizations and companies are exploring the growing use of virtual reality programs in educational settings as well.

VRML and XML describe the geometry and behavior of the virtual world or scene. VRML files can be viewed in Apple *Safari, Netscape Communicator,* and *Internet Explorer* browsers with the necessary plug-in. Creating worlds in VRML also requires building a 3-D model of the environment, as with the traditional VR models described above. This can be accomplished with modeling software, which can then output the VRML code, or students can code the world directly as they would a web page with HTML. Although not as realistic as full immersion VR, web-based VR costs much less to implement. The technical requirements for creating VRML products limited their use in education until the release of online VR environments such as *SecondLife*, an online virtual world created entirely by its users. Users first create an avatar to represent their digital presence; then they explore the digital world to connect and collaborate with others, build houses and communities, and even sell items in the environment in exchange for real money. At present, *SecondLife* is being used in K–12 schools and universities around the world with an assortment of education integration research studies currently in progress. Coffman and Klinger (2008) suggest that immersing students in virtual environments such as *SecondLife* is meaningful and engaging, often leading to an increase in student achievement, improved pedagogical reflection, and enhanced student metacognition.

- **3-D models** — These are made possible with sophisticated software that creates three-dimensional replicas of objects or locations. The products are then viewed on a flat screen computer (as opposed to an immersive environment). Some 3-D models are transferred to VRML and viewed via web browsers, as described above. Steed (2001) describes several educational uses of these models and gives examples of 3-D software.

- **Geospatial technologies and Geographic Information Systems (GIS) (K-12)** — Internet-based tools such as *Google Earth* (see Figure 6.5) and software applications such as *ArcView* are considered **Geographic Information Systems (GIS)**. GIS software is used by teachers, students, and scientists to visualize, measure, and analyze data from the environment, often represented in imagery superimposed on an interactive 3-D model of the Earth. Although it has been noted that GIS, a geospatial technology, is the one technology that can assist students in meeting all of the National Geography Standards (Bednarz, 1999), the actual implementation of GIS within classrooms is far behind expected rates (Kerski, 1999). Research suggests that learning geography with geospatial technologies is best accomplished through the use of problem solving, multiple scaffolds, and guidance (Doering & Veletsianos, 2007). Technology Integration Lesson 6.6 discusses such a lesson.

Technology Integration Lesson 6.6

GeoThentic: Learning Geography Through Geospatial Technologies

Title: Where to build a new hospital in the San Francisco Bay Area?

Grade Level: K–8

Content Area/Topic: Geography, social studies, environmental studies, science

NETS for Students: Standards 1 (Creativity and Innovation), 2 (Communication and Collaboration), 3 (Research and Information Fluency), 4 (Critical Thinking, Problem Solving, and Decision Making), 5 (Digital Citizenship), and 6 (Technology Operations and Concepts)

Description of Standards Applications: This integration lesson offers students the opportunity to use geospatial technologies to analyze authentic data and to provide a justification, based on this data, of where the best place is to build a hospital in the San Francisco Bay Area. This activity encourages students to be creative as they analyze the data, communicate their analysis of the data, critically think about their justifications, and showcase their findings. Students develop critical problem-solving skills as they explore data in a geospatial technology to identify the best location to build a new hospital in the San Francisco Bay Area.

Instruction: How should a K–8 geography teacher use a geospatial technology such as *Google Earth* in the classroom? Most teachers have students pinpoint a series of locations and measure the connecting distances, essentially using the technology as a digital representation of the traditional globe. Alternatively, in this lesson teachers have students solve authentic, ill-structured problems using the data layers available in *Google Earth* and the scaffolding media support available in the *GeoThentic* online environment (i.e., situated movies to present the problem, screen capture videos to demonstrate *Google Earth* tools, online resources and data layers, and a built-in chat tool). *GeoThentic* is built on the premise of providing cognitive apprenticeship (Collins, Brown, & Newman, 1989) by situating students' learning within an authentic setting and the necessary media to help support their exploration of the problem. For example, in the *Build a San Francisco Hospital* module, learn-

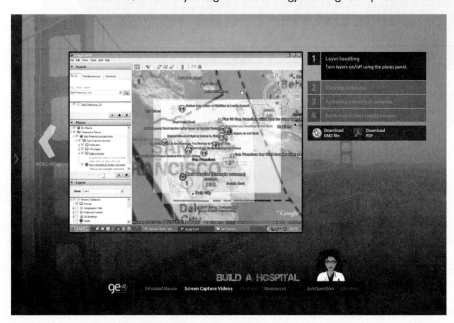

ers analyze socio-scientific data (e.g., seismic activity, population density, existing hospital locations, income, and so on) to identify and justify the best location in the Bay Area to build a new hospital. For more information, see http://geothentic.umn.edu.

Assessment: Rubrics can be used to evaluate the quality of students' identified locations and justifications. Additionally, students can discuss and vote on the best location and justification submitted by their peers.

Source: Doering, A., & Veletsianos, G. (2007). Multi-Scaffolding Learning Environment: An Analysis of Scaffolding and Its Impact on Cognitive Load and Problem-Solving Ability. *Journal of Educational Computing Research, 37*(2), 107–129.

FIGURE 6.5 Geospatial Technology: *Google Earth*

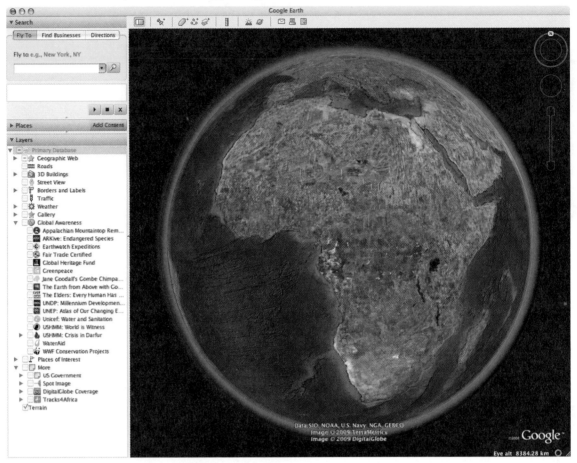

Source: Google™ Earth is a trademark of Google, Inc. Reprinted by permission.

- *QuickTime* VR (QTVR) (K-12) — Originally made possible through the **QuickTime VR Authoring Studio** from Apple, this type of VR is easy to access using the standard *QuickTime* player available free from Apple. It requires much less effort to create than immersion systems, VRML, or 3-D models do. Currently, there are many QTVR authoring tools available. In QTVR, you can take a series of photographs at 360 degrees around a pivotal point. For example, a classroom could be recorded by setting up the camera in the middle of the room on a tripod. A series of 16 photos would be taken at 22.5-degree intervals. The photos are then input into a QTVR authoring software that "stitches" them together into a seamless panoramic view of the room. Because QTVR uses actual photographs to create the panorama, it provides a more realistic representation than computer-generated systems do. QTVR seems to be the most common use of VR in K–12 classrooms.

Integration Strategies for Virtual Environments and Immersion Tools

Though not as commonly used as other forms of hypermedia, VR is generating interest as a tool for many instructional needs. Some common classroom applications of VR resources are described here and summarized in Table 6.8.

- **Imaging for virtual field trips** — Perhaps the most common VR application is *QuickTime* VR panoramas created and used for virtual field trips. Stevenson (2001) describes a variety of virtual field trips that use *Quicktime* VR movies to give tours of locations around the world. She also provides related links on how to create a virtual field trip.

- **3-D models to illustrate how systems work** — Although still limited to more technical topics in the areas of mathematics, science, architecture, and engineering, 3-D modeling is experiencing increasing use in education as a way to help students visualize mathematics and science concepts. Example models are

TABLE 6.8 VR and Immersion Authoring Software Tools

Types of Products	Instructional Uses

• *QuickTime* VR Authoring Tools
   http://www.apple.com/quicktime/resources/tools/qtvr.html
• *VRWorkx*
   http://www.vrtoolbox.com/vrthome.html
• *The Panorama Factory*
   http://www.panoramafactory.com/
• *3DS Max*
   http://www4.discreet.com
	• Imaging for virtual field trips
	• 3-D models to illustrate how systems work
	• Immersion learning environments for exploration, practice, communication, and collaboration

described to study characteristics of the solar system (Bakas & Mikropoulos, 2003; Barab, Hay, & Barnett, 2000) and processes of photosynthesis (Mikropoulos, Katsikis, & Nikolou, 2003).

- **Immersion learning environments for practice, exploration, communication, and collaboration** — Full immersion systems are usually limited to university settings (Comer, 1999; Young, 2000), but they have seen fairly extensive use in special education as a way to allow students to practice skills in a realistic but safe setting. Goldstein (2002) describes one such use with software designed to help students with attention deficit disorders and/or mobility and visual problems. Mohnsen (2003) also described VR systems that would be useful for physical education, but these are currently too expensive to be practical. Becker and Schuetz (2003) describe one VRML-based lesson for modeling groundwater flow for geology students. Orman (2003) describes a virtual environment for training performing musicians to prepare for the pressures of live performance, which she feels has great promise for this purpose. Additionally, virtual environments such as *SecondLife* are quickly finding their way into more and more K–12 classrooms around the world, ultimately diminishing the distances between learners for communication and transforming the traditional boundaries of online collaboration.

Multimedia Authoring Tools, Type 5: Web 2.0 Authoring Tools

Recently, the most rapidly increasing use of hypermedia authoring tools in the classroom comes in the form of technologies that represent significant changes in the traditional model of web content generation and consumption—namely **Web 2.0 authoring tools** (Buffington, 2008; O'Reilly, 2005). Web 2.0 authoring tools are freely available to anyone with an Internet connection (which makes for simple and cost-free integration into most classrooms and schools) and provide users with the powerful capabilities of generating and sharing online content (e.g., photos, text, videos, website links, and so on), creating online portfolios (i.e., personalized spaces to showcase course projects and reflect on learning), social networking (i.e., meeting, connecting, communicating, and collaborating with others online), and tagging or rating other user generated content.

Classroom Potential

Web 2.0 authoring tools are being used in classes ranging from history and art education to science and foreign languages. A prime example of Web 2.0 technology use is in the literacy classroom. Doering, Beach, and O'Brien (2007) suggest that Web 2.0 technologies are "redefining the notions of reading, composing, and performing processes to infuse digital literacies that students use daily into English language arts curriculum" (p. 42). When composing online text through the use of blogs and wikis (see below for descriptions), students are encouraged to think both multimodally and semiotically; in other words, students need to explore which media and modality best represent their ideas in order to communicate their work effectively to others. Additionally, Ellison and Wu (2008) found positive student perceptions of using blogs in the classroom, including the engaging novelty and convenience of the technology; being able to communicate their ideas through a less formal writing voice, which the blog encouraged; and the ability to read and comment on other students' ideas in addition to receiving feedback on their own blogs.

Although there are many Web 2.0 authoring tools currently available (with new and innovative tools arriving on the scene almost daily), the six main types of Web 2.0 technologies are: blogs, wikis, podcasts, e-Portfolios, social networking communities, and video and photo sharing communities. Examples of Web 2.0 authoring tools are listed in Table 6.9.

TABLE 6.9 Web 2.0 Authoring Tools

Items of Each Type	Instructional Uses
• **Blogs** — interactive websites created, designed, managed, and updated by an individual (e.g., *WordPress.com, Blogger.com, MovableType.com*) • **Wikis** — a collection of web pages that encourage collaborative contributing and modifying of content (*Wikipedia.org*) • **Podcasts** — digitized, downloadable audio files shared over the Internet for playback on the computer or personal media devices (e.g., Apple *iPod, ESPNRadio.com* podcenter) • **e-Portfolios** — websites created by students to showcase digital assets they have created (e.g., *ePortfolio.com*) • **Social networking** — online communities that allow for sharing of interests and content and connecting with individuals around the world (e.g., *MySpace.com, Facebook.com*) • **Video and photo sharing** — provide users with easy-to-use tools to upload video and photo files for online sharing (e.g., *YouTube.com, Vimeo.com, Flickr.com*)	• Compose and share reflections on coursework or course topics • Allow students to think collectively about a subject or event and conceptualize where (and how) their personal description or understanding of the concept fits into a larger structure of community-generated knowledge • Encourage students to share and reflect upon their work and lives in the context of a broad community of connected individuals • Potential to connect students to both personal and classroom interactive learning spaces 24 hours a day

 Go to MyEducationLab and select the topic "Emerging Trends." Go to the Weblinks section and review the NCTE Policy Brief entitled 21st Century Literacies.

• **Blogs** — Short for the term "web logs," **blogs** (e.g., *WordPress.com, Blogger.com, MovableType.com*) are interactive websites created, designed, managed, and updated by an individual, with regular entries of event descriptions, opinions, narratives, and commentaries added over time. Essentially a journal of thoughts, ideas, and descriptions, blog authors can upload images, video, links, and other documents to support their content. Users do not have to understand HTML or other authoring languages to create and update blogs; rather, most blogging sites provide a content management system that consists of easy-to-use forms in which users enter their text, images, and content, with the page immediately published online for anyone to see.

• **Wikis** — **Wikis** are a collection of web pages located in an online community that encourage collaboration and communication of ideas by having users contribute or modify content, sometimes on a daily basis. Wikis also promote "meaningful topic associations between different pages by making page link creation almost intuitively easy" and "seek to involve the visitor in an ongoing process of creation and collaboration that

constantly changes the Web site landscape" (quotes extracted from *Wikipedia.org*, the largest and fastest growing reference wiki on the Internet).

• **Podcasts** — Digitized audio files often saved in MP3 file format, **podcasts** are created by users and shared over the Internet for playback on the computer or personal media devices (e.g., Apple *iPod*). What differentiates a podcast from simply uploading an audio file to a website is that podcasts can be syndicated and subscribed to by online users for automatic download. Podcasts typically resemble a radio broadcast or audio interview.

• **e-Portfolios** — **e-Portfolios** (e.g., *ePortfolio.com*) are websites created by students to showcase their work and to organize, revise, and store digital assets they have created inside and outside the classroom. The distinction between an e-Portfolio and a blog often resides in the cleaner, more organized and professional design of an e-Portfolio, as well as in the nature of the content. Whereas blogs may consist of open-ended opinions and rough narratives or ideas, e-Portfolios typically are comprehensive, organized collections of assets, descriptions, and reflections.

• **Social networking sites** — **Social networking** sites (e.g., *MySpace.com, Facebook.com*) focus on building communities of individually designed web pages consisting of personal profiles, blogs, photo slideshows, music and videos, podcasts, and a network of connected friends or supporters. Users can design and upload their content, meet and connect with friends from around the world, and share media and interests in an online, easy-to-use website environment.

- **Video and photo sharing communities** — Video (e.g., *YouTube.com*, *Vimeo.com*) and photo (e.g., *Flickr.com*) sharing communities are websites that provide users with easy-to-use tools to upload video and photo files to a server for online sharing, either public or private, with viewers from around the world. Online viewers can comment on the videos and photos, tag (i.e., provide keywords) the content for increased searchability, and rate the quality of content or artistic vision of the user-generated media.

Integration Strategies for Web 2.0 Authoring Tools

As noted above, Web 2.0 authoring tools are steadily becoming the most-used authoring technologies in the classroom (Doering, Beach, & O'Brien, 2007). Ideas for harnessing the full potential of such technologies are only in their infancy, however, with fresh and innovative integration strategies flourishing throughout Internet education forums and in the pages of recent academic research publications.

Unlike the other four types of hypermedia and multimedia authoring tools, integration strategies are somewhat inherently built into the definitions of each Web 2.0 technology as listed above. For example, whereas blogs encourage students to think critically when composing and sharing reflections on coursework or course topics, wikis encourage students to think collectively about a subject or event and conceptualize where (and how) their personal description or understanding of the concept fits into a larger structure of community-generated knowledge. On the other hand, social networking communities and video/photo sharing communities encourage students to share and reflect upon their work and lives in the context of a broad community of connected individuals (e-Portfolios accomplish a similar task in the classroom, simply through a more organized and professional medium).

Educators must remember that the most important facet of teaching with such technologies is to maintain an open and explorative perspective when developing new integration strategies and adapting (amplifying and transforming) existing lessons. Finally, to open doors to further exciting potential for Web 2.0 integration in the classroom, many of the Web 2.0 authoring tools listed above have already found their way onto the mobile technologies (e.g., Internet-connected cellular phones) that students carry with them nearly all the time. Imagine a world in which students are connected to both personal and classroom interactive learning spaces 24 hours a day without having to sit in the computer lab or be at their home computer. In reality, that world is today.

Interactive Summary

The following is a summary of the main points covered in this chapter.

1. **Definitions of multimedia and hypermedia** — Although *multimedia* means "multiple media," and *hypermedia* means "linked media," the terms have come to be used interchangeably. The hypermedia concept is based on the ideas of Vannevar Bush in his landmark article "As We May Think."

2. **Current and future impact of multimedia/hypermedia** — Multimedia products, already seeing substantial use in education, are predicted to have even greater impact in the future since they mirror the increased emphasis on visual media in the modern world. Educational contributions are being seen in four areas: increased motivation, more flexible learning modes, development of creative and critical thinking skills, and improved writing and process skills.

3. **Research on multimedia/hypermedia** — Research finds that multimedia's benefits center on its ability to offer students multiple channels through which to process information. Several studies have offered recommendations on designing and using multimedia products for instructional purposes.

4. **Five types of multimedia/hypermedia resources in education** — Types of multimedia/hypermedia resources include commercial multimedia/hypermedia software packages and four kinds of multimedia/hypermedia authoring tools: presentation software (e.g., Microsoft's *PowerPoint*), video production and editing systems (e.g., Apple's *iMovie*), hypermedia design and development software (e.g., *Adobe Flash*), virtual reality (VR) environments (e.g.,

Apple's *QuickTime VR*), and Web 2.0 authoring tools (e.g. *Google's Blogger*).

5. **Commercial multimedia/hypermedia resources** — These include instructional software (e.g., tutorials, drills, simulations), interactive books and ebooks, reference materials, and collections of development materials. Educators use criteria under the following headings when selecting these materials: instructional planning and support, instructional design, content, interface design and navigation, and feedback and interactivity.

6. **Authoring resources, procedures, and skills** — When teachers or students create their own multimedia/hypermedia materials, they need a variety of digital resources (e.g., audio, video, photos, graphics, and text) and hardware (e.g., computers, scanners, digital cameras, camcorders, microphones, audio speakers) at their disposal as well as design and authoring skills, which they can develop over time.

7. **General authoring procedures** — These include reviewing existing products, performing background research, storyboarding, creating individual frames or segments, adding links and/or scripts, and testing and revising the final product.

8. **Authoring with presentation software** — Integration strategies for *PowerPoint-* or *Keynote*-type presentations include support for lectures or presentations of content, practice screens (e.g., spelling words, new vocabulary), assessment screens (e.g., identification of objects), brief tutorials, book reports, and student-created presentations. Rubrics help assess presentations.

9. **Authoring with video production and editing systems** — Integration strategies include demonstrations of procedures (e.g., science experiments), student-created presentations, video lectures, video portfolios, video decision-making/problem-solving simulations, documenting school activities (e.g., yearbooks), visual literacy demonstrations, and teaching video production. Rubrics are available to assess video products.

10. **Authoring with hypermedia development software** — Integration strategies include brief tutorials, student-created presentations, interactive storybooks, and website design. Rubrics and checklists are available to assess hypermedia projects.

11. **Authoring with virtual reality and other immersion resources** — These tools include full immersion environments, web-based VRML (e.g., *SecondLife*), 3-D software, geospatial technologies and Geographic Information Systems (GIS), and *QuickTime VR*. Integration strategies include imaging for virtual field trips, 3-D models to illustrate how systems work, and immersive learning environments for exploration, communication, and collaboration.

12. **Authoring with Web 2.0 design tools** — These tools include online user-generated content websites and tools such as blogs (e.g., *WordPress.com*), wikis (e.g., *Wikipedia.org*), podcasts (Apple's *iTunes*), e-Portfolios (e.g., *ePortfolio.org*), social networking communities (e.g., *Facebook.com*), and video and photo sharing communities (e.g., *YouTube.com, Vimeo.com, Flickr.com*).

Key Terms

- aesthetics
- Audio Video Interleave (AVI) format
- avatar
- blog
- electronic slide show
- e-Portfolio
- Extensible Mark-up Language (XML)
- *Flash*
- full immersion system
- geospatial technology
- Geographic Information Systems (GIS)
- haptic interface
- head-mounted display (HMD)
- hypermedia
- interaction design
- Moving Picture Experts Group (MPEG) format
- multimedia
- podcast
- *QuickTime* movie format (MOV)
- *QuickTime VR Authoring Studio*
- social networking
- storyboard
- usability
- utility
- video editing software
- virtual reality (VR)
- Virtual Reality Modeling Language (VRML)
- Web 2.0 authoring tools
- wiki

Web-Enrichment Activities

1. Thinkport.org provides a list of multimedia simulations. Go to the Think Technology section at http://www.thinkport.org/Technology/simulations.tp, and investigate some of the simulations demonstrated there. Identify two that you think would be valuable for teaching, and explain how you would incorporate the site or materials into your instruction.

2. Go online to *The Atlantic* (http://www.theatlantic.com/doc/194507/bush) to read Vannevar Bush's article "As We May Think." Do a search online of Vannevar Bush to find out more about him. Why is he considered a pioneer in technology? Explain the basic premise of his article in *The Atlantic*.

3. **Software Skill-Builder Tutorial** Access practical tutorial and skill-building activities, and build your skills using popular software and hardware online. Go to Apple.com (http://www.apple.com/quicktime/tutorials), and explore the different QTVR tutorials you can take online. Choose one to complete. Explain which tutorial you completed and what you learned from it. How might you incorporate this program into your instruction?

Go to MyEducationLab to complete the following exercises.

Video Select the topic "Instructional Planning," and go to the "Assignments, Activities, and Applications" section. Access the video "PowerPoint Guides and Prompts Teaching" to see how one teacher stimulates student interest by incorporating technology in her presentations. Complete the activity that follows the video.

Tutorials Select the topic "Software," and access the practical tutorial and skill-building activity titled "Adobe Flash, Basics." Use the tutorial to learn how to use a hypermedia tool. This skill will be reviewed again in the Technology Integration Workshop.

Technology Integration Workshop

The TIP Model in Action

Read each of the following scenarios related to implementing the TIP Model, and answer the questions that follow it based on your Chapter 6 reading and activities.

TIP MODEL SCENARIO #1   Mr. Joaquin is looking for a more motivating alternative to traditional written book reports. His fifth-grade students do not especially like reading books or writing book reports. Mr. Joaquin was talking to a colleague who uses *Adobe Flash* multimedia software to make doing book reports more appealing to students.

1.1 Describe how you think using *Adobe Flash* multimedia software would make it more likely that Mr. Joaquin's students would enjoy doing book reports.

1.2 What would be the relative advantage of using this software tool?

1.3 Would it be better to have the students work individually or in groups to do the exercises? How would you arrange the computer systems to carry out this strategy?

TIP MODEL SCENARIO #2   Mr. Clint and Ms. Snyder, two junior high school social studies teachers, plan a schoolwide project to document the history of the local area by focusing on the families whose personal histories are intertwined with the history of the region. They plan to have students interview many individual family members and research local sources of historical information. Then they want the students to organize all of the information into a book about the history of the local region.

2.1 What multimedia tools could the teachers use to enhance and support this project?

2.2 What would be the relative advantage of using such multimedia tools?

2.3 This kind of project would require a lot of work in researching, organizing information, and producing the final product. Suggest some ways that the work could be divided up and accomplished among classes so as to model for students how to organize work tasks in large, complex projects.

TIP MODEL SCENARIO #3   Mr. Eliott is a fourth-grade teacher and has several students in his class who speak English as a second language. He works on increasing the comprehension skills of all his students, encouraging them to read books and stories to practice their skills. His students who speak English as their second language have trouble reading independently, and Mr. Eliott does not have the time to read to each of them individually. He would like to find a way they can have books read aloud to them in an enjoyable way and also answer comprehension questions about what they have heard and read.

3.1 What type of multimedia tool could help Mr. Eliott address this problem?

3.2 What would be the relative advantages of using this tool with his students who speak English as a second language?

3.3 How would it be possible for these students to use this tool in class without disturbing or distracting other students?

TIP MODEL SCENARIO #4   Ms. Warnick is a high school curriculum coordinator who wants the students to prepare an electronic portfolio they can take with them to display the quality of their work and what they have accomplished throughout their courses. She would like this to include film footage of them giving class presentations as well as digital samples of their work. The completed portfolio for graduating seniors would be placed on a CD they could take with them.

4.1 What multimedia tool would you recommend that Ms. Warnick use to address this problem?

4.2 What would be the relative advantage of using this tool?

4.3 If she wanted teachers to assist with this activity, what would she have to make sure was done before the portfolio concept was introduced to students?

TIP MODEL SCENARIO #5   Ms. Bradley's eighth-grade language arts students have a spelling test every Friday. Spelling counts for 10% of their overall semester grade. There is no time during the regular class period during the week for students to practice, and it is obvious from their grades that many students do not study the words outside class. Ms. Bradley thought of a way to use Microsoft *PowerPoint* software to make sure her students see all the spelling words and hear them pronounced every time they come in the classroom and every time they leave.

5.1 How do you think Ms. Bradley uses *PowerPoint* software to address this problem?

5.2 What would be the relative advantage of using *PowerPoint* software for this purpose?

5.3 Which of *PowerPoint*'s multimedia benefits is Ms. Bradley using for this activity?

TIE into Practice: Technology Integration Examples

The Technology Integration Example that opened this chapter (*Interactive Multimedia Storybooks*) showed how a teacher might use hypermedia authoring software to help produce the annual literary anthology of student work. With the knowledge you have gained from Chapter 6, do the following with this example:

1. Ms. Dubey's students created an interactive storybook similar to the one below using *Adobe Flash*. Create your own interactive storybook using *Adobe Flash*.

Source: Courtesy of HyperStudio/Sunburst.

2. Answer the following questions about the *Interactive Storybook* example:
   • Phase 2 — How would having the middle school students work on an interactive storybook for younger students offer relative advantage for language develop-

ment in comparison with other reading-related activities the teachers could do?
   • Phase 3 — One of the desired outcomes of this project was effective cooperative group work skills. Look at Kathy Schrock's website, Discovery Education, (http://school.discovery.com/schrockguide/assess.html) to locate two different rubrics to help assess this kind of outcome.
   • Phase 4 — Why does the technology coordinator have the students do small projects (e.g., an interactive map of their school) before getting started on the interactive storybooks? Why is storyboarding such an important part of the hypermedia development sequence?
   • Phase 5 — If no money were available to purchase a lab-pack of *Adobe Flash* copies, could the technology coordinator make temporary copies to be used just for this project and then destroy them afterward?
   • Phase 6 — Can you think of strategies Ms. Dubey might use to coordinate group work on the project and to cope with student absences?

3. What NETS for Students skills would students learn by working on the *Interactive Storybook* project? (See the front of this book for a list of NETS for students.)

Technology Integration Lesson Planning

Complete the following exercise using sample lesson plans found on MyEducationLab.

1. Locate lesson ideas — Go to MyEducationLab, and select the topic, "Instructional Planning." Under "Lesson Plans" review examples of lessons that use *Adobe Flash*, video development, 3-D modeling, and virtual field trips with *QuickTime* movies. Choose two of the following integration lessons:
   • Holocaust Video Histories
   • A Monarch Butterfly Movie Project
   • Video Helps Teach History and Writing

2. Evaluate the lessons — Use the *Evaluation Checklist for a Technology-Integrated Lesson* (located on MyEducationLab under the topic, "Instructional Planning.") to evaluate each of the lessons you chose.

3. Modify a lesson — Select one of the lesson ideas, and adapt its strategies to meet a need in your own content area. You may choose to use the same multimedia software as in the original or a different one.

4. Add descriptors — Create descriptors for your new lesson like those found within the sample lessons (e.g., grade level, content and topic areas, technologies used, relative advantage, objectives, NETS standards).

5. Save your new lesson — Save your modified lesson with all of its descriptors.

For Your Teaching Portfolio

For this chapter's contribution to your teaching portfolio, add the following products you created in the Technology Integration Workshop:

- The *Adobe Flash®* product you created for the *Interactive Storybook* project

- The evaluations you did using the *Evaluation Checklist for a Technology-Integrated Lesson*

- The new lesson plan you developed, based on the one you found on MyEducationLab.

Part 3

Linking to Learn: Tools and Strategies

Thanks to microcomputers, the last 25 years have seen an explosion of computer technology–related activity in schools and classrooms. But the emergence of a graphically oriented Internet in 1994 suddenly and dramatically shifted the spotlight from stand-alone microcomputers to the importance of linking with others: other people, other cultures, other points of view. The chapters in this section focus on the resources and strategies that link students and teachers with each other and with the world outside the classroom.

Part 3

Required Background for Teachers

In Part 3, two chapters help teachers build the skills they will need to take advantage of the potential of distance learning resources.

Chapter 7   **Distance Learning Tools and the Role of the Internet in Education**

This chapter reviews web-based and other tools and methods that link learners with each other and with needed resources. It also describes and gives practice in skills and techniques needed to implement distance learning strategies.

Chapter 8   **Integrating the Internet into the Curriculum**

This chapter goes one step further and focuses on uses of the Internet that address current educational needs. It describes the unique capabilities of web-based tools and gives examples and practice in applying them in various instructional situations. Finally, it focuses on how to design effective web-based lessons and on the websites to support teaching and learning.

Chapter 7

Distance Learning Tools and the Role of the Internet in Education

The World Wide Web has transformed the way people live, work and play. People can play travel agent and book all the elements of a vacation online. They can arrange for their bills to be paid automatically while they are gone. They can put a hold on mail delivery, find directions to tourist attractions and get a long-term weather forecast before they pack.

CNN.com

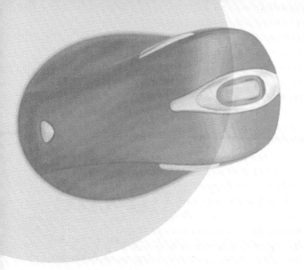

Technology Integration Example

A Research Paper Website

Based on: "So You Have to Do a Research Project?" at http://www.ri.net/schools/East_Greenwich/research.html.

Grade Level: High school • Content Area / Topic: Research, study skills • Length of Time: Nine weeks

Phases 1 and 2: Assess technological pedagogical content knowledge; Determine relative advantage

Ms. Almon was the library media specialist at Werebest High School. One of her tasks was to help all teachers and students use the library's resources effectively for students' research paper assignments. Over the years, she had compiled a substantial collection of handouts, lists of sources, and assessment materials, which she copied, placed in notebooks, and updated periodically. However, she and the teachers agreed it was difficult to get students to use these notebooks. The students' study skills and organizational strategies left a lot to be desired, and each teacher seemed to have a different approach to teaching these important skills. As she and the teachers talked about this situation, they agreed that it would be better to have these materials available in a website, so that students could access them wherever they were, the materials could be easily updated, and the approach for doing research would be consistent across all classes. They decided to work together to create a research paper resource website. They also decided they would use this site and a set of video tutorials to structure a series of teaching activities to help students complete research paper assignments. Ms. Almon knew the content very well (content knowledge), but she did not know how to design a website (technology knowledge) just yet. However, two of the teachers she was working with knew how to use Google Pages very well (technology knowledge), and they all knew that if they collaborated and taught each other, they could easily create a website for the research papers. Furthermore, another teacher who was collaborating had used numerous videos in his classroom to teach social studies (pedagogical knowledge), so they felt that as a team they would be successful.

Phase 3: Decide on objectives and assessments

Ms. Almon and the teachers decided they would structure their assessments around the "Big Six" information literacy

skills as well as around the quality of content in the students' research papers. To make sure that all teachers structured students' learning in the same way, they agreed on objectives for each of these skill areas and created assessment methods to measure each of them. They also decided to measure student attitudes toward research and writing. The outcomes, objectives, and assessments they decided on were as follows:

- **Big Six information skills #1–#3:** Defining, searching for, and acquiring information. **Objective:** Students will identify a topic for a research paper, use the project website to identify published sources of information related to the topic, and locate the items of information. **Assessment:** Checklist of required tasks and products from information searches.

- **Big Six information skills #4–#6:** Analyze, synthesize, and evaluate information. **Objective:** Students will write summary analyses of the information in each item they locate, write a synthesis across all information, and prepare an outline of the points they will emphasize in their research papers. **Assessment:** Checklist of required tasks and products from information analyses.

- **Final paper:** Write a research paper. **Objective:** Students will achieve a rubric score of at least 15 of 20 possible points on an assigned research paper. **Assessment:** Rubric on research paper content, structure, mechanics, and creativity.

- **Attitudes toward writing and research: Objective:** The students will demonstrate a good attitude toward the writing approach and research used in the project by reporting a rating of at least 45 of 50 possible points on an attitude survey. **Assessment:** Likert scale attitude survey.

Phase 4: Design integration strategies

Ms. Almon and the teachers worked together to determine what they would place on the resource website and how students would use it. They decided the site would be most useful if it provided links to other helpful sites and a structure to help students work through the process of doing their searches and writing their papers. They also decided they should create short video tutorials on key points in the process, such as how to select a research paper topic and how to use a graphic organizer to create a visual outline. The website and the tutorials should also help make the teaching process more consistent across classes. They decided to recommend the following time frame for the research paper project:

- **Week 1: Introducing the project and identifying a topic:** All teachers introduce the research paper project by displaying the website to the whole class, using a large monitor or projection system. They review the steps, discuss the process (displaying some of the links at each step), show the first video tutorial, and help students select their research paper topics.

- **Weeks 2–3: Helping students obtain information:** The teachers show students how to use website links to search for information related to their topic. One of the activities is deciding which type of resource to use. For resources that can best be found in the library, Ms. Almon arranges to show students how to access these resources in the library media center, using a video tutorial as an overview. Students use the website resources at the classroom workstation or in the computer center, depending on what else the teacher is doing in the classroom during this time.

- **Weeks 4–6: Helping students analyze and synthesize information:** The teachers help students review their information and make decisions on how to structure their paper and what to include in it. They show videos on doing graphic organizers and let students practice using these techniques.

- **Weeks 7–8: Writing the papers:** During this time, students complete most of the writing on their papers at home or in the library media center after school. Some teachers allocate class time for students to work in class and to review and give feedback on students' word-processed drafts.

- **Week 9: Presentations:** Students present their papers using the strategy selected by their teacher. Some prepare *PowerPoint* presentations to accompany their oral presentations; others create a video or a web page with links to other resources.

Phase 5: Prepare the instructional environment

The main preparation task for the project was creating the website and video tutorials and deciding what to include in each. However, Ms. Almon also had to coordinate the students' trips to the library media center. Preparation tasks included:

- **Creation of website content:** Ms. Almon and the teachers decided on the sections of content to include. Then each of them searched for the best links to include, made a Bookmark/Favorites file of the sites they found, and wrote the content for that section of the site. Ms. Almon compiled the materials into a website and uploaded the site to the school server.

- **Video development:** The teachers also decided on four topics that would support the teaching of research paper strategies and could be presented well via video. Ms. Almon worked with the district media department to create the four brief video tutorials—how to select a research paper topic, how to create a graphic organizer, how to use the library media center resources, and strategies for presenting a research paper. These were placed on the school computers and on a DVD, and copies were given to each teacher.

- **Handout:** To make sure students understood the assignment and had access to all resources, Ms. Almon created a handout that all teachers could give their students. She also posted this handout on the website so that students could **download** it (transfer it from the Internet to their computer) whenever they wished.

- **Library media center and computer lab scheduling:** Before students began work on the projects, the teachers scheduled time for their students in the lab and in the library media center.

Phase 6: Evaluate and revise

After all students had completed their research papers, the teachers met to review the data students had collected. Students did very well on the first set of information skills but less well on the second set. Student attitudes toward the writing process were generally high: About 75% of students rated it 20 points or more. Comments volunteered by students on their surveys indicated they would like more in-class time to revise their products and more individual assistance with the revision process. Rubric scores on research papers were also generally good, with noticeable improvement in the areas of structure and content. Scores were lowest on mechanics. The teachers decided to create a set of writing exercises to give students more concentrated practice on analysis and synthesis skills before doing their own written summaries. They also decided to target one or two mechanics skills for special practice with word-processed exercises. All the teachers agreed that the website and video tutorials had been critical focal points in making instruction across classes more consistent and easier to follow.

Objectives

After reading this chapter and completing the learning activities for it, you should be able to:

1. Define *distance learning*.

2. Describe two ways of classifying distance learning delivery systems.

3. Describe four kinds of distance learning activities.

4. Describe how each of the following current major issues related to distance learning helps shape its impact and future directions: Digital Divide, child development and socialization, impact on school reform, virtual schooling.

5. Describe strategies teachers can use to address each of the following potential pitfalls related to Internet use: access to inappropriate materials, threats to safety and privacy, viruses and hacking, copyright and plagiarism problems.

6. Describe findings from research on distance learning that can help shape practice and enhance impact.

7. Use each of the following: URLs, site navigation strategies, bookmarks or favorites, search engines.

8. Evaluate website content for quality and usefulness.

9. Troubleshoot basic problems with Internet use.

10. Describe the purpose of each of the following Internet resources, and identify how it would meet a specific communications need: email, listservs, bulletin boards, blogs, chatrooms, instant messaging (IM), videoconferencing, MUDs/MOOs/avatar spaces.

11. Identify the materials and effective procedures needed to design and evaluate online courses.

Introducing the Internet

A Brief History of the Internet in Education

The Internet has made such a difference in our society that it is difficult to remember when we did not depend on it for communications, instruction, and even entertainment. There is so much to learn about the uses of the Internet in education that many educators find it difficult to know where to begin. Yet today's educational uses of the Internet bear little resemblance to its original purpose. The U.S. Department of Defense (DOD) developed the first version of the Internet during the 1970s to allow quick communication among researchers working on DOD projects in about 30 locations. The DOD also saw it as a way to continue communications among these important defense sites in the event of a worldwide catastrophe such as a nuclear attack. Because these projects were funded by the DOD's Advanced Research Projects Agency (ARPA), the network was originally called **ARPAnet**.

In the 1980s, just as desktop computers were becoming common, the National Science Foundation funded a high-speed connection among university centers based on the ARPAnet structure. By connecting their individual networks, universities could communicate and exchange information in the same way the DOD's projects had. However, these new connections had an additional, unexpected benefit. A person accessing a university network from home or school could also get access to any site connected to that network. This connection began to be called a gateway to all networks, and what we now call the Internet was born.

Networks connect computers to allow users to share resources and exchange information easily. The Internet, or the Net, as it is commonly known, has been called the ultimate network or "the mother of all networks" because it is a network of networks. It is a way for people in network sites all over the world to communicate with each other as though they were on the same local-area network. The name *Internet* means literally "between or among networks." Though most people think of the Internet as synonymous with the **World Wide Web (WWW)**, the latter really is a subset of the Internet system. The WWW is an Internet service that links sites around the world through hypertext, texts that contain links to other texts. You use a program called a **web browser** to bring up one of these hypertext or web page documents, and you can click on text or graphics linked from it to other pages in other locations. In this way, you "travel" around the Internet from site to site. (See the Navigating the Net section later in this chapter.)

The very first web browser was **Mosaic**, introduced in 1993. It was its highly graphic nature that caused an explosion of Internet use by the following year. The most common current web browsers are *Firefox* and *Internet Explorer,* although others such as Apple's *Safari* are also used.

FIGURE 7.1 URL in a Browser window

Address line for URL

Three required parts of every URL (although it can have more optional ones):

http://www.nasa.gov
①   ② ③

① Each web page address begins with **http://**, which stands for **HyperText Transfer Protocol (HTTP)**.
The "http://" shows it is an Internet address.
(Most, but not all, addresses contain **www**, which stands for **World Wide Web**.)

② The next part of the address here is **nasa**, the name of the computer or *server* to which you connect. Every server on the Internet has an assigned label called the *domain name*.
nasa shows that this computer belongs to the National Aeronautics and Space Administration, a government agency with a wealth of resources on its website.

③ Finally, another required part of the domain name, the *domain designator*, tells what kind of group owns the server. Some example domain designators are:

org = organization
gov = government agency
k12._.us = public schools
mil = military agency

com = business
edu = university
net = network
aus = Australia

Using Uniform Resource Locators (URLs)

Our use of the Internet depends on the use of common procedures or Internet protocols that allow computers to communicate with each other despite differences in programs or operating systems. One important protocol is the manner of listing website addresses. Just about every home in the world has an address so that people can find it and make deliveries of mail and other items. Each place you "visit" on the Internet also has an address, for many of the same reasons. However, the Internet is less tolerant of mistakes in an address than is the U.S. Post Office! Each address must be entered exactly, with every punctuation mark in place, or it will not work.

Internet addresses are called **uniform resource locators**, or **URLs**. Look at the example URL shown in a browser window in Figure 7.1. The line where the URL is entered is called the *address line*. The last three letters in the address line constitute what is called a **domain designator**, which typically indicates the type of content one would find at the website. The most common designators are: .com (commercial site), .gov (government), .net (networks, Internet service providers), .edu (higher education institu-

tions), and .org (non-commercial organizations). Sometimes, the line between the names gets blurry. For example, *.net* is often used instead of *.org* for many schools and other organizations. There are many more designators, and more are being added all the time as the need arises. The U.S. nonprofit organization that sets up domain names is the Internet Corporation for Assigned Names and Numbers (ICANN). You can learn more about ICANN at http://www.icann.org.

Optional parts of a URL.   If an organization is a large one, it may have more than one server, or it may split up a large computer into sections. When this is done, the domain name will have more parts. For example, the College of Education and Human Development at the University of Minnesota (umn) has a college web site:

http://cehd.umn.edu/

Optional parts called *suffixes* can come after a domain designator. Suffixes show locations on the server that are set aside for specific purposes. For example, the College of Education and Human Development's Curriculum and Instruction site is shown at a certain location on the UMN server indicated by the suffix after the slash (shown here as the underlined part):

http://cehd.umn.edu/CI

Three URL uses. Three things to learn about URLs are how to locate them, how to read them, and how to "fix" errors in them.

- **Locating URLs** — If you want to visit a site, but you don't know its URL, one way to find it is to make an educated guess. For example, let's say you want to find the website for the National Council of Social Studies. Since you know it probably will have an "org" designator, and organizations usually use their initials in URLs, a good guess would be http://www.ncss.org.

- **Reading URLs** — If someone gives you a URL, very often you can tell what and where it is by reading its parts. Look at an example:

http://www.noaa.gov

If you knew that the URL someone gave you was one on the subject of weather, you might guess this is for the National Oceanic and Atmospheric Administration (NOAA), a government agency that offers students and teachers a wealth of up-to-date information on the weather.

- **Fixing errors in URLs** — Someone may give you a URL with an error in it (or you may write it down incorrectly). Five common errors you can look for and correct are:

  - Error #1: Omitting one of the parts — The most common omission is the www.
  - Error #2: Wrong domain designator — For example, using .com instead of .org.
  - Error #3: Punctuation errors — Confusing back slashes (\) with forward slashes (/); including a space between letters.
  - Error #4: Omitting punctuation — Leaving out a dot (.) or underscore (_).
  - Error #5: Misspellings — Most misspellings in URLs occur in suffixes.

Navigating the Net

You can move around from web page to web page on the Internet by using three different options: clicking on links, using the Forward and Back buttons, and using the History bar or button.

Method #1: Navigating with links. You can "travel" on the Internet by using your mouse to click **links** (also known as **hot links** or *hot spots*), text or images that have been programmed into the web page to send your browser to another location on the Internet, either within the site or to another site, when you click on them.

How do you know when images are links? When you pass a mouse pointer, or cursor, over an image (without clicking) and the pointer turns into a "browser hand," that image is a link. For example, visit NASA online at (http://www.nasa.gov), and pass the pointer across the page. Any part of a web page can be programmed to be a link. Point to the button labeled "For Educators," and click on it to bring up a page that looks similar to Figure 7.2.

Method #2: Navigating with buttons. Forward and Back buttons are available on your browser menu bars. As indicated in the NASA web page example in Figure 7.2, you can use the Back button to return to a page you were just on (in this example, back to the NASA home page from the "For Educators" page). If you want to return to the "For Educators" page, you can use the Forward button.

Method #3: Navigating with the "History." Every browser has a History section where a user can navigate randomly (rather than just forward or back) to previously visited sites without having to retype a URL address into the address bar. Simply open the address bar and scroll down to select and visit any of the pages listed there.

Using Bookmarks, Favorites, and Online Organizers

You can visit so many sites on the Internet that you quickly lose track of where you found a valuable site on a certain topic. You could write all of them down, but a quicker way to go to such sites is to let a feature in your browser help you create a list or use an online organizational tool. This browser-based list is called a **Bookmark file** (in *Firefox*) or **Favorites file** (in *Internet Explorer*).

Adding a Bookmark or Favorite. Making a Bookmark or Favorite is very simple. Just travel to the site, and when it is on the screen, go to the Bookmarks or Favorites menu at the top of the browser frame and select Bookmark This Page in *Firefox* or Add Page to Favorites in *Internet Explorer*. (The names of these options may vary, depending on the version of the browser.)

Organizing a Bookmarks or Favorites file. Harris (1998a) says that "well-prepared bookmarks files are great resources for teachers and should be shared with others who have similar interests." But what is a "well-prepared bookmarks file"? For a Bookmark collection to be most useful to you and others, it should be organized into sections, much like a library or any

FIGURE 7.2 Navigating with Forward and Back Buttons

Browser Menu Bar

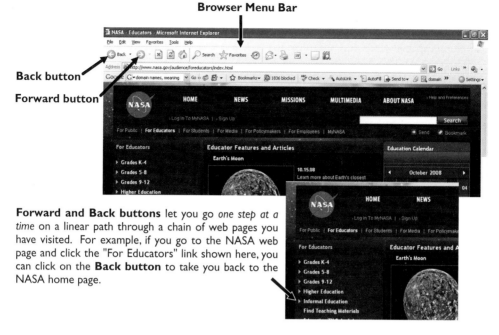

Back button

Forward button

Forward and Back buttons let you go *one step at a time* on a linear path through a chain of web pages you have visited. For example, if you go to the NASA web page and click the "For Educators" link shown here, you can click on the **Back button** to take you back to the NASA home page.

FIGURE 7.3 Social Bookmarking

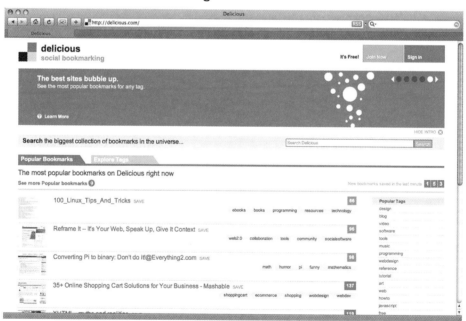

Source: Reproduced with permission of Yahoo! Inc.® 2008 by Yahoo! Inc. YAHOO! and the YAHOO! logo are trademarks of Yahoo! Inc.

collection of materials. After you create Bookmarks, you can organize them into categories of related items.

Go to MyEducationLab and select the topic "Internet." Go to the "Tutorial" section and complete the tutorial entitled, "Bookmarking in Web Browser."

Using an Online Organizer. The website *del.icio.us* (see http://del.icio.us/) allows you to access your Bookmarks at any location by saving your websites online in one place. At this site, you can also bookmark pages for your friends and see what other people are bookmarking. Figure 7.3 shows an example of online bookmarking.

Starting Up Search Engines

Before the Internet, it was difficult to locate specific resources or items of information. Now there is so much information that companies have developed special searching programs to help us locate things. These searching programs are called *search engines*. Some popular search engines and how to use them are described here.

Types of search engines. According to SearchEngineWatch, a site with information on all available search engines, there are many kinds of search engines. Check out SearchEngineWatch to learn about various types of sites (e.g., filtered ones for kids, multimedia search engines). Two commonly cited types of search engines are:

- **Major search engines** — The most popular ones cited by SearchEngineWatch are:
  - **Google** http://www.google.com
  - **Yahoo!** http://www.yahoo.com
  - **Ask Network** http://www.ask.com
- **Metacrawlers** — These programs use more than one search engine at the same time to locate things. The top five cited by SearchEngineWatch are:
  - **Dog Pile** http://www.dogpile.com
  - **Clusty** http://clusty.com
  - **HotBot** http://www.hotbot.com
  - **Kartoo** http://www.kartoo.com
  - **Mamma** http://www.mamma.com

Search Strategies. Search engines can be used in two ways:

- **For subject index searches** — The search engine site provides a list of topics you can click on. See an example in Figure 7.4.
- **For keyword searches** — Type in a combination of words that could be found in the URLs of the sites or documents you want. When searching Google, you are doing a keyword search. Just type in the search word or phrase, and the search engine displays a list of websites whose URLs contain the word or phrase. The pages listed as results of the search are sometimes called **hits**. Try out a keyword search in the Figure 7.5 exercise.

Evaluating Internet Information

At a time when everything in the world seems so high tech and highly controlled, the Internet is, in some ways, a wild frontier. While there are oversight agencies that set up and monitor general items such as domain designators (see earlier section on Using Uniform Resource Locators), no one controls who posts web pages or the quality of their content.

Three kinds of problems arise from this lack of control. One of these, the hazards of offensive or dangerous subject matter or illegal activities, is discussed at various points in this

FIGURE 7.4 Yahoo Subject Index

Yahoo! Directory

Arts & Humanities
Photography, History, Literature...

Business & Economy
B2B, Finance, Shopping, Jobs...

Computers & Internet
Software, Web, Blogs, Games...

Education
Colleges, K-12, Distance Learning...

Entertainment
Movies, TV Shows, Music, Humor...

Government
Elections, Military, Law, Taxes...

Health
Diseases, Drugs, Fitness, Nutrition...

News & Media
Newspapers, Radio, Weather...

Recreation & Sports
Sports, Travel, Autos, Outdoors...

Reference
Phone Numbers, Dictionaries, Quotes...

Regional
Countries, Regions, U.S. States...

Science
Animals, Astronomy, Earth Science...

Social Science
Languages, Archaeology, Psychology...

Society & Culture
Sexuality, Religion, Food & Drink...

New Additions
4/6, 4/5, 4/4, 4/3, 4/2...

Source: Reproduced with permission of Yahoo! Inc.® 2008 by Yahoo! Inc. YAHOO! and the YAHOO! logo are trademarks of Yahoo! Inc.

chapter. The other two problems are less perilous but still have serious implications for teachers and students. Web pages can be less than useful for reasons related to content and design.

Content. The Internet's vast information storehouse, unfortunately, contains some information that is incomplete, inaccurate, and/or out of date. It even has some sites that are works of complete fiction presenting themselves as fact. Students frequently accept as authoritative any information they find on the Internet. However, young people must learn that blind acceptance of any information (on the Internet or elsewhere) is a risky practice. An essential skill for the Information Age is being able to evaluate information critically and to look for indications that content is accurate and reliable. Figure 7.6 shows a checklist of criteria to use when evaluating website content.

Design. We have learned a great deal in recent years about what makes a website functional and easy to use. However, some sites are so poorly designed that people may find it difficult or impossible to locate or read the information they have to offer. (Design criteria are discussed along with web page/website design procedures in Chapter 8.)

Basic Internet Troubleshooting

Like most technologies, the Internet presents its share of "head scratchers." The majority of these errors and problems can be corrected easily; others require more complicated fixes

FIGURE 7.5 Search Engine Strategy: Using Keywords

Using keywords

Problem: You want to know about literary criticism on the novel *Showboat* by Edna Ferber. A keyword search with the phrase Ed na Ferber's Showboat" yields hundreds of hits on the music and the movie. However, you want to know ONLY about the book. Try the following:

- Go to the Google search engine site: http://www.google.com.
- Click the Advanced Search button on the right.
- Fill in the terms *Showboat* and *Edna Ferber*, separated by commas, as shown below in the **all these words** box.
- Fill in the terms *musical, theater,* and *movie,* separated by commas, as shown below, in the **any of these unwanted words** box.
- Review the list of results.

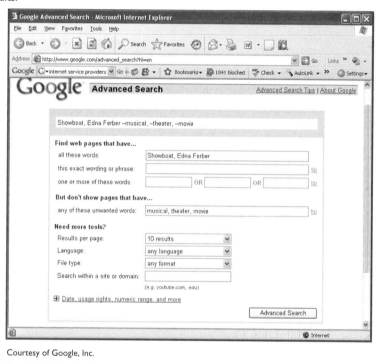

Courtesy of Google, Inc.

Source: Google™ is a trademark of Google, Inc. Reprinted by permission.

or adjustments. Two of the most common difficulties for Internet users are discussed here.

Problem type #1: Site connection failures. After you enter the URL, the site won't come up on the screen. This is the most common problem people encounter; it may occur because of URL syntax errors, problems with the local or domain server, bad links, or firewall issues. The error message for each problem indicates the cause.

- **URL syntax errors** — As mentioned earlier, each dot, punctuation mark, and letter in a URL has to be correct, or the site will not load. The most common error message for this problem is: "… unable to locate the server. Please check the server name and try again." If this message appears, check the URL syntax and make sure you have not done any of the following:
  - Confused the letter "l" with the number "1"

- Confused the letter "O" with the number "0"
- Confused the hyphen "-" with the underscore "_"
- Confused the forward slash "/" with the backward slash "\" in "http://" or in suffixes
- Omitted a required punctuation mark
- Misspelled a part of the URL
- Used the wrong domain designator (e.g., edu instead of org).

- Many URL errors occur in suffixes that follow the domain designator. Try omitting all suffixes beyond the slash and going directly to the main part of the URL. The main page may show the links you want, or the site may have a built-in search engine you can use.

- **Local or domain server down** — If you have checked the URL syntax and are positive it is correct, it may be

FIGURE 7.6 Criteria for Evaluating Website Content

WWW CYBERGUIDE RATINGS FOR CONTENT EVALUATION

Site Title: _____ Subject: _____

URL: _____ Audience: _____

Purpose for exploring this site: _____

Notes on possible uses of this site and URLs for useful linked sites: _____

_____

_____

To determine the worth of the website you are considering, evaluate its content according to the criteria described below. Circle Y for Yes, N for No, NA for Not Applicable.

1. First look			
A. User is able to quickly determine the basic content of the site.	Y	N	NA
B. User is able to determine the intended audience of the site.	Y	N	NA
2. Information Providers	ˋ		
A. The author(s) of the material on the site is clearly identified.	Y	N	NA
B. Information about the author(s) is available.	Y	N	NA
C. According to the info given, author(s) appear(s) qualified to present information on this topic.	Y	N	NA
D. The sponsor of the site is clearly identified.	Y	N	NA
E. A contact person or address is available so the user can ask questions or verify information.	Y	N	NA
3. Information Currency			
A. Latest revision date is provided. Date last revised_____	Y	N	NA
B. Latest revision date is appropriate to material.	Y	N	NA
C. Content is updated frequently.	Y	N	NA
D. Links to other sites are current and working properly.	Y	N	NA
4. Information Quality			
A. The purpose of this site is clear: business/commercial— entertainment — informational — news—personal page—persuasion.	Y	N	NA
B. The content achieves this intended purpose effectively.	Y	N	NA
C. The content appears to be complete (no "under construction" signs, for example).	Y	N	NA
D. The content of this site is well organized.	Y	N	NA
E. The information in this site is easy to understand.	Y	N	NA
F. This site offers sufficient information related to my needs/purposes.	Y	N	NA
G. The content is free of bias, or the bias can be easily detected.	Y	N	NA
H. This site provides interactivity that increases its value.	Y	N	NA
I. The information appears to be accurate based on the user's previous knowledge of the subject.	Y	N	NA
J. The information is consistent with similar information in other sources.	Y	N	NA
K. Grammar and spelling are correct.	Y	N	NA
5. Further Information			
A. There are links to other sites that are related to my needs/purposes.	Y	N	NA
B. The content of linked sites is worthwhile and appropriate to my needs/purposes.	Y	N	NA
Totals			

Based on the total of Yes and No answers and your overall observations, rate the content of this site as:

__ Very useful for my information needs __ Worth bookmarking for future reference __ Not worth coming back to

Comments:

©Karen McLachlan, 7/31/2002   East Knox High School   Howard, Ohio

Source: Reprinted courtesy of Karen B. McLachlan.

that the server that hosts the website is not working temporarily. It may have a technical problem, or it simply may be down for regular maintenance. In this case, you may get an error message like the one shown previously. Wait a day or two, and try it again.

- **Server traffic** — A rarer cause of connection failures is that the server handling Internet traffic for the network or for users in the geographic region is not working properly. Error messages say: "Failure to resolve domain error. Try this site again later" or "Page has no content."

- **Bad or dead links** — If a URL repeatedly fails to connect and you are sure the syntax is correct, the site may have been taken off the Internet. This is known as a *bad* or *dead link.* If this is the case, you may get the same error message given previously, or the site may provide a message that says: "Bad link."

- **Firewalls** — Sometimes a site will not connect because a network's firewall blocks it. If you think your network's firewall is blocking your access to a site in error, contact your network administrator and request that this be adjusted.

Problem type #2: Feature on the site will not work. If an Internet site indicates that it has a special feature such as an animation, a movie, or sound but it will not work for you, there are three possible causes:

- **Plug-in required** — It may be that your computer does not have the special program or plug-in required to play the movie or sound. Usually, if a special plug-in is needed, the site will have a link to a location where you can download the plug-in and install it on your computer (see Chapter 8).

- **Compatibility errors** — The Internet works because there are agreements in place about how to make various machines and programs "talk" to each other. However, sometimes differences exist between operating systems or versions of software that make them incompatible. Unfortunately, some sites can be seen only with Apple's *Safari,* with *Firefox,* or with *Internet Explorer.* The web page usually indicates if it requires a specific browser.

- **Java and other program errors** — Internet web pages usually are written in a combination of three programming languages: HyperText Markup Language (HTML), Java, and less often, Perl. HTML is the basic language that sets up and formats a page, Java is used for special features like counters or chatrooms, and Perl is used to write *CGI scripts,* which are used when the site wants people to enter information into the web page (e.g., a survey). If you get a Javascript error message, make sure Java is enabled (select *Preferences* under the *Edit* menu) and/or download a newer version of Java. If you have an enabled, up-to-date version but still get a Javascript error message, there really may be an error in the Java or Perl language of the program or script. In this case, the only thing you can do is to contact the site and alert them to the error.

Current Pitfalls in Internet Use

As it has become a society-wide tool, the Internet also has spawned its share of society-wide debates and problems. In many ways, it is a reflection of the best and worst qualities of our society. Problems with equity and human behavior (and misbehavior) have already begun to emerge. Five kinds of potential problem areas are discussed here, along with strategies that educators can use to make the Internet a safer, more worry-free place for teaching and learning.

Potential pitfall #1: Accessing sites with inappropriate materials. Like a big-city bookstore, the Internet has materials that parents and teachers may not want students to see, either because they are inappropriate for an age level or because they contain information or images considered objectionable. Yet the Internet is designed to make information easily obtainable, and unfortunately, such materials can be accessed all too easily by accident. For example, for years only the domain designator differentiated the website for our nation's Executive Branch (http://www.whitehouse.gov) from one with X-rated images and materials. Because it is so easy to access these sites, preventing students from accidentally landing on them can be difficult.

The Children's Internet Protection Act, signed into law December 21, 2000, is designed to ensure that libraries receiving federal e-rate funds take measures to keep children away from Internet materials that could be harmful to them (McNabb, 2001). Most schools have found that the best way to prevent access to sites with inappropriate materials is to install **firewall software** and/or **filtering software** on individual computers or on the school or district network that connects them to the Internet. Firewall software protects a computer from attempts by others to gain unauthorized access to it and also prevents access to certain sites (e.g., Norton Internet Security & SpyWare Doctor). Filtering software limits access to sites on the basis of keywords, a list of off-limit sites, or a combination of these (e.g., Cyber Patrol & Net Nanny).

Potential pitfall #2: Safety and privacy issues for students. Although most social networking sites are blocked in schools today, the dominance of them outside of school and the lack of experience most students have, put young people at special risk on the Internet in three ways:

- **Online predators** — Some people get on the Internet to seek out and take advantage of vulnerable young people. Young people tend to believe what they hear and read. Therefore, in a **chatroom** (an online location where people can drop in and exchange messages), they may not consider the possibility that a 12-year-old

FIGURE 7.7   Strategies to Increase Privacy and Safety on the Internet

SafeKids.Com

Go to **the SafeKids site** to explore these and other strategies:
http://www.safekids.com/child_safety.htm/
Created by site founder Lawrence J. Magid. Used with permission.

Strategy #1:   Teach the rules—Review the following *Kids' Rules for Online Safety* with students. Think of some ways you could teach these online rules to students. For example, have students create a multimedia presentation of the rules or role-play how they would react if they encountered one of these problems:

1. I will not give out personal information such as my address, telephone number, parents' work address/telephone number, or the name and location of my school without my parents' permission.

2. I will tell my parents right away if I come across any information that makes me feel uncomfortable.

3. I will never agree to get together with someone I "meet" online without first checking with my parents. If my parents agree to the meeting, I will be sure that it is in a public place and bring my mother or father along.

4. I will never send a person my picture or anything else without first checking with my parents.

5. I will not respond to any messages that are mean or in any way make me feel uncomfortable. It is not my fault if I get a message like that. If I do I will tell my parents right away so that they can contact the service provider.

6. I will talk with my parents so that we can set up rules for going online. We will decide on the time of day that I can be online, the length of time I can be online, and appropriate areas for me to visit. I will not access other areas or break these rules without their permission.

7. I will not give out my Internet password to anyone (even my best friends) other than my parents.

8. I will be a good online citizen and not do anything that hurts other people or is against the law.

Strategy #2:   Manage cookies—Do the following:

- Set your browser to prevent or limit cookies.

- Use a "cookie manager" program to control the information given to cookies (see list of cookie managers at http://www.spychecker.com/software/cookiemanager.html).

Cookie Pal

http://www.kburra.com/cpal.html

---

named "Mary" may actually be a 50-year-old man. Mitchell, Finkelhor, and Wolak (2007) encouragingly report that the percentage of Internet-using youth (ages 10 to 17) who are exposed to unwanted sexual solicitation has declined from 19% in 2000 to 13% in 2005; however, incidents of harassment and unwanted exposure to pornography has increased. Students should be told never to provide their complete names, addresses, or telephone numbers to any stranger they "meet" on the Internet, and they should report to teachers any people who try to get them to do so.

- **Sales pitches aimed at children** — This is a problem similar to that posed by television commercials. Many Internet sites have colorful, compelling images that encourage people to buy. Young people may make purchase commitments they cannot fulfill.

- **Privacy issues** — As Ross and Bailey (1996) note, "Student privacy in public education is a credo enforced by the Family Rights and Privacy Act" (p. 51). In their web products, teachers should be careful not to identify students with last names, addresses, and other personal information. Another privacy issue surrounds the use of **cookies**, or small text files placed on a hard drive by a web server contacted on the Internet. The purpose of cookies is to provide the server with information that can help personalize web activity to your needs. But cookies also may track behavior on the Internet in ways that violate privacy. See Figure 7.7 for a summary of strategies to address privacy and safety issues.

Potential pitfall #3: Fraud on the Internet.   Teachers may find that the fastest, easiest way to order computer products and/or teaching materials is to go to a company's

FIGURE 7.8 Strategies to Prevent Computer Viruses

Strategy #1: Keep virus protection software up to date—Maintain, use, and frequently update your virus protection software.

Strategy #2: Download only from reputable sites—Avoid shareware programs, a frequent source of attached viruses.

Strategy #3: Never open email attachments from unknown senders.

Strategy #4: Never open email attachments until you confirm their intent—Some viruses are programmed to send emails and attachments automatically through someone's email program and infect the computers of the recipients. If you weren't expecting a file from the person, do not open the attachment until you can confirm they sent it.

website and order them online. However, most areas of the Internet are not secure. That is, what you do on the Internet can be monitored by others. Some people use this monitoring capability to look for a credit card number or other information they can use fraudulently. As online consumers, teachers and even students must be sure to purchase products only from well-known, reputable sites that offer a secure server. Secure servers have special programs to prevent outside monitoring of transactions. The URL for a secure server usually begins with "https" instead of the usual "http" and has a symbol of a lock in the web browser.

Potential pitfall #4: Computer viruses and hacking. Viruses are programs written for malicious purposes. They come in several varieties and are named according to the way they work—for example, worms, logic bombs, and Trojan horses. Two ways to get viruses on your computer from the Internet are through email attachments and downloaded files.

- **Email attachments with viruses** — An increasingly popular way to send files and programs to friends or colleagues is to attach them to email messages. However, if a computer contains a virus programmed to attach itself to files, the virus can inadvertently be sent along with the file. When the person receiving the attachment opens it, the virus transfers to his or her computer.

- **Downloaded files and programs with viruses** — As with email attachments, viruses can attach themselves to files and programs and be received along with the

item being downloaded. Figure 7.8 identifies strategies to address these virus problems.

An additional problem is attacks by **hackers**, those who seek to gain unauthorized access to computer systems for the purpose of stealing and corrupting data. Using effective firewalls can prevent hackers from entering the system. However, many schools are finding that firewall software designed to protect users from harmful sites also can have the undesirable side effect of preventing students and teachers from accessing harmless, useful sites. Occasionally, firewalls also can prevent those outside a network from reaching users of the network. School systems find firewalls to be an essential, but problematic, component of being part of the web community and a topic of debate as far as who makes the call regarding what should and should not be blocked and the impact it has on teaching and learning.

Potential pitfall #5: Copyright and plagiarism issues. The Internet is such a rich and easy-to-access source of documents, images, and other resources that it sometimes is easy to forget that many of these resources are copyrighted and protected by U.S. copyright laws. Also, the growing wealth of written products available on the Internet makes it all too easy for students to locate material and cite it without crediting the author or even to turn in whole papers as their own. See Figure 7.9 for strategies to address these concerns.

FIGURE 7.9 Strategies to Address Copyright and Plagiarism Problems

Strategy #1: Teach the rules—Teach students what plagiarism is, why it is wrong, what is permitted, and what is not.

- **If the site clearly is copyrighted,** request permission from owners.
- **If the site has no copyright statement,** reference the site by its URL and owner name.

Strategy #2: Use sites to check for and prevent plagiarism.

Courtesy of iParadigms, LLC.

- **Plagiarism prevention website:** (http://www.turnitin.com)
- **MyDropBox.com website** (http://www.mydropbox.com/)

TABLE 7.1 Resources for Communicating on the Internet

Type of Resource	Resource Name	Description
Asynchronous (left message) communications	Email	Electronic messages sent to individuals.
	Listserv	An electronic list of email addresses, everyone on the list gets a copy of the email sent to the list address.
	Bulletin board (BB)	Electronic area set up in a distance course to post messages and hold asynchronous discussions.
	Blogs	Short for *web log*. A publicly accessible web page set up and hosted by an individual or group for the purpose of discussing a topic or issue.
Synchronous (live interaction) communications	Chatrooms	Internet locations that allow "live" communications between two or more users.
	Instant messaging	A private chatroom in which members alert each other when they wish to chat, then may send messages that are received immediately; like a telephone conversation but with text messages.
	Videoconferencing	A form of two-way, interactive communication that allows those involved to see and hear each other. Requires a camera, audio input device (e.g., a microphone), an output device (e.g., speakers), and a shared program such as Microsoft's *NetMeeting*.
Cyber collaborations	MUDs, MOOs, avatar spaces	MUD is an acronym for multiuser dungeons (or dimensions or domains), and MOO stands for MUDs object-oriented, programs that allow many users at different sites to interact at the same time via avatars and typed text in a graphical, VR-like environment.

Communicating on the Internet

Increasingly, the Internet has become a primary form of communication for teachers and students, replacing traditional channels such as sending letters and making telephone calls. Described here and summarized in Table 7.1 are a variety of written and visual Internet resources that make this communication possible and support many instructional strategies.

Email

Electronic mail (email) is the most common way to exchange personal, written messages between individuals or small groups. Email may be sent via a program (e.g., Microsoft's *Outlook Express*) or through capability built into an Internet browser. This versatile medium supports a variety of classroom activities. Researchers have found that email not only has great potential to improve communications among students, teachers, and parents (Boulware & Tao, 2002), but it can also improve students'

writing. For example, Berkson and Britsch (1997) found that having students email others gave more immediate purpose for their writing, motivated them to write more frequently and produce longer passages, and gave them greater confidence in their writing. See some examples hosted by the ePals Classroom Exchange in Technology Integration Lesson 7.1.

The etiquette guidelines that govern behavior when communicating on the Internet have become known as **netiquette**. Netiquette covers not only rules of behavior during discussions but also guidelines that reflect the unique electronic nature of the medium. Netiquette usually is enforced by fellow users who are quick to point out infractions of netiquette rules. The summary of email rules in Figure 7.10 on page 222 is based on published sources such as Shea's (2004) online book, *Netiquette*.

Listservs, Bulletin Boards, and Blogs

Three kinds of communication take the form of asynchronous (not in real time) messages rather than synchronous (real-time) exchanges: listservs, bulletin boards, and blogs.

Technology Integration Lesson 7.1

Distance Learning via Email Communications

Title: Keypal Collaborations   **Grade Level:** All grades
Content Area/Topic: All content areas

NETS for Students: Standards 1 (Creativity and Innovation), 2 (Communication and Collaboration), and 3 (Research and Information Fluency)

Description of Standards Applications: This integration lesson offers students the opportunity to communicate synchronously and asynchronously online as they explore partnerships and discuss content. After choosing an investigation, students use their creativity and research skills to discuss various topics. The exchanging of messages with students at distant sites, "keypals," has long been recognized as a way to motivate students to use language. The activities described here show that keypal exchanges also can help students learn a variety of topics, ranging from Spanish to multicultural education.

Instruction: Begin by contacting a site such as the ePals Classroom Exchange (http://www.epals.com) or Teaching.com (http://www.iecc.org/), organizations designed to host projects that encourage email collaborations. Some example activities from the ePals website are as follows:

- *Space day* — In partnership with Space Day(SM), an initiative of the Space Day Foundation, fourth- to eighth-grade students collaborate with other students around the world via email on real challenges encountered by people living and working in space.
- *Healthy wetlands* — High school students around the world work together via email to make the connection between clean, safe drinking water and the wetlands located in their own communities. Teachers and students use research manuals to guide them through the water cycle, watersheds, wetland types, and other topics. They visit a wetland to record their observations and meet with guests and experts in environmental science.
- *The way we are* — Students work together to break down commonly held stereotypes about people in other regions of the world. After exchanging information and becoming familiar with an individual, a culture, and a community, student partners reexamine their beliefs about that culture and community.
- *EPals book club* — Students from around the world talk about and post comments, writings, surveys, and reviews on their favorite books and authors.

Sources: Baugh, I., and Baugh, J. (1997). Global classrooms: E-mail learning communities. *Learning and Leading with Technology, 25*(3), 38–41; and the ePals Classroom Exchange website, http://www.epals.com.

Listservs. **Listservs** or **lists** are discussion groups that feature ongoing emailed "conversations" among groups of individuals who belong to an organization or share common interests. When an email message is addressed to a listserv mailing list, it is automatically duplicated and sent to everyone on the list. Replies to a listserv also go to everyone on the list.

Bulletin boards. Like listservs, **bulletin boards (BBs)** are electronic message centers but are used for posting messages of interest to group members who visit the BB rather than for emailed notices that all members receive at once. Bulletin board members must go to the BB location to review and leave messages. Bulletin board communications are sometimes known as "threaded discussions."

Blogs. Short for *web log,* a **blog** is a web page that serves as a publicly accessible location for discussing a topic or issue. Each is usually set up and maintained by an individual.

FIGURE 7.10 Netiquette: Rules of Behavior on the Internet

- **Identify yourself:**
  —Begin messages with a salutation and end them with your name.
  —Use a signature (a footer with your identifying information) at the end of a message

- **Include a subject line.** Give a descriptive phrase in the subject line of the message header that tells the topic of the message (not just "Hi, there!").
- **Avoid sarcasm.** People who don't know you may misinterpret its meaning.
- **Respect others' privacy.** Do not quote or forward personal email without the original author's permission.
- **Acknowledge and return messages promptly.**
- **Copy with caution.** Don't copy everyone you know on each message.
- **No spam (a.k.a. junk mail).** Don't contribute to worthless information on the Internet by sending or responding to mass postings of chain letters, rumors, etc.
- **Be concise.** Keep messages concise—about one screen, as a rule of thumb.
- **Use appropriate language:**
  —Avoid coarse, rough, or rude language.
  —Observe good grammar and spelling.
- **Use appropriate emoticons (emotion icons) to help convey meaning.** Use "smiley's" or punctuation such as :-) to convey emotions. See website list of emoticons at http://netlingo.com/smiley.cfm and http://www.robelle.com/smugbook/smiley.html.
- **Use appropriate intensifiers to help convey meaning.**
  —Avoid "flaming" (online "screaming") or sentences typed in all caps.
  —Use asterisks surrounding words to indicate italics used for emphasis (*at last*).
  —Use words in brackets, such as (grin), to show a state of mind.
  —Use common acronyms (e.g., LOL for "laugh out loud").

Blogs began as personal journals, but their use rapidly expanded to a public discussion forum in which anyone could give opinions on the topic. Kajder, Bull, and Van Noy (2004) find that blogs have revived journaling as a way to encourage students to write more.

Chatrooms, Instant Messaging, and Videoconferencing

Three kinds of synchronous communications are chatrooms, instant messaging (IM), and videoconferencing.

Chatrooms. Chatrooms are Internet locations that allow "live" communications between two or more users. As users in a chatroom type in their comments, everyone in the "room" sees what they type.

Users of chatrooms sometimes use **avatars**, moving 3-D figures that represent people in virtual environments. Avatars may or may not actually look like the person they represent. This use is more common in higher education than in K–12 environments.

Instant messaging. One type of Internet communication is **instant messaging (IM)**, a service that allows users to use private chatrooms in which members alert each other when they wish to chat. Members then may send messages that are received immediately—like a telephone conversation but with text messages. The IM system alerts a person when someone wishes to chat with him or her. IMs are usually live, but they also may be left as messages to be read later, and the person notified can then initiate a chat session. IM communications make frequent use of abbreviations such as RUOK for "Are you okay?" and CUL for "See you later." Students are natural IMers, and schools are finding ways to make instructional use of this versatile communication tool. Lewis and Fabos (2005) provided a detailed account of student uses of instant messaging and described the changing epistemologies and attendant practices associated with IM use (multivocality, performativity, resourcefulness, hybrid textuality, and new forms of circulation and surveillance).

OMG! The proliferation of cell phones and the ease of IM'ing puts you in touch with your BFF ASAP.

FIGURE 7.11 The Virtual World of Second Life®

Videoconferencing. This form of two-way interactive communication allows those involved to see and hear each other. Each person must have a camera, an audio input device such as a microphone, and an output device such as speakers. In addition, each participant must use a program such as *Skype* or *NetMeeting*. It is also helpful to have a high-speed connection so the video will move smoothly. Those who want to videoconference may also subscribe to a free hosting service such as *Yahoo! Messenger*, Apple's *iChat*, or *Skype*. Videoconferencing is used more in higher education than in K–12 schools, but it is becoming more common as high-speed connections in schools become more common.

Cyber Collaborations: MUDs and MOOs, and Avatar Spaces

Odasz (1999–2000) recommends two resources to support online collaboration, usually for older and more sophisticated learners: multiuser dungeons (or dimensions or domains) or **MUDs**, and a MUDs object-oriented (**MOOs**), a MUD whose code is available and is, therefore, free. These whimsical-sounding resources are programs that allow many users at different sites to interact at the same time. The environment is graphical but, unlike virtual reality, interaction is through typed text or, less often, voice. Odasz says that

sample applications include "interactive fiction" or having students role-play characters from literature. An example MUD may be seen at http://angalon.tamu.edu/.

The future of the Internet will be increasingly visual, and one feature contributing to this is the use of **avatar spaces**, MUD locations where users can interact through their graphic representations. (Also see avatars described earlier in the Chatrooms section.) The widespread use of avatars on the Internet was proposed in Neal Stephenson's 1992 science fiction novel *Snow Crash*. These figures can be made to look much like the person they represent, or they may be complete fantasy figures, selected by a user to project a certain aura or point of view. The uses of avatar spaces in education are limited but have great potential for fostering visual literacy, motivating students to develop writing and other communication skills, and helping teach skills that involve visual design. The most popular avatar-based environment is Second Life® (see Figure 7.11), where a virtual world is giving thousands of individuals literally a second life. Numerous higher education schools are teaching courses within Second Life® and organizations such as Reuter's Press now deliver the news within this environment. At the University of Minnesota, instructors are teaching courses and the College of Education and Human Development is developing its own "island" to deliver such courses within Second Life®.

Distance Learning: Placing the Internet in Context

Many of you reading this text cannot remember a time when cell phones and text messaging were not the norm. A time when we "googled" something we did not understand or needed more information about. A time when emailing was not a daily activity. Technology is changing every aspect of society as we know it. The technological norms are no longer the typewriter and the telephone, but the laptop and the cell phone. Even in the rapid environment of technological evolution, remarkable changes in communications, in particular, have come about with incredible speed; some resources have developed from possible to pervasive in only a few years. These changes are by no means completed or even slowing down. The primary reason for this breathtaking revolution in communications is society's recognition of the importance of ready access to people and resources. If "knowledge is power," as Francis Bacon said, then communication is freedom—freedom for people to reach information they need in order to acquire knowledge that can empower them. This heady freedom permeates the atmosphere of an Information Society. This freedom in communication is pervasive, as many of us are always "connected."

Background on Distance Education

Rapid developments in communication technologies have brought about what Moore (1995), quoting an issue of *The Economist,* called "the death of distance," which happens "when the cost of communications comes down to next to nothing, as seems likely in the first decade of the next century" (p. 1). But the death of distance seems to have given new life to education in the form of **distance learning (DL)**. The United States Distance Learning Association (USDLA) defines *distance learning* as:

> *The acquisition of knowledge and skills through mediated information and instruction, encompassing all technologies and other forms of learning at a distance.*

Distance learning has not only changed how quickly educators and students can exchange and access information; it also has altered the educational equation in fundamental ways. Thanks to distance technologies such as broadcast systems and the Internet, learning has escaped the physical boundaries of the classroom and the school, and students and teachers have become part of a virtual classroom they share with counterparts around the world. Our society is just beginning to understand and take advantage of the potential of this new classroom. From our first life of interacting with the Internet as a resource that we use on a sporadic basis, to our "SecondLife" within online environments, the times are changing, and it is time to get moving!

Making the Case for Technology Integration

Use the following questions to reflect on issues in technology integration and to guide discussions within your class.

1. Durden (2001) says that "...no existing form of distance learning can similarly affirm students as individuals and also force them to acknowledge the ideas of others.... Disenfranchised students, as much as their affluent and advantaged peers, deserve a chance at a residential, liberal education—not an unproven alternative." What evidence can you cite to contradict Durden's belief that distance learning cannot help students acknowledge each other's ideas? How would you respond to Durden's criticisms of distance learning as an unproven alternative to face-to-face education?

2. The following is a quote from the report *Fools Gold: A Critical Look at Computers and Childhood* by the Alliance for Childhood: "Those who place their faith in technology to solve the problems of education should look more deeply into the needs of children. The renewal of education requires personal attention to students from good teachers and active parents, strongly supported by their communities. It requires commitment to developmentally appropriate education and attention to the full range of children's real low-tech needs—physical, emotional, and social, as well as cognitive" (Cordes & Miller, 2000, p. 4). In light of the increasing importance of the Internet as an information resource and an instrument for students' research, how would you respond to this statement?

The Internet burst on the scene in our society and in education a relatively short time ago, but it quickly set fire to the interest and imagination of even the least technical teachers, students, and parents. Almost all DL applications involve some Internet resource or activity, and many rely exclusively on Internet materials. As the example at the beginning of this chapter shows, distance learning is not just the delivery of whole courses. DL also refers to the use of the Internet and other resources to play key roles in all kinds of classroom communications. For example, Doering, Hughes, and Scharber (2007) provide a framework to highlight the range of technology resources available for integration that showcase how social studies teachers are utilizing specific online resources. The online resources, on a continuum from being used in face-to-face classrooms to completely online, are integrated in four ways: (1) *individual lesson plans* distributed online that enhance existing face-to-face curriculum; (2) online *lesson enhancements* that augment individual face-to-face lessons; (3) *completely online courses and curriculum* where current face-to-face courses and curriculum are supplanted; and (4) an *all-inclusive online course, curriculum* and online learning environment where, depending on the pedagogy, the online learning environment flexibly provides all three earlier forms—individual lessons, lesson enhancements, and completely online courses and curriculum.

The USDLA's definition of distance learning leaves open the door to more constructivist views of learning, including the possibility that, though learning is taking place, there may not be an instructor at all, and no formal or organized instruction may be offered. The USDLA definition says simply that learning may take place where learners are connected with information resources, with each other, with instructors, or with any combinations of these resources. Because the Internet figures so prominently in many distance learning activities, the rest of this chapter focuses primarily on this rapidly growing and evolving force in education.

Distance Learning Delivery Systems

Although the Internet was the catalyst for an unprecedented interest in distance learning, it is by no means the only delivery system for distance learning. Indeed, distance learning can be done without any electronic assistance at all. Distance learning has been done by correspondence study via postal mail (a.k.a. snail mail) since the 19th century. Changes in our technological capabilities have brought about gradual changes to our methods of delivering instruction at a distance. The first major change to correspondence courses came when presentations were placed on videotape and mailed along with print materials. Later, improvements in the quality and availability of broadcast technologies made it possible to send audio and video information, either live or taped.

Distance delivery systems can be classified in any of several ways. Simonson, Smaldino, Albright, and Zvacek (2000) suggested a classification scheme based on Dale's cone of experience, a system designed by Edgar Dale to categorize media according to their degree of realism. Dale said media range from concrete (e.g., hands-on or multisensory experience) to abstract (verbal symbols such as text descriptions) and that younger or less experienced students require more concrete experiences before they can understand abstract ones. Thus, distance delivery systems can be classified according to the degree to which they approximate reality. However, this classification system also may be overlaid with the methods and technologies used to deliver them.

Sometimes several of the technologies listed in Table 7.2 are used in combination to achieve the desired level of realism. Currently, two of the most popular arrangements for distance learning are video courses or *telecourses* and web-based courses. Telecourses are still more common in higher education than they are in K–12 levels, but some K–12 curriculum materials are also delivered in this way (e.g., integrated science units broadcast from the University of Alabama to schools). **Videoconferencing** (live video and audio communications) via the Internet unfortunately is still not as frequent today as hoped, but it is increasing. Videoconferencing is being used in many adventure learning programs such as the GoNorth! Adventure Learning

TABLE 7.2 Classification System for Distance Learning Delivery

	Types of Interaction	Delivery Methods
Most abstract, least realistic	One-way, print-based	Correspondence courses via postal mail and/or fax
	Tape or broadcast audio mailed or downloaded to students	Prerecorded audio or video
	One-way, synchronous audio from instructor to students	Broadcast radio
	Two-way, synchronous audio between students and instructor	Audioconferencing telephone systems
	Taped or broadcast video mailed or downloaded to students (no synchronous interaction with instructor)	Broadcast television: microwave or satellite link
Most realistic, least abstract	Text and multimedia interactions	Web-based course management systems
	Live video from instructor to students (with synchronous audio interaction)	Teleconferencing
	Two-way, synchronous video between instructor and students	Videoconferencing

Top Ten Ways Distance Resources Support Learning

The following characteristics of distance resources have the ability to enhance teaching and learning activities in unique ways.

1. **Fast access to information** — Students use the Internet to locate information quickly for classroom research and development projects and educational opportunities.

2. **Access to experts not available locally** — Internet projects let students tap the expertise of experts at a distance.

3. **Fast communication to groups** — Internet pages, email, and listservs help teachers and students send updates and stay in touch with each other and with parents and community members.

4. **Communication resources to support collaboration** — Email, bulletin boards/conferences, blogs, chats, web pages, and other resources make it easier for students and teachers to work together and share products, whether they are in the same physical location or at a distance.

5. **Access to learning materials** — Teachers download prepared handouts, tests, images, and other materials to use with students; students can use online self-instructional tutorials to surge ahead on a topic.

6. **Access to courses and lessons not locally available** — Teachers and students can take courses on topics for which teachers are not available at their sites.

7. **Access to education for homebound students** — Students who are home-bound due to illness, disability, or discipline can take courses and complete degree programs online.

8. **Learning communities support collaboration** — Teachers and students support and encourage each other and share ideas and materials to advance learning.

9. **Lesson ideas from multiple sources** — Teachers can locate teaching ideas on any topic from a variety of Internet sites set up for this purpose.

10. **Increased interaction among students and between students and teachers** — Many educators and students feel that the communication options available in distance courses make it possible for them to interact more than is possible in face-to-face environments.

Series, where students can talk with educators and explorers as they cross the Arctic by dogsled. Other programs have linked students to NASA's astronauts and scientists and to the divers who explored the Titanic. Podcasts, audio and digital video files delivered via the Internet, are becoming increasingly popular as more teachers and students learn how to develop and deliver podcasts.

Types of Distance Learning Activities

Once a rarity in education, distance activities have become a mainstream alternative to and supplement for face-to-face learning. As Table 7.2 indicates, some distance activities are carried out via broadcast and stored video and audio (e.g., videoconferencing and podcasts), but the Internet has become the primary medium for most distance learning. Although most educators think of distance learning only as courses, there are actually numerous ways to integrate the Internet into the classroom in support of learning. Just as Doering, Hughes, and Scharber (2007) provided a framework in the social studies for integrating Internet resources, Allen and Seaman (2006) identified three types of online courses: online, where most or all of the content is delivered online; blended/hybrid, where the course is a mixture of online and face-to-face delivery; and web-facilitated, where a course uses web-based technology in a face-to-face setting. There are four types of general activities that fall under these frameworks: student research, online classroom materials, web-based lessons, and virtual courses and programs. A summary of the instructional benefits of these activities is given in the *Top Ten* feature.

Student research. Students use the Internet to search for materials and information to support their research and production work. Although search engines have become easier and more productive to use for this purpose, students still need help applying what Ms. Almon in the *Technology Integration Example* referred to as the "Big Six" skills. These skills are an important foundation to ensure that students make best use of this form of distance learning. The "Big Six" are:

1. Task Definition
2. Information-Seeking Strategies
3. Location and Access
4. Use of Information
5. Synthesis
6. Evaluation

(Courtesy of http://www.big6.com)

Online classroom materials. In this type of distance learning, teachers use online materials to help teach themselves and/or their students a topic or skill. The example at the beginning of this chapter is illustrative of this approach. Online tutorials such as those available at the Internet4Classrooms website are the most common example of this type.

Web-based lessons. In this type of learning, teachers use website resources to structure a curriculum lesson. Harris (1998b) lists 18 different kinds of these lessons, which she calls *activity structures.* This type of distance learning will be covered in more depth in Chapter 8.

Virtual courses and programs. Distance courses were popular in higher education long before they caught on at K–12 levels. Since 1996, virtual courses and diploma programs have sprung up around the United States and in other countries (Clark, 2001; Loupe, 2001; Roblyer & Marshall, 2002–2003; Zucker & Kozma, 2003).

Current Issues in Distance Learning

When communications became more global and accessible, many in education hoped it would mean better access to high-quality education for all students, regardless of location and economic status. These hopes have not been universally realized, and unexpected problems have occurred,

including the widening of the Digital Divide, socialization issues, and impact on educational reform.

Digital Divide issues. As discussed in Chapter 1, greater dependence on the Internet has served to widen still further the Digital Divide. Recent studies show that while more students are using the Internet and other distance resources, children from underserved populations (i.e., low-income and some minority students) still have far less access at home and school than other students do (Corporation for Public Broadcasting, 2003). If this gap persists, it augurs future problems in providing equitable access to the resources distance learning offers.

Development and socialization issues. Spending too much time on computers has been cited as harmful to children's development of relationships and social skills. The American Academy of Pediatricians, recognizing these potentially harmful effects of overexposure to mass media (including the Internet), calls for limiting children's use of media to 1 to 2 hours per day (McNabb, 2001). In light of increasing dependence on virtual courses at high school levels, this advice will be difficult to heed.

Positive and negative impact on education reform. Many educators predict that distance learning will reform teaching methods and increase access to quality education. Advocates have been optimistic that the distance learning movement would alter traditional, teacher-centered methods and bring about richer, more constructivist ones. However, recent reports at higher education levels dispute this belief (Zemsky & Massey, 2004), finding that distance resources are usually used to support traditional approaches. Virtual K–12 schools are a growing phenomenon, but their impact on educational reform is often hampered by issues such as high dropout rates and funding disputes. Virtual schooling has also become a political issue, since some educators and parents fear that virtual schools could become the primary vehicle that would allow federal and state funding for private and home-schooled students (Roblyer, 2004).

Virtual schooling issues. Although an increasingly popular strategy, K–12 virtual courses and programs present the following ongoing challenges:

- **Curriculum alignment** — To be awarded credit, virtual school curriculum standards have to be aligned to state and local standards where the students reside. This is especially difficult when students from a given virtual school come from more than one state.
- **Teacher certification** — To ensure they are qualified, online teachers must receive certification from a state agency. Schools must either identify one agency or accept teachers from several different certifying agencies.
- **Accreditation** — Course credit can be granted either by the virtual school or the school district.

Adapting for Special Needs

Given the importance of the Internet in K–12 education, it is essential that students with disabilities have access to the web. Standard web browsers can be problematic for some types of computer users—for example, individuals who are blind or have poor vision and individuals who are unable to use a mouse for screen navigation.

One example of an alternative web browser that is designed to be responsive to physical and sensory disabilities is *Opera* (http://www.opera.com). Valuable features of this browser include single-key navigation, which makes it possible to browse the web using only the keyboard, and visual presentation control to zoom in and enlarge the content and change the font and colors. The research and development that went into this product have contributed to making the web more accessible for individuals with disabilities as well as those in the non-handicapped population who might need simpler interfaces for searching the web via palm devices and cell phones. This software may be downloaded free for Windows, Macintosh, Linux, and the Smartphone/PDA.

Contributed by Dave Edyburn

Accrediting agencies have emerged to certify online schools, but it is sometimes difficult to tell if the agency itself is reliable.

- **Funding** — Lawsuits have arisen over whether virtual schools should be authorized to use public funds. Some people believe that virtual schools are an attempt to implement home schooling at public expense.

- **Possible negative consequences** — There is an ongoing dialog on the possible negative effects of virtual schooling on students' socialization. Also, the dropout rate is usually higher for online courses, and it has become clear that not all students can succeed in online environments (Roblyer & Marshall, 2002–2003). Successful online students seem to need more than the usual degree of organization skills and self-motivation, as well as better-than-average computer skills.

Current Research in Distance Learning

Though fueled by the popularity of the Internet, the current wellspring of support for distance learning seems unlikely be just a passing fad. Years of research have confirmed the effectiveness of some forms of distance learning, and studies of other strategies are on the increase. This section captures some current research that indicates how distance learning is helping shape the future of teaching and learning. In the past, the most popular kind of research compared a distance learning method with a traditional one. However, several other kinds of questions also are proving useful in shaping the impact of distance learning. Findings on these topics are described here and summarized in Table 7.3 on page 229.

Effectiveness of distance learning compared with face-to-face (FTF) learning. Some distance learning methods are among the most well studied in education. For example, course delivery via instructional television has long been considered equivalent to FTF instruction in its impact on achievement and on attitudes of students (Russell, 1992). A more recent review (Russell, 1997) comparing distance education with traditional classroom instruction also found no overall difference, although there was significant variation. In addition, **asynchronous** courses, in which information and messages are left for the receiver to read later, tended to show greater gains than **synchronous** ones, in which communications are sent and received immediately (Bernard et al., 2004). There is also no doubt that distance students tend to drop out at higher rates than students in FTF courses do (Oblender, 2002; Zucker & Kozma, 2003).

Machtmes and Asher's (2000) meta-analysis of video-based distance courses, or telecourses, found that courses with two-way interaction between instructor and students were more effective than traditional courses. Peterson and Bond (2004) found no differences in achievement between preservice teachers' learning of instructional planning in online and FTF courses. In the latter study, data also suggested an FTF advantage for lower performing students, but the authors said further research in this area was needed to explore this finding. When Zucker and Kozma (2003) compared virtual high school courses with face-to-face ones, they found comparable frequency of interaction with teachers, but lower interaction among students and a slightly higher dropout rate in virtual courses. While they did not report achievement comparisons, Zucker and Kozma did note special challenges for virtual courses in presenting and solving visual problems (e.g., designing a structure) and in teacher inspection of hands-on work. They said that, while virtual courses could be successful with these activities, they would require substantially more planning than face-to-face ones would.

Course characteristics that affect success. Some studies focus on course factors that correlate directly to dropout rates

TABLE 7.3 Summary of Research Findings and Major Reports on Distance Learning

Research Topic	Research Questions	Findings
Effectiveness and impact	• Are distance courses as effective as FTF courses?	• No significant overall differences in achievement between distance and FTF courses. • Asynchronous courses reflect higher achievement than synchronous ones. • Dropout rate usually higher in distance courses. • Harder to teach topics that have visual problems and solutions in distance courses.
Course quality	• What are the characteristics of effective distance courses?	The most successful courses have: • High interaction • Instructor and other support throughout the course • Fewer technical problems and good technical support when problems occur.
Effective distance learners	• What are the characteristics of students who are effective distance learners?	• Mixed evidence on whether single cognitive factors (e.g., self-efficacy) predict success. • Combination of achievement beliefs, responsibility, self-organization ability, and technology skill/access appears to predict student success.
Effective distance instructors	• What are the characteristics of effective distance instructors?	Effective distance instructors have good: • Course planning and organizational skills specific to distance environments • Verbal and nonverbal presentation skills specific to distance learning situations • Ability to involve and coordinate student activities among several sites • Communication and classroom organizational skills • Collaborative work with others to produce effective courses • Ability to use questioning strategies
Cost effectiveness	• What cost factors enter into preparing and implementing distance education programs? • How do we determine cost effectiveness?	• Costs factors include technology, transmission, maintenance, infrastructure, production, support, and personnel. • Distance education becomes more cost effective when resources are used more efficiently and with more courses.

in distance learning courses (Bernard & Amundsen, 1989; Gibson & Graf, 1992). However, many researchers agree with Wilkes and Burnham (1991) that course success should be measured by more than just endurance and achievement, since "highly motivated learners may be willing to endure almost (anything) to achieve a passing grade" (p. 43). Therefore, the majority of studies in this area focus on attitude surveys of students who complete distance learning courses. Researchers agree that the handful of factors described here are the major contributors to course satisfaction (Biner, 1993; Bolliger & Martindale, 2004; Cheng, Lehman, & Armstrong, 1991; and Hardy & Boaz, 1997):

• **High interaction** — Though some studies find that the convenience of distance learning means more to students than teacher interaction does (Klesius, Homan, & Thompson, 1997), the single greatest determinant of satisfaction across studies is the amount of interaction between instructor and students (Fulford & Zhang, 1993; Furst-Bowie, 1997; Roblyer & Wiencke, 2003, 2004; Smith, 1996; Thompson, 1990; Westbrook, 1997; Zirken & Sumler, 1995). McHenry and Bozik (1997) found that lack of "classroom community" among distance learners can decrease interaction and affect course satisfaction. But, as is typical of distance learning and traditional classes alike, smaller class size can determine student perception of interactivity and, therefore, satisfaction with distance learning instruction. Riddle (1990) suggests that meeting students face to face for the first class meeting helps establish a rapport that can lead to better interaction throughout the course. Roblyer and Ekhaml (2000) created an interaction rubric to help define what interaction means in practical terms and to help instructors reflect on how they can make their courses more interactive. Roblyer and Wiencke (2003, 2004) offer an updated version of the rubric.

- **Support during course** — Many studies show that students value and profit from instructor and other support during their course experiences, from registration through course activities and evaluation (Gibson & Graf, 1992; Hardy & Boaz, 1997; Zucker & Kozma, 2003). McHenry and Bozik (1997) find that lack of library resources and slow transfer of paperwork are among the support problems that negatively affect course satisfaction.
- **Minimal technical problems** — Consistent evidence exists that technical problems can doom the best planned course (Cheng, Lehman, & Armstrong, 1991; Thomerson & Smith, 1996; Zucker & Kozma, 2003). Successful courses are those that minimize technical problems so that the student can focus on the learning rather than on computer and technical issues.

Characteristics of successful distance learners. Some researchers have tried to identify student capabilities or other factors that could predict whether a student might drop out, be less satisfied, or do less than others in an online activity. Hypothesized characteristics include self-motivation and ability to structure one's own learning (Gibson & Graf, 1992; Hardy & Boaz, 1997), previous experience with technology (Richards & Ridley, 1997), good attitude toward course subject matter (Coussement, 1995), and locus of control (Dille & Mezack, 1991). Studies disagree on whether single cognitive factors can predict success. Wang and Newlin (2000) and Osborn (2001) found that higher internal locus of control and spending more time online can predict whether students will be successful in online learning environments. Also, Lim (2001) found that students' computer self-efficacy (i.e., belief in their ability to use computers effectively) could predict their degree of satisfaction in online courses. However, DeTure (2004) found that self-efficacy and cognitive style

were poor predictors of higher grades. Roblyer and Marshall (2002–2003) found that a set of four characteristics working in combination (achievement beliefs, responsibility, self-organization ability, and technology skill/access) offered a better prediction of whether virtual high school students will succeed in online courses.

Characteristics of effective distance learning instructors. Cyrs (1997) emphasizes that distance learning instructors need different skills than instructors for traditional courses do. His review of research reveals several areas of unique competence, all of which require experience with distance learning environments:

- Course planning and organization that capitalize on distance learning strengths and minimize constraints
- Verbal and nonverbal presentation skills specific to distance learning situations
- Collaborative work with others to produce effective courses
- Ability to use questioning strategies
- Ability to involve and coordinate student activities among several sites.

Moskal, Martin, and Foshee (1997) refer to these skills in general as instructional design skills specific to distance learning. In their review of studies in this area, Roblyer and McKenzie (2000) found that many of the factors that make for a successful online instructor are the same as those for any successful instructor: good communication and classroom organization skills.

Research on cost effectiveness of distance learning. Threlkeld and Brzoska (1994) noted several categories of cost factors involved with offering a distance learning course:

- **Technology** — Hardware and software
- **Transmission** — Ongoing expenses of leasing transmission access (e.g., T1 lines, satellite)
- **Maintenance** — Repairing and updating equipment
- **Infrastructure** — Foundational network and telecommunications infrastructure located at originating and receiving sites
- **Production** — Technical and personnel support to develop/adapt teaching materials
- **Support** — Expenses needed to keep the system working successfully—for example, costs of administration, registration, advising/counseling, local support, facilities, and overhead
- **Personnel** — Instructors and support staff.

Although studies show that the initial costs of starting distance learning programs are high, research also suggests that as course management strategies become more efficient and are used over more courses, program costs should decrease (Ludlow, 1994).

Offering Courses and Programs with Distance Technologies

As described earlier in this chapter (see the Types of Distance Learning Activities section), web-based courses and degree programs, although problematic, are becoming increasingly common in K–12 education. More and more teachers are participating in the design and delivery of these activities. Various tools and information can be useful when designing course and online instruction.

Web Course Development and Support Tools

Developing and hosting web courses require an array of online and offline tools. Distance courses are made possible by a **course management system (CMS)**, an online collection of web course design and delivery tools. Other helpful tools used in the design and delivery of web-based courses include site capturing software, intranets, and whiteboards (a.k.a. smartboards).

- **Course management systems** — Since around 1997, course management systems have become the most common means of designing and delivering web-based courses. A school or district usually buys a license for a system such as WebCT or Blackboard, and its personnel use the system's features (e.g., graphics, conferences, chatrooms, email, links to PDFs and web pages) to design and deliver courses hosted by its servers. The course management system also includes gradekeeping and student tracking features such as an electronic portfolio for each student. More recently, **open-source** (software that is freely distributed) CMSs have become available and are becoming extremely popular. Software programs such as *Joomla* and *Moodle* are changing the landscape of CMS use for distance learning development.

- **Site capturing software** — On a high-traffic day, the Internet can be as slow as a highway traffic jam. Slow-moving screens can play havoc with teachers and students trying to carry out learning activities. An alternative is to use a product such as Blue Squirrel's *Web Whacker* software, which downloads pages or sites to a computer's hard drive where they later can be run through a browser without the need for an Internet connection. The popularity of this software created the term *site whacking*.

- **Intranets** — Another way to speed up access to the Internet is through an internal network called an **intranet**. This network, like the Internet, is based on communications protocols, but it belongs to an organization and can be accessed only by the organization's members. An intranet's websites look and act just like other websites, but the network has a firewall that will not allow unauthorized access. A school might maintain its own intranet of selected sites for use in courses while allowing access to the larger Internet for other sites. More information about creating and maintaining intranets is available from online magazines such as *Intranet Journal* (http://www.intranetjournal.com).

- **Electronic whiteboards (or smartboards)** — **Electronic whiteboards** are interactive display screens connected to a computer that multiple users can write or draw on. *Whiteboard* is the generic name, and *Smartboard* is the trade name of SMART Technologies, Inc. Whiteboards are often used along with videoconferencing and course management systems because they make it possible for everyone to see illustrations and demonstrations of concepts and products as they are being drawn and revised.

Characteristics of Effective Distance Courses and Programs

Effective online courses have been offered in every content area from math to music and from physics to physical education. A review of these courses yields the following four common, essential characteristics: effective course structure and design, engaging learning activities, interactive learning communities, and effective assessment strategies.

Well-designed and structured to support learning. Just as with any course, effective online courses must be well planned and systematically designed to take advantage of the unique capabilities and constraints of the learning environment. Alley and Jansek (2001) list 10 characteristics of a high-quality online learning environment:

- Knowledge is constructed, not transmitted.
- Students can take full responsibility for their own learning.
- Students are motivated to want to learn.
- The course provides "mental white space" for reflection.
- Learning activities appropriately match student learning styles.
- Experiential, active learning augments the website environment.
- Solitary and interpersonal learning activities are interspersed.
- Inaccurate prior learning is identified and corrected.
- "Spiral learning" provides for revisiting and expanding prior lessons.
- The master teacher is able to guide the overall learning process.

Many distance learning classes are taught via interactive video systems.

Engaging, collaborative activities. Although some students prefer courses to be individual, tutorial-like ones in which they work at their own pace through a sequence of tasks, the most enjoyable courses seem to be those in which students are highly engaged in discussion and collaboration. Many online courses encourage this kind of engagement through the bulletin boards or conferences provided by CMSs. Klemm (1998) described eight ways of achieving more student engagement through online conferences:

- **Require participation** — Participation in each conference should be a required, graded activity rather than an optional one.

- **Form learning teams** — If handled properly, collaborative activities can encourage a "team spirit" toward learning.

- **Make activity interesting** — Consider student backgrounds, experiences, interests, and concerns.

- **Don't settle for opinions** — Student contributions should be based on their readings and research.

- **Structure the activity** — Have a specific set of tasks and a definite beginning and end to each.

- **Require a deliverable** — The activity should revolve around a product to develop and turn in.

- **Know what you are aiming for** — Set up expectations for adequate participation, and communicate them clearly to students. Instructors should provide consistent, ongoing critiques and feedback to encourage involvement.

- **Use peer grading** — Ask students to rate each other on their contributions to the conference. (This is the most controversial of Klemm's recommendations; not all experts agree this is feasible.)

An interactive learning community. Teachers and students agree that online courses are more motivating if they simulate the community one finds in a good face-to-face course. Solloway and Harris (1999) say that so-called **learning communities** (groups of people who "meet" via email or web pages to support each other's learning) in web-based courses are the result of careful planning and strong support by the instructor and a support team. However, it is apparent that learning communities require more than just well-designed instruction. They also involve strategic, ongoing efforts by the instructor to encourage student-to-student interaction, as well as student-to-instructor interaction, and to have students get to know each other as learners and as people. They are communities in the truest, most culture-based sense of the word.

Effective assessment strategies for online courses and programs. While alternative assessments are popular in online lessons, many online learning course systems also offer traditional assessment options. WebCT, for example, has a test module with which instructors can develop objective tests, have students take them online, grade them automatically, and summarize test results across the class.

Assessing the Quality of Distance Courses

Two rubrics on MyEducationLab (under the topic, "Assessment") lay out the elements that teachers and students can use to assess the overall quality and usefulness of a distance learning course. The *Rubric for Online Instruction,* designed and hosted online by California State University–Chico, focuses on the characteristics shown in Figure 7.12 and allows courses to be assessed prior to delivering or taking them.

The other rubric *(Rubric for Assessing Interactive Qualities of Distance Courses),* developed by the author of this textbook, is useful as a post-course evaluation instrument. It focuses on the following characteristics:

- Social/rapport-building designs for interaction
- Instructional designs for interaction
- Interactivity of instructional resources
- Evidence of learner engagement
- Evidence of instructor engagement

FIGURE 7.12 Rubric for Online Instruction

Learner Support & Resource	**Online Organization & Design**
Course contains extensive information about being an online learner and links to campus resources. It also provides a variety of course-specific resources, contact information..<u>More</u>	Course is well-organized and easy to navigate. Students can clearly understand all components and structure of the course. The syllabus identifies..<u>More</u>
Instructional Design & Delivery	**Assessment & Evaluation of Student Learning**
Course offers ample opportunities for interaction and communication student to student, student to instructor and student to content. Goals are clearly defined and aligned..<u>More</u>	Course has multiple timely and appropriate activities to assess student readiness for course content and mode of delivery. Learning objectives, instruct..<u>More</u>
Innovative Teaching with Technology	**Faculty Use of Student Feedback**
Course uses a variety of technology tools to appropriately facilitate communication and learning. New teaching methods are applied and innovative enhance..<u>More</u>	Instructor offers multiple opportunities for students to give feedback on course content. Instructor offers multiple opportunities for students to give feedback on..<u>More</u>

Source: Reproduced with permission of Academic Technologies and the Center for Excellence in Learning and Teaching, California State University, Chico; http://www.csuchico.edu.

Interactive Summary

The following is a summary of the main points covered in this chapter.

1. **Internet basics:**
   - **Internet concepts** — Students and teachers who use the Internet should know how to use URLs, site navigation strategies, bookmarks or favorites, and search engines.
   - **Internet strategies** — Students and teachers should also know how to evaluate website content and do basic Internet troubleshooting.

2. **Communicating on the Internet** — Online communication resources include email, listservs, bulletin boards, blogs, chatrooms, instant messaging, videoconferencing, and MUDs/MOOs/avatar spaces.

3. **Distance learning:**
   - **Distance learning is defined by the** United States Distance Learning Association (USDLA) as "The acquisition of knowledge and skills through mediated information and instruction, encompassing all technologies and other forms of learning at a distance."
   - **Distance learning delivery systems may be classified as most abstract to most realistic,** according to types of interaction (from one-way, print-based to two-way video) and delivery methods (from correspondence courses to videoconferencing).
   - **Types of distance activities include** student research, online materials, web-based lessons, and virtual courses and programs.

   - **Current distance learning issues include** the widening Digital Divide, concerns about children's development and socialization, impact on school reform, and virtual schooling issues.
   - **Types of Internet pitfalls include** accessing inappropriate materials, threats to safety and privacy, Internet fraud, viruses and hacking, and copyright and plagiarism problems.
   - **Findings from current research on distance learning include** distance learning and face-to-face learning can yield equivalent results; successful distance courses are those that have high interaction, good support, and minimal technical problems; successful learners are those who have achievement beliefs, responsibility, self-organization ability, and technology skill/access; successful instructors are those who have good communication and classroom organization skills; and distance learning programs are more cost effective when they are used with more courses.

4. **Distance courses and programs** — To design and use distance courses and programs, teachers and students use web course development and support tools such as course management systems (e.g., WebCT and Blackboard), site capturing software, intranets, and whiteboards.

5. **Effective course design requires** structure designed to support learning; engaging, collaborative activities; supportive online learning communities; and good assessment strategies.

6. **Distance course quality may be assessed** during design using the Rubric for Online Instruction and after a course through the Rubric for Assessing Interactive Qualities of Distance Courses.

Key Terms

- ARPAnet
- asynchronous
- avatar
- avatar space
- blog
- Bookmarks file
- bulletin board (BB)
- chatroom
- cookie
- course management system (CMS)
- distance learning (DL)

- domain designator
- download
- electronic whiteboard
- Favorites file
- filtering software
- firewall software
- hacker
- hit
- instant messaging (IM)
- intranet
- learning community

- link/hot link
- listserv (list)
- *Mosaic*
- MUD/MOO
- netiquette
- open-source software
- synchronous
- uniform resource locator (URL)
- videoconferencing
- web browser
- World Wide Web (WWW)

Web-Enrichment Activities

1. Browse the links below, and then choose one of the following topics on virtual school issues: curriculum alignment, teacher certification, accreditation, funding, possible negative consequences. Present your evidence for your views on the issue. State, based on your reading, whether you support or oppose virtual schooling.

   - NCREL Virtual Schools Policy Report

     http://www.ncrel.org/policy/pubs/html/pivol11/apr2002c.htm

   - The Effects of Distance Education on K–12 Student Outcomes

     http://www.ncrel.org/tech/distance/index.html

   - Distance Education Courses for Public Elementary and Secondary School Students

     http://nces.ed.gov/pubsearch/pubsinfo.asp?pubid=2005010

   - Education World Virtual High School Article

     http://www.education-world.com/a_curr/curr119.shtml

2. Go to the following sites, and use Figure 7.6 to evaluate their content accuracy:

   - http://city-mankato.us/
   - http://descy.50megs.com/NewHartford/newhtfd.html

   Is the website accuracy acceptable? Is there any reason to believe the content should not be used?

3. Go to Website 101 (http://website101.com/RSS-Blogs-Blogging), and choose an article to read on a topic about blogging or RSS feeds that you were not familiar with up to this point. Write a brief summary of the key points of the article. Can you think of how you might use blogs or RSS feeds in a K–12 classroom?

PEARSON
myeducationlab
The Power of Classroom Practice
www.myeducationlab.com

Go to MyEducationLab to complete the following exercises.

Video   Select the topic "Distance Education," and go to the "Assignments, Activities, and Applications" section. Access the video "Florida Virtual Teachers" to hear two teachers discuss their experiences teaching within the Florida Virtual School. Complete the activity that follows the video.

Building Teaching Skills   Select the topic "Distance Education," and go to the "Building Teaching Skills and Dispositions" section. Access the activity "Building an Effective Online Learning Environment" and complete the activity that follows.

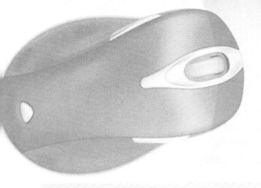

Technology Integration Workshop

The TIP Model in Action

Read each of the following scenarios related to implementing the TIP Model, and answer the questions that follow it based on your Chapter 7 reading and activities.

TIP MODEL SCENARIO #1   Ms. Eltona was very pleased when her school placed a three-computer workstation in each classroom so that students could do Internet research for classroom assignments. However, she finds that when students have a research paper to do for her class, they do a quick keyword search, locate a number of web pages on the topic, copy down what each page says, and put that in their research papers. She tells other teachers that she thinks using the Internet makes her students' papers worse instead of better because it makes it too easy to find information that may be unreliable.

1.1   What skills do Ms. Eltona's students need to learn to be able to realize better benefits from their Internet use?

1.2   How could Ms. Eltona help teach these skills as a part of her research paper assignments?

1.3   What criteria should she include in her research paper rubric to make sure students are using appropriately the information they locate in their Internet searches?

TIP MODEL SCENARIO #2   Mr. Omrey is a high school business education teacher and is teaching a unit on software tools. He finds that nearly all of his senior students come into his classes knowing something about word processing and spreadsheets; a few even know about databases. Since they are at so many different levels of knowledge, he would like a way to individualize students' instruction, allowing them to start with what they know and then to build more skills on each tool. Yet he has no funds for tutorial workbooks or software.

2.1   What distance learning tools available on the Internet may be useful to address Mr. Omrey's needs?

2.2   If he used such tools, what strategies and materials could Mr. Omrey use to track his students' skill development?

2.3   If Mr. Omrey has 15 computers in his classroom and 25 students, how might he give his students equitable access to the distance resources?

TIP MODEL SCENARIO #3   Ms. Pomeroy has heard that students tend to want to write better and observe more spelling, grammar, and usage rules when they write for distance audiences. She would like to have her students exchange messages with students in other English-speaking countries.

3.1   How could Ms. Pomeroy identify students in other countries for her students to correspond with via email?

3.2   Since Ms. Pomeroy would like to make sure students behave courteously during their email exchanges, she would like to create a classroom poster of the "Top Ten Rules" to observe when emailing. What could she use as the basis for these rules? What ten items would you suggest she include on the poster?

3.3   What elements should be included in a rubric to assess students' email messages?

TIP MODEL SCENARIO #4   Mr. Sloan is a high school principal in a small, rural community. Several parents have complained to him that the school does not offer advanced placement courses in several areas (e.g., physics, foreign languages). He knows his district cannot afford to hire teachers for these subjects. He has heard about virtual courses in these topics offered by a consortium in another state, and he thinks this would be a good idea for his district. He tells the superintendent that since the more advanced students would be the ones taking these courses, they should do well in them.

4.1   If the district could make these courses available to the students, what would be the relative advantage of offering them via distance learning?

4.2   What does research show about Mr. Sloan's assumption that more advanced students would do well in virtual courses?

4.3   Assuming that these courses could be made available to students in his school, what strategies could Mr. Sloan implement to support the students' access to and use of them?

TIP MODEL SCENARIO #5   Ms. Courtney's students are working in groups to do research projects. However, each group wants to bookmark many websites for their projects, and the list of bookmarks is so long that students cannot locate theirs anymore; it takes too long to find them.

5.1   If you were Ms. Courtney, what browser resource would you recommend students use to address this logistical problem?

5.2   What would be the relative advantage of using this resource, as compared to writing down all the URLs or placing them in a word-processed file?

5.3   How could you add use of this resource to the list of things you assess for students' projects?

TIE into Practice: Technology Integration Examples

The Technology Integration Example that opened this chapter (*A Research Paper Website*) showed how a teacher might collect web resources on doing research and create a website to support students' research projects. With the knowledge you have gained from Chapter 7, do the following with this example:

1. To organize the online resources they found to act as links from their research project website, Ms. Almon and the teachers would need to create a Bookmark/Favorites folder like the one shown here. Create a Bookmark/Favorites folder by following the hands-on tutorial located on MyEducationLab under the topic "Internet."

2. Answer the following questions about the *Research Paper Website* example:

   • Phases 1 and 2 — How does Ms. Almon view her technological pedagogical content knowledge? How does her TPACK affect the project? How do her colleagues' TPACKs complement the project? What are the relative advantages to students and to Ms. Almon and the teachers of having the research paper website? of the video tutorials?

   • Phase 3 — One of the outcomes from this project is a Likert scale measuring student attitudes toward the writing approach used in the project. Prepare a Likert scale with items that address these attitudes. (See Chapter 2 for an explanation and example of Likert scales.)

   • Phase 4 — Would it be a good idea to have students work individually, in pairs, or in small groups on the learning tasks outlined for Phase 3? Explain.

   • Phase 5 — To create a handout that would stay in the format in which it was created (word processing) when downloaded from the website, in what format would Ms. Almon have to save it after she created it? (*Hint:* See the discussion of materials generators software tools in Chapter 5.) How could she send this file to someone who did not have access to the Internet?

   • Phase 6 — What might Ms. Almon and the teachers do to improve student performance on the second set of research skills?

3. What NETS for Students skills would students learn by working on the *Research Paper Website* project? (See the front of this book for a list of NETS for Students.)

Technology Integration Lesson Planning

Complete the following exercises using sample lesson plans found on MyEducationLab.

1. Locate lesson ideas — Go to MyEducationLab under the topic "Distance Education." Go to "Lesson Plans" to review examples of lessons that use email and student resource websites. Choose two of the following integration lessons:
   • Online and Face-to-Face High School
   • Virtual School Advantages
   • Learning Online
   • Virtual School Teacher Skills
   • Virtual English Course
   • Virtual Geometry Course
   • Virtual School Philosophy

2. Evaluate the lessons — Use the *Evaluation Checklist for a Technology-Integrated Lesson* (located on MyEducationLab under the topic, "Instructional Planning.") to evaluate each of these lessons.

3. Modify a lesson — Select one of the lesson ideas, and adapt its strategies to meet a need in your own content area. You may choose to use the same multimedia software as in the original or a different one.

4. Add descriptors — Create descriptors for your new lesson similar to those found within the sample lessons (e.g., grade level, content and topic areas, technologies used, relative advantage, objectives, NETS standards).

For Your Teaching Portfolio

For this chapter's contribution to your teaching portfolio, add the following products you created in the Technology Integration Workshop:

• The Bookmark/Favorites file and the Likert scale you created for the research paper project

• The evaluations you did using the *Evaluation Checklist for a Technology-Integrated Lesson*

• The new lesson plan you developed, based on the one you found on MyEducationLab.

Sample Bookmarks File (Create this product using the tutorial section of MyEducationLab)

Chapter 8
Integrating the Internet into the Curriculum

The Internet has had a profound impact on the social, economic, and political life of America . . . we have seen enormous changes in the way we conduct research, make purchases, learn about the world, live our lives.

Jeffrey Cole, in *The Chronicle of Higher Education* (April 2004)

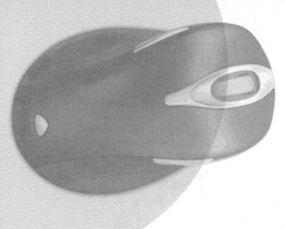

Technology Integration Example

Agayu: Adventure Learning in Chukotka, Russia

Based on: *Agayu* at *http://www.polarhusky.com/2007*

Phases 1 and 2: Assess technological pedagogical content knowledge; Determine relative advantage

Ms. Anderson was upset at how her students were reacting to the activities she taught in her geography course. She was using a recent geography textbook and many accompanying activities, but still her students were not motivated. A colleague of Ms. Anderson's, Mr. Clay, was using a hybrid online adventure learning program entitled "GoNorth!" in which his students were studying geography while following a group of scientists, explorers, and educators as they dog sled across the Arctic while using an online K–12 curriculum interacting and collaborating with literally millions of students worldwide. Mr. Clay's students had covered the walls in the school with pictures they made that represent the Polar Huskies, dog sleds, and activities from the online learning environment. In fact, Ms. Anderson's students were always hearing about the program from Mr. Clay's students during lunch, and they asked if they could get involved with the program too. She decided she would take a closer look at the online environment to see what the real advantage of the program would be. She went to the "GoNorth!" website (http://www.polarhusky.com/2007/), obtained her username and password, and logged in. The program was free, so she decided she would definitely check out the curriculum and the online activities. Ms. Anderson soon came to realize that her students could learn about the geography of numerous places around the world as if she and her students were actually there. In addition to the authentic nature of the activities, her students could collaborate with other students worldwide, interact with the online games, send a note to the team in the Arctic, and truly become part of the experience. She also realized by watching Mr. Clay's students that her students would probably be motivated to learn. Ms. Anderson checked out the curriculum online and decided to start with the "Agayu" lesson of Module 2.

Before immediately jumping into the project, Ms. Anderson assessed her technological pedagogical content knowledge to see where she might be deficient and also where she could capitalize on her strengths. She realized her technology and pedagogical knowledge were very strong compared to her content knowledge. However, given the comprehensive curriculum that was part of the GoNorth! project, she decided to go ahead and integrate it within her classroom.

Phase 3: Decide on objectives and assessments

Ms. Anderson wanted her students to feel more motivated to study geography, but she also wanted to make sure they were reaching the necessary goals of the established school curriculum. To make sure they achieved the goals, she wrote down the following outcomes and objectives and designed assessments matched to each one, as follows:

- **Outcome:** The understanding and appreciation of culture. **Objective:** Students will achieve a 90% rubric score to show they can describe how culture is experienced through language and how the people with whom Team GoNorth! interact are the same and different than themselves. Students will work cooperatively to complete the GoNorth! Agayu lesson on storytelling, reading traditional stories from the Yu'pik people of Chukotka, Russia. **Assessment:** Rubric covering completion of required tasks, search strategies, locating required information, cooperative group work, and discussion.

- **Outcome:** Improved attitudes about studying geography and cultures around the world. **Objective:** Students will demonstrate increased motivation to learn geography by scoring at least 25% higher on an attitude survey after the instruction compared with before and being able to communicate how people from around the world are similar. **Assessment:** Likert scale attitude instrument.

Phase 4: Design integration strategies

Ms. Anderson felt it would be best if the students did some exploratory research at the beginning of the activity by spending time within the GoNorth! online learning environment and then following up the exploration with the activity written within the GoNorth! curriculum, as it effectively integrated the Internet within the curriculum.

- **Day 1:** Introduce the project and the website; give the pre-instruction attitude survey. Using the classroom computer with an electronic whiteboard, show the GoNorth! website and the many areas students can explore to become part of the project. These areas include web pages such as the Yaranga, Polar Husky A to Z, collaboration zones, expert chats, the online game Wumpa's World, and the Polar Husky dogyard.

- **Day 2:** Brainstorm as a class to create a concept map about what an oral tradition is. Share with the students that Native Arctic cultures such as the Yu'pik and the Chukchi people in Chukotka have been preserving their history and culture through various oral traditions and that written accounts are only very recent (beginning in the 1960s). Explain as well that oral tradition includes storytelling in many formats. After the discussion and brainstorming, watch "The Drums of Winter," available in *Classroom Movies* for Module 2 in *Scrapbook* of the *Explore* section at PolarHusky.com/2007/. Share with students that this was filmed in Alaska on the coast of the Bering Strait but that the Yu'pik population extends to both sides of the Bering Strait, from Chukotka to Alaska. Discuss the role of drum dancing to the Yu'pik culture. How is this a form of storytelling? Who would be considered the storyteller?

- **Day 3:** Pass out the student page titled "Being Fox." In pairs or individually, students first read about the fox mask, then read the story associated with the fox mask as told by Yu'pik Elder Alma Keyes, read about the animal itself, and answer the two associated questions. Yu'piks believe that each animal has a special person within. How does this story illustrate that belief? How does the story of the fox mask represent Yu'pik culture?

- **Day 4:** In teams of two or more, students read a traditional Yu'pik story assigned from the list below. The stories can be accessed from *Your Study Resources* for Module 2 in the *Investigate* section of *Logistics* at PolarHusky.com under the title "Yu'pik Stories & Masks."

–Snowy owl story	–Death mask story
–Plant masks story	–Half-face mask story
–Red fox mask story	–Clam mask story
–Beetle mask story	–Common loon mask story
–Caribou mask story	–Crow mask (I) story
–Simple mask story	–Crow mask (II) story
–Salmon berry mask story	

From the assigned story, students develop a mask or several masks for all team members. A mask can be as simple or elaborate as they wish to make it. Students then dance or act out the story. Depending on students' preference, one student can read the story aloud while others illustrate it. If possible, film or document the students' enactments in pictures or even in audio. End each performance by talking as a class about the message of the story and its delivery.

- **Day 5:** Have students go to *Collaboration Zone 02: Culture Zone* to upload pictures of their masks or the video of their mask presentations. Make sure the word "masks" is included as part of the title. While there, have students explore posts from other students and communicate their responses.

Phase 5: Prepare the instructional environment

Ms. Anderson spent time exploring the online learning environment, preparing herself on how to effectively integrate the Internet within her classroom. Preparation tasks included the following:

- **Understanding of website content in general:** Ms. Anderson spent a few hours on the GoNorth! website to read the curriculum and activity guide so as to obtain a full understanding of the online learning environment and curriculum.

- **Research lesson and activities:** Ms. Anderson acquired the Agayu lesson from the online curriculum and downloaded the activities and handouts that complemented the online learning environment.

- **Collaboration zones:** Ms. Anderson spent time exploring the collaboration zones, reading what other students and teachers had posted in the past and getting ready to scaffold her students' participation within the zones.

- **Computer lab scheduling:** Ms. Anderson scheduled time for her students in the lab so that they could complete the online activities. She also allowed them to do some of the work at home, if they liked.

Phase 6: Evaluate and revise

After students had completed their masks and uploaded them to the collaboration zones, Ms. Anderson reviewed the data from the activities. As she had hoped, she found attitudes toward studying geography had much improved after the project. Many students made unsolicited comments such as "Why can't we learn everything this way?" and "I love Polar Husky!" Her rubrics revealed considerable variation in the understanding of culture. She decided she would continue using the GoNorth! learning environment with her students. As a result of implementing GoNorth!, exam scores were much improved over what she had seen in the past. Students told her that both the online activities and the making of the masks helped a great deal. It was evident that students who had home computers knew much more about the online learning environment and the GoNorth! Team and Polar Huskies than students who had access only at school. She decided to research ways she could give all students more Internet access at school.

http://2007.polarhusky.com/explore/trail_reports/week_13.html

Chukotka 2007

Explore   Logistics   Support

G❄North!

Trail Reports   Scrapbook   Timber Tales   Zones   Map It!   Read It!   Send-A-Note   Q & A   Chat   Quiz   Challenge

Wk 01   Wk 02   Wk 03   Wk 04   Wk 05   Wk 06   Wk 07   Wk 08   Wk 09   Wk 10   Wk 11   Wk 12   Week 13

Log Out

Week 13 ● The End: Spacibo!

Date Posted: 5.14.2007
Location: 64°5'N 165°4'W
Nome, Alaska, United States
Weather Conditions: Sunshine and blue sky, 10° F (−12°C)

A 25–30 feet wide span of water separated us from land. We were back on the banks of the bay in Provideniya where we set off a little less than a month ago. As we arrived back in Provideniya some 360 miles of dogsledding later, rocks and dirt where the dogs had been staked out in deep snow, swans flying in formation above and scorching temperatures in the mid-forties (3–5 Celsius) signaled the end of this year's adventure learning expedition GoNorth! Chukotka 2007. It is time to wrap it up, time for the last howl, and time to extend our most heartfelt thank you to all of those that made this year's program a huge success. The heartfelt thank you goes to GoNorth! learners of all ages, teachers, sponsors, partners, friends, family, the entire crew at Education Basecamp and throughout the campus at the University of Minnesota, the true superstars of GoNorth! – the Polar Huskies and most especially, the people of Chukotka. It has not been our typical 'long-haul' expedition – but what a haul!

In Provideniya.

Source: From *GoNorth! Adventure Learning Series* courtesy of PolarHusky.com.

Objectives

After reading this chapter and completing the learning activities for it, you should be able to:

1. Apply criteria to determine if a web-based activity could enhance learning for a given topic or skill.

2. Describe types of web-based learning activities and match them with appropriate integration strategies.

3. Create web-based learning activities that meet the criteria for effective lessons.

4. Match web-based authoring and development tools with the products they are designed to create.

5. Demonstrate how to download images, programs, and plug-ins for use in web page development and use.

6. Give examples of the functions websites serve in web-based projects and learning activities.

7. Identify resources and procedures for developing web pages and websites.

8. Follow effective procedures to design and create web-based products.

9. Select and apply instruments to assess the quality of web-based lessons and products.

Background on Web-Based Learning Activities

Web-based activities have great potential to enhance learning, but they are time consuming to develop and implement and difficult to design in ways that have substantial, positive impact on students' learning (Coulter, Feldman, & Konold, 2000; Fabos & Young, 1999; Harris, 2000). Coulter et al. point out that "The Internet is no silver bullet for improving education" (p. 43). They encourage teachers considering web-based activities to ask themselves several questions before deciding to do an online project. They are, in effect, asking teachers to document the relative advantage of online activities in comparison with other strategies they might use to accomplish the same purposes. The following questions are based on those outlined by Coulter et al. (2000) and can form the basis of an integration plan for web-based activities:

- **What is the curriculum-related purpose of the activity?** Using the Internet should not be thought of as an end in itself. The activity should accomplish some objective or purpose in the required school curriculum.

- **Does the Internet enhance the activity?** The rule of thumb is that if the activity could be done without the Internet, it probably should be.

- **How will students use online resources (as opposed to just locating them)?** The object of the activity should be for students to do something with what they locate on the Internet. Once they locate information, they should be asked to determine its meaning, compile and synthesize various sources, or critique its usefulness.

- **Do students have the necessary information analysis/ information synthesis skills, or am I including these in the instruction?** To make sure the project doesn't become an "information locating" exercise, it should call for additional, higher level tasks *after* the students find the information. However, teachers must be sure their students have the prerequisite skills to do these higher level tasks.

- **Do I have the necessary time and support for the activity?** Harris points out two problems that are frequently cited in the failure of online activities. First, online projects can take longer than other learning strategies, and teachers often do not allow sufficient time. Harris recommends doubling the original time estimate. Second, any number of technical problems can and do occur during an online project. Teachers must make sure they have the technical support to resolve these problems in an efficient way so as not to slow down the momentum of the project.

Types and Examples of Web-Based Lessons and Projects

Some of the most exciting distance learning applications call for students to use technology as a means of collaboration so they can address significant problems or issues or communicate with people in other cultures throughout the world. In recent years, the depth and breadth of collaboration has dramatically improved (see Doering, 2006, 2007).

Making the Case for Technology Integration

Use the following questions to reflect on issues in technology integration and to guide discussions within your class.

1. In a 1998 debate in *Time* magazine, powerful representatives of two sides squared off. The following quotes are in response to the question "Should schools be connected to the Internet?"

   Vice President Al Gore: "Access to the basic tools of the information society is no longer a luxury for our children. It is a necessity.... We must give our children ... the chance to succeed in the information age, and that means giving them access to the tools that are shaping the world in which they live" (Tumulty & Dickerson, 1998, p. 54).
   David Gelernter (victim of the Unibomber): "First learn reading, writing, history, and arithmetic. Then play Frisbee, go fishing, or surf the Internet. Lessons first, fun second.... If children are turned loose to surf, then Internet in the schools won't be a minor educational improvement, it will be a major disaster" (Tumulty & Dickerson, 1998, p. 55). Using information in this chapter combined with other readings, which of these positions is more plausible? How would you respond to each of these statements?

2. Speaking of distance courses via the Internet, Hartley and Bendixen (2001) warned that " ... most would agree that learning on the web is troublesome for the less motivated student. If web learning is dependent on motivation and motivation is correlated with socioeconomic status, we may be contributing to an expansion of the digital divide" (p. 25). What ways would you suggest to counteract the effects they refer to and to ensure that better access means more equitable access to learning opportunities, especially in today's world when so many students are "connected" be it through the computer or cell phone?

Harris (1998, 2002) refers to these efforts as "telecollaborations" and describes three general application categories:

1. **Interpersonal exchanges** — Students communicating via technology with other students or with teachers/experts

2. **Information collection and analysis** — Using information collections that provide data and information on request

3. **Problem solving** — Student-oriented and cooperative problem-solving projects.

TABLE 8.1 Types and Examples of Web-Based Lessons and Projects

Type of Web-based Activity	Sample Sites	Description
Electronic pen pals (keypals)	• **ePals** http://www.epals.com • **International E-Mail Classroom Connections (IECC)** http://www.iecc.org/	Links students at a distance to exchange information.
Electronic mentoring	• **International Telementor Program** http://www.telementor.org/ • **Chats with NASA Personnel** http://quest.arc.nasa.gov/sso/chats/	Links students with experts to answer questions and support learning.
Electronic (virtual) field trips	• **Tramline Virtual Field Trips** http://www.tramline.com • **National Health Museum** http://www.accessexcellence.org/RC/virtual.html • **Go North!** http://www.polarhusky.com	Visit sites to view people, places, and resources not locally available.
Electronic publishing	• **Children's Express** http://www.childrens-express.org/ • *Midlink* **Magazine** http://www.cs.ucf.edu/∼MidLink/ • **Voicethread** http://voicethread.com/	Share written and artistic products on websites.
Group product development	• **CIESE Online Classroom Projects** http://www.ciese.org/collabprojs.html	Work on written or artistic products with students at different sites.
Problem-based learning	• **The GLOBE Program** http://www.globe.gov • **Pathfinder Science projects** http://kancm.org/ • **International Schools CyberFair** http://www.gsn.org/gsh/cf/index.html • **MIDI Music Relay** http://www.kidlink.org/KIDPROJ/Midi/ • **Project Mars Millennium** http://www.projectpioneer.com/mars	Explore topics, obtain and analyze data, or participate in simulated problem solving with other students.
Social action projects	• **IEARN Network** http://www.iearn.org/ • **Cranes for Peace Project** http://www.cranesforpeace.org/ • **I Have a Dream Project** http://www.kidlink.org/dream/ • **Earth Day Groceries** http://www.earthdaybags.org	Discuss and create solutions for social or environmental problems with other students.

Harris lists strategies she calls *activity structures* that fall under these three categories. Lessons based on a given activity structure all follow the same basic design, even though their content and objectives may vary. Detailed descriptions of these activity structures may be found in Harris's book, *Virtual architecture: Designing and directing curriculum-based telecomputing* (1998). Some forms these models can take are described here, and examples of each are given in Table 8.1.

Electronic penpals or "keypals." Teachers link up each student with a partner or penpal in a distant location to whom the student writes letters or diary-type entries. As discussed in Chapter 7, a good resource for locating classroom keypals is http://www.ePals.com.

Electronic mentoring. Dyrli (1994) referred to subject matter experts who volunteer to work closely with students online as **electronic mentors** (p. 34). Guidance may be one-to-one links between students and expert resources or may take the form of chats, discussion groups (e.g., in blogs), or learning communities. (See Technology Integration Lesson 4.2 in Chapter 4.)

Electronic (or virtual) field trips. An **electronic field trip** in its simplest form fills classroom screens with visual images of a place considered to offer some educational value and to which students would not routinely be able to travel. As Tuthill and Klemm (2002) note, real field trips enhance learning but are seldom used due to logistical problems. They describe premade electronic field trips as ways to circumvent these problems and bring real-world situations into the classroom. These activities explore unique locations around the world, and by involving learners at those sites, students share the experience with other learners at remote locations. An example of this is the GoNorth! adventure learning series that was discussed in the Technology Integration Example (Doering, 2007).

Electronic publishing. When students submit their written or artistic products to a website, it is called **electronic publishing**. This allows their work to be shared with other students and visitors to the site and can be done quite easily with products such as **Google Docs**.

Group product development. Teachers have developed many variations of online group development of products. For example, students may use email to solicit and offer feedback on an evolving literary project, sometimes involving advice from professional authors. Or students may work independently toward an agreed-on goal, each student or group adding a portion of the final product. This is sometimes called *chain writing*.

Problem-based learning. Sage (2000) described **problem-based learning (PBL)** as "learning organized around the investigation and resolution of an authentic, ill-structured problem" (p. 10). This kind of problem solving can take many forms, four of which are described here:

- **Collaborative problem solving** — This model involves several students or student groups working together to solve a problem. These kinds of lessons were dubbed **webquests** by Bernie Dodge and Tom March at San Diego State University and became a model for teachers across the country in creating their own lessons. All of these lessons give students a scenario and a task to do in response to that scenario; usually they have a problem to solve or a project to complete.

- **Parallel problem solving** — In this strategy, students in a number of different locations work on similar problems. They solve a problem independently and then compare their methods and results or build a database or other product with information gathered during the activity.

- **Data analysis** — These activities give students access to data from real phenomena such as weather or solar activity. Using these data, students are able to answer questions and solve problems posed by their teachers, their peers, and themselves.

- **Simulated activities** — These are the web equivalent of simulation software. For example, Hartley (2000) describes sites with a variety of virtual "labs" in which students can learn chemistry, physics, and math principles.

Social action projects. In **social action projects**, students are responsible for learning about and addressing important global social, economic, political, or environmental conditions. For example, students collaborating on a peace project might write congressional representatives to voice concerns and present their viewpoints. The emphasis in this kind of project is collaboration to offer solutions to an issue of practical community (global or local) concern.

Integration Strategies for Web-Based Activities

These types of projects help address a variety of classroom needs, and it is this match of activity types with needs that defines and shapes integration strategies. Web-based projects are so rich in resources and learning possibilities that each one can usually be used with more than one of the integration strategies discussed next. Table 8.2 identifies good sources of award-winning, web-based lesson plans, activities, and collaborative projects.

TABLE 8.2 Sites with Collections of Web-Based Lessons and Projects

Source	Description	Content Areas
Annenberg Channel http://www.learner.org/interactives/	"Exhibits" or web-based explorations of concepts or themes depicted in the Annenberg video resources	All content areas—mostly science, geography, and history
Camp Silos http://www.campsilos.org/	Interactive lessons	Farming and prairie life
Center for Improved Engineering and Science Education (CIESE) http://www.stevens.edu/currichome.html	Collaborative projects that use real-time data available from the Internet	Science and mathematics
Co-Nect teleprojects http://exchange.co-nect.net/Teleprojects	Interactive data collection projects	All content areas
Consumer Jungle http://www.consumerjungle.org/	Interactive lessons from the Young Adult Consumer Education Trust	Consumer skills
Exploratorium: The Museum of Science, Art, and Human Perception http://www.exploratorium.edu/educate/index.html	How-to descriptions of classroom projects	Science
Eyes on Art Lessons http://www.kn.pacbell.com/wired/art2/index.html	How-to lessons and activities	Art
The Franklin Institute Online http://www.$$.edu/fellows	Lesson plans and classroom activities	Science
The Global Schoolhouse http://www.globalschoolnet.org/	Clearinghouse for more than 2,000 online collaborative projects, organized by topic, grade, and project date	All content areas
GoNorth! Adventure Learning Series http://www.polarhusky.com	Comprehensive K–12 curriculum and online activities	Science, social studies, literacy, elementary, math, physical education
Knowledge Network Explorer http://www.kn.pacbell.com/wired	Online curriculum, webquests, and other materials	All content areas
National Geographic Xpeditions http://www.nationalgeographic.com/xpeditions/	Geography lesson plans for grades K–12	Geography, social studies, science
National Geographic lessons and resource sites http://www.nationalgeographic.com/features/	More than 100 website "explorations" of various topics	Science, geography, history
National Geophysical Data Center http://www.ngdc.noaa.gov/education/education.html	Collections of resources on various topics	Science and geography
Teacher's Desk Lesson Plans http://www.teachersdesk.com/lessons/lessons.htm	Classroom lesson and projects	All content areas
Tramline's Virtual Field Trips http://www.tramline.com	Structures and guided teacher-designed "field trips" through a series of websites and dozens of topics	All content areas

Support for student research. Students frequently use websites and web-based video resources and videoconferencing to gain insights into topics they are studying and to locate information for research papers and presentations. This work may be in the form of individual or group-based research projects or electronic mentoring. (See Technology Integration Lesson 8.1.)

Motivation for writing. As discussed in Chapter 7, strategies in which students write for distance audiences help motivate them to write more and to do their best writing. Activities might include forming keypals and electronic publishing. (See Technology Integration Lesson 8.2.)

Practice for information literacy skills. Locating and using information from Internet sources has become a key part of classroom learning. It is important that students have opportunities to learn how to use web resources efficiently and effectively. Possible activities include individual and cooperative research projects. (See Technology Integration Lesson 8.3.)

Visual learning problems and solutions. Many sites provide access to data, images, animations, and videos that help students understand complex problems and guide them in creating their own solutions. Possible activities include individual and cooperative research projects as well as problem-based learning projects. (See Technology Integration Lesson 8.4.)

Development of collaboration skills. Web-based projects provide rich opportunities for students to learn how to work together to solve problems. Many web-based projects call for students to produce a product, such as a brochure, web page, or multimedia presentation. McGrath (2004) describes ways to help make these collaborative projects most productive. Projects that promote collaboration skills

Technology Integration Lesson 8.1

Support for Student Research

Title: Connecting Science Students with NASA Resources

Grade Levels: All grades

Content Area/Topic: Earth science

NETS for Students: Standards 1 (Creativity and Innovation), 2 (Communication and Collaboration), 3 (Research and Information Fluency), and 4 (Critical Thinking, Problem Solving, and Decision Making)

Description of Standards Applications: The Earth According to WORF (World Observation Research Facility) is an interdisciplinary project that takes advantage of some of the resources available from NASA to support education. This integration lesson offers students the opportunity to learn how to analyze NASA imagery, ask questions about the photographic detail to NASA officials, and participate in a videoconference. Students need to be innovative as they select the photography and to use their critical thinking skills when they analyze and communicate their findings.

Instruction: The project begins by having students learn how to analyze photographic detail. Then they obtain WORF images from four Earth locations, analyze them, and document their findings. Each student develops five questions he or she would like to ask in a videoconference with NASA experts. Each class involved in the project forwards its best 10 questions, which the experts address in the videoconference.

Assessment: Students take pre- and post-tests on earth science and image analysis concepts.

Source: Peterson, R., Starr, B., & Anderson, S. (2003). Real NASA inspiration in virtual space. *Learning and Leading with Technology, 31*(1), 14–19.

Technology Integration Lesson 8.2

Motivation for Writing

Title: Choose Your Own Adventure: A Hypertext Writing Experience

Grade Levels: 6 through 8

Content Area/Topic: English, writing

NETS for Students: Standards 1 (Creativity and Innovation) and 2 (Communication and Collaboration)

Description of Standards Applications: This integration lesson offers students the opportunity to participate in the development of an adventure story with their peers. Each student will use his or her creativity as the group writes each phase of the adventure and an individual ending. The groups publish their stories and communicate about them with their peers.

Instruction: After exploring the concept of "choose your own adventure" stories, the teacher divides students into small groups of three to four and has them brainstorm ideas for their own stories. Next, each group maps the first part of the story using a graphical organizer (e.g., *Inspiration*). The group decides who is going to write each phase of the adventure, and each student writes an individual ending to his or her group adventure. Each group publishes its story on a hyperlinked website that group members develop (e.g., *Google Pages*) where each student ending is hyperlinked. Students can share their stories with each other as well as with other classes and can vote on the best ending and story.

Assessment: Teacher-developed rubric (student reflection, creativity, participation).

Source: Modified from Wilhelm, J., & Friedemann, P. (1998). *Hyperlearning: Where projects, inquiry, and technology meet.* York, ME: Stenhouse. (View the lesson plan at http://www.readwritethink.org.)

Technology Integration Lesson 8.3

Practice for Information Literacy Skills

Title: The American Dream

Grade Levels: 4 through 10

Content Area/Topic: Social studies

NETS for Students: Standards 1 (Creativity and Innovation), 2 (Communication and Collaboration), 3 (Research and Information Fluency), and 4 (Critical Thinking, Problem Solving, and Decision Making)

Description of Standards Applications: This integration lesson offers students the opportunity to use a webquest to investigate the concept of the American dream. Through the creativity, collaboration, and research among students, they present what they believe the American dream is, based on their prior knowledge and the data found at the American Memory Collection at http://memory.loc.gov.

Instruction: The teacher begins by discussing the concept of the American dream. Then students write about their visions of what the dream means to them personally and for the country. The teacher introduces the American Memory Collection and reviews research techniques for using it. Students assume roles within small groups to create a product that documents their vision of the American dream.

Assessment: Teacher-developed rubric on students' use of research techniques and their final product documenting their vision.

Source: Donlan, L. (1999). Come dream with us: America dreams. *Learning and Leading with Technology, 24*(5), 26–28.

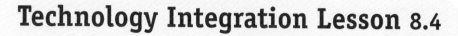

Technology Integration Lesson 8.4

Visual Learning Problems and Solutions

Title: Bringing the Planets Closer to Home

Grade Levels: 5 through 8

Content Area/Topic: Science and mathematics: Astronomy, measurement

NETS for Students: Standards 1 (Creativity and Innovation), 3 (Research and Information Fluency), and 4 (Critical Thinking, Problem Solving, and Decision Making)

Description of Standards Applications: This integration lesson offers students the opportunity to use NASA photos in an image editing program as they research and calibrate images and compare them to Mars. After analysis, students compare features that change over time. This activity is designed to make the connection between science and mathematics more hands-on and meaningful for students by having them analyze real data in the form of images.

Instruction: Students begin by downloading NASA photos from the Internet (e.g., images of the solar system) and converting them to an uncompressed TIF format using an image processing program such as Adobe *Photoshop*. Their task is to learn how to measure the images. First, they use the software to calibrate the images (determine the scale) by comparing the size of the image to a known measure such as the diameter of Mars. Then they multiply the measured distance by the scale to determine the size of other features they have downloaded. In this way, students can measure and compare features that change, such as the Martian and Earth polar ice caps. These measurements can be the basis of many projects to study space phenomena.

Assessment: Teacher-developed exercise to assess students' ability to measure and determine the scale of various images.

Source: Slater, T., & Beaudrie, B. (2000). Far out measurements: Bringing the planets closer to home using image processing techniques. *Learning and Leading with Technology, 27*(5), 36–41.

Technology Integration Lesson 8.5

Collaborative Skills Development

Title: Working Together to Build Worlds

Grade Levels: 9 through 12

Content Area/Topic: Astronomy, geology, biology, meteorology

NETS for Students: Standards 1 (Creativity and Innovation), 2 (Communication and Collaboration), 3 (Research and Information Fluency), and 4 (Critical Thinking, Problem Solving, and Decision Making)

Description of Standards Applications: This integration lesson offers students the opportunity to develop a world by using their creative, collaborative, research, and problem solving skills. Students use knowledge from ten content areas as they develop a world that is as good or better than Earth is today. Content areas include: astronomy (design a solar system), geology (make maps), meteorology (define topography and weather), microbiology (create cellular life forms), marine biology (define sea plants), marine zoology (define sea creatures), marine ecology (design ocean ecosystems), botany (define land plants), zoology (define land animals), and land ecology (design land ecosystems).

Instruction: As students work in groups that are created by combining students' content expertise (science, astronomy, etc..), the teacher helps students brainstorm about the kind of planet they want to develop. Then students use the project website to work through the ten units on the concepts related to building various parts of their world. Finally, students create a web page or *PowerPoint* presentation to display their world.

Assessment: Teacher-created rubrics on group work skills and the quality of science concepts reflected in the final product presentation.

Source: Viau, E. (2004). Building a world. *Learning and Leading with Technology, 31*(5), 18–21.

Technology Integration Lesson 8.6

Multicultural Experiences

Title: Connecting with the Past—A Native American Memory Box Project

Content Area/Topic: History, multicultural education

Grade Level: Middle school

NETS for Students: Standards 1 (Creativity and Innovation), 2 (Communication and Collaboration), 3 (Research and Information Fluency), 4 (Critical Thinking, Problem Solving, and Decision Making), 5 (Digital Citizenship), and 6 (Technology Operations and Concepts)

Description of Standards Applications: Artists across cultures and throughout time have sought to incorporate the multifaceted connections between past and present in their artworks. George Catlin visited more than 140 Native American tribes and painted in excess of 325 portraits and 200 scenes of American Indian life. This site presents and interprets Catlin's artworks from the Smithsonian American Art Museum's permanent collection. Catlin viewed his subjects as a "vanishing race" and sought to preserve their images for future generations. This integration lesson offers students the opportunity to research George Catlin's life and to appreciate his ability to connect the present to the past with images that will last for generations to come. Upon completing the investigation of the Smithsonian American Art Museum, students use a multitude of skills and talents to develop a memory box that holds personal significance.

Instruction: Acquaint students with artworks that have dealt with issues of memory and the connection of the past and present. Use resources on the *Artifacts and Memory—For Students* page of the Campfire Stories website to guide the activity. Discuss the ways these artworks make an effort to connect elements of past and present cultures. Students then each create their own memory box, using objects that hold personal significance for them. On completion of the project, have students present their boxes to other class members for constructive feedback on the project.

Assessment: Use a checklist to assess completion of tasks.

Source: Campfire Stories with George Catlin. Available from http://catlinclassroom.si.edu.

---

include individual and cooperative research projects, electronic publishing, group development of products, problem-based learning, and social action projects. (See Technology Integration Lesson 8.5.)

Multicultural experiences. Many web-based projects focus on broadening students' perspectives on their own and other cultures and providing insights into how their culture relates to others in the world. Appropriate web-based activities include electronic (virtual) field trips and social action projects. (See Technology Integration Lesson 8.6.)

Website Support for Web-Based Learning Activities

Harris (1998) pointed out that websites can perform several functions to support distance learning activities. The following discussion of website support functions is based on Harris's description. Note that a single website can serve one or more of these functions. (See Table 8.3 for a summary of these functions and example sites that fulfill them.)

Function #1: Project overview, announcement, and application. Sites can introduce the goals and purposes of existing projects and invite people to participate. For example, the Westward Ho! website provides an overview of available projects and gives participants a place to sign up, as shown in Figure 8.1.

Function #2: Tutorial instruction. A website can serve to deliver actual instruction and information on a topic or project. For example, CalTech's Cool Cosmos website, shown in Figure 8.2, has web tutorials about

TABLE 8.3 Website Support Functions

Function	Description	Sample Site
1. Project overview, announcement, and application	Describes existing projects and offers signup location.	**Westward Ho!** http://www.cyberbee.com/wwho
2. Tutorial instruction	Offers instruction and information on topics.	**Cool Cosmos** http://www.coolcosmos.ipac.caltech.edu/
3. Information summaries and exchanges	Allows information to be added to a collection that will be shared with others.	**KIDLINK Multicultural calendar** http://www.kidlink.org/KIDPROJ/MCC/
4. Communication and support	Provides virtual meeting places to support students' communications and resources to support project work.	**Math Forum** http://mathforum.org/
5. Displays of past and current student work	Shows examples of students' work in web publications centers.	**Kid Plus** http://www.kidplus.org
6. Project development centers	Invites the creation of new distance learning projects.	**Global SchoolNet Foundation** http://www.gsh.org

topics such as multiple-wavelength astronomy as well as resources such as a multiple-wavelength gallery that shows celestial objects observed in different wavelengths.

Function #3: Information summaries and exchanges. Students can use websites to add information to a collection that will be shared with others. For example, KIDLINK's Multicultural Calendar database (see Figure 8.3) is a collection of descriptions written by students of holidays and festivals around the world. Students use the site to enter summaries, and they can search the resulting database by month, holiday, country, and author.

Function #4: Communication and support. A website can serve as a virtual meeting place to support students'

FIGURE 8.1 Example of Project Overview, Announcement, and Application Website Function

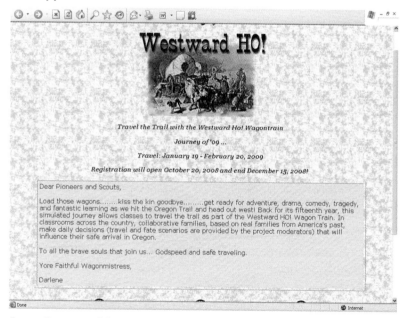

Source: Courtesy of CyberBee.

FIGURE 8.2   Example of Tutorial Instruction Website Function

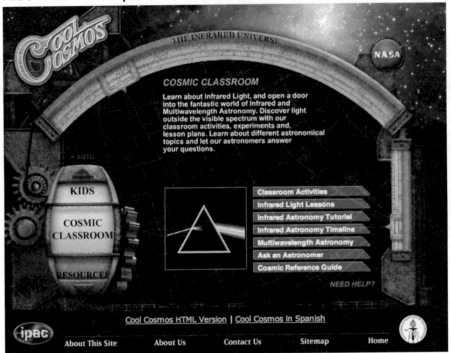

Source: Courtesy of NASA/JPL-Caltech

communications as they work together at distant locations. These websites can be even more helpful if they build in streaming video or videoconferencing. They may also offer links to resources to support project activities and make gathering information for project work more efficient. See an example in Figure 8.4.

FIGURE 8.3   Example of Information Summary and Exchange Website Function

Source: Courtesy of the Kidlink Society.

FIGURE 8.4 Example of Communication and Support Website Function

Source: Reproduced with permission from Drexel University, copyright © 2009 by The Math Forum@Drexel.

Function #5: Displays of past and current student work. Websites can be used as web publication centers in which students show examples of their poems, stories, pictures, and multimedia products. Some sites also show ongoing descriptions of past, current, and planned project activities. See an example in Figure 8.5.

Function #6: Project development centers. Websites sometimes are set up for the specific purpose of inviting new distance learning projects. The Global SchoolNet Foundation has hundreds of existing projects and invites teachers around the world to register new ones. See an example in Figure 8.6.

FIGURE 8.5 Example of Student Work Website Function

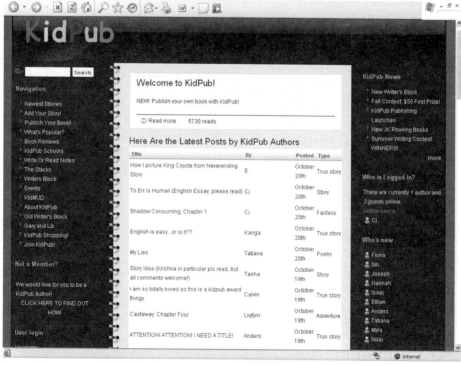

Source: Courtesy of KidPub Worldwide Publishing, www.kidpub.com.

FIGURE 8.6   Example of Project Development Center Website Function

Source: Copyright GlobalSchoolNet.org. Reprinted by permission.

Assessing the Quality of Web-Based Lessons

Hundreds of web-based activities are available for teachers to use in their classrooms or join online; some work better than others. How can teachers evaluate the quality of given activities and select those that will work best for their students? One useful assessment instrument is the *Rubric for Evaluating WebQuests*, shown in Table 8.4. Although webquests represent just one of many possible types of web-based lessons, the elements of this rubric apply to most web-based lessons.

Resources for Web Page and Website Development

Developing personal, professional, school, and project web pages and websites has become an excellent way for both teachers and students to learn the power of the Internet, participate in cooperative projects, and display project results.

This section describes the resources needed to develop a web product and outlines procedures required to create effective web page products.

Web Page and Website Authoring Tools

Only a few years ago, web pages could not be developed without program authoring languages and scripting tools. Now, thanks to web page development software, it is possible to develop whole sites without writing a line of code or script. However, even if one uses a web development tool such as Macromedia *Dreamweaver* that generates code automatically, it is good to know enough about each of the major program authoring languages to make minor adjustments to developed pages or to troubleshoot problems as they occur. Program authoring languages include Hypertext Markup Language (HTML), Java, Virtual Reality Modeling Language (VRML), ActionScript in Adobe **Flash,** Practical Extraction and Report Language (PERL), and many more. Also described here are web page and website software tools that allow developers to create web products without programming.

Top Ten

Strategies for Integrating the Internet into the Curriculum

The following powerful web-based lessons and projects have proven successful in classrooms around the country.

1. Writing with Writers http://teacher.scholastic.com/writewit — In this series of writing projects, students work with authors, editors, and illustrators to develop their skills in various genres. They then publish their work online to share with other young writers at this Scholastic-sponsored website.

2. Hello Dolly! A Webquest on Cloning http://www.pusd.info/projects/dolly/main.htm — Because governments around the world are currently debating the potential impact of cloning on society, this website asks students to propose how to legislate cloning. They use resources at the site to learn about the issues, create a proposal, and present their findings during a "cloning summit."

3. GoNorth! Adventure Learning Series http://www.polarhusky.com and http://cehd.umn.edu/adventure/ — In these projects, students explore a different Arctic location annually while following a team of explorers, scientists, and educators as they dogsled throughout the Arctic. There is a comprehensive K–12 curriculum teachers can employ while their students collaborate in the *collaboration zones*, participate in the *expert chats*, send a note of encouragement to Team GoNorth! through the *send-a-note* feature, participate in the weekly trivia game, and adopt a Polar Husky sled dog. There are over 3,000 educational web pages to be explored.

4. WeatherScope: An Investigative Study of Weather and Climate http://www.k12science.org/curriculum/weatherproj2/en — Schools pretend that they have been selected by a world-famous meteorological institution to conduct an investigation and report on local and world weather and climate. To complete the assignment, they are shown how to create weather instruments and how to access the Internet to locate real-time weather information from around the world.

5. Journey North http://www.learner.org/jnorth — Students study wildlife migration and seasonal change by sharing their field observations with classmates across North America. They track the coming of spring through the migration patterns of animals such as monarch butterflies, bald eagles, robins, hummingbirds, whooping cranes, the budding of plants, changing sunlight, and other natural events.

6. Unsung Heroes: An ePals project http://www.epals.com/projects/unsung_heroes — ePals invites classes around the world to exchange information about students, teachers, and others in their communities whose positive actions are making a difference in the quality of life of those around them. Students exchange email and contribute to the ePals Unsung Heroes discussion board.

7. ReadWriteThink http://www.readwritethink.org — This website provides lessons, standards, web resources, and student materials for supporting literacy in K–12 reading and language arts classrooms. A plethora of resources are at this site, providing educators and students with access to free, high-quality, Internet-based content.

8. GeoThentic: Authentic Online Geography http://www.geothentic.umn.edu — In this exciting online environment, students use multiple scaffolds to solve authentic geographic problems using geospatial technologies such as *Google Earth*. Ranging from situated movies that announce the problem as if it were a live television broadcast to screen-capture videos, collaboration zones, and intelligent agents, students and teachers alike can use the environment to assist in all aspects of using geospatial technologies within social studies and science classrooms.

9. Global Grocery List Project http://www.landmark-project.com/ggl/index.html — In this ongoing email project, students visit their local grocery stores, record the prices of items on the grocery list, and share their prices with classes all over the world. The result is a growing table of current, peer-collected data that can be used in math, social studies, science, and health classes.

10. The National Math Trail http://www.nationalmathtrail.org — To illustrate that "math is all around you," this project challenges K–12 teachers and teams of students to observe their surroundings and create math problems about what they see and what they would like to figure out. The site provides examples of math trail projects and other resources, and students can submit their class's math trails to the site for posting.

To visit these web links online, go to MyEducationLab.

TABLE 8.4   Rubric for Evaluating Webquests

The webquest format can be applied to a variety of teaching situations. If you take advantage of all the possibilities inherent in the format, your students will have a rich and powerful experience. This rubric will help you pinpoint the ways in which your webquest isn't doing everything it could do. If a page seems to fall between categories, feel free to score it with in-between points.

	Beginning	Developing	Accomplished	Score
Overall Aesthetics (This refers to the webquest page itself, not the external resources linked to it.)				
Overall Visual Appeal	0 points There are few or no graphic elements. No variation in layout or typography. OR Color is garish and/or typographic variations are overused and legibility suffers. Background interferes with the readability.	2 points Graphic elements sometimes, but not always, contribute to the understanding of concepts, ideas, and relationships. There is some variation in type size, color, and layout.	4 points Appropriate and thematic graphic elements are used to make visual connections that contribute to the understanding of concepts, ideas, and relationships. Differences in type size and/or color are used well and consistently. See Fine Points Checklist.	
Navigation and Flow	0 points Getting through the lesson is confusing and unconventional. Pages can't be found easily and/or the way back isn't clear.	2 points There are a few places where the learner can get lost and not know where to go next.	4 points Navigation is seamless. It is always clear to the learner what all the pieces are and how to get to them.	
Mechanical Aspects	0 points There are more than 5 broken links, misplaced or missing images, badly sized tables, misspellings, and/or grammatical errors.	1 point There are a few broken links, misplaced or missing images, badly sized tables, misspellings, and/or grammatical errors.	2 points No mechanical problems noted. See Fine Points Checklist.	
Introduction				
Motivational Effectiveness of Introduction	0 points The Introduction is purely factual, with no appeal to relevance or social importance. OR The scenario posed is transparently bogus and doesn't respect the media literacy of today's learners.	1 point The Introduction relates somewhat to the learner's interests and/or describes a compelling question or problem.	2 points The Introduction draws the reader into the lesson by relating to the learner's interests or goals and/or engagingly describing a compelling question or problem.	
Cognitive Effectiveness of Introduction	0 points The Introduction doesn't prepare the reader for what is to come, or build on what the learner already knows.	1 point The Introduction makes some reference to learner's prior knowledge and previews to some extent what the lesson is about.	2 points The Introduction builds on the learner's prior knowledge and effectively prepares the learner by foreshadowing what the lesson is about.	
Task (The task is the end result of student efforts . . . not the steps involved in getting there.)				

	Beginning	Developing	Accomplished	Score
Connection of Task to Standards	0 points The task is not related to standards.	2 points The task is referenced to standards but is not clearly connected to what students must know and be able to do to achieve proficiency of those standards.	4 points The task is referenced to standards and is clearly connected to what students must know and be able to do to achieve proficiency of those standards.	
Cognitive Level of Task	0 points Task requires simply comprehending or retelling of information found on web pages and answering factual questions.	3 points Task is doable but is limited in its significance to students' lives. The task requires analysis of information and/or putting together information from several sources.	6 points Task is doable and engaging, and elicits thinking that goes beyond rote comprehension. The task requires synthesis of multiple sources of information, and/or taking a position, and/or going beyond the data given and making a generalization or creative product. See WebQuest Taskonomy.	

Process (The process is the step-by-step description of how students will accomplish the task.)

	Beginning	Developing	Accomplished	Score
Clarity of Process	0 points Process is not clearly stated. Students would not know exactly what they were supposed to do just from reading this.	2 points Some directions are given, but there is missing information. Students might be confused.	4 points Every step is clearly stated. Most students would know exactly where they are at each step of the process and what to do next.	
Scaffolding of Process	0 points The process lacks strategies and organizational tools needed for students to gain the knowledge needed to complete the task. Activities are of little significance to one another and/or to the accomplishment of the task.	3 points Strategies and organizational tools embedded in the process are insufficient to ensure that all students will gain the knowledge needed to complete the task. Some of the activities do not relate specifically to the accomplishment of the task.	6 points The process provides students coming in at different entry levels with strategies and organizational tools to access and gain the knowledge needed to complete the task. Activities are clearly related and designed to take the students from basic knowledge to higher level thinking. Checks for understanding are built in to assess whether students are getting it. See: • Process Guides • A Taxonomy of Information Patterns • Language Arts Standards and Technology • WebQuest Enhancement Tools • Reception, Transformation and Production Scaffolds	

(continued)

TABLE 8.4 (*continued*)

	Beginning	Developing	Accomplished	Score
Richness of Process	0 Points Few steps; no separate roles assigned.	1 point Some separate tasks or roles assigned. More complex activities required.	2 points Different roles are assigned to help students understand different perspectives and/or share responsibility in accomplishing the task.	
Resources (Note: you should evaluate all resources linked to the page, even if they are in sections other than the Process block. Also note that books, video, and other off-line resources can and should be used where appropriate.)				
Relevance and Quantity of Resources	0 points Resources provided are not sufficient for students to accomplish the task. OR There are too many resources for learners to look at in a reasonable time.	2 points There is some connection between the resources and the information needed for students to accomplish the task. Some resources don't add anything new.	4 points There is a clear and meaningful connection between all the resources and the information needed for students to accomplish the task. Every resource carries its weight.	
Quality of Resources	0 points Links are mundane. They lead to information that could be found in a classroom encyclopedia.	2 points Some links carry information not ordinarily found in a classroom.	4 points Links make excellent use of the Web's timeliness and colorfulness. Varied resources provide enough meaningful information for students to think deeply.	
Evaluation				
Clarity of Evaluation Criteria	0 points Criteria for success are not described.	3 points Criteria for success are at least partially described.	6 points Criteria for success are clearly stated in the form of a rubric. Criteria include qualitative as well as quantitative descriptors. The evaluation instrument clearly measures what students must know and be able to do to accomplish the task. See <u>Creating a Rubric</u>.	
Total Score				*150*

Source: Original WebQuest rubric by Bernie Dodge. This is Version 1.03. Modified by Laura Bellofatto, Nick Bohl, Mike Casey, Marsha Krill, and Bernie Dodge and last updated on June 19, 2001; http://webquest.sdsu.edu/webquestrubric.html. Reprinted with permission.

HTML. **HTML** is the Internet standard for how web pages are formatted and displayed. An example of HTML and the beginning of the page it generates is shown in Figure 8.7. (Note that the example displays only the beginning of the complete code.) Beginners can find a variety of HTML tutorials, tips, and tools on the Internet.

Java. Originally called OAK, **Java** is a high-level programming language developed by Sun Microsystems. An object-oriented language similar to C++, it was originally developed for more general use but has become popular because of its ability to allow users to create interactive graphic and animation activities on web pages. Many predeveloped Java applications, called **Java**

FIGURE 8.7 Sample Web Page with Partial HTML Source Code

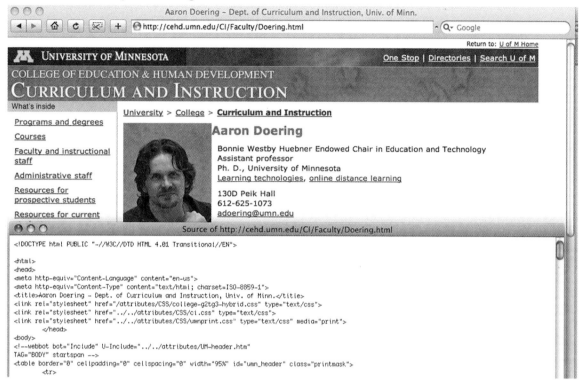

Source: Courtesy of University of Minnesota College of Education & Human Development.

applets, are available for downloading from a web server (http://java.sun.com/applets) and can be run on any computer that has a Java-compatible web browser. As Bull, Bull, and Bull (2000) note, Java applets make possible web page features such as animations and special effects, graphics and buttons, interactive displays, and web data collection forms.

VRML.   Although not in common use by most developers, **VRML** develops and displays 3-D objects on web pages. These objects give the illusion of being "real" much more than videos or animations do, and they can be used to create virtual worlds. VRML has great potential for making web pages very interactive and lifelike (Skipton, 1997). Skipton notes that most VRML packages let developers create basic shapes (primitives) such as cubes, spheres, and cylinders and include polygon-based modeling tools for creating more complex objects. Some offer further modeling features—free-form or cutouts—that enable users to extrude or cut out shapes to create more complicated models. Skipton adds that, in combination with other programs, VRML can create "a multi-user avatar space" like that in the science fiction novel *Snow Crash* (Stephenson, 1993).

PERL and other programming languages.   Developers can use **PERL** or another programming language (e.g.,

Adapting for Special Needs

The Internet has important instructional applications for all students. Students with disabilities can particularly benefit from web resources that expand the palette of available information resources. For example, students who cannot read a textbook may be directed to websites where the reading/interest level can be adjusted (Windows on the Universe, http://www.windows.ucar.edu). Tools such as TrackStar (http://trackstar.4teachers.org/) offer a useful alternative to report writing for many students as they gather and organize web links into a web page known as a *track*, which is subsequently published on the web. A variety of tools are available to assist teachers of students with special needs in designing instructional lessons and units that integrate the Internet into the curriculum. Two useful starting points are:

- Cheryl Wissick's Web Toolboxes, http://www.ed.sc.edu/caw/toolbox.html

- TeAch-nology, http://www.teach-nology.com/.

Contributed by Dave Edyburn

Java, C++, Visual Basic) to write **Common Gateway Interface (CGI)** programs that create *dynamic documents*. That is, web page users can insert their comments or answers into active web pages as they run on a server. Many web pages contain forms that use a CGI program to process the form's data once it is submitted. All the information entered at these sites is gathered and processed by a CGI server, which prepares a summary of the information using a database software such as *FileMaker Pro* (FileMaker, Inc.). Repp (1999) described some uses of CGI scripts for education, including sites for handing in student assignments, dynamic calendars that can be updated regularly, and online surveys and other research instruments for gathering and storing data.

ActionScript in Adobe® Flash®. ActionScript within Adobe *Flash* software provides an advanced authoring environment for creating content for the web, a mobile, or virtually any digital platform. Ranging from instructional media and games to interactive websites, *Flash* can take a typical HTML-designed website and make it into an interactive experience. An example of education software using *Flash* is the University of Minnesota's VideoANT software developed by Brad Hosack. VideoANT is an online environment synchronizing web-based video with timeline-based text annotations (see Figure 8.8).

Web development software. Web development tools generate HTML, CGI scripts, and other code so that users can develop web page and website products without having to know programming languages. Web development tools range from simple programs for development (e.g., *Google Sites* and *TeacherWeb*) to complex, full-featured packages (e.g., Adobe's *Dreamweaver*) that allow development of

FIGURE 8.8 Example of a *Flash*-Based Learning Environment
VideoANT: Online Environment Synchronizing Web-Based Videos with Timeline-Based Text Annotations using Adobe *Flash* at http://ant.umn.edu
Academic Technology Services, University of Minnesota — http://cehd.umn.edu/ats/

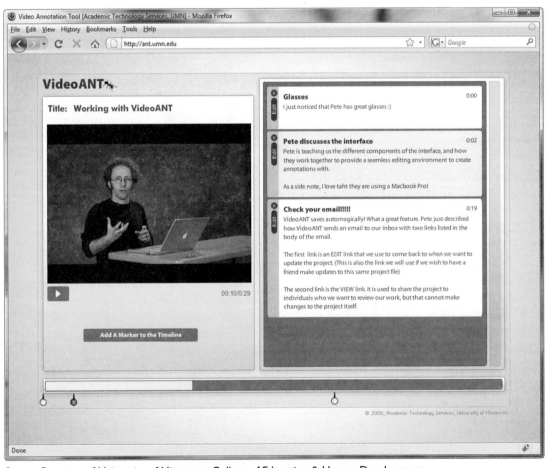

Source: Courtesy of University of Minnesota College of Education & Human Development.

multiple-page websites with sophisticated multimedia components.

Downloading Images, Programs, and Plug-ins

Several of the resources that are useful in both developing and using web pages can be **downloaded**—that is, transferred from a website to your computer—for free from company sites. Some of these downloadable resources are images, programs (e.g., updated versions of browsers), and *plug-ins* or "player" programs that allow you to play audio and video clips in web pages. Most of today's browsers come with the plug-ins already installed when you download the browser.

Downloading images. The Internet has been around in text format since 1969. However, it became the society-wide phenomenon we know today only when the first web browser, *Mosaic*, made it possible for the Internet to appear on computer screens as images. Why do images make such a difference? There may be two reasons. First, pictures are an "information shortcut." The old adage that "a picture is worth a thousand words" points to the reality that people grasp many concepts more quickly when they are presented as images rather than as text. Second, people seem able to remember a great deal of information visually.

But it is possible to take advantage of the visual tapestry of the Internet in ways other than receiving information. You can use your browser to "capture" or download almost any image you see from a web page and store it on your computer. Once you download an image, you can use it in your own web pages. Try downloading an image in the exercise given in Figure 8.9. Downloading an image from the Internet is easy, but remember that many images you find on web pages are copyrighted. Their legal use is determined by copyright law and by the owner of the website. If you are not sure if you can use an image legally, contact the website owner to request permission.

After you save an image on your computer, you can insert it in documents or other web pages. However, you may need to change the image format from the original file format. Several **image formats**, or ways of storing images, have been developed over the years to serve various purposes: either a certain computer or operating system required it, or certain formats were found to deal better with differences among image types (e.g., photos rather than drawn images or clip art). You can tell the format of an image by the suffix in its filename. The most common formats follow:

- **BMP** — Stands for "bitmapped." Originally developed for use on Disk Operating System (DOS) and Windows-compatible computers.

- **EPS** — Stands for "Encapsulated PostScript." Allows transfer of artwork between any software packages that use PostScript printing files.

- **PDF** — Stands for "Portable Document Format." Stores document pages as images.

- **PICT** — Short for "Picture" format. Originally developed for use on Macintosh computers.

- **TIF** — Stands for "Tagged Image File." A flexible format used to exchange files among various software applications and computers.

- **GIF** — Stands for "Graphics Interchange Format." Used for drawn images, illustrations, clip art, or animations.

- **JPEG** — Stands for "Joint Photographic Experts Group," and the filename extension is jpg. Used for photographs.

Images downloaded from web pages will be in either GIF or JPEG format. If you want to use images in your own web pages, they must be in one of these two formats. If you want to change an image to one of these formats, you need to bring it into an image manipulation program (e.g., Adobe *Photoshop*) and save it in either GIF or JPEG format.

Downloading programs and plug-ins. Web browsers made the Internet visual, but subsequent developments gave it sound and motion. Special programs called **plug-ins** have been created to allow people to see and hear the multimedia features that make the Internet increasingly lifelike. Although plug-ins tend to change and update frequently, the Internet has a built-in way of allowing people to take full advantage of its multimedia features and to keep up with advancements required for their use. Instead of buying the programs or plug-ins on disk or CD, Internet users can download many of them directly from the company sites. Five of the most commonly downloaded programs and plug-ins are described here and summarized in Table 8.5.

- **Updated browser versions** — Most new computers come with a browser program stored on the hard drive. However, browsers update frequently, constantly adding new features and capabilities. It is necessary to use an up-to-date version in order to see newer Internet features. You can download newer versions of browsers from the Apple, Firefox, and Microsoft websites.

- **PDF reader** — This program lets you see Portable Document Format files. These are pages stored as images so they may be printed out with a page appearance identical to

FIGURE 8.9 **Downloading Images Exercise**

Problem: Let's say you want to have students use word processing to make an illustrated booklet of the three branches of the U.S. government. You might go to sites for each of these branches and capture images for them to use in their booklets. Do the following:

- Go to the White House website for kids located at http://www.whitehouse.gov/kids/timeline/.

- Click (on a PC, right-click) on the image of the 1777 flag you see here, but instead of letting up the mouse after you click, hold it down until a menu like one of the following appears:

Freedom Timeline
Historical Stories of Freedom

intelligence
1777
An Unlikely Spy

liberty
1831
Underground Railroad

diplomacy
1886
Statue of Liberty

giving
1938
March of Dimes

relief
1948
Berlin Airlift: Candy Bomber

Open Link in New Window
Open Link in New Tab

Download Linked File
Download Linked File As...
Add Link to Bookmarks...

Copy Link

Open Image in New Window
Open Image in New Tab

Save Image to the Desktop
Save Image As...
Add Image to iPhoto Library
Use Image as Desktop Picture

Copy Image Address
Copy Image

Macintosh *Safari*
Image Capture

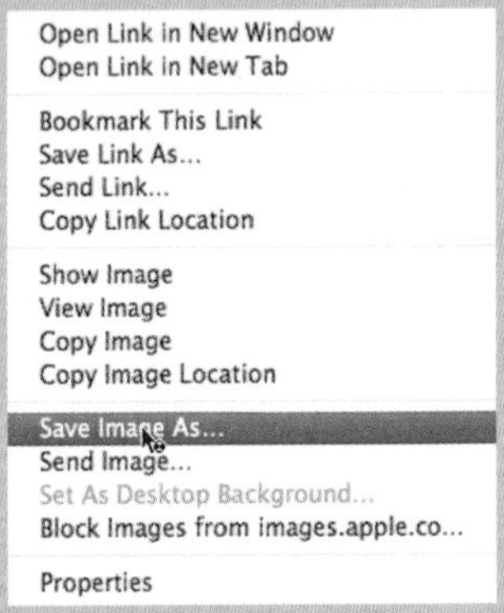

Open Link in New Window
Open Link in New Tab

Bookmark This Link
Save Link As...
Send Link...
Copy Link Location

Show Image
View Image
Copy Image
Copy Image Location

Save Image As...
Send Image...
Set As Desktop Background...
Block Images from images.apple.co...

Properties

Macintosh *Firefox*
Image Capture

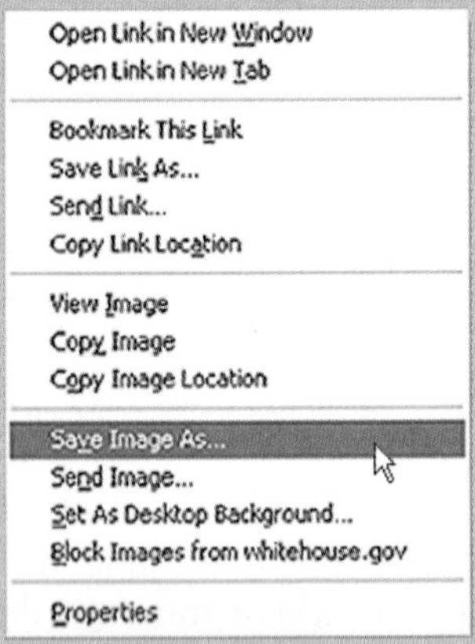

Open Link in New Window
Open Link in New Tab

Bookmark This Link
Save Link As...
Send Link...
Copy Link Location

View Image
Copy Image
Copy Image Location

Save Image As...
Send Image...
Set As Desktop Background...
Block Images from whitehouse.gov

Properties

Windows PC
Firefox **Image Capture**

Netscape and the "N" logo are registered trademarks of Netscape Communications Corporation. Netscape content © 2005 Netscape Communications Corporation. Used with permission.

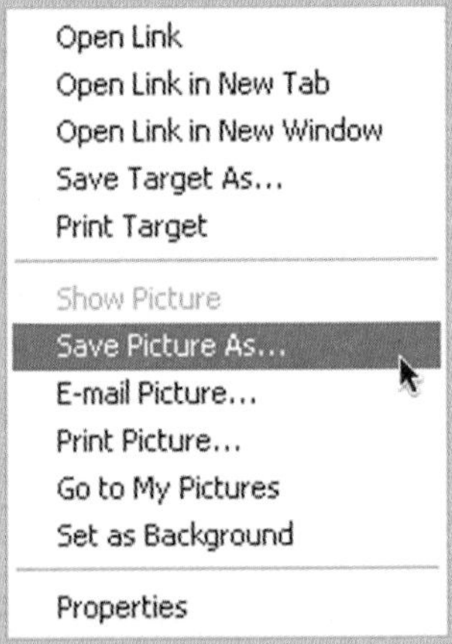

Open Link
Open Link in New Tab
Open Link in New Window
Save Target As...
Print Target

Show Picture
Save Picture As...
E-mail Picture...
Print Picture...
Go to My Pictures
Set as Background

Properties

Windows PC *Internet*
Explorer **Capture**

Internet *Explorer* screen shots reprinted by permission from Microsoft Corporation.

- Drag down and select the option to save the image to your computer.

- Depending on whether you have a Macintosh or PC computer, this box will look something like the following. The file name is the one under which it was stored when it was put on the web page: **timeline1_r2_c1.gif**:

Save As: timeline1_r2_c1.gif

- Change this name to something you may find easier to remember and save it. For example:

Save As: flag.gif

TABLE 8.5   Popular Programs to Download for Web Page Development and Use

Type of Program	Program Name	Download Source
Browsers	Safari	• **Apple** http://www.apple.com/safari
	Firefox	• **Mozilla** http://www.mozilla.com
	Internet Explorer®	• **Microsoft** http://www.microsoft.com/ie
PDF reader	Adobe *Reader®*	• **Adobe** http://www.adobe.com/products/ acrobat/readstep2.html
Streaming video and audio players	RealPlayer (audio/video)	• **RealNetworks** http://www.real.com/
Movie players	*Quick Time®* movie player	• **Apple Computer** http://www.apple.com/quicktime/
Animation players	*Flash®* animations player Adobe *Flash*	• **Adobe** http://www.adobe.com/products/flashplayer

Source: Courtesy of Apple Inc. Courtesy of Mozilla. Courtesy of Microsoft Corporation. Courtesy of Adobe, Inc.

the original document. A PDF format is particularly important when the original text contains both print and images or when one wants to see the appearance of the original document. For example, one might photograph and store the pages of the Declaration of Independence so that history students could see them. Numerous companies have developed software for creating your own PDF files from any type of file you may have. For example, if you own an Apple computer using a recent operating system (OS 10.5 and higher), you can create a PDF file from the Print menu. You can also purchase a program to create PDF files from Adobe, Inc., but the Adobe *Reader* viewer plug-in required to see already-stored PDF files is available free from Adobe, Inc., and Apple has its own program called *Preview.*

- **Streaming video and audio player plug-ins** — An exciting Internet capability is being able to see action or hear sounds live on the Internet. **Streamed video and audio** is so called because it sends or "streams" images and sounds a little at a time so one need not download the files completely before using the contents. This is especially useful for large videos that take a long time to download. Video quality is dependent on the quality and speed of the line connecting the computer to the Internet. Knee, Musgrove, and Musgrove (2000) describe methods of producing streamed video for classroom use. Once these files are seen and stored on a computer, they also may be seen and/or heard later. *Real Player* is one common example.

- **Movie player plug-ins** — Videos that have been digitized and stored as movie files may be viewed through a plug-in. Programs such as Apple's *QuickTime* are used to create these movies, which usually are shot with a camcorder and stored in a Moving Picture Experts Group (MPEG) or MP3 format. To see them, one needs a *QuickTime* or MPEG player plug-in. Although originally designed as a movie player, more recent versions of *QuickTime* can also be used with streaming video and audio.

- **Animation plug-ins** — Special programs that create animated content (e.g., sliding menus, games, movies) for the web also come with their own players such as Adobe's *Flash.*

File Transfer Options: Email Attachments and FTP Programs

When teachers and students engage in distance collaborations, they often need to exchange files of their work. Two ways to transfer large written documents, graphic files, and programs from one computer to another include email attachments and **File Transfer Protocol (FTP)**.

Sending files as email attachments.   One easy way to send files is merely to attach them to email messages.

FIGURE 8.10 Sample FTP Window in *WS_FTP* Software

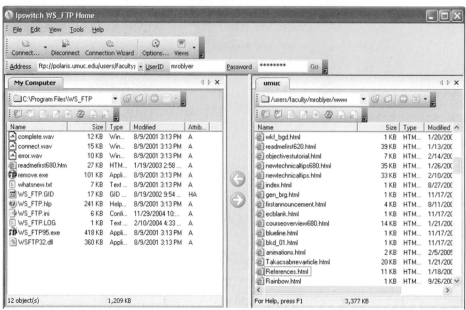

Source: Courtesy of Ipswitch, Inc.

Browsers and email programs have built-in options for selecting files to send as attachments. Usually, it's as easy as selecting the attachment option from a menu while preparing an email message. The receiver must have the appropriate software to view these files. Files are sometimes sent in compressed (stuffed) format and the user must decompress (unstuff) them with a utility program such as *Stuffit Expander* (Allume Systems). Although transferring files is rapidly getting easier, a few technical issues remain concerning the compatibility of files prepared in one program and sent to another and the size of the files that may be rejected by some mail servers. Compatibility problems often can be overcome by sending files as PDF documents (described earlier in this chapter) or by using a service such as yousendit (http://www.yousendit.com), which allows you to upload files to a server and have a recipient download it, thus, removing the email component.

Sending files via File Transfer Protocol (FTP). A common procedure for uploading files to servers on the Internet is using a file transfer protocol (FTP). FTP requires software (e.g., *WS_FTP, Cyberduck*) and a server set up to receive files. (Most computer systems also have built-in FTP capabilities, but they must be compatible with the server to which the files are being sent.) After teachers and students create web pages, they usually use FTP software to send the files to the school or district server. FTP software allows them to both send files and to view, move, or delete files that they have already sent.

Figure 8.10 shows a sample FTP program window with files that have been uploaded from a computer hard drive to a server.

Most schools or districts that have their own server also have their own FTP software and procedures they want teachers to follow for uploading new files. However, if they use another site (e.g., one made available to them by an Internet service provider or ISP), they have to contact the web administrator of that server for the usernames and passwords required to send files via FTP.

Procedures for Developing and Evaluating Web Pages and Websites

Required Development Resources

Teachers and students can use two different strategies in creating their own web pages and websites:

- Creating pages from scratch and linking them
- Downloading, or "grabbing," existing pages and modifying them for their own use.

To implement either of these strategies, you will need three different resources:

1. **Web development software** — Although you can create pages by programming them in HTML code, teachers will find that using web page development software is preferable; it is easier and faster, and it requires much less

technical skill. As with most tool software, web page development software packages vary considerably as to features and prices. A package such as Adobe's *Dreamweaver* is full featured and must be purchased. However, using a program such as *Google Sites* (http://sites.google.com) is quite easy, efficient, and rewarding.

2. **FTP software** — Depending on the type of web development software, after developing the web pages for your site, some automatically upload your web pages to the server while others require you to transfer or upload them to a server manually to be viewed publicly. To do this, you need FTP software, as discussed in the preceding section. If your website will be housed on your school or district server, technical personnel there may provide an FTP package, or they may want to upload your pages for you. If your site will be on another server, contact that server's web administrator to determine the required procedures. *Google Sites* (http://sites.google.com) stores your website on Google's server and thus, FTP as described is not needed.

As students become more familiar with various websites, you can work with them to use design and content criteria to evaluate website quality and begin to develop their own sites.

3. **Server to house the website** — Your website must have a "home," that is, a computer or server on which it resides. Most teachers choose to have their website on their school or district server. In this case, you may want to learn about the procedures that have been established in your school or district for obtaining required permissions and for uploading pages to the server.

Caveats When Creating Web Page Information

Before you begin developing pages, consider these items:

- **Limit sharing of personal information** — Because so many people will have access to your website, you may wish to limit personal information such as pictures and telephone numbers. For example, most educational websites include only first names and email addresses rather than full names and street addresses.
- **Limit photos and large graphics** — These take a long time to load, which can be frustrating to users (e.g., parents) who wish to see the information on your site.
- **Address web page criteria** — Use the same criteria for your own page that you wish to see in other sites. Review the criteria for effective web pages presented later in this chapter. You may want to review educational sites you like and follow their structure.

Recommended Web Page Development Sequence

The following eight steps are recommended as a sequence for web page development (also see Figure 8.11).

Step 1: Plan and storyboard. Planning and design, the first steps in developing a website, are the most difficult and important—and most frequently neglected—of all the steps. Though most people want to get to the fun of development, planning is critical to a well-designed website. Create storyboards (i.e., make a rough sketch of each page) for the site by using cognitive mapping software such as *Inspiration* or 3- by 5-in. sticky notes placed on large pieces of poster board to represent the web pages.

Step 2: Develop pages with text. The next step is to create blank web pages and insert text elements such as titles, paragraphs of description, and any text labels that will later serve as links. There are three kinds of page structures: basic, basic with **anchors** (locations on the page to link to), and **frames**. Frames are sections on a web page; the contents of each frame are actually different web pages. Frames are useful for showing different kinds of information side

FIGURE 8.11 Recommended Eight-Step Website Development Sequence

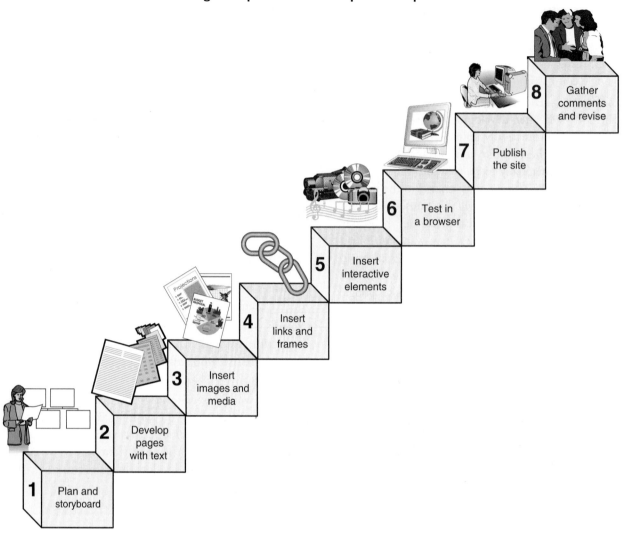

by side on the same page, but not all browsers support them. Designers of frame-based pages usually also give viewers a no-frames option.

Step 3: Insert images and media. Pictures, animations, photos, and movies come next. Images and animations must be in GIF or JPEG format; movies and sounds must be in MPEG format. If movies or audio are to be streamed, the page should inform the user of that and provide a way to obtain the plug-in needed to see or hear the item.

Step 4: Insert links and frames. After all pages are designed, insert links or "hot spots" from text and images to other pages in the site and locations on the Internet.

Step 5: Insert interactive elements. If desired, make the web page "interactive" by inserting Java applets, interactive forms, and mail-to commands to gather comments from users who visit your site.

Step 6: Test in a browser. Many development programs have a built-in preview system, but it is essential to test the site with an actual browser to observe how it will work when it is published on the web.

Step 7: Publish (upload) the site. For others to see created web pages, developers must place the pages on a server. This is called *publishing the site.* If the user can sit down at the keyboard of the computer acting as the server, the files may be moved over from a disk to the hard drive. For servers that are not nearby, the user may upload the pages to the server as FTP files.

Step 8: Gather evaluation comments, revise, and maintain the site. The best websites are those that are updated regularly based on user comments and the continuing insights of the developers. Obtaining user feedback may be done through interactive forms built into the page (see step 5) or simply through inviting emailed comments.

FIGURE 8.12 **Sample Option Bar to Aid Website Navigation**

Criteria for Evaluating Web Pages and Website Design

Chapter 7 included a description of criteria and procedures for evaluating website content (see Figure 7.6). Another way to evaluate a web page is by its design. As teachers and students do their own web page products, they can use the following characteristics to judge design quality:

• **Good structure and organization** — The first page of the site indicates clearly how to get to its various parts. Some sites do this with an option bar that appears at the top, bottom, or side of every page in the site.

Option bars allow you to move easily around the site. See an example option bar from the United States Department of Education in Figure 8.12.

• **Clear text and/or graphic links** — Branches are organized so that you can get back to the main page in no more than three clicks. One device for large sites provides a link to a **site map** or an at-a-glance guide to the contents. Figure 8.13 provides an example of a site map for the National Oceanic and Atmospheric Administration website.

• **Good visual design** — Pages are designed for good readability. A limited number of colors and fonts are used; fonts are easy to read, and colors are selected for

FIGURE 8.13 **Sample Site Map**

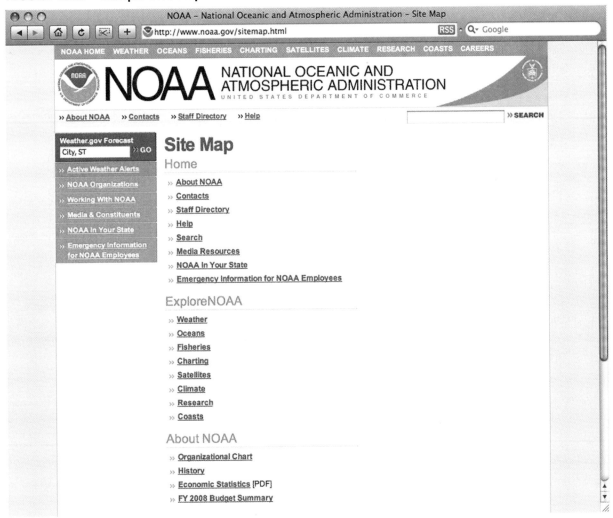

contrast with the background. Graphics do not distract from reading the content. You can tell from looking at an icon what information you will get when you click it.

- **Easy navigation** — Pages load quickly. It's easy to get around in the site. Links are provided so you can get back to the main page from any part of the site. The most important information is given at the top of the page. All links work as they should. Larger sites have their own built-in search engine.

A checklist of criteria based on the items described in this chapter is shown in Table 8.6. This checklist is also on MyEducationLab under the topic "Internet." This can be used to evaluate your own and others' website designs.

Go to MyEducationLab and select the topic "Internet." Go to the "Assignments, Activities, and Applications" section and watch the video, "Using the Internet" and complete the activity that follows.

Criteria for Evaluating Student Web Products

As students begin to create their own web page products, it is helpful to give them criteria in the form of rubrics that describe the quality they are aiming for in each of several aspects. Many such web page rubrics are available. Two of the best are shown in Table 8.7 and Figure 8.14. Table 8.7 shows a rubric designed especially for young learners, and Figure 8.14 shows one for older students.

TABLE 8.6 Web Page Evaluation Checklist

1. Content

_____ All information is accurate. The "last time updated" date is given.

_____ Information is complete but not excessive or redundant.

_____ Information is well organized and clearly labeled.

_____ Information is interesting, informative, and worthwhile.

_____ Information is not redundant to other sources; there is a reason to put it on the web.

_____ All text has correct spelling, grammar, and punctuation.

_____ Level of content and vocabulary are appropriate for intended audience.

_____ Content is free from stereotyping, coarse or vulgar language, or matter that could be offensive to typical users.

_____ Author(s) of the page are clearly identified.

_____ The page gives an email address or other way to contact authors.

2. Visual and Audio Design

_____ The site has a consistent, common look and feel across pages.

_____ Graphics, animations, videos, and sounds make an important contribution.

_____ Pages have only one or two fonts.

_____ Each page uses limited numbers of colors, especially for text.

_____ Type colors/styles and text-to-background contrast were selected for readability.

_____ Each graphic is designed to fit 640 × 480 pixel screens (allowing for scroll bars/toolbars).

_____ Each page is limited to two to three screens; the most important information is at the top.

_____ The pages are simply and attractively designed and make a user want to read them.

3. Navigation

_____ Pages load quickly.

_____ Pages have simple, consistent navigation scheme for quick, easy navigation.

_____ The first page shows clearly how the site is organized and how to get to all items.

_____ Text and icon links are easy to identify. Graphics and sounds are clearly identified.

_____ Icons have been well chosen to represent the information they link to.

_____ Each supporting page has a link back to the home page.

4. Miscellaneous (for larger sites and pages)

_____ Requests for private information are secured.

_____ Page information is kept short enough that it can be printed quickly.

_____ Users can choose to load alternate versions of pages (e.g., text only, smaller images).

_____ The site has its own search engine for locating things within the pages.

_____ Branching is organized so all content is three clicks or fewer from the home page.

Use the following tips to make your sites and pages easier to design and use:

_____ Organize the site on paper ahead of time before inputting it into the computer.

_____ To speed loading, limit graphics to no more than 50K and reuse images whenever possible.

_____ Use GIFs for line art or graphics with limited colors and sharp edges; use JPEGs for photos with many colors and smooth gradients. Avoid PICT and other formats that must be converted by users.

_____ Test out your page in a real browser.

_____ Use a GIF spacer (1 × 1 transparent GIF) to space paragraphs, indents, or alignments on pages.

TABLE 8.7 Rubric for Assessing Young Learners' Web Pages

Excellent	Very Good	Fair	Unacceptable
_____ directions followed	_____ directions followed	_____ directions mostly followed	_____ directions not followed
_____ visually pleasing	_____ visually pleasing	_____ visually distracting	_____ visually confusing
_____ excellent organization of information	_____ mostly clear writing	_____ writing occasionally unclear	_____ writing unclear
_____ information grammatically sound (French and English)	_____ few grammatical and/or spelling mistakes	_____ many grammatical errors and/or misspellings	_____ many grammatical errors and/or misspellings
_____ all words are correctly spelled	_____ font shows accent marks	_____ font does not display accents	_____ font does not display accents
_____ font shows accent marks	_____ links and anchors work	_____ not all links and anchors work	_____ links and anchors do not work
_____ links and anchors work	_____ special effects usually enhance, not detract		_____ special effects distract
_____ special effects enhance, not detract			

Source: From "Cyber traveling through the Loire Valley," by Jane Chenuau as appeared in *Learning and Leading with Technology.* Reprinted by permission of the author.

FIGURE 8.14 Rubric for Evaluation of Older Learners' Web Pages

Criteria	Standards				
	Level 1	Level 2	Level 3	Level 4	Level 5
Development Process	Handwritten proposal sheet submitted to teacher	Text for page entered into simple word processor or HTML-creation program (BBEdit, PageMill, Claris HomePage, FrontPage)	Draft page is printed out from within Netscape; text on page partially achieves proposal	Evidence of revision of page in web browser (Netscape, Explorer); substantially achieves (or explains changes to) proposal	Critical reflection of development process is submitted in writing (individually)
Network Skill	Student has problems bring up their Web Page within a web browser (Netscape, Explorer)	Text is in a program other than the word processor; Images not saved in .gif or .jpg format; One or more files in wrong location or have wrong file name	All .html files in simple word-processor of HTML-creation program; All images .gif or .jpg; All file names and group numbers correct	Running word-processor or HTML-creation program and web browser (Netscape or Explorer) simultaneously; efficient use of Internet access programs	Efficient revision: testing changes by switching between word-processor or HTML-creation program and web browser (Netscape or Explorer)
Thinking Process	Disconnected and unrelated thoughts; vague ideas	Concrete description and evaluation; no analysis of causes, no meaning	Description, analysis, meaning, evaluation; identifies problems and solution	Integrates multiple sources of information to assess issue; balances personal and external	Identifies and examines root causes as well as immediate issue; persuasive and convicted
Writing Process	Difficult to understand, tangents, spelling and other errors	Many errors but consistent line of thought	Easy to understand; perfect spelling; one or two grammar, syntax, or semantic problems	Same as Level 3 but no errors	Clear, concise, well written
HTML Skill	No HTML formatting tags; Text is not broken into paragraphs	Text is broken in paragraphs; Headings are used; no other tags	Paragraphs; headings; title ; and the following tags as appropriate: preformatted text ; styles ; centered text ; horiz. rule	Same as Level 3 plus images > and links	Same as Level 4 plus at least two lists, images as Links, "Return to..." links, colored text/background, background image
Layout	Layout has no structure or organization	Text broken into paragraphs and/or sections	Headings label sections and create hierarchy; some consistency	Hierarchy closely follows meaning; Headings and styles are consistent within pages; Text, images, and links flow together	Consistent format extends page-to-page; design is intentional; attention to different browsers and monitor size
Navigation	One Page	One Page with TITLE, Heading	2 pages (or one page with links to other resources)	3 pages with clear order, labeling and navigation between pages; all links work	Title Page with other pages branching off, and at least four pages total; Navigation path is clear and logical, all links work
Images	No images	Images are unrelated to page/text/proposal; most images were recycled from other pages on the Internet; Images too big/small in size or resolution; Images poorly cropped or have color problems	Images have strong relation to text; some Images are student produced; Images have proper size, resolution, colors, and cropping	Same as Level 3 plus images are from 3 or more sources (scan, CD-ROM, QuickCam, ZapShot, video tape, net, SuperPaint, PhotoShop, LogoMotion, etc.)	Same as Level 4 with either: more advanced Photoshop, PhotoDeluxe or Illustrator work

Source: This Rubric is a modified version of that created by John Pilgrim, technology resource teacher, Fall 1995, Horace Mann Middle School, SFUSD. Found at edtech.sandi.net/rubric. Reprinted by permission.

Interactive Summary

The following is a summary of the main points covered in this chapter.

1. **Types and examples of web-based lessons and projects** — Types of web-based activities include electronic pen pals (keypals), electronic mentoring, electronic (virtual) field trips, electronic publishing, group development projects, problem-based learning, and social action projects.

2. **Integration strategies for web-based lessons** — These include support for student research, motivation for writing, practice for information literacy skills, visual learning problems and solutions, development of collaboration skills, and multicultural experiences.

3. **Website functions to support web-based learning activities** — These include project overview, announcement, and application; tutorial instruction; information summaries and exchanges; communication and support; displays of past and current student work; and project development centers.

4. **Assessment of web-based lessons** — The quality of web-based lessons such as webquests may be assessed with a webquest rubric developed by webquest originator Bernie Dodge.

5. **Web page and website software tools** — Programmers and other technical experts use tools such as HTML, VRML, PERL, ActionScript, and other programming/authoring tools to develop web pages and websites. Teachers and students are among those who use web development tools such as *Google Pages* and Adobe *Dreamweaver* and *Flash*, which produce the same web products but require less technical expertise.

6. **Downloading images, programs, and plug-ins** — Resources that may be downloaded for web page development and use include browser versions, PDF readers, and players for movies and other web media.

7. **File transfer options** — When developing web products, teachers and students use email attachments to send files to each other and FTP programs (e.g., *WS_FTP*) to upload completed pages to the servers on which they will reside.

8. **Web page development procedures** — A recommended eight-step process for developing web products is (1) plan and storyboard, (2) develop pages with text, (3) insert images and media, (4) insert links and frames, (5) insert interactive elements, (6) test in a browser, (7) publish the site, (8) gather comments and revise.

9. **Web page evaluation and assessment resources** — Criteria for evaluating web page/website design include good structure and organization, clear text and/or graphic links, good visual design, and easy navigation. Teachers and students may use rubrics to assess the quality of their products.

Key Terms

- anchor
- BMP (format)
- Common Gateway Interface (CGI)
- download
- electronic field trip
- electronic mentor
- electronic publishing
- EPS (format)
- File Transfer Protocol (FTP)
- *Flash*
- frame
- GIF (format)
- Google Docs
- HTML
- image format
- Java
- Java applet
- JPEG (format)
- PERL
- PICT (format)
- plug-in
- Portable Document Format (PDF)
- problem-based learning (PBL)
- site map
- social action project
- streamed video and audio
- TIF (format)
- VRML
- webquest

Web-Enrichment Activities

1. Choose a webquest from the WebQuest Portal at http://webquest.org or by doing a web search for a webquest about a specific topic. Evaluate the webquest using the rubric in Table 8.4.

2. Go to Edutopia to view the video "Beginning the journey: Five-year-olds drive their own PBL projects" (http://www.edutopia.org/beginning-journey-five-year-olds-drive-their-own-pbl-projects). The video explores problem-based learning and how it motivates children. Why are the students energized, interested, and engaged? How can technology help launch young children on a journey of lifelong learning? What are the main elements of a project-based learning unit?

3. Go to W3 Schools at http://www.w3schools.com/default.asp and explore some of the tutorials offered on the site. In particular, search for the Web Building Tutorial or the Tutorial on Adding Multimedia (sound and video). Rate the quality of the tutorials for their appropriateness and ease of use for educators.

Go to MyEducationLab to complete the following exercises.

Video   Select the topic "Instructional Strategies," and go to the "Assignments, Activities, and Applications" section. Access the video "Scholarly Writings Online Engage Students" to see how one teacher uses online articles to broaden students' perspectives in History. Complete the activity that follows the video.

Video   Select the topic "Math Integration" and go to the "Assignments, Activities, and Applications" section. In the video "E-Z Geometry Website Supports Student Work," one teacher explains how a class website has become a valuable resource for student learning. Complete the activity that follows.

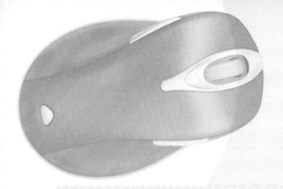

Technology Integration Workshop

The TIP Model in Action

Read each of the following scenarios related to implementing the TIP Model, and answer the questions that follow it based on your Chapter 8 reading and activities.

TIP MODEL SCENARIO #1 Each year, Mr. Gill has his fifth-grade students identify an issue of current popular concern—for example, local pollution problems, homeless or migrant people, or quality of education for students with English as a second language. Mr. Gill has them use the Internet to research what other communities and groups are saying and doing about the problem. Then the students develop a position statement with a proposed solution and post it on the school's Internet site. They request that feedback on their site be emailed to the teacher.

   1.1 What relative advantage does Mr. Gill see for using the Internet as opposed to other resources for this project?

   1.2 According to the textbook, what is the name for this kind of problem-based learning?

   1.3 Why does Mr. Gill have people email feedback to him rather than to the students?

TIP MODEL SCENARIO #2 Mr. LeDoux is trying to get his high school English students to think about possible careers in journalism or other areas that require writing. He has his students contact one or more of the people he knows in these areas who have agreed to be interviewed online. They answer students' questions about how they entered the field, what they do on a daily basis, and what they do and don't like about their work. When they have completed the interview(s), students write a summary and present it to the class.

   2.1 What relative advantage does Mr. LeDoux see for using the Internet as opposed to other resources for this project?

   2.2 According to the textbook, what is the name for this kind of online activity?

   2.3 Why doesn't Mr. LeDoux let his students research and find their own people to be their online information sources?

TIP MODEL SCENARIO #3 Each year, Dr. Prida has her ninth-grade students do a project in which they interview ninth graders at other schools and create a newsletter documenting their current shared views and concerns they feel are noteworthy. The newsletter is posted on the school's web page. When the newsletter is done, Dr. Prida contacts the teachers of the cooperating ninth-grade classrooms and gives them the URL for the newsletter. The teachers ask their students to create and email Dr. Prida "Letters to the Editor," giving their comments and opinions about the newsletter stories.

   3.1 What relative advantage does Dr. Prida see for using the Internet as opposed to other resources for this project?

   3.2 What relative advantage do the other teachers see for having their students use the Internet and email as opposed to other resources?

   3.3 What outcomes might Dr. Prida assess for this project, and how would she assess them?

TIP MODEL SCENARIO #4 To introduce his unit on the Constitution, Mr. Lorrie has his students do a web-based scavenger hunt. He gives them a list of questions about presidents and a list of websites with annotations about the kinds of information they supply about historical figures. As well as answering the questions, the students document the search method they used to locate each of their answers. Mr. Lorrie then asks them to write a brief description of other noteworthy facts/data they found in the course of the hunt. He awards several kinds of prizes for the hunt: for the most correct answers at the end of the allotted time, the most efficient/organized search techniques, and the best "other information" found.

   4.1 What relative advantage does Mr. Lorrie see for using the Internet as opposed to other resources for this project?

   4.2 Why do you think Mr. Lorrie recognizes three different aspects about the hunt in awarding the prizes?

   4.3 Do you think Mr. Lorrie should have his students work individually, in pairs, or in small groups to do this kind of activity? Explain your answer.

TIP MODEL SCENARIO #5 Each semester two science teachers in two different schools give their high school students an ecological problem to solve related to conditions in their local area. After each class has collected data from online sources provided by the teachers, each student has to analyze the data, figure out the cause of the problem, and create a proposed solution. Students use the project website to display their collected data and solutions. Local scientists and interested citizens are asked to judge the solutions and to write an analysis of the feasibility of each. Then the students discuss their solutions and how they might improve them, based on the judges' input.

5.1 What relative advantage does the teachers see for using the Internet as opposed to other resources for this project?

5.2 According to the textbook, what is the name for this kind of problem-based learning?

5.3 Why would the teachers have judges assess the answers rather than evaluating the solutions themselves?

TIE into Practice: Technology Integration Examples

The Technology Integration Example that opened this chapter (*Agayu: Adventure Learning in Chukotka, Russia*) showed how a teacher might integrate an adventure learning program within his or her classroom to meet the national standards while interacting with authentic resources. With the knowledge you have gained from Chapter 8, do the following with this example:

1. Answer the following questions about the *Agayu: Adventure Learning* example:

   • Phases 1 and 2: What relative advantage did Ms. Anderson hope the adventure learning program would have for learning about geography? How would the adventure learning approach be a better strategy than the usual way of studying geography from the textbook?

   • Phase 3: One of the desired outcomes Ms. Anderson hoped for was that her students would have a better understanding and appreciation of culture, which she planned to assess with a rubric. Create a rubric that she might use to assess this as well as completion of required tasks, knowledge of search strategies, ability to locate required information, and quality of cooperative group work.

   • Phase 4: Ms. Anderson has students working in groups of two or three to complete the mask activity. What are the advantages and disadvantages of having

students work in groups as opposed to working individually on an activity like this?

   • Phase 5: One of the strategies Ms. Anderson plans to use as part of her website is setting up online collaboration zones. Explain the strategies you would use to get students to share their work online so it would proceed smoothly and involve all of the students.

   • Phase 6: In evaluating the results of the adventure learning activity, Ms. Anderson found that students who had home computers did better than students who only had access to computers at school. In what ways might she improve access to the Internet so that all students would do better?

2. What NETS for Students skills would students learn by working on the adventure learning activity? (See the front of this book for a list of NETS for Students.)

Technology Integration Lesson Planning

Complete the following exercises using sample lesson plans found on MyEducationLab.

1. Locate lesson ideas — MyEducationLab has several examples of lessons that use the integration strategies described in this chapter: support for student research, motivation for writing, practice for information literacy skills, visual learning problems and solutions, development of collaboration skills, and multicultural experiences. Locate an example integration idea for each of these strategies. Go to MyEducationLab under the topic "Internet" and go to "Lesson Plans" to review example lessons. Choose two of the following integration lessons:

   • Learning About Each Other at a Distance

   • Gathering Information by Email

   • Online Opportunities for Problem-Solving Projects

   • Authors in Residence and Online Mentors

   • Using Technology to Study Biospheres

   • Tuskegee Tragedy

2. Evaluate the lessons — Use the *Evaluation Checklist for a Technology-Integrated Lesson* (located on MyEducationLab under the topic "Instructional Planning") to evaluate each of these lessons.

3. Modify a lesson — Select one of the lesson ideas and adapt its strategies to meet a need in your own content area. You may choose to use the same approach as in the original or to adapt it to meet your needs.

4. Add descriptors — Create descriptors for your new lesson similar to those found on the database (e.g., grade level, content and topic areas, technologies used, relative advantage, objectives, NETS standards).

5. Save your new lesson — Save your modified lesson with all its descriptors.

For Your Teaching Portfolio

For this chapter's contribution to your teaching portfolio, add the following products you created in the Technology Integration Workshop:

- The rubric you created for the *Agayu: Adventure Learning* project
- The evaluations you did using the *Evaluation Checklist for a Technology-Integrated Lesson*
- The new lesson plan you developed, based on the one you found on MyEducationLab.

Part 4

Integrating Technology Across the Curriculum

Parts 1 through 3 have introduced the full range of educational technology resources and provided examples and practice with integration strategies for each one. The chapters in Part 4 describe how these resources and strategies are being used in each of six content areas and in special education.

Part 4
Required Background for Teachers

In an effort to model subject-area integration, disciplines are addressed by chapter as described here.

Chapter 9   **Technology in English and Language Arts Instruction**

Language arts in this chapter include the communications skills (reading, listening, speaking) addressed primarily in elementary grades as well as English topics (writing and literature), which are the focus at secondary levels.

Chapter 10   **Technology in Foreign and Second Language Instruction**

This chapter focuses on the learning of foreign languages and on English language learning (ELL) for non-native speakers.

Chapter 11   **Technology in Mathematics and Science Instruction**

Science and mathematics topics are considered closely related, and curricula for them are often intertwined. This chapter looks at how technology applications help integrate the teaching of these topics and how they address the special curriculum needs of each.

Chapter 12   **Technology in Social Studies Instruction**

Technology applications covered in this chapter include those for history, social studies, civics, and geography. Social sciences may be one of the subject areas most influenced by recent technological advances.

Chapter 13   **Technology in Music and Art Instruction**

This chapter focuses on technology applications for the topics in arts instruction to which the majority of K–12 students are exposed: music (appreciation, theory, and performance) and art (drawing, painting, and image production).

Chapter 14   **Technology in Physical Education and Health Education**

The closely related subjects of physical education and health are generally not accorded the status of the more "academic" subject areas. However, the quality of the teaching of these subjects may play a major role in the future success of students. Instructional technology provides a number of resources that may maximize the effectiveness of the limited time that typically is given to these subjects.

Chapter 15   **Technology in Special Education**

Chapter 15 is the only chapter identified by population rather than by topic. Technology applications for students with special needs are addressed in Part 4 because the curriculum for special needs students has many unique characteristics. Needs of special students addressed in this chapter include those for learners with mental disabilities and behavioral/emotional disorders; learners with physical disabilities (e.g., hearing impairments, visual impairments, wheelchairbound); and gifted and talented students.

Chapter 9
Technology in English and Language Arts Instruction

The Internet and other forms of information and communication technology (ICT) such as word processors, Web editors, presentation software, and e-mail are regularly redefining the nature of literacy. To become fully literate in today's world, students must become proficient in the new literacies of ICT. Therefore, literacy educators have a responsibility to effectively integrate these technologies into the literacy curriculum in order to prepare students for the literacy future they deserve.

Position statement of the International Reading Association (2001, p. 2)

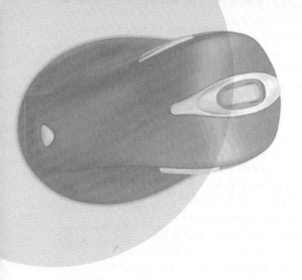

Technology Integration Example

Classroom Revolutions

Based on: Skarecki, E., & Insinnia, E. (1999). **Revolutions in the classroom.** *Learning and Leading with Technology, 26*(7), 22–27.

Grade Levels: 8 through 10 • Content Area/Topic: English literature, information literacy skills • Length of Time: Two weeks

Phases 1 and 2: Assess technological pedagogical content knowledge; Determine relative advantage

As Ms. Skerritt searched the Internet for materials to help teach her literature unit, she was amazed at the rich array of images and background information on Dickens' *A Tale of Two Cities* and the history surrounding the period it depicted. It was always a struggle to get her students interested in books and events from so long ago, but as she looked over the Internet resources, she realized they could make all the difference. Not only would students be able to locate more information much more quickly than they could in the library, the compelling images and vivid personal accounts also could help make the story come alive. It also offered fertile ground for exploring various approaches to literary criticism. She realized how important it was becoming that students learn to use the Internet to locate relevant and reliable information and select items that illustrated their ideas about what they were reading in class. She decided to build the unit around using Internet resources for researching and analyzing information on Dickens' famous book. She would have students work in groups, using laptops checked out from the media center, to research various events and themes in *A Tale of Two Cities*. In the process, she would teach them how to locate and select useful resources on the Internet. Ms. Skerritt was confident in her knowledge of Dickens' work and the historical period in which it was located (content knowledge), but she was less confident about locating the best resources to use (technology knowledge) and teaching students how to find these resources (technology and pedagogy knowledge). She decided to ask the media specialist, Ms. Kermit, to help her locate appropriate websites and to team-teach a mini-lesson on locating relevant and reliable resources.

Phase 3: Decide on objectives and assessments

Ms. Skerritt knew that the goals for this unit would focus on both literary analysis and developing good Internet skills to support that analysis. She decided that the following outcomes,

objectives, and assessments captured what she felt was important for students to learn:

- **Outcome:** Skills in locating reliable information. **Objective:** Students will apply criteria accurately to determine if given Internet sites are reliable. **Assessment:** A checklist of criteria for selecting reliable sites.

- **Outcome:** Literary critique skills. **Objective:** Students will demonstrate abilities to critique events and themes in *A Tale of Two Cities* by researching and preparing a *PowerPoint* presentation of findings on a selected theme. **Assessment:** Rubric to assess the *PowerPoint* presentation.

- **Outcome:** Knowledge about events in history and in the novel. **Objective:** Students will demonstrate that they have learned and remembered key events and characters from the novel and the historical period by answering correctly at least 90% of a set of short-answer questions. **Assessment:** Short-answer exam on events/characters.

Phase 4: Design integration strategies

Ms. Skerritt felt that exploring Internet sites could be done in conjunction with reviewing the novel. That way, students could develop their Internet skills as they discussed the story and the historical events on which it was based. Then they would research and present a theme from the book. Working with Ms. Kermit, she planned the following 2-week timeline for the project:

- **Days 1–4: Reviewing the novel using the Internet:** After introducing the project, Ms. Skerritt begins a review of the book using Internet sites (supplemented by Ms. Kermit). She shows students the set of sites she wants them to use, assigns students to groups, and gives each group a different question to answer for each of three sections of the book. To emphasize the point that not all websites are useful, Ms. Skerritt shows them a site that is not reliable and has them go through the checklist to see why it is not. For every site students use, they have to apply criteria to show why it is reliable.

- **Day 5: Reviewing major themes:** After students complete their reviews, they hold a class discussion on the answers they found and brainstorm the main themes of the book. Ms. Skerritt assigns each group a theme for which they will locate information on the Internet and report on their findings in a *PowerPoint* presentation. She gives the groups a handout on items to include in their research and presentations.

- **Days 6–8: Researching themes and creating *PowerPoint* presentations:** The groups complete their research and develop their *PowerPoint* presentations. They select images and information from the sites they visited to illustrate their points and the events in the book.

- **Days 9–10: Giving *PowerPoint* presentations and taking final test:** Each group gives its presentation, and the class discusses it. Finally, Ms. Skerritt gives them a test covering the main events, characters, and themes within the book.

Phase 5: Prepare the instructional environment

As they prepared for this project, their tasks included:

- **Creation of Bookmark/Favorites file:** As Ms. Skerritt and Ms. Kermit located the sites Ms. Skerritt wanted her students to use, they bookmarked them. Ms. Kermit showed Ms. Skerritt how to upload the Bookmark file to the school's network and transferred it to the computer lab so her students could access it there.

- **Research handout:** During two prep periods, Ms. Skerritt and Ms. Kermit co-created a handout of the checklist for judging website reliability and placed it on the school's website for easy viewing and downloading.

- **Hardware checkout:** The school had a wireless network so that teachers and students could use computers in any classroom. Ms. Skerritt arranged to check out a set of laptops from the library media center so that her students could do their research in the classroom. She also arranged for a projection system on the days Ms. Kermit would demonstrate Internet use and example sites and at times when students would need them to display their *PowerPoint* presentations at the end of the project.

- **Adaptations:** One of Ms. Skerritt's students had cerebral palsy and could not use the keyboard. Ms. Skerritt arranged for an adaptive keyboard and software to allow the girl to use the computer without typing.

- **Development of assessments:** Finally, Ms. Skerritt created the rubrics and tests she needed for the unit.

Phase 6: Evaluate and revise

After the students had completed the unit, Ms. Skerritt talked to them about how they liked the project, and she reviewed their products and test results. It was obvious that they loved this approach to learning about literature. The most common comment she heard was, "I never knew a 'classic' could be so exciting!" The websites seem to have made the events in the book more real and interesting to them. Ms. Skerritt was especially pleased with the results of the test on the novel and the history surrounding it. The only students who had difficulty were two students who were absent for a large portion of the project. She asked Ms. Kermit to help her create a website that described the project and led students through it so that they could do work from home or on their own, if they needed to. Finally, she found that students seemed to have a good grasp of judging web page reliability.

Objectives

After reading this chapter and completing the learning activities for it, you should be able to:

1. Identify and discuss current issues related to the integration of technology into English and language arts curricula.

2. Describe effective ways in which technology can be integrated into English and language arts instruction.

3. Design and implement instructional activities that model effective ways to integrate technology into English and language arts instruction.

Language arts refers to those language-based processes by which we think, learn, and communicate. (See NCTE and IRA standards for English and language arts in Table 9.1.) In the elementary grades, the language arts curriculum focuses primarily on developing the fundamental skills of reading, writing, listening, and speaking. In the later grades, language arts instruction is usually in courses that focus on literature, composition, and formal communication (in either a student's native language or a foreign one). Because literacy skills and processes are fundamental to success in most other disciplines, language arts instruction is often stressed in content-area courses (e.g., social studies, sciences, and mathematics). This latter practice is often referred to as "reading and writing in the content area" or is addressed as study skills and strate-gies. In this chapter, we provide an overview of how technology can be used to enhance language arts instruction in all of the above ways.

What Does TPACK Look Like in English and Language Arts Instruction?

Teaching and learning with technology has been termed a "wicked problem" (Mishra & Koehler, 2007), which is why teachers continue to have questions about how to incorporate technology more meaningfully into their English and language arts teaching and learning. So, what

TABLE 9.1 NCTE/IRA Standards for English/Language Arts

The standards for English/Language Arts were copublished by the National Council for Teachers of English (NCTE) and the International Reading Association (IRA) in 1996. Listed below are summaries of the 12 standards, taken from the NCTE website (http://www.ncte.org/standards).

1. Students read a wide range of print and nonprint texts to build an understanding of texts, of themselves, and of the cultures of the United States and the world; to acquire new information; to respond to the needs and demands of society and the workplace; and for personal fulfillment. Among these texts are fiction and nonfiction, classic and contemporary works.

2. Students read a wide range of literature from many periods in many genres to build an understanding of the many dimensions (e.g., philosophical, ethical, aesthetic) of human experience.

3. Students apply a wide range of strategies to comprehend, interpret, evaluate, and appreciate texts. They draw on their prior experience, their interactions with other readers and writers, their knowledge of word meaning and of other texts, their word identification strategies, and their understanding of textual features (e.g., sound–letter correspondence, sentence structure, context, graphics).

4. Students adjust their use of spoken, written, and visual language (e.g., conventions, style, vocabulary) to communicate effectively with a variety of audiences and for different purposes.

5. Students employ a wide range of strategies as they write and use different writing process elements appropriately to communicate with different audiences for a variety of purposes.

6. Students apply knowledge of language structure, language conventions (e.g., spelling and punctuation), media techniques, figurative language, and genre to create, critique, and discuss print and nonprint texts.

7. Students conduct research on issues and interests by generating ideas and questions, and by posing problems. They gather, evaluate, and synthesize data from a variety of sources (e.g., print and nonprint texts, artifacts, people) to communicate their discoveries in ways that suit their purpose and audience.

8. Students use a variety of technological and information resources (e.g., libraries, databases, computer networks, video) to gather and synthesize information and to create and communicate knowledge.

9. Students develop an understanding of and respect for diversity in language use, patterns, and dialects across cultures, ethnic groups, geographic regions, and social roles.

10. Students whose first language is not English make use of their first language to develop competency in the English language arts and to develop understanding of content across the curriculum.

11. Students participate as knowledgeable, reflective, creative, and critical members of a variety of literacy communities.

12. Students use spoken, written, and visual language to accomplish their own purposes (e.g., for learning, enjoyment, persuasion, and the exchange of information).

Source: Standards for the English Language Arts, by the International Reading Association and the National Council of Teachers of English, Copyright © 1996 by the International Reading Association and the National Council of Teachers of English. Reprinted with permission.

are the implications of knowing about TPACK in the content area of English and language arts (see Figure 9.1)? TPACK, as discussed earlier in this book, is teacher knowledge that is the result of the synergy among three knowledge domains (technology, pedagogy, and content). TPACK's essential features are "(a) the use of appropriate technology (b) in a particular content area (c) as part of a pedagogical strategy (d) within a given educational context (e) to develop students' knowledge of a particular topic or meet an educational objective or student need" (Cox, 2008, p. 40). Specifically within English and language arts, TPACK can be illustrated through an example of how to approach writing and storytelling. In most English and language arts curricula, writing is a focal point. A teacher who exhibits TPACK planning takes note of the curriculum goals and the learning objectives while simultaneously considering how/if technology could add value to the goals and objectives and identifying best practices and pedagogy to use. For example, when teaching a lesson about writing stories, instead of having students write stories using only text (printed or typed), a teacher who thinks from the TPACK perspective considers the added value of having students use a digital medium such as iMovie or VoiceThread to tell their stories. Not only does digital technology extend the story in ways not possible in print (e.g., through the addition of audio or pictures), but a digital medium also expands the potential audience for sharing the story. So, a TPACK teacher considers the pedagogical, technological, and content advantages of having students compose stories in digital spaces where they would be accessible to others, whereas a teacher who does not exhibit strong technology knowledge may have students word process their stories and hand them in to be corrected (an audience of one).

FIGURE 9.1 TPACK and English/Language Arts

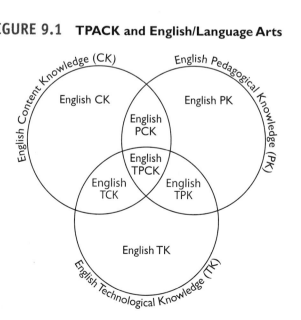

Issues and Problems in English and Language Arts Instruction

Reading, writing, and critically analyzing written texts are considered fundamental skills for a literate person. However, teachers of English and language arts encounter many issues when teaching these skills and integrating technology into the curriculum. Specifically, we as teachers need to understand the importance of expanding the definition of literacy, exploring new instructional practices, making decisions on keyboarding instruction, creating social learning environments, working with diverse learners, motivating students, and teachers' growth as literacy professionals, all of which are discussed in the following subsections.

Expanding the Definition of Literacy

The definition of *literacy* has changed dramatically in the United States over the course of its history, from being able to sign your name, to being familiar with certain canonical texts, to being able to read and write and make meaning from the written word, to being proficient in 21st century skills that are context specific (Kaestel et al., 1989; Myers, 1996; National Adolescent Literacy Coalition, 2007). Our charge as teachers is to recognize that traditional definitions of literacy are no longer sufficient and to shift our conception to new literacies (Kinzer, 2003; Lankshear & Knobel, 2003; Leu, Kinzer, Coiro, & Cammack, 2004). Today, literacy is "no longer an end point to be achieved but rather a process of continuously learning how to be literate" (Leu, 2001, p. 568). As new technologies emerge, the nature, expansion, and definition of literacy change (Coiro, 2003; Karchmer, 2001a; Leu & Kinzer, 2000; Reinking, McKenna, Labbo, & Kieffer, 1998). According to Leu (2002a), "The new literacies include the skills, strategies, and insights needed to successfully exploit the rapidly changing information and communication technologies (ICT) that continuously emerge in our world" (p. 313). Leu (2002a) points out that as new technologies emerge, so does the need for new literacies; therefore, it is critical that *students learn how to learn* **new literacy** *technologies*. This view is supported by the International Reading Association (IRA) in its literacy and technology position statement, which reads (2001): "Traditional definitions of reading, writing, and viewing and traditional definitions of best practice instruction—derived from a long tradition of book and other print media—will be insufficient" (p. 2).

Exploring New Instructional Practices

There is a direct correlation between the emergence of new literacies and the need for new instructional practices. Teachers are expected to provide new forms of literacy instruction so that students know how to locate, critically evaluate, use, and communicate through technology resources. For instance, students need instruction on how to find appropriate electronic information sources to be incorporated into their research products and presentations as well as how to access and use information stored in a variety of sources (e.g., still and moving images, text, sound, and print). This perspective is supported in Standard 8 of the National Council of Teachers of English (NCTE) and IRA *Standards for the English Language Arts* (1996; see Table 9.1), which specifically emphasizes the importance of students' using technology in their learning: "Students use a variety of technological and informational resources (e.g., libraries, databases, computer networks, video) to gather and synthesize information and to create and communicate knowledge" (p. 39).

Students also need knowledge about hardware (e.g., computers, camcorders, digital cameras, webcams) and how to use it to create and present multimedia products. Providing instruction in this area can support the integration of technology across curricular areas and can give students opportunities to integrate information into meaningful learning experiences, projects, and presentations (Toomey & Ketterer, 1995).

In addition, there is a growing need for teachers to instruct students to comprehend language in the context of visual images since images play an increasing role in communication. These images are often in technology-based formats ranging from digital pictures to streaming video. Students need instruction in processing the information and separating out bias and inaccuracies (intentional and otherwise). For example, image manipulation software allows us to alter images in ways that completely change how a person or event is depicted. Students must be taught to be aware of and to search for these changes and the alterations in ideas and concepts that they communicate. Clearly the new literacies require a high level of critical sophistication from our students, and it is only through instruction and experiences with new literacies that they will develop these skills. These expectations can add pressure to an already full curriculum, in terms of both time and material resources.

Fortunately, a growing body of literature illustrates ways to implement new instructional practices. For instance, Myers and Beach (2001) provide examples of how hypermedia fosters critical literacy; Labbo, Eakle, and Montero (2002) discuss how to use digital photographs and software in a language experience approach; Bull, Bull, and Kajder (2003) and Weiler (2003) provide insights on how to use weblogs as student journals; Ohler (2008) offers the "how tos" of digital storytelling; Leu (2002b) tells how to integrate the Internet using an Internet workshop framework; and Labbo et al. (2002) share teacher wisdom in stories about using technology for literacy instruction.

 Making the Case for Technology Integration

Use the following questions to reflect on issues in technology integration and to guide discussions within your class.

1. Many educators believe that with the growth of media and information technology, media literacy is just as important as—or even more important than—print literacy (that is, learning to read and write). What is your position on the relative importance of the two "literacies"? What information from this chapter helps support your position?

2. The emergence of word processing has had the effect of making handwritten schoolwork less important, especially in later grades. Some educators feel that handwriting should be given much less emphasis, even in earlier grades, in favor of teaching keyboarding and computer use. What is your position on this proposal? What are the pluses and minuses of de-emphasizing the teaching of handwriting in favor of keyboarding?

Making Decisions about Keyboarding Instruction

The most common way to write using a computer requires input through a regular **QWERTY keyboard**, so named because of the first six letters in the top letter line of a typewriter keyboard. There is an ongoing discussion of whether we should teach keyboarding instruction as a prerequisite to the use of computers for writing. Those in favor argue that students will learn bad habits if they use the keyboard without proper training, that these bad habits might become permanent, and that failure to learn proper fingering will inhibit fluent and speedy keyboarding. Those against requiring keyboarding instruction as a prerequisite argue that too much student time and computer resources are spent on getting students trained to type quickly, that students need only basic keyboard familiarization, and that keyboarding instruction would likely be a waste of time unless students have real-world applications in which to use the computer. Both arguments are legitimate, and most teachers have resolved the issue, at least temporarily, by favoring keyboarding instruction if it is available and needed but not preventing students from using the computer if they do not yet have good keyboarding skills.

Creating Social Learning Environments

New forms of literacy are much more contingent on social interactions with others than traditional literacies are (Leu,

Adapting for Special Needs

For Literature

Students with reading difficulties often struggle in English classes with literature assignments. Their lack of fluency often interferes with comprehension, and the task may take longer for them than for students who read at grade level. Several strategies are described for making the literature curriculum accessible for struggling students.

Electronic texts (etexts) contain the full text of a book. A wide variety of electronic texts are available—particularly for books with expired copyrights (i.e., many of the classics)—and can simply be downloaded to your computer. Here are a few good websites for locating these etexts:

- Infomotions (http://www.infomotions.com)
- Bibliomania (http://www.bibliomania.com/)
- Electronic Text Center (http://lib.virginia.edu/digital/collections/finding_digital.html)
- Project Gutenberg (http://www.gutenberg.org/)
- The Plays of William Shakespeare (http://www.theplays.org)

Once the etext is on your computer, it is possible to manipulate the text in several ways to make it more accessible for students. First, the font and type size can be enlarged for students with impaired vision. Second, the etext can be copied and pasted into talking word processors (e.g., Don Johnston's *Co:Writer*) or text-to-speech programs (e.g., *ReadPlease*) so that the student can listen to the text as the computer reads it. Finally, for students whose first language is not English, etext can be copied and pasted into a language translation tool (e.g., *Babel*

Fish) to obtain a translation that can be used to assist them in understanding the text.

Another strategy for supporting students who struggle to understand key concepts in literature is to use study aids that provide advanced organizers for their reading—for example, summaries of plots and character descriptions. A number of websites feature complete resource collections for the most popular books taught in school:

- SparkNotes (http://www.sparknotes.com)
- NovelGuide (http://www.novelguide.com)
- Free Book Notes (http://www.freebooknotes.com)
- Pink Monkey (http://www.pinkmonkey.com)

For Writing

Some students struggle with the physical process of handwriting, which interferes with development of their written expression skills. An alternative is dictation. USB handheld digital dictation devices can be purchased at any office supply store (from $50 to $150); these allow the user to dictate information into the handheld device and then to upload the file to the computer. Many students may already have an iPod, a popular portable music and media player that also has dictation capabilities. Currently, the information will still need to be transcribed. However, a second resource may complete the process. iDictate (http://www.iDictate.com) is a transcription service. Users may submit information by dictating it over the telephone, and it will be transcribed and returned via email in 20 minutes to 24 hours at a cost of a one and a quarter cents per word—very affordable! Because supports like this are built into the adult world, it is probably appropriate to begin teaching students how to access and use such tools so that they can evaluate their personal usefulness.

Contributed by Dave Edyburn

Kinzer, Coiro, & Cammack, 2004). According to the *Standards for the English Language Arts* (NCTE/IRA, 1996), teachers should begin "giving students the enjoyment and pride of sometimes being their teachers' teachers" (p. 40). Technology offers a natural setting in which students can be positioned as the experts, helping redefine the student–teacher relationship (Bryan, 2000; Doering, 2006). The new forms of literacy and students becoming experts illustrate the power of people working together and are grounded in the social constructivist theory (Vygotsky, 1962), which asserts that learning occurs through interactions with others.

Another reason that new literacies demand a more social environment is that teaching and learning are no longer confined to a traditional classroom context. Today, thanks to the Internet, the classroom is a worldwide classroom in which networked technologies for literacy enable us to communicate with people around the world. We transmit and receive information in different formats and from different people. These interactions provide a tremendous multicultural benefit to our classrooms that has never existed before.

Working with Diverse Learners

Schools have more diverse student populations today than ever before. This cultural and linguistic diversity creates classrooms that are richer yet more complex. Although we

Special software and hardware can help bridge the learning gap for students with special needs ranging from second language learners to those with emotional or physical challenges.

value and celebrate the opportunity to interact with students of different nationalities, races, and ethnicities, this creates new challenges for English and language arts teachers (Matthews, 2000; Mora, 2000; Mora, 2001). This is especially true when working with ESL and ELL students (see Chapter 10). It is also true when working with struggling readers. Often when students experience literacy problems at a young age, they continue to have reading difficulties throughout their schooling. Students who typically experience this problem include children who begin school without a solid literacy foundation, learn English as a second language, live in literacy-impoverished homes, have attention deficit/hyperactivity disorder, or do not receive appropriate instruction in school. Because many students need additional instruction in literacy, appropriate use of technology (e.g., audio books, websites, and software) can support their growth. Fortunately, numerous Internet resources are available to assist teachers with struggling readers (Johnson, 2001; Johnson, 2002).

Motivating Students

The more students read, the better developed their language and writing skills become. However, we as teachers find it an ongoing challenge to motivate students to read—either for study or for pleasure. Indeed, students rarely choose reading as a free-time activity. Fortunately, one of the encouraging findings from the research is that both students and teachers are highly motivated and interested in the new literacies (Leu, 2002a). Teachers are turning to the interactive and visual qualities of software and websites to increase motivation for reading and writing. Also, computer-based tracking systems such as *Accelerated Reader*

(Lopez, 2000; Poock, 1998) are designed especially to increase the amount of reading students do for enjoyment.

Teachers also find it an ongoing challenge to motivate students to express themselves in writing. Students especially resist the labor involved in revising research papers and compositions. In addition to word processing, which has been in use for many years, a variety of technology tools and strategies have emerged to spur students' desire to write, to improve the quality of their written products (e.g., email projects, blogs), and to provide authentic publication sources. According to the *English Language Arts Standards* (NCTE/IRA, 1996), technology not only enhances students' motivation to write but also encourages them to assume greater responsibility for their learning.

Teachers' Growth as Literacy Professionals

The position statement published by the International Reading Association (2001) clearly states what literacy teachers need to know about integrating technology into the curriculum. According to the IRA, students have the right to:

- Teachers who are skilled in the effective use of technology for teaching and learning;
- A literacy curriculum that integrates the new literacies of technology into instructional programs;
- Instruction that develops the critical literacies essential to effective information use;
- Assessment practices in literacy that include reading and writing with technology tools;
- Opportunities to learn safe and responsible use of information and communication technologies;, and
- Equal access to technology.

Obviously, these visions will not be fully realized unless teachers receive continued and systematic professional development. Unfortunately, at this point in time, this is not happening. Even though the U.S. Department of Education recommends that 30% of a school district's technology budget be spent on professional development, currently only 6% is being appropriated for this endeavor (IRA, 2001). Thus, the burden falls on teachers' shoulders to take responsibility for learning how to integrate ICT effectively into the curriculum. Teachers are expanding their own professional growth through school/university partnership projects (Bauer & Anderson, 2001; Maring, Boxie, & Wiseman, 2000) and "cybermentoring" (Boxie, 2004; Boxie & Maring, 2001), use of online resources for professional development (Johnson & Zufall, 2004), and increased access to and participation in professional organizations such as the International Reading Association (IRA) and the National Council for Teachers of English (NCTE).

Technology Integration Strategies for English and Language Arts Instruction

Perhaps the most creative and prolific array of strategies and applications for enhancing teaching with technology is to be found in English and language arts. Recent publications by NCTE entwine technology and English education: "English language arts and digital technology are now inseparable. Digital technology . . . has significant and lasting consequences for reading, writing, speaking, listening, and teaching" (McGrail & Rozema, 2005). The greatest challenge faced by English educators today is technology integration: "While technology has been implemented in traditional approaches to English language arts instruction . . . such uses, as Lankshear and Knobel (2003) point out, tend only to 'perpetuate the old, rather than to engage with and refine or reinvent the new' " (McGrail & Rozema, 2005, p. 29).

This section focuses on integration strategies that support the following three English and language arts areas: language skills development, literacy development, and the process writing approach. Strategies and resources under these three headings are summarized in Table 9.2. See also the accompanying *Top Ten* feature for additional strategies.

Language Skills Development

Though technology use in English and language arts clearly emphasizes motivation and support for reading fluency and writing production, many programs are also in use that instruct or give practice in individual reading and writing skills. These programs address primarily lower level thinking skills that generally involve rote drill-and-practice activities. Clearly there is a time and place for this type of technology in the classroom, although higher order, problem-solving skills should be emphasized. Here we describe some important strategies for supporting language skills development.

TABLE 9.2 Summary of Technology Integration Strategies for English and Language Arts

Technology Integration Strategies	Benefits	Sample Resources and Activities
Language skills development: decoding/phonics, comprehension, vocabulary	• Gives motivational, individual instruction and/or practice in individual reading and writing skills. • Supplies private, individual feedback to scaffold students' learning.	• Reading instructional systems • Electronic dictionaries and thesauruses • Electronic devices • Talking word processors http://www.educationalinsights/com/
Literacy development	• Helps match books to students' own interests. • Presents reading assignments in ways that students find compelling; helps track reading. • Engages students in reading by helping them visualize the people and places in books. • Supports the reflection and frequent modification called for in process writing.	• Networked literacy projects • Interactive storybooks (electronic or talking books) • Tracking systems • Digital storytelling activities • Online reading materials • Writing in blogs • Script writing in video projects • Threaded discussions in distance tools http://www.ebn.weblogger.com/
Process approach to writing	• Supports students as they produce and revise text; frees them to focus on generating and sharing ideas. • Supports all stages of the writing process: planning, drafting; revising and editing, and publishing.	• Word processing • Planning for writing electronic outliners, concept mapping software, Internet resource sites • Drafting, revising, editing, projected images of word-processed drafts, spell checkers, grammar checkers • Publishing, desktop-published brochures, newspapers, and booklets; electronic slide shows; and web pages http://my.powa.org

Strategies for Technology in English/Language Arts

Take advantage of these ten powerful strategies for using technology to enhance the teaching of reading, writing, and language skills.

1. **Electronic publishing projects to encourage student writing** — Students spend more time writing when they know their work will be displayed on a website or in a print product that others will see.

2. **Electronic penpal (keypal) activities to encourage student writing** — Students are more likely to want to write and to take more care with spelling and language conventions when they have an authentic audience.

3. **Internet resources to engage students in literature** — Internet sites offer examples, background, and analysis to enrich students' study of literary works and help make literature more real and relevant to them.

4. **Online book clubs** — Encourage pleasure reading by having students create an online book club for kids or join an existing one.

5. **Concept mapping software to help students plan their writing** — Concept mapping software (e.g., *Inspiration*) helps students create visual outlines to plan what they want to write about.

6. **Talking books to engage students in reading** — Interactive storybooks or electronic books scaffold students' initial reading skills and draw them into reading activities.

7. **Alternate formats for writing stories** — Students can use a video-editing program such as *iMovie* and an audio-editing program like *Audacity* to develop stories in formats other than simply text — encompassing movies, pictures, and sound.

8. **Threaded discussions to motivate student writing** — These draw students into writing by giving them a supportive, nonjudgmental environment for expressing their ideas.

9. **Blogs and fan fiction websites to motivate student writing** — Students practice written expression as they engage in dialogue with others about topics of mutual interest.

10. **Tracking systems to motivate student reading** — Systems such as *Accelerated Reader* give students opportunities for reading at their own levels and rewards them for improved comprehension.

Teaching decoding skills. We generally teach skills in **decoding** or "sounding out" words in the early primary grades, and according to a limited amount of research, students who have access to digitized speech support increase their decoding abilities (Reitsma, 1988). Several websites offer interactive sites with speech support. Bertelsen, Kauffman, Howard, and Cochran (2003) methodically examined phonics websites and identified four as being the most useful for children. First, *GameGOO: Learning That Sticks* is an interactive site for prekindergarten through grade 3 based on state standards for language arts. Most activities use phonic elements such as letter recognition, letter–sound correspondence, and spelling. It is especially appropriate for students with special needs because it links to the Earobics Literacy site, which provides voice output. Second, *Between the Lions* includes videos, books, and interactive games from PBS's award-winning children's program. This website offers information on phonics skills and word activities and also provides visual and auditory assistance for students who have learning difficulties. Third, *Chateau Meddybemps: Fun with Letters* was named by the International Reading Association as the third best site on the web for helping children learn phonics. In addition to activities that reinforce letter recognition and formation, it includes a writer's workshop area with pages for creating stories. The final identified site, *Words and Pictures*, aligns the United Kingdom's national curriculum standards with the teaching of words through interactive games and activities.

Check it out:

- GameGOO: Learning That Sticks   http://www.cogcon.com/gamegoo/gooeyhome.html
- Between the Lions   http://pbskids.org/lions/
- Chateau Meddybemps: Fun with Letters   http://www.meddybemps.com/letterary/index.html
- Words and Pictures   http://www.bbc.co.uk/education/wordsandpictures/phonics

Developing other reading skills. A variety of other technology resources support teachers as they work to increase students' fluency with phonics, comprehension, and vocabulary skills:

- **Software-based and online systems** — The editors of *Technology and Learning* (2003) recommend several software-based and online systems for providing instruction in phonics, decoding, comprehension, and vocabulary skills to young learners. These systems generally promise individualized, interactive exercises to promote students' literacy development. These include *The Imagination Station* (istation.com), *Balanced Literacy* (Intellitools), *Lexia Early Reading* (Lexia Learning), *OpenBook to Literacy* (OpenBook Learning), *FOCIS Reading and Language* (PLATO), *STAR Early Literacy* (Renaissance Learning), *Destination Reading* (Riverdeep), *Early Reading Program* (Lightspan), *Orchard Language Arts K–3* (Siboney), and *The Literacy Center* (LeapFrog SchoolHouse).

- **Reference resources** — Electronic dictionaries and thesauruses, discussed in Chapter 5, provide support to students as they learn vocabulary and spelling skills. These handy resources are integrated into most word processing software programs, but more complete, full-featured ones are also available as separate software packages.

- **Electronic devices** — These include battery-operated devices such as Educational Insights' GeoSafari Phonics Pad, which has a collection of phonics games for grades preK–2. Rankin-Erickson, Wood, and Beukelman (2003) describe a computer for first graders that comes equipped with a **talking word processor**, a software package that reads typed words aloud. This type of processor helps them "read" words they did not know, thus supporting their vocabulary acquisition. Intellitools' *IntelliTalk* is one example of this versatile type of resource. Other products, such as Alphasmart's *Dana*, are specifically targeted to young learners to encourage more writing without the expense of desktop or laptop computers.

Creating everyday teacher activities. Through his work with teachers across Georgia, Tennessee, and Kentucky, Grant (see Grant, 2002; Hill, Reeves, Grant, Wang, & Hans, 2005) notes how teachers can quickly develop "everyday activities with everyday applications" using word processors, spreadsheets, and electronic presentations to support small phonics, vocabulary, and other literacy lessons. For example, with whole-class instruction, the teacher can use a word processor with large point sizes to have students demonstrate correct verb tenses, correct conjugations, and plurals. The large point size allows the teacher to see student responses at a distance while monitoring the class. For on-screen reading, the teacher can use the commenting feature to add supplemental instruction on unknown words or difficult passages, such as adding definitions. Spreadsheets likewise can be used as a method to keep up with vocabulary words, definitions, and sentence usages. Finally, electronic presentations can be used by teachers or students to develop flash cards for phonics and vocabulary, including in foreign languages, or early childhood teachers can use the slide sorting feature to mix up the order of a story and have students re-sequence it.

Literacy Development

When teachers look for ways to motivate and support students' literacy development, they usually try to tap into students' own interests, present books in ways that students find compelling, and engage students in "book talks" about authors and stories to help them visualize the people and places in books. Teachers can develop telecollaborative inquiry projects that are meaningful and authentic and that promote higher levels of engagement. The following examples are among those designed by teachers to accomplish these purposes:

- **Networked literacy projects** — Activities like the one in the chapter-opening example use Internet sites to engage students in reading books. Also, Helt (2003) describes the use of online literature circles and pairing students with online mentors to discuss literature as ways to spur students' interest in reading. Classroom teachers may also use story starters, having each student write one sentence, paragraph, line, or stanza and then having him or her email it to the next student, who adds to it.

- **Activities with interactive storybooks (electronic books) and talking books** — As described in Chapter 5, these tools are regular literature books that have been placed into an electronic format, usually on CD, DVD, or an Internet site. They are interactive in several ways. First, they often allow stories and/or language elements (e.g., specific words or phrases) to be read aloud to students. Second, they can let students vary the sequence in which they read parts of stories. Finally, they can be formatted to allow students to choose alternate paths or endings. Doty, Popplewell, and Byers (2001) found that these interactive qualities can result in greater comprehension for students than reading in a static format can.

- **Uses of reading management and intervention programs** — *Accelerated Reader*, a popular system from Renaissance Learning, is among the most studied educational technology tools (Lopez, 2000; Poock, 1998). Most teachers use the system to diagnose students' reading levels, provide books and stories for students to read, and track their comprehension by administering questions on each item they read. Studies have shown it to be successful in motivating students to read; however, a review of these studies refutes these findings, citing that increased access to books and time devoted to reading are what increase students' comprehension, not the system itself (Krashen, 2003). Other reading intervention systems are used widely across the United States, including Scholastic's *Read 180 Program*, which is geared toward older struggling readers in grades 4 through 12 and *Reading Recovery*, which is geared towards struggling first-grade readers.

- **Digital storytelling** — Kajder and Swenson (2004) find that good readers create "a mental movie of images evoked by the story" (p. 18). To support this process, they had students produce a series of digital images to visually communicate meaning and provide a narration for the video. They found that this activity helps make the reading process more visual to students and, therefore, easier to understand. Electronic presentation software that includes narration capabilities (e.g., *PowerPoint*) is another tool for students in practicing oral presentations; it may provide additional practice for struggling readers as well.

- **Connections to online reading materials to engage students** — An often-used strategy that teachers use is to locate books, stories, and Internet sites that match up with students' interests and reading levels. Schmar-

Dobler (2003) cautions us to remember that students first need modeling and instruction on how to read on the Internet. This cannot be overemphasized: Internet users typically do not read on-screen in the same way as they read books or magazines. There is emerging research on the nature of reading comprehension on the Internet or with other ICTs (Coiro, 2003; Coiro, 2006; Leu, 2004) that will help us understand more clearly how reading online differs from reading traditional print text.

The Internet offers a wealth of resources for connecting students and literacy. For example, the International Children's Digital Library (http://www.icdlbooks.org/) has more than 2,000 free online books from which students may select. Naturally, teachers use these resources in numerous ways. Karchmer (2000) shares how one teacher used children's literature to support interdisciplinary instruction. Forbes (2004) talks about web-based bookmarking as an important strategy for creating a list of favorite bookmarks and storing them on the web. This process provides structure and content for elementary students and those with special needs by saving time and providing them access to appropriate web materials.

- **Writing in blogs** — One strategy that is currently increasing in popularity is having students respond to blogs (web logs). Introduced in Chapter 6, blogs are web pages that serve as publicly accessible locations for discussing topics or issues. Students can use these either as personal journals or as public discussion forums for trading opinions and interactions (Oravec, 2002). They can create their own blog by using a blog website, such as Blogger, or they can join a blog initiated by others. Kajder and Bull (2003) found that characteristics of blogs, such as immediate feedback and active participation, are very motivational to struggling students. See Technology Integration Lesson 9.1 for a list of activities they recommend for motivating student writing.

- **Motivating writing with video projects** — Just as Kajder and Swenson (2004) found that creating a narrated video parallels the reading process, Scot and Harding (2004) say that "the process of creating a digital video parallels the writing process" (p. 27). Script writing for their videos becomes an excellent way to get students engaged in written communication. The simplicity and intuitiveness of such video production tools as Apple's *iMovie* and Microsoft's *MovieMaker* allow students to focus on the writing content without having to confront a significant software learning curve.

- **Threaded discussions at a distance** — Finally, many teachers find that having students participate in discussion boards instigates both reading and writing. Especially if the topic is one in which they are already interested, students

Technology Integration Lesson 9.1

Motivating Student Writing

Title: Reading and Writing Ideas with Blogs   **Grade Levels:** All grades
Content Area/Topic: English, writing

 NETS for Students: Standards 1 (Creativity and Innovation), 2 (Communication and Collaboration), 4 (Critical Thinking, Problem Solving, and Decision Making), and 6 (Technology Operations and Concepts)

Description of Standards Applications: Blogs are a popular way to help students engage with text and provide opportunities for an authentic writing experience. This integration lesson offers students the opportunity to use the Internet to develop a blog about authentic topics using various instructional activities. Through the instructional activities, students use their creativity as they communicate and critically think using writing and a blog as their media.

Instruction: Ten instructional activities that make use of blogs are (1) character journals (challenging students to write about a fictional character); (2) character roundtable (several students write to each other as they role-play fictional characters); (3) open minds (drawing an outline of an empty head and "filling it" in the blog space with what the character might be thinking); (4) think-aloud postings (students post reflections and analyses of assigned readings; (5) literature circle group responses (sharing and reflecting on reports of reading assignments); (6) nutshelling (posting "most meaningful" lines from literature and using them as prompts for reflective writing); (7) devil's advocate writing (online debates to explore positions on topics for later writing); (8) exploding sentences (adding descriptive detail to posted sentences); (9) photoblogs (using blogs that incorporate images to annotate and write captions for pictures); and (10) storyblogs (class-constructed stories and essays).

Source: Kajder, S., & Bull, G. (2003). Scaffolding for struggling students: Reading and writing with blogs. *Learning and Leading with Technology, 31* (2), 31–35.

---

want to share their thoughts. Course management systems such as *Moodle* and *Blackboard* can provide class-based discussion boards that teachers set up for students' use in threaded discussions. For example, Scharber (2008) proposes the creation of online book clubs to encourage students to read for pleasure via "talking" to students in their class or in other classes or schools via threaded or synchronous discussions using these course management systems.

 Go to MyEducationLab, select the topic "Language Arts Integration." Go to the "Assignments, Activities, and Applications" section and watch the video, "Wireless Webquests" and complete the activity that follows.

The Process Approach to Writing

In reviewing two decades of research on writing skills, Bruning and Horn (2000) found that teaching writing requires special attention to motivational aspects, including fostering engagement by using authentic writing tasks and providing a supportive context for writing. The mid-1980s saw a new approach to writing instruction that focused on writing as a process, as opposed to writing as a tool for learning, such as note taking or journal writing. With the introduction of word processing software, students gained access to electronic tools that supported this new approach, allowing for the reflection and frequent modification called for in process writing. As discussed in Chapter 4, writing in a word processing environment supports students as they produce and revise text, thus freeing them to focus on generating and sharing ideas. Inherent in the process approach is the need to give and receive feedback from others; thus, writing groups are a necessity.

Fortunately, numerous online resources are available to help teachers conduct process writing (Johnson, 2002). For instance, after working with classroom teachers for 5 years to integrate technology into the curriculum, Linda Labbo (2004) provided guidelines for implementing what she coined the *Author's Computer Chair*. The *Author's Computer Chair* encourages students to discuss the computer-related process of meaning making during all stages of the process. Described next are an array of other technology resources that have emerged to support all stages of the writing process.

Prewriting. Getting started is often one of the most difficult aspects of writing, and young writers find it particularly onerous. During the prewriting stage, teachers communicate to students the format, audience, topic, purpose, and assessment method for the writing assignment. It is critical that teachers model the type of writing expected. For instance, when writing poetry, students find it motivational to see samples from other students or to view unusual or experimental forms of poetry for which word processors can facilitate development: dada, sound poems, optophonetic poems, oulipo, snowballing, iceograms, iterative poetry, and transformations. Internet sites offer rich sources of these examples (e.g., the website of the Academy of American Poets at http://www.poets.org/). During this stage, students also need to organize their thoughts graphically. For instance, if students are writing a fictional story, they need to brainstorm ideas for the story line, setting, and major characters; refine and organize those ideas; and generate a plan for presenting each story element in an intriguing manner. If the assignment is to write a report, then students need to gather information on the topic from a variety of sources; synthesize and arrange this information into categories or subtopics; and generate a plan for presenting the information in a logical way. All types of prewriting activities can be facilitated by using information organizing software such as electronic outlining and concept mapping programs.

- **Electronic outlining** — Electronic outlining is now integrated into almost all major word processing programs and is easily accessible as a planning tool. **Electronic outliners** automatically generate headings and subheadings from typed information. The advantages to using them are that new headings/subheadings can be easily inserted anywhere in the outline, headings/subheadings can be shifted around quickly to reflect a student's thinking and planning, and the prefixes serving as organizational clues are automatically changed to reflect revisions to the outline's organization.

- **Concept mapping software** — Also known as *webbing software*, **concept mapping software** is popular as a prewriting planning tool. It allows students to produce an outline as a visual map (see Figure 9.2). The most popular concept mapping programs are *Kidspiration* for grades K–3 and *Inspiration* for grades 4 and above (Inspiration Software, Inc.), products that have electronic tools for both outlining and diagramming. The diagramming side of the program can be used to create a variety of graphic displays, all of which are useful for students who like to think and plan using visual representations of their ideas. For example, students can easily brainstorm a cluster map of ideas for a story and then rearrange or expand on the

FIGURE 9.2 *Inspiration* **Concept Map for** *To Kill a Mockingbird*

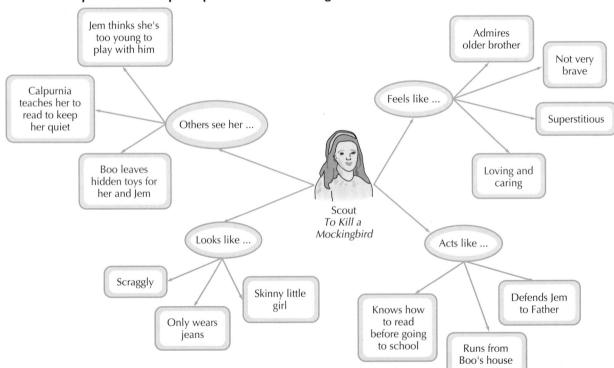

Source: © 2005 Inspiration Software®, Inc. Diagram created in Inspiration® by Inspiration Software, Inc. Used with permission.

Technology has made the tasks of drafting and revising written reports much easier for students ... and teachers.

ideas for later development. Students can also use the program to generate a hierarchical map of key concepts to be explored for a research paper and link those concepts with labels that demonstrate their conceptual relationship. *Inspiration* also has a personal digital assistant (PDA) version to assist students engaged in the trend toward mobile learning.

New strategies to support the prewriting planning process are emerging as new technologies develop. Baumbach, Christopher, Fasimpaur, and Oliver (2004) describe one such strategy: using handhelds as "personal literacy assistants" to aid students with brainstorming, research, and organizing tasks prior to writing.

Drafting. Drafting is the stage of the writing process during which students put ideas and information into words, sentences, and paragraphs. When drafting, the student engages in the act of composing text, a creative act leading to words and sentences that might later be revised or refined. The term *drafting* for this stage implies an impermanence to the product (i.e., a draft), reflecting the notion that students will continue to plan, rethink, and reorganize their ideas, even while producing text. Depending on the availability of equipment, students can either draft directly on the computer using a word processing program or type in their handwritten draft when they reach some level of completion. Electronic note card templates may also assist students—in research and in the transition from research to drafting.

Revising and editing. Revising is the stage during which students make changes in the paper's content or structure that reflect decisions about how to improve its overall quality. To revise well, students have to move from composing

FIGURE 9.3 **Example of Track Changes and Comments Using Microsoft Word**

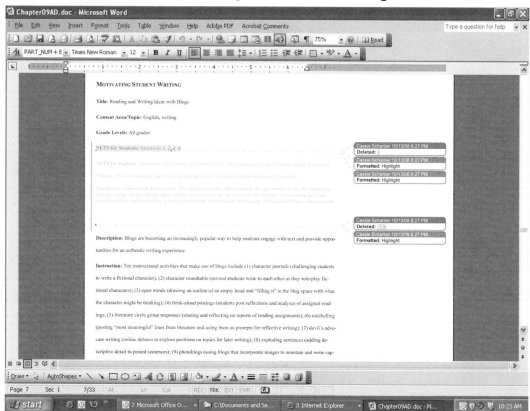

Source: http://www.editorialmanager.com/robohelp/5.0/microsoft_word_track_changes_.htm

text to analyzing it, looking for what needs to be added, deleted, or rearranged. One of the best ways for teachers to assist in this process is to project a student's typed draft onto a screen and then model the thinking and decision making that goes into analyzing and revising the text. If projected from a computer, changes can be made to the text as the students watch. Students consistently report that the writing process is easier when conducted on a computer, and teachers report more and better writing when students use computers (Lowther, Ross, & Morrison, 2003; Russell & Plati, 2000). After teachers model, students revise each other's papers using word processing capabilities such as highlighting in various colors or using the Track Changes feature. Using colors, students can visually identify the thesis sentence, supporting sentences, and transition sentences within a passage. Using Track Changes, students can revise and comment on each other's work with the author having the final say in accepting or ignoring the changes made by others (see Figure 9.3). Editing, as opposed to revising, is the process of refining a paper so that it adheres to standard conventions for spelling, syntax, punctuation, and style. Editing is a far more superficial task than revising but no less important. All word processing programs have features that support the editing process. These include spell checkers and grammar checkers as well as electronic search capabilities to verify consistency of word usage, tone, and tense.

Once again, the teacher can model the editing process, and students can then edit each other's papers.

Publishing. Reports, newspaper articles, brochures, slide shows, and web pages are all publishing formats available to students for sharing their written work with peers, teachers, and the larger community. (See Technology Integration Lesson 9.2 and the chapter-opening example in Chapter 5.) As mentioned earlier in this chapter, publishing writing on the Internet provides students with a wider audience and purpose for their writing (Karchmer, 2001), which increases students' motivation both for writing (Turner & Paris, 1995) and for doing their best work. Teachers can use two types of publishing approaches:

- **Traditional (paper) publishing** — Students produce paper products such as reports, books, newspaper articles, and brochures. Desktop publishing programs are designed to facilitate the production of professional-looking printed products. In the past, there were significant differences between word processing software and the programs used for desktop publishing. As word processing programs have become increasingly sophisticated, however, these distinctions have little significance for most teachers and students. Now, both types of software include features that support layout, design, and high-end graphic manipulation.

Technology Integration Lesson 9.2

Publishing Student Writing

Title: New Millennium Newspapers　　　　**Grade Levels:** 5 through 9
Content Area/Topic: Writing news stories

NETS for Students: Standards 1 (Creativity and Innovation), 2 (Communication and Collaboration), and 6 (Technology Operations and Concepts)

Description of Standards Applications: This integration lesson offers students the opportunity to use web-development software to create a web newspaper about the future. Using their creativity and communications skills, students predict what it will be like in 2030 and beyond.

Instruction: Have students create newspaper-type stories with predictions about the future; then publish these Special Edition stories in a "web newspaper." Some motivating activities to get students writing include creating a sample entertainment newspaper section circa 2030 or writing time capsule predictions about various areas of society in the future—for example, education, fashion, the environment, health, sports, and science.

Source: Reissman, R. (1999). Predicting the future: Students create content for new millennium newspapers. *Learning and Leading with Technology, 27*(2), 18–21.

- **Electronic publishing** — Students can also share their writing in electronic forms such as websites, electronic books, multimedia slide shows, and news broadcasts. Many Internet websites have been set up specifically to allow students to publish their work. Viani (2003– 2004) describes how to set up a site specifically for sharing students' written work in online electronic portfolios, which serve both instructional and assessment purposes. Email and website projects are also a way to connect student writers with distant audiences (Lemkuhl, 2002). Electronic penpal (keypal) projects are growing in popularity and provide creative and authentic opportunities for communication. One handy reference is ePALS Global Community, which connects 4.6 million students and educators in 191 countries. Another example of electronic publishing is to have two or more classrooms work together on a common project, such as a travel brochure or a collection of sayings, stories, or poems.

Interactive Summary

The following is a summary of the main points covered in this chapter.

1. **Issues in English and language arts instruction** — These include:
   - Expanding the definition of literacy
   - Exploring new instructional practices
   - Making decisions on keyboarding instruction
   - Creating social learning environments
   - Working with diverse learners
   - Motivating students
   - Teachers' growth as literacy professionals

2. **Integration strategies for English and language arts** — Strategies for integrating technology into this area include three general areas:
   - Language skills development
   - Literacy development
   - The process writing approach

Key Terms

- concept mapping software
- decoding
- electronic outliner
- new literacy
- QWERTY keyboard
- talking word processor

Web-Enrichment Activities

1. *Digital Storytelling* — Visit the Center for Digital Storytelling at http://www.storycenter.org/index1.html, and watch one of the stories. Refer to the National Standards for English and language arts in Figure 9.1 or online at http://www.ncte.org/about/over/standards/110846.htm. Which of the 12 NCTE standards do you think could be met by using digital storytelling with students?

2. *Software Skill-Builder Tutorials* — Access practical tutorial and skill-building activities, and build your skills using popular software and hardware online. Go to *Kidspiration* (http://www.inspiration.com/popups/kidstutorial/index.cfm), and explore how to use *Kidspiration*. How might you incorporate this program into your instruction?

Go to MyEducationLab to complete the following exercises.

Building Teaching Skills   Select the topic "Language Arts Integration" and go to the "Building Teaching Skills and Dispositions" section. Access the activity "Using Technology in the Writing Process" and complete the activity that follows.

Tutorials   Select the topic "Software" and access one of two practical tutorial and skill-building activities for PowerPoint: "PowerPoint for Mac, Basics" or "PowerPoint for PC." Use the tutorial to learn the basic skills of creating a PowerPoint presentation. This skill will be reviewed again in the Technology Integration Workshop.

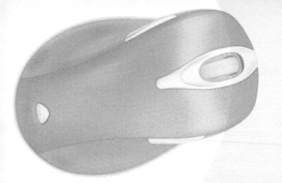

Technology Integration Workshop

The TIP Model in Action

Read each of the following scenarios related to implementing the TIP Model, and answer the questions that follow it based on your Chapter 9 reading and activities.

TIP MODEL SCENARIO #1   Ms. Mirabel has great difficulty getting her students to prepare an outline to plan what they will write for a composition assignment. She has taught them how to do outlines, but they seem unwilling or unable to do them. They have a great deal of trouble organizing information for writing, and she thinks it might be better for them to create a diagram that shows in pictures how concepts are related. She has heard about a software tool that can help them create their outlines more easily and faster.

1.1 What technology resource would help Ms. Mirabel address this problem?

1.2 What would be the relative advantage of using this resource as opposed to others?

1.3 Would it be better to have the students work individually or in groups to do the activity? Explain your answer.

TIP MODEL SCENARIO #2   Mr. Gerard has his class work in small groups to create a short story. As a whole class, they discuss the plot and characters; then each group writes a part of the story. They exchange sections and critique each other's parts. Then they do a final version. After the draft is complete, they post the story on the school's web server, along with stories posted from past classes.

2.1 What would be the relative advantage for Mr. Gerard's students of using word processing for their drafts instead of doing typed or handwritten drafts?

2.2 What would be the relative advantage of posting the story on the Internet when it is completed?

2.3 What outcomes would Mr. Gerard probably want to assess in addition to the quality of the writing in the final product? Suggest a way to carry out this assessment.

TIP MODEL SCENARIO #3   Mr. Norton has noticed that his students write as little as possible, and writing tests show they are badly in need of more practice in this area. He thinks if he can get them to keep weekly journals, it might give them the practice they need to begin improving their written expression.

3.1 What technology resource might provide a motivational environment for students to keep weekly journals?

3.2 If Mr. Norton has only three computers in the room, what are some ways he could manage student access to the resource?

3.3 What kind of assessment might be appropriate for an activity like this?

TIP MODEL SCENARIO #4   Several of Ms. Watts' second-grade students speak English as a second language and have great difficulties with English vocabulary. She wants to give them a fun, motivational way to practice using new vocabulary. Her principal says that he has about $150 to buy some resources to help if she can identify something that would work well.

4.1 What kind of technology resource might be within the budget she has and could help Ms. Watts' students be motivated about the practice they need?

4.2 If Ms. Watts has five students who need help, what would be an effective way to have the students get access to these resources in a way that would not disturb other class members?

4.3 How could Ms. Watts determine if there has been improvement in her students' vocabulary skills?

TIP MODEL SCENARIO #5   Ms. Vignioti's 10th-grade students think poetry is irrelevant and boring. When she asks them to read poems in books and study their forms, they either refuse or do as little as possible. She has heard about an Internet project in which students see poems other students have written, write poems of their own, post them on a shared website, and write critiques of each other's work. She wonders if this might increase students' interest in learning about poetry.

5.1 What might be the relative advantage of using a website project like this?

5.2 How might Ms. Vignioti begin such a project in a way that would capture students' interest?

5.3 How might Ms. Vignioti determine the impact of such a project on students' motivation and knowledge of poetry forms?

TIE into Practice: Technology Integration Examples

The Technology Integration Example that opened this chapter (*Classroom Revolutions*) showed how a teacher might have students use Internet sites to research a novel and report their findings in a *PowerPoint* presentation. Having students use this presentation strategy can be helpful in many kinds of literature projects, ranging from book reports to critical analysis projects. With the knowledge you have gained from Chapter 9, do the following to explore this strategy:

1. Young students can create a *PowerPoint* book report. Having completed a tutorial on the basics of *PowerPoint*, create a sample *PowerPoint* book report.

2. Answer the following questions about the *Classroom Revolutions* example:

   - Phase 1 — How did Ms. Skerritt view her technology, pedagogy, and/or content knowledge? How does her TPACK affect her lesson?

   - Phase 2 — What kinds of relative advantage did Ms. Skerritt feel that Internet use would bring to her students' study of the novel *A Tale of Two Cities?* Why did she choose a *PowerPoint* presentation as the way students would display their findings?

   - Phase 3 — One of the desired outcomes Ms. Skerritt identified for her students was to create a *PowerPoint* presentation on their research findings. Create a rubric she might use to assess this presentation. (*Hint:* Look at Kathy Schrock's Guide for Educators at http://school.discovery.com/schrockguide/assess.html to locate an existing rubric you can modify.)

   - Phase 4 — On days 9 and 10 of the timeline, Ms. Skerritt has students giving their *PowerPoint* presentations. What could she do to make this serve as a review for the test as well as a display of the students' research?

   - Phase 5 — Ms. Kermit uploaded Ms. Skerritt's Bookmark file to the school's network and transferred it to the computer lab so that her stu-

dents could use it. How might she organize this file so that each group had a separate set of Internet sites?

   - Phase 6 — In evaluating the outcomes of the activity, Ms. Skerritt was pleased with the students' learning. Do you have any suggestions on how she could improve this lesson?

3. What NETS for Students skills would students learn by working on the *Classroom Revolutions* project? (See the front of this book for a list of NETS for Students.)

Technology Integration Lesson Planning

Complete the following exercise using sample lesson plans found on MyEducationLab.

1. Locate lesson ideas — MyEducationLab has several examples of lessons that use the integration strategies described in this chapter: generating interest in and support for reading and writing, providing support for learning to write, and computer-supported language skills learning (decoding, comprehension, and vocabulary development). Go to MyEducationLab under the topic "Language Arts Integration" and go to "Lesson Plans" to review example lessons. Choose two of the following integration lessons:

   - All About Me

   - Using Databases, Spreadsheets, and Word Processing to Study Genetics

   - A Class Literary Paper

   - A Cross-Age Collaborative Electronic Book Project

   - Electronic Outlining for Writing and Studying

2. Evaluate the lessons — Use the *Evaluation Checklist for a Technology-Integrated Lesson* (located on MyEducationLab under the topic "Instructional Planning") to evaluate each of these lessons.

3. Modify a lesson — Select one of the lesson ideas, and adapt its strategies to meet a need in your own content area. You may choose to use the same approach as in the original or to adapt it to meet your needs.

4. Add descriptors — Create descriptors for your new lesson similar to those found within the sample lessons (e.g., grade level, content and topic areas, technologies used, relative advantage, objectives, NETS standards).

5. Save your new lesson — Save your modified lesson with all its descriptors.

For Your Teaching Portfolio

For this chapter's contribution to your teaching portfolio, add the following products you created in the Technology Integration Workshop:

- The sample *PowerPoint* book report you created
- The evaluations you did using the *Evaluation Checklist for a Technology-Integrated Lesson*
- The new lesson plan you developed, based on the one you found on MyEducationLab.

Chapter 10
Technology in Foreign and Second Language Instruction

One challenge for language teachers is to shape students' computer using experiences into language learning experiences.

Carol A. Chapelle (2001, p. 2)

The proliferation of authentic texts on the Web is far from enough to guarantee that language learners can profitably delve into texts they have located to help them in their language acquisition.

Robert Godwin-Jones (2007, p. 8)

Technology Integration Example

A Discussion Board en Français

Based on: DeLuca, A., and Hoffman, B. (2003). Vamos a darles algo a discutir (Let's give 'em something to talk about). *Learning and Leading with Technology, 30*(5), 36–41.

Grade Levels: 9 through 12 • Content Area/Topic: French, Art • Length of Time: One semester

Phases 1 and 2: Assess technological pedagogical content knowledge; Determine relative advantage

The French teachers at Sabine High School agreed that their students needed more practice writing in French. They had tried various kinds of writing assignments, but students always seemed to do the minimum required, and their fluency in writing the language remained low. The teachers agreed that students would be more motivated if assignments had greater purpose and a real audience. While visiting another school, one of the teachers saw a project for Spanish language students that seemed to fulfill all of these requirements. The teachers at that school held a Spanish art identification contest using an asynchronous online discussion board. They posted images of Spanish art, and students had to identify the pieces and discuss and describe the art *en Español* on the discussion board. Students who were the first to do these tasks earned points, and students who accumulated the most points won recognition and prizes. The Spanish teachers said that the strategy worked well for students learning English as well. Also, the project exposed students to some important artwork from the Spanish-speaking countries the students were learning about. Because their school had a Blackboard® online course management system that all teachers and students could use via the Internet from any location, the French teachers decided to implement the project using discussion forums on that system.

The Spanish art identification project motivated the teachers to see how a lesson like this might fit into their classrooms. However, the teachers wondered if they had the knowledge to move forward with such a project. They had been exposed to the concept of technological pedagogical content knowledge (TPACK) at a recent workshop and decided to use the TPACK framework to reflect on where they would locate themselves within the model. They wanted to reflect on the model and see what area(s) of their knowledge might need to be enhanced before moving forward with the project.

Phase 3: Decide on objectives and assessments

The French teachers wanted to make sure the expectations for the project were clear to students and teachers alike, so they agreed on the following objectives and assessment methods to measure students' performance:

- **Objective:** All students access each of the forums and post all of the required descriptions. **Assessment:** A checklist of items students were required to post about each artwork, with points for each posting and extra points for being first or second to identify and describe the artwork.

- **Objective:** All students will demonstrate improved writing in French by achieving a 90% rubric score. **Assessment:** A rubric to assess the quality and quantity of students' descriptive writing in French

- **Objective:** Each student must score at least 80% on a short-answer test on art from French-speaking countries. **Assessment:** A test consisting of questions on the art represented in the forums.

Phase 4: Design integration strategies

The teachers knew that it would take some time to review students' French language skills, prepare content and procedures for the forums, and get students used to working with them. They designed the following sequence of activities to prepare for and carry out the project:

- **August–December:** Prepare artwork graphics to place on the forums and do administrative tasks to use online forums. Develop students' descriptive vocabulary related to art (e.g., *nature morte, paysage, croquis, aquarelle, gravure, toile*) and language to express their opinions about art (e.g., *J'aime vraiment cette peinture à l'huile*). Develop students' knowledge about the French-speaking countries and cultures from which the art originates.

- **January:** Introduce the Blackboard environment and the art identification tasks. Assign the first forum as a practice to iron out any logistical problems. Review the items students are required to post about each artwork, and review assessment strategies. Point out to the students that they can see each other's postings and choose to complete the assignment requirements in the context of a reply to a classmate.

- **February–April:** Introduce one online forum for credit each month. Assess each, and review the answers to the forum at the end of the month.

- **May:** Review points won, recognize students, and award prizes.

Phase 5: Prepare the instructional environment

The teachers knew that setting up the activity would require some concerted effort the first time they did it, so they divided the following tasks among themselves to lessen the load on each of them:

- **Setting up forums:** Teachers obtained the required information about how to create discussion forums and set up one forum for each month. Each student needed to have a unique sign-on, so they made a list of students, created usernames and passwords for them, and entered them into the system.

- **Preparing content for assignments:** Teachers selected a set of paintings and sculptures for each forum, making sure they represented various French-speaking countries and cultures they had studied. For each forum, they wrote a set of questions to be answered about the pieces of art.

- **Preparing assessments and handouts:** Teachers created the checklists and rubrics they would use to assess student progress. They also prepared a handout describing the project and giving the URLs for accessing the system.

- **Ensuring student access:** Teachers had already confirmed that most students had Internet access at home. However, to make sure everyone had adequate time and access whenever they wanted it (so they all had equal chance to be first with the correct answers), the teachers designated times in their classrooms and in the language lab when students could get online.

Phase 6: Evaluate and revise

Teachers observed that students posted increasingly faster for each forum and that most wrote more sentences each time. By having a clear purpose for writing that allowed for student choice, the project helped develop students' writing skills. Furthermore, the teachers noticed that there was more interaction between students with each successive forum, which speaks to the benefits of having an interested audience when writing in a foreign language, even if this audience includes students' classmates and other classes in the school. The test on students' knowledge of art and culture showed that students had learned a lot about art from the countries they were studying. When the teachers interviewed the students, it was apparent that all were enthusiastic about the project, with a few exceptions. Some students had no Internet access at home or had to share access with family members. They felt it was unfair that others had more opportunities to look up and post answers. The teachers decided to designate more time in each forum for lab work so that all students would have the access they needed. Students also suggested that the competition be by class instead of across classes, giving more students opportunities for winning awards. The teachers decided that the project had worked so well that they would expand it to include musical works by French-speaking musicians next time.

Objectives

After reading this chapter and completing the learning activities for it, you should be able to:

1. Identify current issues in second and foreign language learning that may inform the selection and use of technology.

2. Describe key strategies for integrating technology into second and foreign language curricula.

3. Identify example software and web resources required to carry out a range of technology integration strategies.

4. Create activities for language instruction that model successful integration strategies.

What Does TPACK Look Like in Second and Foreign Language Instruction?

Questions that many teachers consider with regard to technological pedagogical content knowledge (TPACK) include "How does this relate to me?" and "What are the implications of knowing about TPACK in my content area?" TPACK in any discipline is the perfect union of three knowledge domains: content, pedagogy, and technology to develop a knowledge base from which a teacher can view a lesson and understand how technology can enhance the learning opportunities and experiences for students while also knowing the correct pedagogy to enhance the learning of the content. In second and foreign language instruction, a teacher is incorporating the TPACK principles when he or she plans a lesson and, without hesitation, thinks about not only the content as it relates to student achievement and motivation, but also about the pedagogy and technology needed to allow for student achievement and motivation. The teacher thinks about this marriage of knowledge domains where technology is not an add-on but a unified part. For example, when teaching students about the context in which a language is used within a society, instead of simply lecturing about a country, the social norms, and common phrases one might need to be successful in a situation, teachers using their TPACK think about the lesson goals with not only the content goals and the pedagogy in mind, but also the technology. They immediately think about using technology in unison with the pedagogy and content to assist students in experiencing an authentic environment. This means teachers may use an adventure learning approach in their classroom that gives students the opportunity to discuss, share, and interact with students from cultures around the world. It also may involve having students go to the foreign language lab, where they practice their conversational skills as they watch authentic situations online. (See Figure 10.1.)

Problems of Practice in Second and Foreign Language Instruction

In an English-speaking environment, English is the *second or additional* language for a language learner. When the target language, or language of study, is spoken mainly in other countries, it is referred to as a **foreign language (FL)**. While the underlying processes of learning ESL and a FL are similar, there are also many differences relevant to teaching and technology integration strategies. Key differences are the availability of the language input in the environment and opportunities for using the language in meaningful situations. **English language learners** have much exposure to and opportunities for speaking the language they are learning because they are learning a majority language. They also have urgency to learn the language quickly because they need English for everyday, employment, and educational purposes. Conversely, FL learners typically have fewer opportunities to practice the foreign language, and teachers often go to great lengths to find people and places with whom and where their students can use the target language. FL learning is different than **English as a second language (ESL)** in that it is often seen as enrichment rather than a matter of crucial importance for academic success. Both ESL and FL learning contexts are discussed in this section, along with how technology can address the key problems of practice in each setting.

Common Problems in ESL Teaching and Learning

Developing academic language and background knowledge. A common goal among K–12 ESL teachers is to develop their students' academic language and background knowledge sufficiently for them to participate in mainstream classes. This goal is often challenging because typical grade-level content materials are usually above the proficiency levels of ESL students. Technology offers some helpful solutions to this problem. For example, a high school English language learner who has a low level of proficiency but much knowledge of current events can

FIGURE 10.1   TPACK and Foreign Languages/ESL

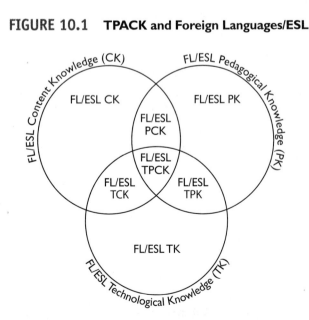

make use of the multimedia available on the websites of newspapers such as the *New York Times* or the *Washington Post*, magazines from across the spectrum of pop culture such as *Sports Illustrated* or *People*, or television stations like ESPN and CNN. On these websites, students can look at photos with short captions, listen to podcasts, and watch videos on topics of their choice. Learning to use this tool affords learners with lower levels of proficiency access to authentic, high-level information on high-interest, current topics and reduces the reading load by offering short captions and high-quality visuals. Initially, students may need guidance in navigating websites such as these. They need to learn what the icons mean, how to use the headings, and how to recognize the key vocabulary words—that is, to acquire the basic media literacy needed to benefit from the tools.

It is often helpful for English language learners to read text designed for native English speakers who are younger than they are, if the materials are not too childish and the task assigned is age-appropriate (e.g., compare and contrast three versions of the Cinderella story through literary and cultural lenses). One useful resource for finding books with relevant academic and cultural content for English language learners is the International Children's Digital Library, a searchable, multilingual children's library. The listed books are appropriate for children from 3 to 13 years of age, but they may also work well for older English language learners, particularly the nonfiction books. There are also many websites that have simplified language and interesting pictures and visuals, such as Desert USA, Whale Times, Discovery, and National Geographic. Theme-based ESL instruction that uses interesting content such as that found on these websites promotes recycling of academic vocabulary and provides exposure to the differing discourses of the academic disciplines that English language learners will be confronted with. For an example of how one middle school ESL teacher achieved sustained content-based instruction, see Bigelow, Ranney, and Hebble (2005).

Differentiating instruction. In many ESL settings, teachers need to deliver instruction across a wide range of proficiency levels. Unlike FL classes, ESL teachers cannot assume their classes have been divided according to proficiency level. Older English language learners come with a range of print literacy skills in English and their native language as well as a wide range of prior formal schooling experiences. It is common at the elementary level to collaborate with a grade-level teacher to deliver ESL services; at the upper levels, students of different needs are of-

Today's classrooms serve as an example of the country's "melting pot." Therefore, teachers have to be prepared for the diverse learning needs of their students.

ten served in stand-alone classes, sheltered content classes, and ESL classes. Technology can help the teacher differentiate instruction through software programs that assist in tracking individual students and can offer ways for students to work independently on developing their reading, writing, speaking, and listening skills. Oral and written language practice programs can offer individuals simulated authentic practice while the teacher is working with other students. With the new multimedia programs that include actual spoken models, ESL students can use the computer to help them practice their oral English language production. In addition, grammar check programs allow students to receive instant feedback on their use of vocabulary and verb tenses as they practice their written English.

Integrating the students' native languages. Efforts to prepare students for mainstream classes in English often require building background knowledge in the content area so that when they are confronted with grade-level content instruction, students have a knowledge base upon which to acquire new knowledge. One of the easiest ways to do this is to use students' native languages. Based on Cummins' Linguistic Interdependence Hypothesis (1979), use of students' native languages also serves to build students' skills in their native languages, which in turn facilitates skills in English. An additional benefit of using the students' native languages to help them gain access to grade-level content is that they come to see that their native languages are valued as a resource at school. This practice creates a more welcoming learning environment for immigrant children and youth (Goldstein, 2003).

Translation Tools

Machine translation tools, when used appropriately, can be a valuable learning and productivity aid. For students learning a second language, language translation tools are helpful for exploring new words and phrases. For students whose first language is not English, language tools are often helpful for converting information in order to help them make sense of the topic when they do not know specific English words. Among the most common free language translation tools on the web are these:

- Babel Fish (http://babelfish.yahoo.com/)
- Free Translator (http://www.free-translator.com)
- Free Translation (http://www.freetranslation.com)
- World Lingo (http://www.worldlingo.com)

In addition, the Google search engine site provides an array of language tools (http://www.google.com/language_tools? hl=en) that can be used for translating text or web pages, and it offers options for presenting the Google interface in a student's native language or accessing a Google search engine in the student's native language.

Technology can assist teachers in using the students' native languages even when the student speaks a less common native language. Many new programs allow teachers to use a vocabulary list specific to future lessons to help prepare students to be more successful in participating in grade-level and content classrooms with few accommodations. Machine translation tools, when used appropriately, can be helpful to teachers and students. Teachers can look up key content words in the students' native languages or translate some simple instructions on a project. For students, the tools function like bilingual dictionaries and help them unlock the meaning of a text both at the word level and the phrase level. Yahoo's *Babel Fish* is one among many of these tools. Google's *Language Tools* search engine site provides an array of language tools that can be used for translating text or web pages, and it offers options for presenting the Google interface in languages other than English. The main limitation of these tools is that they offer translations only in common foreign languages (e.g., French, Spanish, Chinese, Korean), not those of many of our more recent arrivals (e.g., Hmong, Somali, Vietnamese).

There are, however, other ways to bring students' native languages into the ESL class—through electronic newspapers from around the world. It is possible to access newspapers in most languages found among English language learners on the Internet, as long as the computer is set up to read the fonts used in languages that do not use the Roman alphabet. Students can read about many topics relevant to their classes in newspapers in their native language.

Common Problems in Foreign Language Programs

Authentic materials, authentic perspectives. It is common for FL teachers to be nonnative speakers of the language they teach. It is also common for FL teachers—native or nonnative—to have infrequent opportunities to spend extended periods of time in countries where their FL is spoken. Therefore, there is a need to find ways to expose students to both a range of native speakers of the FL, including varieties of the language not spoken by the teacher and to up-to-date examples of how the language is currently used. By bringing these components into a FL curriculum on a regular basis, technology makes it possible for students to experience the cultural, political, and individual perspectives of those who speak the language of study. An increase in authentic perspectives and materials designed for native speakers of the language taps into high-quality teaching of culture using the standards set forth by the American Council on the Teaching of Foreign Languages (National Standards in Foreign Language Education Project, 1999). The standards integrate (1) *perspectives* (e.g., status symbols in Chinese cultures), (2) *products* (e.g., Mexican murals, *Fons Bandusiae*, French hop-hop music), and (3) *practices* (e.g., Tag der Deutchen Einheit) to teach culture. When all three components are integrated into a FL curriculum, they work together to deepen students' cultural competence synergistically. Technology can bring insider voices and authentic materials into the FL classroom to teach culture through perspectives, products, and practices.

One common way to make efficient use of websites in FL classes is with Trakstar.com. This tool for **web-based language learning (WBLL)** allows teachers to expedite students' navigation time to relevant websites and to focus their attention on specific tasks. Jessica Lee, for example, a high school Spanish teacher in Minnesota, has used Trakstar as part of her website for her Spanish I students, to teach them about Mexican holidays such as *El Día de los Muertos* and *Cinco de Mayo*. Jessica identified pertinent websites and resources for her students prior to teaching the units about the Mexican holidays. She annotated each of the sites and organized them, so her students didn't have to take the time to do those steps. The results were that students were more efficient, productive, and motivated.

Creating audience and purpose. Another common problem related to practice opportunities for FL teachers and their students is creating a broader repertoire of individuals to talk with and audiences that wish to read their writing. Silva and Brice (2004), citing Leki (2001), claim that "the greatest ideological challenge . . . is the question of the purpose of FL writing instruction" (p. 80). Technology can assist with the dilemmas of who FL students will communicate with and why. With online video and audio conferencing tools (e.g., *iChat*, *Skype*), students are now able to talk with peers in other countries and interact with presenters who visit their class via these inexpensive online tools. Blogging functions on most class websites also offer more purposes to write to classmates or students in other classes about collaborative projects or reviews of movies or music. *Moodle*, a common open-source course management tool available online to teachers, has collaborative writing tools such as wikis. *Google Docs* offers options for students to create documents with each other or with native speakers anywhere in the world. These technology tools create opportunities for **distributed language learning (DLL)**, in which students learn together and work toward common purposes, with possibilities for negotiating form and meaning as they progress. Online publishing offers students an audience beyond their teachers and can give students an incentive to revise their work. There is a wide array of opportunities for sharing student writing with new audiences. Amphitheater Public Schools in Tucson, Arizona, compiled a helpful list of such opportunities and posted it online at http://www.amphi.com/~pgreenle/EEI/studentpublish.html.

Technology Integration Strategies for ESL and Foreign Language Instruction

One of the most important things students can take away from a language class is the ability and confidence to use the language in everyday interactions with speakers of the language. **Computer-assisted language learning (CALL)** has made great strides in offering students new ways to enhance their speaking and listening skills. There are now a variety of technology-based tools available to support both ESL and foreign language

learners in and out of class. These strategies include support for authentic oral language practice, language sub-skill practice, presentations, text production, virtual field trip immersion experiences, virtual collaborations, and productivity and lesson design support for teachers. Also essential is the capability of teachers to assess oral language skill development in more systematic ways. Technology can take assessment of oral language skills beyond casual monitoring of group work, in-class presentations, and sporadic oral language proficiency tests given by the teacher. See a summary of these strategies and the resources to support them in Table 10.1. See also the *Top Ten* feature for additional strategies on developing the full range of language skills.

Go to MyEducationLab, select the topic "Foreign Language Integration." Go to the "Assignments, Activities, and Applications" section and watch the video, "Tablet Computers in Spanish" and complete the activity that follows.

Support for Authentic Oral Language Practice and Assessment

Resources to support strategies for oral language practice and assessment include the following:

• **Multimedia software and interactive storybooks** — These technologies are designed to support language acquisition and vocabulary development and have several strengths. First, these programs allow teachers to individualize instruction per the students' differing language levels. Second, they give students an opportunity to interact in English authentically in a less stressful environment as compared to a face-to-face environment. Interactive books are a good example of using technology in this manner. These books appear on the screen, and the student can set the program to read the book aloud as he or she follows along, giving the reader the chance to see the word and the illustrations and to hear the words pronounced. The reader can opt to read the story unaided, touching a word with a stylus when a prompt is needed. Many of these programs have additional learning games attached, using the vocabulary and illustrations from the storybook. LeapFrog SchoolHouse has a variety of these books available.

LeapFrog also has programs available in French and Spanish, and another that gives support in five languages, including Lao and Hmong. LeapFrog SchoolHouse's *Language First!*™ program is suitable for grades K–5 and provides 36 theme-based interactive books written at four language development levels. Scholastic has a number of

TABLE 10.1   Summary of Technology Integration Strategies for ELL and Foreign Language Instruction

Technology Integration Strategies	Benefits	Sample Resources and Activities
Support for authentic oral and written practice	• Helps individualize instruction for students' differing language levels. • Helps students internalize word meanings and gives additional practice in using the new words. • Gives practice in following oral English direction and reading and responding in written English. • Builds listening competence.	• *Language First* and other interactive resources from LeapFrog SchoolHouse. http://www.leapfrogschoolhouse.com • Interactive storybooks at BAB Books http://www.sundhagen.com/babbooks • Randall's ESL Cyber Listening Lab http://www.as-lab.com/ • Internet Picture Dictionaries http://www.Enchantedlearning.com/Dictionary.html
Support for practice in language subskills	• Provides intense practice in specific language skills and vocabulary sets. • Corrects common errors being made by students. • Incorporates vocabulary currently being studied in class.	• Practice programs: Rosetta Stone Software (http://www.rosettastone.com/schools) and Transparent Language Software (http://www.shoptransparent.com/) • Idioms and slang http://www.stuff.co.uk/phrasal.htm
Presentation aids	• Helps reduce students stress and focus their presentations. • Teaches valuable skills in making effective presentations. • Makes classroom presentations more understandable and interesting.	• See presentation aids available from the Telus Learning Connection http://www.2learn.ca • Digital cameras and scanners.
Support for text production	• Supports authentic use of language in creating journals, oral reports, and research projects. • Supports correct usage with grammar checks, correct spelling, and style.	• Foreign language word processing and other tools at Translation.net http://www.translation.net • Internet Picture Dictionaries http://www.pdictionary.com
Virtual field trips for modified language immersion experience	• Offers expanded opportunities for language acquisition. • Allows students to "visit" locations and have experiences that wouldn't be available to them otherwise.	• Tramline field trips http://www.tramline.com • The Virtual Geography Department at the University of Wisconsin http://www.trwsp.edu/geo/projects/virtdept/vft.html
Virtual collaborations	• Helps motivate students to use new language skills. • Helps students learn more about the diversity of their own country than they would from textbooks.	See online collaborative projects to join at • The Global School House http://www.globalschoolnet.org • IEARN http://www.iearn.org/projects
Productivity and lesson design support for teachers	• Saves teacher time in locating and preparing lesson ideas and materials.	• ESL.net http://www.esl.net • The ESL Internet Group http://www.esl-group.com/tres.html • Telus Learning Connection http://www.2learn.ca • Ohio University site: http://www.ohiou.edu/esl/english/vocabulary.html • Integrating ESL into the curriculum http://www.teach-nology.com/tutorials/teaching/esl/

titles available in interactive storybook format, including the Clifford books. Many of these interactive book programs emphasize vocabulary games to help students internalize word meanings and to give additional practice in using the new words encountered in the storybooks. Links to these and other interactive storybook resources are listed in Table 10.1.

- **Learning games on handheld computers** — LeapFrog also has learning games appropriate for older language learners. Its series of handheld computers is designed to give elementary, middle, and high school students practice in math, science, social studies, and languages using content from the most common textbooks across the country. (See Figure 10.2.) Students should always be invited to share what they are learning and ask questions after working independently.

- **Language labs** — These have long been a mainstay in ESL and FL instruction. In the 1960s and 1970s, these labs consisted of audiotapes that students listened to and imitated. Since then, we have learned much about the importance of communication, authentic practice, monitoring, and feedback. Language labs look very different these days. Students now have headphones so they can hear themselves and self-monitor their oral production. The new language labs provide students with a recorder, video monitor, and/or a computer in each individual station, and activities are much more interactive. Activities such as recorded dialog journals, in which students speak about an assigned topic or a topic of their choice, give the teacher an opportunity for monitoring, feedback, and authentic verbal interaction. Listening instruction can be built into the lab setting by having students listen to oral instructions while building a project such as a paper airplane, Lego construction, or origami figure.

Additional resources for building listening competence can be found at Randall's Cyber Listening Lab. This site provides short (1- to 3-minute) and long

Language labs offer students the opportunity to practice foreign language skills.

(5- to 10-minute) listening exercises with *RealAudio*, a downloadable player available from www.real.com/.

- **Radio broadcasts** — For more advanced students, National Public Radio (www.npr.org) offers live radio broadcasts on the Internet that provide both news and drama from which teachers can create motivational activities to give the learner practice in oral and written language.

- **Podcasts** — Teachers can now create their own podcasts for listening instruction and practice, but an even more innovative use for podcasts is assessment. Using *Audacity* or another free software tool, teachers can gather oral language samples from students. This use of podcasts gives teachers greater ease in assessing students' individual speaking skills, using a rubric or checklist they design specifically for the task. These digital files can be stored in an online portfolio to assess progress over time and for students' reflection on their own progress.

FIGURE 10.2 **Leapster Handheld Personal Learning Tools (PLTs)**

Source: Courtesy of LeapFrog Enterprises, Inc.

Support for Practice in Language Subskills

Technology can be very useful in providing intense practice in specific language skills and vocabulary sets. Websites such as *English Zone, ESP Bears,* and *Tower of English* provide in-depth practice in areas that often give students great difficulty. For FL teachers, websites exist where students can practice speaking and writing the language. Pinyin Practice, for example, offers Chinese tones online. Dartmouth University's *Kanji Practice* offers an opportunity to practice reading and writing Japanese kanji. Students can even do traditional Spanish grammar drills, but in a new and engaging way (www.columbia.edu/~fms5).

Top Ten

Strategies for Technology in ELL/ Foreign Language Instruction

Take advantage of these ten powerful strategies for using technology to enhance the teaching of both English and foreign languages.

1. **Images downloaded from the Internet help illustrate language concepts** — Illustrations help students learning to use English understand content and offer FL students opportunities set in places where the target language is spoken to discuss, describe, and speculate about what they see.

2. **Interactive storybooks support language acquisition** — Students can strengthen their language skills by hearing the language read to them.

3. **Interactive software and handheld devices provide language skills practice** — Students use these resources to get individual, private feedback as they practice their language skills.

4. **Presentation aids help scaffold students' language use** — The visual formats of presentation software and videos help students demonstrate their range of language skills in nontraditional, collaborative, and engaging ways.

5. **Websites offer exercises for students to practice subskills** — Online exercises are easy to access and provide intense practice in specific language skills and vocabulary sets.

6. **Virtual collaborations provide authentic practice** — Students who work with native speakers of the target language gain both valuable language learning opportunities and intercultural insights.

7. **Virtual field trips provide simulated experiences** — Students see people and places in locations they could not visit otherwise.

8. **Word processing** — Students are able to check spelling and grammar as they practice writing in the target language.

9. **Language labs support language acquisition** — Students get personal instruction with monitoring, feedback, and authentic verbal interaction.

10. **Web-based, authentic content** — Websites designed for native speakers of the target language can offer students written and oral text on topics of interest in the target language and in the students' native language(s).

One value of these types of websites is that the exercises provide models of activities that can be used by teachers to create similar activities to correct common errors being made by the students or to incorporate vocabulary currently being studied in class. Whenever possible, teachers should have students read exercises aloud after completing them to promote the connection between written and oral modalities. This practice promotes balanced skill development.

Presentation Aids

When students are asked to give oral presentations, they can use *PowerPoint* or *Keynote* software or homemade videos to assist them. Visuals, in addition to supporting the concepts being presented, help students using them learn valuable skills in making effective presentations. Visuals also help reduce students' stress and focus their presentations.

The Telus Learning Connection sponsors a website that gives both teachers and students the support they need to make and use technology in presentations. (See Figure 10.3.) Under the Educators Resources section, use the pull-down menu of Our Tools and then Teacher Tools to find many ideas and supports for presentations. This section covers a wide range of application tools, from videoconferencing tools to web development tools to multimedia tools.

In addition to the websites and programs available for creating good oral presentations, digital cameras and scanners can also help create visuals to make the presentations more

Several companies offer software that students can use to practice language skills and vocabulary. Two such providers of these materials are Transparent Software and Rosetta Stone (pictured).

Source: Courtesy of Rosetta Stone Ltd.

FIGURE 10.3 **A Resource Website for Teacher Presentation Tools**

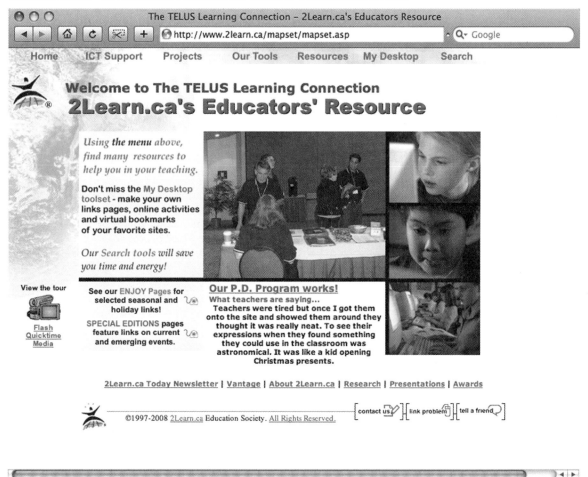

Source: Courtesy of 2Learn.ca Education Society, Edmonton, Alberta, Canada.

understandable and interesting. Scanned or digital pictures can easily be imported into *PowerPoint* or *Keynote* slides and are very effective in supporting student learning. Many teachers of English learners have found it vital to create a file of images for use in their instruction. The slides can be alphabetized, grouped by topic, or organized in any other way that makes them accessible. The Internet serves as a valuable resource for photographs and other images to add to presentations.

Support for Text Production

It is important throughout the process of acquiring a language, no matter which one, that students have multiple opportunities to listen, speak, read, and write using the language. Word processing programs are available in many languages: French, Spanish, Russian—even Chinese. In addition to the authentic use of language in creating journals, descriptions of experiences, oral reports, and research projects, word processing programs support correct usage with grammar checks, correct spelling (spell checks), and reminders to employ good style (e.g., use active rather than passive voice). (See Technology Integration Lesson 10.1 for a sample classroom strategy.) Spell checks and grammar checks are not foolproof, however. Students should always be encouraged to read their writing aloud and to listen for clues that corrections or refinements should be made.

A valuable addition to the writing process is inviting student authors to read their writing aloud to a small group or developing an audio file with a program like *Audacity* to be posted online while structuring opportunities for questions and comments. These processes provide

Technology Integration Lesson 10.1

Support for Text Production

Title: Word Processing in Early Foreign Language Learning

Grade Levels: 7 and 8

Content Area/Topic: ELL writing, foreign language learning

NETS for Students: Standards 1 (Creativity and Innovation), 2 (Communication and Collaboration), 3 (Research and Information Fluency), and 6 (Technology Operations and Concepts)

Description of Standards Applications: This integration lesson offers students the opportunity to use word processing software to develop their writing skills through the creation of an autobiography. Students identify the information they would like to include in an autobiography by interviewing family members and reflecting on their personal lives. They use either word processing or desktop publishing software to write an autobiography to be shared with their peers.

Beginning language students need the practice of writing simple compositions in the language they are studying. Yet students who have limited vocabulary and grammar mastery frequently find it difficult and tedious to accomplish this practice. Word processing lets students make corrections more quickly, and combining their writing with graphics makes the activity more exciting and helps them convey complex thoughts they are not yet able to express.

Instruction: One such writing skills activity is student autobiographies, in which students develop self-portraits using images and their own written text. Students are asked to incorporate items such as name, age, birthday, family members, grandparents and their nationalities, friends, activities they like to do on weekends, religion, favorite TV programs, foods they like to eat, favorite sports, places they have visited, remarks about their school, and languages they speak.

Assessment: Rubric to assess self-portrait.

Source: Lewis, P. (1997). Using productivity software for beginning language learning. *Learning and Leading with Technology, 24*(8), 14–17.

opportunities for oral English practice and listening practice while also giving authors some ideas for revisions. The use of word processors allows the student-author to revise easily without rewriting by hand. The finished, printed copy of the text is also very motivational to the writer because it is highly readable and without penmanship issues.

The presentation and publication programs discussed offer a helpful addition to the production of text across age levels. These programs allow the author to add illustrations, charts, and possibly audio or video text to their projects to make them even more interesting.

Virtual Field Trips for Modified Language Immersion Experience

Field trips provide a wealth of opportunities for language acquisition but are being greatly limited by funding. A good use of technology is the "virtual field trip," in which the teacher or a member of the class takes a field trip, videotapes it, and records running commentary. The narrator strives to make sure that there is a good match between what is being viewed and what is being said. Virtual field trips provide opportunities for students to go places that would be impossible for them to see other-

wise. There are also professionally produced field trips. For example, many of the world's outstanding art museums have virtual tours that can be viewed online. Virtual Tours (http://www.virtualfreesites.com/tours.html) offers a directory of more than 300 virtual free sites, including tours of museums, exhibits, and points of interest around the world. Other examples of virtual tours include:

- GoNorth! — Adventure Learning Series (http://www. polarhusky.com)
- Visible Body — Virtual dissections (http://www. accessexcellence.org/RC/virtual.php)
- Vicki Blackwell's Internet Guide for Educators — A library of the best virtual field trips (http://www. vickiblackwell.com/vft.html).

See Technology Integration Lesson 10.2 for a strategy based on the virtual tour concept.

As with any field trip, students should be prepared ahead of time for their experience, building background knowledge, vocabulary, and expectations. The virtual field trip should be followed with activities that encourage students to use their experiences to practice their oral and written language. Some virtual field trips, such as those that use the adventure learning frame-

Technology Integration Lesson 10.2

Virtual Field Trips for Modified Language Immersion Experiences

Title: Cyber Traveling in the Loire Valley   **Grade Levels:** 5 and 6
Content Area/Topic: French

NETS for Students: Standards 1 (Creativity and Innovation), 2 (Communication and Collaboration), 3 (Research and Information Fluency), and 6 (Technology Operations and Concepts)

Description of Standards Applications: This integration lesson offers students the opportunity to participate in a virtual field trip as they use word processing software and possibly a web development tool to present their research on a *château* in France. Students practice their French language skills by taking a virtual trip to the Loire Valley region of France and writing in French about their findings.

Instruction: Students are asked to prepare a written report on a *château* of their choice, writing (*en français*) facts about it such as when it was built, who built it, the architectural style, its history, its location, and when you can visit it. They can compose the project in *Microsoft Word* or *Google Docs*. When they are done writing, students can create web pages to publish and share their work using *Google Pages*.

Assessment: Rubric to assess web page information.

Source: Chenuau, J. (2000). Cyber traveling through the Loire Valley. *Learning and Leading with Technology, 28*(2), 22–27.

Making the Case for Technology Integration

Use the following questions to reflect on issues in technology integration and to guide discussions within your class.

1. Are virtual trips to foreign countries and virtual conversations with citizens of those countries as good as actually going there or speaking directly to people? If not, what are the differences, and what could teachers do (or not do) to make up for them?

2. Online projects can link students of different backgrounds and allow them to learn more about people of other cultures without meeting them in person. Learning about people in this way presents unique benefits and problems. Can you think of some of each? What are some ways to implement online strategies that maximize the benefits and minimize the problems?

work (Doering, 2006; Doering, 2007) also have complete curricula that support the real-time authentic learning adventure.

Virtual Collaborations

Many teachers have found student collaborations via email to be effective in motivating students to use new language skills (Ybarra & Green, 2003). Using email and numerous other collaborative activities via the Internet, students can work with students of numerous cultures to provide authentic writing and research experiences. These collaborations often start because two teachers establish email connection and begin an exchange of email messages between their students. See sites such as the Global SchoolHouse for help on establishing contacts with distant students (see the links in Table 10.1).

Productivity and Lesson Design Support for Teachers

The Internet holds a wealth of resources to help ESL and FL teachers prepare for and carry out lessons. Some of these are listed in Table 10.1. Projects and programs in ESL and FL instruction are evaluated and discussed at ESL.net. The Intercultural Development Research Association offers a number of teaching resources and professional development opportunities. Many ESL teacher resources and free downloads are available at the ESL Internet Group site. The Telus Learning Connection website also provides a format in which teachers can network and share ideas and concerns. For FL teachers, a wealth of lesson and unit ideas can be found across the Internet on sites hosted by commercial and private groups; university programs are also available at locations such as the Content-Based Language Teaching through Technology (CoBaLTT) website (http://www.carla.umn.edu/cobaltt/).

Interactive Summary

The following is a summary of the main points covered in this chapter.

1. **Issues in ESL and foreign language instruction** — These include:
   - Developing academic language and background knowledge to succeed in mainstream classes
   - Differentiating instruction across proficiency levels
   - Integrating students' native languages
   - Integrating authentic materials and perspectives of native speakers of the target language
   - Developing an audience and purpose for assignments.

2. **Integration strategies for ESL and foreign language instruction** — Strategies for integrating technology into this area cover a number of general topics:
   - Support for authentic oral and written practice.
   - Support for practice in language subskills. See especially products from Rosetta Stone Software and Transparent Language Software.
   - Presentation aids. See especially resources from the Telus Learning Connection.
   - Support for text production. See especially tools at Translation.net.
   - Virtual field trips for modified language immersion experience. See Tramline field trips.
   - Virtual collaborations. See collaborative projects to join at the Global SchoolHouse and IEARN sites.
   - Productivity and lesson design support for teachers. See especially ESL.net.

Key Terms

- computer-assisted language learning (CALL)
- distributed language learning (DLL)
- English as a second language (ESL)
- English language learner
- foreign language (FL)
- web-based language learning (WBLL)

Web-Enrichment Activities

1. Go to http://www.stuff.co.uk/wicked.htm for a list of exercises and activities available online for English language learners. Explore the various options. Which might be most helpful?

2. Choose a translation website from the list below. Type or paste in a short paragraph in English.
   - *Babel Fish* — http://babelfish.yahoo.com/
   - *Free Translator* — http://www.free-translator.com
   - *Free Translation* — http://www.freetranslation.com

   Translate the text into another language, and then translate the translation back into English. How similar is the final result to your original paragraph? Based on this experience, what recommendations do you have for teachers who use translation websites?

3. ***Foreign Language Learning*** — Go to Ñandutí (http://www.cal.org/earlylang/), a comprehensive site on foreign language learning in grades K–8 created by the Center for Applied Linguistics (CAL). Go to the Teaching Resources section, and explore the various Materials and Curricula. Be sure to look at the Teacher-Created Sites. How might a FL teacher gain the most from this site? What technology options are discussed?

Go to MyEducationLab to complete the following exercises.

Video   Select the topic "Foreign Language Integration," and go to the "Assignments, Activities, and Applications" section. Access the video "Using a Class Web Page for Learning" to see how one teacher maximizes content learning in context. Then complete the activity.

Video   Select the topic "Diverse Populations," and go to the "Assignments, Activities, and Applications" section. Access the video "Using Technology to Meet Objectives" and complete the activity.

Tutorials   Select the topic "Software" and access the practical tutorial and skill-building activity for "Microsoft Word for PC." Use the tutorial to learn the basic skills of creating Word documents. This skill will be reviewed again in the Technology Integration Workshop.

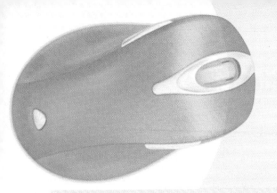

Technology Integration Workshop

The TIP Model in Action

Read each of the following scenarios related to implementing the TIP Model, and answer the questions that follow it based on your Chapter 10 reading and activities.

TIP MODEL SCENARIO #1 Señora Griggs is helping her AP Spanish students prepare for the AP exam. She knows that there will be a lot of vocabulary on the exam many of the students may not have encountered, so she decides to offer them the opportunity to practice vocabulary using a Spanish drill-and-practice program she has available. However, she has only one copy.

1.1 How would you recommend that Sra Griggs have her students use this one copy of the software?

1.2 What would be the relative advantage of using this software?

1.3 What data could Sra Griggs gather to get some indication of whether the program was helping her students be better prepared for the exam?

TIP MODEL SCENARIO #2 Herr Caesar would like to motivate his students to spend more time on their German translations. Students complete the practice exercises he creates for them only under duress. He hears about a website that links individual students to a keypal in a German school so they can communicate in both German and English.

2.1 What would be the relative advantage for Herr Caesar of using this strategy with his students?

2.2 How would you advise Herr Caesar that he structure this project to make it most meaningful for both students in this country and in Germany?

2.3 Would you advise Herr Caesar to encourage students to communicate with their German keypals from their home computers if they have them? Why or why not?

TIP MODEL SCENARIO #3 Señorita Sartori would like the students in her AP Spanish class to have an immersion experience in which they go to a Spanish-speaking country and interact with native speakers. However, the school is in a small, rural community and has no funds for this kind of activity. Srta Sartori has read that virtual collaborations can be a good replacement for immersion experiences, but she does not know how to find school partners for such a project.

3.1 How would you advise Srta Sartori to locate school partners for a virtual collaboration?

3.2 What would be the relative advantage of such a project?

3.3 What kind of assessment might be appropriate for an activity like this?

TIP MODEL SCENARIO #4 Several of Mr. Junita's students are new to the school and speak little English. They seem hesitant to try out their English skills; Mr. Junita thinks they are afraid of being laughed at by the other children. He requests special funds to obtain some iQuest handheld computers for these students so that they can practice using English words and phrases at school and at home.

4.1 What would be the relative advantage of using these handheld computers for practicing English?

4.2. How would you instruct these students to use the handhelds to obtain the maximum benefit from them (i.e., not just to play with them)?

4.3. How would you assess the benefits to the students of using these devices?

TIP MODEL SCENARIO #5 The students in Ms. Liu's Chinese class can recognize many Chinese characters and have strong oral language skills. They are also quite good at writing Chinese in Pinyin; however, Ms. Liu believes they are ready to produce more meaningful writing in Chinese. She has noticed that students tend to make many errors when they write characters by hand and are limited by the number of characters they know. She would like them to generate simple descriptions of themselves and their families through writing and to move beyond the production of single characters to short sentences.

5.1 What resource might Ms. Liu obtain to help her students produce more Chinese writing?

5.2 What would be the best way to have students use this resource: individually, in pairs, or in small groups? Why?

5.3 What would Ms. Liu have to do before she asked students to use this resource for a graded assignment?

TIE into Practice: Technology Integration Examples

The Technology Integration Example that opened this chapter (*A Discussion Board en Français*) showed how a teacher might have students use various technology resources to enhance French language learning. With the knowledge you have gained from Chapter 10, complete the following to explore how the rest of the activities in this lesson would work:

1. Foreign language students might create a menu to practice their skills. Having completed a tutorial on the basics of Word, develop this activity and create an example for students.

2. Answer the following questions about the *Discussion Board en Français* example:

   • Phase 1 — How should teachers assess their technological pedagogical content knowledge, and what should they do if they are deficient in one of the knowledge domains?

   • Phase 2 — The teachers felt that students needed an authentic way to practice their French language skills. What makes an activity "authentic," and what kinds of relative advantage does an authentic approach have?

   • Phase 3 — One of the desired outcomes the teachers want to accomplish with this project is better writing in French. To assess this, they will use a rubric to assess the quality and quantity of students' writing in French. How will they have to handle this assessment if they want to measure *improved* writing ability?

   • Phase 4 — In May, at the end of the project, teachers will recognize students and give awards for correct identifications. What would be a way to use technology to do these recognitions?

   • Phase 5 — One thing that always seems to happen with student usernames and passwords is that students forget them. How should the teachers manage this problem efficiently?

   • Phase 6 — In evaluating the outcomes of the activity, the teachers found that students wrote more with each forum. What would they need to do to determine if quality of writing improved? Which criterion should they have set to gauge "improvement"?

3. What NETS for Students skills would students learn by working on the *Discussion Board en Français* project? (See the front of this book for a list of NETS for Students.)

Technology Integration Lesson Planning

Complete the following exercise using sample lesson plans found on MyEducationLab.

1. Locate lesson ideas — MyEducationLab has several examples of lessons that use the integration strategies described in this chapter: support for authentic oral and written practice, support for practice in language subskills, presentation aids, support for text production, virtual field trips for modified language immersion experience, virtual collaborations, and productivity and lesson design support for teachers. Go to MyEducationLab under the topic "Foreign Language Integration" and go to "Lesson Plans" to review example lessons. Choose two of the following integration lessons:

   • An Online Foreign Language Art Competition

   • Casa de Joanna: Language Learning Resources

   • Productivity Software for Beginning Language Learning

   • Three Days in Munich via the Internet

   • Word Processing in Early Foreign Language Learning

2. Evaluate the lessons — Use the *Evaluation Checklist for a Technology-Integrated Lesson* (located on MyEducationLab under the topic "Instructional Planning") to evaluate each of these lessons.

3. Modify a lesson — Select one of the lesson ideas, and adapt its strategies to meet a need in your own content area. You may choose to use the same approach as in the original or to adapt it to meet your needs.

4. Add descriptors — Create descriptors for your new lesson similar to those found within the sample lessons (e.g., grade level, content and topic areas, technologies used, relative advantage, objectives, NETS standards).

5. Save your new lesson — Save your modified lesson with all its descriptors.

For Your Teaching Portfolio

For this chapter's contribution to your teaching portfolio, add the following products you created in the Technology Integration Workshop:

- The sample French menu activity you did in *Microsoft Word*
- The evaluations you did using the *Evaluation Checklist for a Technology-Integrated Lesson*
- The new lesson plan you developed, based on the one you found on MyEducationLab.

Chapter 11
Technology in Mathematics and Science Instruction

The terms and circumstances of human existence can be expected to change radically during the next human life span. Science, mathematics, and technology will be at the center of that change—causing it, shaping it, responding to it. Therefore, they will be essential to the education of today's children for tomorrow's world.

Benchmarks for Scientific Literacy (American Association for the Advancement of Science, 1993)

Technology Integration Example

Hot and Cold Data

Based on: Caniglia, J. (1997). The heat is on! Using the calculator-based laboratory to integrate math, science, and technology. *Learning and Leading with Technology, 25*(1), 22–27.

Grade Levels: Middle to high school • Content Area/Topic: Physics, graphing, and measurement • Length of Time: Three weeks

Phases 1 and 2: Assess technological pedagogical content knowledge; Determine relative advantage

Ms. Belt and Mr. Alter, the physics and mathematics teachers, respectively, at Pinnacle High School, were excited about the new **calculator-based laboratories (CBLs)** that had just arrived. As they learned about how CBLs can "grab" temperature data and display it in graphs and spreadsheets, they realized that activities with CBLs provide a natural link between science and mathematics studies. Having students use CBLs would be an ideal way to give them hands-on insights into the relationship between these two important skill areas. They also agreed that CBL activities would address the ongoing challenge of making abstract science and math concepts more concrete and visual. Having students collect and analyze their own data, they felt, would give students authentic, hands-on application of these concepts. They decided that a unit on heating and cooling experiments would be a good first activity. Students could take temperature measurements with the CBL probes and then use mathematical procedures to graph and analyze the resulting data.

Prior to implementing the CBL project, both Ms. Belt and Mr. Alter realized they needed to assess their technological pedagogical content knowledge (TPACK) so that they could evaluate their strengths and weaknesses and understand where they were located within the TPACK model. Ms. Belt realized that her knowledge of content and technology was extremely strong but that her pedagogical knowledge related to using the technology in the classroom was very weak. Mr. Alter realized that he was strong in content knowledge but not strong in pedagogical or technological knowledge. Being aware of their strengths and weaknesses in these areas, they decided they would contact the company that developed the CBLs to see if there were professional development opportunities. They learned that there were many professional development opportunities on integrating the CBLs in the classroom.

They immediately enrolled in preparation for their new integration of CBLs into their classrooms.

Phase 3: Decide on objectives and assessments

The teachers decided they would assess student progress in four areas: CBL performance tasks, carrying out scientific experiments, interpreting data from experiments, and completing and reporting on scientific experiments. They decided on the following outcomes and objectives they hoped students would achieve and outlined assessment methods to measure students' performance on them:

- **Outcome 1:** CBL procedures. **Objective:** Each student will score at least 85% on a performance test designed to measure competence with CBL procedures. **Assessment:** A checklist with points assigned for successful completion of each task.

- **Outcome 2:** Completing and reporting on scientific experiments, with teacher assistance. **Objective:** All students demonstrate they can work in groups to carry out the steps in an assigned experiment and to write summaries of their findings by achieving a rubric score of at least 85% on their work. **Assessment:** A checklist with points assigned for each step done correctly; a rubric to assess the quality of written summaries.

- **Outcome 3:** Interpreting data from experiments. **Objective:** All students will demonstrate the ability to review and interpret data derived from experiments by correctly answering at least 8 of 10 questions requiring data interpretation. **Assessment:** A mid-unit test in which each student reviews example charts and answers questions on how to interpret the data.

- **Outcome 4:** Completing and reporting on scientific experiments, without teacher assistance. **Objective:** All students demonstrate they can replicate and interpret data from a CBL experiment by working in pairs to complete the required tasks without assistance. **Assessment:** A checklist with points assigned for each step done correctly; a rubric to assess the quality of written summaries.

Phase 4: Design integration strategies

The teachers decided to team-teach the unit to draw together even more the links between the two content areas. Working together, they designed the following sequence of activities:

- **Week 1:** Introduce unit activities and CBLs, and provide hands-on practice. Introduce the unit with a *Consumer Reports*–type scenario. Makers of camp stoves each claim their product heats water faster than their competitors' do. The various stoves used three different fuels: white gas, kerosene, and butane. The students have to establish which manufacturer is correct and write up their findings for the *CR* magazine. Demonstrate how students can use the CBL to grab data and how it displays temperatures in graph form. Hold a discussion about interpreting CBL data. Students carry out the introductory experiment in three large groups. Using camp stoves borrowed from a local sporting goods store, students use the CBLs to heat water to boiling. They go through the step-by-step procedures for hands-on experiments, write up their findings, and present them to the whole class. Hold a whole-class discussion to interpret results, and write up a summary for *CR*.
- **Week 2:** Carry out heating/cooling experiments, and present findings. As Ms. Belt helps small groups prepare materials for the next set of experiments, Mr. Alter has students do individual performance checks on CBL procedures and provides additional instruction as needed. Each small group is assigned a heating/cooling experiment—for example,

which cup holds heat the longest: styrofoam, paper, or ceramic? Which color container holds heat the longest: white, black, or metallic? Each group completes its assigned experiment, answers the question, writes up its findings, and presents the findings to the class by inserting spreadsheet and graphed data into a *PowerPoint* presentation.

- **Week 3:** Do mathematical analyses and presentations; take final tests. Each group works with the data to explore linear, quadratic, and exponential functions of graphed data. Finally, students work in pairs to do their replication experiment and to answer questions on the meaning of the graphs.

Phase 5: Prepare the instructional environment

The teachers got a local sporting goods store to loan them three different camp stoves for the first experiment/ demonstration. They tested each of the CBLs and calibrated them as needed. They designed and copied each of the performance measures and made copies of lab sheets needed during the experiments.

Phase 6: Evaluate and revise

At the end of the unit, the teachers reviewed the students' products and discussed how the unit had worked. Mr. Alter and Ms. Belt were happy with the overall performance of the class. They were impressed at how engaged students had become in using the CBLs to gather and analyze data. Perhaps most encouraging, two female students seemed especially excited by the work they had done on the scientific experiments; they asked the teachers to give them information on careers in science and mathematics. The teachers concluded that this kind of multidisciplinary unit worked very well. They decided to plan other CBL experiments, to be carried out on a long-term basis and at locations outside the classroom.

Objectives

After reading this chapter and completing the learning activities for it, you should be able to:

1. Identify some of the current issues in mathematics and science instruction that may affect the selection and use of technology.

2. Describe key strategies for integrating technology into mathematics and science curricula.

3. Identify example software and web resources required to carry out each integration strategy.

4. Create instructional activities for mathematics and science instruction that model successful integration strategies.

Science and technology have a unique relationship. Technology supports science and science makes new technology possible. Both will play a critical role in our students' future. Thus, it is not surprising that efforts to reform teaching and learning in these two areas have been at the center of the national standards movement. U.S. elementary students perform well compared to students in other nations, but that performance diminishes as our students progress through school (Beaton et al., 1997–1998). However, numerous programs have been developed with the aim of changing these data. For example, it has been shown that students' performance on math and science assessments improved in almost all age groups when K–12 teachers collaborated with higher education colleagues (NSF, 2007). Technology provides many opportunities to build students' conceptual knowledge of mathematics and science as well as to connect their learning to problems found in our world. This chapter highlights current issues and problems in mathematics and science education and describes strategies for integrating technology into teaching and learning processes for these areas.

What Does TPACK Look Like in Science and Math Education?

The questions surrounding technological pedagogical content knowledge (TPACK) for teachers many times are: "How does this relate to me?" and "What are the implications of knowing about TPACK in my content area?" TPACK in any discipline is the perfect union of three knowledge domains (content, pedagogy, and technology) to develop a knowledge base from which a teacher can view a lesson and understand how tech-

nology can enhance the learning opportunities and experiences for students while also knowing the correct pedagogy to enhance the learning of the content. In science education, for example, a teacher who is fluent within a content area is incorporating TPACK principals when he or she readily introduces students to technologies such as probeware when developing a lesson. As another example, when teaching about magnetic north, instead of simply lecturing on the differences between geographic north and magnetic north, the teacher might have students use a magnetic field sensor and data collection software to monitor the magnetic field intensity as they identify magnetic north. The teacher understands that the correct pedagogy with this technology will engage and motivate students as they explore the content to a greater degree. In math education, a teacher with a TPACK perspective is, like those in the examples related to science education, one who thinks with technology. Thus, when teaching slope and y-intercept, teachers introduce students to graphic calculators, which they can use to enter data and graph equations on lines rather than being limited to sitting through lectures and completing worksheets. (See Figure 11.1.)

Issues and Problems in Mathematics Instruction

Accountability for Standards in Mathematics

The *Principles and Standards for School Mathematics*, released in 2000 by the National Council of Teachers of Mathematics (NCTM), serves as a primary resource and guide for all who make decisions that affect the mathematics education of students in pre-kindergarten through

FIGURE 11.1 TPACK and Math and Science

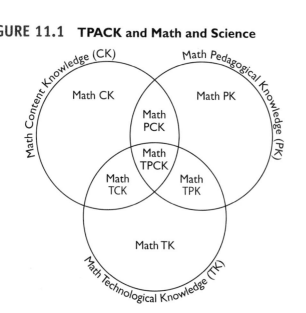

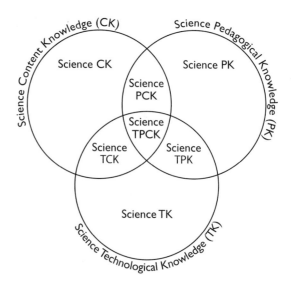

Top Ten

Strategies for Technology in Math and Science Instruction

Take advantage of these ten powerful strategies for using technology to enhance the teaching of mathematics and science.

Mathematics Strategies

1. **Graphing calculators give students hands-on practice in solving mathematical problems** — These handy tools help students do mathematical calculations and visualize algebraic concepts in a manner that enhances understanding and problem-solving skills.

2. **Interactive geometry software such as the *Geometer's Sketchpad* makes abstract concepts easier to understand** — These software tools make geometric concepts more concrete, visual, and interactive so that students with limited mathematical background can understand them more readily and students with more advanced knowledge can explore them more deeply.

3. **Spreadsheets help students carry out "what if" problem solving** — Spreadsheets do the manual calculations involved in solving higher order problems.

4. **Students use the Internet to obtain useful math-related information** — Internet sites are rich sources of data sets and mathematical information to answer questions, and they help students see real-world applications of mathematical principles.

5. **Reasoning and skill-building software increases students' fluency with prerequisite subskills while developing logic and comprehension** — Instructional games, puzzles, and drills offer private, personal feedback in a motivating environment to help students build fluency.

Science Strategies

1. **The GLOBE program offers opportunities for doing authentic science activities** — This web-based resource is a rich collection of hands-on activities in which students can apply science concepts.

2. **NASA Internet sites keep students in touch with scientific events** — Through web-based activities, students participate in events, such as the landing of the Mars Rover, that they would otherwise be unable to observe.

3. **Calculator-based labs give students hands-on practice with scientific data analysis** — These tools let students collect and analyze data to support science experiments.

4. **GPS and GIS tools let students make observations and analyze data to support scientific investigations** — Students use these tools to study the weather, land cover, soil, and hydrology.

5. **Digital imaging tools and simulations slow down or speed up processes for easier observation** — These activities allow students to study phenomena they would otherwise be unable to see or could not see well with the naked eye.

grade 12. Through this document, mathematics educators describe a vision of mathematics teaching and learning. Achieving this vision requires "solid mathematics curriculum, competent and knowledgeable teachers who can integrate instruction with assessment, education policies that enhance and support learning, classrooms with ready access to technology, and a commitment to both equity and excellence" (NCTM, 2000, p. 3). The *Principles and Standards* document calls for a common foundation of mathematics to be learned by all students. Six principles address crucial issues fundamental to all school mathematics programs:

- Equity
- Curriculum
- Teaching
- Learning
- Assessment
- Technology

Within the technology principle, NCTM stresses that "technology is essential in teaching and learning mathematics" and "it influences the mathematics that is taught and enhances students' learning" (NCTM, 2000, p. 24). "In the mathematics classroom envisioned in *Principles and Standards,* every student has access to technology to facilitate his or her mathematics learning under the guidance of a skillful teacher" (NCTM, 2000, p. 25).

There are ten mathematics standards for pre-kindergarten through grade 12:

Content Standards
- Numbers and Operations
- Algebra
- Geometry
- Measurement
- Data Analysis and Probability

Process Standards
- Problem Solving
- Reasoning and Proof
- Communication
- Connections
- Representations

Through these principles and standards, NCTM provides guidance on how to prepare students for a society that requires mathematical knowledge for filling crucial economic, political, and scientific roles in a highly technological workplace.

Adapting for Special Needs

For Mathematics

Students with disabilities and students who are at risk often fail to achieve high levels of competency in math due to problems with completing accurate calculations. This may involve procedural knowledge about what steps to complete in what sequence, and/or there may be a lack of fluency in manipulating numbers during a calculation. An obvious (albeit controversial) solution is to teach students with special needs how to use a calculator. A vast number of online calculators are available:

- Calculator: http://www.calculator.com
- Online Converters: http://onlineconverters.com
- Martindale's Calculators On-line Center: http://www.martindalecenter.com/calculators.html

A different tactic is to combine an online calculation tool with instructional support. WebMath (http://www.webmath.com) provides how-to help and calculating support for students struggling with all levels of math by providing step-by-step guidance on how to complete a specific problem.

For Science

Students with disabilities often struggle in science due to an inability to manipulate the science lab equipment or because they are unable to read the textbook. Recent advances in technology can address both concerns.

The Digital Blue QX5 Digital Microscope (http://digiblue.com/digital_blue/qx5.html) is a powerful microscope that attaches to the computer so that students can view digital images on the microscope slide via the computer or a projection system. For students unable to access the lenses of a microscope, this tool provides an opportunity for students and teachers to point to a specific part of the image to ensure that all students are observing the same phenomena.

BrainPop (http://www.brainpop.com), a subscription-based site, provides instruction in a multimedia format that is helpful for students who are unable to read the textbook. Students select science from a menu of curriculum areas and see a vast array of science instructional topics. After selecting a particular topic, BrainPop offers streaming video, lab activities, and resources to engage students in the topic and provide fundamental information and skills.

Contributed by Dave Edyburn

Challenges in Implementing the *Principles and Standards for School Mathematics*

Helping teachers change their teaching styles to meet the vision described in the NCTM standards is not an easy task. The standards seek a fundamental shift in the way most teachers work (Burrill, 1997). Technology can serve as a catalyst to move teachers toward an instructional style that is more student centered, active, and relevant to the world we live in. Technology also provides learners with the opportunity to visualize and make more concrete the generally abstract world of mathematics.

Research points to three implications for the selection and use of technology related to mathematics education. First, teachers should consider an appropriate combination of off- and on-computer activities. Second, they should consider technology as a mathematical tool rather than as a pedagogical tool. Third, they should view technology as a tool for developing student thinking. One way to accomplish these goals is to use computer software and applications that can be extended for long periods of time across topics to engage students in meaningful problems and projects rather than providing a variety of applications with no internal coherence (Clements, 1998).

In "Great Expectations: Leveraging America's Investment in Educational Technology," researchers at the Benton Foundation concluded that after more than two decades of research on the benefits of technology, mounting evidence exists to document the positive influence of technology on student achievement in mathematics (Benton Foundation Communications Policy Program, 2002). The researchers

concluded that mathematics software, particularly programs that promote experimentation and problem solving, enables students to embrace key mathematical concepts that are otherwise difficult to grasp. This research-based evidence has also been described more metaphorically by mathematics teacher Dan Kennedy (1995) in his article "Climbing the Tree of Mathematics," in which he articulates how technology provides his students with a means of achieving mathematical understanding previously unknown. Through both systematic research and common wisdom derived by accomplished teachers, ample evidence exists to support strategies for integrating technology into the teaching and learning of mathematics to increase student understanding and achievement.

Technology Integration Strategies for Mathematics Instruction

Technology resources have made possible a variety of teaching and learning strategies to help address the *Principles and Standards for School Mathematics*. These include using virtual manipulatives, fostering mathematical problem solving, allowing representation of mathematical principles, implementing data-driven curricula, supporting math-related communications, and motivating skill building and practice. Table 11.1 summarizes these strategies and gives examples of some of the technology resources that make them possible.

Using Virtual Manipulatives

Computer software can play an important role in the way students perceive mathematics. At the elementary level, teachers can display models for numbers and operations on the computer screen so that students can derive and construct their own meaning for mathematical concepts. At higher levels, teachers can use software models to make abstract concepts more concrete. Both of these strategies are called **virtual manipulatives** because students use them to do simulated activities they used to do with real objects (Moyer, Bolyard, & Spikell, 2002). These simulated activities offer more flexibility than activities using actual objects in the way teachers can use them to illustrate concepts.

Mankus (2000) describes and provides several examples of how online interactive manipulatives can be used to develop understanding. Utah State University maintains a library of virtual manipulatives for all grade levels that are tied to each of the standards' content strands. For examples of virtual manipulatives, see the websites listed in Table 11.1.

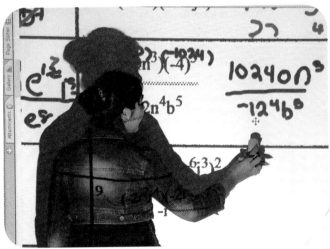

The availability in class of an interactive whiteboard hooked to a laptop computer allows students to work through math problems and then save all their work.

TABLE 11.1 Summary of Technology Integration Strategies for Mathematics

Technology Integration Strategies	Benefits	Sample Resources and Activities
Using virtual manipulatives	• Supports hands-on activities for learning mathematics. • Offers flexible environments for exploring complex concepts. • Provides a concrete representation of abstract concepts.	• **National Library of Virtual Manipulatives for Interactive Mathematics at Utah State University** http://matti.usu.edu/nlvm/index.html • **National Library of Virtual Manipulatives at the Shodor Foundation website** http://www.shodor.org • **Manipula Math with Java** http://www.ies.co.jp/math/java/index.html • **Mathematics, Science, and Technology Education at UIUC** http://www.mste.uiuc.edu/java/default.php
Fostering mathematical problem solving	• Helps students gather data to use in problem solving. • Provides rich, motivating problem-solving environments. • Gives students opportunities to apply mathematical knowledge and skills in meaningful contexts.	• CBLs • Software (e.g., The Learning Company's *Zoombinis: Thinkin' Things*) • Programming languages • Texas Instruments Educational Technology Download Center http://education.ti.com/educationportal/sites/US/sectionHome/download.html
Allowing representation of mathematical principles	• Makes abstract mathematical concepts more visual and easier to understand. • Gives students environments in which to make discoveries and conjectures related to geometry concepts and objects.	• Graphing calculators • Software (e.g., *Geometer's Sketchpad, KaleidoMania*) • Spreadsheets • Key Curriculum Press Software http://www.keypress.com/x6475.xml
Implementing data-driven curriculum	• Provides easy access to many data sets. • Provides real statistics to support investigations that are timely and relevant. • Supports development of student knowledge and skill related to data analysis. • Allows for exploration and presentation of data in a graphical form.	• Software (e.g., *Fathom, Tabletop, Tabletop Jr.*) • U.S. Census http://www.census.gov/ • Spreadsheets • Statistical software (e.g., *StatCrunch,* http://www.statcrunch.com/)
Supporting math-related communications	• Allows easy contacts with experts. • Promotes social interaction and discourse about mathematics. • Allows teachers to reach other teachers for the exchange of ideas.	• Math Forum—Ask Dr. Math http://mathforum.org/dr.math/ • Math Forum—Problems of the Week http://mathforum.org/pow/ • Math Forum—Public Discussions http://mathforum.org/discussions/ • ON-Math, the Online Journal of School Mathematics http://www.nctm.org/onmath
Motivating skill building and practice	• Provides motivating practice in foundation skills needed for higher order learning. • Provides guided instruction within a structured learning environment. • Delivers instruction when teacher may not be available.	• **PLATO Learning** http://www.plato.com • **Waterford Early Science and Math** http://www.pearsondigital.com

Use the following questions to reflect on issues in technology integration and to guide discussions within your class.

1. The Mathematical Sciences Education Board offers a view on reforming mathematics instruction:

   "The national call for reform in mathematics teaching and learning can seem overwhelming, because it requires a complete redesign of the content of school mathematics and the way it is taught. The basis for reform is the widespread belief that the United States must restructure the mathematics curriculum.... Simply producing new texts and retraining teachers will not be sufficient to address the major changes being recommended."

   How might various technologies and technology-based methods be able to shape and support a restructured mathematics curriculum?

2. Cavanagh's (2004) article "NCLB Could Alter Science Teaching" presents contrasting beliefs about effective science instruction:

   Quote #1: "Advocates of discovery learning say direct instruction can easily regress into lecture-style teaching, heavy on rote recitation of scientific facts and memorization. 'It's cheaper, faster, and not as effective,' contended Wayne Carley, the executive director of the National Association of Biology Teachers, in Reston, Va. 'If you want kids to memorize a bunch of facts, it's a great way to learn ... [however] science is not just a set of facts but a process for discovering more facts.'" (p. 12).

   Quote #2: "Directors of the Baltimore Curriculum Project, a nonprofit program that works with three schools serving both elementary and middle school students in that city, have been using direct instruction for the past six years in subjects from reading and language arts to mathematics. Leaders of the project, which largely serves students from low-income families and has seen an improvement in test scores among its participants in recent years, plan to use direct instruction in science over the next few years...." (p. 12).

   Why do these groups have such different beliefs about effective science instruction? How might technology be able to merge these seemingly disparate methodologies?

Fostering Mathematical Problem Solving

NCTM defines problem solving as ". . . engaging in a task for which the solution method is not known in advance. In order to find a solution, students must draw on their knowledge, and through this process, they will often develop new mathematical understandings. Solving problems is not only a goal of learning mathematics but also a major means of doing so" (NCTM, 2000). Regardless of how many mathematical facts, skills, or procedures students learn, the true value of mathematics is realized only when they can apply their knowledge to solve problems. Technology, by its definition, is a tool for solving problems. To prepare mathematically powerful citizens for the future, learning to solve problems using mathematics and appropriate technological tools is essential to education at all levels.

As students acquire number sense, they can begin to make generalizations that lead them to concepts in algebra. Technology tools provide students with a variety of means for exploring the critical concept of functions. (see Figure 11.2).

FIGURE 11.2 Data Gathering and Analysis Devices: (a) Graphing Calculator, (b) CBL, and (c) ImagiProbe Sensor Interface System with PalmOne Handheld Computer

(a)

(b)   **(c)**

Sources: (a, b) Reprinted with permission. © 2006 Texas Instruments; http://education.ti.com. (c) Reprinted with permission of Pasco Scientific; http://www.imagiworks.com.

Using graphing calculators and computer algebra systems, students can graph functions accurately, explore mathematical models of real-life phenomena, and explore symbolic representations and patterns. Calculator-based labs (a.k.a. probeware) provide a means to link either calculators or computers to scientific data–gathering instruments such as thermometers or pH meters, which allows students to gather data and then analyze it. Probes are also available for Palm-powered handheld devices.

As Technology Integration Lesson 11.1 shows, spreadsheets can be a powerful means of supporting problem-solving exercises. Computer programming can also help develop problem-solving abilities by allowing students to analyze and decompose a problem and use systematic trial and error to find solutions. A modern (and free) language such as *Python* (Van Rossum, 2001) can provide students with a means of learning to write computer code for the purpose of solving problems.

Mathematical problem solving does not have to resemble work. To many learners, young and old, it can actually be a form of recreation. Software resources have been developed to create problem-solving environments that require the exercise of mathematical ideas in a context that resembles a game or puzzle. The Learning Company's *Zoombinis Logical Journey* for young learners is made up of numerous puzzles in a colorful and engaging environment that allow students to use logic, data analysis, algebra, and graphing concepts as if they were playing a game. Similarly, software like Edmark's *Thinkin' Things* series integrates mathematics and science into an entertaining problem-solving environment. (See Figure 11.3.) Different titles in the series focus on young (preK–3), elementary (grades 2 through 5), and middle (grades 3 through 8) learners.

Allowing Representation of Mathematical Principles

Mathematics is an abstract subject. Our understanding of mathematical ideas and concepts is closely tied to how we represent the abstractions of mathematics. To some, the concept of "five" is literally five objects (apples, pennies, and so on); to others, it is the numeral 5; to the ancient Romans, it was represented by the numeral V. Technology has greatly enriched the way the abstractions of mathematics can be represented, and today students must learn mathematics using several representations: symbolic (with numerals, variables, equations, and so on), verbal (with words such as "What percent increase is needed to reach $32,000?"), graphical (using two- or three-dimensional graphs), or numerical (using tables of numbers or spreadsheets). For each of these representations, technology resources have been developed to allow learners to explore mathematics within that representation—and to explore the interaction among representations.

FIGURE 11.3 *Thinkin' Things* and *Zoombinis* Problem-Solving Software

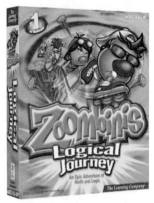

Source: Thinkin' Things: Toony the Loon's Lagoon, Gr 4-8 and *Zoombinis: Logical Journey* Problem-Solving Software packages from Riverdeep Interactive Learning Limited.

Research has shown that the use of graphing calculators can improve students' understanding of functions and graphs as well as the interconnections among the symbolic, graphical, and numerical representations of problems (Dunham & Dick, 1994; Heller, Curtis, Jaffe, & Verboncoeur, 2005). Without technology, it is difficult, if not impossible, for students to move from the symbolic realm of $f(x) = x^2 - 3$ to the equivalent graphical rendering shown in Figure 11.4a to the numerical representation in Figure 11.4b that resembles a spreadsheet.

In addition to calculators, many computer-based programs such as *Green Globs* (Sunburst), *Derive* (Chartwell-Yorke Ltd.), and *TI Interactive* (Texas Instruments) provide learning environments across three different mathematical realms. **Interactive** or **dynamic geometry software** provides students with an environment in which to make discoveries and conjectures related to geometry concepts and objects. Here abstract ideas can be played out on a computer screen, making concepts more real and providing a doorway into mathematical reasoning and proof. As Renne (2000) illustrates, Internet resources also can help students make connections between abstract geometry and real objects in the world around them. (See Technology Integration Lesson 11.2.)

FIGURE 11.4 **(a) Graphical Representation and (b) Table or Numerical Representation of Mathematics Principle** $f(x) = x^2 - 3$

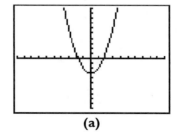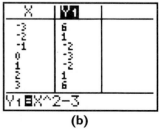

| (a) | (b) |

Source: Courtesy of Edwin M. Dickey.

Technology Integration Lesson 11.1

Fostering Mathematical Problem Solving

Title: What If? Problem Solving with Spreadsheets

Content Area/Topic: Algebra

Grade Levels: 6 through 9

NETS for Students: Standards 3 (Research and Information Fluency) and 4 (Critical Thinking, Problem Solving, and Decision Making)

Description of Standards Applications: Students tend to solve math word problems by using an intuitive "guess and check" strategy. This integration lesson offers students the opportunity to use spreadsheets to research and problem-solve algebra word problems. Spreadsheets are a natural tool to support this strategy because they allow students to find patterns, guess and check, and set up tables. Spreadsheet-based strategies are illustrated for several kinds of algebra word problems, including "How many coins of each kind are there in a given total?" and "What is the temperature when Celsius and degrees Fahrenheit are equal?"

Source: Feicht, L. (2000). Guess and check: A viable problem-solving strategy. *Learning and Leading with Technology, 27*(5), 50–54.

Technology Integration Lesson 11.2

Allowing Representation of Math Principles

Title: Studying Graphs and Functions

Content Area/Topic: Algebra graphs and functions

Grade Levels: 7 through 11

NETS for Students: Standards 1 (Creativity and Innovation), 2 (Communication and Collaboration), 3 (Research and Information Fluency), 4 (Critical Thinking, Problem Solving, and Decision Making)

Description of Standards Applications: This integration lesson offers students the opportunity to collaborate and use spreadsheets and graphing calculators to research and problem-solve the effects of parameters on the behavior of a defined function.

Students graph the pattern in a scenario that describes a morning run taken by a boy named Julio. After each student presents a spreadsheet-generated graph of Julio's run, small groups work together to decide which graph is the best representation of the data in the scenario. This leads to a class investigation of two topics: the best-fit function for the data and the families of curves, and the effects of parameters on the behavior of the defined function. Students use graphing calculators to do these investigations, discussing questions such as "Can a linear function, a quadratic function, a third-degree polynominal, or an equation in exponential form describe the data adequately and accurately?" The activity can be extended by doing the same investigation of other scenarios.

Source: Manoucherhri, A., & Pagnucco, L. (1999–2000). Julio's run: Studying graphs and functions. *Learning and Leading with Technology, 27*(4), 42–45.

Instead of memorizing geometric facts or concepts, students can explore and arrive at conclusions on their own. For instance, using a program like the *Geometer's Sketchpad* (KCP Technologies), students can construct and measure the interior angles of a polygon and determine the formula that relates the measure of the angle to the number of sides.

Software capable of depicting solid or three-dimensional objects on a screen provides learners with a way to visualize objects that are difficult to imagine. Understanding the nature and properties of transformations and symmetry has become increasingly important and can be found in nearly all state mathematics standards. Again, software packages can facilitate learning and instruct students in this area. Websites are available that teach symmetry (Dorsey et al., 2001), and software such as *KaleidoMania!* (KCP Technologies), shown in Figure 11.5, goes further into the process of using symmetry and geometric transformations to create artistic objects.

Go to MyEducationLab, select the topic "Math Integration." Go to the "Assignments, Activities, and Applications" section and watch the video "*Geometer's Sketchpad* for Inductive Reasoning" and complete the activity that follows.

Implementing Data-Driven Curricula

U.S. students scored well in the area of data analysis on the Third International Mathematics Science Study (Beaton et al., 1997–1998). The importance of statistical inference and probability has already had an impact in U.S. schools. Technology provides an ideal means of developing student knowledge and skill related to data analysis. *Fathom* (KCP Technologies), an example of which is shown in Figure 11.6, is a comprehensive package designed for schools that helps analyze and represent statistical data in a wide range of forms.

Computer spreadsheets also provide environments in which children can explore number concepts, operations, and patterns with data they obtain from various sources. (See Technology Integration Lesson 11.3.) Students can work with basic operations, explore "what if" problems, and build a foundation for algebraic thinking. Activities such as planning a fund-raising activity (Zisow, 2001) or analyzing M&Ms data (Drier, 2001) provide teachers with an important software tool to help build students' number sense.

Supporting Math-Related Communications

The Internet offers students the opportunity to communicate with each other or even with experts in different fields. Expressing ideas in written form is essential; therefore, students must convert their mathematical thinking into words. Projects such as those found at the Math Forum @ Drexel's *Problems of the Week* allow teachers to pose problems that their students must solve and then communicate about.

FIGURE 11.5 Illustrating Transformations and Symmetry with *KaleidoMania!*

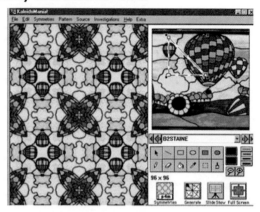

Source: Courtesy of Key Curriculum Press, 1150 65th Street, Emeryville, CA 94608: 1-800-995-MATH, www.keypress.com.

(See Figure 11.7.) *Ask Dr. Math* (also on the Math Forum) provides contacts with experts who can answer questions.

As Technology Integration Lesson 11.4 shows, student-created websites can be a valuable form of communication for student projects. Using computers and calculators in small-group settings also promotes social interaction and discourse. Teachers often find that grouping students in pairs enhances learning, augmenting communication from teacher-to-student or computer-to-student to a richer student-to-student-to-computer type of communication.

Motivating Skill Building and Practice

Although the current emphasis is on learning higher order mathematics skills, students often need more resources to support the practice of basic skills. These skills provide an important foundation on which they can build more advanced skills. Some technology resources that can support this practice include the following:

FIGURE 11.6 *Fathom:* **An Example Data Source for Mathematical Problem Solving**

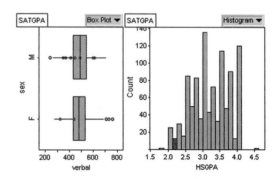

Source: Courtesy of Key Curriculum Press, 1150 65th Street, Emeryville, CA 94608; 1-800-995-MATH, www.keypress.com.

FIGURE 11.7 Math Forum Problems of the Week

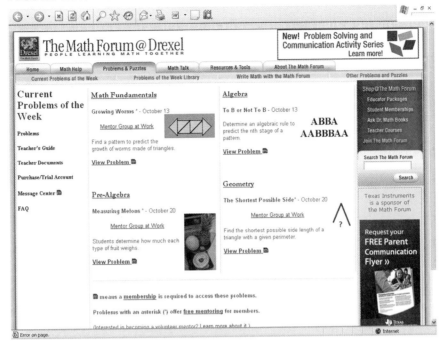

Source: Reproduced with permission from Drexel University, copyright © 2009 by The Math Forum@Drexel.

- Plato Learning has been developing tutorial and skill-building software for more than 40 years, making it one of the longest-standing companies in the computer industry. Courseware is available at all levels, from early childhood to adult, and across numerous content areas. Its mathematics titles address fundamental skills as well as problem solving and explorations.

- Waterford *Early Math and Science* software includes daily instructional activities that address mathematics and science standards for elementary grades. These curriculum materials foster exploration and inquiry while providing a foundation in basic skills, problem solving, and science.

Table 11.2 lists some useful websites for mathematics instruction.

TABLE 11.2 Recommended Websites for Mathematics Instruction

- **National Council of Teachers of Mathematics** (http://www.nctm.org.)—Home page of the professional organization that developed the first curriculum standards. Offers a wide range of resources, including journals, conferences, newsletters, and products, as well as an electronic version of the *Principles and Standards* document (http://standards.nctm.org/).

- **Math Forum** (http://mathforum.org/)—Resources for students, teachers, and anyone interested in mathematics education. Among the best: Ask Dr. Math (to answer questions). Problems of the Week (challenges at all levels and for all math subjects), and Discussion Groups (virtual communities interested in math).

- **Texas Instruments Resources for Educators** (http://education.ti.com/educationportal/)—As one would expect, this site includes numerous resources for using calculators and computers in the classroom. It also includes ideas for parents to help their children develop an interest in and comfort with mathematics.

- **Math World** (http://mathworld.wolfram.com/)—Billed as the "web's most extensive mathematics resource," Math World is a comprehensive, interactive encyclopedia of mathematics. Definitions, diagrams, and explanations of mathematics ideas, concepts, and terms are all explained in detail and with illustrations.

- **History of Mathematics** (http://www.groups.dcs.st-and.ac.uk:80/-history/)—Biographies, historical topics, even "famous curves" can be found at this comprehensive collection, illustrating how mathematics has developed as a human endeavor.

- **PBS Mathline** (http://www.pbs.org/teachers)—High-quality lessons, activities, and professional development for teachers addressing mathematics concepts and connections.

Technology Integration Lesson 11.3

Implementing Data-Driven Curriculum

Title: Measuring Up

Grade Levels: 7 through 10

Content Area/Topic: Measurement: ratios and proportions

NETS for Students: Standards 2 (Communication and Collaboration), 3 (Research and Information Fluency), 4 (Critical Thinking, Problem Solving, and Decision Making), and 6 (Technology Operations and Concepts)

Description of Standards Applications: This integration lesson offers students the opportunity to compare authentic data from students within the class to Leonardo's da Vinci's calculations. Students collaborate as they research and problem-solve ratios and proportions.

Students begin by taking measurements of each student in the class and entering these data into a spreadsheet. They use their own data and compare it to Leonardo da Vinci's calculations based on his 1492 drawing "The Proportions of the Human Figure" to predict "the perfect numbers." After students compare their results, they discuss their conclusions about da Vinci's hypothesized "perfect proportions."

	A	B	C	D	E	F	G
1				Body Proportions Spreadsheet			
2							
3	Student	Sex	Total Height	Height to Belly Button	Arm Span	Ratio of Belly Button Height to Total Height	Ratio of Arm Span to Total Height
4	Suzy Q.	F	64	38.25	63.5	=D4/C4	=E4/C4
5	Martha P.	F	70	42.75	72	=D5/C5	=E5/C5
6	John B.	M	72	48	72	=D6/C6	=E6/C6
7	Sam S.	M	60	35.5	63	=D7/C7	=E7/C7
8							
9	Class Average		=AVERAGE(C4..C7)	=AVERAGE(D4..D7)	=AVERAGE(E4..E7)	=AVERAGE(F4..F7)	=AVERAGE(G4..G7)
10	Male Average		=AVERAGE(C6..C7)	=AVERAGE(D6..D7)	=AVERAGE(E6..E7)	=AVERAGE(F6..F7)	=AVERAGE(G6..G7)
11	Female Average		=AVERAGE(C4..C5)	=AVERAGE(D4..D5)	=AVERAGE(E4..E5)	=AVERAGE(F4..F5)	=AVERAGE(G4..G5)

Source: Morgan, B., & Jernigen, J. (1998–1999). A technology update: Leonardo da Vinci and the search for the perfect body. *Learning and Leading with Technology, 26*(4), 22–25. Reprinted with permission from Morgan and Jernigen, copyright © 1999 ISTE (International Society for Technology in Education), Iste@iste.org, www.iste.org. All rights reserved.

Issues and Problems in Science Instruction

Accountability for Standards in Science

When the American Association for the Advancement of Science (AAAS) published *Science for All Americans* (1989), the document set out recommendations for what all students should know and be able to do in science, mathematics, and technology by the time they graduate from high school. The AAAS (1990) advocates that the goal of K–12 science curriculum is "Science for All." The AAAS also challenges science teachers and educators to ensure that "ALL" students are scientifically literate so that all children can participate in the everyday science discourse.

Technology Integration Lesson 11.4

Supporting Math-Related Communications

Title: Taking Shape—Linking Geometry and Technology

Content Area/Topic: Geometry

Grade Levels: 3 through 5

NETS for Students: Standards 1 (Creativity and Innovation), 2 (Communication and Collaboration), 3 (Research and Information Fluency), 4 (Critical Thinking, Problem Solving, and Decision Making), and 6 (Technology Operations and Concepts)

Description of Standards Applications: This integration lesson offers students the opportunity to take digital photos with which to create and communicate about a virtual book of geometrical shapes from the real world.

Teachers often help students understand geometry concepts by having them make lists and draw items with various shapes in the world around them—for example, basketball hoops for circles and monkey bars for rectangles. This activity expands on that strategy. Students bring in pictures of objects with various geometrical shapes and scan them into files to create a *Geometry in the World* virtual book. Reviewing all of the pictures as a whole class, students create categories to account for all of the pictures—cones, angles, horizontals and verticals, multiple shapes, and circles. Each category becomes a chapter for the book. Students work in small groups to do a web page for their chapter. They end with a class presentation of the whole site and a discussion of the geometry concepts they learned.

Source: Adapted from Renne, C. (2000). Taking shape: Linking geometry and technology. *Learning and Leading with Technology, 27*(7), 58–62.

The *National Science Education Standards* (NSES), released in 1995 by the National Research Council (NRC), outlines the content that all students should know and be able to do; it also provides guidelines for assessing student learning in science. The NSES provides guidance for science teaching strategies, science teacher professional development, and the support necessary to deliver high-quality science education. The NSES also describes the policies to bring coordination, consistency, and coherence to science education programs. Many of the state standards documents have drawn their content from the *Benchmarks for Science Literacy*, published by the AAAS in 1993, and/or the *National Science Education Standards*.

The U.S. Department of Education and the National Science Foundation (1992) endorse mathematics and science curricula that "promote active learning, inquiry, problem solving, cooperative learning, and other instructional methods that motivate students." Similarly, the National Committee on Science Education Standards and Assessment (1992) has stated that "school science education must reflect science as it is practiced," and that

one goal of science education is "to prepare students who understand the modes of reasoning of scientific inquiry and can use them." The basis for inquiry-oriented science instruction is developing varied opportunities for students to learn science process skills such as collecting, sorting, and cataloging; observing, note taking, and sketching; and interviewing, polling, and surveying. In addition, research shows that inquiry-related teaching is effective in developing scientific literacy and the understanding of science processes, vocabulary knowledge, conceptual understanding, critical thinking, positive attitudes toward science, and construction of logico-mathematical knowledge.

Technology can play an important and integral role in inquiry-oriented science instruction. Gee, Hull, and Lankshear (1996) identified four major ways in which technology is utilized in science classrooms:

1. **As a productivity tool** — Technology aids in accomplishing tasks with greater efficiency and allowing

students to spend more time on tasks that support learning and less time on activities that have a lower impact on learning. Students use less time on tasks such as data management and calculations, for example, and more time on interpreting and understanding the science concepts related to those data.

2. **Communicating ideas and information** — Technology facilitates communication in science through written words and illustrations (graphs and pictures). Technology can also enhance communication between and among students.

3. **Investigating with technological tools** — Technology can aid in the fundamental practice of scientific investigation—collecting information and representing that information appropriately. Most commonly, two kinds of technological processes are used in investigations: simulation and data-gathering tools such as the probes.

4. **Creating knowledge products** — Technology can enhance the process of creating knowledge products through computer-generated graphs, pictures, hyperlinks, and web designs. Technology can allow students to synthesize information in complex and more challenging ways.

To integrate technology in the science classroom on a regular basis, one must understand the meaning of technology in the context of science teaching and learning. Two definitions of technology frequently mentioned are provided in the *Benchmarks for Science Literacy* and the *National Science Education Standards*.

[Technology] once meant knowing how to do things—the practical arts or the study of the practical arts. But it has also come to mean innovations such as pencils, television, aspirin, microscopes, etc., that people use for specific purposes, and it refers to human activities such as agriculture or manufacturing and even to processes such as animal breeding or voting or war that change certain aspects of the world. (AAAS, 1993, p. 43)

The central distinguishing characteristic between science and technology is a difference in goal: the goal of science is to understand the natural world, and the goal of technology is to make modifications in the world to meet human needs. Technology as a design is included in the Standards as parallel to science as inquiry. (NRC, 1996, p. 24)

Several needs and problems specific to the teaching of science topics help shape the uses of technology in the sciences. In addition to meeting science standards, these issues include a "narrowing pipeline" of scientific talent, the

increasing need for scientific literacy, difficulties in teaching K–8 science, and a new emphasis on teaching scientific inquiry.

The Narrowing Pipeline of Scientific Talent

For years now, great concern has grown about America's ability to compete in science, mathematics, and technology in the future. With the declining number of students—especially female and minority students—pursuing studies in the math, science, and engineering fields, America faces a growing crisis in leadership for much-needed science/technology/engineering/mathematics (STEM) initiatives. This trend could have serious consequences for the long-term economic and national security of our country. One of the first reports on the issue was presented by EMC Corporation's (2003) *Fueling the Pipeline: Attracting and Educating Math and Science Students*. Since the publication of this seminal report, other organizations—both private and public—have continued to explore the problem.

Go to MyEducationLab, select the topic "Internet." Go to the "Assignments, Activities, and Applications" section, open the Web Activity "Fueling the Pipeline," and complete the exercise on the state of technology in science and math.

Increasing Need for Scientific Literacy

As the science benchmarks and standards reflect, there is a need for all citizens to be scientifically literate in order to make informed decisions that affect our country's future. More than ever before, America's economic and environmental progress depends on the character and quality of the science education that the nation's schools provide.

Difficulties in Teaching K–8 Science

In a study conducted by the Educational Testing Service, Gitomer, Latham, and Ziomek (1999) compared SAT scores for teacher candidates passing the Praxis II exam with the average score for all college graduates. The researchers concluded that elementary education candidates have much lower math and verbal scores than other college graduates do. Part of this problem may stem from the minimal content preparation in mathematics and science. As a result, teaching science for understanding becomes difficult due to the lack of deep understanding of the discipline on the part of the teacher. One way to assist teachers in science is through increased professional development. The Eisenhower National Clearinghouse offers a guide to improving professional development in the areas of math, science, and technology.

New Emphasis on and Controversies about Scientific Inquiry

As many educators place increasing emphasis on hands-on science skills (as opposed to the rote learning of concepts), technology can play a special role in improving classroom practice by teaching **scientific inquiry**, the processes of approaching problems scientifically. Describing this trend, Rubin (undated) says, "When learning with technology focuses on doing inquiry-based learning, the following approaches are commonly adopted in classrooms:

- Technology is viewed as a tool, much like a pencil or pen, but considerably more powerful.
- Use of the technology is primarily taught in the context of solving problems.
- Students help one another with the mechanics of the technology; in fact, in many classrooms, students are the local experts on technological details.
- Talk about and around technology is as important as the technology itself, just as talk about how one finds and uses information is as important as the information itself.
- Technology is used to augment communication by expanding audience (e.g., over networks and by producing hard copy) and expressive options (e.g., mixing graphs and words)."

This new emphasis is not without controversy. Cavanagh (2004) reports on a new study by the Carnegie Mellon University and the University of Pittsburgh that found that students taught through direct instruction (rather than inquiry or discovery learning methods) were more likely on average to become "experts" in designing scientific experiments—an important step in the development of scientific-reasoning skills. Also, Cavanagh notes that "The students who showed expertise in designing those experiments through direct instruction performed just as well as those who developed similar expertise through discovery paths on a separate test of their broader scientific judgment—countering some previous claims that direct instruction produces weaknesses in that area" (p. 1). As a result of such studies, the National Science Teachers Association (NSTA) recommends a combination of direct and inquiry methods.

Technology Integration Strategies for Science Instruction

Technology resources support many kinds of teaching and learning strategies to help address science standards. These strategies include supporting authentic science experiences, supporting scientific inquiry skills, supporting science concept learning, and accessing science information and tools. Table 11.3 summarizes these strategies and gives examples of some of the technology resources that make them possible.

Supporting Authentic Science Experiences

The American Association for the Advancement of Science (AAAS, 1993) called on teachers and schools to engage students in *doing science* rather than just hearing about it or seeing a demonstration. Authentic science not only involves hands-on science; it also includes connecting science to students' lives and life experiences. Involving students in active scientific investigations can improve their attitude towards science as well as their understanding of scientific concepts. Constructivist learning theory and cognitive apprenticeship concepts provide support for authentic science instruction. Authentic science instruction involves the process of scientific inquiry, the process of asking new and novel questions, hypothesizing, collecting data, analyzing, and communicating the results to peers and getting feedback to improve on the model. Scientists use a variety of technologies to create authentic science experiences. Following are some excellent programs, tools, and ideas with which to begin your exploration.

The GLOBE Project. The GLOBE project is an excellent example of utilizing technologies to do authentic science. GLOBE is an environmental science project that utilizes remote sensing and ground-based observations to study the local environment. The project makes use of a number of technologies to conduct local investigations. Teachers and students can investigate the weather, land cover, soil, and hydrology. Students utilize Global Positioning Systems (GPS), Geographic

TABLE 11.3 Summary of Technology Integration Strategies for Science

Technology Integration Strategies	Benefits	Sample Resources and Activities
Supporting authentic science experiences	• Provides resources needed for doing each phase of authentic science activities. • Some internet projects provide environments that support all phases of an authentic science project.	• **The GLOBE Project** http://www.globe.gov • **NASA** http://www.nasa.gov • **Jason Project** http://www.jason.org/ • **Archimedes Laboratory** http://www.archimedes-lab.org/index_optical.html • **Project FeederWatch** http://www.birds.cornell.edu/pfw • **The Association of Science-Technology Centers** www.astc.org • **EarthKAM** http://www.earthkam.ucsd.edu
Supporting scientific inquiry skills	• Helps students locate and obtain information to support inquiry. • Makes data collection and analysis easier and more manageable. • Makes it easier to visualize and understand phenomena. • Supports communicating results of inquiry.	• **GIS Population Data** http://www.esri.com • **Journey North project** http://www.learner.org/jnorth/ • **RedRover Goes to Mars** http://planetary.org/rrgtm/ • **The Exploratorium** http://www.exploratorium.edu • **Digital Library for Earth System Education (DLESE)** www.dlese.org
Supporting science concept learning	• Allows simulating and modeling of scientific processes. • Provides opportunities to engage in problem-solving activities.	• **Web-Based Chemistry Simulations** http://cse.edc.org/products/simulations/default.asp
Accessing science information and tools	• Allows access to unique tools and collections of information. • Expands opportunities for learning.	• Information on space at NASA http://www.nasa.gov/home/index.html • Information on weather at NOAA http://www.noaa.gov • Information on the latest health findings http://www.nih.gov • Exploring the Environment Curriculum http://www.cotf.edu/ete • National Academy Press http://www.nap.edu

Information Systems (GIS), and information technologies to collect and analyze data. Figure 11.8 is an example activity from the GLOBE project.

In this example, students take ground observations using traditional and state-of-the-art technology. They use temperature data-loggers, a GPS unit, and traditional technologies such as a weather shelter and a U-tube thermometer. Then they record their data in a notebook and enter the data into a database at the GLOBE site. They manipulate data with online graphing and visualization

FIGURE 11.8 Carbon Investigation in the GLOBE Environment

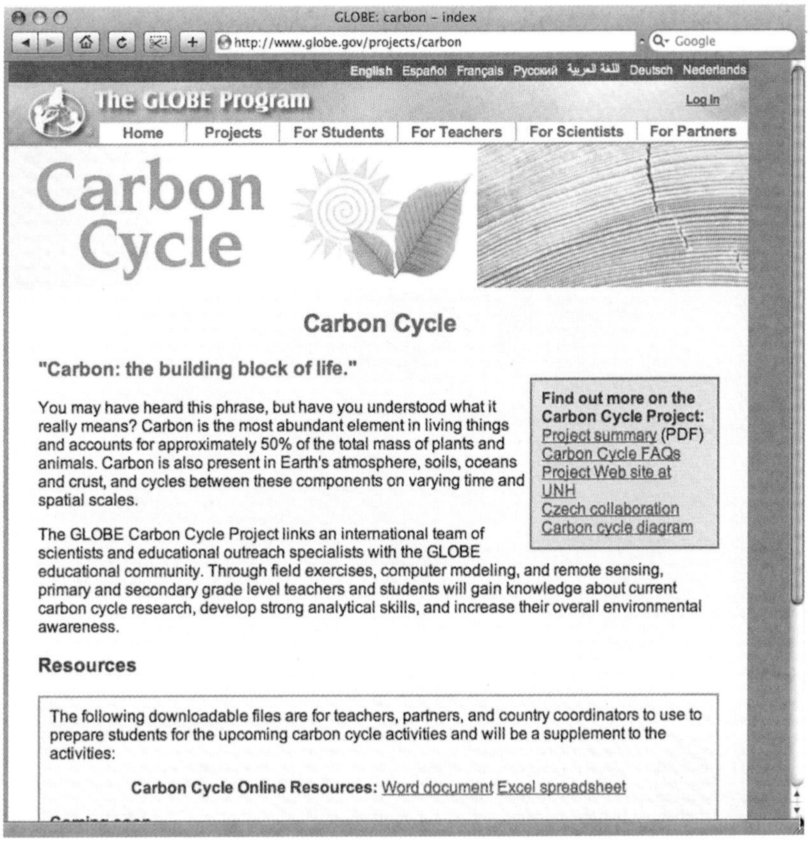

Source: Courtesy of The Globe Program, University Corporation for Atmospheric Research, http://globe.gov.

tools. The data can also be displayed in a graphical form, allowing students to look for patterns over time. To complete the process, students write up their results and post them to the GLOBE Student Research website. In the write-up, students report on their research questions, discuss their procedures, communicate their results using graphs and charts, and make conclusions. Once posted on the website, the report is peer reviewed by GLOBE participants.

GoNorth! Adventure Learning Series. The GoNorth! adventure learning series is driven by the adventure learning model of online learning. Adventure learning (AL) is a hybrid distance education approach that provides students with opportunities to explore real-world issues through authentic learning experiences within collaborative learning environments (Doering, 2006; Doering, 2007; Doering & Veletsianos, 2007). AL provides students with opportunities to explore content by fostering authentic learning experiences within a hybrid online environment; moreover, AL allows learners separated by

distance and time to connect with one another while providing them with access to resources and opportunities for interaction with the real world (Doering, 2006).

AL is based on two major theoretical approaches to learning: inquiry-based learning and experiential learning. Within the AL approach, students pose questions, research problems with experts and colleagues within their classroom and throughout the world, and ultimately share their findings in virtual spaces with colleagues from around the globe (Doering & Veletsianos, 2007; Doering, Miller & Veletsianos, 2008). In other words, students' learning processes involve pursuing answers to their own questions rather than memorizing rote facts. For example, in module 4 of the GoNorth! Fennoscandio 2008 adventure learning program, students study the possible causes of global climate change. Students graph tree ring data collected by "GoNorth! Cool Scientist" Dr. Glenn Juday to predict tree growth and precipitation while working with concepts such as correlated, anti-correlated, and uncorrelated data. Once students analyze and compare their data within their own classroom, they are encouraged to share the project findings

FIGURE 11.9 Climate Zone

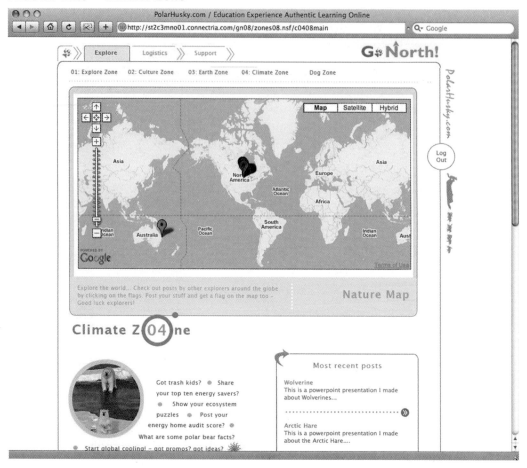

Copyright 2006 PolarHusky.com

Source: From *GoNorth! Adventure Learning Series* courtesy of PolarHusky.com..

online in the Climate Zone collaboration zone, sharing their data and findings with students throughout the world (see Figure 11.9).

Webquests. As initially introduced in Chapter 8, a webquest is designed to connect students with a reasonable sample of Internet resources where they, on their own, decide which resources to use to answer their questions. In its simplest form, a webquest begins with a web page that describes a task and then provides links to guide students to answer questions or find a solution to a problem. An example is a scenario in which a student is to design an experiment for a space mission and convince a group of scientists to fund it. The webquest describes the scenario and then directs the student to sites to learn about prior experiments, the process of designing experiments, evaluation, and presentation of results. All the information is contained in the select links leading from the initial web page.

The variety of webquests ranges from simple to complex. For example, webquests for elementary grade students can consist of a simple workbook, whereas a webquest for middle and high school students can be more thought provoking and engaging. The rubric shown in Table 8.4 on page 254 can be used to evaluate the effectiveness of a webquest. Webquests exclusively use web-based technology that is easy for teachers and students to manage. Because students are linked directly to another site without the need to use a search engine, webquests are supervision friendly. One limitation of webquest exercises is that students depend on secondary data, thus not experiencing the collection of primary data. In general, however, webquests serve as useful tools for encouraging students to read for meaning, understanding, synthesizing, and presenting the product. Webquests reduce the chance of the student doing a simple cut-and-paste exercise.

Project FeederWatch. Project FeederWatch from Cornell University provides teachers with a bird identification key and instructions for stocking a bird feeder, gathering data, and submitting the information to the site. How a teacher or participant wants to use this data is up to him or her. This project provides numerous opportunities for using spreadsheet data and carrying out geographic information system analyses.

Virtual Field Trips. Instead of going on a traditional field trip to a museum, recycling center, or food irradiation plant, a virtual field trip relies on the Internet to allow students to visit an informal learning setting. Two useful Internet sites can help you get started. The website for the Association of Science-Technology Centers allows students and teachers to locate the nearest museums and science centers. They also can use local museum Internet sites to learn about science outreach activities.

An educational program from NASA, EarthKAM (Earth Knowledge Acquired by Middle School Students) offers students the opportunity to find photos of the Earth's surface taken from space. Students and teachers can sort through numerous photos organized by theme, geographic location, or a number of other groupings. This categorization helps them organize thousands of pictures on various educational topics.

Supporting Scientific Inquiry Skills

The preceding section describes several examples of authentic science using a combination of technologies. Teachers do not always have time to incorporate into their schedule long-term investigations that encompass the entire scientific process. However, technology can be used to teach about specific elements of the scientific inquiry process, as discussed next.

Locating information to investigate scientific issues and questions. The Internet has become an indispensable tool for investigating important scientific questions. Science teachers and students have access to a number of exciting resources for teaching and learning science. For many of the science areas, teachers and students can access information from sources such as NASA or museums such as the Exploratorium.

The National Science Foundation (NSF) has funded the creation of digital libraries for science, including the Digital Library for Earth System Education (DLESE), a wonderful resource for teachers and students. The DLESE is a community of educators, students, and scientists working to improve the teaching of and learning about the Earth system at all levels. DLESE provides access to a number of collections of educational and scientific resources. Digital libraries provide a starting point for the investigation of scientific questions.

Collecting data. Data collection and archiving are important parts of the scientific inquiry process. Science bases its conclusions on data. A number of tools are available for data collection and archiving. The calculator or computer-based laboratory (CBL) is an ideal tool for middle school through high school science. CBL sensors collect data, and the data can be downloaded into a computer or calculator and then manipulated in a spreadsheet. By archiving data in a spreadsheet, the data can be used at another time or compiled for long-term investigations. Technology Integration Lesson 11.5 provides an example of how probes can be used to gather data for an inquiry activity.

Journey North projects connect students and scientists in real-life science research. The project identifies itself as the "citizen science" project for children.

Journey North engages students in a global study of wildlife migration and seasonal change. K–12 students share their own field observations with classmates across North America. They track the coming of spring through the migration patterns of monarch butterflies, robins, hummingbirds, whooping cranes, gray whales, bald eagles— and other birds and mammals; the budding of plants; changing sunlight; and other natural events. (From the homepage of Journey North, http://www.learner.org/jnorth/)

Presented with a list of projects, such as the Bald Eagles and the Tulip Gardens, students choose a project that interests them and participate in creating a large database that can be used to study factors such as climate change, migration, and soil and water conditions. Similarly, a Journey South project documents the migration patterns of monarch butterflies to Mexico. All Journey projects correlate directly to *National Science Education Standards*, with an emphasis on science inquiry. The site offers teachers dozens of lesson plans and activities to use with their students.

Science inquiry includes active involvement in collecting data.

Technology Integration Lesson 11.5

Supporting Scientific Inquiry Skills

Title: Measuring with Precision versus Accuracy   **Grade Levels:** 5 through 7
Content Area/Topic: Scientific methods

 NETS for Students: Standards 2 (Communication and Collaboration), 3 (Research and Information Fluency), and 4 (Critical Thinking, Problem Solving, and Decision Making)

Description of Standards Applications: This integration lesson offers students the opportunity to use thermometers with different scales to research temperatures of hot and cold water as they learn about accuracy and precision while sharing their results with their colleagues. As part of their work, students learn the difference between precision and accuracy by comparing the reading of a scale of temperature with its physical meaning.

Instructions: Have a container of hot water and one of cold water to use as high and low reference points. Students make two kinds of readings: one from a scale marked every 10 degrees centigrade, and the other from a scale marked every 1 degree centigrade. Although both readings are accurate, the second reflects greater precision. Have the students work in groups to use the probes to take various readings using each scale. After all groups have completed and recorded their readings, calculate the range for each scale. Half the range is the *precision*. The difference between the reference thermometer and the temperature probe is the *accuracy*. Discuss the difference with students.

Source: Flick, L. (1989). "Probing" temperature and heat. *The Computing Teacher, 17*(2), 15–19.

Visualizing data and phenomena. A number of visualization tools exist that allow students to see representations of data and phenomena that may be difficult to see directly. Computer simulations differ from illustrations and pictures in that students can manipulate elements in them. These include tools that help students visualize macroscopic phenomena, such as the phases of the moon, that are difficult to understand because they cannot be seen directly.

Visualization tools can also be used to examine microscopic or other phenomena that would otherwise be difficult or impossible to observe—for example, molecular structure or growth of plants or animals. Technology Integration Lesson 11.6 illustrates how digital imaging can help students study butterfly metamorphosis.

Some tools make it possible to rotate and examine structures from multiple viewpoints to help students understand them (see, e.g., http://www.reciprocalnet.org). Visualizations can be used in a variety of teaching situations. They can be used by teachers as a tool for a lecture or demonstration, or as a way of inviting students to describe what they see, leading students to explain concepts for themselves. Visualizations can also be used as a remedial tool for tutorials. Visualizations are used in the workplace as well.

Meteorologists regularly show computer-generated visualizations on television to help explain weather phenomena. City planners use GIS to plot population growth.

Analyzing data. Analyzing data can be done with a number of existing programs that come standard on computers. Spreadsheets allow data to be entered and analyzed using simple statistics or algorithms supplied by the students. In the GLOBE project, *MultiSpec* software provides students with the ability to identify land cover types on a LandSat image. GIS software allows students to analyze factors in an image by removing or adding attributes and looking for connections among attributes.

Communicating results. Once data are analyzed, scientists write up the results and submit them for publication using standard productivity software (e.g., word processing). Scientists collaborate on scientific problems, and the Internet facilitates the communication process. In addition to graphs and visualizations, scientists use images from digital cameras and other digital instruments to record data and compare and contrast data over time. This is especially useful in land cover investigations and in astronomy.

Technology Integration Lesson 11.6

Supporting Scientific Inquiry Skills

Title: Digital Imaging on the (Butter)fly   **Grade Levels:** 9 through 12
Content Area/Topic: Biology

 NETS for Students: Standards 2 (Communication and Collaboration), 3 (Research and Information Fluency), 4 (Critical Thinking, Problem Solving, and Decision Making), and 6 (Technology Operations and Concepts)

Description of Standards Applications: This integration lesson offers students the opportunity to use time-lapse photography to research the metamorphosis of a caterpillar as well as to learn about digital imaging.

Students learn how digital imaging can support their scientific inquiry by allowing them to observe phenomena better than they could with the naked eye. To help students better understand the process of metamorphosis, the teacher shows them how to set up a digital camera to take time-lapse images. They focus the camera on the caterpillar as it is about to emerge, and then they take the video. By speeding up the completed footage, students can see and discuss each phase of the process.

Source: Bowen, A., & Bell, R. (2004). Winging it: Using digital imaging to investigate butterfly metamorphosis. *Learning and Leading with Technology, 31*(6), 24–27.

The Internet also provides a medium for communication among scientists. Data can be emailed to researchers around the globe. Classroom teachers can also have scientists interact with students in their classroom by participating in webcasts. For example, the GoNorth! Adventure Learning Series allows students to interact synchronously with scientists and experts around the world on a weekly basis.

Supporting Science Concept Learning

Technology-based strategies that simulate and model scientific processes can help students develop the foundation knowledge and skills they need to engage in inquiry. Students often have difficulty understanding complex scientific concepts, especially when such concepts are presented and explained in text only as nonmoving static images. Simulations and animations can make these concepts clearer by showing how the concepts work in action. These include animations in which students can see and sometimes manipulate applets to learn a scientific concept. For example, mixing colored light is an elementary science activity that is

FIGURE 11.10   Colors Simulator Created by IMITS at the University of Idaho

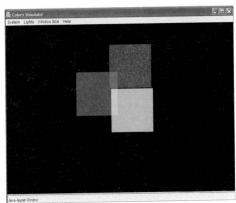

Source: Reprinted with permission from NOVA, University of Idaho, IMITS.

often confusing to students. Utilizing the "color mixer" simulation tool shown in Figure 11.10, learners can use the RGB screen as a mechanism to clarify these abstract concepts.

Other simulations allow students to mix chemicals and simulate the results, saving dollars and providing a safe environment for chemistry and physical science study. Virtual dissections allow students to examine anatomy without coming into contact with preservation chemicals. In physics, students can use simulations to conduct historical experiments.

Accessing Science Information and Tools

The Internet has opened up a world of opportunities for learning beyond the classroom. For example, students can control a rover like the ones on Mars (see Figure 11.11) or operate a telescope or camera from the space shuttle. It is also an unlimited source of data for classroom experiments and investigations. (See Technology Integration Lesson 11.7.)

The Internet also is a valuable resource of up-to-date science information. Science knowledge changes faster than most school libraries can keep up with. Books are out of date the minute they are published. If you want the latest information on space, you can access NASA; the weather, NOAA; medicine, the NIH. Most of these sites provide content targeted for teachers and students. A number of curriculum projects are also available online for teachers and students. NASA's classroom of the future provides a free Exploring the Environment curriculum that integrates science and social studies to examine current issues.

FIGURE 11.11   The Mars Rover Online

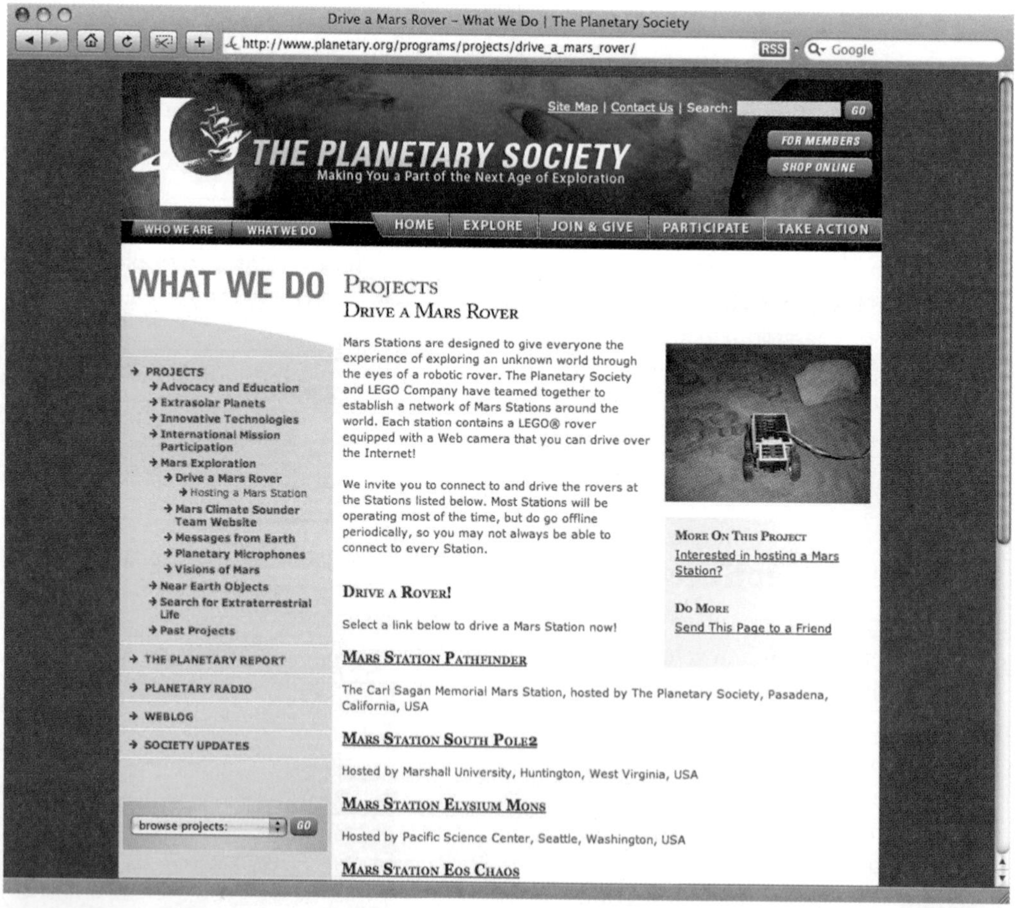

Source: Courtesy of The Planetary Society, plantary.org.

Technology Integration Lesson 11.7

Accessing Science Information and Tools

Title: Cyber Data

Content Area/Topic: Earth science

Grade Levels: 2 through 12

 NETS for Students: Standards 2 (Communication and Collaboration), 3 (Research and Information Fluency), 4 (Critical Thinking, Problem Solving, and Decision Making), and 6 (Technology Operations and Concepts)

Description of Standards Applications: This integration lesson offers students the opportunity to plot authentic data using technologies such as a spreadsheet or a geographic information system for the purpose of analyzing and studying trends of carbon dioxide to study relationships between global and atmospheric conditions.

Students use two Internet sites to obtain data on global temperatures and atmospheric concentrations of carbon dioxide and use the data to answer questions about these topics. Students plot monthly average carbon dioxide concentrations for a given year and observe patterns in increases and decreases. Then they graph the temperature data for a year and compare them with the carbon dioxide data. They discuss possible links between the biosphere and the atmosphere. Finally, they use the Internet to gather other information on global warming, and they discuss the current trends.

Source: Slattery, W., Hundley, S., Finegan-Stoll, C., & Becker, M. (1998). Collecting science in a net. *Learning and Leading with Technology, 26*(1), 25–30.

Teachers can also use the Internet for assistance with content knowledge and for professional development opportunities that may not be available locally. They can also exchange ideas and teaching strategies with other teachers. The Eisenhower National Clearinghouse (ENC) provides a comprehensive website for connecting teachers with resources and training. The ENC provides a number of online publications containing the latest research on teaching and learning science. Teachers can also utilize the National Academy Press website (http://www.nap.edu) to examine the most current publications in science and science education available online for free.

Barriers to Integrating Science and Technology

Although the amount of special resources available to science teachers grows continually, two key barriers exist that pose problems in the extensive utilization of technology in science instruction.

Teacher Resistance to Technology Use in Science Class. The *National Science Education Standards* advocate for professional development for teachers with an emphasis on technology:

> *NSES Professional Development Standard A:* Professional development for teachers of science requires learning essential science content through the perspectives and methods of inquiry. Such science learning experiences must introduce teachers to scientific literature, media, and technological resources that expand their science knowledge and their ability to access further knowledge.

Nonetheless, a survey of public school teachers indicates that teachers feel there is too little time to learn about, plan, and implement instructional technology in their everyday instructions (National Center for Educational Statistics, 2004). Despite investment in equipment and software, there simply is not enough investment in professional development programs to educate teachers in using technology effectively in their instructional practices. Without addressing the concerns of teachers, educational technology will not be an everyday part of teaching and learning.

Equity in Access to Technology. The gaps in availability of educational technology among demographic groups is very clear. In a report from the National Center for Educational Statistics (2003) a stark disparity exists in the amount of Internet and computer access among African American, Hispanic, and White students (see Figure 11.12). The factors that influence the technological divide among racial and ethnic groups are confounded by socioeconomic status, instructional resources available to students, and financial support available to schools. A study out of California suggests that schools lack textbooks for poor and minority students (Oakes & Saunders, 2004). Therefore, despite access to technology being an issue in many areas, more fundamental needs, such as science textbooks for needy students, negatively impact science teachers' ability and desire to integrate technology and science in their everyday instruction.

FIGURE 11.12 Percentage of children in nursery school and students in grades K–12 using computers at home and at school, by race/ethnicity: 2003

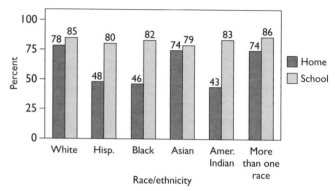

© 2006 National Center for Education Statistics

Source: Computer & Internet Access by Students in 2003. Statistical Analysis Report, U.S. Department of Education, Institute of Education Sciences NCES 2006–065. http://nces.ed.gov/pubs2006/2006065.pdf.

Interactive Summary

The following is a summary of the main points covered in this chapter.

1. **Issues in mathematics instruction** — These include:
   - Accountability for Standards in Mathematics
   - Challenges in implementing the Principles and Standards for School Mathematics.

2. **Integration strategies for mathematics instruction** — Six strategies are described for integrating technology into this area:
   - Using virtual manipulatives
   - Fostering mathematical problem solving
   - Allowing representation of mathematical principles, i.e., *Geometer's Sketchpad*
   - Implementing data-driven curricula, i.e., *Fathom*
   - Supporting math-related communications, i.e., *Ask Dr. Math*
   - Motivating skill building and practice.

3. **Issues in science instruction** — These include:
   - Accountability for standards in science
   - The narrowing pipeline of scientific talent
   - Increasing need for scientific literacy
   - Difficulties teaching K–8 science
   - New emphasis on and controversies about scientific inquiry.

4. **Integration strategies for science instruction** — Four strategies are described for integrating technology into this area:
   - Supporting authentic science experiences, i.e., the GLOBE project
   - Supporting scientific inquiry skills, i.e. the *Exploratorium*
   - Supporting science concept learning
   - Accessing science information and tools.

Key Terms

- calculator-based laboratory (CBL)
- interactive or dynamic geometry software
- scientific inquiry
- virtual manipulative

Web-Enrichment Activities

1. ***Math Problems of the Week*** — Visit the Math Forum Problems of the Week website at http://mathforum .org/pow/. Do one of the current problems, using the help and mentoring features if you need them. Discuss how online problems of the week can be used in classrooms. How can teachers use technology to teach their own problems of the week?

2. ***Virtual Manipulatives for Math and Science*** — Use an online manipulative or interactive applet from one of the sites listed below.

   - Manipula Math with Java—http://www.ies.co.jp/ math/java/index.html

   - Sample Digital Manipulatives—http://arcytech.org/ java/patterns/patterns_j.shtml

   - Applet for 3-D Shapes—http://www.shodor.org/ refdesk/Resources/Models/SurfacePlot

   - Web-Based Chemistry Simulations—http://cse.edc .org/products/simulations/default.asp

   Evaluate the manipulative or applet using the following criteria, and then add an additional criterion to your evaluation.

   a. The manipulative or applet was an accurate reflection of the mathematical or scientific principle.

   b. The manipulative or applet was effective in helping me to understand, visualize, and practice the principle.

   c. The manipulative or applet functioned smoothly and was easy to use.

   d. The manipulative or applet matches with content-area standards for learning.

3. ***Computer Microscope*** — The ProScope digital microscope is demonstrated at a school in the clip at the website listed below.

   http://eagleqt.stillwater.k12.mn.us/~degerb/ promotional/ProScope.mov

   View the clip, and then list the scientific inquiry skills you think are addressed through the use of the technology. What are some other ways you might be able to use such technology in the classroom?

Go to MyEducationLab to complete the following exercises.

Video Select the topic "Science Integration," and go to the "Assignments, Activities, and Applications" section. Access the video "Science Applications" to see how students use technology to demonstrate what they have learned. Complete the activity that follows the video.

Building Teaching Skills Select the topic "Math Integration," and go to the "Building Teaching Skills and Dispositions" section. Access the activity "Technology Supports Student Learning" and complete the full activity.

Tutorials Select the topic "Software" and access the practical tutorial and skill-building activity for "Merging Excel into PowerPoint." Use the tutorial to learn the advance skill of merging Excel graphs into PowerPoint presentations. This skill will be reviewed again in the Technology Integration Workshop.

Tutorials Select the topic "Software" and access the practical tutorials for "Incorporating Excel into a Lesson: Elementary" and "Incorporating Excel into a Lesson: Middle/Secondary." Both tutorials demonstrate how you can incorporate Excel into Math lessons for different grade levels

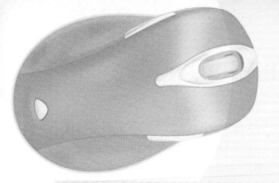

Technology Integration Workshop

The TIP Model in Action

Read each of the following scenarios related to implementing the TIP Model, and answer the questions that follow it based on your Chapter 11 reading and activities.

TIP MODEL SCENARIO #1 Ms. Waldrup, the AP mathematics teacher, wanted to have her students do simple correlations with two data sets to demonstrate the mathematical principles involved. However, it took students too long to do these calculations by hand and there were too many data-entry errors using a calculator.

1.1 What technology-based strategy could Ms. Waldrup use to address this problem?

1.2 What would be the relative advantage of using this strategy?

1.3 Would it be better to carry out this strategy with the whole class or with students working individually or in groups? Explain how you would do it.

TIP MODEL SCENARIO #2 Mr. Brino was trying to show his teenage students in the business education program how they could figure out quickly how much car they could buy with the money they had. He wanted to show them the relationship among the down payment, interest rate, and length of the loan and how this all would affect monthly payments and the total they would spend on the car at the end of the loan period. However, he wanted them to be able to do the calculations quickly, so they could focus on the underlying math concepts.

2.1 What technology-based strategy could Mr. Brino use to address this problem?

2.2 What would be the relative advantage of using this strategy?

2.3 Describe the steps you might use to carry out a simple lesson using this strategy.

TIP MODEL SCENARIO #3 Dr. Ahmed wanted his students to take readings at a local stream as part of an experiment on acid and alkaline substances in water. He wanted to use handheld probeware devices when they went on the field trip. With these devices, students could collect the data, bring the readings back in a data file, and download the file to a computer for analysis. However, he had 27 students and only 15 handhelds.

3.1 What grouping strategy could Dr. Ahmed use to make the available devices work well with this many students?

3.2 What pedagogical strategies would you advise Dr. Ahmed to use with his students when carrying out the data collection?

3.3 What would be the relative advantage of using this strategy as opposed to manual methods of collecting the readings?

TIP MODEL SCENARIO #4 Ms. Lyndia was the school counselor in charge of helping students prepare for the test her school district had developed to select those students eligible for the special math/science magnet program, which offered all expenses paid to those who were selected. She knew a lot about the kinds of items that would be on the test, and she knew that some of the students needed to practice some of the skills.

4.1 What technology-based strategy would you recommend Ms. Lyndia use to address this problem?

4.2 What would be the relative advantage of using this strategy as opposed to a paper-and-pencil format?

4.3 Should students practice individually, in pairs, or in small groups? Explain.

TIP MODEL SCENARIO #5 Mr. Cardillo's ninth-grade students had a lot of problems understanding geometry concepts. They seemed to understand them better when he drew the figures and angles for them as he explained the concepts, but this was not feasible for every problem. It took too long, and he couldn't draw well enough to show everything clearly.

5.1 What technology-based strategy would you recommend Mr. Cardillo use to address this problem?

5.2 What would be the relative advantage of using this strategy?

5.3 If Mr. Cardillo had 32 students in his class and only one computer, what would you recommend he do to carry out this strategy most effectively?

TIE into Practice: Technology Integration Examples

The Technology Integration Example that opened this chapter (*Hot and Cold Data*) showed how a teacher might have students use CBLs and spreadsheet activities to carry out experiments. As each group completed its assigned experiment, it presented the results to the class by displaying the graphed data in a *PowerPoint* presentation. With the knowledge you have gained from Chapter 11, do the following to explore this strategy:

1. Create a spreadsheet graph like the example shown here. Having completed a tutorial on creating a spreadsheet graph and importing it into PowerPoint, create an example graph like the one below.

2. Answer the following questions about the *Hot and Cold Data* example:

   • Phase 2 — What kinds of relative advantage did the teachers feel the use of CBLs would bring to the learning activity? How would using spreadsheets help?

   • Phase 3 — Outcomes 2 and 4 are very similar statements. Why are they stated as separate outcomes?

How would the assessment for them differ? How would it be similar?

   • Phase 4 — Students may not be familiar with *Consumer Reports* and its approach to comparing products. If the teachers did not have access to the magazines themselves, what could they do to help students understand this approach?

   • Phase 5 — What could the teachers do with the performance measures and lab sheets to make them more accessible to students both inside and outside class?

   • Phase 6 — In evaluating the outcomes of the activity, the teachers found that all students showed competence with CBL procedures and were able to carry out the experiments with teacher assistance. However, some students still had difficulty with the final outcome. How might the teachers change the implementation to help students better achieve this outcome?

3. What NETS for Students skills would students learn by working on the *Hot and Cold Data* project? (See the front of this book for a list of NETS for Students.)

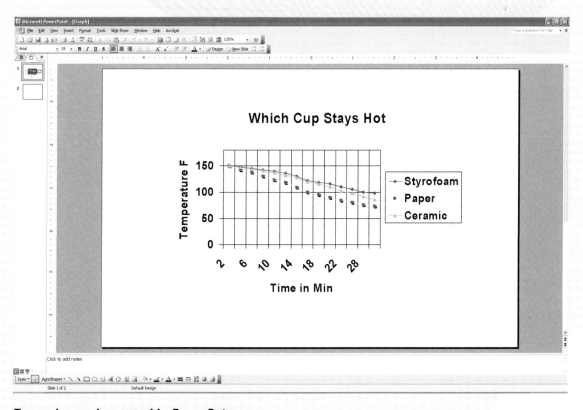

Example graph created in *PowerPoint*.

Technology Integration Lesson Planning

Complete the following exercise using sample lesson plans found on MyEducationLab.

1. Locate lesson ideas — MyEducationLab has several examples of lessons that use the mathematics and science integration strategies described in this chapter. Go to MyEducationLab under the topics "Math Integration" and "Science Integration" and go to the Lesson Plans to review example lessons. Choose two of the following integration lessons:

   - Algebra, Geometry, and Conic Sections
   - Bringing the Planets Closer to Home
   - Code Crackers: A Beginning Algebra Activity
   - Data Analysis for Young Children
   - Using Probeware to Integrate Mathematics and Science
   - Visualize it in 3-D

2. Evaluate the lessons — Use the *Evaluation Checklist for a Technology-Integrated Lesson* (located on MyEducationLab under the topic "Instructional Planning") to evaluate each of these lessons.

3. Modify a lesson — Select one of the lesson ideas and adapt its strategies to meet a need in your own content area. You may choose to use the same approach as in the original or to adapt it to meet your needs.

4. Add descriptors — Create descriptors for your new lesson similar to those found within the sample lessons (e.g., grade level, content and topic areas, technologies used, relative advantage, objectives, NETS standards).

5. Save your new lesson — Save your modified lesson with all its descriptors.

For Your Teaching Portfolio

For this chapter's contribution to your teaching portfolio, add the following products you created in the Technology Integration Workshop:

- The sample graph and *PowerPoint* frame you created
- The evaluations you did using the *Evaluation Checklist for a Technology-Integrated Lesson*
- The new lesson plan you developed, based on the one you found on MyEducationLab.

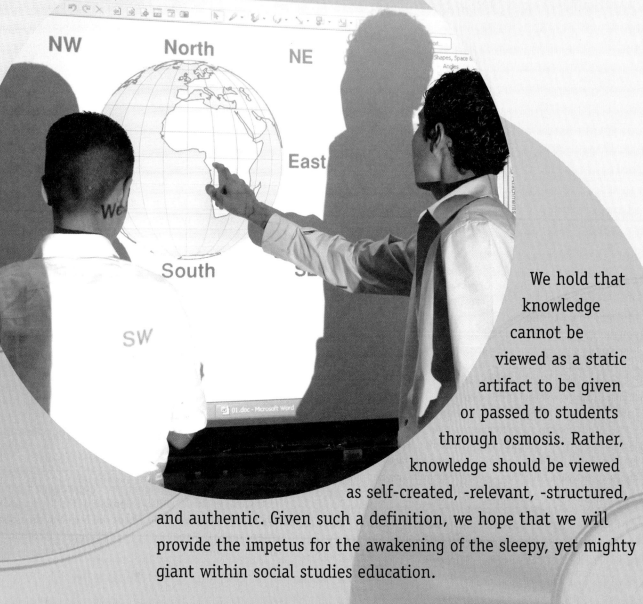

Chapter 12

Technology in Social Studies Instruction

We hold that knowledge cannot be viewed as a static artifact to be given or passed to students through osmosis. Rather, knowledge should be viewed as self-created, -relevant, -structured, and authentic. Given such a definition, we hope that we will provide the impetus for the awakening of the sleepy, yet mighty giant within social studies education.

Aaron Doering, George Veletsianos, & Cassandra Scharber (2007)

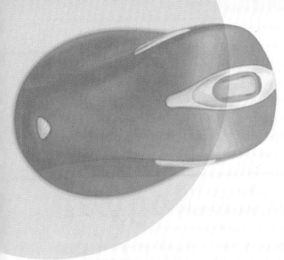

Technology Integration Example

Studying Our Past, Mapping Our Future

Based on: Parmenter, B., & Burns, M. (2001). GIS in the classroom: Challenges, opportunities, and alternatives. *Learning and Leading with Technology, 28*(7), 10–17.

Grade Levels: 7 through 8 • Content Area/Topic: Geography, civics, and history • Length of Time: Six weeks

Phases 1 and 2: Assess technological pedagogical content knowledge; Determine relative advantage

Mr. McVee taught the state and local studies classes for his school's eighth-grade students. He had always felt that one of his most important tasks as a **social studies** teacher at this level was to help his students see that people shape the history and growth of an area and that the students themselves could have a major role in shaping the future of areas in which they live. He knew this was important preparation and background for the civics and history courses they would take in high school. However, he also knew how difficult it was to get students to grasp complex, abstract concepts like the relationship between past history, current conditions, and future developments. He decided that this concept would become more meaningful to students if they gathered information from local citizens about the history of their local area and used their findings to hypothesize plans for the area's future.

As he brainstormed activities, he looked for resources that could make historical and geographical concepts more real and compelling to students and that would emphasize their ability to shape their future. In a recent district workshop, he had learned that the Environmental Systems Research Institute (ESRI; http://www.esri.com) provides a free **Geographic Information System (GIS)** viewer on its website through which students can see actual maps overlaid with census data. GISs are software systems that house database collections of graphic and text information about the surface of the Earth and also provide tools for viewing, manipulating, and analyzing these data. He read about a project in which students created "life maps" of people and places on GIS maps of the area during different periods of time (Audet & Ludwig, 2000). He also had experimented with simulation software that gave students an active role in decision making about social issues. He decided to integrate these and other resources into a 6-week unit around three major activities: identifying events that shaped the history and growth of the area, creating life

maps of people from the history of the local area, and developing a "growth scenario" for the future.

Before Mr. McVee decided to implement this unit that he read about, he thought he should have some idea of how to use the GIS and how it might be integrated into the K–12 classroom. He had played around with other forms of GISs such as *Google Earth*, but he had never used ESRI's new viewer. Thus, Mr. McVee decided to assess his own own technological pedagogical content knowledge (TPACK) so that he could evaluate his strengths and weaknesses and understand where he fit within the TPACK model. His location within the model indicated that he was very strong in content knowledge but that he lacked knowledge of both technology and pedagogy. In response to this, Mr. McVee went on to ESRI's website and found a number of lessons and teaching ideas. He downloaded some "starter" lessons to help him and his students become familiar with the software. He also downloaded some ready-made presentations to help him showcase the idea to his students and get them involved.

Phase 3: Decide on objectives and assessments

Mr. McVee decided that each activity in the unit should result in a graded, small-group product. The products would be timelines showing local events and population growth; life maps of people, places, and events in the local area; and a map presentation of their growth scenario for the future. The following outcomes, objectives, and assessments would help identify and measure students' achievement:

- **Outcome:** Timelines and population growth. **Objective:** Each group will complete all tasks to produce a timeline of the major phases of development in the local area, with events and population figures noted for each time period. **Assessment:** Ratings checklist of required components and characteristics.

- **Outcome:** Life maps. **Objective:** Each group will complete all tasks to produce a life map of a well-known figure from each time period in the area's history.

Assessment: Ratings checklist of required components and characteristics.

- **Outcome:** Future growth plans. **Objective:** Each group will achieve at least 90% on a rubric covering their plan for future growth of the area, which they create based on their analysis of past and current events and growth. **Assessment:** Rubric to cover quality of research, required components, and cooperative group work.

Phase 4: Design integration strategies

After spending a great deal of time on ESRI's website and talking with other teachers within the online bulletin boards, Mr. McVee decided he would use the following sequence to accomplish the goals of the unit:

- **Week 1: Introduce the unit:** Introduce the unit to the class as *Our Area: Past, Present, and Future.* Show actual photos of the same local area at different periods of time. Compare the photos and discuss what kinds of things changed and why. Tell them about the products they will create during their study of the evolution of their area. Ask students to "volunteer" parents, grandparents, or great grandparents who would come to school so the class could interview them and gather information about events that shaped the local area. Have the class brainstorm questions to ask during interviews with their "senior authorities." Demonstrate the Tom Snyder *TimeLiner* software. Form small groups, and assign each small group a time period. Give each some background history materials on the time period, and have them experiment with creating a timeline of events that occurred in the United States and the world during their particular time period.

- **Week 2: Gather information and create timelines:** Have student groups interview the local expert(s) for their assigned time period. Have them visit websites that give general information about the time period. After compiling their notes on the answers to the interview questions, have each group use the *TimeLiner* software to create a timeline of events during their time period. From local newspaper records, library records, and local "historians," students obtain pictures to illustrate world, national, and local events. Each group presents its timeline and describes how the people and events they learned about helped shape the local area.

- **Weeks 3–4: Create life maps:** Demonstrate ESRI's GIS viewer. Show students how they can get census data on their local area from the U.S. Census Bureau site, and use the ESRI *ArcExplorer* viewer to see maps of census data for their area. Form small working groups, and have each group experiment with displaying a different kind of data on the same area. They also answer questions such as "Why are congressional districts drawn as they are?" and "Have they changed over time?" Have them present their data analysis to the whole class. Discuss how the "life map" will look and how to go about creating it.

Group members import the GIS map they produced earlier into a graphics package and create a "life map" of the person they interviewed, showing places and events the person discussed and the boundaries of the town at that time. They present their maps to the class.

- **Weeks 5–6: Create future scenarios with GIS data:** Introduce this phase of the unit by having student groups use the Tom Snyder *Decisions, Decisions: Town Government* software to explore citizens' roles in governing the local community. Lead a discussion comparing the findings of each of the group. Then tell students to imagine they are part of a citizen's action committee assigned the task of planning a growth scenario for their community for the next decade. Have each group look at a different area of growth (e.g., housing, transportation, recreational areas, services such as waste disposal and water). As a whole class, students download historical census data from the U.S. Census Bureau website, put it in a spreadsheet, and use it to project population statistics for the area during the next 10 years. In small groups, they discuss the implications of this population growth for their area of concern. Using the maps they created for their life maps, they show what would need to be planned and developed to keep up with the area's growth. Mr. McVee helps them print their maps on transparency sheets. Using an overhead projector, they overlay the maps and "negotiate" to resolve any conflicts they see (e.g., new housing vs. a larger city park). As a whole class, they merge the maps into one to represent their plan for the future. They end the unit by reflecting on their decisions and the implications they would have for the area.

Phase 5: Prepare the instructional environment

In the weeks before the project began, Mr. McVee had to organize several kinds of resources. First, with the help of students, he had to obtain historical photos and data on the community. Then he had to identify the resource people who could serve as authorities on each decade from 1950 through 2000 and set up interview times. To have his students see and discuss the U.S. Census Bureau website and GIS maps as a whole class, Mr. McVee needed to schedule the use of a large-screen projection system and obtain permission to print transparencies on the computer lab's laser printer. He also had to locate and set up websites on the historical periods for the students to view. Finally, he had to make sure the two software packages worked on his classroom computers.

Phase 6: Evaluate and revise

Mr. McVee tried out the lesson and administered the following self-assessment to review how it worked for him:

- Did students' products reflect growth in their thinking about people's roles in shaping their future?
- Did the students become engaged in each of the tasks?

- Did each of the software and web resources and small groups work as smoothly as expected?
- Did most students score well on the checklists and rubric?

Also, he interviewed students about their perceptions of the unit. As expected, they were most positive about the interviews of local people and the hands-on work with the website. They were less enthusiastic about having to work in small groups. After considering students' work on all the outcomes, Mr. McVee decided the unit was a success. He resolved to contact the state GIS office for more local data for various time periods that students could use in their work. He also decided to look for strategies to make his students feel more positive about working in groups.

Objectives

After reading this chapter and completing the learning activities for it, you should be able to:

1. Identify current issues in social studies instruction that may impact the selection and use of technology.

2. Describe key strategies for integrating technology into social studies curricula.

3. Create instructional activities for social studies instruction that model successful integration strategies.

Since the Industrial Revolution, science and technology have shaped the world in fundamental ways. In the 1990s, computer technologies and the emergence of the Internet have accelerated this influence. Better, faster, worldwide communications have made the world at once smaller and more complex. Life was simpler—and less informed—when people were not able to know so much about themselves and others so quickly. Now, with so much information at hand, we have much to discover about our world and its people. But it is through this exploration that we make our world more like the place we want it to be—be it for better or for worse. Just 30 years ago, the Internet, cell phones, DVDs, computers, and public transportation as we know it today did not exist. Think how fast technology is changing our life and how our life is changing the environment.

The National Council for the Social Studies (NCSS) has adopted the following formal definition for the social studies:

> Social studies is the integrated study of the social sciences and humanities to promote civic competence. Within the school program, social studies provides coordinated, systemic study drawing upon such disciplines as anthropology, archaeology, economics, geography, history, law, philosophy, political science, psychology, religion, and sociology, as well as appropriate content from the humanities, mathematics, and the natural sciences. The primary purpose of social studies is to help young people develop the ability to make informed and reasoned decisions for the public good as citizens of a culturally diverse, democratic society in an interdependent world. (NCSS, 1994, p. 3)

As an area that focuses on the interconnections of people and the earth, social studies education has been affected by the impact of technology perhaps more than any other content area. Not only is there more to learn about the world than ever before, but also the information is changing constantly and dramatically. Fortunately, the same technologies that created this more complex world also can help teach about it. Unfortunately, Martorella's (1997) comment that technology within the social studies is a "sleeping giant" has not yet been realized. Bolick, however, (2004) argues that the "giant is waking" in certain areas within the social studies and calls for collaboration between social studies teacher educators, instructional designers, and technology specialists to realize the potential of technology within social studies education.

What Does TPACK Look Like in Social Studies Education?

Questions surrounding technological pedagogical content knowledge (TPACK) for teachers include "How does this relate to me?" and "What are the implications of knowing about TPACK in my content area?" TPACK in any discipline is the perfect union of three knowledge domains (content, pedagogy, and technology) to develop a knowledge base from which a teacher can view a lesson and understand how technology can enhance the learning opportunities and experiences for the students while also knowing the correct pedagogy to enhance the learning of the content. In social studies education, a teacher is incorporating the

FIGURE 12.1 **TPACK and Social Studies**

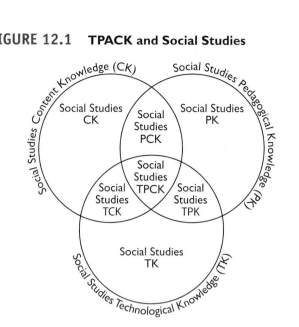

TPACK principles when he or she plans a lesson and, without hesitation, thinks about the student accomplishment that must be achieved and understands the content that can be taught through the correct pedagogy and technology. For example, when teaching a lesson in geography about climate change, instead of simply lecturing about the current data—ice core, traditional ecological knowledge, and the melting of the Arctic ice sheets—teachers who possess TPACK think about technology and how students can learn in a way that they could not without the technology. Thus, a teacher thinks about how students could collect climate change data for locations around the world and have students analyze change over time using a geospatial technology such as *ArcExplorer* or *Google Earth*. A teacher thinks about the relative advantage of having students use this real-time authentic data and uses various pedagogical approaches to scaffold learners to answer difficult questions. (See Figure 12.1.)

Issues and Problems in Social Studies Instruction

Methods of Addressing Social Studies Instruction Standards

The *National Social Studies Standards,* released by the NCSS in 1994, address overall curriculum design and comprehensive student performance expectations. However, standards also exist for each of the social studies disciplines—such as civics, economics, geography, government, and history—which provide more specific content detail for each discipline. The social studies teacher often needs to be a "jack of all trades" and hopefully a master of more than one content area. Unfortunately, many preservice teachers who are social

studies majors get tracked into areas, such as history, where it is felt they most likely can get a job, leaving courses in content areas such as economics and geography last on their list.

NCSS hopes that curriculum designers will use the NCSS social studies standards for creating the overall framework and then fill in the detail using the discipline standards. Ten themes form the framework of the social studies standards; those, along with a brief description of each, are presented next (NCSS, 1994; http://www.socialstudies.org/standards). At the elementary and middle school levels, school systems usually address the social studies curriculum by teaching a variety of topics from these strands. In high school, social studies tends to become divided into more specific areas, such as history and civics. Thus, when referring to a course, the term *social studies* is more commonly used to describe K–8 classes than high school classes.

- **Theme 1: Culture** — The study of culture prepares students to answer questions such as these: What are the common characteristics of different cultures? How do belief systems, such as religion or political ideals, influence other parts of the culture? This theme typically appears in units and courses dealing with geography, history, sociology, and anthropology as well as multicultural topics across the curriculum.

- **Theme 2: Time, continuity, and change** — Humans seek to understand their historical roots and to locate themselves in time. Knowing how to read and reconstruct the past allows one to develop a historical perspective and to answer questions such as these: Who am I? What happened in the past? How am I connected to those in the past? How has the world changed, and how might it change in the future? Why does our personal sense of relatedness to the past change? This theme typically appears in courses in history and others that draw on historical knowledge and habits.

- **Theme 3: People, places, and environments** — The study of people, places, and human–environment interactions assists students as they create their spatial views and geographic perspectives of the world beyond their personal locations. Students need the knowledge, skills, and understanding to answer questions such as these: Where are things located? Why are they located where they are? What do we mean by "region"? How do landforms change? What implications do these changes have for people? This theme typically appears in units and courses dealing with area studies and geography.

- **Theme 4: Individual development and identity** — Personal identity is shaped by culture, groups, and institutional influences. Students should consider such questions as these: How do people learn? Why do people

Collaborative projects promote communication and reflection, as well as provide information to support research.

behave as they do? What influences how people learn, perceive, and grow? How do people meet their basic needs in a variety of contexts? How do individuals develop from youth to adulthood? This theme typically appears in units and courses dealing with psychology and anthropology.

- **Theme 5: Individuals, groups, and institutions** — Institutions such as schools, churches, families, government agencies, and the courts play an integral role in our lives. It is important that students learn how institutions are formed, what controls and influences them, how they influence individuals and culture, and how they are maintained or changed. Students may address questions such as these: What is the role of institutions in this or other societies? How am I influenced by institutions? How do institutions change? What is my role in institutional change? This theme typically appears in units and courses dealing with sociology, anthropology, psychology, political science, and history.

- **Theme 6: Power, authority, and governance** — Understanding the historical development of power, authority, and governance and their evolving functions in contemporary U.S. society and other parts of the world is essential for developing civic competence. In exploring this theme, students confront questions such as these: What is power? What forms does it take? Who holds it? How is it gained, used, and justified? What is legitimate authority? How are governments created, structured, maintained, and changed? How can individual rights be protected within the context of majority rule? This theme typically appears in units

and courses dealing with government, politics, political science, history, and law.

- **Theme 7: Production, distribution, and consumption** — Because people have wants that often exceed available resources, a variety of ways have evolved to answer these questions: What is to be produced? How is production organized? How are goods and services distributed? What is the most effective allocation of factors of production such as land, labor, capital, and management? This theme typically appears in units and courses dealing with economic concepts and issues.

- **Theme 8: Science, technology, and society** — Modern life would be impossible without technology and the science that supports it. But technology raises many questions: Is new technology always better than old? What can we learn from the past about how new technologies result in broader social change, some of which is unanticipated? How can we cope with the ever-increasing pace of change? How can we preserve our fundamental values and beliefs in the midst of technological change? This theme draws on the natural and physical sciences, social studies, and the humanities and appears in a variety of social studies courses, including history, geography, economics, civics, and government.

- **Theme 9: Global connections** — The realities of global interdependence require an understanding of the increasingly important and diverse global connections among world societies and the frequent tension between national interests and global priorities. Students need to be able to address such international issues as health care, the environment, human rights, economic competition and interdependence, age-old ethnic hostilities, and political and military alliances. This theme typically appears in units or courses dealing with geography, culture, and economics, but it may also draw on the natural and physical sciences and the humanities.

- **Theme 10: Civic ideals and practices** — An understanding of civic ideals and practices of citizenship is critical to full participation in society and is a central purpose of the social studies. Students confront questions such as these: What is civic participation, and how can we be involved? How has the meaning of citizenship evolved? What is the balance between rights and responsibilities? What is the role of the citizen in the community and the nation and as a member of the world community? This theme typically appears in units or courses dealing with history, political science, and cultural anthropology and fields such as global studies, law-related education, and the humanities.

Adapting for Special Needs

The study of current events is an important strand in social studies. Although teachers increasingly use video tools to engage students, print materials continue to be an important resource for learning about current events. One innovative tool for engaging students in news media stories is creating a personalized newspaper. Using technology known as selective dissemination of information (SDI), users create a set of filters that allow topics of interest to be presented. One of the most popular personalized newspaper services is known as Crayon (http://crayon.net). Personalized news services also can be found in some web hosting systems (http://my.yahoo.com) that even allow the presentation of selected daily comics. The value to students is that they take responsibility for deciding what types of stories they want to monitor, which typically helps engage them in reading. This also can be an excellent way to prepare students for writing following a period of monitoring the news. For students who have difficulty reading, web-based plug-ins like the ReadingBar (http://www.readplease.com) can be installed in the web browser. Students click on individual words or whole sections of text, and these are read to them.

For students with mild or moderate cognitive impairments, specially designed resources are available to provide current events information at an appropriate level. News-2-You (http://www.news-2-you.com) is a subscription-based service that prepares an 8-page current events reader each week that is downloaded in PDF format and copied for distribution to students. These specially written resources feature high-interest, low-vocabulary stories with each word accompanied by a rebus image.

Contributed by Dave Edyburn

Dilemmas in Teaching Social Studies Effectively

Despite their obvious value and relevance to future citizens, social studies themes and topics are not usually among those included in statewide assessments. Many states limit their graduation tests to language arts (i.e., reading and writing) and mathematics. Since many teachers tend to focus instruction primarily on tested topics, social studies areas are often placed on the back burner (Flannery, 2004). Consequently, school resources such as technology materials tend to be directed toward other content areas.

The sheer amount of material to review in many social studies topic areas is also a concern. A good example is a world history course, which often covers the period from the dawn of civilization to the present day. The amount of content, coupled with the de-emphasis on social studies topics, creates an ongoing challenge to schools to teach social studies in a meaningful way. A longstanding joke within social studies circles goes like this, "Did you get past World War I this year?"—referring to the large amount of content to be covered and the short amount of time in a school year to do so. Unfortunately, in many cases, this old joke reflects the reality of the challenge social studies teachers face.

Adding to this challenge is the changing role of technology itself. At first, teachers looked at technology resources as a collection of tools to help teach specific content and skills. However, as teachers began to see technology making profound changes in social, civic, and economic functioning, they saw value in more constructivist uses (Berson & Balyta, 2004; Doering & Veletsianos, 2007). Unfortunately, using technology in constructivist ways, while potentially powerful, is also more time consuming than using it for directed uses, which further adds to the dilemma of how to use technology effectively in teaching social studies.

Finally, there is the issue of costs for high-quality resources. For example, it costs $900 to equip 30 computers with *TimeLiner* software. Social studies teachers have to make the case that the expense of these resources is worthwhile due to increased achievement or other benefits while also understanding how to use constructivist technologies effectively. However, a number of free constructivist technologies are available, such as *Google Earth*, ESRI's *ArcExplorer Java Edition for Educators*, *Google Documents*, and *VoiceThread*.

The "History Wars" and Other Debates on the Content and Focus of Social Studies

Social studies has attracted more debate and criticism than perhaps any other content area, and much of this discussion centers around the appropriate role of history in the curriculum (Evans, 2004). Schools have struggled to give proper emphasis to all of the social studies topics. However, some critics feel strongly that schools should focus squarely on teaching history and civics rather than taking a broader approach and covering a number of social studies topics. In recent years, leaders in the field of social studies have made the case that students should be aware of the broad array of influences that have shaped our country's history. Critics of this approach feel that the content of history courses has become diluted—that courses focus too much on topics they consider to be outside the mainstream, traditional historical themes and important events that shaped the United States. These critics feel that teachers who are not well prepared in the latter approach are ill equipped to teach history effectively.

Perils of the Information Explosion

The ready availability of information on the Internet has created several concerns for social studies educators. Some believe that Internet information has the potential to alter the traditional relationship between student and teacher since teachers are no longer the primary source of facts or opinions. Teachers tell of students bringing printed web pages to school that contradict what the textbook says or even what the teacher says. In the past, most information that students received was sifted through a reliable filter; today, those filters often are nonexistent. Students can find sites that profess Nazi and Ku Klux Klan ideology, treat rumor as fact, and promote conspiracy theories that range from UFO landings in Roswell, New Mexico, to the CIA selling drugs in American cities. Many students have been drawn to these types of sites without questioning their accuracy.

Many educators believe we need information literacy or media literacy now more than ever. Some believe that rather than shying away from the hate or conspiracy sites, we should be using them as demonstration tools to teach our students how to become critical consumers of information. As Harp (1996) puts it, schools must "mobilize their curriculum leaders into quality management" (p. 38) to monitor and help students become more analytical about the information they receive.

Technology Integration Strategies for Social Studies Instruction

Technology tools make possible a variety of strategies to enhance learning for the varied topics and concepts that comprise social studies content. Some of the nine strategies described here support more traditional, directed approaches to teaching social studies topics. Most of these strategies, however, make possible what many social studies educators feel is a more meaningful, dynamic way of learning key concepts (Whitworth & Berson, 2003). The following integration strategies suggest activities to address each of the 10 themes in the NCSS *National Social Studies Standards*.

Simulated Problem-Solving Environments

Many social studies topics present issues, concepts, or procedures that at first are complex and confusing to students. Simulations, or electronic environments that allow students to interact with simulated events or locations, can help make these concepts more clear and meaningful.

It is for this reason that simulations have been a popular resource in social studies learning since the early days of microcomputers in schools. Some simulations allow students to take an active part in historical situations that would not otherwise be possible due to historical or physical distance. Other problem-solving environments situate learning in authentic situations using real-world data and situated movies to motivate students (Doering & Veletsianos, 2007). Most such products are designed to immerse students in problem-solving scenarios where they must make decisions and apply information they have learned.

Updated versions of some of the early simulations (e.g., *The Oregon Trail*) are still being used, and other, more sophisticated simulations have emerged as technology has become more capable (e.g., *GeoThentic*, Muzzy Lane's *Making History*). By placing students in the role of decision makers in these simulations, they not only see the relevance of social studies in their daily lives, but they also develop better problem-solving skills. Some popular examples of simulated problem-solving environments that address various social studies themes are listed in Table 12.1.

Making the Case for Technology Integration

Use the following questions to reflect on issues in technology integration and to guide discussions within your class.

1. Harp's 1996 article, "The History Wars," described the conflict that resulted when some historians proposed altering the "traditional" treatments of American and world history to include emphasis on multicultural influences. He said, "While some are still fighting hard for a set, traditional curriculum—with standards to match—technology has opened the history classroom door to a dizzying array of data, artifacts, and perspectives. Helping teachers to make sense of it all is more than half the battle."

   What role has technology played in causing "the history wars"? What needs to be done to help teachers "make sense of it all"?

2. The National Council for the Social Studies said, "Powerful social studies teaching is integrative across time and space, connecting with past experiences and looking ahead to the future. It helps students appreciate how aspects of the social world function, not only in their local community but also in the past and in other cultures" (1994, p. 33).

   What are some ways in which technology can enable teaching strategies with these characteristics?

Top Ten

Strategies for Technology in Social Studies Instruction

Take advantage of these ten powerful strategies for using technology to enhance the teaching of social studies topics.

1. **Adventure learning provides students with opportunities to collaborate with other students, teachers, and experts** — Students use a research-based curriculum as they study authentic real-time adventures taking place around the world. Students learn from the curriculum and each other as they are part of an unfolding narrative.

2. **Virtual field trips help students learn about other cultures** — The wealth of information and images available about other cultures enriches students' study of other lands and ways of life.

3. **Send students on a geocaching treasure hunt with GPS devices** — These motivating activities get students to spend more time studying geographical information and techniques.

4. **"Live through" history with *Muzzy Lane*'s simulated immersion experience** — Students play the role of decision maker in historical situations in order to see the relevance of these events in their daily lives and to develop better problem-solving skills.

5. **Do webquests to learn the history behind political issues** — Students do Internet research to learn that current issues have historical roots in past events and debates.

6. **Integrate geospatial technologies to study the earth, people, and the symbiotic nature between the two** — Geospatial technologies such as *Google Earth* allow for real-world analysis as students study content such as history, economics, and geography.

7. **Students learn economic principles with stock market simulation games** — The complexities of the stock market become easier to understand when students play the role of stockbroker, investing "their own" money and seeing the return over time.

8. **Teach local and other history with electronic storytelling** — Images and audio make the stories of lives, events, or eras come alive for students and play a key role in helping students prepare oral histories.

9. **Use software such as *VoiceThread* to allow for real-time collaboration around numerous forms of content** — This kind of hands-on software allows students to post content (e.g., photos, videos, pdfs) and comment on each other's work in an online learning environment.

10. **Use digital cameras to explore community-based history and current issues** — Digital photography allows students to capture images from their vantage point, participate in the construction of knowledge, and learn how diverse perspectives can be shaped.

TABLE 12.1 Resources and Social Studies Themes: Simulated Problem-Solving Environments

Sample Sites	Social Studies Themes
Muzzy Lane's *Making History* http://www.muzzylane.com/ml/making_history	Theme 2: Time, continuity, and change Theme 6: Power, authority, and governance
Riverdeep's *The Oregon Trail* http://web.riverdeep.net/portal/page?_pageid=818,1380671, 818_1380706&_dad=portal&_schema=PORTAL	Theme 2: Time, continuity, and change Theme 7: Production, distribution, and consumption
Tom Snyder's *Decisions, Decisions 5.0* http://www.tomsnyder.com	Theme 6: Power, authority, and governance Theme 10: Civic ideals and practices
GeoThentic http://geothentic.umn.edu iearn Collaboration Center http://media.iearn.org/projects	Theme 3: People, places, and environments Theme 9: Global connections Theme 1: Culture Theme 9: Global connections
The International Communication and Negotiation Simulations (ICONS) http://www.icons.umd.edu/	Theme 9: Global connections
Who Killed William Robinson? http://web.uvic.ca/history-robinson/indexmsn.html	Theme 1: Culture Theme 4: Individual development and identity

Graphic Representations

Students often have problems visualizing abstract concepts such as timelines and maps. Teachers can use various technologies to represent these concepts graphically, which can enable even novices to understand and apply them. Products such as graphing software and spreadsheets (e.g., Microsoft's *Excel*) put data into a concrete form for easier analysis and representation of concepts and allow geographic concepts to be depicted visually. Graphic representation products (see Table 12.2) such as timeline generators allow students to understand time sequences and track change over time.

Virtual Trips

Virtual trips are "visits" students make to Internet sites to see places they could not easily go to in real life or that can help them get more out of trips they are able to take. Virtual trips do not have the interactive qualities of the simulated environments described earlier, but they have some of the same instructional benefits. Visiting foreign locations gives students a richer, more comprehensive perspective on the world around them and makes the world a living part of their classroom. For students who may travel little, the wealth of images and information from virtual trips helps them see and understand the variety of cultures, sights, and events outside their own communities. To best explain methods of using virtual trips in the middle school classroom, Beal and Mason (1999) have described four objectives of virtual field trips such as those listed in Table 12.3:

1. To help students synthesize what they learned on a class field trip
2. To prepare students for an upcoming class field trip
3. To provide students with information about areas they are unable to visit as a class
4. To provide students with information about areas their teacher visited.

TABLE 12.2 Resources and Social Studies Themes: Graphic Representation Products

Sample Sites	Social Studies Themes
Tom Snyder's *Neighborhood MopMachine 2.0* http://www.tomsnyder.com	Theme 3: People, places, and environments
Tom Snyder's *TimeLiner 5.0* http://www.tomsnyder.com	Theme 2: Time, continuity, and change
Tom Snyder's *The Graph Club* and *GraphMaster* http://www.tomsnyder.com	All themes

TABLE 12.3   Resources and Social Studies Themes: Virtual Field Trips

Sample Sites	Social Studies Themes
Bodie, California, a gold mining boomtown in the 1800s http://www.bodie.com	Theme 3: People, places, and environments
Virtual Tour of Israel http://www.3disrael.com/	Theme 2: Time, continuity, and change
Colonial House, a tour of life in the Colonial Era http://www.pbs.org/wnet/colonialhouse/history/index.html	Theme 2: Time, continuity, and change
Paris Yellow Pages with photos http://photos.pagesjaunes.fr/	Theme 1: Culture Theme 4: Individual development and identity

Adventure Learning

Adventure learning (AL) is a hybrid distance education approach that provides students with opportunities to explore real-world issues through authentic learning experiences within collaborative learning environments (Doering, 2006; Doering, 2007; Doering & Veletsianos, 2007). Specifically, this hybrid approach includes a K–12 curriculum designed with activities that work in conjunction with an authentic activity. For example, in the GoNorth! adventure learning series, Team GoNorth! annually dogsleds throughout circumpolar Arctic regions while students experience the travels with them virtually. The all-inclusive curriculum, the travel experiences and observations of Team GoNorth!, and the online learning environment are delivered concomitantly so that students are able to make connections among what is happening in the real world, their studies, and the collaboration and interaction within the online learning environment. As students collaborate to study a topic or to create a product, these projects promote communication, encourage reflection, and provide a wealth of information to support students' research. The sites listed in Table 12.4 are good sources for adventure learning projects.

Digital Storytelling

Digital storytelling is the process of using images and audio to tell the stories of lives, events, or eras. In this technique, students use personal narrative to explore community-based

history, politics, economics, and geography. These projects offer students the opportunity to make their own lives a part of their scholarly research. The use of digital images in the social studies can accomplish many purposes (Berson, 2004; Berson & Berson, 2003; Lee, 2008; Lee & Clark, 2004):

1. Assist students in comparing and contrasting the past and the present
2. Sensitize students to diverse perspectives and biases
3. Provide visual cues that reinforce geographic concepts
4. Represent abstract and concrete social studies concepts (e.g., democracy, liberty, needs and wants)
5. Foster skills in analysis and critical thinking
6. Facilitate greater connections to the community
7. Personalize associations with the study of geography, history, economics, government, and other related disciplines.

With the exploding world of Web 2.0 technologies, many digital tools can be used to create digital stories. Using technologies such as Apple's *iMovie*, camcorders, digital cameras, and voice recorders, student can create amazing stories. By sending students into their world with a digital camera in hand, teachers provide opportunities for them to bring their lives into the classroom, creating a rich, authentic authoring space. Writing text and arranging pictures as artifacts within a digital space allows students to explore events from multiple perspectives. As an extension or adaptation, students might create digital movies about an event, place, or individual, using

TABLE 12.4   Resources and Social Studies Themes: Adventure Learning

Sample Sites	Social Studies Themes
GoNorth! Adventure Learning Series http://www.polarhusky.com	All themes
The Jason Project http://www.jason.org/public/home.aspx	Theme 3: People, places, and environments Theme 8: Science, technology, and society

FIGURE 12.2 Digital Story

Emilystory
Added by Emily Olson at 8:58am on July 1st, 2008
✉ Send Message   View Videos

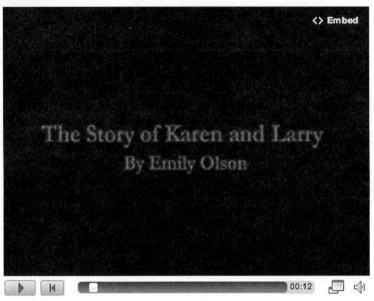

OK...one more try. Check out the Digital Story I created for my other class this semester. What a great way to bring technology into the classroom!

the camera to capture scenes and artifacts that could be woven together to tell a particular story. Figure 12.2 shows a digital story about a student's parents growing up. After creating the digital story, the student posted it onto the Ning website that was created for the class for her colleagues to watch. Table 12.5 lists websites that support digital storytelling.

Digital Information Critiques

History is replete with examples of the use of manipulated images to control people's impressions and opinions. As citizens in the Digital Age, students need to develop skills in critically evaluating digital information— how to analyze images and tell fact from fiction. Social studies activities provide a context for simultaneously exploring the social impact of images and developing

TABLE 12.5 Resources and Social Studies Themes: Digital Storytelling

Sample Sites	Social Studies Themes
Voice Thread www.voicethread.com	All themes
Center for Digital Storytelling http://www.storycenter.org	All themes
Digital Documentaries http://www.digitales.us/resources/documentary.php	All themes
PBS Civil War http://www.pbs.org/civilwar/	Theme 2: Time, continuity, and change
National Archives and Records Administration http://www.archives.gov/	Theme 2: Time, continuity, and change
Digital Resource Centers (DRC) http://www.teacherlink.org/content/social/digresources/	Theme 2: Time, continuity, and change Theme 3: People, places, and environments
The Oral History Society Home Page http://www.ohs.org.uk/	Theme 2: Time, continuity, and change Theme 3: People, places, and environments

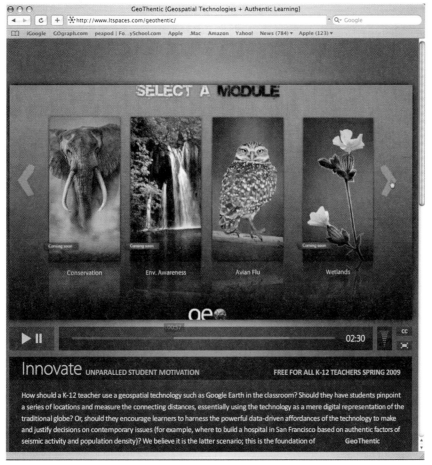

Sites like GeoThentic allow students to use real-world authentic data to solve environmental problems using geospatial technologies.

Source: Courtesy of GeoThentic: Learning Technologies, University of Minnesota.

media literacy skills (Van Hover, Swann, & Berson, 2004). (See Table 12.6.)

Electronic Research

As students study areas such as politics, economics, and current events, information is likely to change quickly and frequently. Internet sources give students and teachers up-to-date information they could not obtain easily from other sources. Also, access to information summaries and examples of data "pictures" on the Internet help students learn to analyze information in both graphic and text forms. Since we are relying more and more on Internet sources for reliable,

TABLE 12.6   Resources and Social Studies Themes: Digital Information Critiques

Sample Sites	Social Studies Themes
Jeff Stare's *The Camera Always Lies: Breaking the Myth of Objectivity* http://www.media.it.org/reading_room/article639.html	Theme 8: Science, technology, and society
Media Construction of War: A Critical Reading of History (Project Look Sharp) http://www.ithaca.edu/looksharp/	Theme 8: Science, technology, and society
DoKorne and Chin's *Photo Forgery Getting to the Heart of* *a Photojournalist's Code of Ethics* http://www.nytimes.com/learning/teachers/lessons/20040311/thursday	Theme 8: Science, technology, and society
Don't Buy It http://pbskids.org/dontbuyit/	Theme 8: Science, technology, and society

Technology Integration Lesson 12.1

Electronic Research

Title: Invention Events

Content Area/Topic: Technology education, history

Grade Levels: 5 through 8

NETS for Students: Standards 2 (Communication and Collaboration), 3 (Research and Information Fluency), and 4 (Critical Thinking, Problem Solving, and Decision Making)

Description of Standards Applications: This integration lesson offers students the opportunity to use the Internet to research inventions, develop a database of their findings, and communicate their findings to their peers. Students select an invention of interest to them. Just about anything, ranging from the telephone to the Internet, can be researched easily online. Students peruse a series of relevant websites, gathering information and background on their inventions. After they complete their research, students enter the inventions and the information about them into a database. Fields include items such as invention name, category, date of patent or invention, inventor, and significant effect of invention. After discussion about the inventions selected and researched by the class members, students each create a timeline to position their invention historically with reference to events surrounding the introduction of their inventions.

Source: Barrett, J. (2001). Indispensable inventions. *Learning and Leading with Technology, 29*(1), 22–26.

up-to-date information, students must learn where they can look for various kinds of data and facts they need to complete research in school and, later, at work. Technology Integration Lesson 12.1 provides an example of this strategy, and Table 12.7 lists sample products that support electronic research.

GIS and GPS Lessons

Geospatial technologies, such as *Google Earth (GE)* and *ArcExplorer,* allow individuals to view and examine the world through multiple layering of data within a spatial environment (see Figure 12.3). Although access

TABLE 12.7   Resources and Social Studies Themes: Electronic Research

Sample Sites	Social Studies Themes
Democratic and Republican Party websites http://www.democrats.org/ http://www.mc.org	Theme 6: Power, authority, and governance Theme 10: Civic ideals and practices
U.S. Congress http://thomas.loc.gov	Theme 6: Power, authority, and governance Theme 10: Civic ideals and practices
U.S. Information Agency http://clvnet.org	Theme 10: Civic ideals and practices
The White House http://www.whitehouse.gov	Theme 6: Power, authority, and governance Theme 10: Civic ideals and practices
Census in Schools http://www.census.gov/dmd/www/teachers.html http://www.census.gov/main/www/cen2000.html	Theme 1: Culture Theme 10: Civic ideals and practices
Ellis Island Records http://www.ellisisland.org/?google_ad5 http://www.ellisislandimmigrants.org/	Theme 1: Culture Theme 2: Time, continuity, and change
Multiculturalpedia http://www.netlaputa.ne.jp/~tokyo3/e/	Theme 1: Culture

FIGURE 12.3 A GIS Example

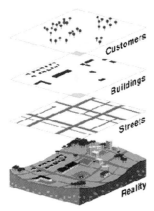

nologies within the classroom has been alarmingly slow (Baker & Bednarz, 2003; Kerski, 1999). Reasons for the delay include a dearth of research on its effectiveness (Baker & Bednarz, 2003), design issues related to Geographic Information Systems (GIS) and web-based geospatial technologies (Green, 2001), a general lack of geographic pedagogical content models (Doering, Veletsianos, & Scharber, 2007), a shortage of related curricula, low dissemination of geospatial technology into K–12 schools (Bednarz & Schee, 2006), and nonexistent and/or ineffective teacher training models (Doering, 2006).

to and use of such technology was previously limited by steep costs and demanding hardware, recently geospatial technologies have become increasingly popular with the general public. For example, the newcomer to geospatial technologies, Google Inc., reported that in 2006, *Google Earth* was downloaded more than 100 million times (Google, 2006). Nor is Google Inc. the only company providing new geospatial technologies: Microsoft recently introduced *Virtual Earth 3D*, and the Environmental Systems Research Institute (ESRI) introduced *ArcWeb Explorer*. The popularity of geospatial technologies is due to improvements in computers' computational power as well as to easier access and a reduction in the cost of geospatial technologies and data (Milla, Lorenzo, & Brown, 2005). Although geospatial technologies have become widely used and access costs have declined, integration of such tech-

 Go to MyEducationLab, select the topic "Social Studies Integration." Go to the "Assignments, Activities, and Applications" section and view the video "Using Authoring Software" to see how one teacher uses technology to extend a social studies concept. Complete the activity that follows.

Another tool that allows students to look at geography from many different perspectives is a **Global Positioning System (GPS)**. Lary (2004) describes a popular GPS classroom activity called **geocaching**, which Lary calls a "high-tech, worldwide treasure hunt . . . where a person hides a cache for others to find" (p. 15). Students look at a database of caches at the geocaching website (http://www.geocaching.com), decide on a cache to hunt for, and use a GPS to help them locate it. Table 12.8 lists good sources of other GIS and GPS lessons. Gauthier (2004) also describes a science and social studies project that uses GIS and GPS together and may be done at any grade level. See Technology Integration Lesson 12.2, which is based on Gauthier's description.

TABLE 12.8 Resources and Social Studies Themes: GIS and GPS Lessons

Sample Sites	Social Studies Themes
Teaching with GIS http://www.esri.com/industries/k-12/index.html	Theme 3: People, places, and environments
GIS in the Classroom: Using Geographic Information Systems in Social Studies and Environmental Science http://books.heinemann.com/products/E00479.aspx	Theme 3: People, places, and environments
Math lessons with GPS http://www.teacherlink.org/content/math/activities/gps.html	Theme 3: People, places, and environments
Science/geography lessons with GIS and GPS http://sciencespot.net/Pages/classgpslsn.html	Theme 3: People, places, and environments

Technology Integration Lesson 12.2

GIS and GPS Lessons

Title: Disaster Preparedness with GIS and GPS Tools

Grade Levels: All grade levels

Content Area/Topic: Social studies, civics

 NETS for Students: Standards 2 (Communication and Collaboration), 3 (Research and Information Fluency), 4 (Critical Thinking, Problem Solving, and Decision Making), and 6 (Technology Operations and Concepts)

Description of Standards Applications: This integration lesson offers students the opportunity to use GPS and GIS technologies to research and analyze local data, critically think and make decisions about these data, and communicate these findings to their peers.

Students use GIS and GPS tools to help plan how they and their community will respond in the event of a natural or human-made disaster. Students must have access to GIS data on the geography of their local areas. They begin by using their GPS receivers to find the school's latitude/longitude location. They can also locate their streets and houses to get practice with the tools. The teacher divides the class into groups and assigns them information to gather about their school (e.g., capacity of the building, number of classrooms, large rooms such as gymnasiums). They also collect information to determine whether their school or other local sites would be good shelters in the event of emergencies (e.g., if there is availability of food storage, medical supplies, electrical generators). They use GIS imagery to analyze what areas are in danger from which kinds of disasters (e.g., floods) and decide where the people in these areas might go for shelter.

Source: Gauthier, S. (2004). GIS helps prepare students for emergencies. *Learning and Leading with Technology, 32*(3), 22–25.

Practice of Factual Information

A more traditional, but still useful, integration strategy is having students use drill-and-practice, instructional game software, or pay-to-view Internet sites (e.g., Princeton Review's AP/SAT tutorials) to help them learn and remember important facts, such as states and capitals or dates of famous events. For example, Educational Insights' *Classroom Jeopardy* game (see Table 12.9) provides a unique and highly motivational approach to this kind of practice by placing it in the context of a quiz show game in which the whole class can participate.

TABLE 12.9 Resources and Social Studies Themes: Practice of Factual Information

Sample Sites	Social Studies Themes
States Web Games http://www.sheppardsoftware.com/web_games.htm	Theme 3: People, places, and environments
Educational Insights' *Classroom Jeopardy* social studies game http://www.edin.com/	All themes

Interactive Summary

The following is a summary of the main points covered in this chapter. Additional examples and information on these points can be found by visiting the recommended websites at MyEducationLab.

1. **Issues in social studies instruction** — These include:
   - Methods of addressing social studies standards
   - Dilemmas in teaching social studies effectively
   - Perils of the information explosion.

2. **Integration strategies for social studies instruction** — Nine strategies are described for integrating technology into this area:
   - Simulated immersion experiences
   - Graphic representations
   - Virtual trips
   - Adventure learning
   - Digital storytelling
   - Digital information critiques
   - Electronic research
   - GIS and GPS lessons
   - Practice of factual information.

Key Terms

- digital storytelling
- geocaching
- Geographic Information System (GIS)
- geospatial technologies
- Global Positioning System (GPS)
- social studies

Web-Enrichment Activities

1. **News-2-You** — View the sample paper at the News-2-You website (http://www.news-2-you.com). This current events publication is created for young students and students who have reading difficulties. Give examples from the sample issue of activities that would help students learn about cultures, democratic society, and the world.

2. **Social studies webquest** — Select a social studies webquest from http://webquest.org. Identify components of the WebQuest that you think are examples of the ten NCSS social studies standards themes.

3. **Geocaching tutorial** — Visit the geocaching website at http://www.geocaching.com/about/, and learn about using geocaching in the classroom. Come up with a plan for using geocaching in the classroom with your students. What could you "cache"?

Go to MyEducationLab to complete the following exercises.

Video   Select the topic "Professional Development," and go to the "Assignments, Activities, and Applications" section. Access the video "GIS Training" to see how teachers are trained to use this problem-solving software in their classes. Then complete the activity that follows.

Video   Select the topic "Social Studies Integration," and go to the "Assignments, Activities, and Applications" section. View the video "Using GIS Software" and consider how GIS technologies can help motivate learning. Complete the full activity.

Tutorials   Select the topic "Internet" and access the practical tutorial and skill-building activity for "Trackstar." Use the tutorial to learn the basic skills of this online management system. This skill will be used later in the Technology Integration Workshop.

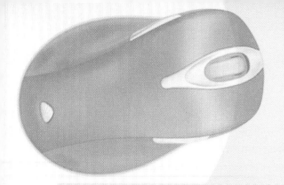

Technology Integration Workshop

The TIP Model in Action

Read each of the following scenarios related to implementing the TIP Model, and answer the questions that follow it based on your Chapter 12 reading activities.

TIP MODEL SCENARIO #1 Mr. Daley wanted to show his sociology students how they could test hypotheses about correlations among social factors such as population centers and crime statistics. He had heard of a technology tool that would allow students to do this with maps so that they could see at a glance if their hypotheses were correct.

    1.1 What technology-based strategy could Mr. Daley use to address this need?

    1.2 What would be the relative advantage of using this strategy?

    1.3 What would you suggest that Mr. Daley have his students produce to show the results of their work? How might he assess this product?

TIP MODEL SCENARIO #2 Dr. France's students were going to be studying the Early American period in our country's history in the spring semester, and she wanted to make the class more engaging than it had been in the past. She wished she could have her students visit places like Williamsburg, Philadelphia, and Monticello, but they did not live near any of these sites.

    2.1 What technology-based strategy could Dr. France use to address this problem?

    2.2 What would be the relative advantage of using this strategy?

    2.3 What could Dr. France's students produce to show what they had learned? How might she assess their products?

TIP MODEL SCENARIO #3 Ms. Rodrigues's social studies students were about to study the U.S. Constitution. She not only wanted to show them what was included in our Constitution, but she also wanted them to see all the factors that must be considered when any new country creates a charter to guide its development and reflect its national

principles. She had heard about software that allowed students to do this in a role-playing way.

    3.1 What technology-based tool could Ms. Rodrigues use to address this need?

    3.2 What would be the relative advantage of using this strategy instead of holding a class discussion on this topic?

    3.3 Should students work individually, in pairs, in small groups, or as a whole class on this activity? Explain.

TIP MODEL SCENARIO #4 Ms. Fernanda wanted to have her students study their local area, so she arranged to have them work via email with a class of students in another state. They exchanged background information about their own locations, their weather conditions, favorite spots to visit, and other items of interest to both. Finally, they each worked on a travel brochure based on each other's locations that included a local map and summarized the information they had gathered. They ended the project by emailing each other a copy of the brochure.

    4.1 What problems did Ms. Fernanda address with this technology-based strategy?

    4.2 What would be the relative advantage of using this strategy as opposed to having students do a brochure without contacting other students?

    4.3 What outcomes should be assessed in such a project, and how might they be assessed?

TIP MODEL SCENARIO #5 Dr. Levar's students were studying how the stock market both reflects our country's economy and helps shape it. He asked them to track five stocks over the course of 2 months and to chart their value. At the same time, they tracked events in the country and the world that might affect stock market performance for the stocks they picked. They ended the project by describing the events that corresponded with major dips and peaks and why they thought these events affected the stocks.

    5.1 What problems is Dr. Levar addressing with this technology-based strategy?

    5.2 If he had students work in small groups on this activity, explain how this strategy might best be carried out in the classroom.

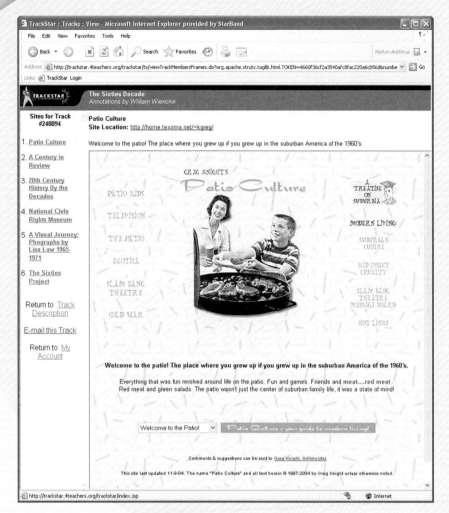

Source: Example from the TrackStar Website at http://trackstar.4teachers.org. Courtesy of Greg Knight's Patio Culture.

5.3 What would be a good way for Dr. Levar to have students present their findings? Explain why this presentation strategy would be effective.

TIE into Practice: Technology Integration Examples

The Technology Integration Example that opened this chapter (*Studying Our Past, Mapping Our Future*) showed how teachers might use a variety of technology tools to study the history of their local area. Since each group has to visit assigned websites, you may want to consider using an online management system such as *TrackStar* to organize these sites and give students quick access to them. With the knowledge you have gained from Chapter 12, do the following to explore this strategy:

1. Having completed a tutorial on working in *TrackStar*, use the *TrackStar* website to organize the project like the example shown.

2. Answer the following questions about the *Studying Our Past, Mapping Our Future* example:

- Phases 1 and 2 — What were the kinds of relative advantage that Mr. McVee felt this project would have for his students' study of their local area? What would the use of GIS add to this study? What is Mr. McVee's TPACK? Is he ready to move forward successfully with this project?

- Phase 3 — Mr. McVee also has to grade his students with percentage grades that will add to their class average. If his rubric has a total of 35 points, how will he translate a rubric score into a percentage grade?

- Phase 4 — What technology resources could be helpful as student groups interview the local expert(s) for their assigned time period?

- Phase 5 — One important task to prepare for the unit was obtaining historical photos and data on the community. Where might he obtain these?

- Phase 6 — One of the end-of-project questions Mr. McVee asked was if most students "scored well" on the checklists and rubric. What would he have to do at the beginning of the project in order to ascertain this?

3. What NETS for Students skills would students learn by working on the *Studying Our Past, Mapping Our Future* project? (See the front of this book for a list of NETS for Students.)

Technology Integration Lesson Planning

Complete the following exercise using sample lesson plans found on MyEducationLab:

1. Locate lesson ideas — MyEducationLab has several examples of lessons that use the social studies integration strategies described in this chapter. Go to MyEducationLab under the topic "Social Studies Integration" and go to the Lesson Plans to review example lessons. Choose two of the following integration lessons:
   - A Hypertext Study of the Fall of Communism
   - Black History Past to Present
   - Building a Simulated City
   - Presidential Pardon & Proclamation: Port Chicago Disaster

2. Evaluate the lessons — Use the *Evaluation Checklist for a Technology-Integrated Lesson* (located on MyEducationLab under the topic "Instructional Planning") to evaluate each of these lessons.

3. Modify a lesson — Select one of the lesson ideas, and adapt its strategies to meet a need in your own content area. You may choose to use the same approach in the original or adapt it to meet your needs.

4. Add descriptors — Create descriptors for your new lesson similar to those found within the sample lessons (e.g., grade level, content and topic areas, technologies used, relative advantage, objectives, NETS standards).

5. Save your new lesson — Save your modified lesson with all its descriptors.

For Your Teaching Portfolio

For this chapter's contribution to your teaching portfolio, add the following products you created in the Technology Integration Workshop:

- PDFs of pages you created using the tutorial on the *TrackStar* system
- The evaluations you did using the *Evaluation Checklist for a Technology-Integrated Lesson*
- The new lesson plan you developed, based on the one you found on MyEducationLab.

Chapter 13
Technology in Music and Art Instruction

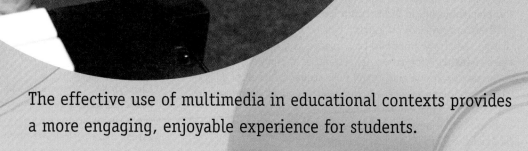

The effective use of multimedia in educational contexts provides a more engaging, enjoyable experience for students.

Lipscomb & Walls, 2005

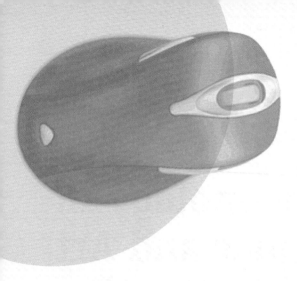

Technology Integration Example

The Fine Art of Electronic Portfolios

Based on: Duxbury, D. (2000). Make sweet music with electronic portfolios. *Learning and Leading with Technology, 28*(3), 28–31, 41.

Grade Levels: Middle to high school• Content Area/Topic: Music and art composition, technology • Length of Time: Ongoing

Phases 1 and 2: Assess technological pedagogical content knowledge; Determine relative advantage

The music, arts, and technology resource teachers at Eureka High School were discussing the new block scheduling plan in which music, art, and technology credits would share one of the four 90-minute units students would attend each day. The teachers realized that a logical thread among these three curricula would be to have students develop a web-based portfolio of their music and art. They felt this would meet several needs. First, it would be a way of working with each student at individual levels of musical and artistic expertise. This was important because students in their classes would range from beginners at musical composition or art skills to advanced musicians or artists who were active in choir, band, orchestra, and/or art studios. Second, it had always been difficult to find an audience for student work; the teachers knew that having others view their work was motivating and provided helpful feedback to students at all levels. A web-based format would make it easier to share students' works. Third, it would be easy to create projects that linked skills across the disciplines—for example, having students use a **Musical Instrument Digital Interface (MIDI)** keyboard and music editor to prepare a musical composition expressing the feeling or mood of a painting. (MIDI refers to a standard that has been adopted by the electronic music industry for controlling devices, such as synthesizers and sound cards.) Finally, the teachers realized that an electronic portfolio could serve as a valuable, ongoing assessment tool for students' art, music, technology, and language development, and would help students develop skills in using technology to present their work and to communicate and share information with others.

Prior to the beginning of the project the resource teachers realized they should assess their own technological pedagogical content knowledge (TPACK) so they could evaluate their strengths and weaknesses and understand where they might locate themselves within the TPACK model. The music and technology teachers felt very comfortable and knowledgeable

with all three domains of technology, pedagogy, and content knowledge. It was only the art teacher who felt behind in his technology knowledge and how to effectively use web-based and image-editing tools within the classroom. As the three discussed their weaknesses and strengths, it was refreshing for them to see how they could help each other to be at the center of the TPACK model. They decided they would move forward together to make it a success for their students.

Phase 3: Decide on objectives and assessments

The teachers decided they each would use a component of the portfolio as the basis of student assessment each grading period. The art and music teachers would assign each student individual benchmarks to achieve in their composition and skill development, and the technology teacher would use the website the students produced to assess their production skills. Students' grades would be a combination of the three assessments, with each content area weighted according to which one was being emphasized during the grading period. They decided on the following outcomes, objectives, and assessment strategies:

- **Outcome:** Progress in art. **Objective:** Students will meet their assigned benchmark for progress in art skills. **Assessment:** Rubric to assess this portfolio component.
- **Outcome:** Progress in music. **Objective:** Students will meet their assigned benchmark for progress in music skills. **Assessment:** Rubric to assess this portfolio component.
- **Outcome:** Progress in language expression. **Objective:** Students will meet their assigned benchmark for development in written expression. **Assessment:** Rubric to assess this portfolio component.
- **Outcome:** Technology skills. **Objective:** Students will demonstrate competence in each required web page development skill by completing assigned tasks. **Assessment:** Web production checklist.

Phase 4: Design integration strategies

The teachers decided they would follow the same sequence of activities for each grading period:

- **Review skill levels and set benchmarks:** The art and music teachers meet with each student, review accomplishments to date, and set benchmarks for individual skill development. Some students with lower skill levels are placed in small groups so that teachers can spend more time working with them.

- **Review portfolio requirements:** The technology teacher meets with each student, reviews the requirements for the portfolio, and sets tasks and expectations to assist students to develop a more clear and aesthetically-pleasing presentation.

- **Decide on projects:** A different project is set for each grading period. For example, for the first project, the teachers decide to have students use their MIDI keyboards and notation software to write a musical composition based on the music of a period they have been studying in their history classes. Then the students use image manipulation software to create a collage of colors and images that come to mind as they listen to the music composition they or their fellow students have created. The technology teacher helps them add their sound and graphics creations to their portfolios.

- **Determine group presentations:** Each teacher identifies whole-group presentations that they need to offer. For example, the music teacher needs to demonstrate techniques with the MIDI keyboard and music notation software. The art teacher designs a presentation on how to use layering techniques in *Adobe Photoshop* to create a graphic collage. The technology teacher develops demonstrations of video and audio editing techniques. After their group presentations, the teachers work with each student as needed to complete the required products.

- **Arrange reviews and final presentations:** The teachers arrange for various experts in other locations to do online reviews of the students' creations and to give them feedback. Students will revise their products as time permits and as they feel appropriate. The teachers arrange for an "Evening at Eureka" to be given at the end of the grading period, at which computers would be set up in a lab to display each student's work. Parents and friends are to be invited via the school website and via desktop-published invitations created by the art students.

Phase 5: Prepare the instructional environment

The technology teacher creates a main page for the student portfolios, with links to each student's work. He or she also creates a link from the school's main page to the portfolio section. The music teacher has a MIDI keyboard classroom, but there aren't enough keyboards for each student to have one for a whole period. The teachers arrange the schedule so that half the class attends band, choir, or orchestra practice, works in the art studio, or works on their individual portfolios in the computer lab, while the other half works on composition.

Phase 6: Evaluate and revise

At the end of each grading period, the teachers reviewed the students' portfolios, assessed progress, and discussed ways to make the work go more smoothly. Some of the questions they asked were:

- Did most students meet the individual benchmarks set for them?
- Were students actively engaged in the project work?
- Did the group demonstrations provide adequate initial instruction before students began work on their own?
- Were the classrooms and lab times organized for efficient work?

The teachers were gratified to see that most students seemed motivated by the idea of using a multimedia web format to display their work and were making good progress on their benchmarks. However, it was apparent that many students needed more individual instruction than the demonstrations could provide. The teachers decided to videotape a series of short demos so that students could view them individually or in small groups, as needed, after the initial presentation. They agreed that the scheduling proved to be a challenge. They decided to request that additional MIDI keyboards and software be obtained to support this work. Also, English and history teachers approached them about coordinating the portfolio work with students' writing and research projects. The teachers agreed to work together to merge these skill areas into students' portfolio assessments.

Objectives

After reading this chapter and completing the learning activities for it, you should be able to:

1. Identify some of the current issues in music and art education that may affect the selection and use of technology.

2. Describe key strategies for integrating technology into music and art curricula.

3. Create instructional activities for music and art instruction that model successful integration strategies.

The Arts
in the Information Age

Many arts educators have resisted pressure to use computers and other instructional technologies, complaining about the contradiction inherent in blending impersonal machines with traditionally humanistic endeavors. In reality, however, technology has always played a part in the arts. Over the centuries, technology has provided tools, materials, and processes that aided artists' creative expression. In more recent times, the phonograph in music and the camera in visual arts have changed people's definitions of art. The integration of computers and other forms of electronic technology represents the next logical step in the evolution of the arts.

Many educators and members of the community question the need for instructional technology in the arts curriculum. Even some proponents of technology applications in other disciplines balk at investments in technology for the arts. Robinson and Roland (1994) offer four reasons for linking the goals of a school arts program with rapidly developing instructional technologies:

1. **Expanded modes of expression** — By integrating new technologies into the arts curriculum, instructors expose students to new and exciting modes of artistic expression. All media have a place in the curriculum if they enable students to achieve desired instructional outcomes. New technologies warrant special attention because they constitute entirely new genres that may alter paradigms about art.

2. **Literacies for the Information Age** — The new technological culture requires today's students to develop a whole new set of literacies that go far beyond computer literacy. Arts instruction provides many unique opportunities for students to hone analytical skills to critically evaluate the flood of messages that fill a technologically saturated environment. The communicative language of the new technologies—sound, animation, music, drama, video, graphics, text, and voice—is also the language of the arts. Thus, arts teachers are particularly well positioned to help students develop skills as both critical producers and critical consumers of electronic media.

3. **Creative approaches to modern problems** — In the workplace of tomorrow, workers often will have to generate creative solutions to problems. An arts program that develops students' potential for innovation in the areas of music, animation, graphics, multimedia, desktop publishing, and other emerging technologies will enable those students to compete in tomorrow's global business environment.

4. **Arts as aesthetic balance** — The arts counterbalance the massive infusion of technological change that society is experiencing. Technology can be seductive, and people need to keep in mind that there are unique human abilities. Citizens of tomorrow's world will need coping skills that enable them to retain their aesthetic sensibilities in the face of breathtaking technological advances. Arts education will help develop and maintain these skills.

Another version of this view, which calls for an understanding of "appropriate technologies," is described as follows in the *National Standards for Arts Education* (Music Educators National Conference [MENC], 1994):

For the arts, technology thus offers means to accomplish artistic, scholarly, production, and performance goals. But the mere availability of technology cannot ensure a specific artistic result: the pencil in a student's hand ensures neither drawing competency nor a competent drawing. Nor, by itself, will exchanging the pencil for an airbrush or a computer graphics program create a change in the student.

What Does TPACK
Look Like in Art
and Music Education?

The questions surrounding technological pedagogical content knowledge (TPACK) for teachers often include "How does this relate to me?" and "What are the implications of knowing about TPACK in my content area?" TPACK in any discipline is the perfect union of three knowledge domains (content, pedagogy, and technology) to develop a knowledge base from which a teacher can view a lesson and see how technology can enhance learning opportunities and experiences for students while also knowing the correct pedagogy to enhance the learning of the content. In art education, for instance, a teacher is incorporating the TPACK principles when he or she, fluent within a content area, readily introduces students to image editing tools such as *Photoshop,* thereby allowing them to develop their own pieces of art. At the same time, this teacher knows the correct pedagogy for introducing the content and the technology to the students in a way that is seamless. In music education, as another example, teachers fluent in content knowledge and using the TPACK perspective might readily introduce *GarageBand* to allow students to develop their own compositions. Again, the teacher knows the correct pedagogy for employing this technology that enables students to learn composition through *GarageBand.* (See Figure 13.1.)

Issues and Problems
in Music Instruction
Redefining Music Literacy

In music education, the term **music literacy** usually means an ability to read standard music notation. But the computer

FIGURE 13.1 TPACK and Music and Art

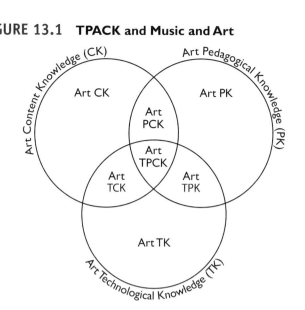

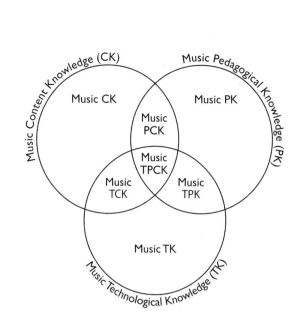

enables—if not encourages—experimentation with alternative ways to represent music. The earliest sequencers, even those with notation capability, have always included a "graphic" or "matrix" editor, a window in which the user could edit music by dragging, deleting, or expanding small rectangles on a grid. Composer Morton Subotnick authored *Making Music,* a software package that allows children to draw lines that are then rendered into melodies with a similar contour. More recently, Tod Machover of the MIT Media Lab has developed numerous projects for children and adults, such as *Hyperscore,* that require no formal training or music literacy.

Today, the desktop music production software industry (e.g., Apple, Emagic, Cakewalk, Propellerheads, Cubase) is helping accelerate a trend away from reliance on printed sheets and toward a sound artifact. This means that many students discouraged by a requirement to learn notation-based theory can now participate in the school music program as both composers and performers with little, if any, ability to read music.

Training Teachers to Meet Music Standards

Until states begin requiring that teacher candidates demonstrate proficiency with technology, teacher preparation programs will have a difficult time making a case for including required technology courses in their curricula. Teacher preparation programs, already overloaded with content, would be reluctant to displace a more traditional course with one whose skills remain in the "optional" category with respect to licensure.

TABLE 13.1 Standards in Music Technology and Music Education

Areas of Competency in Music Technology (http://www.ti.me.org/standards/section2.html)	MENC Standards (http://www.menc.org/publication/books/standards.html)
1. Electronic musical instruments (keyboards, controllers, synthesizers, samplers, sound reinforcement equipment)	1. Singing, alone and with others, a varied repertoire of music.
2. Music production: data types (MIDI, digital audio); processes (sequencing, looping, signal processing, sound design)	2. Performing on instruments, alone and with others, a varied repertoire of music.
3. Music notation software	3. Improvising melodies, variations, and accompaniments.
4. Technology assisted learning (instructional software, accompaniment/practice tools, Internet-based learning)	4. Composing and arranging music within specified guidelines.
5. Multimedia: authoring (web pages, presentations, digital video); digital image capturing (scanning, still/video camera); Internet; electronic portfolios	5. Reading and notating music.
	6. Listening to, analyzing, and describing music.
	7. Evaluating music and music performances.
6. Productivity tools, classroom and lab management: productivity tools (word processing, spreadsheet, database); computer systems (CPU, I/O devices, storage devices/media); lab management systems; networks	8. Understanding relationships among music, the other arts, and disciplines outside the arts.
	9. Understanding music in relation to history and culture.

Making the Case for Technology Integration

Use the following questions to reflect on issues in technology integration and to guide discussions within your class.

1. Consider the following quote from *The Electronic Word: Democracy, Technology, and the Arts* by Richard Lanham (1995): "Many areas of endeavor in America pressured by technological change have already had to decide what business they were really in, and those making the narrow choice have usually not fared well. The railroads had to decide whether they were in the transportation business or the railroad business; they chose the latter and gradual extinction. Newspapers had to decide whether they were in the information business or only the newspaper business; most who chose the newspaper business are no longer in it. A fascinating instance of this choice is now taking place in the piano industry. Steinway used to own the market, and it has decided to stay in the piano business. Yamaha decided it was in the keyboard business—acoustic and electronic—and has, with Roland, Korg, and other manufacturers, redefined the instrument. Time has yet to tell who will win, financially or musically" (p. 64).

   Following Lanham's examples of the newspaper, railroad, and musical instrument industries, what "businesses" were music educators in before the advent of the "electronic word," and has this development forced a similar reassessment? Do you see the "business" of teaching music facing redefinition with the emergence, proliferation, and dominance of computerized technologies?

2. In her discussion of issues and problems in arts education, Janis Boyd (undated) cites the following quote: "Excellence and innovation are critical to our collective future in generating the industries we require to enhance the nation's economic and social well-being. Creativity and innovation drive not only the cultural industries, but also developments in science, technology, industrial and management practices, all major contributors to our continuing socioeconomic growth."

   How does this intersection between technology and art education help make the case for including technology in art education?

However, in its publication, *The School Music Program: A New Vision,* the music professional organization **Music Educators National Conference (MENC)** said: "The K–12 music curriculum that was established by the 1930s has evolved only gradually since that time. . . . [T]he curricula that were acceptable in the past will be inadequate to prepare students for the 21st century" (1994, p. 3). The pamphlet goes on to designate technology as one of seven areas in which the new music curriculum is fundamentally different from the traditional curriculum. Table 13.1 lists music technology and music education standards.

The Intersection of Popular Music, Technology, and Music Instruction

In 2004, MENC published a collection of essays addressing the issue of popular music. *Bridging the Gap: Popular Music and Music Education* made very little mention of popular music's heavy reliance on technology for both production (composition) and live performance. Any music teacher seeking to start and sustain a program component dedicated to rock, hip hop, or other pop genres must have (or have access to) extensive knowledge of desktop music production and live sound reinforcement—not to mention a credible familiarity with pop music's complex web of music, culture, and traditions.

The Music Director as Small Business Administrator

A typical secondary school music program involves hundreds of students, rooms full of instruments and other equipment, wardrobes of uniforms and choral robes, libraries of sheet music, methods books and other print resources, and large budgets. The music director usually oversees the largest inventory of physical assets outside the athletic department. The music director is responsible for tracking students' academic progress and other duties common to all classroom teachers. In addition, the music director must be his or her own director of development, constantly on the lookout for continuing or increased funding. All of these issues make knowledge of information management software a high priority—if not a stated requirement—for the efficient operation of a successful music program.

Technology Integration Strategies for Music Instruction

In a superb review of research related to technology and music learning, Peter Webster (2002) identifies several categories of music experience that have been the focus of technology integration: music listening, performance, and com-

Top Ten

Strategies for Technology in Music and Art Instruction

Take advantage of these ten powerful strategies for using technology to enhance the teaching of music and art.

Music Strategies

1. **Students use software like Apple's *GarageBand* as a personal recording studio** — Students have the flexibility and resources they need to support their own creative musical explorations.

2. **Teachers use an electronic keyboard lab to develop students' skills in keyboarding, theory, and harmony** — Networked systems allow the teacher to monitor individual students as they build their skills.

3. **Software such as *Practica Musica* serves as a tutorial in music fundamentals** — Interactive software gives students hands-on practice in music theory and ear training.

4. ***Music Ace's* "Doodle Pad" teaches young students about parts for different instruments** — The software makes it easy for young learners to "write" music with parts for different instruments.

5. **Students build a website to help teach music history** — The wealth of images and information on the Internet gives students the material they need to research composers, compositions, and periods of musical history and to share their findings on the web.

Art Strategies

1. **Students take virtual field trips to art museums** — Through virtual tours available at many sites, students can "visit" museums and see great works of art that serve as illustrations of artists' work and models for their own work.

2. **Students create electronic portfolios to illustrate their creative products** — *PowerPoint* presentations, videos, electronic books, and websites offer versatile venues for students to document and share their work.

3. **Illustrate artworks/techniques with digital slide shows** — Teachers can store large collections in very little space and show parts of collections to illustrate techniques and products of various artists.

4. **Teacher-created websites give short tutorials on art concepts** — The Internet offers an easy, motivating way to let students develop background knowledge of art concepts on their own.

5. **Students create an illustrated desktop-published brochure or newsletter** — This activity is a great way for students to practice writing as well as visual design skills.

position. He also acknowledges the crucial role that technology plays in research and assessment within the educational environment. In addition to general-purpose software (e.g., word processing, spreadsheet, web authoring), two broad categories of computer-based tools play a primary role in serving the needs of music teachers: *instructional software* (programs developed primarily for teaching music skills) and *music production software* (programs that facilitate music composition, recording, and performance). Muro (1994), Rudolph (2004), and Mauricio (2000) conclude that the most effective technology for music classrooms is not necessarily the computer. The first step in the process of integrating music technology may well be the purchase of an electronic keyboard or a synthesizer. For financial reasons, many schools that have to choose between a *computer* lab or a *keyboard* lab for their music programs choose the latter. Another relatively recent entry into the music performance realm is the "intelligent"

accompaniment system (*SmartMusic*). With a library of over 30,000 compositions at the time of this writing, students can select a piece from either the ensemble or solo literacy and practice with an accompaniment system that follows their performance as tempo is varied for expressive purposes. In a school or university with little or no budget to provide accompanists, such technologies provide significant opportunity. Strategies that make use of all these resources include support for music composition and production, music performance, self-paced learning and practice, teaching music history, and interdisciplinary strategies. These are summarized in Table 13.2 and discussed next.

 Go to MyEducationLab, select the topic "Internet." Go to the "Assignments, Activities, and Applications" section and view the video "A Web-based Music Project" to see how one teacher uses the Internet to expand students' awareness and appreciation of music and art. Complete the activity that follows.

TABLE 13.2   Summary of Technology Integration Strategies for Music

Technology Integration Strategies	Benefits	Sample Resources and Activities
Support for music composition and production	• Offers a range of mixing and sound design options to support composition for students of any age. • Supports both traditional and nontraditional composition. • Offers teachers maximum flexibility in designing music curriculum.	• Apple/Emagic Logic http://www.apple.com/logic/ • Apple's *GarageBand* http://www.apple.com/ilife/garageband/ • Reason (Propellerhead) Software http://www.propellerheads.se/ • BubbleMachine http://www.lipscomb.umn.edu/bubblemachine
Support for music performance	• Expedites preparation for performance (e.g., rearranging music for alternate instrumentations, re-creating lost or missing parts from the score, transposing parts, and simplifying difficult passages). • Helps teachers with theory lessons, quizzes, and other handouts to aid student performance.	• *Sibelius* notation software http://www.sibelius.com • *Finale* and *Print Music* software http://www.finalemusic.com/ • *MidiNotate* http://www.notation.com/
Support for self-paced learning and practice	• Offers individual, personal help with needed skills, ear training, or music theory.	• *Practice Musica* http://www.ars-nova.com/
Support for teaching music history	• Internet sites provide easy-to-access background information on composers and musical periods/compositions. • Website generation offers a venue for students to share their research.	• Classic Motown timeline http://classic.motown.com/timeline/ • See also pbs.org for other interactive and educational timelines and music history resources.
Support for interdisciplinary strategies	• Builds on natural relationships between music and other topics (e.g., physics). • Helps promote musical literacy while teaching related concepts.	• *Math & Music* http://www.wildridge.com/

Support for Music Composition and Production

For the purposes of this chapter, music production and music composition mean the same thing. The two essential tools in this process are **sequencers** and **notation software**, and each can contribute substantially to teaching both production and performance. Sequencers allow the user to record, edit, and play back digital audio and MIDI data. Notation programs generally have fewer recording and playback options but offer more flexibility in score and page setup, part extraction, text formatting, and other print-related issues. In other words, a sequencer facilitates music making in the *aural* domain, whereas notation facilitates music making in the *visual* domain.

Sequencers and notation software allow students to compose music in both traditional and nontraditional ways. With either tool, they can enter music with the mouse, play it with a MIDI-equipped keyboard or other input device (e.g., guitar or wind controller) or import it by opening standard MIDI files created by others (e.g., their fellow students, their teachers, or files found on the Internet). Designed *primarily* for desktop music production, the sequencer typically offers more options for creating a *sonic* artifact: more sophisticated mixing and sound design features. Notation software is designed *primarily* to facilitate the production of music as a *visual* artifact, music on paper or on screen that can then be performed by a live musician. Note, however, that almost all sequencers now offer at least a basic notation component, and notation software programs are giving the user more and more playback options.

Music production software includes sequencing (MIDI and digital audio), digital audio editing (often a component of a sequencing program), and music notation. Although these programs offer teachers maximum flexibility in designing curriculum, they require more involvement from the teacher in creating curricula, directing instruction, assessment, training, and technological maintenance.

Sequencers are available in both hardware and software form. The hardware sequencer is usually found as an integrated component of a synthesizer workstation—a synthesizer with the ability to record multiple tracks of MIDI information. Software sequencers run as an application on a computer and therefore require a more complete MIDI workstation (computer, MIDI controller, sound module, and a MIDI interface) but are exponentially more powerful, with increased processing speed, storage capacity, and a bigger screen on which to display data.

Most sequencing programs simulate the functions of the physical recording studio. Music is recorded on tracks and assigned to channels for playback and editing. Software plug-ins are digital equivalents of outboard (hardware) signal modifiers such as echo chambers and compressors and, depending on the processing power of the computer being used, provide the composer with a desktop recording studio equipped with virtually unlimited mixing options. Many sequencers offer the ability to record sound directly onto the computer's hard drive with the use of a microphone. Live, simultaneous multichannel recording is possible with an external digital audio interface. After recording, digital audio data, as represented by a wave shape, can be manipulated (edited) with the ease and precision of text in a word processor.

With software programs like *Finale*, teachers, musicians, and arrangers can compose and arrange music to meet their needs. The playback feature allows you to hear the chord structures and make changes as necessary.

With very few exceptions, all sequencers support both step- and real-time recording of MIDI data. Once MIDI notes are entered, they can be edited like any other data on the computer: cut, copied, and pasted. All performance parameters of MIDI data can be controlled by the user independently of one another—including pitch, tempo, volume, and dynamics.

Some programs designed for young children have sequencing components that enable composition. The "Doodle Pad" component of *Music Ace,* for example, allows the user to drag different-shaped happy faces (representing notes of different rhythmic values) onto a staff. In addition, the user can assign each note to one of several different sounds (e.g., piano, violin) as represented by a different color. With proper direction, however, elementary school students can be taught the basic operations of even the most sophisticated professional software. By middle school, many students possess the instrumental technique and/or the computer skills necessary to take advantage of more complicated processes, such as digital audio editing and adding musical expression to their MIDI data (Ohler, 1998). (See Technology Integration Lesson 13.1.)

Projects that begin at a computer workstation in a lab can be used in other situations throughout the music program. Students can create notation files that are then used to facilitate performance in the rehearsal room or at a concert. Students who are especially proficient on an instrument (including voice) can create a sequenced instrumental "bed" to accompany a live performance or group or individual rehearsal.

Desktop music systems (e.g., the MIDI sequencer) have prompted new definitions of musicianship that recognize alternative tracks to musical creativity, as well as the traditional conservatory model of preparation. As suggested earlier, students with little or no "formal" musical training or keyboard skills can create and edit compositions using a sequencing program with step-entry capability. Students can also perform analyses of music using pre-existing MIDI files and/or digital audio imported from a CD. Once the pieces have been imported into a sequencer, students can explore all aspects of musical form, harmony, orchestration, and other parameters. Sequencers and audio editing software offer students the ability not only to *listen* to prerecorded music but also to *manipulate* it. Students can demonstrate their understanding of musical form by literally separating a piece of recorded music into its structural components. In this way, expositions, recapitulations, second choruses, guitar solos, all become discrete audio events, which in turn can be rearranged—resequenced—into new formal configurations. Apple's

Technology Integration Lesson 13.1

Technology in Music Instruction

Title: Play the Recorder on the Computer   **Grade Levels:** K–5
Content Area/Topic: Music composition

 NETS for Students: Standards 2 (Communication and Collaboration) and 3 (Research and Information Fluency)

Description of Standards Applications: This integration lesson offers students the opportunity to learn music composition using *Recorder Teacher* software. Students interact with the tutorial as they enhance their note reading and tonguing and blowing.

Studying the recorder is often used as a way of teaching and reinforcing music composition concepts to students at all levels. In this lesson, students use *Recorder Teacher* software to learn how to play the recorder. The teacher demonstrates the fingering for various notes by showing the software tutorial. As students try playing notes, the program plays them as well, to let students check that they are playing them correctly. Tonguing and blowing concepts also are demonstrated. As students begin to write their own musical compositions, the computer plays them. Finally, students test their skills in two different ways: fingering or note reading. *Recorder Teacher* and other similar programs are available at http://www.theshops.co.uk/childsplay.

Source: Dillon, R. (1998). In the key of "see and hear": How students can learn to play the recorder by playing musical computers. *Learning and Leading with Technology, 26*(2), 15–17.

FIGURE 13.2 Frame from Apple Computer's *GarageBand*

Source: Screen shot reprinted with permission from Apple Inc.

GarageBand has become popular among young people for mixing and playing their own music. (See the example in Figure 13.2.) Multimedia authoring programs like *Flash* and *Director* exemplify another type of technological tools that can be used to facilitate the understanding and exploration of musical form. *BubbleMachine*, a *Flash*-based program developed by Scott Lipscomb and Marc Jacoby is available for free download to educators and allows the user to create interactive listening guides for any audio MP3 file (http://lipscomb.umn.edu/bubblemachine/index.htm). Also available from this same website are a variety of template files that can be used to create interactive listening guides for any composition falling into the following established musical forms: sonata form, AABA, and 12-bar blues.

Students with performance skills can record MIDI data over their favorite audio recordings using different kinds of MIDI controllers. More advanced analysis projects, such as those that might take place in an advanced placement music theory class, can now be undertaken using music software as a presentation tool. Consequently, the general music class can accomplish a great deal more than simply providing those students who are supposed to be unmusical or at least untrained with a passive listening experience.

While the preceding scenarios lend themselves best to a lab environment with multiple computers, even a single computer can provide valuable support for a general music curriculum. Rudolph and Peters (1996) have demonstrated how a computer running sequencing software can support music instruction with **Orff instruments**. These are instruments for children developed by K. Maendler

Adapting for Special Needs

For students with physical disabilities, determining physical motions and manipulations that are feasible and the types of interface controls (switches, sliders, potentiometers, and so on) that can be used is often the first step in making art and music activities accessible. Several assistive technology companies specialize in products that allow individuals with disabilities to use switches to operate electronic devices, providing access to tools for creating music and art products. For example, Enabling Devices (http://enablingdevices.com) makes a variety of adapted toys that allow switch users to operate moving toys, fans, radios, and games. AbleNet, Inc. (http://www.ablenetinc.com/) is another company that specializes in products that allow individuals with disabilities access to activities through switch-activated devices. Also see the following sites for a summary of issues and answers related to making music and art more accessible to individuals with special needs:

- Disabilities, Visual Impairment & Music (http://www.palatine.org.uk/directory/index.php/Music/MusDis/)

- The Drake Music Project (http://www.drakemusicproject.org/)

- The Liverpool Institute for Performing Arts—Learning Resources Online (http://www.lipa.ac.uk/lronline/support_for_students/disableinfo.htm)

Contributed by Dave Edyburn

under the direction of composer Carl Orff. Modeled after a wooden African instrument, they were specially designed to provide a successful and fun first experience with making music.

Support for Music Performance

Software like *Finale* and *Sibelius* offers all of the power and flexibility of word processing applied to music notation. In a school music program, this category of software expedites many of the tasks related to ensuring that each student has something to play, allowing the teacher (or students) to re-arrange music for alternate instrumentations, transpose parts into more accessible keys for performance, and simplify difficult passages. When printed, notation documents are legible and have a professional look, eliminating the lack of clarity and potential confusion that can result from handwritten parts. And, as is the case with all computer-generated data, existing documents can be corrected and/or revised without having to reenter the music from scratch. Notation files are small in comparison to digital audio, video, and graphics files, so entire libraries (hundreds of scores, parts, and handouts) can be stored using an insignificant amount of disk space.

With notation software, teachers can create theory lessons, quizzes, and other handouts that combine notation with text and other graphics. In fact, the most recent versions of these programs often include templates or wizards to greatly facilitate the creation of such informational documents and assessments. The capability of exporting sections of a musical score in a graphic format (GIF, JPG, or EPS) makes the insertion of these images into word processing documents very easy to accomplish. Even when such capabilities are not built into the notation software, screen captures of short passages can be created from the notation document and then inserted into a word processing document. Advanced notation programs also allow for maximum flexibility in generating unusual or irregular layouts.

In clarifying the roles of the sequencer and the notation program in the teaching of music performance, analysis, and composition, it is helpful to consider the hypothetical scenario of an ensemble class. To support sectional or individual practice, the teacher could enter the score of a piece into a sequencer. Once the music had been entered, the student or teacher could choose which parts needed to be heard, creating a "music-minus-one" type of accompaniment. In this way, for instance, the clarinet section could rehearse to a sequence consisting of the entire ensemble minus the clarinets. Or the second clarinet player could practice sectional passages by selecting only the clarinet parts for playback, but muting the second clarinet part. Meanwhile, the notation program could be used to edit any parts that need to be revised in order to match better the performance level of the students. These techniques have been demonstrated effectively by Rudolph and Peters (1996).

During the past decade, the piano lab has given way to the electronic *keyboard* lab, where students can develop keyboard skills as well as learn theory and harmony (Mark, 1996). Keyboard labs can now be networked with devices that allow the teacher to communicate with individual students or groups of students by means of a microphone and headphones.

Support for Self-Paced Learning and Practice

Most CD-ROM–based programs can accommodate both self-paced learning and activities more closely directed and monitored by the teacher. *Practica Musica,* for example, can be used as a tutorial in music fundamentals with little or no input from the teacher. It can also serve as a drill program when a student needs help with a particular topic related to ear training or music theory. Teachers need to consider multiple integration strategies when evaluating and using instructional software. While interactivity and multimedia make instructional software a *potentially* more powerful teaching aid than an inert, linear textbook, these programs cannot replace a teacher's careful supervision. In the end, the responsibility for effective teaching—with or without technology—rests with the teacher.

Almost all music instructional software packages either have a designated drill component or can be utilized as such. They are probably the easiest programs to install and to learn. Many have the capability of maintaining assessment information and other important data for multiple students on the same computer, accessible only to the instructor through use of a password-protected account. Companies generally provide online demos or trial downloads of these programs so that teachers can sample them before they buy.

Support for Teaching Music History

Of the nine national standards for music education, the only one that refers specifically to music history is the last one: "Understanding music in relation to history and culture." General music teachers have long sought to foster a deep understanding of musical works by situating them in their social and historical context. This is an excellent way to introduce young students to the practice of research, while offering more mature students unlimited opportunities for independent projects. The Internet is rapidly becoming the most powerful research tool available to students and teachers at all levels of education. Students and teachers can access card catalogs, electronic books, online journals, archived and current newspaper articles, audio and MIDI files, video clips, databases of thousands of out-of-print books, and discussion groups on almost any topic imaginable. Productive educational use of the Internet is limited only by the user and, to some extent, the connection speed and processing power of the computer. The effective use of such powerful tools requires clear instruction, guidance, and supervision by the teacher.

Building a website can be a perfect culminating activity for a general music class. Students can do much of the planning in groups—even offline, if computer access is limited. Within each group, students can assign themselves areas of the site according to individual strengths and literacies: A student who can't read music may be proficient with a web page authoring tool; some students can search the Internet for relevant graphics while others look for text or sound. Videos and DVDs continue to be a source of valuable historical reference material, many in the form of informative documentaries. Use of DVDs is highly advantageous for the user since they provide random access to content through the designation of chapter markers. Excerpts from these media can be captured on a computer's hard drive and incorporated into a student- or teacher-authored web page or software presentation as long as care is taken to clearly understand and follow existing copyright laws. With the advent of digital music files, the understanding of the copyright law as it relates to digital media is a very important aspect of a student's education. Finished projects can be viewed locally on a single computer, burned to a CD for multiple computers, posted on a school intranet, or uploaded to an Internet site so that parents or other students around the world can see it, link to it, and perhaps even contribute their own material.

Finally, a compelling general music class has the potential to be a highly effective recruiting tool. Students who initially feel out of place in their school's traditional music program dominated by instrumental and/or choral ensembles may find an exciting and challenging alternative role for themselves by enrolling in a technology-enhanced general music class. Often, it is access to music technology that attracts these students, who typically constitute 80% to 85% of the secondary school population (Edwards, 2006).

Support for Interdisciplinary Strategies

Beyond the opportunities for interdisciplinary study that will inevitably present themselves in a general music class, student-produced music and research can enhance a variety of other aspects of school life. Multimedia-based research projects in the humanities can easily include music that underscores a presentation or that is itself the object of study. A sequencer can facilitate the work of student composers who want to supply music for dance projects or video footage of athletic events. The close relationship between music and physics calls for projects that examine the science of sound. Identifying the existence of shared fundamental concepts across disciplines (e.g., ratios represented in math as fractions and in music as note durations) opens the door to a new world of learning potential within which multiple representations of these basic concepts and their connections are used to deepen student understanding (Scripp, 2007).

Issues and Problems in Art Instruction
Funding for Art Instruction

As a result of lean economic times and the ever-increasing emphasis on accountability in mathematics and reading as reflected in standardized testing related to the No Child Left Behind Act, funding for arts education is at an all-time low. Teachers and school administrators must increasingly find ways to stretch funds available for arts education. In light of this reality, funding for technology in art is especially difficult; updating technology resources and buying electronic supplies present continuing problems. For example, production of graphics is a popular art activity, but the cost of expensive ink for printers and specialized paper supplies quickly depletes an annual budget. Teachers are forced to take measures such as password-protecting printers and putting software print controls in place to limit the number of pages a student may print for free.

Ethical Issues Associated with the Use of Images and Other Materials

Since it is becoming easy to use images from the Internet and other sources, it is increasingly important to teach students that they must cite sources and request permission to use information, images, or other sourced materials. When students are carrying out research or creating artwork on the computers for websites or graphic design or other art projects, it is important to instruct them about issues of appropriation and repurposing of images and how this use intersects with plagiarism. Discussions should take place about issues of copyright law and what constitutes infringement. Perhaps a short assignment early in the term could require students to identify the specific issues and how they feel about copying someone else's work, whether text, image, or sound.

Accessing Images Used in Art Instruction

If schools use filtering software on computers to protect students from unsavory materials (e.g., pornography), many great works of art are also likely to be filtered out, unless the filter is carefully constructed. Care should be taken to allow these important artworks to be visible and accessible to students. The works of lesser known, more contemporary artists can sometimes blur the line between what is generally considered to be art and what is not. In photography, the nude figure has been a common subject. Some of the great artists have used the nude as metaphor for beauty, nature, and life. Limiting access by allowing only the names of the most famous artists to pass through a filter will not solve the problem. Strategies must be designed for allowing complete access to images of artworks for students to use. If all else fails, teachers must make sure the school library has a good collection of art and art history books. Also, many museums are making available images from their collections on CD or DVD for purchase.

The Challenge of Meeting Standards in Arts Instruction

Despite the limited funding for the arts and arts education, a group of professional organizations joined with the Consortium of National Arts Education Associations to promote a vision of K–12 arts education as described in the *National Standards for Arts Education* (http://www.ed.gov/pubs/ArtsStandards.html). The standards suggest that students know and be able to do the following by the time they have completed secondary school:

- Be able to communicate at a basic level in the four arts disciplines—dance, music, theatre, and the visual arts. This includes knowledge and skills in the use of the basic vocabularies, materials, tools, techniques, and intellectual methods of each arts discipline.

- Be able to communicate proficiently in at least one art form, including the ability to define and solve artistic problems with insight, reason, and technical proficiency.

- Be able to develop and present basic analyses of works of art from structural, historical, and cultural perspectives, and from combinations of those perspectives. This includes the ability to understand and evaluate work in the various arts disciplines.

- Have an informed acquaintance with exemplary works of art from a variety of cultures and historical periods, and a basic understanding of historical development in the arts disciplines, across the arts as a whole and within cultures.

- Be able to relate various types of arts knowledge and skills within and across the arts disciplines. This includes mixing and matching competencies and understandings in art making, history and culture, and analysis in any arts-related project.

Schools are challenged to find ways of meeting these standards in an educational climate in which the role of the arts is often not a priority.

Technology Integration Strategies for Art Instruction

As with music instruction, technology resources in art instruction support a variety of classroom strategies—from simple demonstrations of materials to student production techniques. Strategies include accessing art examples for classroom use, using teaching examples and materials, producing and manipulating digitized images, supporting graphic design and 3-D modeling, supporting desktop publishing with graphics, virtual field trips to art museums, creating movies as an art form, using computerized kilns, and sharing students' creative and research works. These are summarized in Table 13.3.

Go to MyEducationLab, select the topic "Music and Art Integration." Go to the "Assignments, Activities, and Applications" section and view the video "Website and Photoshop in Photography." Then complete the activity that follows.

Accessing Art Examples for Classroom Use

Internet sites and DVD collections are rich sources of artworks that students can use as illustrations of artists' work and as models for their own work. Teachers can generate a set of sites to bookmark for regular use in classes (see Table 13.4). They can also get students involved in these searches. For example, they might give students an assignment that asks them to find sources for paintings that use still life as subject matter, that use the technique of chiaroscuro, or that are 15th-century Florentine. As a result of students' actively looking and

TABLE 13.3 Summary of Technology Integration Strategies for Art

Technology Integration Strategies	Benefits	Sample Resources and Activities
Accessing art examples for classroom use	• Internet and CD collections provide ready access to works of art to use as samples, illustrations, and models.	• *Masters of Photography* CD http://www.masters-of-photography.com • World Wide Arts resources art history section http://www.ar.com/artists • Kinder Art's Multicultural Art resources http://www.kinderart.com/multic
Using teaching examples and materials	• Multimedia slide lectures are easier to use than slides and allow quick, random access to examples, illustrations. • Teacher-created websites can provide easy-to-access exercises in color theory, design theory, and photography techniques.	• *PowerPoint, HyperStudio*, Apple's *Keynote* • Teacher-created websites, e.g., http://www.nku.edu/~houghton/docent
Producing and manipulating digitized images	• Offers an easy, flexible system for creating images. • Lets novice artists create high-quality products. • Lets novice artists scan found objects to use in compositions.	• Camcorders, VCRs, digital cameras, scanners • Digitizing software, e.g., *FotoFinish* http://www.fotofinish.com • Paint programs, e.g., Riverdeep's *Kidpix*, Adobe's *Photoshop Elements*
Supporting graphic design and 3-D modeling	• Makes possible graphic techniques that can be done only on the computer with this software. • Offers many opportunities for artistic expression. • Demonstrates how easily images can be altered, thus fostering visual literacy skills.	• Image manipulation software, e.g., *Adobe Photoshop* http://www.adobe.com • Morphing software, e.g., *Morpheus* http://www.morpheussoftware.net/ • 3-D modeling software, e.g., *Ulead COOL 3D* http://www.ulead.com
Supporting desktop publishing with graphics	• Lets students illustrate their brochures, newsletters, and other documents with high-quality graphics.	• *Adobe Photoshop* http://www.adobe.com
Virtual field trips to art museums	• Allows students to see models and examples of artworks not locally available. • Makes possible multicultural "field trips" to gather examples of art and music from around the world.	• Virtual Tour of the Louvre Museum, Paris http://www.louvre.fr/anglais/visite/vis_f.htm • Art Institute of Chicago http://www.artic.edu/ • Museum of Modern Art http://www.moma.org • Metropolitan Museum of Art http://www.metmuseum.org/ • Smithsonian museums http://www.si.edu/ • National Gallery of Art http://www.nga.gov/
Creating movies as an art form	• Students can produce their own creative works for research, reports, assignments, and entertainment.	• Apple Computer offers *iMovie* and *GarageBand* http://www.apple.com • ArcSoft's *VideoImpression* http://www.arcsoft.com/ • Microsoft's *Movie Maker* http://microsoft.com

TABLE 13.3 *(continued)*

Technology Integration Strategies	Benefits	Sample Resources and Activities
Using computerized kilns	• Automatic monitoring frees student and teacher time during production of ceramic works. • Allows for more precise control of processes and repeatable results. • Involves easy preset programs with multizone controls and advanced capabilities. • Takes care of monitoring for non-school hours.	• Cress kilns http://www.ceramicssf.com • Bailey kilns http://www.baileypottery.com
Sharing students' creative and research works	• Allows students many ways of documenting work and easily sharing it with others.	• *PowerPoint* presentations • Videos • Electronic books • Websites

sharing, more learning will take place. Other example activities include:

- Have students use the school library to find specific works of art, and then challenge them to locate on the Internet other examples of the artist's work or work from the same period.
- To teach about the work of contemporary artists, have students look at galleries and exhibitions online to see the new work.
- For instructional reinforcement, use DVD collections on art techniques.
- Create a digital library to use for slide shows and presentations. Assign students who are traveling during the school year or during the summer to visit galleries and museums and bring back pamphlets, postcards, or examples of artwork they see. Scan the examples to create images for the classroom digital library.
- Obtain and use resources such as the *Masters of Photography* CD.

Using Teaching Examples and Materials

Computers can be used by teachers to create *PowerPoint* slide lectures (Gleeson, 1997) and to bring in images either by scanning or photographing with digital cameras. Also, faculty who are web savvy can create interactive websites to help students learn color theory, design theory, and photography techniques.

Producing and Manipulating Digitized Images

The most common type of hardware resource in art instruction is image digitizing equipment. Graphic scanners are com-

puter peripherals that transfer print materials into digital images on a computer. A scanner can transfer images, photographs, line drawings, or text into graphics files in a cost-

Employing computer graphics as part of art instruction can result in some amazing creations by students. Senior Jabari Walker's "Village Warrior" serves as a perfect example."

(Courtesy of Digital Media Instructor Karin Gunn, West Port High School, Ocala, FL)

TABLE 13.4   Recommended Websites for Museums and Virtual Field Trips

- Virtual Tour of the Louvre Museum, Paris (http://www.louvre.fr/anglais/visite/vis_f.htm)
- Art Institute of Chicago (http://www.artic.edu/)
- Museum of Modern Art (http://www.moma.org)
- Metropolitan Museum of Art (http://www.metmuseum.org/)
- Smithsonian Museums (http://www.st.edu/)
- National Gallery of Art (http://www.nga.gov/)
- Whitney Museum of American Art (http://www.whitney.org/)
- Andy Warhol Museum (http://www.warhol.org/warhol/)
- Art Museum Image Consortium (http://www.amico.org/)
- Tour of Florence Cathedral (http://www.nku.edu/~houghton/duomoweb)
- Photography Exhibition of the work of Douglas Prince (http://www.nku.edu/~photo/prince/index.html)
- Great Artists: DaVinci to Picasso (http://www.theartgallery.com.au/ArtEducation/greatartists/)
- Fine Art History Quick Reference (http://www.theartgallery.com.au/ArtEducation/greatartists/)
- Masters of Photography (http://www.masters-of-photography.com/)
- Photography of Henri Cartier-Bresson from NPR (http://www.npr.org/display_pages/features/feature_1318621.html)
- International Sculpture Center (http://www.sculpture.org/)
- Architect Frank Lloyd Wright Foundation (http://www.franklloydwright.org/)
- Architect Zaha Hadid (http://www.zaha-hadid.com/)
- Great Buildings Online (http://www.GreatBuildings.com/gbc.html)
- Non-Western art listings at Penn State Library (http://www.libraries.psu.edu/artshumanities/art/nonwestern.html)
- Non-Western art links (http://www.bc.edu/bc_org/avp/cas/fnart/links/non_Western.html)
- Non-Western art links on *The Educator*, online magazine for the professional in education (http://www.the-educator.co.uk/mainsite/links/art/nonwes.htm)
- Science, Art and Technology course from Art Institute of Chicago for science teachers (http://www.artic.edu/aic/students/sciarttech/)

effective and efficient manner. An artist can also capture an image from a video source (camcorder or VCR) using digitizing software like *iMovie, Final Cut*, or *Premiere*. Finally, a digital camera allows direct transfer of images to the computer hard drive. This equipment provides the user with a flexible system for capturing and manipulating digital images using computer software like *Photoshop*. This is a good example of using technology to foster creativity. Indeed, the ability to digitize still images and video has opened up a whole new genre of art.

A wide variety of software is available to teachers and students who are interested in producing computer art. Simple paint programs (*Microsoft Paint, Paintbrush*, or *KidPix*) are available for very young students; in fact, teachers often use these types of programs when first introducing students to the computer. Integrated software and hypermedia authoring programs (*Flash* or *Director*) always include fairly sophisticated draw or paint tools—good intermediate tools for the developing computer artist. High-level pro-

grams (*Photoshop*) suitable to the advanced artist would be used primarily at the high school level. One way a student might use paint or draw software would be to design the layout for a hypermedia project. Using these tools, a student who does not possess highly developed artistic techniques can produce a very attractive design.

Supporting Graphic Design and 3-D Modeling

Art educators can choose from among a number of software options to let students explore graphic design. A range of animation programs is available, from simple cell-type animation to more advanced programs that offer features like **tweening** or **morphing**. These graphic techniques can be done only with computer software. Other programs are specifically geared toward cartoon production and allow artists to add music and sound.

Technology Integration Lesson 13.2

Technology in Art Instruction

Title: Visualize It in 3-D

Grade Levels: 7 through 12

Content Area/Topic: Art, astronomy

 NETS for Students: Standards 2 (Communication and Collaboration), 3 (Research and Information Fluency), and 4 (Critical Thinking, Problem Solving, and Decision Making)

Description of Standards Applications: This integration lesson offers students the opportunity to work together to make what was once a very difficult idea into a realistic 3-D model. These models can be exported as a *QuickTime* movie and shared within a website. The model creation allows students to critically think about the impact of visualization on meaning.

Many concepts in school learning are symbolic rather than concrete, and students spend a great deal of time learning to code and decode relevant symbols. A good way to make many symbolic concepts more understandable is making them visual by creating 3-D models. To depict a solar eclipse, for example, students might discuss what a solar eclipse is and view a video or photos of such an event. After viewing and discussing, they can collaborate to create a 3-D model of the sun and moon. Then they can use animation effects to demonstrate how the eclipse takes place and store the animation as a *QuickTime* movie. Models created by various groups can be presented for comparison and discussion. Other subject areas in which learning can be enhanced through 3-D models include cell structures and air flow patterns in science, volume problems in math, choreography in the performing arts, and virtual sculptures in art.

Source: Steed, M. (2001). 3-D visualization: Using 3-D software to represent curricular concepts. *Learning and Leading with Technology, 29*(3), 14–20.

An art studio would not be complete without an image manipulation program like *Adobe Photoshop,* which enables students to edit clip art or digital photos. High-end programs provide hundreds of options and special effects for altering images. Morphing software enables the user to transform images smoothly from one shape or image to another. This technique offers tremendous potential for artistic expression and, by demonstrating how easily images can be altered, helps foster the development of visual literacy skills.

Finally, as Quesada (1998) and Steed (2001) describe, students can use 3-D, modeling, and animation software to communicate ideas visually through computer-generated models, animation, and imagery. One such activity is part of an interdisciplinary assignment called "Pocket Lint Project." Students use whatever they can pull out of their purses or pockets as the basis for developing a character. They use 3-D and animation software to create a model for their character and use geometry to "convey a sense of emotion" (Quesada, 1998, p. 54). Other good curriculum uses are described in Technology Integration Lesson 13.2.

Supporting Desktop Publishing with Graphics

Many schools look to their own graphics arts programs for the creation of brochures and newsletters as part of student learning activities. Because students gain valuable experience through creating and producing these publications, the activities can be considered a kind of internship to prepare for actual jobs as graphic artists for newspapers or other companies.

Virtual Field Trips to Art Museums

Many museums around the world have sites that allow a virtual tour through the museum. Although clearly this is not the same as viewing the works in person, virtual tours do offer a way for students to explore and expand their knowledge base. Some sites make their server available for students to post their own creations and to learn to create art using a certain medium like papier maché, batik, or origami. These sites also can be the basis for multicultural "field trips" to gather examples of art and music from around the world (Quesada, 1998). When using the Internet for arts instruction, it is important to remember that the images are reproductions; students will need to be made aware of the idea of scale and be reminded that they need to keep in mind the limitations of digital imagery.

Creating Movies as an Art Form

Students can now make short digital movies with software that often comes with the computer. For example, Mac-intosh computers come with *iMovie,* and Windows computers come with *Movie Maker,* both of which allow students to produce their own creative works using images, digital video, and sound for the purpose of reports, assignments, and entertainment. These inexpensive-to-create movies can be shared across platforms by saving them in *QuickTime* or *Flash Video* format. Not too long ago, creating video projects was expensive and difficult, but with the new generation of video editing software, it is affordable and relatively easy to accomplish.

Using Computerized Kilns

Art teachers who work in fired pottery media can use computerized electric kilns to save student time and assure better-quality products. **Computerized kilns** automatically set required temperatures, monitor lengths of time, and begin the process of cooling down and shutting off. Without the computer, teachers and students must keep a careful eye on the kiln and check the temperature by using cone indicators viewed through a peephole in the door of the kiln. The process of firing a kiln can take days, depending on the type and size of the kiln and its load, so this represents a considerable time savings.

FIGURE 13.3 **Sample Teacher-Created Website for Art Instruction**

Source: Academic website design. Courtesy of Barbara Houghton.

Sharing Students' Creative and Research Works

Through electronic publishing, videos, and presentation software, students can share their art creations with others. (See Figure 13.3.) Portfolios have long been a way for art students to demonstrate their achievements and abilities, and electronic portfolios are a natural extension of this strategy. Students can create *PowerPoint* presentations, videos, electronic books, blogs, and websites to show their research and creative work. Artists' books can be created and printed using desktop publishing and color inkjet printers.

Interactive Summary

The following is a summary of the main points covered in this chapter.

1. **A rationale for teaching arts in the Information Age** — Four parts of the justification for including art and music in school curriculum are expanded modes of expression, literacies for an Information Age, creative approaches to modern problems, and arts as aesthetic balance.

2. **Issues and problems in music instruction** — These include:
   - Redefining music literacy
   - Training teachers to meet music standards (see music standards and music technology standards)
   - The intersection of popular music, technology, and music education
   - The music director as small business administrator.

3. **Integration strategies for music education** — Five strategies are described for integrating technology into this area:
   - Support for music composition and production (see Apple's *GarageBand*)
   - Support for music performance (see *Sibelius* notation software)
   - Support for self-paced learning and practice (see *Practica Musica*)
   - Support for teaching music history (see example at Classic Motown timeline)
   - Support for interdisciplinary strategies (see math and music strategies).

4. **Issues and problems in art instruction** — These include:
   - Funding for art education
   - Ethical issues with using images
   - Accessing images used in art education
   - The challenge of meeting standards in arts education.

5. **Integration strategies for art instruction** — Nine strategies are described for integrating technology into this area:
   - Accessing art examples for classroom use
   - Using teaching examples and materials
   - Producing and manipulating digitized images
   - Supporting graphic design and 3-D modeling
   - Supporting desktop publishing with graphics
   - Virtual field trips to art museums
   - Creating movies as an art form
   - Using computerized kilns
   - Sharing students' creative and research works.

Key Terms

- computerized kiln
- morphing
- Music Educators National Conference (MENC)
- Musical Instrument Digital Interface (MIDI)
- music literacy
- notation software
- Orff instruments
- sequencer
- tweening

Web-Enrichment Activities

1. **Creative Online Music Environment** — Try the music tools at http://www.creatingmusic.com/mmm/mmm.html, such as the Musical Sketchpads, Rhythm Band, Playing with Music, or Melodic Contours. Using these activities, students can creatively express themselves. They can also make observations about the sounds that result from their actions. List three questions to ask students to consider while they use one of the tools at the website. The questions should guide students' thinking about musical concepts.

2. **Visit the Louvre** — Take a virtual tour of the Louvre Museum, one of the world's most famous museums, by going to http://www.louvre.fr/llv/musee/visite_virtuelle.jsp?bmLocale=en. Identify some ways you could incorporate such a tour into your instruction. How can virtual tours help enhance art instruction?

3. ***iMovie* Tutorial** — Go to Atomic Learning at http://movies.atomiclearning.com/k12/imovie2x.shtml to take a tutorial on using *iMovie*. Using the tutorial, create your own movie incorporating your favorite music and images. Pick a theme for the movie and build around that theme.

Go to MyEducationLab to complete the following exercises.

Video   Select the topic "Music and Art Integration," and go to the "Assignments, Activities, and Applications" section. Access the video "Composition Software and MIDI in Music" to see how teachers use special software to help students learn music. Then complete the activity that follows.

Tutorials   Select the topic "Software" and access the practical tutorial and skill-building activity for "Adobe Photoshop, Basics." Use the tutorial to learn the basic skills of this software. This skill will be used later in the Technology Integration Workshop.

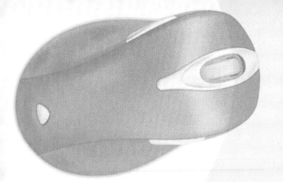

Technology Integration Workshop

The TIP Model in Action

Read each of the following scenarios related to implementing the TIP Model, and answer the questions that follow it based on your Chapter 13 reading activities.

TIP MODEL SCENARIO #1 Mr. Orson, a music performance teacher, has been talking to his friend and colleague, Mr. Niesson, who is a music teacher in Dublin, Ireland. Mr. Orson and Mr. Niesson would like to have their students work together on creating new musical pieces based on a series of Irish folk tunes that Mr. Niesson has collected in the rural areas near the city. Mr. Niesson would send recordings of the tunes, and the students would play them and work on variations based on them. However, the teachers and students need a way to make both the music production tasks and communicating their products faster and easier.

    1.1 What technology-based strategies could the teachers use to address these needs?

    1.2 What would be the relative advantage of using these strategies?

    1.3 What would be a good way to display their products, once they are created?

TIP MODEL SCENARIO #2 Mr. Daniel, the school's music teacher, is interested in collaborating on the development of an interdisciplinary project with Ms. Merrill, the history teacher. They plan to have Ms. Merrill's students research the backgrounds of the musical composers of the Romantic period, listen to some of their works, and locate information on the events of the times that helped shape their perspectives and, consequently, the music they created. At the same, Mr. Daniel's students will be researching and practicing the musical works of the composers of the Romantic period. When the students from both classes have finished their research, they will be paired together to create a blog that showcases their final products using media such as podcasts, photos, and videos.

    2.1 What technology-based strategy could the teachers use to carry out such a project?

    2.2 What would be the relative advantage of using this strategy?

    2.3 If they wanted to have Ms. Merrill's students work in small groups, how would they implement this in the class?

TIP MODEL SCENARIO #3 Students in Dr. Hadley's music appreciation class are preparing for their end-of-semester recitals. There is a variety of musical pieces to be performed, and Dr. Hadley plans to accompany each student during his or her recital. He wants students to be able to practice individually with accompaniment, but he did not have time to accompany each of them as they practiced.

    3.1 What technology-based tool could Dr. Hadley use to address this need?

    3.2 What would be the relative advantage of using this strategy rather than allowing students to practice without accompaniment?

    3.3 If Dr. Hadley has 30 music students and only eight music stations, what strategy could he use to allow each student to practice individually?

TIP MODEL SCENARIO #4 Mr. Lucien wanted to teach his art students some visual literacy skills he had been reading about. He had heard that these skills were becoming increasingly important for students as consumers of news information and potential buyers of products. He wanted to show them how easy it is to create fictional images that look real or to alter real images to create false impressions.

    4.1 What technology-based strategy could Mr. Lucien use to address this need?

    4.2 Why could this skill probably not be taught in a nontechnology way?

    4.3 How could Mr. Lucien arrange this activity so that students could work on it in groups?

TIP MODEL SCENARIO #5 Ms. Samda was an art resource teacher in a small, rural school district. She wanted her students to have opportunities to look at and appreciate various works of art and to learn something about the artists. However, they were far from any art museum, and there was no money for field trips even if there were one close by.

5.1 What technology-based strategy could Ms. Samda use to address this need?

5.2 What planning would Ms. Samda have to do before she introduced this activity to students?

5.3 What could she do to help structure this activity to keep students on task?

TIE into Practice: Technology Integration Examples

The Technology Integration Example that opened this chapter *(The Fine Art of Electronic Portfolios)* showed how a teacher might conduct an interdisciplinary unit combining music, art, and technology. One activity students were asked to do to demonstrate their skills was to use image manipulation software to create a collage of colors and images that came to mind as they listened to the music composition they or their fellow students created. With the knowledge you have gained from Chapter 13, do the following to explore this strategy:

1. Using *Adobe Photoshop* software, create a graphic collage like the example shown below.
2. Answer the following questions about *The Fine Art of Electronic Portfolios* example:

Example of a Graphic Collage

- Phases 1 and 2 — What kinds of relative advantage did the teachers feel the intersection of arts and technology offered for student portfolios? Do the instructors have the required TPACK to teach this lesson? If not, how do they acquire it?
- Phase 3 — The teachers will measure each student's progress in meeting assigned benchmarks in their composition and skill development. How will they set these benchmarks?
- Phase 4 — What is the purpose of having the "Evening at Eureka" show at the end of the grading period? What could teachers do to ensure that this event has the greatest possible positive instructional impact on students?
- Phase 5 — There are a lot of activities going on at the same time for these students. What could the teachers create or use to keep track of what each student is doing and what level they are on at a given time?
- Phase 6 — One of the end-of-project questions the teachers asked was if students were actively engaged in the project work. How might they ascertain this?

3. What NETS for Students skills would students learn by working on *The Fine Art of Electronic Portfolios* project? (See the front of this book for a list of NETS for the students.)

Technology Integration Lesson Planning

Complete the following exercise using sample lesson plans found on MyEducationLab.

1. Locate lesson ideas — MyEducationLab has several examples of lessons that use the art and music integration strategies described in this chapter. Go to MyEducationLab under the topic "Music and Art Integration" and go to the Lesson Plans to review example lessons. Choose two of the following integration lessons:
   - Technology and Music in the Middle School
   - Computers, Art, and Music at the Elementary Level
   - MusicLand Theme Park
   - Play the Recorder on the Computer
   - Exploring Tessellations with Computer Art
2. Evaluate the lessons — Use the *Evaluation Checklist for a Technology-Integrated Lesson* (located on MyEducationLab under the topic "Instructional Planning") to evaluate each of these lessons.

3. Modify a lesson — Select one of the lesson ideas and adapt its strategies to meet a need in your own content area. You may choose to use the same approach as in the original or to adapt it to meet your needs.

4. Add descriptors — Create descriptors for your new lesson similar to those found within the sample lessons (e.g., grade level, content and topic areas, technologies used, relative advantage, objectives, NETS standards).

5. Save your new lesson — Save your modified lesson with all its descriptors.

For Your Teaching Portfolio

For this chapter's contribution to your teaching portfolio, add the following products you created in the Technology Integration Workshop:

- The sample *Adobe Photoshop* collage you created
- The evaluations you did using the *Evaluation Checklist for a Technology-Integrated Lesson*
- The new lesson plan you developed, based on the one you found on MyEducationLab.

Chapter 14
Technology in Physical Education and Health Education

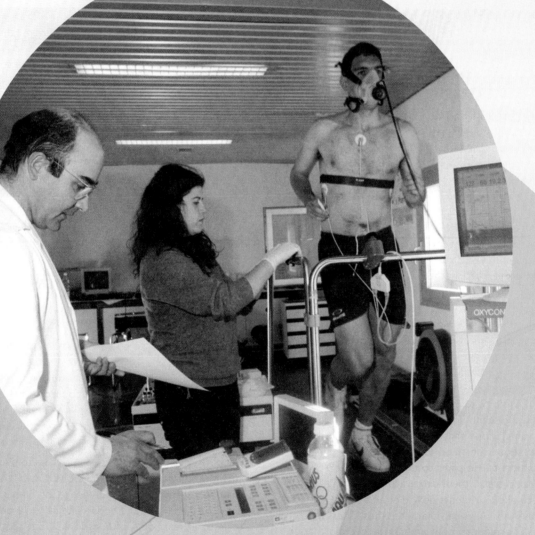

With obesity at near epidemic proportions among our young people, you'd think physical education would be at the top of schools' priority lists. But you'd be wrong.

CBS *Early Show*, January 27, 2005

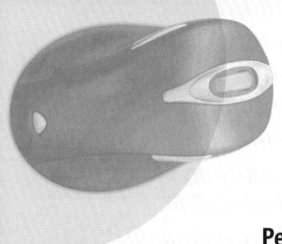

Technology Integration Example

Personal Fitness Plans You Can Live With

Based on: Manteno (Illinois) Community Unit No. 5 School District webquest at http://www.manteno.k12.il.us/lweedon/webquest.htm

Grade Level: 9 through 12 • Content Area/Topic: Biology, health, physical education, and technology • Length of Time: Three weeks

Phases 1 and 2: Assess technological pedagogical content knowledge; Determine relative advantage

Mr. Martinez, a high school physical education/health teacher, is concerned that not all students are choosing to take health or physical education courses and that there is a national trend toward low exercise levels and poor eating habits among teenagers. He talks to the biology teacher and the technology education (TE) teacher about a project the three of them could do on eating habits and exercise that would meet requirements for courses in physical education/health, biology, and technology. They agree that the project would have more impact for current and future students if it could be presented in the form of videos. That way, it could be more easily presented to many students, it would be in a visually compelling format, and it could serve as a resource for future classes.

The teachers decide to write descriptions of various "example teenagers" and to have their students work in pairs and small groups to design health and fitness plans appropriate for each example. The plans the students develop will relate to human growth and development concepts they are covering in biology, and the video design will address skills required in the technology education class. Mr. Martinez shows several simulations that the teachers agree will help make concepts about the need for fitness more visual and compelling to students. He plans to demonstrate heart monitors, devices that track the heart rate of the individuals wearing them, to show students how diet and exercise affect heart rate and other physical characteristics. Then he will show students how to document and track this information on a spreadsheet.

Before starting this lesson, the three teachers reflected on their technological pedagogical and content knowledge (TPACK), both individually and as a group that could support each other. Mr. Martinez reflected on his knowledge and felt he was close to the center of the TPACK model as he had experience with various technologies that could be used in the physical education/health classroom and various pedagogical strategies. He had also taught the same course for over 15 years and felt he had strong content knowledge. Within this specific realm of using technology in the physical education/health classroom, the technology teacher was not well versed within the appropriate pedagogies or content, but he felt he could assist in the learning and teaching of the technology. It was much different for the biology teacher. The biology teacher was just beginning to learn the various technologies that could be used in a classroom, how those technologies relate to teaching content, and what pedagogies would be appropriate. Thus, he felt that he leaned towards being strong in content but weak in technology and pedagogy. Although the three teachers had very different backgrounds and different strengths, they felt that if they collaborated and spoke frequently, they could be a successful team.

Phase 3: Decide on objectives and assessments

The teachers decide on three outcomes and assessments:

- **Outcome:** Video production/group work. **Objective:** Students will demonstrate video production skills and group work skills by achieving at least an 85% rubric score on the videos they produce. **Assessment:** Rubric to evaluate videos and cooperative work skills.

- **Outcome:** Knowledge of human anatomy/physiology, nutrition, and body system functions. **Objective:** All students will demonstrate knowledge of human anatomy/physiology, nutrition, and body systems by responding correctly to at least 90% of questions about these systems. **Assessment:** List of questions requesting example images and written descriptions as responses.

- **Outcome:** Feasible lifestyle plans. **Objective:** Students will achieve a rubric score of at least 85% on the plans they produce, including specific and appropriate recommendations for lifestyle changes, exercises, and eating habits. **Assessment:** Rubric adapted from one at the Manteno website.

Pre-Fitness Report

Mohammed   Period __5__   Age __17__ Grade __7__

	Pre Score	Minimum	Met/ Not Met	Suggested Change	Goal
Curl Ups	12	18	Not Met	2-5	13
Flexed Arm Hang	1	8	Not Met	1-4	2
Mile Run	7.30	10	Met	30-60 sec	7.28
Pacer	1	41	Not Met	4-6	2˚
Walk Test	122	35	Met	1-2	130
Trunk Lift	12	9	Met	0-1	12
Sit/Reach	12 12	12	Met Met	0-1	12 12
Shoulder	1 1	1	Met Met	T	2 2
BMI	33.79	17.5-26.0	Not Met	reduce	27.8
Skinfolds	19	17-32	Met	maintain	17

Comments: Met minimum standards on 6   test items

Health-Related Fitness Tutorial/Portfolio
Source: Courtesy of Bonnie's Fitware, Inc.

Phase 4: Design integration strategies

The three teachers agree on the following sequence of instruction and activities:

- **Week 1: Assign the project and collect information —** In each class, describe and discuss the requirements for the project and the learning activities that will take place. **Biology class:** Assign readings and hold class discussions about body systems. To review concepts, use assignment sheets from *A.D.A.M.: The Inside Story* (A.D.A.M.), *InnerBody Works* (Tom Snyder Communications), and *Muscle Flash* (Bonnie's Fitware). **PE/Health class:** Show the video *Personal Fitness: Looking Good/Feeling Good* (Kendall-Hunt). Review concepts about diet and exercise. Analyze the impact of diet with simulations such as *Pyramid Challenge* and *DINE Healthy* (DINE Systems), and analyze fitness performance and prepare fitness plans using *Health-Related Fitness* (Bonnie's Fitware). **Technology class:** The teacher works with the whole class to design the video structure and then forms small groups and assigns each group to work on a video depicting each student.
- **Week 2: Prepare information and materials — Biology class:** The teacher assists as students finish

working on their simulation assignments and as they take notes and gather materials to answer the biology questions. **PE/Health class:** Students begin their word-processed descriptions of appropriate fitness plans for their "example teenagers." **Technology class:** The small groups work on video production techniques and learning the video editing software.

- **Week 3: Prepare and display video products — Technology class:** The small groups storyboard their videos and prepare scripts based on information from the word-processed descriptions. They complete work on their videos and edit them as needed. Students present their videos to each of the classes, and teachers use their checklists and rubrics to assess the work.

Phase 5: Prepare the instructional environment

The teachers check out the software and videos from the Media Center and gather the assignment sheets to be used with them. Each teacher prepares copies of the rubrics and checklists. The TE teacher agrees to put these on the website so that students can look at them online. The biology teacher decides to have students do most computer simulations at the computer lab, so he schedules times for it. Mr. Martinez coordinates which students can work in pairs or small groups and prepares materials to communicate this information to the students.

Phase 6: Evaluate and revise

After they completed the unit, the three teachers reviewed the videos, looked at summary data from the checklists and rubrics, and discussed how the activities progressed. They agreed that the project worked well and determined how they might share class time in the future to make the work easier to coordinate. They agreed that, although students loved the body and nutrition simulations, they were time consuming. They decided to limit the number of simulations done inside class time and to allow students to do more on their own time for extra credit. They also found that some groups took more time with script writing than was originally planned, so their videos took more than a week to complete; this would need to be built into the plan for next time.

Objectives

After reading this chapter and completing the learning activities for it, you should be able to:

1. Discuss the role of technological pedagogical knowledge when preparing to teach lessons that integrate technology effectively in the K–12 classroom.

2. Identify some of the current issues in physical education and health education that might impact the selection and use of technology.

3. Describe some popular uses for technology in physical education and health education.

4. Identify exemplary Internet sites for physical education and health.

5. Create instructional activities for physical education and health education that model successful integration strategies.

Today, the health of young people—and the adults they will become—is critically linked to the health-related behaviors they choose to adopt. Because strong evidence exists that participation in health and physical education classes can help develop healthy behaviors in children, many schools, like the one in the *Personal Fitness Plans You Can Live With* example at the beginning of this chapter, are trying to find ways that all students can realize these benefits.

As the example shows, educational technology offers teachers valuable resources for informing and empowering students to make the right health choices. The most effective methods of instruction are student-centered approaches like the ones in *Personal Fitness Plans You Can Live With*: hands-on, cooperative learning activities that include problem solving and peer instruction to help students develop skills in decision making, communications, goal setting, resistance to peer pressure, and stress management (Kane, 1993; Seffrin, 1990). This chapter provides more details and examples of technology resources and integration strategies that teachers can use to help prepare students to lead longer and healthier lives.

What Does TPACK Look Like in Physical and Health Education?

The questions that many teachers consider with regard to technological pedagogical content knowledge (TPACK) include "How does this relate to me?" and "What are the implications of knowing about TPACK in my content area?" TPACK in any discipline is the perfect union of three knowledge domains (content, pedagogy, and technology) to develop

a knowledge base from which a teacher can view a lesson and understand how technology can enhance the learning opportunities and experiences for students while also knowing the correct pedagogy to enhance the learning of the content. In physical education/health, a teacher is incorporating the TPACK principals when he or she plans a lesson and, without hesitation, thinks about the student achievement that must be attained and understands the content that can be taught through the correct pedagogy and technology. For example, when teaching a lesson in physical education, instead of simply asking students to run the mile and to take times with a stopwatch to measure gains and achievement, a teacher with a TPACK perspective thinks about technology and how students can learn the content in a way that they could not without technology. Thus, a physical education/health teacher might request a class set of heart rate monitors that their students could use. Prior to running the mile, students would learn about the technological operations of a heart rate monitor and how heart rate is a better indicator than just speed for understanding one's body as one works on getting into shape. As they run the mile, students learn that some of the students may be in the middle of the pack, but their heart rate is higher than others. They learn what this means for future training and improvement. (See Figure 14.1.)

Issues and Problems in Physical Education and Health Education

Physical Inactivity

Today's headlines on television and in newspapers frequently remind us of the ever-increasing problem of obesity and lack of physical activity. Ewing et al. (2008) have linked a decrease in physical activity and obesity to urban sprawl. Graham, Holt-Hale, and Parker (1998) point out that children are less physically active in part because they spend more of their free time indoors watching television and playing computer games rather than outside in physical play. This inactivity has also recently been discussed in terms of gender. For example, while the benefits of physical activity (bone-mass increase, decrease in blood pressure, psychological well-being, and so on) have been well known for years, many young people (especially girls) fail to meet minimum guidelines set forth by the Surgeon General (Marcus, Williams, Dubbert, et al., 2006; Parker, Jacobs, Schreiner, Schmitz & Dengel, 2007). "Low and declining levels of physical activity are a particular concern among preadolescent and adolescent girls, as population-based surveys consistently report that girls are significantly less active than their male counterparts" (Ransdell & Petlichkoff, 2005, p. 4). This society-wide trend affects both the motor

FIGURE 14.1 TPACK and Physical Education/Health

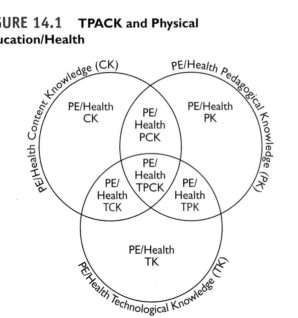

development and the health of our country's youth. Although technology may be partially responsible for the current decline in physical activity, it also holds the potential for motivating youngsters to increase their levels of physical activity. Several of the computer games available in arcades, such as *Downhill Skier, Dance Dance Revolution, Wii,* and golf games, require participants to be physically engaged in order to be successful in the game. However, this activity is not a substitute for mandatory physical education during school hours.

Instructional Time for Health and Physical Education

With schools currently refocusing their priorities on meeting standards in content areas and increasing scores on state and national tests, programs like health instruction and physical education have suffered. This is unfortunate, because three out of four deaths are due to preventable chronic conditions (U.S. Department of Health and Human Services, 1996a). In addition, cognitive functioning is related to proper nutrition and physical activity (Caine & Caine, 1995). Also, children's self-concept and self-esteem (Payne & Issacs, 1995), as well as their prosocial skills (Borba, 1989), are positively affected by their involvement in physical activities.

To achieve desired results, experts recommend 50 hours of health instruction per school year and 150 minutes of physical education instruction per week for grades K–5 and 225 minutes for grades 6 through 12. However, the actual amount of time contributed to health and physical education in most schools is far less than that. One solution may be the kind of technology-enabled curriculum integration shown in the *Personal Fitness Plans You Can Live With* example. Teachers can address several subject areas simultaneously while allowing students to see the connections between what they learn in school and real-life situations. Technology resources improve communication among and the productivity of students and teachers; allow more hands-on, visual learning experiences; help motivate students to spend more time on activities; and serve as a platform for students' products.

Accuracy of Health and Physical Education Resources

To be information literate, a person must be able to recognize when information is needed and know how to locate, evaluate, and use effectively the needed information. The national health standards speak directly to this issue. Because anyone can post anything on the Internet, students need to become more information literate so that they can be good consumers of health and fitness products and information. Specifically, they must be able to differentiate between accurate and inaccurate information in the context of health and fitness education.

Making the Case for Technology Integration

Use the following questions to reflect on issues in technology integration and to guide discussions within your class.

1. What type of support do you think the author is talking about in the following quote? "Support is greatly needed if physical activity is going to be increased in a society as technologically advanced as ours. Most Americans today are spared the burden of excessive physical labor. Indeed, few occupations today require significant physical activity, and most people use motorized transportation to get to work and to perform routine errands and tasks" (Satcher, 1997, foreword).

   Is instructional technology part of the problem, part of the solution, or neutral? Is the problem likely to get worse or better? With the help of computer technology, more and more people are now working from their homes. Will this trend lead to more or less physical activity?

2. Is there a way to turn the passive activities discussed in the following quote into ones that require physical activity? "Even leisure time is increasingly filled with sedentary behaviors, such as watching television, surfing the Internet, and playing video games" (Satcher, 1997, foreword).

   Can any of these activities be used to promote physical activity? What role can schools play in changing the amount of leisure time spent on sedentary activities?

Addressing the Standards

School physical education has come far from its early emphasis on physical training and calisthenics. It evolved into sports education; then lifetime activities; and now its current focus is on health-related fitness, behavioral competencies, and motor skills needed for lifelong engagement in enjoyable physical activity. This current shift is due, in part, to the national physical education standards (see Table 14.1), first introduced in 1995 and updated in 2004 by the National Association for Sport and Physical Education (NASPE). The AAHE national health education standards (see Table 14.2) were also published in 1995 (American Alliance for Health, Physical Education, Recreation, and Dance). The focus of the health education standards is health literacy—the capacity of individuals to obtain, interpret, and understand basic health information along with the competence to use such information to enhance health.

TABLE 14.1 NASPE Standards for Physical Education

1. Demonstrates competency in motor skills and movement patterns needed to perform a variety of physical activities.

2. Demonstrates understanding of movement concepts, principles, strategies, and tactics as they apply to the learning and performance of physical activities.

3. Participates regularly in physical activity.

4. Achieves and maintains a health-enhancing level of physical fitness.

5. Exhibits responsible personal and social behavior that respects self and others in physical activity settings.

6. Values physical activity for health, enjoyment, challenge, self-expression, and/or social interaction.

Source: Reprinted from *Moving into the Future: National Standards for Physical Education, 2nd Edition* (2004) with permission from the National Association for Sport and Physical Education, 1900 Association Drive, Reston, VA 20191-1599.

Drawing on the findings from the School Health Policies and Programs Study (SHIPPS), Pate and Small (1995) state: "Instruction practices in physical education often do not reflect the goals set by either the national health objectives or the National Physical Education Standards" (p. 312). This has not changed much since the introduction of the national standards. Although there has been some movement in certain areas of the country, there is certainly a need for greater implementation of the standards. Technology can play a role by making it easier to post and share key information. As health and physical educators share their successful standards-based curricula on the Internet, this may encourage broader implementation of standards. In addition, standards-based software now provides teachers with resources for increasing and measuring student learning related to the standards.

Handling Controversial Health Issues

Controversial subject matter has proven to be another challenge for health education. Many special interest groups press for inclusion of their particular issue in the health education curriculum. But including too many such issues actually can water down a curriculum and make it less effective. One area of particular concern is human sexuality. Many experts believe information and guidance on sexual decisions are essential; others feel students should be taught that abstinence is the only choice and that teaching about a controversial subject tends to legitimize it in the mind of the student. Other controversial topics include date rape, suicide, drugs, violence, and character education. Technology resources such as videos and well-chosen websites can provide valuable insights into these topics as well as help facilitate the logistics of instruction when only a subset of the total class is involved.

TABLE 14.2 AAHE Standards for Health Education

1. Students will comprehend concepts related to health promotion and disease prevention to enhance health.

2. Students will analyze the influence of family, peers, culture, media, technology, and other factors on health behaviors.

3. Students will demonstrate the ability to access valid information and products and services to enhance health.

4. Students will demonstrate the ability to use interpersonal communication skills to enhance health and avoid or reduce health risks.

5. Students will demonstrate the ability to use decision-making skills to enhance health.

6. Students will demonstrate the ability to use goal-setting skills to enhance health.

7. Students will demonstrate the ability to practice health-enhancing behaviors and avoid or reduce health risks.

8. Students will demonstrate the ability to advocate for personal, family, and community health.

Source: Reprinted, with permission, from the American Cancer Society. *National Health Education Standards: Achieving Excellence, Second Edition.* Atlanta, GA: American Cancer Society; 2007, www.cancer.org bookstore.

Top Ten

Websites for Physical Education and Health Education

Teachers can find information and resources for enhancing the teaching of physical education and health at the following ten websites.

1. American Alliance for Health, Physical Education, Recreation, and Dance http://www.aahperd.org   The professional organization for educators in these areas.

2. American School Health Association   http://www.ashaweb.org/   The professional organization for health educators.

3. Centers for Disease Control and Prevention   http://www.cdc.gov   This site offers a broad range of current information on health and wellness and is an excellent source of quality information for students and teachers.

4. Go Ask Alice   http://www.goaskalice.columbia.edu/   Students or teachers ask questions about health and wellness issues. Visitors simply send in their questions; they are answered by a team of experts from the Columbia University Health Question & Answer Service.

5. Kids Health   http://www.kidshealth.org/   Parents, children, teens, and professionals find answers to commonly asked health questions. Topics include the benefits of different types of vitamins, the food pyramid, healthy children's recipes, how to read food labels, and keeping fit.

6. Health Teacher   http://www.healthteacher.com/   Subscription-based site that offers a comprehensive, sequential K–12 health education curriculum consisting of almost 300 lesson guides that meet national health education standards and provide skills-based assessment methods.

7. University of Alberta Health Centre Health Information Page   http://www.ualberta.ca/ healthinfo   Provides access to free interactive software that teaches about various health topics relevant to young adults.

8. Science of Sport   http://www.exploratorium.com/sport/index.html   Interactive site addresses the science of sport—specifically baseball, cycling, skateboarding, and hockey.

9. P.E. Links 4U   http://www.pelinks4u.org   Provides information on adapted physical education, coaching and sports, elementary physical education, health and nutrition, fitness, interdisciplinary secondary physical education, and technology in physical education. Also has links to other major physical education websites.

10. Using Technology in Physical Education Newsletter   http://www.pesoftware.com/ technews/news.html   Newsletter provides physical educators and health educators with the latest information on using technology in physical education.

Technology Integration Strategies for Physical Education and Health Education

This section is aligned with the national physical education (PE) and health education (HE) standards, as noted in parentheses in the following list:

1. Technology to Support Improvements in Fitness (PE 3, 4)

2. Technology to Develop and Improve Motor Skill Performance (PE 1, 2)

3. Technology to Improve Students' Beliefs and Interactions Related to Physical Activity (PE 5, 6)

4. Technology to Assess and Enhance Personal Health (HE 3, 6)

5. Technology to Support the Procurement of Valid Health Information (HE 1, 2, 4)

6. Technology to Influence Others' Health Behaviors (HE 5, 7)

7. Technology to Support Interdisciplinary Instruction.

Technology Integration Lesson 14.1 illustrates how the following integration strategies can be implemented. For a summary of the strategies described here and technology resources that can help implement them, see Table 14.3.

Technology Integration Lesson 14.1

Technology-Enabled Physical Education

Title: Integrating Technology into Middle School Physical Education

Content Area/Topic: Physical fitness and social skills

Grade Level: 6 through 8

NETS for Students: Standards 2 (Communication and Collaboration), 3 (Research and Information Fluency), 4 (Critical Thinking, Problem Solving, and Decision Making), and 6 (Technology Operations and Concepts)

Description of Standards Applications: This integration lesson offers students the opportunity to use physical education technologies such as heart rate monitors to collect data on their personal fitness, develop media that communicate their findings, and share it with their peers.

To make it possible for schools to spend needed time on physical education and health courses in grades 6 through 8, technology-based strategies can help teachers integrate these topics into other content areas to create interdisciplinary lessons. Technology can help make time spent on physical education and health more hands-on and productive.

Instruction: Students can keep personal fitness goals and achievements as part of their electronic portfolios; analyze and graph data from their use of heart monitors; view videos that demonstrate model performances, various sports, and other motor activities to learn more about how the body works; and use the Internet to research sports and physical activities in other countries and historical periods. Another physical activity that is ideal as the basis for an interdisciplinary topic is orienteering, a combination of walking, running, and hiking while following a map and using a compass or GPS.

Assessment: Assessment for these strategies will depend on teacher goals for the activities. Most plans call for students to complete portfolio components, which are then graded by rubric.

Source: Mohnsen, B. (2000). Vaughn, Nekomi, and Luis: What they were doing in middle school physical education. *Learning and Leading with Technology, 27*(5), 22–27.

TABLE 14.3 Summary of Technology Integration Strategies for Physical Education and Health Education

Technology Integration Strategies	Benefits	Sample Resources and Activities
Supporting improved fitness	• Devices help analyze, monitor, and improve fitness. • Displaying students' data on the Internet allows competition between students across the country. • Devices help monitor heart rate as students work toward fitness goals. • Helps students develop and track their fitness goals and plans.	• Treadmills, stair steppers, and stationary bikes • Heart monitors • Electronic portfolio and spreadsheet software
Developing and improving motor skill performance	• Displays model performances. • Supports self-analysis and monitoring of improvement. • Gives students visual feedback on performances. • Helps teachers organize data collection and report on students' progress.	• Instructional broadcasts on motor skills • Video cameras • Handheld computers • Biomechanical analysis programs: *SportsCAD Motion Analysis* http://www.sportscad.com
Shaping students' beliefs and interactions related to physical activity	• Connects students of various backgrounds to allow interactions related to physical activity. • Students learn about the history of sports and dances.	• Televised shows and specials • Internet-based epals programs • Internet and electronic encyclopedias
Helping students assess and enhance personal health	• Guides students through the process of making changes to enhance their health.	• Nutritional analysis programs: *DINE Healthy* and *Pyramid Challenge* (DINE Systems) • Risk assessment programs
Helping students obtain valid health information	• Provides current information for researching health topics.	• Internet sites: Web MD http://www.webmd.com • Software: *My Amazing Human Body* (DK Multimedia), *A.D.A.M.: The Inside Story* (A.D.A.M.)
Influencing health behaviors	• Webquests allow students to collaborate on health-related issues. • Presents health issues in real-life settings to foster decision-making and critical thinking skills.	• Internet webquest sites: *Addiction* (http://technoteacher.com/WebQuests/ADDICTION/) • Video-based simulations: *Science Sleuths* (Science Kit and Boreal Labs–http://sciencekit.com)
Supporting interdisciplinary instruction	• Shows relationships between physical education/health-related topics and other subject areas.	• Bonnie's Fitware www.pesoftware.com

Supporting Improved Fitness

Technology devices and software are available to help analyze, monitor, and improve fitness. Exercise equipment, such as treadmills, stair steppers, and stationary bikes, meet the criteria of a technology device designed to improve fitness. Used in combination with monitors, these devices can show students the results of their efforts in terms of heart rate, speed, and power. Life Cycle Rowers, for example, show a small boat moving across the screen; the faster the student rows, the faster the boat moves. Connecting two Concept II rowers together provides the opportunity for indoor rowing races. Displaying the output of monitoring equipment to the Internet provides for competition between students across the country.

Electronic **blood pressure devices** (to monitor blood pressure), **body composition analyzers** (to determine the percent of body fat), **pedometers** (to monitor the number of steps one takes), **accelerometers** (to count calories, e.g., Cal Trac), and **spirometers** (to measure lung volume) are devices

Heart-rate monitors provide immediate feedback and promote self-awareness.

that assist with analyzing and monitoring fitness levels. Each device measures a different aspect of health and fitness, allowing students to use their own bodies for data collection and analysis. The most popular device in this category is the **heart monitor** (e.g., Cardio Sport Ultima) (see photo above). Students wear the heart watches around their wrists while an elastic band holds the transmitters to their chests (see photo). The transmitter senses the heartbeat from the heart's electrical impulses and transmits each beat to the wristwatch receiver through radio transmission. Younger children benefit from using the HeartTalker, with which instead of reading their heart rates on a wristwatch receiver, they receive audio feedback regarding their heart rate and exercise time from headphones attached to the transmitter. Heart monitors are especially effective for providing students with feedback as to whether they are in their target heart rate zones and benefiting from the training effect for cardiorespiratory endurance.

Students also can be put in charge of their own learning along with the development of fitness goals and plans. *Health-Related Fitness Tutorial/Portfolio* (Bonnie's Fitware) guides students through the five areas of health-related fitness: flexibility, muscular strength, muscular endurance, body composition, and cardiorespiratory endurance. The electronic portfolio portion of this software allows students to enter fitness plans, exercises, drawings or video clips, journal entries, caloric input/output, and fitness scores, which are then analyzed by the software. **Nutritional analysis programs** (to analyze calorie intake and monitor portions of required food groups), fitness analysis programs, and spreadsheet applications also can be used to calculate and graph individual nutrition and fitness goals. *Muscle Flash* (Bonnie's Fitware), with grade-specific versions, teaches and quizzes students about the names, locations, functions, and exercises for a variety of muscles through a flash card simulation. The learning from this program allows students to select the appropriate exercise(s) for specific muscle groups.

Adapting for Special Needs

As with all people, students with disabilities are paying increased attention to exercise, health, and wellness issues. As a result, a variety of resources are available to assist in understanding the unique challenges associated with health and disability:

- The President's Challenge Physical Activity and Fitness Awards Program: Accommodating Students with Disabilities (http://www.presidentschallenge.org/educators/disabilities.aspx)
- Be Fit for Life—Creating Healthy Lifestyles for People with Disabilities (http://www.health.state.ny.us/nysdoh/prevent/target7.htm#fit)
- Health and Wellness Information (http://www.ilru.org/healthwellness/healthinfo/).

Assistive technology and adapted sports equipment compose a specialized area of rehabilitation engineering that is critical to many applications of fitness and participation in sports for persons with disabilities. See the DRM WebWatcher-Sports and Recreation website at http://www.disabilityresources.org/SPORTS.html.

Contributed by Dave Edyburn

Developing and Improving Motor Skill Performance

Technology can provide students with information, model performances, and feedback, along with opportunities for self-analysis and monitoring of improvement in the area of motor skill performance. In order for students to develop a new motor skill, they must first understand and observe a model performance. Instructional broadcasts on motor skills provide a model demonstration of the skill to be learned. Software (e.g., Bonnie's Fitware's *VolleyballComplete* and *Elementary Physical Education Dictionary*, Ball Hog's *Soccer*) also provides learners with model skill performances and a description of not only the *how*, but also the *why*. Knowing why a skill is performed in a certain manner is beneficial to the learning of new skills and, more significantly, to the transfer of that learning to new movement experiences.

Asking students to set personal goals and then monitoring their progress on motor skill acquisition is motivational to the student but often a paperwork nightmare for a physical educator responsible for 200 to 600 students. Handheld computers help physical educators organize their data collection (e.g., grades, attendance, fitness scores) during the instructional period. Once the data have been transferred to a desktop or

Electronic portfolios can be used to record and monitor personal data.

notebook computer, they can be analyzed and reported to students and parents in a variety of formats. Electronic portfolios (e.g., Bonnie's Fitware's *Physical Education Portfolio*) can put students in charge of collecting, recording, and analyzing their motor skill achievement, fitness performance, social interactions, and cognitive learning. The electronic portfolios can be accessed using notebook, tablet, or even handheld computers (see photo above).

Once students begin to practice motor skills, feedback becomes the significant component for perfecting performance. Digital video cameras record performance and allow for replay and analysis. The use of video is most effective when it is shown to the student immediately after the performance, along with external verbal feedback and cues (Darden

& Shimon, 2000; Doering, 2000). Video replay is best used with students beyond a beginner skill level. (See Figure 14.2.) Students need some knowledge and viable mental image of the skill in order to use the information these images provide. For students with advanced skills, replay also is useful for strategy and tactics. Because advanced movement is so fast and sometimes difficult to analyze at normal speed, slow motion replay and freeze-frame capabilities are essential.

To provide for student self-analysis, a digital video camera (see photo on page 398) should be placed at one station in a learning circuit (e.g., for tennis skills). Each phase of the skill is modeled while students work in pairs to identify critical features, patterns, and concepts associated with the skill. Then students rotate through the stations in small groups, with one group beginning at the digital camcorder station. One student hits the ball, the second student provides feedback, and the third person records the skill performance. The student-coach uses the first set of columns on a criteria sheet to provide specific feedback. On the rotation after the video station, the students review the images. The instant replay provides immediate feedback for the performer, who uses the second set of columns on the criteria sheet to self-assess performance.

Student projects can be used to assess and further develop their understanding and performance of motor skills. All motor skills fall into a general movement pattern category (e.g., overhand pattern, kicking pattern). Understanding the relationship between skills using the same movement pattern helps when transferring knowledge and experience from one motor skill to another (e.g., overhand throw to volleyball serve). Students working in small groups can investigate one movement pattern

FIGURE 14.2 **Developing and Improving Motor Skill Performance**

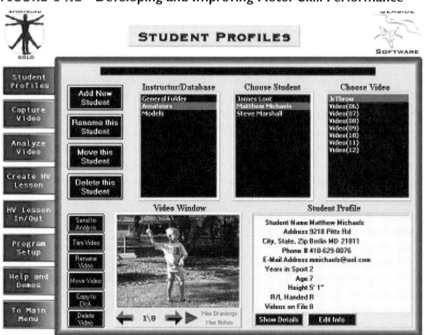

Video footage allows a teacher, coach, or the individual to go back and review a performance and break down stages in the skill.

and record their findings on video. Next they can visit other classes and record examples of their particular movement pattern. Each group then shares its video with the rest of the class.

The examples so far in this section have targeted standard 1; however, standard 2 also addresses motor skill improvement. Students must analyze their own movement performance using scientific principles of movement and create their own practice plan in order to improve performance. Physical educators often have believed that this learning would occur through the process of osmosis—that simply participating in sport would transfer this learning to students. We now understand that for students to see the connection between sports and science or sports and improvement, they must understand some basic cognitive concepts and principles.

Broadcasts, such as *SportsFigures* (ESPN), provide information on the science of sports. Each lesson includes step-by-step explanations of the scientific principles. ESPN has launched a companion website (http://www.sportsticker.com/sportsfigures) that is designed for teachers, students, and parents. It contains interactive components such as educational games, video clips, and curriculum information to support student learning.

Software packages, such as *Biomechanics Made Easy* (Bonnie's Fitware) and *SimAthlete* (Bonnie's Fitware), provide reference information on the important biomechanical and motor learning concepts (e.g., goal setting, feedback, stability, force production). *Biomechanics Made Easy* then quizzes students on their understanding and application of the concepts, whereas *SimAthlete* goes a step further by asking students to create a practice plan (coach) for different athletes. The better the practice plan, the better the athlete performs during competition. *Measurement in Motion* (Learning in Motion) and *Dart Trainer* (Dartfish) take biomechanical analysis to another level by encouraging open-ended exploration. The software packages use video clips (supplied by the teacher or captured using stu-

dent subjects) and allow for ease of measurement and analysis of movement performance (e.g., ball rotation, limb speed).

Shaping Students' Beliefs and Interactions Related to Physical Activity

Standards 5 and 6 of the national physical education standards address primarily the affective domain. Although software to address this area is limited, videos and the Internet can provide opportunities to address these areas. Televised shows, such as *Gossip Girls* and after-school specials, often focus on social and self-esteem issues related to physical activity or appearance. Physical educators can use recordings of shows or portions of pertinent programs as prompts for journal writing when asking students how they would feel if presented with the situation addressed in the recording.

The Internet offers an ideal medium for connecting students with different backgrounds and beliefs and providing them with the opportunity for interactions related to physical activity. Many of us had pen pals when we were students. Today, students have keypals (a.k.a. epals). Keypals are students who connect with one another via electronic mail. They can share ideas, concerns, physical education/activity experiences, information, written assignments, and research. Through these connections, they learn to accept individuals from other communities and cultures. Sites such as http://www.pesoftware.com/pepals.html or http://www.epals.com are available to help teachers get started with this type of activity. They can visit one of the sites to find other physical educators interested in teaming for this type of project.

Students also can access an array of individuals with knowledge and expertise related to physical education, sports, and fitness. Olympic athletes, professional athletes, biomechanists, medical doctors, exercise physiologists, and motor learning specialists can provide students with insights regarding real-life experiences related to physical activity. Bonnie's Fitware sponsors the Olympic Athlete Project. This project began in 1995, when an Olympic rower was identified to share his trip to the Olympics with students. Steven Segaloff was a potential Olympic coxswain when he began communicating with students across the United States. He sent email messages every other week that dealt with his sport, his training program, the selection process, his relationship with the other rowers (teamwork), and his feelings about training and participating in the Olympics. Students, in turn, emailed back asking specific questions of interest to them.

Appreciation for a sport or dance can be enhanced through an understanding of its origins. The Internet and electronic encyclopedias provide students with access to a wealth of information, including the history of sports and dances. However, it is important that students are prepared to use this research tool. They must learn to double-check all references, examine author credentials, and cite resources.

Helping Students Assess and Enhance Personal Health

When studying health, students are motivated when they can see a connection between what they are studying and their own bodies. When attempting to motivate individuals to change their lifestyles and adopt a wellness approach toward their health, information alone is not enough. Fortunately, software is available to guide students through the process of making changes. These programs (e.g., Ripple Effects' *Relate for Kids* and *Relate for Teens*) help students apply their knowledge to problem-solving situations. Record keeping, visual representation, and data analysis are all components of these programs.

Many nutritional analysis programs are currently available. These programs (e.g., DINE Systems' *DINE Healthy* and *Pyramid Challenge*) ask the user for data on age, weight, height, gender, and amount of physical activity, and then calculate the individual's nutritional needs. The user records the types and amounts of foods eaten daily, and the program creates a report that lists the calories ingested, the nutrient values for all foods, and the total of all nutrients ingested. These reports then are used to determine if the student has met the recommended dietary allowances and whether the number of calories ingested was excessive. These programs expose poor nutritional and fitness behaviors through their analysis of daily food intake and physical activity. Appropriate menus and exercises are recommended for a healthier lifestyle. The software packages serve as personal trainers for fitness and nutrition.

Another type of program along these lines is the risk assessment program. These programs ask the user to input data regarding his or her lifestyle. Questions include height, weight, gender, age, cholesterol level, blood pressure, smoking habits, alcohol usage, physical activity habits, family medical history, nutritional information, and use of seat belts. Based on the data received, the program determines the individual's life expectancy, cardiovascular disease risk, and/or cancer risk. Several shareware programs on risk assessment are available as well as web-based software at sites such as http://hin.nhlbi.nih.gov/atpiii/calculator.asp.

Helping Students Obtain Valid Health Information

Historically, the health education textbook has been the primary source of information and reading material in health education classes. Today, students have access to a wide variety of Internet sites and software. As noted earlier,

FIGURE 14.3   KidsHealth Website

Source: © 2004 www.KidsHealth.org. Reprinted with permission.

students need instruction on how to distinguish between accurate and inaccurate information.

KidsHealth (see Figure 14.3) is an example of a health-related site targeted at K–12 students. High-quality software includes *Body Fun* (Bonnie's Fitware) for elementary students and *BARNS Multimedia Series I* and *II* (Learning Multi-Systems) for middle and high school students. Children and teenagers can use these and other resources to research health topics, including the side effects of commonly used medicines or symptoms of major medical illnesses.

Influencing Health Behaviors

When dealing with all of the complex issues in health education, a mentoring relationship offers great potential for promoting self-analysis and metacognition on the part of the older student. Email and videoconferencing may also be used to set up online projects with other classes around the world. For example, fifth-grade classes in different parts of the world collaborate on studying local safety issues. When they complete their research, they work together on developing a web page that promotes environmental health. Students also are able to discuss the differences between various cultures with regard to subjects such as drug use or government-sponsored health care.

Using the webquest strategy (see http://webquest.org/index.php), students are given an authentic problem to solve, along with web resources on the topic. Students typically work in collaborative teams. Each student explores the linked sites related to a specific role to which they have been assigned on the team. Students then teach what they have learned to the other team members. Finally, higher level questions guide students toward more challenging thinking and a deeper understanding of the topic being explored.

 Go to MyEducationLab, and select the topic "Internet." Go to the "Assignments, Activities, and Applications" section and open the Web Activity "Health and Fitness Online." Then complete the activity that follows.

Video resources also are an efficient way to remove logistical hurdles when teaching health-related issues. Videos allow students to hear information and advice from a voice other than the teacher's. They also allow students to see health issues in real-life settings.

Some resources let students see the consequences of ill-advised choices, whether it be smoking, drugs, or poor nutrition. These resources include video-based simulations that foster decision-making and critical thinking skills. Simulation programs place students in situations where they have to apply their knowledge to solve medical or health mysteries. A popular simulation website, *Science Sleuths* (Science Kit and Boreal Labs), uses humorous mysteries to engage students in the process of problem solving and critical thinking. The mystery episodes are fictitious but introduce important health concepts and processes. Students can access video interviews; conduct science experiments; and examine photos, articles, charts, graphs, and much more. Topics related to health education include Blood Components and Function, Human Development and Heredity, and The Nervous System.

Finally, simulations and diagnostic tools are available to help students think through health and social situations. Software available from Psychological Enterprises (http://www.eqparenting.com/ppsg.htm) helps students work through social decisions that can affect their physical and emotional health. For an example use of this product, see Technology Integration Lesson 14.2.

Technology Integration Lesson 14.2

Technology-Supported Health Instruction

Title: Reinforcing Healthy Social Problem Solving   **Grade Level:** K–6
Content Area/Topic: Health and social skills

 NETS for Students: Standards 2 (Communication and Collaboration), 3 (Research and Information Fluency), and 4 (Critical Thinking, Problem Solving, and Decision Making)

Description of Standards Applications: This integration lesson offers students the opportunity to use research and communication skills such as speaking, listening, and making new friends using technology that coaches and assesses them. The authors of this article (see source entry) say, "Social and emotional skills are learned skills, like riding a bike or tying your shoes" (p. 19).

Instruction: Begin by pretesting students with instruments such as *Piers Harris* (to measure self-esteem), *Health Locus of Control* (to measure how much control students feel they have over health issues), and *Group Social Problem Solving Assessment* (to measure knowledge of social problem-solving strategies). Teach students concrete skills such as speaker power, listening position, keeping calm, active listening skills, and making new friends. (See source article for further information on these strategies.) This gives all students a common language for discussing social problems. Administer the instruments to each student; once students identify a problem, the software helps them work through the process of reflecting on feelings and setting a goal for solving the problem.

Assessment: After using these processes for at least 6 months, post-test each student.

Source: Poedubicky, V., Brown, L., Hoover, H., & Elias, M. (2000–2001). Using technology to promote health decision making. *Learning and Leading with Technology, 28*(4), 18–21, 56.

Supporting Interdisciplinary Instruction

The popular opinion regarding interdisciplinary instruction for health and physical education is that these subject areas support learning in other subjects. However, the perspective of health and physical educators is that interdisciplinary instruction requires a symbiotic relationship—where subject areas support each other. Mohnsen (2003) offers an example of an interdisciplinary health-related fitness unit in which the physical education teacher focuses on the benefits of physical training and conditioning and the health education teacher focuses on health issues related to diet and physical activity. The science teacher explores how the digestive system works, and the mathematics teacher provides word problems on the input and output of calories. See Technology Integration Lesson 14.1 earlier in this chapter for another example of an interdisciplinary lesson that integrates physical education, science, and math, along with the use of computers. Technology teachers can help with these interdisciplinary units by providing Internet research support and multimedia project development tools that let students demonstrate their health and physical education learning.

Physical Education and Health Education Online

A recent trend is for physical education and health education courses to be taught online. As the number of K–12 schools offering courses online grows exponentially through the United States, the opportunities for reaching students in an online format are becoming increasingly popular (Doering, 2006; Doering, Hughes, & Scharber, 2007). Although online courses are now available in brick and mortar schools, one of the most popular completely online schools is the Florida Virtual School (FVS). FVS demographics indicate that 61% of students are female and 39% male compared to a 51% and 49% demographic in brick and mortar schools (Florida TaxWatch, 2007). Of these demographics, physical education and health education courses had the highest enrollment (21.7%), and 30.4% of the grades earned in these courses were 80% or higher (Florida TaxWatch, 2007). One might wonder what an online physical education course looks like. As with any course, the design and pedagogy differ greatly from class to class. However, they most commonly consist of a goal or goals, such as walking 4 miles, that students need to accomplish in a week. Students keep a log of their physical activity—sharing their data with other students while they keep a journal about their experiences.

Interactive Summary

The following is a summary of the main points covered in this chapter.

1. **Issues in physical education and health education** include physical inactivity; limited instructional time for health and physical education; accuracy of health and physical education resources; addressing the standards; and handling controversial health issues.

2. **Integration strategies for physical education and health education** are in seven general areas:
   - Supporting improved fitness
   - Developing and improving motor skill performance
   - Shaping students' beliefs about physical activity
   - Helping students assess and enhance personal health (e.g., http://www.dinesystems.com)
   - Helping students obtain valid health information (e.g., http://www.webmd.com)
   - Influencing health behaviors
   - Supporting interdisciplinary instruction.

Key Terms

- accelerometer
- blood pressure device
- body composition analyzer
- heart monitor
- nutritional analysis program
- pedometer
- spirometer

Web-Enrichment Activities

1. **Risk assessment tool for estimating your 10-year risk of having a heart attack** http://hin.nhlbi.nih.gov/atpiii/calculator.asp — The risk assessment tool uses information from the Framingham Heart Study to predict a person's chance of having a heart attack in the next 10 years. If you know your cholesterol levels, you can use the tool. Read the information provided and describe the type of health concepts that students can learn by using the tool to try various scenarios.

2. **KidsHealth** (http://www.kidshealth.org) — KidsHealth, created by the Nemours Foundation, provides doctor-approved health information about children from before birth through adolescence. Use the Kid's Site link on this web page, and try one or more of the games. Identify the health or physical education standards that are addressed by the game.

3. **Nutritional analysis program** — Use the Nutrition Analysis Tool (http://www.ag.uiuc.edu/~food-lab/nat/mainnat.html) to analyze a meal or a day's food intake.

PEARSON
myeducationlab
The Power of Classroom Practice
www.myeducationlab.com

Go to MyEducationLab to complete the following exercises.

Video Select the topic "PE/Health Integration," and go to the "Assignments, Activities, and Applications" section. Access the video "Nutrition Quest" to see how one school uses technology to expand students' understanding and knowledge of nutrition. Then complete the activity that follows.

Tutorials Select the topic "Software" and access the practical tutorial and skill-building activity for "*iMovie* for Mac, Basics" or "*MovieMaker* for PC, Basics." Use the tutorial to learn the basic skills of creating your own movies on your computer. This skill will be used later in the Technology Integration Workshop.

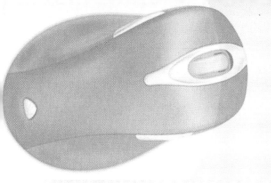

Technology Integration Workshop

The TIP Model in Action

Read each of the following scenarios related to implementing the TIP Model, and answer the questions that follow it based on your Chapter 14 reading activities.

TIP MODEL SCENARIO #1 Ms. Hayward wants all of her physical education students to keep a "fitness portfolio." She wants them to enter weekly entries on what they have accomplished in their own fitness plans and in assigned exercises and activities, their entries in a fitness journal, and video clips of their performances. She wants them to be able to update it and share it easily with other students and their parents and friends.

1.1 What technology-based strategies could Ms. Hayward use to address these needs?

1.2 What would be the relative advantages of using these strategies?

1.3 Why does Ms. Hayward want students to be able to share the portfolio easily with parents and friends?

TIP MODEL SCENARIO #2 Whenever his tennis students are practicing various new skills he has just introduced, Mr. Larue takes videos of their performances with his digital camera. Later that day, he and the students look at the students' performances together and analyze how they could improve their techniques.

2.1 What problem(s) does this technology-based strategy address?

2.2 What is the relative advantage of using this strategy?

2.3 What are two reasons Mr. Larue may want to use a digital video camera as opposed to a regular video camera to record students' performances?

TIP MODEL SCENARIO #3 Ms. Escarcega wants her students to be prepared for drug-related situations they may encounter outside school. She knows that it does no good to talk to them about what they should do in these situations. She has found a software package that includes a set of short videos, each with a different drug-related scenario. At the end of each scenario, students have the opportunity to choose from a list of responses and to see what might happen after each choice.

3.1 What problem(s) does this technology-based strategy address?

3.2 What is the relative advantage of using this strategy?

3.3 Should students work individually, in pairs, in small groups, or as a whole class on this activity? Explain your answer.

TIP MODEL SCENARIO #4 Mr. Decker knows that his 10th- and 11th-grade students have and will have a lot of questions about issues related to drugs, sex, and domestic violence. They will be graduating soon, and he wants to make sure they know some of the places they can go for accurate, reliable information from health agencies and other authoritative sources. He decides to have them do an in-class scavenger hunt to locate answers to various questions by looking at some of the key sites.

4.1 What problem(s) does Mr. Decker's technology-based strategy address?

4.2 What is the relative advantage of using this strategy as opposed to just giving the students a list of the websites?

4.3 Should students work individually, in pairs, in small groups, or as a whole class on this activity? Explain your answer.

TIP MODEL SCENARIO #5 Mrs. Norgaard is a physical education teacher who wants each of her students to set fitness goals for him- or herself. She has students decide how many exercises of each kind they will do each week and what their target heart rate should be. She has them keep track of how well they have met their goals. However, keeping this information in the notebook she has set up for each class is becoming cumbersome and difficult to update. In addition, she cannot easily calculate averages across the class or how much a student has fallen short of or exceeded a goal.

5.1 What technology-based strategy could Mrs. Norgaard use to address this need?

5.2 What would be a good way to organize the ongoing task of entering and updating student information? Should Mrs. Norgaard do the updating, or should the students do it? Explain your answer.

5.3 What could Mrs. Norgaard do to help structure this activity to keep students on task?

TIE into Practice: Technology Integration Examples

The Technology Integration Example that opened this chapter *(Personal Fitness Plans You Can Live With)* showed how a teacher might have students create videos that depict healthy lifestyles. This strategy can be helpful in many kinds of health and physical education activities. With the knowledge you have gained from Chapter 14, do the following to explore this example:

1. Create part of a video example like the one described in the chapter. A sample frame from the video is shown here. Shoot your own video or digital images of yourself or a friend performing a physical skill. Then transfer your video or images to *iMovie* or *MovieMaker*.

2. Answer the following questions about the *Personal Fitness Plans You Can Live With* example:

   • Phase 1 — Why would the use of videos be an especially powerful way to display this health-related information?

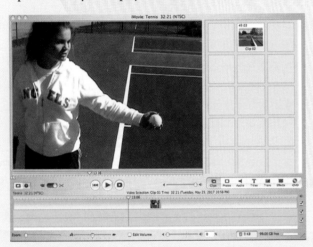

Source: Sample *iMovie* video. Screen shot reprinted with permission from Apple Inc.

   • Phase 2 — One of the desired outcomes for this project is to create a video of lifestyle recommendations for each example teenager. Create a rubric that the teachers might use to assess these videos. (*Hint:* Look at Kathy Schrock's Guide for Educators at http://school.discoveryeducation.com/schrockguide/ to locate an existing rubric you can modify.)

   • Phase 3 — What are the benefits of an interdisciplinary approach to this project? Why is this especially important when considering ways of teaching physical education and health skills in today's schools?

   • Phase 4 — Work and information from three different subject-area classes must be coordinated so that one builds on the other. Name one way to facilitate the sharing of these student products among the classes as students complete them.

   • Phase 5 — One finding from the post-project assessment was that script writing took more time in the Technology Education class than had been originally anticipated. Can you think of a way to make this work go more quickly? (*Hint:* Script writing is an English/language arts skill.)

3. What NETS for Students skills would students learn by doing the *Personal Fitness Plans You Can Live With* project? (See the front of this book for a list of NETS for students.)

Technology Integration Lesson Planning

Complete the following exercise, using sample lesson plans found on MyEducationLab:

1. Locate lesson ideas — MyEducationLab has several examples of lessons that use some of the integration strategies described in this chapter. Go to MyEducationLab under the topic "PE/Health Integration" and go to the Lesson Plans to review example lessons. Choose two of the following integration lessons:

   • A Nutrition Database

   • Create an Athlete

   • Personal Trainer

2. Evaluate the lessons — Use the *Evaluation Checklist for a Technology-Integrated Lesson* (located on MyEducationLab under the topic "Instructional Planning") to evaluate each of these lessons.

3. Modify a lesson — Select one of the lesson ideas and adapt its strategies to meet a need in your own content area. You may choose to use the same approach as in the original or to adapt it to meet your needs.

4. Add descriptors — Create descriptors for your new lesson similar to those found within the sample lessons (e.g., grade level, content and topic areas, technologies used, relative advantage, objectives, NETS standards).

5. Save your new lesson — Save your modified lesson with all its descriptors.

For Your Teaching Portfolio

For this chapter's contribution to your teaching portfolio, add the following products you created in the Technology Integration Workshop:

   • The sample *iMovie* video you created

   • The evaluations you did using the *Evaluation Checklist for a Technology-Integrated Lesson*

   • The new lesson plan you developed, based on the one you found on MyEducationLab.

Chapter 15
Technology in Special Education

For most of us, technology makes things easier. For a person with a disability, it makes things possible.

Judy Heumann, Assistant Secretary, U.S. Department of Education, Office of Special Education Programs

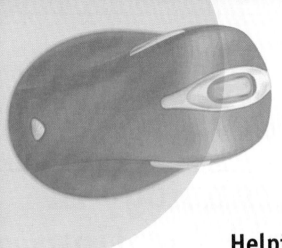

Technology Integration Example

Helping Students with Disabilities Blend In

Based on: Judd-Wall, J. (1996). Curriculum blending: Computerized surveying activities for everyone. *Learning and Leading with Technology, 23*(8), 61–64.

Grade Level: All grade levels • Content Area/Topic: Research methods, data analysis, charting, graphing • Length of Time: Three weeks

Phases 1 and 2: Assess technological pedagogical content knowledge; Determine relative advantage

Three of the students in Ms. Montoya's sixth-grade class had special needs. Dorothy had cerebral palsy and came to class in her motorized wheelchair. Although bright and enthusiastic, she had difficulty with fine-motor skills and could not write or use the computer keyboard and mouse. Ralph was a shy, sweet boy with mild mental deficits. Geraldo had hearing impairments and was reluctant to speak in class. Ms. Montoya made special efforts to involve Dorothy, Ralph, and Geraldo in all class activities and had shown the other students how to welcome them into their work and play. She consulted with the school district's Special Education Resource Office to obtain an alternate keyboard and input software for Dorothy and special speech development software for Geraldo. She tried several resources and strategies to help develop Ralph's reading skills and found that he especially liked working with interactive books. However, she wanted to organize a class project that would involve all her students and show that each one of them could make a valuable contribution to the work despite their varying talents and ability levels. She learned in a district workshop about curriculum blending or curriculum overlapping, the practice of having students at all ability levels (including those with physical or learning disabilities) work on the same activities, but grading them differently. She decided to do a curriculum blending project that involved having the class do a survey of students in the school. Dorothy and Geraldo and others would be put in charge of gathering the data using an alternative input and spoken word processor system recommended by the Special Education Resource Office. The system could voice the questions, and students could enter their responses directly onto a touch panel on the computer screen. Ralph could work in the group that did initial tasks in the data analysis, and the whole class could learn how to do research and ask different levels of "what if" questions from compiled data. She correlated several required math skills with these activities.

Ms. Montoya really wanted to make a difference, but she was stressed about her ability to infuse technology, pedagogy, and content into her classroom. Thus, she did a TPACK self-assessment of her knowledge to see where she was deficient and how she might capitalize on her strengths. She realized that her technology and content knowledge were very strong compared to her pedagogical knowledge. However, because she would have the assistance of the individuals who held the district workshop on curriculum blending, she felt it was fine to move forward with her plan.

Phase 3: Decide on objectives and assessments

Ms. Montoya developed an assignment sheet for each student that indicated which tasks they would be required to do and how they would be graded. The sheets were tailored to the ability and skill levels of each student. Although tasks were different, criteria were similar and included accomplishing all tasks, working with others in the group, and completing a required product. Ms. Montoya stated the outcome as follows:

- **Outcome:** Survey completion and data analysis.
- **Objective:** Students will complete each of their assigned tasks to complete the survey activity, analyze and display the data, and complete a bulletin board showing their work.
- **Assessment:** Checklist of survey/product tasks with points assigned to each task.

Phase 4: Design integration strategies

Ms. Montoya designed the following sequence of activities around a survey of the students in the school.

- **Week 1:** Introduce the survey project, and train students. Give students the assignment sheets, and discuss the purposes and uses of survey research. Work with them to design a simple "script" for the survey and to enter it into the voice word processor, and show them how the input system works to collect data. Have them discuss methods of getting students to stop and complete the survey (e.g., offer them a sticker that says "I voted!" as some voting places do on election days). Have students rehearse the sequence in advance so that it will move quickly when they actually begin the survey.

- **Week 2:** Do the survey. Select a location (e.g., near the library) for data collection. Ask Geraldo to be in charge of encouraging students who pass by to participate in the survey. Place Dorothy in charge of demonstrating how the system input works. To get the question presented, a student touches a question icon, and the computer gives a typed and a voice response that states the question. Then the student answers the question by touching answer icons.

- **Week 3:** Show the whole class how to analyze the results, and do a summary product (e.g., a bar graph) based on the results. For example, ask students to calculate percentages (e.g., What percentage of the population is male? female?) and query the data (Do male students tend to prefer a certain sport?). Have Ralph work on the computer to sort and organize the responses for each query. Divide students into small groups, and have them do their own queries and bar graphs. Have all the students help prepare a bulletin board to post their findings for the school to see. Place pictures of the students around the bulletin board, identifying the roles they played in the survey activity.

Phase 5: Prepare the instructional environment

Ms. Montoya worked closely with the special education personnel to set up the special computer system and learn how to use it. She obtained permission to have the "survey station" in the hall outside the library and asked the main office to publicize the survey in the morning announcements. She spent extra time with Geraldo and Ralph to prepare them for their roles.

Phase 6: Evaluate and revise

At the end of the unit, Ms. Montoya reviewed the project and reflected on its impact. Some of the questions she asked were the following:

- Did students at all ability levels accomplish their required tasks?

- Did students (including those with special needs) seem engaged in the learning?

- Did students (including those with special needs) seem to acknowledge that all of them had made a valuable contribution to the class?

- Did the alternative computer system work smoothly?

Ms. Montoya was happy with how involved the students were in the survey. Parents of all three students with special needs came by to see the bulletin board and to express their pride in their children's work. Ms. Montoya and the principal agreed that they would have to work on relocating the computer station so as not to disrupt hall traffic, since the "talking computer" drew quite a crowd. However, the principal also asked her to share her project with other teachers who had students with special needs.

Objectives

After reading this chapter and completing the learning activities for it, you should be able to:

1. Differentiate among the terms *impairment, disability,* and *handicap.*

2. Identify current issues affecting the acquisition and use of technology in special education.

3. Explore applications of assistive, instructional, and productivity technologies commonly used by students with disabilities and their teachers.

Introduction

Education for students with special needs encompasses strategies for both those with physical and/or mental deficits and those with special gifts or talents. Although technology can be used to enhance education for both populations, this chapter addresses primarily applications for students with disabilities.

While the terms *impairment, disability,* and *handicap* are often used synonymously, differences among these concepts have important implications for the use of technology in classrooms. An **impairment** involves an abnormality or loss of function in a physical, anatomical, or psychological structure. Impairments to human function may be congenital (present at birth) or acquired through accident or disease. It is important not to make assumptions concerning a person's ability or limitations simply because he or she has an impairment.

When an impairment limits an individual from performing an activity in a manner normally expected for human beings (communicating with others, hearing, movement, manipulating objects, and so on), we refer to this as a **disability**. A student who has lost the function of his right arm has an impairment; this condition will have little or no impact on a variety of life functions. However, this student may encounter situations where the inability to use two arms places him at a disadvantage with others. A **handicap** arises when an individual is unable to fulfill a role due to an impairment or disability. It is critical to understand that a handicap is not a characteristic of an individual. Rather, a handicap results from the mismatch between one's abilities and the demands of an environment (Cook & Hussey, 1995).

In the United States, federal law recognizes several types of disabilities. Most citizens are likely to know one or more individuals whose life function has been affected by disability in some form: deaf, deaf-blind, hard of hearing, mental retardation, multihandicapped, orthopedically impaired, other health impaired, seriously emotionally disturbed, specific learning disability, speech impaired, or visually handicapped.

The fields of special education and rehabilitation have had a long-standing interest in technology. Special education technology has been a part of the United States educational system since at least 1879, when the United States Congress made a $10,000 grant for the production of Braille materials by the American Printing House for the Blind. In 1958, funding was provided for captioning films for the deaf. These are just two examples of laws whose purpose was to improve instruction via technology for people with disabilities. As technology became more visible within the educational setting, the federal government established two Special Education Instructional Materials Centers (SEIMCs), whose purpose was to explore ways to make educational technologies more accessible to special education teachers. The two original SEIMCs eventually expanded to a network of 14 regional SEIMCs, the Council for Exceptional Children ERIC Clearinghouse, four Regional Media Centers for the Deaf, and a Network Coordinating Office. Thanks to the establishment of SEIMCs (although they were later disbanded), we have today the Council for Exceptional Children's (CEC) Technology and Media Division (TAM), which publishes the *Journal for Special Education Technology (JSET)* (Blackhurst & Edyburn, 2000). Historically, the emphasis on technology for individuals with disabilities has been thought of as **assistive technology**—that is, extending the abilities of an individual in ways that provide physical access (e.g., wheelchairs, braces) and sensory access (e.g., Braille, closed captioning). However, technology can also help address special teaching and learning needs. In this chapter, we use the term *special education technology* to cover both dimensions—assistive technology and instructional technology.

Regardless of the specific application of technology, the general goal is always the same: to harness the potential of technology in ways that offer an individual with a disability increased opportunities for learning, productivity, and independence—opportunities that otherwise would not be available. In the section Issues and Problems in Special Education, we explore several issues involved in capturing the potential of technology for individuals with disabilities.

What Does TPACK Look Like in Special Education?

The questions surrounding technological pedagogical content knowledge (TPACK) for special education teachers include "How does this relate to me?" and "What are the implications of knowing about TPACK in special education?" TPACK in any discipline is the perfect union of three knowledge domains (content, pedagogy, and technology) to develop a knowledge base from which a teacher can view a lesson and understand how technology can enhance the learning opportunities and experiences for the students while also knowing the correct pedagogy to enhance the learning of the content. In special education, a teacher is incorporating the TPACK principles when he or she reviews a lesson plan and, without hesitation, thinks about the pedagogy and technology that can be used to meet the unique needs of each student in his or her caseload and what adaptations might be needed to be made to that pedagogy and technology. For example, when reviewing a language arts lesson plan, a special education teacher using the TPACK perspective thinks about technology and how his or her students can learn and achieve content in a way they could not without the technology and relevant adaptations. Thus, a teacher thinks about how he or she can

FIGURE 15.1 TPACK and Special Education

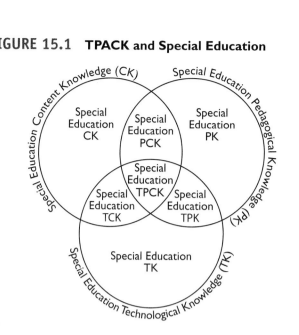

use software products like *Reader Rabbit* (Broderbund) to provide remedial reading help and also considers voice recognition software to allow students who are unable or have difficulty writing by hand to express themselves in written form. (See Figure 15.1.)

Issues and Problems in Special Education

A number of issues affect the delivery of special education services. The following sections briefly identify six current issues that have an impact on uses of technology in special education.

Legal and Policy Directives

Special education, more than other areas of education, is governed by laws and policies. This means that teachers, administrators, and special education technology specialists must be well versed in federal and state laws, policies, and procedures. To learn more about the legal and policy foundations of the field of special education technology, consult the following resources: Blackhurst (1997), Blackhurst and Edyburn (2000), U.S. Department of Education (2000).

The following federal laws promote the use of technology by individuals with disabilities:

• The Technology-Related Assistance Act for Individuals with Disabilities (Public Law 100–407), passed in 1988, provides funding for statewide systems and services to provide assistive technology devices and services to individuals with disabilities.

• Reauthorization of the Individuals with Disabilities Education Act (IDEA) in 1997 (Public Law 105–17)

mandates that every individualized education program (IEP) team "consider" assistive technology when planning the educational program of an individual with a disability. The most current reauthorization in 2004 contains no new technology information, but serves to reemphasize to schools the importance of academic achievement by students with disabilities and the need to help each student meet achievement goals.

Implications of the No Child Left Behind Act for Special Education

The No Child Left Behind (NCLB) Act has had a significant influence in special education, as it has in all other areas of education. Perhaps one of the most important components of the law focuses on Annual Yearly Progress (AYP), which requires documentation that each school is meeting specific performance criteria established in the law. One benefit of these new AYP requirements is that they focus public attention on the persistent underachievement of students with physical disabilities.

Need for Trained Personnel

Considerable effort has been devoted to identifying the knowledge and skills needed by teachers (Lahm & Nickels, 1999) and specialists (Lahm, 2000) to use technology in special education. Individuals can use the NETS competency statements to document their experience, knowledge, and skills in their own teaching portfolio. University teacher preparation programs and inservice workshop providers can review the NETS competency frameworks and align individual competency statements with specific courses and training events in order to communicate the specific outcomes participants will gain.

Despite the efforts on the part of most universities to improve the preparation of teachers to use technology in the classroom, most teachers begin their career with minimal experience using technology in ways that (1) enhance their own productivity, (2) enhance the effectiveness of instruction and the success of all students, and/or (3) enable them to acquire and use assistive technology for students in need of performance support. The common three-credit course, first developed in the 1980s, continues to be the norm for preparing teachers; unfortunately, it is generally inadequate in exploiting the power and possibilities that technology offers.

Another issue regarding the adequacy of training in special education technology centers on the use of interdisciplinary teams for evaluating the need for assistive technology and decision making in the selection of appropriate devices and services. The current assistive technology delivery system was originally developed to respond to the needs of students with low-incidence disabilities (approximately 1.4

Use the following questions to reflect on issues in technology integration and to guide discussions within your class.

1. The following quote highlights critical professional development needs regarding using technology to enhance the academic performance of students with disabilities: "Given pressures exerted by regulations from IDEA and No Child Left Behind (2001), the need to develop specific methods that address general curriculum standards for special education students cannot be overstated. Special education professional training opportunities and experiences should be restructured to include methods that promote access to the general curriculum through the support possible by classroom uses of technology. This technology training must be curriculum specific, integrated across subject areas, and actively engage learners" (Puckett, 2004, p. 15).

   Do you feel you have adequate preparation for using technology to enhance the learning of all students in your classroom? In which areas do you feel most confident in your technology skills for differentiating instruction? In which areas do you feel most uncomfortable with your current skills, and how might these deficits affect student achievement in specific content areas?

2. The following quote summarizes some of the current challenges associated with measuring the outcomes of assistive technology: "The continued scarcity of funding resources for assistive technology assessments, equipment, and training portends the need for predictive algorithms that can facilitate decision making by practitioners, reimbursement agencies, and consumers" (Lenker & Paquet, 2003, p. 13).

   What do these authors mean by "predictive algorithms"? What decision making can these algorithms help facilitate?

Requirements for Inclusive Classrooms

During the 1990s, a major change occurred in how special education services were delivered. Rather than placing students with disabilities in separate classrooms (self-contained special education) and allowing them to participate in selected classes in general education, a process called **mainstreaming**, efforts were made to include them in the general education classroom, an activity known as **inclusion**. This philosophical shift has been controversial. Nonetheless, students with disabilities now spend the majority of the school day in general education classrooms and receive a variety of support services (U.S. Department of Education, 2000).

Although students with disabilities have gained physical inclusion into general education, access to the general education curriculum is still limited. That is, without appropriate modifications, for instance, a student in a wheelchair cannot conduct the same science experiment as everyone else because her wheelchair cannot get close enough to the lab bench for the student to manipulate the chemicals and beakers. Likewise, when the bulk of subject matter content is contained in teacher-made materials and textbooks, a significant portion of special education students do not have access to the information they are expected to learn (e.g., students who are blind, have learning disabilities, or cannot read at grade level). With the NCLB expectation that all students will achieve high academic standards, there is an urgent need for assistive technology to help students in the general education classroom succeed.

Universal Design for Learning

Principles of **universal design** have emerged from our understanding of the design of physical environments for individuals with disabilities. Perhaps the best example of the success of universal design principles is curb cuts. Originally designed to improve mobility for people with disabilities

Adaptive input devices allow students with physical disabilities to use computers for learning.

million students in the United States). The sheer size of the high incidence population requires a rethinking of service delivery systems. The first step in accessing assistive technology services is not a referral for a comprehensive multidisciplinary evaluation (Edyburn, 2003). Instead, many students who have access to assistive technology have that access as the result of advocacy efforts that have challenged the system rather than through a systemic process that ensures that all students in need of devices have them (Edyburn, 2000).

FIGURE 15.2   Universal Design for Learning Guidelines

Universal Design for Learning Guidelines

I. Representation

Use multiple means of representation

1. Provide options for perception
- Options that customize the display of information
- Options that provide alternatives for auditory information
- Options that provide alternatives for visual information

2. Provide options for language and symbols
- Options that define vocabulary and symbols
- Options that clarify syntax and structure
- Options for decoding text or mathematical notation
- Options that promote cross-linguistic understanding
- Options that illustrate key concepts nonlinguistically

3. Provide options for comprehension
- Options that provide or activate background knowledge
- Options that highlight critical features, big ideas, and relationships
- Options that guide information processing
- Options that support memory and transfer

II. Expression

Use multiple means of expression

4. Provide options for physical action
- Options in the mode of physical response
- Options in the means of navigation
- Options for accessing tools and assistive technologies

5. Provide options for expressive skills and fluency
- Options in the media for communication
- Options in the tools for composition and problem solving
- Options in the scaffolds for practice and performance

6. Provide options for executive functions
- Options that guide effective goal setting
- Options that support planning and strategy development
- Options that facilitate managing information and resources
- Options that enhance capacity for monitoring progress

III. Engagement

Use multiple means of engagement

7. Provide options for recruiting interest
- Options that increase individual choice and autonomy
- Options that enhance relevance, value, and authenticity
- Options that reduce threats and distractions

8. Provide options for sustaining effort and persistence
- Options that heighten salience of goals and objectives
- Options that vary levels of challenge and support
- Options that foster collaboration and communication
- Options that increase mastery-oriented feedback

9. Provide options for self-regulation
- Options that guide personal goal setting and expectations
- Options that scaffold coping skills and strategies
- Options that develop self-assessment and reflection

CAST
Universal Design for Learning

within our communities, curb cuts not only accomplish that but also improve access for people with baby strollers, roller blades, bikes, and so on. More recently, universal design concepts have been applied to computers by including disability accessibility software as part of the operating system so that access is provided as the computer comes out of the box (rather than requiring that an individual track down assistive technology specialists to make specialized modifications). Today, accessibility control panels are available on every computer.

In the past few years, a concerted effort has been made to apply universal design principles to learning. A leader in the area of universal design for learning has been the Center for Applied Special Technology (CAST). CAST considers universal design to be a critical issue if students with disabilities are going to be able to access the general education curriculum. In 1999, CAST, in collaboration with the U.S. Department of Education's Office of Special Programs, established the National Center on Accessing the General Curriculum

(NCAC) to help create practical approaches for improved access to the general curriculum by weaving together new curricula, teaching practices, and policies. NCAC completed its funded work in November, 2004, but its publications are available through CAST. To learn more about universal design and access to the general curriculum, visit the National Center for Accessing the General Curriculum online.

Teachers working with students within inclusion settings face a relentless demand to modify curricular, instructional, and assessment materials. Modifications will always be necessary as a result of technology, media, and materials that are not designed with an understanding of the range of diversity found in every classroom. It is also important to note that modifications are always reactive, meaning that students with disabilities experience a delay in obtaining information that is readily available to their peers without disabilities. Universal design seeks to alter this paradigm by providing a new way of thinking about access that is proactive rather than reactive. Figure 15.2 outlines the three principles that guide universal design for learning: representation, expression, and engagement (CAST, 2008; Dolan, 2000; Edyburn, 2001; Grogan & Ruzic, 2000; McGuire, Scott, & Shaw, 2006; Orkwis & McLane, 1998; Rose, 2000; Rose & Meyer, 2006; Rose, Meyer, & Hitchcock, 2005; Rose, Sethuraman, & Meo, 2000; Wright, 2006).

Go to MyEducationLab, select the topic "Diverse Populations." Go to the "Assignments, Activities, and Applications" section and open the video "Universal Design for Special Needs." Then complete the activity that follows.

Web Accessibility

There has been a recent push to make websites more usable by people with various disabilities. This practice is referred to as **web accessibility** and consists of designing websites with a set of criteria in mind. Criteria, such as using text equivalents with screen readers, using large or enlargeable images for people with low vision, underlining links as well as coloring them for users with colorblindness, and making pages navigable using the keyboard only. Like universal design for learning, the intention of web accessibility is to provide greater access to information for all users by designing websites for accessibility from the ground up. Resources are available online to provide guidelines for web accessibility, including the following:

- Web Accessibility Initiative — http://www.w3.org/WAI/
- the Illinois Center for Information Technology Accessibility — http://html.cita.uiuc.edu/
- *Building Accessible Websites* by Joe Clark — http://joeclark.org/book/

Technology Integration Strategies for Special Education

This section provides information about general approaches to using assistive and instructional technology for students with special needs and describes specific products that are commonly integrated into curricula for helping achieve academic, behavioral, or social goals. Table 15.1 summarizes all these strategies.

Foundations of Integration Strategies

Special educators must be concerned with two types of technology: assistive technology and instructional technology. Technology integration efforts must include both types of technology. Historically, the emphasis on technology for individuals with disabilities has been in the area of assistive technology. Indeed, the legal definition of assistive technology is considerably broad:

> **§300.5 Assistive technology device.** As used in this part, *assistive technology device* means any item, piece of equipment, or product system, whether acquired commercially off the shelf, modified, or customized, that is used to increase, maintain, or improve the functional capabilities of a child with a disability. (Authority: 20 U.S.C. 1401(1))

The assistive technology evaluation process generally seeks to identify solutions on a continuum involving no-technology ("no-tech"), low-technology ("low-tech"), and advanced technology ("high-tech"). No-tech solutions are strategies such as teaching a person to use his or her body in a different manner to minimize the impact of an impairment (e.g., one-handed typing). The obvious advantage to solutions involving no technology is that they are available in any environment at any time. Low-tech solutions are generally considered to be nonelectrical. Personal word lists, highlighting markers, and organizing systems are all examples of low-technology solutions that can provide a person with appropriate levels of support to be successful in specific tasks. These solutions tend to be relatively inexpensive but quite flexible for enhancing individual performance. High-tech solutions are complex electrical or hydraulic systems (e.g., stair lift, powered wheelchair, voice-activated environmental control). Clearly, high-tech solutions tend to be the most costly and have the greatest number of restrictions regarding their use (e.g., user skill level, limited portability).

Professional practice in special education calls for the evaluation of potential solutions beginning with no-tech, continuing to low-tech, and then going to high-tech, as the needs dictate. For example, spelling words is most efficient when they are committed to memory. However, if a person displays persistent difficulty in spelling from memory (no-tech), low-tech options such as personal word lists or portable dictionaries may be helpful. High-tech solutions such as electronic spelling checkers should be considered only after other options have proved less satisfactory because of dependency on batteries, fragility, and so on.

Two common approaches for technology use by individuals with disabilities involve remediation and compensation (King, 1999). Remediation involves helping an individual learn or improve performance, often the focus of education, training, and therapy. Compensation focuses on using technology to accommodate difficulties performing specific tasks (e.g., providing for the use of a calculator in recognition that a child has been unable to learn the multiplication facts). Both approaches can be used when integrating technology into instruction or therapy.

TABLE 15.1 Summary of Technology Integration Strategies for Special Education

Target Groups	Sample Technology Integration Strategies	Sample Resources and Activities
Students with mild and moderate to severe disabilities	**For individuals with mild cognitive disabilities:** • *Reading:* Use reading skill software, text-to-speech products, interactive storybooks. • *Writing:* Use voice recognition software and word prediction software. • *Mathematics:* Use graphing software, drills, games, and tutorials. **For individuals with moderate to severe cognitive disabilities:** • Software helps teach/reinforce functional skills (e.g., money management, daily living, employability). • Videos enhance acquisition, maintenance, and transfer of functional and community-based behaviors.	• WizCom's Quicktionary Reading Pen http://www.wizcomtech.com/ • Don Johnston's *Co: Writer* and *Write: OutLoud* http://donjohnston.com • Dragon Talk's *Dragon Naturally Speaking* http://www.dragontalk.com/ • Freedom Scientific's WYNN word processing software http://www.freedomscientific.com • AbleNet, Inc. www.ablenetinc.com • Attainment Company http://www.attainmentcompany.com
Students with physical disabilities	• Provide alternative methods of accessing keyboard, mouse, and/or monitor. • Determine the best placement of adaptive technologies, and provide training to ensure the student is able to operate it independently. • Monitor function to ensure maximum level of participation is obtained without undue physical demands.	• AbleNet, Inc. http://www.ablenetinc.com • Adaptivation, Inc. http://www.adaptivation.com • Enabling devices http://www.enablingdevices.com • Intellitools http://www.intellitools.com • ORCCA technology http://www.orcca.com
Students with sensory disabilities	**For individuals who are blind:** • Use canes and sensor technologies to assist movement. • Use text-to-Braille converters. • Use screenreaders. **For individuals who are visually impaired:** • Use closed-circuit television (CCTV) magnification systems. • Use built-in computer screen magnification control panels. **For individuals who are hearing impaired:** • Use FM amplification systems (assistive listening devices).	• VisionCue http://www.visioncue.com/ • Dolphin Computer Access, LLC http://www.yourdolphin.com/ • Freedom Scientific Blind/ Low Vision Group http://www.freedomscientific.com • TeleSensory http://www.telesensory.com • AudioEnhancement http://www.audioenhancement.com/
At-risk students	• Locate software and websites that provide powerful and motivating opportunities to engage in learning activities. • Utilize electronic quizzes and other instructional materials that provide immediate feedback on performance.	• BrainPop http://www.brainpop.com • Don Johnston, Inc. http://www.donjohnston.com • Tom Snyder, Inc. http://www.tomsnyder.com
Students with gifts and talents	• Locate starting point web pages to launch them into content with appropriate challenges. • Provide tools for engaging in self-directed research. • Provide tools such as multimedia presentations, web page design, and electronic portfolios to document learning experiences.	• Duke TIP program http://www.tip.duke.edu/ • Hoagies' Gifted Education Page http://www.hoagiesgifted.org

Top Ten

Strategies for Special Education Instruction

Take advantage of these ten strategies for using technology to enhance education for students with special needs in the following categories.

Students with Physical Disabilities

1. **Use alternative keyboards such as Intellitools' IntelliKeys** — Students with limited manual dexterity need alternatives to the standard keyboard that let them use the computer independently.

2. **Use joysticks or switches instead of keyboards** — Students with severe physical disabilities need ways other than a keyboard to get input to the computer.

3. **Use voice recognition software such as DragonTalk's *Dragon Naturally Speaking*** — Students who are unable to write by hand, who have illegible handwriting, or who find handwriting extremely tedious can use this software to create text from their speech.

Students with Sensory Disabilities

4. **Use text-to-speech readers such as JAWS for Windows** — Students with visual disabilities can use these to have text read to them from a computer screen.

5. **Use optical character recognition (OCR) software or CCTV** — This strategy helps enlarge text for students who are partially sighted.

Students with Communication Difficulties

6. **Use text-to-speech products such as WizCom's Quicktionary pen** — These devices and materials assist students who have difficulty speaking.

7. **Provide a range of tools to support student writers** — Some students need simplified word processing tools such as Tom Snyder's *Scholastic Key*, or specialized word prediction word processors such as Don Johnston's *Co:Writer*.

8. **Use talking word processors such as Don Johnston's *Write:OutLoud*** — Provides speech synthesis to allow students to hear what they have written.

Students with Cognitive Disabilities

9. **Use digital cameras to capture images of objects and environments** — Students with cognitive disabilities sometimes need concrete examples as cues and prompts for learning.

10. **Use specialized calculators such as Programming Concepts' Coin-U-Lator®** — These handheld devices help students learn numerical concepts like making change.

General Integration Strategies for All Students

All of the technology integration strategies discussed in this book have important applications for students with disabilities. However, an essential consideration for all educators when planning for the needs of students with disabilities involves ensuring that the curriculum is accessible. When technology is used to make the curriculum accessible, students with disabilities have the same opportunities to learn as their peers without disabilities (Metheny, 2003; Scleef, 2003). Because some applications of technology in special education are commonly associated with specific disabilities, the following information will provide a brief overview of specific examples of technology used by people with disabilities.

Strategies for Students with Cognitive Disabilities

A variety of conditions may impair an individual's cognitive abilities. Such disabilities are often referred to as cognitive disabilities, developmental disabilities, or mental retardation.

Mild Cognitive Disabilities. Mild disabilities are considered to be the most prevalent type of disability. They include learning disabilities, serious emotional disabilities, and mental retardation. Current estimates indicate that 3.8 million students, ages 6 to 21, have a mild disability (U.S. Department of Education, 2000), representing more than 71% of the students receiving special education services. Meese (2001) describes the following characteristics as being associated with mild disabilities: cognitive (i.e., intellectual ability, attentional deficits, memory and thinking skills), academic (i.e., reading, language arts, mathematics), and social-emotional.

Typically, the important issue for these students is not physical access to the technology, but reading, writing, memory, and retention of information. While these students often have some learning difficulties (e.g., the inability to read at grade level), many have difficulty in learning in only one aspect of the curriculum. As a result, educators planning for the needs of students with mild disabilities often use productivity software as well as other software materials and online resources that can be used with many low-performing students. (See Technology Integration Lesson 15.1.) These may include materials for developing reading, writing, and mathematics skills. The

Technology Integration Lesson 15.1

Using Multimedia to Help Meet Students' Special Needs

Title: A Multimedia Drivers' Training Manual **Grade Level:** 4 through 6
Content Area/Topic: Language arts: reading

NETS for Students: Standards 3 (Research and Information Fluency), 4 (Critical Thinking, Problem Solving, and Decision Making), and 6 (Technology Operations and Concepts)

Description of Standards Applications: This integration lesson offers students with learning disabilities the opportunity to use multimedia development software to create a guide that will help them study for the driver's exam. Many adolescents with learning disabilities are highly motivated to get their driver's license but have difficulty with the written portion of the exam. Not only does the activity help them with language and study skills, it also helps them use computers in a way that empowers them instead of merely drilling or tutoring them.

Instruction: Divide the class into pairs of students, and give each a portion of the total booklet to analyze and present in the product. Students who are nonreaders or who have very low reading levels are paired with those who are better readers. When the entire product is completed, students present it to other classes and use it to study for the driver's examination.

Source: Speziale, M., & La France, L. (1992). Multimedia and students with learning disabilities. *The Computing Teacher, 20*(3), 31–34.

FIGURE 15.3　Quicktionary Reading Pen

Source: Courtesy of WizCom Technologies, Inc.

key with all of these uses is to balance remediation of skill deficits with activities that help develop more creative, higher level thinking skills.

 Go to MyEducationLab, select the topic "Diverse Populations." Go to the "Assignments, Activities, and Applications" section and open the video "Making It Happen." Then complete the activity that follows.

Reading skills.　A characteristic associated with many disabilities is difficulty in learning how to read and in developing grade-level reading skills. As a result, special education teachers tend to devote a great deal of time and energy to the teaching of reading and are likely to use a variety of software products to remediate students' reading abilities. Software products such as *Bailey's Book House* (Riverdeep), *JumpStart Kindergarten Reading* (Knowledge Adventure), and *Reader Rabbit* (Broderbund) are commonly used in classrooms where emergent readers are working on acquiring specific skills. Interactive story-

books are another commonly used resource. Text-to-speech products that help students with communications disabilities include CAST eReader (CAST), the Quicktionary Reading Pen (WizCom) shown in Figure 15.3, and *L&H Kurzweil 3000* (Lernout & Hauspie Speech Products). If teachers provide all instructional text in a digital format, students with disabilities and other struggling readers will be able to copy and paste the information into talking word processors and other text-to-speech software programs so that they can listen to information they cannot read.

Writing skills.　Many tools have been developed to support students who struggle in various phases of the writing process. For students who are unable to write by hand, who have illegible handwriting, or who find handwriting extremely tedious, voice recognition software such as Dragon Talk's *Dragon Naturally Speaking* may be an option. Some students who are slow typists or have difficulty spelling can benefit from word prediction software such as Renaissance Learning's *NEO² Writer*, which offers word choices to complete the first few letters the student types. (See the example in Figure 15.4.) Talking word processors, such as Don Johnston's *Write:OutLoud*, feature speech synthesis to allow students to hear what they have written. (See Figure 15.5.) *WYNN* (Freedom Scientific) is a specialized word processor that provides an array of support tools to students with learning disabilities. Finally, tools such as *Project Poster* and Tom Snyder's *Hollywood High* provide students with alternative writing environments that engage academically struggling students in the writing process in ways that traditional paper and pencil do not.

FIGURE 15.4　NEO Writer

Source: Courtesy of WizCom Technologies, Inc.

FIGURE 15.5　*Write: OutLoud* Word Processor

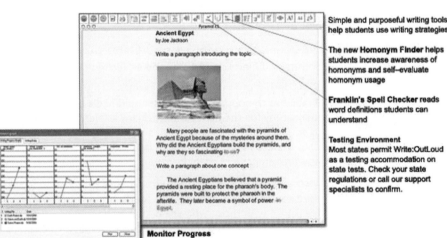

Source: Write:OutLoud © Don Johnston, Inc. Reprinted by permission. To purchase this product, contact Don Johnston, Inc. at 1-800-999-4660 (www.donjohnston.com).

Math skills. Calculators are an important intervention for students with disabilities. A specialized calculator, the Coin-U-Lator® (Programming Concepts, Inc.), was developed to assist students having difficulty counting coins and making change. Other strategies have been developed around simple graphing software materials, as well as drills, games, and tutorials.

Moderate and Severe Cognitive Disabilities. For individuals with moderate and severe cognitive disabilities, considerable effort is devoted to ensuring that they acquire daily living skills such as personal hygiene, shopping (Wissick, 1999b), and use of public transportation. In addition, software is available to help teach functional skills such as money management (Browder & Grasso, 1999), and employability skills (Fisher & Gardner, 1999) must also be taught. (See Technology Integration Lesson 15.2.)

A promising line of research has focused on the creation of video-based instructional materials to enhance the acquisition, maintenance, and transfer of functional and community-based behaviors (Mechling, Gast, & Langone, 2002; Mechling & Langone, 2000; Wissick, 1999a, 1999b).

Teachers working with students with moderate and severe cognitive disabilities need to be familiar with an array of devices that provide an alternative means for accessing the computer since the typical keyboard may be problematic for many students. To simplify the physical or cognitive demands of interacting with the computer, **alternative keyboards**, such as the Intellikeys keyboard (Intellitools), can be used to create customized keyboards. For instance, keys can be enlarged to provide more space for the student to press a key; keys that are not relevant for a given software program can be removed; and multistep functions such as save, print, or quit can be programmed into a single key press. Companies such as AbleNet assist teachers in integrating the assistive technology into instruction.

Technology Integration Lesson 15.2

Using Email and Desktop Publishing to Help Meet Students' Special Needs

Title: Teaching the Concept of Adaptation **Grade Level:** 10 through 12
Content Area/Topic: Language arts: reading

 NETS for Students: Standards 3 (Research and Information Fluency), 4 (Critical Thinking, Problem Solving, and Decision Making), and 6 (Technology Operations and Concepts)

Description of Standards Applications: This integration lesson offers students with mental deficits the opportunity to learn the mental and physical skills needed for careers in the food service industry. A key concept in their vocational training is learning to adapt what they learn in a lab setting to the varied situations they would encounter in the workplace. In this project, students learn this concept through a hands-on activity.

Instruction: Begin by introducing the concept of adaptation by discussing the variations in hamburgers served in major fast-food restaurants. Then talk about how workers at each location must prepare the same basic food (hamburger) according to that restaurant's recipes. After students have gathered email addresses from family and friends around the world, the instructor helps them compose an email message requesting the recipient's favorite meatloaf recipe. As recipes come in, students compile them into a cookbook using desktop publishing software. They finish the project by preparing several of the recipes and talking about how people make meatloaf in many different ways.

Source: Ervin, A. (2002). Meatloaf around the world. *Learning and Leading with Technology, 29*(5), 18–21, 62.

Strategies for Students with Physical Disabilities

Physical disabilities typically affect a person's mobility and agility. Difficulties with motor movements may involve gross- or fine-motor movement and frequently exist concurrently with other disabilities. Assistive technology for individuals with severe physical disabilities may take the form of a power wheelchair operated by a **joystick**, a device with a handle that moves in all directions. Joysticks can also control the movement of the cursor or pointer on a computer screen. To provide access to a computer, it is often necessary to offer an alternative to the typical keyboard. **Switches** are also commonly used for controlling and getting input to the computer as well as activating environmental control systems.

Assessing the need for assistive technology involves a team of specialists including occupational therapists, physical therapists, rehabilitation engineers, and assistive technology specialists. The goal is to identify appropriate tools for access and control that will allow the individual to function across environments: home, school, community, and eventually work.

Strategies for Students with Sensory Disabilities

Sensory disabilities involve impairments associated with the loss of hearing or vision. If there is a complete loss of vision, a person is considered *blind*. An individual is considered *partially sighted* if there is some visual acuity. Similarly, if there is a complete loss of hearing, a person is considered *deaf*. *Hearing impaired* is the term used to describe an individual with some hearing.

Special keyboards have opened up the lines of communication for many people with all forms of disabilities.

For the blind. For an individual who is blind, three kinds of technology facilitate independence and access to environments and information:

- **Canes and sensor technology** — These are used to provide the person with mobility and orientation information when navigating various environments.

- **Tools to convert printed information** — Other essential tools convert printed information into audio so that a person who is blind can gain information by listening rather than reading. This is accomplished through the use of a scanner, **optical character recognition (OCR)** software to scan and translate print into a word-processed file, and speech synthesis. It works by placing text material on the scanner and scanning the material into the computer. The OCR software then converts the scanned information into text, and the speech synthesis tools read the material aloud. *L & H Kurzweil 3000* (Lernout & Hauspie Speech Products) and *Scan and Read Pro* (Premier Programming Solutions) are common text-to-speech systems used by individuals who are blind.

- **Screen readers** — **Screen readers** work as utility software, operating in the background of the computer operating system and reading any text that appears on the screen—for example, menus, text, or web pages. Examples of screen readers include *Hal Screen Reader* (Dolphin Computer Access), *Home Page Reader for Windows* (IBM Special Needs Systems), *JAWS for Windows* (Freedom Scientific), and *OutSPOKEN* (Alca Access Group).

For the partially sighted. Partially sighted individuals must have text information enlarged, or the contrast altered, in order to perceive printed information. When information is in printed form (e.g., books, magazines, flyers) a **closed-circuit television (CCTV)** magnification system can be used. CCTV is a video camera mounted on a frame with a television monitor. Users place materials on the desktop below the camera, set the desired magnification level and move the materials around as necessary such that the information appears on the monitor in a size that can be read comfortably. Many partially sighted individuals can see print on a computer screen by simply activating the built-in screen magnification control panel. This function allows users to select the desired magnification of everything appearing on the screen. This not only helps people with disabilities but also those with failing eyesight associated with aging.

For the deaf. Individuals who are deaf often can use most technologies without significant modifications. However, two problematic areas involve the use of audio feedback (i.e., error messages) and the reliance on sound in multimedia software. When designers provide essential information only in audio form, this information is inaccessible to deaf

Screen Reader software translates the content of a computer screen for the visually impaired.

as well as an auditory signal; multimedia software that includes closed captioning of audio tracks).

Individuals with hearing impairments need few modifications to be able to use computers. A new technology is finding increasing acceptance in classrooms: **FM amplification systems** (Easterbrooks, 1999). These systems involve the teacher wearing a wireless microphone and students with hearing impairments and some students with learning disabilities involving auditory processing difficulties wearing receivers that amplify the teacher's voice and serve to focus attention. These devices are also referred to as *assistive listening devices* and are increasingly found in movie theaters as an accommodation for patrons of all ages.

Strategies for At-Risk Students

individuals. As a result, advocacy and design initiatives encourage that all information be available in multiple formats (e.g., error messages that produce a message on screen

Students at risk for school failure are not considered disabled in the sense of the federal definition of disability. However, their lack of success in school often parallels the low performance of students with disabilities. The use of assistive technology by students with disabilities has helped the profession understand the types of academic challenges students face and the kinds of technology tools that allow them to be successful. The impact of the NCLB Act may cause the profession to consider the application of these tools for other students who struggle to achieve in school. Table 15.2 shows how selected assistive and

TABLE 15.2 Matching Technology Resources to the Needs of At-Risk Students

Learning Difficulties	Strategies
Difficulty remembering things to do, sequence of tasks	• Provide a reminder service: http://www.iping.com. • Use a specialized prompting device: Job Coach at http://www.attainmentcompany.com.
Inability to read and comprehend at grade level	• Provide digital text in a text-to-speech program: ReadPlease at http://www.readplease.com. • Provide instructional materials with multiple levels: http://www.windows.ucar.edu.
Difficulties in written expression	• Use a predictive word processor; e.g., *Co:Writer* (http://www.donjohnston.com) or *WordQ* (http://www.wordq.com) • Offer support for dictation: http://www.idictate.com.
Difficulties in math computations and concepts	• Use online calculators: WebMath at http://www.webmath.com • Use teaching tools such as Virtual Math Manipulatives at http://matti.usu.edu/nlvm/nav/vlibrary.html.
Lack of motivation to engage in school work	• Shift power and control for the student to take responsibility; e.g., clipping services like Crayon (http://crayon.net) to create their own newspaper or My.Yahoo (http://my.yahoo.com) to manage a personal calendar and to-do list. • Use TrackStar (http://trackstar.4teachers.org) to organize engaging instructional activities that parallel the curriculum.

instructional technology products can match the various needs of at-risk students.

Strategies for Students with Gifts and Talents

Heward (2000) says that, according to the Gifted and Talented Children's Act of 1978, gifted and talented students are those "possessing demonstrated or potential abilities that give evidence of high performance capability in such areas as intellectual, creative, specific academic or leadership ability, or in the performing or visual arts, and why by reason thereof require services or activities not ordinarily provided by the school" (PL 95;-561, Title IX, Section 902, p. 534). The primary issue surrounding and shaping education for gifted students is how to identify students who merit these special "services or activities not ordinarily provided by the school." Heward gives a comprehensive discussion of these issues and describes criteria schools use to identify students who qualify as gifted and talented.

Heward (2000) also observes that ". . . the increasingly sophisticated use of technological tools and related methods will provide gifted students with greater connectivity and independence in the future" (p. 572). Citing work by Howell (1994), he finds that technology integration for gifted and talented students should revolve primarily around three strategies (p. 572):

- **Electronic communities** — Communicating with people from distant and differing cultures and languages encourages and provides new avenues for expression.
- **Research** — Using global resources (e.g., on the Internet) to research topics allows gifted students to explore ideas and events more quickly and in greater depth.

- **Interactive and multimedia presentations** — Developing presentations based on their research allows students to display their discoveries in ways that make them more independent learners.

Finally, when gifted students engage in cooperative group work on products such as websites and multimedia presentations, they are working in a motivational environment in which they can learn important social skills required for them to be effective and productive in the world of work.

Final Tips for Teachers

Teachers in non–special education classrooms face a constant challenge to meet the needs of students with disabilities. The following are suggestions for finding ways to apply the power of technology to meet these needs:

- Routinely use web accessibility checkers, like *Wave*, to ensure that all web pages are accessible for students with sensory and physical disabilities. Web accessibility is a critical consideration for those designing instructional web pages as well as all of us who use them.
- Constantly be on guard for new solutions for academic performance problems. Resources such as Closing the Gap's *Solutions* database provide an excellent means of locating new tools for students with disabilities and other struggling students.
- Access professional development resources, such as Assistive Technology Training Online, to support your continuing professional development. Regardless of how much time and energy you have devoted to learning about special education technology, there is always more to learn. Reserve some time to regularly update your knowledge and skills.

Interactive Summary

The following is a summary of the main points covered in this chapter.

1. **Issues in special education** — These include:
   - Legal and policy directives
   - Implications of the NCLB Act for special education
   - Need for trained personnel
   - Requirements for inclusive classrooms
   - Universal design for learning (i.e., the Center for Accessing the General Education Curriculum).

2. **Strategies are described for integrating technology into instruction for all students with special needs, including students with**:
   - Mild disabilities
   - Moderate and severe disabilities
   - Physical disabilities
   - Sensory disabilities
   - At-risk behaviors/situations
   - Gifts and talents.

Key Terms

- alternative keyboard
- assistive technology
- closed-circuit television (CCTV)
- disability
- FM amplification system
- handicap

- impairment
- inclusion
- joystick
- mainstreaming
- optical character recognition (OCR)

- screen reader
- sensory disability
- switch
- universal design
- web accessibility

Web-Enrichment Activities

1. **Website accessibility check** — Use the Cynthiasays web accessibility checker to evaluate the accessibility of a website. Cynthiasays checks whether websites are accessible to people with disabilities. It uses two standards: the Web Content Accessibility Guidelines developed by the World Wide Web Consortium (http://www.w3.org/TR/WAI-WEBCONTENT) and the U.S. Section 508 Guidelines developed by the U.S. government (http://www.section508.gov). Visit the Cynthiasays site at http://www.cynthiasays.com. Enter the address of a website into the URL text box, and use the Test Your Site button to begin the check of the website. Review the results of the accessibility check.

2. **Web accessibility simulations** — Use one of the simulations on the following website: http://www.webaim.org/simulations. Screen Reader Simulation—Experience a screen reader, and learn how inaccessible content affects screen reader users. Low-Vision Simulation—View web content through several types of vision disabilities. Learn how to design content to best work with screen enlarging software. Distractability Simulation—Experience frustrations similar to what someone with a cognitive disability might experience on the web. What understanding do you now have of the experience of a person with a disability? Explain how technology increases a user's abilities.

PEARSON
myeducationlab
The Power of Classroom Practice
www.myeducationlab.com

Go to MyEducationLab to complete the following exercises.

Video Select the topic "Diverse Populations," and go to the "Assignments, Activities, and Applications" section. Access the video "The Landmark Way" to hear about a school of higher education dedicated to students with learning disorders. Then complete the activity that follows.

Building Teaching Skills Select the topic "Diverse Populations," and go to the "Building Teaching Skills and Dispositions" section. Access the activity "Creating an Inclusive Classroom" and complete the full activity.

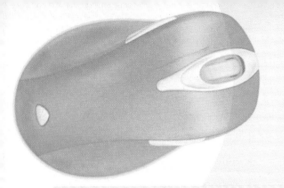

Technology Integration Workshop

The TIP Model in Action

Read each of the following scenarios related to implementing the TIP Model, and answer the questions that follow it based on your Chapter 15 reading activities.

TIP MODEL SCENARIO #1   Ms. Cinqela has a student with cerebral palsy who cannot control her hands enough to write or use a computer keyboard. Ms. Cinqela believes her student is bright; she contributes some valuable things verbally and seems interested in everything the class does. However, she is unable to complete most class assignments.

1.1 What technology-based strategies could Ms. Cinqela use to address these needs?

1.2 What would be the relative advantages of using these strategies?

1.3 Should Ms. Cinqela have her student with cerebral palsy work alone or with other students? Explain your answer.

TIP MODEL SCENARIO #2   Mr. Allgood is a science teacher who has been assigned to teach a group of gifted students. The principal asked Mr. Allgood to create learning activities that would challenge and motivate these students to learn science and mathematics and offer a way they each could demonstrate individual learning using particular kinds of intelligence.

2.1 What technology-based strategy could Mr. Allgood use to carry out such a project?

2.2 What would be the relative advantage of using this strategy?

2.3 Describe how Mr. Allgood might manage this kind of activity in a classroom.

TIP MODEL SCENARIO #3   Mr. Bartle is a fifth-grade teacher who has three low-achieving students with very low mathematics test scores. It is clear that they each lack basic skills in math facts and operations. Mr. Bartle has no time to work with each of these students individually, but he knows they need practice in the skills they lack. They also need motivation to practice the skills, since each has failed frequently in previous classes.

3.1 What technology-based strategy could Mr. Bartle use to address these needs?

3.2 What would be the relative advantage of using this strategy?

3.3 Should these students work individually, in pairs, or as a small group on this activity? Explain your answer.

TIP MODEL SCENARIO #4   Mr. Tindel is a seventh-grade social studies teacher who has two students with learning disabilities. Neither student can read or write very well. However, both have talents—one is an avid photographer, and the other likes to draw and paint. Mr. Tindel wants to create an activity that allows them to participate fully in classroom projects and to have their talents recognized. He feels this recognition would help motivate them to spend time on other learning activities.

4.1 What technology-based strategy could Mr. Tindel use to address this need?

4.2 What would be the relative advantage of using this strategy?

4.3 How could Mr. Tindel determine whether these two students felt more positive about other class work as a result of participation in this activity?

TIP MODEL SCENARIO #5   Mr. Zircone is a fifth-grade teacher. He has a nonverbal student whose vocal cords were injured in a traffic accident. The student is very intelligent, but he is depressed and discouraged because he cannot communicate with his teachers or his classmates. Mr. Zircone overheard some of the children referring to this student as "The Dummy." He wants to find a way to allow this student to communicate in class to show the other students he is not a "dummy" and to allow him to participate more fully in learning activities.

5.1 What technology-based tool could Mr. Zircone use to address this need?

5.2 What would be the relative advantage of using this tool?

5.3 Give an example of a learning activity in a content area (e.g., language arts, science, social studies) that could make use of this tool.

TIE into Practice: Technology Integration Examples

The Technology Integration Example that opened this chapter (*Helping Students with Disabilities Blend In*) showed how a teacher might have students with disabilities help complete a survey. To do the survey activity described in the example, the teacher has to create an online survey document using *Adobe Acrobat* software (see figure below). With the knowledge you have gained from Chapter 15, do the following to explore this strategy:

1. Answer the following questions about the *Helping Students with Disabilities Blend In* example:

   • Phase 1 — Does the teacher have the necessary technological pedagogical content knowledge to teach this activity? Please explain your answer and give possible solutions to assist a teacher who needs more training in technology, content or pedagogy.

   • Phase 2 — What is the relative advantage for the teacher in using the alternative input and spoken word processor system for this survey activity? Does it matter how comfortable a teacher is with technology, content, or pedagogy?

   • Phase 3 — To adapt classroom requirements to the capabilities of each student, the teacher creates a separate set of requirements for the students with disabilities. How does this kind of project make it feasible to accomplish such adaptations?

   • Phase 4 — Why is it important to give Ralph, Dorothy, and Geraldo highly visible roles in this project?

   • Phase 5 — In what other ways could Ms. Montoya have students use technologies to advertise the upcoming survey?

   • Phase 6 — One of the end-of-project questions Ms. Montoya asked was if students acknowledged that each one had made an important contribution. How might she ascertain this?

2. What NETS for Students skills would students learn by working on the *Helping Students with Disabilities Blend In* project? (See the front of this book for a list of NETS for Students.)

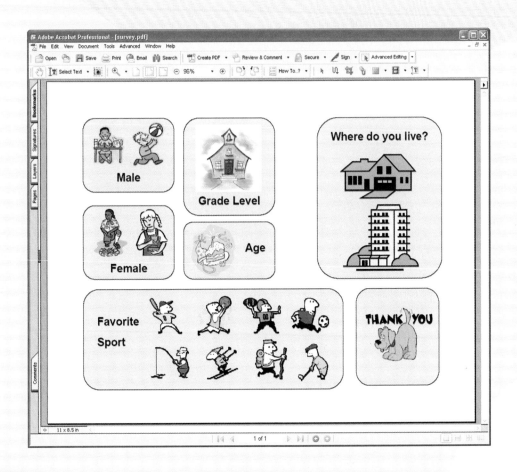

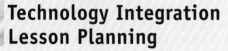

Technology Integration Lesson Planning

Complete the following exercise using sample lesson plans found on MyEducationLab:

1. Locate lesson ideas — The MyEducationLab has several examples of lessons that use technology-based strategies to meet students' special needs as described in this chapter. Go to MyEducationLab under the topic "Diverse Populations" and go to the Lesson Plans to review the following integration lessons:

   - Competitive Creative Activities for Kids with Physical Handicaps
   - Surveying Activities for All Ability Levels

2. Evaluate the lessons — Use the *Evaluation Checklist for a Technology-Integrated Lesson* (located on MyEducationLab under the topic "Instructional Planning") to evaluate each of these lessons.

3. Modify a lesson — Select one of the lesson ideas and adapt its strategies to meet a need in your own content area. You may choose to use the same approach as in the original or to adapt it to meet your needs.

4. Add descriptors — Create descriptors for your new lesson similar to those found within the sample lessons (e.g., grade level, content and topic areas, technologies used, relative advantage, objectives, NETS standards).

5. Save your new lesson — Save your modified lesson with all its descriptors.

For Your Teaching Portfolio

For this chapter's contribution to your teaching portfolio, add the following products you created in the Technology Integration Workshop:

- The evaluations you did using the *Evaluation Checklist for a Technology-Integrated Lesson*
- The new lesson plan you developed, based on the one you found on MyEducationLab.

Glossary

accelerometer—A device that assists with analyzing and monitoring physical fitness levels by counting calories

Acceptable Use Policy (AUP)—An agreement created by a school or other educational organization that stipulates the risks involved in Internet use; outlines appropriate, safe student behavior on the Internet; asks students if they agree to use the Internet under these conditions; and asks if they agree to information about themselves being posted on the school's website

accommodation—Piagetian view of how children change their views of the world by incorporating new experiences

aesthetics—Elements of design in hypermedia or multimedia applications that enhance and heighten the learner experience, such as the graphic or visual design of the system, the pleasure of use between the learner and the materials, and/or the personal satisfaction or reflection experienced by the learner when using and learning with the system

alternative keyboard—Customized keyboards created for users with special needs (e.g., enlarging the keys to provide more space for the student to press a key; removing keys that are not relevant for a given software; programming multi-step functions like *save, print, quit* into a single key press)

anchor—A link inserted on a web page to allow a link to that location from within the page

anchored instruction—Constructivist term for learning environments that reflect situated cognition, or instruction anchored in meaningful, real-life problems and activities

applications programs—Computer software written to support tasks that are useful to a computer user (e.g., word processing) in contrast with systems software

applications software—(See applications programs.)

Archie—A program that allows users to locate a file on the Internet

ARPAnet—A network created in 1969 by the U.S. government–funded Advanced Research Projects Agency (ARPA) to enable communications among important defense sites in the event of a worldwide catastrophe such as a nuclear attack; later became the Internet

artificial intelligence (AI)—Computer programs that try to emulate the decision-making capabilities of the human mind

assimilation—Piagetian view of how children learn by fitting new experiences into their existing view of the world

assistive technology—Devices that extend the abilities of an individual in ways that provide physical access (i.e., wheelchairs, braces) and sensory access (i.e., Braille, closed captioning)

asynchronous—Form of distance communications in which information and messages are left for the receiver to read later; contrasts with synchronous communications, in which information and messages are sent and received immediately

Audio Video Interleave (AVI) format—One of several digital formats for video that are able to be used with video editing software

automaticity—A level of skill that allows a person to respond immediately (i.e., automatically) with the correct answer to a problem

avatar—A graphic representation of a real person in cyberspace; a three-dimensional image that a person can choose to represent himself or herself in a virtual reality environment

avatar spaces—Multi-user dungeons (or dimensions or domains) or MUDs in which users can interact through their graphic representations (i.e., avatars)

blog—Short for "web log," a web page that serves as a publicly accessible location for discussing a topic or issue; began as personal journals and expanded to become public discussion forums in which anyone can give opinions on a topic

blood pressure devices—Devices that assist with analyzing and monitoring physical fitness levels by monitoring and reporting blood pressure

BMP—Stands for "bitmapped." Developed originally for use on Disk Operating System (DOS) and Windows-compatible computers, an image format used for drawn images, illustrations, clip art, or animations

body composition analyzer—A device that assists with analyzing and monitoring physical fitness levels by determining the percent of body fat

Bookmarks file—In the *Netscape* browser, a set of Internet locations or URLs organized so that a user can return to them quickly (See also Favorites file.)

bulletin board (BB)—A computer system set up to allow notices to be posted and viewed by anyone who has access to the network

calculator-based lab (CBL)—Calculator with probes or sensors connected to it to allow gathering of numerical data

cell—In a spreadsheet, a row–column location that may contain numerical values, words, or character data, and formulas or calculation commands

Center for Applied Research in Educational Technology (CARET)—A funded project of the International Society for Technology in Education (ISTE) that has the most comprehensive review of research evidence available on the impact of technology in education (http://caret.iste.edu)

charting/graphing tools—Software tools that automatically draw and print desired charts or graphs from data entered by users

chatroom—A location on the Internet set up to allow people to converse in real time by typing in messages or allowing their avatars to meet and "talk" to each other

classical conditioning—Pavlovian view of learning as involuntary physical responses to outside stimuli (e.g., dogs salivate at the sight of a dog food can)

clip art—One or more pieces of professionally prepared art work, stored as files and designed to be inserted into a document or web page

closed circuit television (CCTV)—A magnification system in which a video camera is mounted on a frame with a television monitor. Users place materials on the desktop below the camera, set the desired magnification level, move the materials around as necessary, and information appears on the monitor in a size that can be read comfortably by an individual with visual impairments

command—One instruction to a computer written in a computer language

Common Gateway Interface (CGI)—An authoring specification on the Internet for how data will be collected at a website; CGI programs are written in a language such as PERL

computer adaptive testing (CAT)—Computer software that continuously analyzes a student's test responses and presents more or less difficult questions based on the student's performance (See also computer-assisted testing.)

computer-assisted design (CAD)—Software used by architects and others to aid in the design of structures such as houses and cars

computer-assisted instruction (CAI)—Software designed to help teach information and/or skills related to a topic; also known as instructional software or courseware

computer-assisted language learning (CALL)—A strategy that utilizes a variety of technology-based tools to support both ESL and foreign language learners in and out of class.

computer-assisted testing (CAT)—Using a computer system to administer and score assessment measures; also, computer adaptive testing

computerized kiln—Oven for firing ceramic products that uses computers to automatically set required temperature, monitor length of time, and begin the process of cooling down and shutting off

computer-managed instruction systems (CMI)—Computer software systems designed to keep track of student performance data, either as part of CAI programs or by themselves

computer platforms—Types of computer systems identified by their operating systems, e.g., PCs with Windows operating systems or Macintoshes with Mac-OS operating systems

computer programs—(See software.)

concept mapping software—Tools designed to help people think through and explore ideas or topics by developing concept maps (i.e., visual outlines of ideas)

constructivists—People who believe that humans construct all knowledge in their minds by participating in certain experiences. Knowledge is the result of constructing both mechanisms for learning and one's own unique version of the knowledge, colored by background, experiences, and aptitudes

constructivist learning—Teaching/learning model based on cognitive learning theory; holds that learners should generate their own knowledge through experience-based activities rather than being taught it by teachers (See also directed instruction.)

contingencies of reinforcement—According to learning theorist B. F. Skinner, experiences (positive reinforcement, negative reinforcement, punishment) that shape desired behavioral responses

cookie—A small piece of text transferred to a web browser through an Internet server for the purpose of tracking the Internet usage habits of the person using the browser

course management system (CMS)—An online collection of web course design and delivery tools; WebCT and BlackBoard are examples

data mining—The practice of collecting data from all the information available and searching it to see relationships among the data elements

data warehouses—Central collection points for data collected through data mining (See also data mining.)

database—A collection of information systematized by computer software to allow storage and easy retrieval through keyword searching; the program designed to accomplish these tasks

decoding—In reading, the act of "sounding out" words

desktop publishing—Term coined in 1984 by the president of the Aldus Corporation to refer to the activity of using software to produce documents with elaborate control of the form and appearance of individual pages

Digital Divide—Term coined by Lloyd Morrisett, former president of the Markle Foundation, to mean a discrepancy in access to technology resources among socioeconomic groups

digital storytelling—Using images and audio to tell the stories of lives, events, or eras

directed instruction—A teaching and learning model based on behavioral and cognitive theories; students receive information from teachers and do teacher-directed activities (See also constructivist learning.)

disability—Condition that occurs when an impairment limits an individual from performing an activity in a manner normally expected for human beings (communicating with others, hearing, movement, manipulating objects, etc.)

disaggregation—Taking student data from a general database and grouping it according to desired characteristics

discovery learning—According to learning theorist Jerome Bruner, a more effective way of children learning concepts by discovering them during their interaction with the environment

distance learning—A form of education in which some means, electronic or otherwise, is used to connect people with instructors and/or resources that can help them acquire knowledge and skills

distributed language learning (DLL)—An online publishing strategy where students share their writings and learn together and work toward common purposes, with possibilities for negotiating form and meaning of a language as they progress

domain designator—A required part of a Uniform Resource Locator (URL) that indicates what kind of group owns the server; examples include ".edu," ".com," and ".org."

download—To bring information (e.g., text files, images) to a computer from the Internet or other network or from a computer to a disc

DreamWeaver—A type of hypermedia authoring software from Adobe

drill and practice—An instructional software function that presents items for students to work on (usually one at a time) and gives feedback on correctness; designed to help users remember isolated facts or concepts and recall them quickly

educational technology—A combination of the processes and tools involved in addressing educational needs and problems, with an emphasis on applying the most current tools: computers and other electronic technologies

electronic field trip (virtual field trip)—Online activities in which students explore unique locations around the world and/or communicate with learners at those sites

electronic gradebook—Software designed to maintain and calculate student grades

electronic mentor—Subject matter expert who volunteers to work closely with students online

electronic outliner—Software features that automatically generate headings and subheadings from typed information

electronic portfolio—A collection of a person's work products over time, arranged so that he or she and others can see how skills have developed and progressed, and presented in an electronic format such as a website or multimedia product

electronic publishing—Activity when students submit their written or artistic products to a website

electronic slide shows—Sequences of frames shown in a linear way with presentation software (e.g., *PowerPoint*)

electronic whiteboard—A device connected to a computer to allow users at different sites to see what the instructor writes or draws during demonstrations; stores demonstrations as computer files

English as a Second Language (ESL)—Designates a student who is learning English after achieving proficiency in another, native language

English Language Learners—Individuals who are learning English as their majority language for everyday uses, employment, and educational purposes

e-Portfolio—Websites created by students to showcase their work and organize, revise, and store digital assets that they have created inside and outside the classroom

EPS (Encapsulated PostScript)—An image format that allows transfer of artwork between any software packages that use PostScript printing files

Events of Instruction, Gagné's—The nine kinds of activities identified by learning theorist Robert Gagné as being involved in teaching and learning

Extensible Mark-up Language—(See XML.)

Favorites file—In the *Internet Explorer* browser, a set of Internet locations or URLs organized so that a user can return to them quickly (See also Bookmarks file.)

field—The smallest unit of information in a database

files—The products created by a database program; any collection of data stored on a computer medium

filtering software—Program stored on individual computers or on the school or district network in order to prevent access to Internet sites with inappropriate materials

firewall—Software that protects a school's or company's entire computer system from attempts by others to gain unauthorized access to it and also prevents access to certain sites

firewall software—A system set up to prevent someone from going to certain locations on the Internet; may be implemented by keyword or by site name

Flash—A type of hypermedia authoring software from Adobe that has become the industry standard for creating interactive web-based animations, websites, interactive storybooks, and online software tools

FM amplification system—Resource for students with hearing impairments in which the teacher wears a wireless microphone and students with auditory processing learning disabilities wear receivers that amplify the teacher's voice and serve to focus attention

foreign language (FL)—A target language, or language of study, spoken mainly in other countries

forms makers—Software tools that create documents and web pages with "fillable" forms

formula—In a spreadsheet, commands used to do calculations on data

frame—Sections programmed to display on a web page; the contents of each frame are actually different web pages displayed on one screen

FTP (File Transfer Protocol)—On the Internet, a way of transferring files from one computer to another using common settings and transmission procedures; also, to transfer files

full immersion systems—Type of virtual reality (VR) system in which a user places a headset (e.g., goggles or a helmet) over the eyes to provide a channel through which the wearer "sees" (i.e., is immersed in) a computer-generated environment

geocaching—An online activity in which students look at a database of caches at the geocaching website (http://www.geocaching.com), decide on a cache to hunt for, and use GPSs to help them locate it

geographic information system (GIS)—A computer system that is able to store in a database a variety of information about geographic locations and display the data in map form

geospatial technologies—Systems that allow individuals to view and examine the world through multiple layering of geographic data within a spatial environment

GIF (Graphics Interchange Format)—An image format used for drawn images, illustrations, clip art, or animations

global positioning system (GPS)—An instrument that uses a worldwide radio-navigation system made possible by a bank of 24 satellites and their ground stations to pinpoint the exact geographic location where the GPS signal originates, cross-references it with mapping software, and shows the location to a user

Google Docs—Tools offered through a special Google site that provide users access to online programs for word processing, spreadsheets, and presentations; the site offers easy storage and sorting of documents online and allows for sharing of documents among multiple users

graphic document makers—Software tools that simplify the activity of making highly graphic materials such as awards certificates and greeting cards by offering sets of clip art and pre-designed templates to which people add their own content

graphing calculator—A calculator with advanced functions and an LED display; allows users to enter equations and shows graphs that result from those equations

hacker—Computer user who demonstrates an unusual, obsessive interest in using the computer; a computer user who engages in unauthorized use of a computer system (See also cracker.)

handheld computer—A small, portable computing device (See also personal digital assistant (PDA).)

handicap—A condition that arises when an individual is unable to fulfill a role due to an impairment or disability

haptic interface—One of the devices (e.g., a data glove) that allow users to experience a full immersion virtual reality system by providing tactile or touch input

hardware—The devices or equipment in a computer system (in contrast with software or computer programs)

head-mounted display (HMD)—In a full immersion virtual reality (VR) system, a headset that provides the sensory channel through which the wearer "sees" a computer-generated environment

heart monitor—Device consisting of a transmitter, which senses the heartbeat from the heart's electrical impulses, and a wristwatch receiver, which receives and records each beat through radio transmission from the transmitter

hits—Pages or items listed as results of an Internet or database search

(HTML) Hypertext Markup Language—The primary authoring language used to develop web pages

hypermedia—Software that connects elements of a computer system (e.g., text, movies, pictures, and other graphics) through hypertext links

IEP generator—Software that assists teachers in preparing individual educational plans (IEPs) required by law for students with special needs by providing on-screen prompts that remind teachers of the required components in the plan

image editing programs—Software tools used to enhance and format photos that are then imported into desktop publishing systems or web page products

image formats—Ways of storing digitized images for use in web pages and multimedia products, e.g., GIF, JPEG

impairment—An abnormality or loss of function in a physical, anatomical, or psychological structure; may be congenital (present at birth) or acquired through accident or disease

inclusion—Activity in which students with disabilities are included in the general education classroom

individual educational plan (IEP)—The educational program required by law to be designed for each student with a disability

information and communication technology (ICT)—New term for "information technology" that now expands to incorporate the Web 2.0 concept "communication and sharing"

inquiry-based learning—(See constructivist learning.)

instant messaging (IM)—A communications service that allows users to create a private chat room which only members of a mutually agreed-upon list may enter; the system alerts a user when someone from the IM list is online; IM also designates the act of instant messaging, as in "to IM"

instructional game—Type of software function designed to increase motivation by adding game rules to a learning activity

instructional software—Applications software that is designed specifically to deliver or assist with student instruction on a topic (See also courseware.)

instructional technology—The subset of educational technology that deals directly with teaching and learning applications (as opposed to educational administrative applications)

integrated learning system (ILS)—Networked or online system that provides both computer-based instruction and summary reports of student progress

integrated packages—Software products (e.g., *Microsoft Works* and *AppleWorks*) that have several applications in a single package (e.g., word processing, database, spreadsheet, and drawing functions)

interaction design—An online design framework focused on creating pleasurable experiences that appeal to and benefit the learner

interactive or dynamic geometry software—Programs that provide students with environments in which to make discoveries and conjectures related to geometry concepts and objects

intranet—An internal network or a subset of the Internet, usually available only to the members of the organization that set it up

Java—Originally called OAK, a high-level programming language developed by Sun Microsystems. An object-oriented language similar to C++, it has become popular for its ability to do interactive graphic and animation activities on web pages.

Java applets—Pre-developed applications created with the Java programming language; make possible web page features such as animations and special effects, graphics and buttons, interactive displays, web data collection forms; and chatrooms

joystick—Input device, used primarily with games, that moves on-screen figures or a cursor

JPEG (also JPG)—Stands for "Joint Photographic Experts Group," an image format used for photographs

laptop computer—Small, stand-alone, portable personal computer system

learning communities—Groups of people who "meet," usually via email, web pages, or other electronic means, to support each other's learning

learning hierarchies—According to learning theorist Robert Gagné, a set of building block skills a student must learn in order to learn a higher-order skill

Likert scale—An assessment instrument consisting of a series of statements with which students indicate their degree of agreement or disagreement

link—Also known as a hot link or hot spot. On the Internet, a piece of text or an image that has been programmed into a web page to send the browser to another Internet location; in a multimedia product, a piece of text or an image that has been programmed to send the user to another location in the product

listserv (list)—On the Internet, a program that stores and maintains mailing lists and allows a message to be sent simultaneously to everyone on the list

Logo—A high-level programming language originally designed as an artificial intelligence (AI) language but later popularized by Seymour Papert as an environment to allow children to learn problem-solving behaviors and skills

long-term memory (LTM)—According to information-processing learning theorists, one of the three kinds of memory or "stores" the brain uses to process information, much like a computer; LTM can hold information indefinitely after it is linked to prior knowledge already in LTM

mainstreaming—An activity in which students with disabilities participate in selected classes in general education

mastery learning—According to learning theorists Benjamin Bloom and B. F. Skinner, an instructional approach in which students learn a sequence of objectives that define mastery of the subject; students pass tests on each objective to demonstrate they have mastered a skill before proceeding to the next one

microcomputer-based laboratory (MBL)—A type of instructional software tool consisting of hardware devices (probes) and software (probeware) to allow scientific data to be gathered and processed by a computer

morphing—Short for *metamorphosing*, refers to an animation technique in which one image gradually turns into another; also known as tweening

Mosaic—One of the first browser programs designed to allow Internet resources to be displayed graphically rather than just in text

Motion Picture Experts Group (MPEG)—A file format for storing and sending video sequences on a network

MUD—Multiuser dungeon (or dimension or domain); a location on the Internet where several users at a time can interact with each other's avatars (graphic representations of each other); see also MOO

multimedia—A computer system or computer system product that incorporates text, sound, pictures/graphics, and/or video

multiple intelligences—According to learning theorist Howard Gardner, nine different and relatively independent types of intelligence that may be fostered by differentiated instruction and assessment

Musical Educators National Conference (MENC)—Professional organization for music educators

Musical Instrument Digital Interface (MIDI)—A standard adopted by the electronic music industry for controlling devices that play music

Musical Instrument Digital Interface (MIDI) device—Equipment that works with specially designed software to allow a computer to control music-producing devices (e.g., sequencers, synthesizers)

music editor—Software that provides on-screen blank musical bars on which the user enters the musical key, time, and individual notes that constitute a piece of sheet music

music literacy—The ability to read standard music notation

music sequencer—Can be either software that supports the on-screen creation of music scores with several parts or tracks, or a hardware component of a music synthesizer workstation

music synthesizer—Music-making equipment controlled by a Musical Instrument Digital Interface (MIDI) device

National Education Technology Standards (NETS)—Benchmark technology skills created by the International Society for Technology in Education (ISTE) for teachers (NETS-T), students (NETS-S), and educational administrators (NETS-A)

netiquette—Etiquette guidelines for posting messages to online services, especially in email

new literacies—The new skills, strategies, and insights necessary to utilize the rapidly changing and emerging technologies in the world

No Child Left Behind (NCLB) Act of 2001—Federal law that put in place accountability measures of all U.S. students, teachers, and schools; requires schools to demonstrate adequate yearly progress (AYP) toward target goals, as demonstrated by test scores, attendance, and other quality indicators

notation software—Software that facilitates music making in the visual domain by allowing flexibility in music score and page setup, part extraction, text formatting, and other print-related issues

nutritional analysis program—Software that analyzes calorie intake and monitors portions of required food groups

objectivism—Knowledge obtained from objectivism is based on observation and experimentation. Objectivism focuses on teaching facts and quantified data and is known to be decontextualized and exists independently of the teacher or knower. Within teaching, the objectivist teaching method assumes that content is presented from the teacher to the student and the student is told if the answer is correct and given positive reinforcement if it is. Students memorize the external truths and knowledge.

objectivists—People who believe that knowledge has a separate existence outside human perception and that it must be transmitted through directed instructional methods, based on behavioral, cognitive-behavioral, and information processing theories

open source software—Computer software available online in which the source code is made available in the public domain and permits users to use, change, and improve the software, and to redistribute it in modified or unmodified form

operant conditioning—According to learning theorist B. F. Skinner, a way of shaping human behavior in which the consequences of people's past actions can act as stimuli to shape future behaviors

optical character recognition (OCR)—Software that allows text to be scanned and placed in a word processing file

Orff instruments—Musical instruments developed for children by K. Maendler under the direction of composer Carl Orff; modeled after a wooden African instrument, they were specially designed to provide a successful and fun first experience with making music

outlining tools—Software designed to prompt writers as they develop outlines to structure documents they plan to write

pedometer—Device that assists with analyzing and monitoring physical fitness levels by monitoring the number of steps one takes

PERL—Practical Extraction and Report Language; one of the programming languages (e.g., Java, C, Visual Basic) used to write Common Gateway Interface (CGI) programs that create "dynamic documents," or documents that allow interaction with users

PICT (picture)—An image format developed originally for use on Macintosh computers

plug-in—A program that adds a specific feature or service to a computer system; many types of audio and video messages are played through plug-ins

podcast—Digitized audio files typically resembling a radio broadcast or audio interview that are often saved in MP3 file format; files can then be shared over the Internet for playback on the computer or personal media devices; podcasts can be syndicated and subscribed to by online users for automatic download

portable document format (PDF)—Format that allows documents to be seen and sent with all the formatting and design elements (e.g., margins, graphics) of the original document without requiring the desktop publishing or word processing software used to create it

probeware—(See MBL.)

problem-based learning (PBL)—According to Sage (2000), learning organized around the investigation and resolution of an authentic, ill-structured problem

problem solving—Problem solving is a complex intellectual function where the learner uses high-order cognitive processes to solve problems and issues one does not initially know.

problem-solving software—Instructional software function that either teaches specific steps for solving certain problems (e.g., math word problems) or helps the student learn general problem-solving behaviors for a class of problems

programmed learning—Techniques for training and instruction based on learning theorist B. F. Skinner's reinforcement principles

puzzle generator—Software tool that automatically formats and creates crossword puzzles, word search puzzles, and similar game-like activities, based on content entered by a user

QuickTime® movie format—Video sequences that may be viewed on a computer screen by a program designed by Apple Computer Company (i.e., *QuickTime*)

QuickTime VR Authoring Studio®—Software that creates a type of virtual reality (VR) environment by using a series of photographs taken at 360 degrees around a pivotal point and "stitching" them together into a seamless panorama view

QWERTY keyboard—Traditional typewriter-like keyboard, so named because of the first six letters in the first line of a typewriter keyboard

radio frequency identification (RFID)—An electronic monitoring system that tracks the location of a person or object with an embedded computer chip and can update information on the chip; RFID devices are being field-tested to track student attendance, increase school security, and monitor the location of library resources

record—In a database file, several related fields (e.g., all the information on one person)

relative advantage—Term coined by Everett Rogers to refer to the perception by potential adopters of an innovation of the degree to which the new method or resource has advantages over the old one; major factor in determining whether the innovation is adopted

rubric—An assessment instrument designed to measure complex behaviors such as writing; consists of a set of elements that define the behavior and ratings that describe levels of performance for each element

sans serif typeface—Typeface in which letters have no small curves (serifs or "hands and feet") at the ends of the lines that make them up; usually used for short titles rather than the main text of a document

scaffolding—Term associated with learning theorist Vygotsky's belief that teachers can provide good instruction by finding out where each child is in his or her development and building on the child's experiences

scientific inquiry—The processes of approaching problems scientifically

screen reader—Utility software that operates in the background of the computer operating system, reading aloud any text that appears on the screen (e.g., menus, text, web pages)

semantic differential—Type of assessment instrument in which students respond to a topic or question by checking a line between each of several sets of bipolar adjectives to indicate their level of feeling about the topic

sensory disabilities—Impairments associated with the loss of hearing or vision

sensory registers—According to information-processing learning theorists, the parts of the brain that receive information a person senses through receptors (i.e., eyes, ears, nose, mouth, and/or hands) and, after a second or so, is either lost or transferred to short-term memory (STM) or working memory

sequencer—A device that facilitates music making in the aural domain by allowing users to record, edit, and play back digital audio and MIDI data

serif typeface—Typeface in which letters have small curves (serifs or "hands and feet") at the ends of the lines that make them up; usually used for the main text of a document

short-term memory (STM)—According to information-processing learning theorists, one of the three kinds of memory or "stores" the brain uses to process information, much like a computer; STM can hold information for about 5-20 seconds, after which it is either transferred to long-term memory (LTM) or lost

simulation—Type of software that models a real or imaginary system in order to teach the principles on which the system is based

site map—An at-a-glance guide to the contents of a website

social action project—Web-based project in which students are responsible for learning about and addressing important global social, economic, political, or environmental conditions

social activism—Characteristic agenda of renowned educator John Dewey that shaped his views about teaching and learning; resulted in the belief that social consciousness was the ultimate aim of all education, and learning was useful only in the context of social experience

social networking—Sites that focus on building communities of individually designed web pages that allow users to upload their content, meet and connect with friends from around the world, and share media and interests in an online, easy-to-use website environment

social studies—According to the National Council for the Social Studies (NCSS), the integrated study of the social sciences and humanities to promote civic competence

software—Programs written in a computer language (in contrast with hardware or equipment)

software piracy—Illegally copying and using a copyrighted software package without buying it

software suite—Software sold as one package but containing several different, unintegrated programs such as Microsoft *Office* (See also integrated packages.)

spirometer—A device that assists with analyzing and monitoring physical fitness levels by measuring lung volume

spreadsheet—Software designed to store data (usually, but not always, numeric) by row–column positions known as cells; can also do calculations on the data

statistical software packages—Software tools that help with qualitative data collection and analysis of student performance on tests by performing the calculations involved in any of these kinds of procedures

storyboard—A frame that serves as part of a planning blueprint from which a multimedia product or web page can be designed

streaming video/audio—A way of transmitting video or audio on the Internet so that it can be seen or heard as the file downloads

structured query language (SQL)—A type of high-level language used to locate desired information from a relational database

student information systems (SIS)—Networked software systems that help educators keep track of student, class, and school data (e.g., attendance, test scores) in order to maintain records and support decision making

student response systems (SRS)—(A.k.a., personal response systems or classroom response systems) a combination of handheld hardware and software that permits each student in the classroom to answer a question simultaneously and lets the teacher see and display a summary of results immediately

switches—Equipment to compress data in order for information to be transmitted at higher speeds [e.g., Asynchronous Transfer Mode (ATM) switches]; also devices that allow an alternative to the typical keyboard and thus allow easier input to the computer by a person with a disability

synchronous—Form of distance communications in which messages are sent and received immediately; contrasts with asynchronous communications, in which information and messages are left for the receiver to read later

systems approaches—Methods originated by educational psychologists such as Robert Gagné and Leslie Briggs, who applied principles from military and industrial training to developing curriculum and instruction for schools; methods used to create a carefully designed system of instruction or instructional design

systems software—Programs designed to manage the basic operations of a computer system (e.g., recognizing input devices, storing applications program commands)

talking word processor—A software package that reads typed words aloud

Technological Pedagogical Content Knowledge (TPACK)— TPACK attempts to capture some of the essential qualities of knowledge <http://www.tpck.org/tpck/index.php?title=Knowledge> required by teachers for technology integration in their teaching, while addressing the complex, multifaceted and situated nature of teacher knowledge <http://www.tpck.org/tpck/index.php?title=Teacher_knowledge> . At the heart of the TPACK framework is the complex interplay of three primary forms of knowledge: Content (CK) <http://www.tpck.org/tpck/index.php?title=Content_%28CK%29> , Pedagogy (PK) <http://www.tpck.org/tpck/index.php?title=Pedagogy_%28PK%29> , and Technology (TK) <http://www.tpck.org/tpck/index.php?title=Technology_%28TK%29>

technology education—A view of technology in education that originated with industry trainers and vocational educators in the 1980s and is currently represented by the International Technology Education Association (ITEA); holds that (1) school learning should prepare students for the world of work in which they will use technology, and (2) vocational training can help teach all content areas such as math, science, and language

test generator—Software designed to help teachers prepare and/or administer tests

test item bank—Pre-made pools of questions that can be used by test generator software to create various versions of the same test

TIF (Tagged Image File)—An image format designed to allow exchange of image files among various software applications and computers

tutorial—Type of instructional software that offers a complete sequence of instruction on a given topic, including explanation, examples, embedded practice and feedback, and, usually, also assessment

tweening—(See morphing.)

universal design—Adjustments made to physical environments as a result of understanding the special needs of individuals with disabilities, e.g., curb cuts in sidewalks to allow wheelchair access

URL (Uniform Resource Locator)—A series of letters and/or symbols that acts as an address for a site on the Internet

usability—A system's ease-of-use, defined as the effectiveness, efficiency, and satisfaction with which learners can accomplish a series of tasks in the hypermedia application

utility—Utility is concerned with the assortment of functionalities and features incorporated in a hypermedia system or application that satisfy the outlined pedagogical objectives and requirements

videoconferencing—An online "meeting" between two or more participants at different sites using: a computer or network with appropriate software; video cameras, microphone, and speakers; and telephone lines or other cabling to transmit audio and video signals

video editing software—Package such as *iMovie* that allows a user to make additions and changes to a selection of digital video

virtual field trip—(See electronic field trip.)

virtual manipulative—Software that students use to do simulated activities they used to do with real objects but which offers more flexibility than actual objects in the ways it can be used to illustrate concepts; often used in learning mathematics

virtual reality (VR)—A computer-generated environment designed to provide a lifelike simulation of actual settings; often uses a data glove and/or headgear that covers the eyes in order to immerse the user in the simulated environment

virtual reality modeling language (VRML)—A programming language that allows the creation and display of 3-dimensional objects on a computer screen and allows users to have the illusion of moving around the objects

virtual system—An instructional environment in which the students learns through immersion in simulated or distance education experiences that take the place of face-to-face ones

virus—A program written with the purpose of doing harm or mischief to programs, data, and/or hardware components of a computer system (See logic bomb, Trojan Horse, worm.)

virus protection software—Software put into place to protect computers from hackers and virus attacks (See hacker, virus.)

VRML (Virtual Reality Modeling Language)—An authoring specification for displaying three-dimensional objects on the Internet

web accessibility—The level to which a website is designed following a set of criteria that make it usable by people with various disabilities

web-based language learning (WBLL)—A strategy in which a teacher identifies pertinent web sites and resources for students to use to aid in their learning of a new language and related cultural lessons

Web 2.0 authoring tools—Authoring tools that are freely available to anyone with an Internet connection and provide users with the powerful capabilities of generating and sharing online content, creating online portfolios, social networking, and tagging or rating other user-generated content

webbing software—(See concept mapping software.)

web browser—(See browser.)

webquest—A curriculum project in which students explore websites to find and analyze information on a topic

wiki—A collection of web pages located in an online community that encourage collaboration and communication of ideas by having users contribute or modify content, sometimes on a daily basis

wireless connectivity—A computer network that reduces the number of required cables and allows greater freedom of movement by computer users; has one drop or cabled access point to the network through which many computer devices can access the network

word atlas—Electronic dictionaries and thesauruses that give pronunciations, definitions, and example uses for each word entry, and offer search and multimedia features similar to those of encyclopedias and atlases

worksheet—Another name besides "spreadsheet" for the product of a spreadsheet program

worksheet generator—Software tool that helps teachers produce exercises for practice (rather than for assessment) by prompting them to enter questions of various kinds

World Wide Web (WWW)—On the Internet, a system that connects sites through hypertext links; now often used as synonymous with "Internet"

XML—Acronym for Extensible Mark-up Language, a language that describes the geometry and behavior of a virtual world or scene

zone of proximal development (ZPD)—Term coined by learning theorist Vygotsky to refer to the difference between two levels of cognitive functioning: adult or expert and child or novice

References

Adams, C. (1998). Teaching and learning with SimCity 2000. *Journal of Geography, 97*(2), 47–55.

Albrecht, B., & Firedrake, G. (1997). New adventures in hands-on and far-out physics. *Learning and Leading with Technology, 25*(2), 34–37.

Alessi, S., & Trollip, S. (2001). *Multimedia for learning: Methods and development.* Needham Heights, MA: Allyn & Bacon.

Allen, D. (1993). Exploring the earth through software: Teaching with technology. *Teaching PreK–8, 24*(2), 22–26.

Allen, I. E., & Seaman, J. (2006). *Making the grade: Online learning in the United States, 2006.* Needham, MA: The Sloan Consortium.

Alley, L., & Jansek, K. (2001). The ten keys to quality assurance and assessment in online learning. *Journal of Interactive Instructional Development, 13*(3), 3–18.

Alliance for Childhood. (1999). *Fool's gold: A critical look at computers and childhood.* Retrieved from http//www.allianceforchildhood.net/projects/computers/computers_reports.htm

American Alliance for Health, Physical Education, Recreation, and Dance. (1995). *National health education standards: Achieving health literacy.* Reston, VA: Author.

American Association for the Advancement of Science. (1989). *Science for all Americans.* Cary, NC: Oxford University Press.

American Association for the Advancement of Science. (1993). *Benchmarks for scientific literacy.* Cary, NC: Oxford University Press.

American Association of University Women. (2000). *Tech-savvy: Educating girls in the new computer age.* Washington, DC: Author. Retrieved from http://www.aauw.org/research/girls_education/techsavvy.cfm

Andaloro, G. (1991). Modeling in physics teaching: The role of computer simulation. *International Journal of Science Education, 13*(3), 243–254.

Anderson-Inman, L., & Zeitz, L. (1993). Computer-based concept mapping: Active studying for active learners. *The Computing Teacher, 21*(1), 6–8, 10–11.

Armstrong, S. (1999). *A framework for evaluating integrated learning systems/multimedia instructional systems.* Modesto, CA: California Instructional Technology Clearinghouse.

Arnett, P. (2000). Mastering reading and writing with technology. *Media & Methods, 37*(1), 12–14.

Ashby, F., Isen, A., & Turken, A. (1999). A neuropsychological theory of positive affect and its influence on cognition. *Psychological Review, 106*, 529–550.

Assistive technologies. (2003). *eSchool News online, 5*(5). Retrieved from http://www.eschoolnews.org/news/showstory.cfm?ArticleID=3693

Atkinson, R., & Shiffrin, R. (1968). Human memory: A proposed system and its control processes. In K. Spence & J. Spence (Eds.), *The psychology of learning and motivation* (Vol. 2). New York: Academic Press.

Audet, R., & Ludwig, G. (2000). *GIS in schools.* Redlands, CA: Environmental Systems Research Institute.

Augmented reality soon could enhance learning. (2002). *eSchool News online, 6*(3). Retrieved from http://www.eschoolnews.org/news/showstory.cfm?ArticleID=4294

Ausubel, D. (1968). *Educational psychology: A cognitive view.* New York: Holt, Rinehart & Winston.

Baek, Y., & Layne, B. (1988). Color, graphics, and animation in a computer-assisted learning tutorial lesson. *Journal of Computer-Based Instruction, 15*(4), 31–35.

Bagui, S. (1998). Reasons for increased learning using multimedia. *Journal of Educational Multimedia and Hypermedia, 7*(1), 3–18.

Bailey, G., & Lumley, D. (1991). Supervising teachers who use integrated learning systems. *Educational Technology, 31*(7), 21–24.

Baines, L., & Stanley, G. (2000). We want to see the teacher. *Phi Delta Kappan, 82*(4), 327–330.

Bakas, C., & Mikropoulos, T. (2003). Design of virtual environments for the comprehension of planetary phenomena based on students' ideas. *International Journal of Science Education, 25*(8), 949–967.

Baker, T., & Bednarz, S. 2003. Lessons learned from reviewing research in GIS education. *Journal of Geography, 102*, 231–233.

Bangert-Drowns, R. (1993). The word processor as an instructional tool: A meta-analysis of word processing in writing instruction. *Review of Educational Research, 63*(1), 69–93.

Barab, S., Hay, K., & Barnett, M. (2000). Virtual solar system project: Building understanding through model building. *Journal of Research in Science Teaching, 37*(7), 719–756.

Barrett, H. C. (2000). Create your own electronic portfolio. *Learning and Leading with Technology, 27*(7), 14–21.

Bauer, J. F., & Anderson, R. S. (2001). A constructive stretch: Preservice teachers meet preteens in a technology-based literacy project. *Reading Online, 5*(5).

Baumbach, D., Christopher, T., Fasimpaur, K., & Oliver, K. (2004). Personal literacy assistants: Using handhelds for literacy instruction. *Learning and Leading with Technology, 32*(2), 16–21.

Beal, C., & Mason, C. (1999, January). Virtual fieldtripping: No permission notes needed. Creating a middle school classroom without walls. *Meridian Middle School Technologies Journal.* Retrieved November 1, 2004, from: http://www.ncsu.edu/meridian/jan99/vfieldtrip/

Bearden, D., & Martin, K. (1998). My make believe castle: An epic adventure in problem solving. *Learning and Leading with Technology, 25*(5), 21–25.

Beaton, A. E., et al. (1997–1998). Mathematics achievement in the middle school years, Mathematics achievement in the primary years, Mathematics achievement in the final year of secondary school. *IEA's Third International Mathematics and Science Study.* Chestnut Hill, MA: Boston College.

Becker, H. (1986a). *Instructional uses of school computers. Reports from the 1985 National Survey.* Issue No. 1. (ERIC Document Reproduction Service No. ED274319)

Becker, H. (1986b). *Instructional uses of school computers. Reports from the 1985 National Survey.* Issue No. 3. (ERIC Document Reproduction Service No. ED279303)

Becker, H. (1992). Computer-based integrated learning systems in the elementary and middle grades: A critical review and synthesis of evaluation reports. *Journal of Educational Computing Research, 8*(1), 1–41.

Becker, H. (1994). Mindless or mindful use of integrated learning systems. *International Journal of Educational Research, 21*(1), 65–79.

Becker, M., & Schuetz, J. (2003). An introduction to ground-water modeling using Virtual Reality Modeling Language (VRML). *Journal of Geoscience Education, 51*(5), 506–511.

Bednarz, S. W. (1999). *Reaching new standards: GIS and K-12 geography.* Retrieved April 10, 2001, from: http://www.odyseey.maine.edu/gisweb/spatdb/gislis95/gi95006.html

Bednarz, S., & Schee, J. 2006. Europe and the United States: The implementation of geographic information systems in secondary education in two contexts. *Technology, Pedagogy and Education, 15*(2), 191–205.

Behrmann, M., & Jerome, M. (2002). Assistive technology for students with mild disabilities. *ERIC Digest.* (ERIC Document Reproduction Service No. ED463595)

Bender, P. (1991). The effectiveness of integrated computer learning systems in the elementary school. *Contemporary Education, 63*(1), 19–23.

Bennett, N., & Diener, K. (1997). Habits of mind: Using multimedia to enhance learning skills. *Learning and Leading with Technology, 24*(6), 18–21.

Benson, D. (1997). Technology training: Meeting teacher's changing needs. *Principal, 76*(3), 17–19.

Benton Foundation Communications Policy Program. (2002). *Great expectations: Leveraging America's investment in educational technology.* Washington, DC: Benton Foundation. Retrieved from http://www.benton.org/publibrary/e-rate/greatexpectations.pdf

Berkson, R., & Britsch, S. (1997). "I am that kid tha [sic] acts weird": Developing e-mail education in a third-grade classroom. *Teaching Education, 8,* 97–104.

Bernard, R., Abrami, P., Lou, Y., Borokhovski, E., Wade, A., et al. (2004). How does distance education compare with classroom instruction? A meta-analysis of the empirical literature. *Review of Educational Research, 74*(3), 379–439.

Bernard, R., & Amundsen, C. (1989). Antecedents to dropout in distance education: Does one model fit all?. *The Journal of Distance Education, 4*(2), 25–46.

Berson, I. R., & Berson, M. J. (2003). Digital literacy for cybersafety, digital awareness, and media literacy. *Social Education, 67*(3), 164–168.

Berson, M. (1996). Effectiveness of computer technology in the social studies. *Journal of Research on Computing in Education, 28*(4), 486–499.

Berson, M. J. (2004). Digital images: Capturing America's past with the technology of today. *Social Education, 68*(3), 214–219.

Berson, M. J., & Balyta, P. (2004). Technological thinking and practice in the social studies: Transcending the tumultuous adolescence of reform. *Journal of Computing and Teacher Education, 20*(4), 141–152.

Bertelsen, C. D., Kauffman, S., Howard, K., & Cochran, L. L. (2003, July/August). Web watch: Phonics websites. *Reading Online, 7*(1).

Bigelow, M. H., Ranney, S., & Hebble, A. (2005). Choosing depth over breadth in a content-based ESL class. In J. Crandall & D. Kaufman (Eds.), *Content-based language instruction in the K–12 setting* (pp. 179–193). Washington, DC: TESOL.

Biner, P. (1993). The development of an instrument to measure student attitudes toward televised courses. *The American Journal of Distance Education, 7*(1), 62–73.

Bitter, G., Camuse, R., & Durbin, V. (1993). *Using a microcomputer in the classroom* (3rd ed.). Boston: Allyn & Bacon.

Black, T. R. (1999). Simulations on spreadsheets for complex concepts: Teaching statistical power as an example. *Journal of Mathematics, Education, and Science Technology, 30*(4), 473–481.

Blackhurst, A. E. (1997). Perspectives on technology in special education. *Teaching Exceptional Children, 29*(5), 41–48.

Blackhurst, A. E., & Edyburn, D. L. (2000). A brief history of special education technology. *Special Education Technology Practice, 2*(1), 21–36.

Bloom, B. (1986). Automaticity. *Educational Leadership, 43*(5), 70–77.

Blosser, P. (1988). *Teaching problem solving—Secondary school science.* (ERIC Document Reproduction No. ED309049)

Bolick, C. (2004). The Giant is Waking! *Journal of Computing in Teacher Education, 20*(4), 130–132.

Bolliger, D., & Martindale, T. (2004). Key factors for determining student satisfaction in online courses. *International Journal on E-Learning, 3*(1), 61–67.

Borba, M. (1989). *Self-esteem builders resources.* Torrance, CA: Jalmar Press.

Borenstein, M. (1997). Mathematics in the real world. *Learning and Leading with Technology, 24*(7), 30–39.

Boulware, B., & Tao, L. (2002). E-mail: Instructional potentials and learning opportunities. *Reading and Writing Quarterly, 18*(3), 285–288.

Boxie, P. (2004). Cybermentoring: An online literacy project in teacher education. *THE Journal.* Retrieved from http://thejournal.com/articles/16922

Boxie, P., & Maring, G. H. (2001). Cybermentoring: The relationship between preservice teachers' use of online literacy strategies and student achievement. *Reading Online, 4*(10). Retrieved from http://www.readingonline.org

Boyd, J. (n.d.). *Myths, misconceptions, problems and issues in arts education.* Retrieved November 18, 2004, from http://www.qsa.qld.edu.au/

Boyle, T. (1997). *Design for multimedia learning.* London: Prentice Hall.

Bozeman, W. (1992). Spreadsheets. In G. Bitter (Ed.), *Macmillan encyclopedia of computers.* New York: Macmillan.

Bracy, G. (1992). The bright future of integrated learning systems. *Educational Technology, 32*(9), 60–62.

Brangwin, N. (2002, Spring). Your personal cyberlibrarian. *Edutopia.* Retrieved from http://www.glef.org

Branigan, C. (2000, December 4). Pennsylvania tests essay-grading computer program for its statewide exam. *eSchool News online, 3*(12). Retrieved from http://www.eschoolnews.com/news/showstory.cfm?ArticleID=1994

Brangian, C. (2002a). Study touts classroom benefits of handheld computers. *eSchool News online, 5*(5). Retrieved from http://www.eschoolnews.org/news/showstory.cfm?ArticleID=3693

Branigan, C. (2002b). Virtual reality gives these students a boost. *eSchool News online, 5*(9). Retrieved from http://www.eschoolnews.org/news/showstory.cfm?ArticleID=3961

Browder, D. M., & Grasso, E. (1999). Teaching money skills to individuals with mental retardation: A research review with practical applications. *Remedial and Special Education, 20,* 297–308.

Brown, C. (2007). Learning through multimedia construction—a complex strategy. *Journal of Educational Multimedia and Hypermedia, 16*(2), 93–124.

Brown, J. S., Collins, A., & Duguid, P. (1989). Situated cognition and the culture of learning. *Educational Researcher, 18*(1), 32–41.

Bruce, B. (2000). Dewey and technology. *The Journal of Adolescent and Adult Literacy, 42*(3), 222–226.

Bruner, J. (1973). *The relevance of education.* New York: W. W. Norton & Company.

Bruning, R., & Horn, C. (2000). Developing motivation to write. *Educational Psychologist, 35*(1), 25–37.

Brunner, C. (1996). Judging student multimedia. *Electronic Learning, 15*(6), 14–15.

Brush, T. (1998). Embedding cooperative learning into the design of integrated learning systems: Rationale and guidelines. *Educational Technology Research and Development, 46*(3), 5–18.

Brush, T., Armstrong, J., & Barbrow, D. (1999). Design and delivery of integrated learning systems: Their impact on student achievement and attitudes. *Journal of Educational Computing Research, 21*(4), 475–486.

Bryan, S. (2000, May 1). *SWAT savvy: A model for effective classroom technology using student experts.* Retrieved June 26, 2003, from http://www.techlearning.com/db_area/archives/WCF/archives/bryan.htm

Buffington, M. (2008). What is Web 2.0 and how can it further art education? *Art Education, 61*(3), 36–41.

Bull, G., Bull, G., & Bull, S. (2000). Java applets. *Learning and Leading with Technology, 27*(8), 42–54.

Bull, G., Bull, G., & Kajder, S. B. (2003). Writing with weblogs: Reinventing student journals. *Learning and Leading with Technology, 31*(1), 32–35.

Bull, G., Bull, G., & Lewis, D. (1998). Introducing dynamic HTML. *Learning and Leading with Technology, 26*(2), 43–45.

Burrill, G. (1997). The NCTM standards: Eight years later. *School Science and Mathematics, 97*(6), 335–339.

Bush, V. (1986). As we may think. In S. Lambert & S. Ropiequet (Eds.), *CD-ROM: The new papyrus.* Redmond, WA: Microsoft Press. [Reprinted from *The Atlantic Monthly*, 1945, *176*(1), 101–108.]

CAI in music. (1994). *Teaching Music, 1*(6), 34–35.

Caine, R. N., & Caine, G. (1995). Reinventing schools through brain-based learning. *Educational Leadership, 52*(7), 43–47.

Caniglia, J. (1997). The heat is on: Using the calculator-based laboratory to integrate math, science, and technology. *Learning and Leading with Technology, 25*(1), 22–27.

Cann, A., & Seale, J. (1999). Using computer tutorials to encourage reflection. *Journal of Biological Education, 33*(3), 130–132.

Cannon, L. (2001). *National library of virtual manipulatives for interactive mathematics.* Retrieved January 5, 2001, from http://matti.usu.edu/nlvm/index.html

Carlin-Menter, S., & Shuell, T. (2003). Teaching writing strategies through multimedia authorship. *Journal of Educational Multimedia and Hypermedia, 12*(4), 315–334.

Carnine, D. (1993). Effective teaching for higher cognitive functioning. *Educational Technology, 33*(10), 29–33.

Carnine, D., Silbert, J., & Kameenui, E. (1997). *Direct instruction reading* (3rd ed.). Upper Saddle River, NJ: Merrill/Prentice Hall.

Carpenter, C. (1996). Online ethics: What's a teacher to do? *Learning and Leading with Technology, 23*(6), 40–41, 60.

Catchings, M., & MacGregor, K. (1998). Stoking creative fires: Young authors use software for writing and illustrating. *Learning and Leading with Technology, 25*(6), 20–23.

Cavallo, J. (2002, Fall). The virtual art museum. *Edutopia.* Retrieved from http://www.glef.org

Cavanagh, S. (2004, November 10). NCLB could alter science teaching. *EdWeek, 24*(11), 1, 12–13. Retrieved November 15, 2004, from http://www.edweek.org

Center for Educational Policy Research. (2003). *Understanding university success: A report from the Standards for Success Project.* Eugene, OR: University of Oregon. Retrieved from http://www.s4s.org/understanding.php

Chapelle, C. A. (2001). *Computer applications in second language acquisition.* Cambridge: Cambridge University Press.

Chen, M. (2001, Winter). Project-based learning transforms curriculum and assessment. *Edutopia.* Retrieved from http://www.glef.org

Cheng, H., Lehman, J., & Armstrong, P. (1991). Comparison of performance and attitude in traditional and computer conferencing classes. *The American Journal of Distance Education, 5*(3), 51–64.

Chrisman, G. (1992). Seven steps to ILS procurement. *Media and Methods, 28*(4), 14–15.

Christopherson, J. (1997). The growing need for visual literacy at the university. *Proceedings of the International Visual Literacy Association 1996 Annual Meeting*, Cheyenne, WY. (ERIC Document Reproduction No. ED408963)

Clark, J. (1996). Bells and whistles . . . but where are the references: Setting standards for hypermedia projects. *Learning and Leading with Technology, 23*(5), 22–24.

Clark, R. (1983). Reconsidering research on learning from media. *Review of Educational Research, 53*(4), 445–459.

Clark, R. (1985). Evidence for confounding in computer-based instruction studies: Analyzing the meta-analyses. *Educational Communications and Technology Journal, 33*(4), 249–262.

Clark, R. (1991). When researchers swim upstream: Reflections on an unpopular argument about learning from media. *Educational Technology, 31*(2), 34–40.

Clark, R. (2007). Learning from serious games? Arguments, evidence, and research suggestions. *Educational Technology, 47*(3), 56–59

Clark, R. E. (1994). Media will never influence learning. *Educational Technology Research and Development, 42*(2), 21–29.

Clark, T. (2001, October). *Virtual schools: Trends and issues.* Report commissioned by the Distance Learning Resource Network, a WestEd Project. Cosponsored by the Centre for the Application of Information Technologies at Western Illinois University. Retrieved from http://www.dlrn.org/trends.html

Clements, D. H. (1998). *From exercises and tasks to problems and projects: Unique contributions of computers to innovative mathematics education.* Retrieved January 3, 2001, from http://forum.swarthmore.edu/technology/papers/papers/clements/clements.html

Clinton, J. (1991). Decisions, decisions. *The Florida Technology in Education Quarterly, 3*(2), 93–96.

Coffman, T., & Klinger, M. (2008). Utilizing virtual worlds in education: The implications for practice. *International Journal of Social Sciences, 2*(1), 29–33.

Cognition and Technology Group at Vanderbilt. (1990). Anchored instruction and its relationship to situated cognition. *Educational Researcher, 19*(6), 2–10.

Cognition and Technology Group at Vanderbilt. (1991, May). Integrated media: Toward a theoretical framework for utilizing their potential. *Proceedings of the Multimedia Technology Seminar*, Washington, DC.

Cohen, M., & Riel, M. (1989). The effect of distant audiences on children's writing. *American Educational Research Journal, 26*(2), 143–159.

Coiro, J. (2003). Reading comprehension on the Internet: Expanding our understanding of reading comprehension to encompass new literacies. *The Reading Teacher, 56*(5), 458–464.

Coiro, J. (2006). Exploring changes to reading comprehension on the Internet: Paradoxes and possibilities for diverse adolescent readers. Dissertation, University of Connecticut, Storrs, CT.

Coiro, J., & Dobler, E. (2007, April/May/June). Exploring the online reading comprehension strategies used by sixth-grade skilled readers to search for and locate information on the Internet. *Reading Research Quarterly, 42*(2), 214–257.

Cole, J. (2004, April 2). Now is the time to start studying the Internet Age. *The Chronicle of Higher Education, 50*(30), B18.

Collins, A., Brown, J., & Newman, S. (1989). Cognitive apprenticeship: Teaching the craft of reading, writing, and mathematics. In L. Resnick (Ed.), *Knowing, learning, and instruction: Essays in honor of Robert Glaser* (pp. 453–494). Hillsdale, NJ: Lawrence Erlbaum Associates.

Collis, B. (1990). *The best of research windows: Trends and issues in educational computing.* Eugene, OR: International Society for Technology in Education. (ERIC Document Reproduction No. ED323993)

Comer, R., & Geissler, C. (1998). *A methodology for software evaluation.* Paper presented at the 1998 meeting of the Society for Information Technology and Teacher Education, Washington, DC, March 10–14. (ERIC Document Reproduction No. ED421140)

Comer, S. (1999). Immersive imaging technology: VR for the web in academia. *Syllabus, 13*(1), 22–26.

Cook, A. M., & Hussey, S. M. (1995). *Assistive technologies: Principles and practice.* St. Louis, MO: Mosby.

Cordes, C., & Miller, E. (2000). *Fool's gold: A critical look at computers and childhood.* College Park, MD: Alliance for Childhood.

Corporation for Public Broadcasting. (2003). *Connected to the future: A report on children's Internet use from Corporation for Public Broadcasting.* Retrieved September 26, 2004, from http://cpb.org/ed/resources/connected

Coulter, B., Feldman, A., & Konold, C. (2000). Rethinking online adventures. *Learning and Leading with Technology, 28*(1), 42–47.

Coussement, S. (1995). *Educational telecommunication: Does it work? An attitude study.* (ERIC Document Reproduction No. ED391465)

Cradler, J. (2003). Technology's impact on teaching and learning. *Learning and Leading with Technology, 30*(7), 54–57.

Crews, K. (2003). Copyright and distance education: Making sense of the Teach Act. *Change, 35*(6), 34–39.

Cuban, L. (1986). *Teachers and machines: The classroom use of technology since the 1920s.* New York: Teachers College Press.

Cuban, L. (2001). *Oversold and underused.* Boston: Harvard University Press.

Cuban, L., Kirkpatrick, H., & Peck, C. (2001). High access and low use of technologies in high school classrooms: Explaining an apparent paradox. *American Educational Research Journal, 38*(4), 813–834.

Cummins, J. (1979). Cognitive/academic language proficiency, linguistic interdependence, the optimal age question and other matters. *Working Papers on Bilingualism, 19,* 197–205.

Cummins, J. (1986). Empowering minority students: A framework for interaction. *Harvard Review, 50,* 18–36.

Curtis, M., Williams, B., Norris, C., O'Leary, D., & Soloway, E. (2003). *Palm handheld computers: A complete resource guide for teachers.* Eugene, OR: International Society for Technology in Education.

Cyrs, T. E. (1997). Competence in teaching at a distance. In T. E. Cyrs (Ed.), *Teaching and learning at a distance: What it takes to effectively design, deliver, and evaluate programs.* San Francisco: Jossey-Bass.

Dabbagh, N. (2001). Concept mapping as a mind tool for critical thinking. *Journal of Computing in Teacher Education, 17*(2), 16–23.

Darden, G., & Shimon, J. (2000). Revisit an "old" technology: Videotape feedback for motor skill learning and performance. *Strategies, 13*(4), 17–21.

Davydov, V. (1995). The influence of L. S. Vygotsky on education theory, research, and practice. *Educational Researcher, 24*(3), 12–21.

DeTure, M. (2004). Cognitive style and self-efficacy: Predicting student success in online distance education. *American Journal of Distance Education, 18*(1), 21–38.

Dille, B., & Mezack, M. (1991). Identifying predictors of high risk among community college telecourse students. *The American Journal of Distance Education, 5*(1), 24–35.

Dillon, A., & Gabbard, R. (1998). Hypermedia as an educational technology: A review of the quantitative research literature on learner comprehension, control, and style. *Review of Educational Research, 68*(3), 322–349.

Dillon, R. (1998). In the key of "see and hear": How students can learn to play the recorder by playing musical computers. *Learning and Leading with Technology, 26*(2), 15–17.

DiPietro, M., Ferdig, R., Boyer, J., & Black, E. (2007). Towards a framework for understanding electronic educational gaming. *Journal of Educational Multimedia and Hypermedia, 16*(3), 225–248. Chesapeake, VA: AACE.

Dipinto, V., & Turner, S. (1995). Zapping the hypermedia zoo: Assessing the students' hypermedia projects. *The Computing Teacher, 22*(7), 8–11.

Dixon, J. K., & Falba, C. J. (1997). Graphing in the information age: Using data from the World Wide Web. *Mathematics Teaching in the Middle School, 2*(5), 298–304.

Doering, A. (2004). *GIS in education: An examination of pedagogy.* Unpublished doctoral dissertation, University of Minnesota, Minneapolis.

Doering, A. (2006a). Adventure learning: Transformative hybrid online education. *Distance Education 27*(2), 197–215.

Doering, A. (2006b). Technology and teacher education: An investigation into pedagogy. Manuscript submitted for publication.

Doering, A. (2007). Adventure learning: Situating learning in an authentic context. *Innovate—Journal of Online Education, 3*(6). Retrieved on July 17, 2008, from http://www.innovateonline.info/index.php?view=article&id=342

Doering, N. (2000). Measuring student understanding with a videotape performance assessment. *Journal of Physical Education, Recreation, and Dance, 71*(7), 47–52.

Doering, A., & Beach, R. (2002). Preservice English teachers acquiring literacy practices through technology tools in a practicum experience. *Language, Learning and Technology, 6*(3), 127–146.

Doering, A., Beach, R., & O'Brien, C. (2007). Infusing multi-modal tools and literacies into an English education program. *English Education, 40*(1), 41–60.

Doering, A., Hughes, J., & Scharber, C. (2007). Teaching and Learning Social Studies Online. In C. Cavanaugh, & R. Blomeyer (Eds.), *What works in K–12 online learning* (pp. 91–103). International Society for Technology in Education.

Doering, A., Hughes, J., & Scharber, C. (2007). Teaching and learning social studies online. In C. Cavanaugh & R. Blomeyer (Eds.), *What works in K–12 online learning* (pp. 91–103), International Society for Technology in Education.

Doering, A., Miller, C., & Veletsianos, G. (2008). Adventure learning: Educational, social, and technological affordances for collaborative hybrid distance education. *Quarterly Review of Distance Education, 9*(1), 249–266.

Doering, A., & Veletsianos, G. (2007a). An investigation of the use of real-time, authentic geo-spatial data in the K–12 classroom. *Journal of Geography,* Special issue on using geo-spatial data in geographic education, *106*(6), 217–225.

Doering, A., & Veletsianos, G. (2007b). Multi-scaffolding learning environment: An analysis of scaffolding and its impact on cognitive load and problem-solving ability. *Journal of Educational Computing Research, 37*(2), 107–129.

Doering, A., & Veletsianos, G. (2008). Hybrid online education: Identifying integration models using adventure learning. *Journal of Research on Technology in Education, 41*(1), 101–119.

Doering, A., Veletsianos, G., & Scharber, C. (2007). Coming of Age: Research and Pedagogy on Geospatial Technologies within K–12 Social Studies Education. In A. J. Milson & M. Alibrandi (Eds.), *Digital Geography: Geo-Spatial Technologies in the Social Studies Classroom* (pp. 213–226). Charlotte, NC: Information Age Publishing.

Doering, A., Veletsianos, G., & Scharber, C. (2007). Coming of age: Research and pedagogy on geo-spatial technologies within K–12 social studies education. In A. J. Milson & M. Alibrandi (Eds.), *Digital geography: Geo-Spatial technologies in the social studies classroom* (pp. 213–226). Charlotte, NC: Information Age.

Dolan, B. (2000). Universal design for learning. *Journal of Special Education Technology, 15*(4), 44–51.

Dorsey, M., et al. (2001). An introduction to symmetry. Retrieved January 4, 2001, from http://www.geom.umn.edu/demo5337/s97a/

Doty, D., Popplewell, S., & Byers, G. (2001). Interactive CD-ROM storybooks and young readers' reading comprehension. *Journal of Research on Computing in Education, 33*(4), 374–384.

Drier, H. (2001). *Collecting and numerically analyzing M&M's data.* Retrieved January 4, 2001, from http://curry.edschool.virginia.edu/teacherlink/math/activities/excel/M&Mnumerical/home.html

Dunham, P. H., & Dick, T. P. (1994). Research on graphing calculators. *Mathematics Teacher, 87,* 440–445.

Durden, W. (2001, October 19). Liberal arts for all, not just the rich. *Chronicle of Higher Education.* Retrieved from http://chronicle.com

Dyrli, O. (1994). Riding the Internet schoolbus: Places to go and things to do. *Technology and Learning, 15*(2), 32–40.

Eagleton, M. (1999). The benefits and challenges of a student-designed school website. Retrieved October 14, 2008, from http://www.readingonline.org/articles/eagleton/text.html

Easterbrooks, S. (1999). Improving practices for students with hearing impairments. *Exceptional Children, 65*, 537–554.

Editors. (2003). Early reading software. *Technology & Learning, 23*(11), 32, 34, 36.

Educational Technology Magazine. (1991a, May). *31*(5). Special issue on constructivist versus directed approaches.

Educational Technology Magazine. (1991b, September). *31*(9). Special issue on constructivist versus directed approaches.

Edwards, N. (2006). *Non-traditional music students: A new population of music student for the 21st Century.* Unpublished manuscript, Illinois State University.

Edyburn, D. L. (2000). Assistive technology and students with mild disabilities. *Focus on Exceptional Children, 32*(9), 1–24.

Edyburn, D. L. (2001). Technology integration strategies: Universal design and technology integration, finding the connections. *Closing the Gap, 20*(1), 21–22.

Edyburn, D. L. (2003). Measuring assistive technology outcomes: Key concepts. *Journal of Special Education Technology, 18*(1), 53–55.

Eggen, P., & Kauchak, D. (2004). *Educational psychology: Windows on classrooms* (5th ed.). Upper Saddle River, NJ: Merrill/Prentice Hall.

Ehman, L., Glenn, A., Johnson, V., & White, C. (1992). Using computer databases in student problem solving: A study of eight social studies teachers' classrooms. *Theory and Research in Social Education, 20*(2), 179–206.

Eiser, L. (1988). What makes a good tutorial? *Classroom Computer Learning, 8*(4), 44–47.

Ellison, N., & Wu, Y. (2008). Blogging in the classroom: A preliminary exploration of student attitudes and impact on comprehension. *Journal of Educational Multimedia and Hypermedia, 17*(1), 99–122.

EMC Corporation. (2003). *Fueling the pipeline: Attracting and educating math and science students.* Hopkinton, MA: Author. Retrieved November 15, 2004, from http://www.emc.com/about/emc_philanthropy/mmi/

Ervin, A. (2002). Meatloaf around the world. *Learning and Leading with Technology, 29*(5), 18–21, 62.

Estep, S., McInerney, W., & Vockell, E. (1999–2000). An investigation of the relationship between integrated learning systems and academic achievement. *Journal of Educational Technology Systems, 28*(1), 5–19.

Estes, C. (1994). The real-world connection. *Simulation and Gaming, 25*(4), 456–463.

Evans, R. (2004). *The social studies wars: What should we teach the children?* New York: The Teachers College Press.

Ewing, R., Schmid, T., Killingsworth, R., Zlot, A., & Raudenbush, S. (2008). Relationship between urban sprawl and physical activity, obesity, and morbidity. In J. Marzluff, E. Shulenberger, W. Endlicher, M. Alberti, G. Bradley, C. Ryan, U. Simon & C. ZumBrunnen (Eds.), *Urban ecology: An international perspective on the interaction between humans and nature* (567–582). Springer, US.

Fabos, B., & Young, M. (1999). Telecommunication in the classroom: Rhetoric versus reality. *Review of Educational Research, 69*(3), 217–259.

Ferris, T. (1988). *Coming of age in the Milky Way.* New York: Doubleday.

Feurer, M., Towne, L., & Shavelson, R. (2002). Scientific culture and educational research. *Educational Researcher, 31*(8), 4–14.

Finzer, W., & Jackiw, N. (1998). Dynamic manipulation of mathematical objects. Retrieved January 5, 2001, from http://forum.swarthmore.edu/technology/papers/papers/s2k/

Fisher, S. K., & Gardner, J. E. (1999). Introduction to technology in transition. *Career Development for Exceptional Individuals, 22*, 131–151.

Flannery, M. (2004, February 22). FCAT puts less stress on study of history. *Miami Herald.* Retrieved from http://www.miami.com

Flores, A. (1998). *Electronic technology and NCTM standards.* Retrieved January 30, 2001, from http://forum.swarthmore.edu/technology/papers/papers/flores.html

Florida TaxWatch (2007). *Final report: A comprehensive assessment of Florida Virtual School.* Tallahassee, FL.

Flowers, R. (1993). New teaching tools for new teaching practices. *Instructor, 102*(5), 42–45.

Forbes, L. S. (2004, October). Using web-based bookmarks in K–8 settings: Linking the Internet to instruction. *The Reading Teacher, 58*(2), 148–153.

Forest, J. (1993). Music and the arts: Keys to a next-century school. *The Computing Teacher, 21*(3), 24–26.

Franklin, S. (1991). Breathing life into reluctant writers: The Seattle Public Schools laptop project. *Writing Notebook, 84*(4), 40–42.

Frederickson, S. (1997). Interactive multimedia storybooks. *Learning and Leading with Technology, 25*(1), 6–10.

Fulford, C., & Zhang, S. (1993). Perceptions of interaction: The critical predictor in distance education. *American Journal of Distance Education, 7*(3), 8–21.

Funkhouser, C., & Dennis, J. (1992). The effects of problem-solving software on problem-solving ability. *Journal of Research on Computing in Education, 24*(3), 338–347.

Furger, R. (2002, Fall). A sampler of designs for teaching and learning. *Edutopia* (http://www.glef.org).

Furger, R. (2003, Fall). The write stuff. *Edutopia* (http://www.glef.org).

Furst-Bowie, J. (1997). Comparison of student reactions in traditional and videoconferencing courses in training and development. *International Journal of Instructional Media, 24*(3), 197–205.

Gagné, R. (1982). Developments in learning psychology: Implications for instructional design. *Educational Technology, 22*(6), 11–15.

Gagné, R. (1985). *The conditions of learning.* New York: Holt, Rinehart & Winston.

Gagné, R., Wager, W., & Rojas, A. (1981). Planning and authoring computer-assisted instruction lessons. *Educational Technology, 21*(9), 17–26.

Galas, P. (1998). From presentation to programming. *Learning and Leading with Technology, 25*(4), 18–21.

Gardiner, S. (2001). Cybercheating: A new twist on an old problem. *Phi Delta Kappan, 83*(2), 172–176.

Gauthier, S. (2004). GIS helps prepare students for emergencies. *Learning and Leading with Technology, 32*(3), 22–25.

Gay, L. R. (1993). *Educational research: Competencies for analysis and application* (4th ed.). Upper Saddle River, NJ: Merrill/Prentice Hall.

Gee, J. P. (2004). *What video games have to teach us about learning and literacy.* New York: Palgrave Macmillan.

Gee, J. P., Hull, G., & Lankshear, C. (1996). *The new work order: Behind the language of the new capitalism.* Sydney: Allen and Unwin.

Gibbs, W., Graves, P., & Bernas, R. (2000). Identifying important criteria for multimedia instructional courseware evaluation. *Journal of Computing in Higher Education, 12*(1), 84–106.

Gibson, C., & Graf, A. (1992). Impact of adults' preferred learning styles and perception of barriers on completion of external baccalaureate degree programs. *Journal of Distance Education, 7*(1), 39–51.

Gill, B., Dick, W., Reiser, R., & Zahner, J. (1992). A new model for evaluating instructional software. *Educational Technology, 32*(3), 39–48.

Gitomer, D. H., Latham, A., & Ziomek, R. (1999). *The academic quality of prospective teachers: The impact of admissions and licensure testing.* Princeton, NJ: Teaching and Learning Division, Educational Testing Service.

Glasgow, J. (1996). Part I: It's my turn! Motivating young readers. *Learning and Leading with Technology, 24*(3), 20–23.

Glasgow, J. (1996–1997). Part II: It's my turn! Motivating young readers using CD-ROM storybooks. *Learning and Leading with Technology, 24*(4), 18–22.

Glasgow, J. (1997). Keep up the good work! Using multimedia to build reading fluency and enjoyment. *Learning and Leading with Technology, 24*(5), 22–25.

Gleeson, L. (1997). An interactive multimedia computer program on art history. In D. Gregory (Ed.), *New technologies in art education: Implications for theory, research, and practice*. Reston, VA: The National Art Education Association.

GLEF staff. (2003, Spring). A passion for projects. *Edutopia* (http://www.glef.org).

Godwin-Jones, R. (2007). Emerging technologies: E-texts, mobile browsing, and rich Internet applications. *Language Learning & Technology, 11*(3), 8–13.

Goldberg, A., Russell, M., & Cook, A. (2003). The effects of computers on student writing: A meta-analysis of studies from 1992–2002. *Journal of Technology, Learning, and Assessment, 2*(1), 1–51.

Goldstein, L. (2002). Virtual reality researchers target special education classes. *Education Week, 22*(3), 8.

Goldstein, T. (2003). *Teaching and learning in a multilingual school: Choices, risks, and dilemmas*. Mahwah, NJ: Lawrence Erlbaum Associates.

Gonsalves, D., & Lopez, J. (1998). Catch your students with microworlds games. *Learning and Leading with Technology, 26*(3), 19–21.

Google. (2006). Google announces major imagery update for Google Earth: New tools and innovations in mapping. Retrieved October 26, 2006, from http://www.google.com/press/pressrel/geoday.html

Goslee, S. (1998, June). *Losing ground bit by bit: Low-income communities in the information age*. Washington, DC: The Benton Foundation and the National Urban League. Retrieved from http://www.benton.org/Library/Low-Income/home.html

Graham, G., Holt-Hale, S., & Parker, M. (1998). *Children moving: A reflective approach to teaching physical education*. Mountain View, CA: Mayfield Publishing Co.

Graham, R. (1994). A computer tutorial for psychology of learning courses. *Teaching of Psychology, 21*(2), 116–166.

Graham, R. (1998). A computer tutorial on the principles of stimulus generalization. *Teaching of Psychology, 25*(2), 149–151.

Grant, M. M. (2002). *Individual differences in constructivist learning environments: Qualitative inquiry into computer mediated learning artifacts*. Unpublished doctoral dissertation, The University of Georgia, Athens, GA.

Green, D. R. (2001). *GIS: A sourcebook for schools*. London: Taylor & Francis.

Grimshaw, S. (2007). Electronic books: Children's reading and comprehension. *British Journal of Educational Technology, 38*(4), 583–599.

Grogan, D., & Ruzic, R. (2000). Walking the walk: Universal design on the web. *Journal of Special Education Technology, 15*(3), 45–49.

Handler, M. (1992). Preparing new teachers to use technology: Perceptions and suggestions for teacher educators. *Computers in Education, 20*(2), 147–156.

Hanfland, P. (1999). Electronic portfolios. *Learning and Leading with Technology, 26*(6), 54–57.

Hardy, D. W., & Boaz, M. H. (1997). Learner development: Beyond the technology. In T. E. Cyrs (Ed.), *Teaching and learning at a distance: What it takes to effectively design, deliver, and evaluate programs*. San Francisco: Jossey-Bass.

Harp, L. (1996, October). The history wars: How technology changes everything. *Electronic Learning, 16*, 32–39.

Harris, J. (1985). Student writers and word processing. *College Composition and Communication, 36*(3), 323–330.

Harris, J. (1998a). Assistive annotations: The art of recommending web sites. *Learning and Leading with Technology, 25*(6), 58–61.

Harris, J. (1998b). *Virtual architecture: Designing and directing curriculum-based telecomputing*. Eugene, OR: International Society for Technology in Education.

Harris, J. (2000). Taboo topic no longer: Why telecollaborative projects sometimes fail. *Learning and Leading with Technology, 27*(5), 36–41.

Harris, J. (2002). Wherefore art thou, Telecollaboration? *Learning and Leading with Technology, 29*(3), 36–41.

Hartley, K. (2000). Online simulations. *Learning and Leading with Technology, 28*(3), 32–35.

Hartley, K., & Bendixon, L. (2001). Educational research in the Internet age: Examining the role of individual characteristics. *Educational Researcher, 30*(9), 22–26.

Hasselbring, T. (1988). Developing math automaticity in learning-handicapped children. *Focus on Exceptional Children, 20*(6), 1–7.

Hasselbring, T., & Goin, L. (1993). Integrating technology and media. In E. Polloway & J. Patton (Eds.), *Strategies for teaching learners with special needs* (5th ed.). New York: Merrill.

Hassenzahl, M. (2004b). The interplay of beauty, goodness, and usability in interactive products. *Human-Computer Interaction, 19*, 319–349.

Hauger, G. (2000). Instantaneous rate of change: A numerical approach. *International Journal of Mathematical Education in Science and Technology, 31*(6), 891–897.

Hawisher, G. (1989). Research and recommendations for computers and compositions. In G. Hawisher & C. Selfe (Eds.), *Critical perspectives on computers and composition instruction*. New York: Teachers College Press.

Healy, J. (1998). *Failure to connect: How computers affect our children's minds—for better or worse*. New York: Simon & Schuster.

Heller, J., Curtis, D., Jaffe, R., & Verboncoeur, C. Impact of handheld graphing calculator use on student achievement in Algebra 1. Retrieved September 3, 2008, from http://education.ti.com/sites/US/downloads/pdf/heller_grcalcreport_2005.pdf

Helt, M. (2003). Writing the book on online literature circles. *Learning and Leading with Technology, 30*(7), 28–31, 58.

Henderson, L., Klemes, J., & Eshet, Y. (2000). Just playing a game? Educational simulation software and cognitive outcomes. *Journal of Educational Computing Research, 22*(1), 105–129.

Hermann, A. (1988). *Desktop publishing in high school: Empowering students as readers and writers*. (ERIC Document Reproduction No. ED300837)

Herrell, A., & Jordan, M. (2003). *Fifty strategies for teaching English language learners* (2nd ed.). Upper Saddle River, NJ: Merrill/Prentice Hall.

Heward, W. (2000). *Exceptional children: An introduction to special education* (6th ed.). Upper Saddle River, NJ: Prentice Hall.

Higgins, K., & Boone, R. (1993). Technology as a tutor, tools, and agent for reading. *Journal of Special Education Technology, 12*(1), 28–37.

Hirsch, E. D. (2002). Classroom research and cargo cults. *Policy Review, 115*. Retrieved from http://www.policyreview.org/OCT02/hirsch.html

Hmelo-Silver, C. E. (2004). Problem-based learning: What and how do students learn? *Educational Psychology Review, 16*(3), 235–266.

Hoffenburg, H., & Handler, M. (2001). Digital video goes to school. *Learning and Leading with Technology, 29*(2), 10–15.

Hoffman, D., & Novak, T. (1998, April 17). Bridging the racial divide on the Internet. *Science, 280*(5362), 390–391.

Hoffman, J. L., & Lyons, D. L. (1997). Evaluating instructional software. *Learning and Leading with Technology, 25*(2), 52–56.

Howard, B. (2001, May 8). Lights! Camera! Learning curve! *PC Magazine*. Retrieved September 6, 2004, from http://www.pcmag.com/article2/0,1759,24860,00.asp

Howell, R. D. (1994). Technological innovations in the education of gifted and talented students. In J. L. Genschaft, M. Mirely, & C. L. Hollinger (Eds.), *Serving gifted and talented students*. Austin, TX: PRO-ED.

Hudgins, B. (2001). Leveraging handheld technology in the classroom. *T.H.E. Journal Online*. Retrieved from http://www.thejournal.com/magazine/vault/A3809.cfm

Hughes, J. E. (2000). *Teaching English with technology: Exploring teacher learning and practice.* Unpublished doctoral dissertation, Michigan State University, East Lansing, MI.

Hughes, J. E., & Scharber, C. (2008). Leveraging the development of English-technology pedagogical content knowledge within the deictic nature of literacy. In *Handbook of technological pedagogical content knowledge for teaching and teacher education.* Monograph by AACTE's Committee on Innovation and Technology. Mahwah, NJ: Lawrence Erlbaum Associates.

Humphries, D. (1989). A computer training program for teachers. In C. Selfe, D. Rodrigues, & W. Oates (Eds.), *Computers in English and the language arts.* Urbana, IL: National Council of Teachers of English.

International Reading Association. (2001). *Integrating literacy and technology in the curriculum: A position statement of the international reading association.* Newark, DE: Author.

International Society for Technology in Education. (2000). *National educational technology standards for students.* Eugene, OR: Author.

International Society for Technology in Education. (2002). *National educational technology standards for teachers: Preparing teachers to use technology.* Eugene, OR: Author.

International Society for Technology in Education. (2008). *National educational technology standards for teachers* (2nd ed.). Eugene, OR: Author.

Jacobsen, J., Moore, M., & Brown, L. (2002). Chemistry comes alive! *Journal of Chemical Education, 79*(11), 1381–1384.

Johnson, D. (2001, April). Web watch: Internet resources to assist teachers with struggling readers. *Reading Online, 4*(9). Retrieved from http://www.readingonline.org/electronic/elec_index.asp?HREF=/electronic/webwatch/struggling/index.html

Johnson, D. (2002). Web watch: Writing resources. *Reading Online, 5*(7).

Johnson, D. (2003). Choosing the right books for struggling readers. *Learning and Leading with Technology, 31*(1), 22–27.

Johnson, D., & Eisenberg, M. (1996). Computer literacy and information literacy: A natural combination. *Emergency Librarian, 23*(5), 12–16.

Johnson, D., & McLeod, S. (2004–2005). Get answers: Using student response systems to see students' thinking. *Learning and Leading with Technology, 32*(4), 18–23.

Johnson, D., & Zufall, L. (2004). Web watch—Not just for kids anymore: WebQuests for professional development. *Reading Online, 7*(5).

Johnson, D. W., & Johnson, R. T. (2004). Cooperation and the use of technology. In D. Jonassen (Ed.), *Handbook of research on educational communications and technology* (2nd ed., pp. 785–811). Mahwah, NJ: Lawrence Erlbaum Associates.

Johnson, D.W., & Johnson, R.T. (2005). New developments in social interdependence theory. *Genetic, Social, and General Psychology Monographs, 131*(4), 285–358.

Johnson, D. W., Johnson, R. T., & Holubec, E. (1992). *Advanced cooperative learning.* Edina, MN: Interaction Book Company.

Jonassen, D. (2000). *Computers as mindtools for schools: Engaging critical thinking.* Columbus, OH: Prentice Hall.

Jordan, P. (2000). *Designing pleasurable products: An introduction to the new human factors.* London: Taylor & Francis.

Kaestle, C., Damon-Moore, H., Stedman, L.C., & Tinsely, K. (1989). *Literacy in the United States: Readers and reading since 1880.* New Haven, CT: Yale.

Kahn, J. (1997a). Scaffolding in the classroom: Using CD-ROM storybooks at a computer reading center. *Learning and Leading with Technology, 25*(2), 17, 19.

Kahn, J. (1997b). Well begun is half done: Teaching students to use concept-mapping software. *Learning and Leading with Technology, 24*(5), 39–40.

Kahn, J. (1998–1999). The same but different: The computer as an alternate medium. *Learning and Leading with Technology, 26*(4), 15–18.

Kajder, S., & Bull, G. (2003). Scaffolding for struggling students: Reading and writing with blogs. *Learning and Leading with Technology, 31*(2), 31–35.

Kajder, S., Bull, G., & Van Noy, E. (2004). A space for "writing without writing": Blogs in the language arts classroom. *Learning and Leading with Technology, 31*(6), 32–35.

Kajder, S., & Swenson, J. (2004). Digital images in the language arts classroom. *Learning and Leading with Technology, 31*(8), 18–21, 46.

Kane, W. M. (1993). *Step-by-step to comprehensive school health: The program planning guide.* Santa Cruz, CA: ETR Associates.

Karchmer, R. A. (2000). Using the Internet and children's literature to support interdisciplinary instruction. *The Reading Teacher, 54*(1), 100–104.

Karchmer, R. A. (2001a). Gaining a new, wider audience: Publishing student work on the Internet. *Reading Online, 4*(10). Retrieved from http://www.readingonline.org

Karchmer, R. A. (2001b). The journey ahead: Thirteen teachers report how the Internet influences literacy and literacy instruction in their K–12 classrooms. *Reading Research Quarterly, 36*, 442–466.

Keizer, G. (1997). Which software works? *Family PC, 4*(5), 117–121.

Kennedy, D. (1995). Climbing the tree of mathematics. *Mathematics Teacher, 88*(6), 640–645.

Kerski, J. (1999). *A nationwide analysis of the implementation of GIS in high school education.* In Proceedings of the 21st Annual ESRI User Conference, San Diego, California. Retrieved August 11, 2006, from http://gis.esri.com/library/userconf/proc99/proceed/papers/pap202/p202.htm

Kim, P. (2006). Effects of 3D virtual reality of plate tectonics on fifth-grade students' achievement and attitude toward science. *Interactive Learning Environments, 14*(1), 25–34.

Kimball, C., & Sibley, P. (1997–1998). Am I on the mark? Technology planning for the e-rate. *Learning and Leading with Technology, 25*(4), 52–57.

King, T. W. (1999). *Assistive technology: Essential human factors.* Boston: Allyn & Bacon.

Kinzer, C. K. (2003). The importance of recognizing the expanding boundaries of literacy. *Reading Online, 6*(10).

Kirschner, P., Strijbos, J., Kreijns, K., & Beers, P. J. (2004). Designing electronic collaborative learning environments. *Educational Technology Research and Development, 52*(3), 47–66.

Kirschner, P.A. (2001). Using integrated learning environments for collaborative teaching/learning. *Research Dialogue in Learning and Instruction, 2*, 1–9.

Kirschner, P. A., Sweller, J., & Clark, R. E. (2006). Why minimal guidance during instruction does not work: An analysis of the failure of constructivist, discovery, problem-based experiential and inquiry-based teaching. *Educational Psychologist, 41*(2), 75–86.

Kleiner, A., & Lewis, L. (2003). *Internet Access in U.S. public schools and classrooms: 1994–2002* (NCES Report No. 2004–011). Washington, DC: U.S. Department of Education, Institute of Education Science.

Klemm, W. (1998). Eight ways to get students more engaged in online conferences. *T.H.E. Journal, 26*(1), 62–64.

Klesius, J., Homan, S., & Thompson, T. (1997). Distance education compared to traditional instruction: The students' view. *International Journal of Instructional Media, 24*(3), 207–220.

Knee, R., Musgrove, A., & Musgrove, J. (2000). Lights, camera, action: Streaming video on your web site. *Learning and Leading with Technology, 28*(1), 50–53.

Knupfer, N., & McIsaac, M. (1989). Desktop publishing software: The effects of computerized formats on reading speed and comprehension. *Journal of Research Computing in Education, 22*(2), 127–136.

Koehler, M. J., & Mishra, P. (2008). Introducing technological pedagogical content knowledge. In AACTE Committee on Innovation and Technology (Eds.), *The handbook of technological pedagogical content knowledge for educators.* Hillsdale, NJ: Lawrence Erlbaum Associates.

Kozma, R. (1991). Learning with media. *Review of Educational Research, 61*(2), 179–211.

Kozma, R. (1994). Will media influence learning? Reframing the debate. *Educational Technology Research and Development, 42*(2), 5–17.

Kozma, R., Zucker, A., & Espinoza, C. (1998, October). *An evaluation of the virtual high school after one year of operation.* Arlington, VA: SRI International. Retrieved from http://vhs.concord.org/

Kraemer, K. (1990). SEEN: Tutorials for critical reading. *Writing Notebook, 7*(3), 31–32.

Krashen, S. (1982). *Principles and practices in second language acquisition.* Oxford: Pergamon Press.

Krashen, S. (2003). The (lack of) experimental evidence supporting the use of Accelerated Reader. *Journal of Children's Literature, 29*(2), 16–30.

Kuhn, D. (2007). Is direct instruction an answer to the right question? *Educational Psychologist, 42*(2), 109–113. Retrieved October 31, 2007, from http://www.cogtech.usc.edu/publications/kuhn_ep_07.pdf

Kulik, J. (2003). *Effects of using instructional technology in elementary and secondary schools: What controlled evaluation studies say.* Arlington, VA: SRI International. Retrieved June 26, 2004, from http://www.sri.com/policy/csted/reports/sandt/it/Kulik_ITinK–12_Main_Report.pdf

Kurzweil, R. (2003). The end of handicaps. *eSchool News online, 6*(7). Retrieved from http://www.eschoolnews.org/news/showstory.cfm?ArticleID=4491

Kwajewski, K. (1997a). Memories in living color: Multimedia yearbooks. *Learning and Leading with Technology, 25*(2), 20–21.

Kwajewski, K. (1997b). Technology as a core value. *Learning and Leading with Technology, 24*(5), 54–56.

Labbo, L. D. (2004). Author's computer chair [Technology in Literacy Department]. *The Reading Teacher, 57*(7), 688–691.

Labbo, L. D., Eakle, A. J., & Montero, M. K. (2002). Digital language experience approach: Using digital photographs and software as a language experience approach innovation. *Reading Online, 5*(8).

Labbo, L. D., Leu, D. L., Kinzer, C. K., Teale, W. H., Cammack, D., et al. (2003). Teacher wisdom stories: Cautions and recommendations for using computer-related technologies for literacy instruction [Technology in Literacy Department]. *The Reading Teacher, 57*(3), 300–304.

Labbo, L. D., Sprague, I., Montero, M. K., & Font, G. (2000). Connecting a computer center to themes, literature, and kindergartners' literacy needs. *Reading Online, 4*(1).

Ladelson, L. (1994). Calibrating probeware: Making in line. *The Computing Teacher, 21*(6), 46–47.

Lahm, E. A. (2000). Special education technology: Defining the specialist. *Special Education Technology Practice, 2*(3), 22–27.

Lahm, E. A., & Nickels, B. L. (1999). What do you know? Assistive technology competencies for special educators. *Teaching Exceptional Children, 32*(1), 56–63.

Lanham, R. (1995). *The electronic word: Democracy, technology, and the arts.* Chicago: University of Chicago Press.

Lankshear, C., & Knobel, M. (2003). *New literacies, changing knowledge and classroom learning.* Philadelphia: Open University Press.

Lary, L. (2004). Hide and seek: GPS and geocaching in the classroom. *Learning and Leading with Technology, 31*(6), 14–18.

Lavie, T., & Tractinsky, N. (2004). Assessing dimensions of perceived visual aesthetics of web sites. *International Journal of Human-Computer Studies, 60*, 269–298.

Lee, J. K. (2008). Toward democracy: Social studies and TPCK. In AACTE's Committee on Innovation and Technology (Eds.), *Handbook of technological pedagogical content knowledge for educators* (129–144). Mahwah, NJ: Routledge.

Lee, J. K., & Clark, W. G. (2004). Studying local history in the digital age: The story of Asaph Perry. *Social Education, 68*(3), 203–207.

Leki, I. (2001). Material, educational, and ideological challenges of teaching EFL writing at the turn of the century, *International Journal of English Studies, 1*, 197–209.

Lemkuhl, M. (2002). Teaching ideas: Pen-pal letters: The cross-curricular experience. *The Reading Teacher, 55*(8), 720–729.

Lenker, J. A., & Paquet, V. L. (2003). A review of conceptual models for assistive technology outcomes research and practice. *Assistive Technology, 15*, 1–15.

Leu, D. (2001). Emerging literacy on the Internet. *The Reading Teacher 54*(6), 568–572.

Leu, D. J., Jr. (2002a). The new literacies: Research on reading instruction with the Internet. In A. E. Farstrup & S. J. Samuels (Eds.), *What research has to say about reading instruction* (3rd ed., pp. 310–336). Newark, DE: International Reading Association.

Leu, D. J., Jr. (2002b). Internet workshop: Making time for literacy. *The Reading Teacher, 55*(5), 466–472.

Leu, D. J., Jr., & Kinzer, C. K. (2000). The convergence of literacy instruction with networked technologies for information and communication. *Reading Research Quarterly, 35*, 108–127.

Leu, D. J., Jr., Kinzer, C. K., Coiro, J. L., & Cammack, D. W. (2004). Toward a theory of new literacies emerging from the Internet and other information and communication technologies. In R. B. Ruddell & N. J. Unrau (Eds.), *Theoretical models and processes of reading* (5th ed., pp. 1570–1613). Newark, DE: International Reading Association.

Leu, D. J., Jr., & Leu, D. D. (2000). *Teaching with the Internet: Lessons from the classroom* (3rd ed.). Norwood, MA: Christopher-Gordon.

Leu, D. J., Jr., Leu, D. D., & Coiro, J. (2004). *Teaching with the Internet: New literacies for new times* (4th ed.), Norwood, MA: Christopher-Gordon.

Lewis, C., & Fabos, B. (2005). Instant messaging, literacies and social identities. *Reading Research Quarterly, 40*(4), 470–501.

Lewis, P. (2001). *Spreadsheet magic: Forty lessons using spreadsheets to teach curriculum in K–8 classrooms.* Eugene, OR: International Society for Technology in Education.

Lewis, R. (1993). *Special education technology.* Pacific Grove, CA: Brooks/Cole.

Lim, C. (2001). Computer self-efficacy, academic self-concept, and other predictors of satisfaction and future participation of adult distance learners. *The American Journal of Distance Education, 15*(2), 41–52.

Linn, R., Baker, E., & Betebenner, D. (2002). Accountability systems: Implications of requirements of the No Child Left Behind Act. *Educational Researcher, 31*(6), 3–16.

Litchfield, B. (1992). Science: Evaluation of inquiry-based science software and interactive multimedia programs. *The Computing Teacher, 19*(6), 41–43.

Litchfield, B. (1995). Helping your students plan computer projects. *The Computing Teacher, 22*(7), 37–43.

Lockard, J., & Abrams, P. (2001). *Computers for twenty-first century educators* (5th ed.). New York: Longman.

Lopez, S. (2000). Cat in the hat and all that. *Time Magazine, 156*(17), 6.

Loupe, D. (2001). Virtual schooling: A new dimension to learning brings new challenges for educators. *eSchool News Online, 4*(6), 41–47.

Lowther, D. L., Ross, S. M., & Morrison, G. M. (2003). When each one has one: The influences on teaching strategies and student achievement of using laptops in the classroom. *Educational Technology Research & Development, 51*(3), 23–44.

Lucas, G. (2003, Spring). Technology as a force for change. *Edutopia* (http://www.glef.org).

Ludlow, B. L. (1994). A comparison of traditional and distance education models. In *Proceedings of the Annual National Conference of the American Council on Rural Special Education,* Austin, TX. (ERIC Document Reproduction No. ED369599)

Lunce, L., & Bailey, B. (2007). Using online simulations to enhance preservice teacher understanding of science concepts. In C. Montgomerie & J. Seale (Eds.), *Proceedings of World Conference on Educational Multimedia, Hypermedia and Telecommunications 2007* (pp. 2892–2899). Chesapeake, VA: AACE.

Machtmes, K., & Asher, J. W. (2000). A meta-analysis of the effectiveness of telecourses in distance education. *American Journal of Distance Education, 14*(1), 27–46. (ERIC Document Reproduction No. ED613342)

Mageau, T. (1990). ILS: Its new role in schools. *Electronic Learning, 10*(1), 22–24.

Mallott, R. (1993). The three-contingency model of performance management and support in higher education. *Educational Technology, 33*(10), 21–28.

Malone, T. (1980). *What makes things fun to learn? A study of intrinsically motivating computer games.* Palo Alto, CA: Xerox Palo Alto Research Center.

Mankus, M. L. (2000). *Using virtual manipulatives on the web to develop number sense.* NCTM Annual Meeting in Chicago. Retrieved from http://mason.gmu.edu/~mmankus/talks/nctm2000/nctmch00.htm

Manouchehri, A., Enderson, M. C., & Pagnucco, L. A. (1998). Exploring geometry with technology. *Mathematics Teaching in the Middle School, 3*(6), 436–442.

Manouchehri, A., & Pagnucco, L. (1999–2000). Julio's run: Studying graphs and functions. *Learning and Leading with Technology, 27*(4), 42–45.

Maor, D. (1991, April). *Development of student inquiry skills: A constructivist approach in a computerized classroom environment.* Paper presented at the Annual Meeting of the National Association for Research in Science Teaching, Lake Geneva, WI, April 7–10, 1991. (ERIC Document Reproduction No. ED326261)

Marcus, B. H., Williams, D. M., Dubbert, P. M., Sallis, J. F., King, A. C., Yancey, A. K., et al. (2006). Physical activity intervention studies. *Circulation, 114,* 2739–2752.

Margolis, J., & Fisher, A. (2002). *Unlocking the clubhouse: Women in computing.* Cambridge, MA: The MIT Press.

Maring, G. H., Boxie, P., & Wiseman, B. J. (2000). School-university partnership through online pattern books. *Reading Online, 4*(5).

Mark, M. (1996). *Contemporary music education* (3rd ed.). New York: Schirmer Books.

Martin, K., & Bearden, D. (1998). Listserv learning. *Learning and Leading with Technology, 26*(3), 39–41.

Martorella, P. (1997). Technology and the social studies: Which way to the sleeping giant? *Theory and Research in Social Education, 25*(4), 511–514.

Martorella, P. H. (Ed.) (1997). *Interactive technologies and the social studies: Emerging issues and applications.* Albany, NY: State University of New York Press.

Matthews, M. S. (2000). Electronic literacy and the limited English proficient student. *Reading Online.* Retrieved from http://www.readingonline.org/electronic/matthews

Mauricio, D. (2000). See Music Tech Ensemble information at http://hhs.suhsd.k12.ca.us/musictech/index.html

Mayer, R. (1997). Multimedia learning: Are we asking the right questions? *Educational Psychologist, 32*(4), 1–19.

Mayer, R., Fennell, S., & Farmer, L. (2004). A personalization effect in multimedia learning: Students learn better when words are in conversational style rather than formal style. *Journal of Educational Psychology, 96*(2), 389–395.

Mayer, R., & Moreno, R. (1998). A split attention effect in multimedia learning: Evidence for dual processing systems in working memory. *Journal of Educational Psychology, 90*(2), 312–320.

Mayer, R., & Moreno, R. (2003). Nine ways to reduce cognitive load in multimedia learning. *Educational Psychologist, 38*(1), 43–52.

Mayes, R. (1992). The effects of using software tools on mathematics problem solving in secondary school. *School Science and Mathematics, 92*(5), 243–248.

McCarthy, R. (1998). Stop the presses: An update on desktop publishing. *Electronic Learning, 7*(6), 24–30.

McCoy, L. (1990). *Does the Supposer improve problem solving in geometry?* (ERIC Document Reproduction No. ED320775)

McCullen, C. (2001). Going the distance . . . with technology. *Technology & Learning, 21*(7), 45–47.

McGrail, E., & Rozema, R. (2005). Envisioning effective technology integration: A scenario for English education doctoral programs. *Contemporary Issues in Technology and Teacher Education* [online serial], *5*(3/4). Retrieved from http://www.citejournal.org/vol5/iss3/languagearts/article2.cfm

McGrath, D. (2004). Strengthening collaborative work. *Learning and Leading with Technology, 31*(5), 3–33.

McGuire, J. M., Scott, S. S., & Shaw, S. F. (2006). Universal design and its applications in educational environments. *Remedial and Special Education, 27*(3), 166–175.

McHenry, L., & Bozik, M. (1997). From a distance: Student voices from the interactive video classroom. *TechTrends, 42*(6), 20–24.

McNabb, M. (2001). In search of appropriate usage guidelines. *Learning and Leading with Technology, 29*(2), 50–54.

Mechling, L., & Langone, J. (2000). The effects of computer-based instructional program with video anchors on the use of photographs for prompting augmentative communication. *Education and Training in Mental Retardation and Developmental Disabilities, 35*(1), 90–105.

Mechling, L. C., Gast, D. L., & Langone, J. (2002). Computer-based video instruction to teach persons with moderate intellectual disabilities to read grocery aisle signs and locate items. *Journal of Special Education, 35*(4), 224–240.

Meese, R. L. (2001). *Teaching learners with mild disabilities: Integrating research and practice.* Belmont, CA: Wadsworth/Thomson Learning.

Merrill, D., & Salisbury, D. (1984). Research on drill and practice strategies. *Journal of Computer-Based Instruction, 11*(1), 19–21.

Metheny, R. (2003). Pre-K 2003: Inclusive, not assistive technology. *Closing the Gap, 22*(5), 1, 24–25.

Microsoft, schools mull security improvements. (2003). *eSchool News online, 5*(8). Retrieved from http://www.eschoolnews.org/news/showstory.cfm?ArticleID=4582

Mikropoulos, T., Katsikis, A., & Nikolou, E. (2003). Virtual environments in biology teaching. *Journal of Biological Education, 37*(4), 176–181.

Milla, K., Lorenzo, A., & Brown, C. 2005. GIS, GPS, and remote sensing technologies in extension services: Where to start, what to know. *Journal of Extension, 43*(3). Retrieved from http://www.joe.org/joe/2005june/a6.shtml

Miller, H. L. (1997). The New York City Public Schools Integrated Learning Systems Project. *International Journal of Educational Research, 27*(2), 91–183.

Mintz, R. (1993). Computerized simulation as an inquiry tool. *School Science and Mathematics, 93*(2), 76–80.

Mishra, P., & Koehler, M. (2006). Technological pedagogical content knowledge: A framework for teacher knowledge. *Teachers College Record, 108*(6), 1017–1054.

Mitchell, K., Finkelhor, D., & Wolak, J. (2001). Risk factors for and impact of online sexual solicitation of youth. *Journal of the American Medical Association, 285*(23), 3011–3014.

Mitchell, K., Wolak, J., & Finkelhor, D. (2007). Trends in youth reports of unwanted sexual solicitations, harassment and unwanted exposure to pornography on the Internet. *Journal of Adolescent Health, 40*, 116–126.

Moersch, C. (1995). Choose the right graph. *The Computing Teacher, 22*(5), 31–35.

Mohnsen, B. (2000). Vaughn, Nekomi, and Luis: What they were doing in middle school physical education. *Learning and Leading with Technology, 27*(5), 22–27.

Mohnsen, B. (2003). *Concepts and principles of physical education: What every student needs to know.* Reston, VA: National Association for Sport and Physical Education.

Molenda, M. (1991). A philosophical critique on the claims of "constructivism." *Educational Technology, 31*(9), 44–48.

Molnar, A. (1978). The next great crisis in American education: Computer literacy. *AEDS Journal, 12*(1), 11–20.

Moore, M. (1995). The death of distance. *The American Journal of Distance Education, 9*(3), 1–4.

Moore, M., Myers, R., & Burton, J. (1994). What multimedia might do . . . and what we know about what it does. In *Multimedia and learning: A school leader's guide.* Alexandria, VA: National School Boards Association.

Mora, J. K. (2000/2001). Responding to the demographic challenge: An Internet classroom for teachers of language-minority students. *Reading Online, 4*(5).

Moreno, R., & Mayer, R. (2002). Verbal redundancy in multimedia learning: When reading helps listening. *Journal of Educational Psychology, 94*(1), 156–163.

Morkes, J., & Nielson, J. (1997). *Concise, scannable, and objective: How to write for the Web.* Retrieved March 1, 2005, from http://www.useit.com/papers/webwriting/writing.html

Moskal, P., Martin, B., & Foshee, N. (1997). Educational technology and distance education in central Florida: An assessment of capabilities. *The American Journal of Distance Education, 11*(1), 6–22.

Moyer, P. S., Bolyard, J. J., & Spikell, M. A. (2002). What are virtual manipulatives? *Teaching Children Mathematics, 8*(6), 372–377.

Muckerheide, P., Mogill, A., & Mogill, H. (1999). In search of a fair game. *Mathematics and Computer Education, 33*(2), 142–150.

Muffoletto, R. (1994). Technology and restructuring education: Constructing a context. *Educational Technology, 34*(2), 24–28.

Muro, D. (1994). *The art of sequencing* [video]. Miami, FL: CPP/Belwin.

Murray, C. (2003a, June). Budget ax falls on school tech programs. *eSchool News Online, 6*(6), 1, 29.

Murray, C. (2003b, November 18). Controversial radio ID tags keep track of kids. *eSchool News online, 6*(11).

Murray, T., et al. (1988). An analogy-based computer tutorial for remediating physics misconceptions. (ERIC Document Reproduction No. ED299172)

Music Educators National Conference. (1994). *Standards for arts education.* Reston, VA: Author. Retrieved March 16, 2005, from the Kennedy Center ArtsEdge website: http://artsedge.kennedy-center.org/teach/standards/

Music Educators National Conference. (2004). *Bridging the gap: Popular music and music education.* Reston, VA: Author.

Myers, M. (1996). *Changing our minds: Negotiating English and literacy.* Urbana, IL: National Council of Teachers of English.

Myers, J., & Beach, R. (2001). Hypermedia authoring as critical literacy. *Journal of Adolescent & Adult Literacy, 44*(6), 538–546.

Naisbitt, J. (1984). *MegaTrends.* New York: Warner Books.

Nathan, J. (1985). *Micro-myths: Exploring the limits of learning with computers.* Minneapolis, MN: Winston Press.

National Adolescent Literacy Coalition. (2007, September). *Foundational and emergent questions: Smart people talk about adolescent literacy.* Washington, DC: Author.

National Association for Sport and Physical Education. (2004). *Moving into the future: National standards for physical education* (2nd ed.). Reston, VA: Author.

National Council for Accreditation of Teacher Education. (1997). *Technology and the new professional teacher. Preparing for the 21st century classroom.* Washington, DC: Author.

National Council for the Social Studies. (1994). *Expectations of excellence: Curriculum standards for social studies.* Silver Springs, MD: Author.

National Council of Teachers of English & International Reading Association. (1996). *Standards for the English language arts.* Urbana, IL: Author.

National Council of Teachers of Mathematics. (2000). *Principles and standards for school mathematics.* Reston, VA: Author.

National Council of Teachers of Mathematics. (2001). *E-Example 5.4: Accessing and investigating data using the World Wide Web; E-Example 5.5: Collecting, representing, and interpreting data.* Retrieved January 5, 2001, http://standards.nctm.org/document/eexamples/chap5/5.4/index.htm and http://standards.nctm.org/document/eexamples/chap5/5.5/index.htm

National Research Council (1996). *National science education standards.* Washington, DC: National Academy Press.

National Science Foundation. (2007). Student results show benefits of math and science partnerships. Retrieved September 3, 2008, from http://www.nsf.gov/news/news_summ.jsp?cntn_id=109725

National Standards in Foreign Language Education Project. (1999). *Standards for foreign language learning in the 21st century.* Lawrence, KS: Allen Press, Inc.

Newman, J. (1988). Online: Classroom publishing. *Language Arts, 65*(7), 727–732.

Niemiec, R., & Walberg, R. (1989). From teaching machines to microcomputers: Some milestones in the history of computer-based instruction. *Journal of Research on Computing in Education, 21*(3), 263–276.

Norman, D. (2004). *Emotional design: Why we love (or hate) everyday things.* New York: Basic Books.

Norris, C., Sullivan, T., Poirot, J., & Soloway, E. (2003). No access, no use, no impact: Snapshot surveys of educational technology in K–12. *Journal of Research on Technology in Education, 36*(1), 15–27.

Norris, W. (1977). Via technology to a new era in education. *Phi Delta Kappan, 58*(6), 451–459.

North American Council for Online Learning. (2008). Fast facts about online learning. Retrieved from http://www.nacol.org/media/nacol_fast_facts.pdf

Norvelle, R. (1992). Desktop publishing. In G. Bitter (Ed.), *Macmillan encyclopedia of computers.* New York: Macmillan.

Oakes, J., & Saunders, M. (2004). Education's most basic tools: Access to textbooks and instructional materials in California's public schools. *Teachers College Record, 106*(10), 1967–1988.

O'Bannon, B., Krolak, B., Harkelroad, M., & Dick, D. (1999). Awesome graphics: Using *Photoshop* for web graphics. *Learning and Leading with Technology, 26*(5), 54–57.

Oblender, T. (2002). A hybrid course model: One solution to the high online drop-out rate. *Learning and Leading with Technology, 29*(6), 42–46.

Odasz, F. (1999–2000). Collaborative Internet tools. *Learning and Leading with Technology, 27*(4), 11–15.

Office of Technology Assessment. (1995). *Teachers and technology: Making the connection* (OTA-EHR-616). Washington, DC: U.S. Government Printing Office.

Ohler, J. (1998). The promise of MIDI technology: A reflection on musical intelligence. *Learning and Leading with Technology, 25*(6), 6–15.

Ohler, J. (2008) *Digital storytelling in the classroom: New media pathways to literacy, learning, and creativity.* Thousand Oaks, CA: Corwin Press.

Okolo, C. (1992). The effect of computer-assisted instruction format and initial attitude on the arithmetic facts proficiency and continuing motivation of students with learning disabilities. *Exceptionality: A Research Journal, 3*(4), 195–211.

Oliver, H. (1994). Book review. Education and informatics worldwide: The state of the art and beyond. *Journal of Research on Computing in Education, 26*(2), 285–290.

Oppenheimer, T. (2003). *The flickering mind: The false promise of technology in the classroom and how learning can be saved.* New York: Random House.

Oravec, J. A. (2002). Bookmarking the world: Weblog applications in education. *Journal of Adolescent & Adult Literacy, 45*(7), 616–621.

O'Reilly, T. (2005). What is Web 2.0: Design patterns and business models for the next generation of software. Retrieved June 30, 2008, from http://www.oreillynet.com/pub/a/oreilly/tim/news/2005/09/30/what-is-web-20.html

Orkwis, R., & McLane, K. (1998). *A curriculum every student can use: Design principles for student access.* OSEP topical brief. Reston, VA: Council for Exceptional Children. Also available from http://www.cec.sped.org/osep/udsign.htm

Orman, E. (2003). Effect of virtual reality graded exposure on heart rate and self-reported anxiety levels of performing saxophonists. *Journal of Research in Music Education, 51*(4), 302–315.

Ormrod, J. (2001). *Educational psychology: Developing learners* (3rd ed.). Upper Saddle River, NJ: Merrill/Prentice Hall.

Osborn, V. (2001) Identifying at-risk students in videoconferencing and web-based distance education. *American Journal of Distance Education, 15*(1), 41–54.

Papert, S. (1980). *Mindstorms: Children, computers, and powerful ideas.* New York: Basic Books.

Papert, S. (1987). Computer criticism vs. technocentric thinking. *Educational Researcher, 16*(1), 22–30.

Parham, C. (2003). Virtual skies. *Technology and Learning, 24*(4), 34–35.

Parker, E., Jacobs, D., Jr, Schreiner, P., Schmitz, K., & Dengel, D. (2007). Physical activity in young adults and incident hypertension over 15 years of follow-up: The CARDIA study. *American Journal of Public Health, 97*(4), 703–709.

Parker, E. D., David, J., Schreiner, P., Schmitz, K., & Dengel, D. (2007). Physical activity in young adults and incident hypertension over 15 years of follow-up: The CARDIA Study. *American Journal of Public Health, 97*(4), 703–709s.

Parker, R. C. (1989). Ten common desktop design pitfalls. *Currents, 15*(1), 24–26.

Parmenter, B., & Burns, M. (2001). GIS in the classroom: Challenges, opportunities, and alternatives. *Learning and Leading with Technology, 28*(7), 10–17.

Pate, R. R., & Small, M. L. (1995). School physical education. *Journal of School Health, 65*(8), 312–317.

Paterson, W., Henry, J., & O'Quin, K. (2003). Investigating the effectiveness of an integrated learning system on early emergent readers. *Reading Research Quarterly, 38*(2), 172–207.

Payne, V. G., & Issacs, L. D. (1995). *Human motor development: A lifespan approach* (3rd ed.). Mountain View, CA: Mayfield Publishing Co.

Perkins, D. (1991). Technology meets constructivism: Do they make a marriage? *Educational Technology, 31*(5), 18–23.

Peterson, C., & Bond, N. (2004). Online compared to face-to-face teacher preparation for learning standards-based planning skills. *Journal of Research on Technology in Education, 36*(4), 345–360.

Phillips, D. C. (1995). The good, the bad, and the ugly: The many faces of constructivism. *Educational Researcher, 24*(7), 5–12.

Ploger, D., Rooney, M., & Klingler, L. (1996). Applying spreadsheets and draw programs in the classroom. *Tech Trends, 41*(3), 26–29.

Ploger, D., & Vedova, T. (1999). Programming dynamic charts in the elementary classroom. *Learning and Leading with Technology, 26*(5), 38–41.

Plymate, L. (1998). Is it linear? *Learning and Leading with Technology, 26*(1), 16–22.

Poedubicky, V., Brown, L., Hoover, H., & Elias, M. J. (2000). Using technology to promote health. *Learning and Leading with Technology, 28*(4), 18–21, 56.

Poock, M. (1998). The Accelerated Reader: An analysis of the software's strengths and weaknesses and how it can be used to best potential. *School Library Media Activities Monthly, 14*(9), 32–35.

Pope, C., & Golub, J. (2000). Preparing tomorrow's English language arts teachers today: Principles and practices for infusing technology. *Contemporary Issues in Technology and Teacher Education.* Retrieved January 28, 2002, from http://www.citejournal.org/vol1/iss1/currentissues/english/article1.htm

Puckett, K. S. (2004). Project ACCESS: Field testing an assistive technology toolkit for students with mild disabilities. *Journal of Special Education Technology, 19*(2), 5–17.

Pugalee, D., & Robinson, R. (1998). A study of the impact of teacher training in using Internet resources for mathematics and science instruction. *The Journal of Research on Computing in Education, 31*(1), 78–88.

Quesada, A. (1998). The arts connection. *Technology and Learning, 19*(2), 52–58.

Raessens, J., & Goldstein, J. (Eds.). (2005). *Handbook of computer game studies.* Cambridge, MA: The MIT Press.

Randel, J., Morris, B., Wetzel, C., & Whitehill, B. (1992). The effectiveness of games for educational purposes: A review of recent research. *Simulation and Gaming, 23*(3), 261–276.

Rankin-Erickson, J., Wood, L., & Beukelman, D. (2003). Early computer literacy: First graders use the "talking" computer. *Reading Improvement, 40*(3), 132–144.

Ransdell, L. B., & Petlichkoff, L. (Eds.) (2005). *Ensuring the health of active and athletic girls and women.* Reston, VA: AAHPERD Press.

Readers' choice awards. (2004). *eSchool News online, 7*(4), 32–33.

Reeves, B., & Nass, C. (1996). *The media equation: How people treat computers, television, and new media as real people and places.* Cambridge: Cambridge University Press/CSLI.

Reigeluth, C., & Schwartz, E. (1989). An instructional theory for the design of computer-based simulations. *Journal of Computer-Based Instruction, 16*(1), 1–10.

Reinking, D., McKeena, M. C., Labbo, L. D., & Kieffer, R. F. (Eds.). (1998). *Handbook of literacy and technology: Transformations in a post-typographic world.* Mahwah, NJ: Lawrence Erlbaum Associates.

Reiser, R., & Dempsey, J. V. (Eds.). (2006). *Trends and issues in instructional design and technology.* NJ: Prentice Hall.

Reissman, R. (2000). Priceless gifts. *Learning and Leading with Technology, 28*(2), 28–31.

Reitsma, P. (1988). Reading practice for beginners: Effects of guided reading, reading-while-listening, and independent reading with computer-based speech feedback. *Reading Research Quarterly, 23*, 219–235.

Rembelinsky, I. (1997–1998). Us and them: Multimedia explorations of prejudice and intolerance in American history. *Learning and Leading with Technology, 25*(4), 42–47.

Renne, C. (2000). Taking shape: Linking geometry and technology. *Learning and Leading with Technology, 27*(7), 58–62.

Repp, R. (1999). The World Wide Web: Interfaces, databases, and applications to education. *Learning and Leading with Technology, 26*(6), 40–41, 60–61.

Revenaugh, M. (1997). *Productivity in the classroom.* Redmond, WA: Microsoft Corporation. Retrieved from http://www.microsoft.com/education/k12/resource/lessons.htm

Richards, C., & Ridley, D. (1997). Factors affecting college students' persistence in online computer-managed instruction. *College Student Journal, 31*, 490–495.

Richards, J. (1992). Computer simulations in the science classroom. *Journal of Science Education and Technology, 1*(1), 67–80.

Riddle, J. (1990). *Measuring affective change: Students in a distance learning class.* Paper presented at the Annual Meeting of the Northern Rocky Mountain Educational Research Association, Greeley, CO. (ERIC Document Reproduction No. ED325514)

Rieber, L., Smith, L., & Noah, D. (1998). The value of serious play. *Educational Technology, 38*(6), 29–37.

Rifkin, J. (2000). *The age of access.* New York: Tarcher/Putnam.

Ringstaff, C., & Kelley, L. (2002). *The learning return on our technology investment: A review of findings from research.* San Francisco: WestEd RTEC. Retrieved from http://www.wsetedrtec.org

Ringstaff, C., & Yocam, K. (1995). *Creating an alternative context for teacher development: The ACOT teacher development centers* (ACOT Report, H#18). Cupertino, CA: Apple Computer Co.

Ritchie, D., & Boyle, K. (1998). Finding the bucks for technology. *Learning and Leading with Technology, 26*(2), 46–50.

Robinson, L. (2003). Technology as a scaffold for emergent literacy: Interactive storybooks for toddlers. *Young Children, 58*(6), 42–48.

Robinson, R., & Roland, C. (1994). *Technology and arts education.* Tallahassee, FL: Florida Department of Education.

Roblyer, M. (1983). How to evaluate software reviews. *Executive Educator, 5*(9), 34–39.

Roblyer, M. (1990). The glitz factor. *Educational Technology, 30*(10), 34–36.

Roblyer, M. (1992). Computers in education. In G. Bitter (Ed.), *Macmillan encyclopedia of computers.* New York: Macmillan.

Roblyer, M., Castine, W., & King, F. J. (1988). *Assessing the impact of computer-based instruction: A review of recent research.* New York: Haworth Press.

Roblyer, M. D. (1991). Electronic hands across the ocean: The Florida–England connection. *The Computing Teacher, 19*(5), 16–19.

Roblyer, M. D. (1996). The constructivist/objectivist debate: Implications for instructional technology research. *Learning and Leading with Technology, 24*(2), 12–17.

Roblyer, M. D. (1997). Technology and the oops! effect: Finding a bias against word processing. *Learning and Leading with Technology, 24*(7), 14–16.

Roblyer, M. D. (1998). Visual literacy: Seeing a new rationale for teaching with technology. *Learning and Leading with Technology, 26*(2), 51–54.

Roblyer, M. D. (1999). Our multimedia future: Recent research on multimedia's impact on education. *Learning and Leading with Technology, 26*(6), 51–53.

Roblyer, M. D. (2000). Digital desperation: Research reports on a growing technology and equity crisis. *Learning and Leading with Technology, 27*(8), 50–53, 61.

Roblyer, M. D. (2003a). Getting our NETS worth: The role of ISTE's National Educational Technology Standards (NETS). *Learning and Leading with Technology, 30*(8), 6–13.

Roblyer, M. D. (2003b). Virtual high schools in the United States: Current views, future visions. In J. Bradley (Ed.), *The open classroom: Distance learning in and out of schools.* London: Kogan Page.

Roblyer, M. D. (2004). Virtual schools, real issues. *The International Principal, 8*(3). Retrieved September 28, 2004, from http://www.readnow.info/

Roblyer, M. D., & Ekhaml, L. (2000). How interactive are your distance courses? A rubric for assessing interactivity in distance learning. *Online Journal of Distance Learning Administration, 3*(2). Retrieved from http://www.westga.edu/~distance/summer32.htm

Roblyer, M. D., & Erlanger, W. (1998). Preparing Internet-ready teachers: Which methods work best? *Learning and Leading with Technology, 26*(4), 59–61.

Roblyer, M. D., & Marshall, J. (2002–2003). Predicting success of virtual high school distance learners: Preliminary results from an educational success prediction instrument (ESPRI). *Journal of Research on Technology in Education, 35*(2), 241–255.

Roblyer, M. D., & McKenzie, B. (2000). Distant but not out-of-touch: What makes an effective distance learning instructor? *Learning and Leading with Technology, 27*(6), 50–53.

Roblyer, M. D., & Wiencke, W. (2003). Design and use of a rubric to assess and encourage interactive qualities in distance courses. *The American Journal of Distance Education, 17*(2), 77–98.

Roblyer, M. D., & Wiencke, W. (2004). Exploring the interaction equation: Validating a rubric to assess and encourage interaction in distance courses. *The Journal of Asynchronous Learning Networks, 9*(1). Available from http://www.sloan-c.org/publications/jaln/index.asp

Rogers, E. (2004). *Diffusion of innovations.* New York: The Free Press.

Ronen, M. (1992). Integrating computer simulations into high school physics teaching. *Journal of Computers in Mathematics and Science Teaching, 11*(3–4), 319–329.

Rose, D. (2000). Universal design for learning. *Journal of Special Education Technology, 15*(1), 67–70.

Rose, D., Sethuraman, S., & Meo, G. J. (2000). Universal design for learning. *Journal of Special Education Technology, 15*(2), 56–60.

Rose, D. H., & Meyer, A. (Eds.). (2006). *A practical reader in universal design for learning.* Boston: Harvard Education Press.

Rose, D. H., Meyer, A., & Hitchcock, C. (Eds.). (2005). *The universally designed classroom: Accessible curriculum and digital technologies.* Boston: Harvard Education Press.

Rose, S. (1988). A desktop publishing primer. *The Computing Teacher, 15*(9), 13–15.

Ross, T. W., & Bailey, G. D. (1996). Creating safe Internet access. *Learning and Leading with Technology, 24*(1), 51–53.

Royer, R., & Royer, J. (2002). Developing understanding with multimedia. *Learning and Leading with Technology, 29*(7), 40–45.

Rubin, A. (undated). *Educational technology: Support for inquiry-based learning.* Retrieved November 15, 2004, from http://ra.terc.edu/publications/

Rudolph, T. (2004). *Technology strategies for music education.* Wyncote, PA: Technology Institute for Music Educators.

Rudolph, T., & Peters, K. (1996). The MIDI sequencer in the music classroom [video]. Chicago: GIA Publications.

Russell, M., & Plati, T. (2000). *Mode of administration effects on MCAS composition performance for grades four, eight, and ten.* Retrieved February 1, 2001, from http://nbetpp.bc.edu/reports.html

Russell, T. L. (1992). Television's indelible impact on distance education: What we should have learned from comparative research. *Research in Distance Education, 4*(4), 2–4.

Russell, T. L. (1997). *The "no significant difference" phenomenon as reported in research reports, summaries, and papers.* Raleigh: Office of Instructional Telecommunications, North Carolina State University.

Saettler, P. (1990). *The evolution of American educational technology.* Englewood, CO: Libraries Unlimited.

Sage, S. (2000). A natural fit: Problem-based learning and technology standards. *Learning and Leading with Technology, 28*(1), 6–12.

Salden, R., Paas, F., & van Merriënboer, J. (2006). A comparison of task selection approaches. *Computers in Human Behavior 22*, 321–333.

Salisbury, D. (1990). Cognitive psychology and its implications for designing drill and practice programs for computers. *Journal of Computer-Based Instruction, 17*(1), 23–30.

Salpeter, J. (2004). Data mining with a mission. *Technology and Learning, 24*(8), 30–34.

Satcher, D. (1997). *Physical activity and health: A report of the surgeon general.* Washington, DC: U.S. Government Printing Office.

Scharber, C. (2008). Online book clubs for the Net generation. Dissertation, University of Minnesota, Minneapolis.

Scharber, C., Dexter, S., & Riedel, E. (2005, April). Formative feedback via an automated essay scorer: Its impact on learners. Paper session for the annual meeting of the American Educational Research Association, Montreal, Québec, Canada.

Scharf, E., & Cramer, J. (2002). Desktop poetry project. *Learning and Leading with Technology, 29*(6), 28–31, 50–51.

Schmar-Dobler, E. (2003). Reading on the Internet: The link between literacy and technology. *Journal of Adolescent & Adult Literacy, 47*(1), 80–85.

Schmidt, H. G., Loyens, S. M. M., van Gog, T., & Paas, F. (2007). Problem-based learning is compatible with human cognitive architecture: Commentary on Kirschner, Sweller, and Clark (2006). *Educational Psychologist, 42*(2), 91–97. Retrieved October 31, 2007, from http://www.cogtech.usc.edu/publications/schmidt_etal_ep07.pdf

Scholten, B., & Whitmer, J. (1996). Hypermedia projects: Metastacks increase content focus. *Learning and Leading with Technology, 24*(3), 59–62.

Schwan, S., & Riempp, R. (2004). The cognitive benefits of interactive videos: Learning to tie nautical knots. *Learning and Instruction, 14*(3), 293–305.

Scleef, L. (2003). Inclusive school communities: Accessible learning environments for all. *Closing the Gap, 22*(3), 1, 14–15, 28.

Scot, T., & Harding, D. (2004). Splicing video into the writing process. *Learning and Leading with Technology, 32*(1), 26–31.

Scripp, L. (2007). A Music-in-Education case study: The Conservatory Lab Charter School—NEC Research Center "Learning Through Music" partnership (1999-2003). In L. Scripp, P. Keppel, & R. Wong (Eds.), *Journal for Music-in-Education: Advancing music for changing times* (pp. 202–223). Boston, MA: New England Conservatory.

Seffrin, J. R. (1990). The comprehensive school health curriculum. *Journal of School Health, 60*(4), 151–156.

Setzer, J., Lewis, L., & Greene, B. (2005) Distance education courses for public elementary and secondary school students: 2002–2003. (NCES No. 2005-010). Washington, DC: National Center for Educational Statistics. Retrieved from http://nces.ed.gov/pubsearch/pubsinfo.asp%3Fpubid%3D2005010

Sfard, A. (1998). One–two metaphors for learning and the dangers of choosing just one. *Educational Researcher, 27*(2), 4–13.

Shea, V. (2004). *Netiquette.* Available from http://www.albion.com/netiquette/book/index.html

Sheingold, K. (1991). Restructuring for learning with technology: The potential for synergy. *Phi Delta Kappan, 73*(1), 17–27.

Sherman, T. (1987–1988). A brief review of developments in problem solving. *Computers in the Schools, 4*(3–4), 171–178.

Shore, A., & Johnson, M. (1992). Integrated learning systems: A vision for the future. *Educational Technology, 32*(9), 36–39.

Shulman, L. S. (1986). Those who understand: Knowledge growth in teaching. *Educational Researcher, 15*(2), 4–14.

Silva, T., & Brice, C. (2004). Research in teaching writing. *Annual Review of Applied Linguistics, 24*, 70–106.

Simmons, P., & Lunetta, V. (1993). Problem-solving behaviors during a genetics computer simulation. *Journal of Research in Science Teaching, 30*(2), 153–173.

Simonson, M., Smaldino, S., Albright, M., & Zvacek, S. (2000). *Teaching and learning at a distance: Foundations of distance education.* Upper Saddle River, NJ: Merrill/Prentice Hall.

Simonson, M. R., & Thompson, A. (1994). *Educational computing foundations.* New York: Merrill.

Simpson, C. M. (2001). *Copyright for schools: A practical guide* (2nd ed.). Worthington, OH: Linworth Publishing.

Skipton, C. (1997, May 5). As the worlds turn: VRML authoring and modeling software. *New Media, 7*(6).

Smith, C. K. (1996). *Convenience vs. connection: Commuter students' views on distance learning.* Paper presented at the Annual Forum of the Association for Institutional Research, Albuquerque, NM. (ERIC Document Reproduction No. ED397725)

Smith, K. (1992). Earthquake! *The Florida Technology in Education Quarterly, 4*(2), 68–70.

Smith, R. A., & Sclafani, S. (1989). Integrated teaching systems: Guidelines for evaluation. *The Computing Teacher, 17*(3), 36–38.

Snyder, I. (1993). Writing with word processors: A research overview. *Educational Research, 35*(1), 49–68.

Solloway, S., & Harris, E. (1999). Creating community online. *Educom Review, 34*(2). Available from http://www.educause.edu/ir/library/html/erm99021.html

Soloman, G. (2001). Deconstructing a grant. *Technology & Learning, 21*(11), 44–52.

Spence, I., & Hively, W. (1993). What makes Chris practice? *Educational Technology, 35*(6), 5–23.

Speziale, M., & La France, L. (1992). Multimedia and students with learning disabilities. *The Computing Teacher, 20*(3), 31–34.

Squire, K. (2005). Changing the game: What happens when video games enter the classroom? *Innovate, 1*(6). Available from http://www.innovateonline.info/index.php?view=article&id=82

Stanton, D. (1992). Microcomputer-based labs. *Electronic Learning Special Edition (Buyers Guide), 12*(1), 16–17.

Steed, M. (2001). 3-D visualization: Using 3-D software to represent curricular concepts. *Learning and Leading with Technology, 29*(3), 14–20.

Stein, M., Silbert, J., & Carnine, D. (1997). *Designing effective mathematics instruction: Direct instruction mathematics* (3rd ed.). Upper Saddle River, NJ: Merrill/Prentice Hall.

Steinburg, R., & Oberem, G. (2000). Research-based instructional software in modern physics. *Journal of Computers in Mathematics and Science Teaching, 19*(2), 115–136.

Steinhaus, K. (1986–1987). Putting the music composition tool to work. *The Computing Teacher, 14*(4), 16–18.

Stemler, L. (1997). Educational characteristics of multimedia: A literature review. *Journal of Educational Multimedia and Hypermedia, 6*(3–4), 339–359.

Stephenson, N. (1993). *Snow crash.* New York: Bantam Books.

Stevenson, S. (2001). Discover and create your own field trips. *Multimedia Schools, 8*(4), 40–45.

Stokes, J. (1999). Problem solving software, equity, and allocation of roles. *Learning and Leading with Technology, 26*(5), 6–9, 30.

Stoll, C. (1999). *High-tech heretic: Why computers don't belong in the classroom and other reflections by a computer contrarian.* New York: Doubleday.

Strommen, E. (1994). Can technology change the test? *Electronic Learning, 14*(1), 44–53.

Stuhlmann, J. (1997). Butterflies! Using multimedia to capture a unique science project. *Learning and Leading with Technology, 25*(3), 22–27.

Sullivan, J. (1995). Exciting ways to use videodiscs. *Media and Methods, 31*(3), S8–S10.

Sumrall, W., & Forslev, W. (1994). Spreadsheet meteorology. *Science Scope, 18*, 36–38.

Sutherland, R. (1993). A spreadsheet approach to solving algebra problems. *Journal of Mathematical Behavior, 12*(4), 353–383.

Swain, M. (1993). The output hypothesis: Just reading and writing aren't enough. *The Canadian Modern Language Review, 50*, 158–164.

Swan, K., & Meskill, C. (1996). Using hypermedia in response- based literature classrooms: A critical review of commercial applications. *Journal of Research on Computing in Education, 29*(2), 167–192.

Taylor, D. (1989). Communications technology for literacy work with isolated learners. *Journal of Reading, 32*(7), 634–639.

Taylor, R. (1980). *The computer in the school: Tutor, tool, tutee.* New York: Teachers College Press.

Tergan, S. (1998). Checklists for the evaluation of education software: Critical review and prospects. *Innovations in Education and Training, 35*(1), 9–20.

Thatcher, M. (2003). Building 3-D worlds. *Technology and Learning, 24*(4), 34.

Thomerson, D., & Smith, C. (1996). Student perceptions of the affective experiences encountered in distance learning courses. *The American Journal of Distance Education, 10*(3), 37–48.

Thompson, A., & Mishra, P. (Winter 2007–2008). Breaking News: TPCK becomes TPACK! *Journal of Computing in Teacher Education, 24*(2). Accessed January 23, 2008, at http://www.iste.org/Content/Navigation-Menu/Membership/SIGs/SIGTETeacherEducators/JCTE/PastIssues/Volume24/Number2Winter20072008/jcte-24-2-038-tho.pdf

Thompson, G. (1990). How can correspondence-based distance learning be improved? A survey of attitudes of students who are not well disposed toward correspondence study. *Journal of Distance Education, 5*(1), 53–65.

Threlkeld, R., & Brzoska, K. (1994). Research in distance education. In B. Willis (Ed.), *Distance education: Strategies and tools.* Englewood Cliffs, NJ: Educational Technology Publications.

Tibbs, P. (1989). Video creation for junior high language arts. *Journal of Reading, 32*(6), 558–559.

Tichon, J., Hall, R., Hilgers, M., Leu, M., & Agarwal, S. (2003). Education and training in virtual environments for disaster management. In D. Lassner & C. McNaught (Eds.), *Proceedings of World Conference on Educational Multimedia, Hypermedia and Telecommunications 2003* (pp. 1191–1194). Chesapeake, VA: AACE.

Tinker, B., Staudt, C., & Walton, D. (2002). The handheld computer as field guide. *Learning and Leading with Technology, 30*(1), 36–41.

Tinker, R. (1998, Winter). Teaching and learning in the knowledge society. *The Concord Consortium Newsletter* (1–2), 14.

Tolhurst, D. (1995). Hypertext, hypermedia, multimedia defined? *Educational Technology, 35*(2), 21–26.

Toomey, R., & Ketterer, K. (1995). Using multimedia as a cognitive tool. *Journal of Research on Computing in Education, 27*(4), 472–481.

Topping, K., & Paul, T. (1999). Computer-assisted assessment of practice at reading: A large scale survey using Accelerated Reader data. *Reading & Writing Quarterly, 15*(3), 213–232.

Trend, D. (2001). *Welcome to cyberschool.* Lanham, MD: Rowman and Littlefield.

Trotter, A. (1991). In the school game, your options abound. *Executive Educator, 13*(6), 23.

Truett, C. (1993). CD-ROM storybooks bring children's literature to life. *The Computing Teacher, 21*(1), 20–21.

Tufte, E. (2003). *PowerPoint* is evil. Power corrupts. *PowerPoint* corrupts absolutely. *Wired Magazine, 11*(9). Retrieved September 6, 2004, from http://www.wired.com/wired/archive/11.09/ppt2.html

Tumulty, K., & Dickerson, J. (1998). Gore's costly high-wire act. *Time, 151*(20), 52–55.

Turkle, S. (2004, January 30). How computers change the way we think. *The Chronicle of Higher Education,* B26–B28.

Turner, J., & Paris, S. (1995). How literacy tasks influence children's motivation for literacy. *The Reading Teacher, 48,* 662–673.

Turner, S. V., & Dipinto, V. M. (1992). Students as hypermedia authors: Themes emerging from a qualitative study. *Journal of Research on Computing in Education, 25*(2), 187–199.

Tuthill, G., & Klemm, B. (2002). Virtual field trips: Alternatives to actual trips. *International Journal of Instructional Media, 29*(4), 453–468.

University of Delaware AUP website: http://www.ash.udel.edu/ash/teacher/AUP.html

University of California-Davis website (2007): http://scg.ucdavis.edu/bitsbytes/022207.cfm

U.S. Department of Education. (2000). *Twenty-second annual report to Congress on the implementation of the Individuals with Disabilities Education Act.* Washington, DC: Author. Available from http://www.ed.gov/offices/OSERS/OSEP/OSEP2000AnlRpt/

U.S. Department of Health and Human Services. (1996a). *Physical activity and health: A report of the Surgeon General.* Atlanta, GA: U.S. Department of Health and Human Services, Centers for Disease Control and Prevention, National Center for Chronic Disease Prevention and Health Promotion.

U.S. Department of Health and Human Services. (1996b). *Physical activity and health: Adolescents and young adults.* Atlanta, GA: U.S. Department of Health and Human Services, Centers for Disease Control and Prevention, National Center for Chronic Disease Prevention and Health Promotion.

U.S. Department of Labor. (1992). *SCANS (The Secretary's Commission on Achieving Necessary Skills) Report.* Washington, DC: U.S. Government Printing Office.

Vaille, J., & Hall, J. (1998). *Guidelines for the evaluation of instructional technology resources.* Eugene, OR: International Society for Technology in Education.

van Buren, C., & Aufdenspring, D. (1998). Quilting our history: An integrated schoolwide project. *Learning and Leading with Technology, 26*(2), 22–27.

Van Dusen, L., & Worthen, B. (1995). Can integrated instructional technology transform the classroom? *Educational Leadership, 53*(2), 28–33.

van Hover, S., Swann, K. O., & Berson, M. J. (2004). Digital images in social studies curriculum. *Learning & Leading with Technology, 31*(8), 22–25.

Van Rossum, G. (2001). *Python language website.* Retrieved January 5, 2001, from http://www.python.org/

Viani, N. (2003–2004). The right write site. *Learning and Leading with Technology, 31*(4), 24–27.

Viau, E. (1998). Color me a writer: Teaching students to think critically. *Learning and Leading with Technology, 25*(5), 17–20.

Volker, R. (1992). Applications of constructivist theory to the use of hypermedia. *Proceedings of Selected Research Presentations at the Annual Convention of the AECT.* (ERIC Document Reproduction No. ED348037)

Vygotsky, L. S. (1962). *Thought and language.* Cambridge, MA: The MIT Press.

Walsh, J. (1999). Edison Project, now Edison Schools Inc., plans to go public. *Education Week, 19*(1), 6.

Walsh, T. (2001). SAMDADs for your classroom. *Learning and Leading with Technology, 28*(6), 32–35, 60.

Wang, A., & Newlin, M. (2000). Characteristics of students who enroll and succeed in web-based classes. *Journal of Educational Psychology, 92*(1), 137–143.

Watson, J. (1993). *Teaching thinking skills with databases.* Eugene, OR: International Society for Technology in Education.

Watt, D. (1992). Logo. In G. Bitter (Ed.), *Macmillan encyclopedia of computers.* New York: Macmillan.

Weiler, G. (2003). Using weblogs in the classroom. *English Journal, 92*(5), 73–75.

Weinstein, P. (1999). Computer programming revisited. *Technology & Learning, 19*(8), 38–42.

Weizenbaum, J. (1976). *Computer power and human reason.* San Francisco: W. H. Freeman & Co.

Westbrook, T. (1997). Changes in students' attitudes toward graduate business instruction via interactive television. *The American Journal of Distance Education, 11*(1), 55–69.

Wetzel, K. (1993). Teacher educators' use of computers in teaching. *Journal of Technology and Teacher Education, 1*(4), 335–352.

White, M. (1992). Are ILSs good for education? *Educational Technology, 32*(9), 49–50.

Whitworth, S. A., & Berson, M. J. (2003). Computer technology in the social studies: An examination of the effectiveness literature (1996–2001). *Contemporary Issues in Technology and Teacher Education* [online serial], *2*(4). Available from http://www.citejournal.org/vol2/iss4/socialstudies/article1.cfm

Wilkerson, T. (2001). Reading and writing the digital way. *Learning and Leading with Technology, 29*(3), 42–24, 60–61.

Wilkes, C., & Burnham, B. (1991). Adult learner motivations and electronic distance education. *The American Journal of Distance Education, 5*(1), 43–51.

Willinsky, J., & Bradley, S. (1990). Desktop publishing in remedial language arts settings: Let them eat cake. *Journal of Teaching Writing, 9*(2), 223–238.

Wilson, B. (2005). Broadening our foundation for instructional design: Four pillars of practice, *Educational Technology, 45*(2), 10–15.

Wissick, C. A. (1999a). Quickstarts: Developing functional literacy skills around food. *Special Education Technology Practice, 1*(3), 22–25.

Wissick, C. A. (1999b). Quickstarts: Let's go grocery shopping. *Special Education Technology Practice, 1*(4), 33–36.

Wood, D., Underwood, J., & Avis, P. (1999). Integrated learning systems in the classroom. *Computers and Education, 33*(2–3), 91–108.

Wright, J. (2006). Learning interventions for struggling students. *Education Digest: Essential Readings Condensed for Quick Review, 71*(5), 35–39.

Ybarra, R., & Green, T. (2003). Using technology to help ESL/EFL students develop language skills. *The Internet TESL Journal, 9*(3). Available from http://iteslj.org/

Young, J. (2000, October 6). Virtual reality on a desktop hailed as new tool in distance education. *The Chronicle of Higher Education,* p. A43.

Zemsky, R., & Massey, W. (2004). *Thwarted innovation: What happened to e-learning and why.* Philadelphia: The Learning Alliance at the University of Pennsylvania.

Zirkin, B., & Sumler, D. (1995). Interactive or non-interactive: That is the question!!! An annotated bibliography. *Journal of Distance Education, 10*(1), 95–112.

Zisow, Marcie A. (2001). Fundraising with technology. *Learning and Leading with Technology, 28*(4), 36–41.

Zucker, A., & Kozma, R. (2003). *The virtual high school: Teaching generation V.* New York: Teachers College Press.

Name Index

AAAS (American Association for the Advancement of Science), 326, 328, 329
AAUW (American Association of University Women), 29
Adams, C., 87
Albrecht, B., 161
Albright, M., 225
Alessi, S., 83, 85, 86, 88
Allen, D., 87
Allen, I. F., 226
Alley, L., 231
American Association for the Advancement of Science (AAAS), 326, 328, 329
American Association of University Women (AAUW), 29
Amundsen, C., 229
Andaloro, G., 87
Anderson, R. S., 282
Anderson, S., 245
Anderson-Inman, L., 154
Armstrong, J., 101
Armstrong, P., 229, 230
Armstrong, S., 102
Arnett, P., 84
Ashbacher, C., 87
Ashby, F., 174
Asher, J. W., 228
Assistive technologies, 24
Atkinson, R., 36
Audet, R., 344
Aufdenspring, D., 192
Augmented reality, 24
Auston, J., 155
Ausubel, D., 5
Avis, P., 101

Baek, Y., 84
Bagui, S., 172
Bailey, B., 87
Bailey, G. D., 98, 218
Baines, L., 43
Bakas, C., 197
Baker, T., 357
Balyta, P., 349
Bangert-Drowns, R., 115, 116
Barab, S., 197
Barbrow, D., 101
Barnett, M., 197
Barrett, H. C., 26
Barrett, J., 356
Bauer, J. F., 282
Baugh, I., 221
Baugh, J., 221
Beach, R., 14, 197, 199, 280
Beal, C., 352
Bearden, D., 97
Beaton, A. E., 316, 324
Beaudrie, B., 152, 247
Becker, H., 100, 101
Becker, M., 197, 337
Bednarz, S., 194, 357
Beers, P. J., 173
Bell, R., 335
Bellofatto, L., 256
Bender, P., 100
Bendixon, L., 241
Bennett, N., 193
Benson, D., 65, 66
Benton Foundation Communications Policy Program, 319
Bernard, R., 228, 229
Bernas, R., 178

Berson, I. R., 349, 353
Berson, M. J., 127, 350, 353, 355
Bertelsen, C. D., 284
Beukelman, D., 285
Bigelow, M. H., 299
Biner, P., 229
Bitter, G., 160
Black, E., 92
Black, T. R., 121, 122
Blackhurst, A. E., 408, 409
Bloom, B., 46, 80
Blosser, P., 96
Boaz, M. H., 229, 230
Boehm, D., 153
Bohl, N., 256
Bolick, C., 346
Bolliger, D., 229
Bolyard, J. J., 319
Bond, N., 228
Boone, R., 80
Borba, M., 391
Borenstein, M., 161
Boulware, B., 220
Bowen, A., 335
Boxie, P., 282
Boyd, J., 368
Boyer, J., 92
Boyle, K., 64
Boyle, T., 170
Bozeman, W., 118
Bozik, M., 230
Bracy, G., 100
Bradley, S., 143
Branigan, C., 24
Brice, C., 301
Browder, D. M., 417
Brown, C., 357
Brown, J., 195
Brown, J. S., 41
Brown, L., 190, 400
Brown, S., 123
Bruner, J., 41
Bruning, R., 287
Brunner, C., 185
Brush, T., 100, 101–102
Bryan, S., 281
Brzoska, K., 230
Buffington, M., 197
Bull, G., 257, 280, 286, 287
Bull, S., 257, 286, 287
Burnham, B., 229
Burns, M., 162
Burrill, G., 319
Burton, J., 170
Bush, V., 170
Byers, G., 176, 286

CAI in Music, 84
Caine, G., 391
Caine, R. N., 391
Cammack, D. W., 279, 281
Camuse, R., 160
Cann, A., 84
CARET (Center for Applied Research in Educational Technology), 15
Carlin-Menter, S., 171
Carnine, D., 38
Casey, M., 256
CAST (Center for Applied Special Technology), 412
Castine, W., 13
Catchings, M., 150
Cavanagh, S., 321, 329

Center for Applied Research in Educational Technology (CARET), 15
Center for Applied Special Technology (CAST), 412
Charters, W. W., 6
Chenau, J., 267, 307
Cheng, H., 229, 230
Chrisman, G., 102
Christopherson, J., 16
Clark, J., 185
Clark, R., 13, 14, 92
Clark, R. E., 38, 43, 79
Clark, T., 227
Clark, W. G., 353
Clements, D. H., 319
Clinton, J., 87
Cochran, L. L., 284
Coffman, T., 194
Cognition and Technology Group at Vanderbilt (CTGV), 41, 47
Cohen, M., 14
Coiro, J., 281, 286
Coiro, J. L., 279, 281
Collins, A., 41, 195
Collis, B., 127
Comer, S., 197
Cook, A. M., 115, 116, 408
Cordes, C., 224
Corporation for Public Broadcasting, 19, 227
Coulter, B., 240, 241
Coussement, S., 230
Cradler, J., 13
Cramer, J., 145
CTGV (Cognition and Technology Group at Vanderbilt), 41, 47
Cuban, L., 6, 11, 13, 66
Cummins, J., 299
Curtis, D., 322
Curtis, M., 24
Cyrs, T. E., 230

Dabbagh, N., 154
Darden, G., 397
Davis, J., 161
Davydov, V., 40
Dempsey, J. V., 6
Dengel, D., 390
DeTure, M., 230
Dexter, S., 24
Dick, D., 150
Dick, T. P., 322
Dickerson, J., 241
Diener, K., 193
Dille, B., 230
Dillon, A., 172
Dillon, R., 372
DiPietro, M., 92
Dipinto, V. M., 185
Dodge, B., 256
Doering, A., 14, 38, 49, 50, 94, 194, 195, 197, 199, 224, 226, 243, 281, 308, 331, 349, 350, 353, 357, 401
Doering, N., 397
Dolan, B., 412
Donlan, L., 246
Dorsey, M., 324
Doty, D., 176, 286
Drier, H., 324
Dubbert, P. M., 390
Duguid, P., 41
Dunham, P. H., 322

Subject Index